W9-ARO-001

Down to Earth Sociology

Introductory Readings
ELEVENTH EDITION

JAMES M. HENSLIN
Editor

THE FREE PRESS

New York London Toronto Sydney Singapore

THE FREE PRESS

*f*P   A Division of Simon & Schuster, Inc.
1230 Avenue of the Americas
New York, NY 10020

Copyright © 1991, 1993, 1995, 1997, 1999, 2001 by James M. Henslin

Copyright © 1972, 1976, 1981, 1985, 1988 by The Free Press

All rights reserved,
including the right of reproduction
in whole or in part in any form.

THE FREE PRESS and colophon are trademarks
of Simon & Schuster.

Manufactured in the United States of America

10 9 8 7 6 5 4 3 2 1

Library of Congress Cataloging-in-Publication Data

Down to earth sociology : introductory readings / James M. Henslin, editor.—11th ed.
    p. cm.
    Includes bibliographical references and index.
    1. Sociology. 2. United States—Social conditions. I. Henslin, James M.

HM586.D68 2001
301—dc21

00-067693

ISBN 0-7432-1208-8

Credits
and Acknowledgments

Grateful acknowledgment is made to the authors and publishers who have granted permission to reprint these selections:

ARTICLE
NUMBER
1   Excerpts from *Invitation to Sociology* by Peter L. Berger. Copyright © 1963 by Peter L. Berger. Reprinted by permission of Bantam Doubleday Dell Publishing Group, Inc.

2   Copyright © 2001 by James M. Henslin.

3   From *The Sociological Imagination* by C. Wright Mills. Copyright © 1959 by Oxford University Press, Inc.: renewed by Yaraslava Mills. Reprinted by permission of Oxford University Press, Inc.

4   Copyright © 2001 by James M. Henslin.

5   Copyright © 1985 by the Society for the Study of Social Problems. Reprinted from *Social Problems*, Vol. 32, No. 3, February 1985, pp. 251–63, by permission.

6   Reprinted by permission of the author and publisher from *Street Corner Society*, University of Chicago Press. Copyright © 1981, 1993. All rights reserved.

7   Reproduced by permission of the American Anthropological Association from *American Anthropologist*, 58:3, June 1956. Not for further reproduction.

8   Excerpts from *The Yąnomamö: The Fierce People*, 2nd Edition, by Napoleon A. Chagnon, copyright © 1977 by Holt, Rinehart and Winston, Inc. Reproduced by permission of the publisher.

9   "The Sounds of Silence" by Edward T. Hall and Mildred R. Hall. Reprinted by permission of the authors from *Playboy*, June 1971, pp. 139–40, 204, 206. Copyright © by Edward T. Hall and Mildred Reed Hall.

10   Reprinted by permission of the author and publisher from *American Journal of Sociology*, University of Chicago Press. Copyright © 1984. All rights reserved.

11   Reprinted by permission of Doubleday & Co., Inc., and Penguin Books Ltd., London, from *The Presentation of Self in Everyday Life*, pp. 1–15. Copyright © 1959 by Erving Goffman.

12   Reprinted by permission of the author.

13   Copyright © 2001 by James M. Henslin.

14   Eder, Donna, *School Talk*, copyright © 1995 by Donna Eder. Reprinted by permission of Rutgers University Press.

15   Copyright © 1986 by the Society for the Study of Social Problems. Reprinted from *Social Problems*, Vol. 33, No. 3, February 1986, pp. 176–90, by permission.

16   This article was originally published in *Redbook*, October 1994, pp. 91–93, 145–47. Adapted from *Talking from 9 to 5: How Women's and Men's Conversational Styles Affect Who Gets Heard, Who Gets Credit, and What Gets Done at Work* by Deborah Tannen. © 1994 by Deborah Tannen. Reprinted by permission of William Morrow & Company, Inc.

17   Reprinted by permission of the author.

18   Copyright © 2001 by James M. Henslin.

19   From *New York* Magazine, February 21, 1982. Reprinted by permission of the author.

20   Published by permission of Transaction Publishers, "Collective Trauma at Buffalo Creek," by Kai Erikson, *Society*, Sept.–Oct. 1976. Copyright © 1976 by Transaction Publishers. All rights reserved.

21   "If Hitler Asked You to Electrocute a Stranger, Would You? Probably" by Philip Meyer, from *Esquire* Magazine. Copyright ©1970 by Hearst Corp.

22   Copyright © 2000 by James M. Henslin.

23   From *Code of the Street: Decency, Violence, and the Moral Life of the Inner City* by Elijah Anderson. Copyright © 1999 by Elijah Anderson. Used by permission of W.W. Norton and Company, Inc.

24   Published by permission of Transaction Publishers, from *Society*, Vol. 11, No. 1. Copyright © 1973 by Transaction Publishers.

25   Published by permission of Transaction Publishers, from *Society*, Vol. 9, No. 6. Copyright © 1972 by Transaction Publishers.

26   Reprinted by permission of the author and publisher from *Science*, Vol. 179 (January 19, 1973), pp. 250–58. Copyright © 1973 by AAAS.

27   Reprinted by permission of the author.

28   From *Gender and Society*, 3 (4), Copyright © 1989 by Sage Publications. Reprinted by permission of Sage Publications, Inc.

29   Reprinted by permission of the author.

30   From *Social Policy*, July/August 1971, pp. 20–24. Published by Social Policy Corporation, New York, NY 10036. Copyright © 1971 by Social Policy Corporation.

31   From *Savage Inequalities* by Jonathan Kozol. Copyright © 1991 by Jonathan Kozol. Reprinted by permission of Crown Publishers, Inc.

32   Reprinted by permission of Rowman & Littlefield.

33   Excerpted from "Life on the Global Assembly Line" by Barbara Ehrenreich and Annette Fuentes, *Ms.* magazine, January 1981. Copyright © 1981 by Barbara Ehrenreich and Annette Fuentes.

34   Reprinted by permission of the author.

35   Adapted from "The Great American Football Ritual: Reproducing Race, Class and Gender Inequality" by D. E. Foley, 1990, *Sociology of Sport*

Journal (Vol. 7, No. 2), pp. 111–35. Copyright © 1990 by Human Kinetics Publishers, Inc. Reprinted by permission.

36 Reprinted by permission of Center for Media Literacy.

37 From *The Second Shift* by Arlie Hochschild and Anne Machung. Copyright © 1989 by Arlie Hochschild. Used by permission of Viking Penguin, a division of Penguin Books USA Inc.

38 From *Human Nature Magazine* 1 (2), pp. 28, 30–36, February 1978. Copyright © by Human Nature, Inc.

39 Reprinted by permission of the author and publisher from *Beyond Caring: Hospitals, Nurses and the Social Organization of Ethics*, University of Chicago Press. Copyright © 1996. All rights reserved.

40 Jennifer Hunt, *Urban Life*, Vol. 13, No. 4 (January 1985) Copyright © 1985 by Sage Publications, Inc. Reprinted by permission of Sage Publications, Inc.

41 Reprinted by permission, from Kelman and Hamilton, *Crimes of Obedience*, 1989. Yale University Press.

42 From *The McDonaldization of Society* by George Ritzer. Copyright © 1992 by Pine Forge Press. Reprinted by permission of Pine Forge Press.

43 Reprinted by permission of the Lancaster Mennonite Historical Society, from *Pennsylvania Mennonite Heritage*, Vol. 13, No. 3, July 1990.

44 "Not Just Weapons of the Weak" by Laura L. Miller. Reprinted by permission of the author and publisher from *Social Psychology Quarterly*, 60 (1), March 1997, excerpts from various pages. Copyright © 1997 by the American Sociological Association.

45 From *Journal of Contemporary Ethnography*, 24 (3). Copyright ©1995 by Sage Publications. Reprinted by permission.

In Memory of

Erving Goffman
1922–1982

and

William Foote Whyte
1914–2000

Whose Examples Are Our Legacy

Contents

Preface to the Eleventh Edition

Sociology has the marvelous capacity to open new windows of perception on our familiar worlds, leaving no aspect of our lives untouched.

IT IS WITH PLEASURE that I introduce the eleventh edition of *Down to Earth Sociology*, a pleasure akin to seeing a dear friend reach another cheerful milestone in his or her life. Adopters of earlier editions will find themselves at home, I believe, in this latest edition. They will see many selections that they have already used successfully in the classroom, and I trust they will welcome the many newcomers.

Following the suggestions of those who have used earlier editions of *Down to Earth Sociology*, I have strived to continue to present down-to-earth articles in order to make the student's introduction to sociology enjoyable as well as meaningful. These selections narrate the first-hand experiences of their authors—researchers who put a human voice on sociological experiences—those who have "been there" and who, with a minimum of jargon and quantification, insightfully share their experiences with the reader.

Focusing on social interaction in everyday activities and situations, these selections share some of the fascination of sociology. They reflect both the individualistic and the structural emphases of our discipline. They make clear how social structure is not simply an abstract fact of life, but vitally affects our lives. These selections help students become more aware of how the decisions of the rich, the politically powerful, and the bureaucrats provide social constraints that augment those dictated by birth, social class, and other circumstances. They help students understand how their location in a social structure lifts or limits their vision of life, closes or opens their chances of success, and, ultimately, brings tears and laughter, hope and despair.

So much of sociology, however, goes about its business as though data were unconnected to people, as though the world consisted of abstract social facts. Yet from our own experiences in social life, we know how far these suppositions are from the truth—how divorced they are from real life. Consequently, I have sought to include authors who are able to share the realities that directly affect people's lives. As I see it, sociology is the most fascinating of the social sciences, and it is this fascination that these selections are designed to convey.

It is my hope that I have succeeded in accomplishing this goal, because sociology has the marvelous capacity to open new windows of perception on our familiar worlds, leaving no aspect of our lives untouched. If these readings even come close to this goal, I am indebted to the many adopters of earlier editions, whose reactions and suggestions have helped give shape to this one. To all of you, a sincere and fond thank you.

I owe a special debt of gratitude to the instructors who shared with me their experiences with the tenth edition. Their sharing proved invaluable in shaping this present version. I wish to acknowledge the help of

Richard Ambler, Southern Arkansas University
Julie E. Artis, DePaul University
Joe Bishop, Dakota State University
John Bowman, University of North Carolina at Pembroke
Tom Boyd, Berea College
Suzanne Brandon, College of St. Catherine
John C. Bridges, Immaculata College
Grace Budrys, DePaul University
Meryl Cozart, Towson University
Rolf Diamon, University of Southern Maine
Merl Dirksen, Lee University
Robert B. Enright, Jr., University of Wisconsin–Stevens Point
David C. Erickson, Northwest College
Kerry Ferris, Bradley University
Richard Gendron, Assumption College
Frank Glamser, University of Southern Mississippi
Peter R. Grahame, Mount Saint Mary's College
Susan F. Greenwood, University of Maine–Orono
Larry D. Hall, Spring Hill College
Terrell A. Hayes, Davis & Elkins College
Ines W. Jindra, Bethany Lutheran College
Cathryn Johnson, Emory University
Susan L. Johnson, Carl Sandburg College
James W. Jordan, Longwood College
Quintus Joubeve, Rutgers University
Mariame Kaba, Northeastern Illinois University
Meg Wilkes Karraker, University of St. Thomas
Margot Kempers, Fitchburg State College

Marilyn Krogh, Loyola University of Chicago
Anthony Lack, Lee College
Helene M. Lawson, University of Pittsburgh
Bill Lockhart, New Mexico State University
Jerry Lowney, Carroll College
Philip Luck, Georgia State University
Kristin Marsh, Emory University
Tina Martinez, Blue Mountain Community College
R. Robin Miller, Drury University
Sharon L. Miller, Hope College
Janine Minkler, Northern Arizona University
Elizabeth J. Mitchell, Rutgers University
Thomas S. Moore, University of Wisconsin–Milwaukee
Christopher W. Mullins, Southwestern Illinois College
Peter F. Parilla, University of St. Thomas
Kristin Park, Westminster College
Tim Pippert, Augsburg College
Paul-Jahi Price, Pasadena City College
Pam Rosenberg, Gettysburg College
Richard Rubinson, Emory University
Ross T. Runfola, Medaille College
Allen Scarboro, Augusta State University
Richard Senter, Jr., Central Michigan University
Ryan Sheppard, King's College
Rick L. Shifley, Montserrat College of Art
Thomas Soltis, Westmoreland County Community College
Marybeth C. Stalp, University of Georgia
Judith Stepan-Norris, University of California–Irvine
Jordan J. Titus, University of Alaska
Kathy Trosen, Muscatine Community College
Suzanne Tuthill, Delaware Technical and Community College
Judy C. Vaughan, Arkansas Tech University
Anita Veit, University of North Carolina
Abram Lawrence Wehmiller, Greenhill School
Clovis L. White, Oberlin College
Fred Zampa, Macon State College

One of the more interesting tasks in preparing this book is to gather information on the contributors' backgrounds. In addition to biographical data concerning their education, teaching, and publishing, this section also contains their statements telling us why they like sociology or became sociologists. You may want to assign this section with the articles to help personalize the readings and increase the student's awareness of biographical factors that go into the choice to become a sociologist.

The selections in this edition continue to be organized to make them compatible with most introductory textbooks. Through subjects that are inherently interesting, we cover the major substantive areas of sociology. Part I, an introduction to the sociological perspective, invites students to view the world in a new way by participating in this exciting enterprise we call sociology. Part II is designed to answer the basic question of how sociologists do research. Part III examines the cultural underpinnings of social life, those taken-for-granted assumptions and contexts that provide the contours of our everyday lives. Part IV focuses on that essential component of our beings, gender and sexuality. There we look at both the process by which we assume the social identity of male or female and how those identities provide the basis for interaction among adults.

In Part V, we examine social groups and social structure, looking behind the scenes to reveal how people's assumptions, their location on social hierarchies, and the features of social settings establish both constraints and freedoms in human relationships. In Part VI, we consider the process of becoming deviant, especially the social context that shapes deviance. We also examine features of social control, those aspects of social groups that are designed to minimize deviance. In Part VII, we focus on social stratification, beginning with the micro level of physical appearance and then looking at gender, race–ethnicity, poverty, education, wealth, and power as dimensions of social inequality. In Part VIII, we analyze the social institutions of economics, politics, education, sports, marriage and family, religion, medicine, law, and the military. In this edition, we add an analysis of the mass media, examining how they influence our ideas and behavior. We conclude the book with a look at social change, the focus of Part IX. After examining how everyday life is being rationalized in a process called McDonaldization, we look at resistance to social change—how the Amish withdraw from mainstream society and how male soldiers undermine the integration of women in the military. We then conclude the book with a look at how people adjust to the aftermath of a hurricane.

These selections bring the reader face-to-face with the dual emphases of contemporary sociological research: the focus on the individual's experiences, and the analysis of social structure. Uncovering the basic expectations that underlie routine social interactions, these articles emphasize the ways in which social institutions are interrelated. It is to their authors' credit that we lose sight of neither the people who are interacting nor the structural base that so directly influences the form and content of their interactions.

J.M.H.
November 2000

About the Contributors

Elijah Anderson (article 23) received his Ph.D. in Sociology at Northwestern University and is the Charles and William Day Professor of Social Sciences at the University of Pennsylvania. He is the author of *A Place on the Corner: Identity and Rank Among Black Streetcorner Men; Streetwise: Race, Class, and Change in an Urban Community;* and *Code of the Street: Decency, Violence and the Moral Life of the Inner City,* the book from which his selection is taken.

Anderson says, "I have always been interested in how individuals relate to society and how society relates to the individual. My interest in the social conditions that people experience—especially the marginality that so many blacks feel and how they relate to the wider social system—motivated me to go into sociology to look for some of the answers. I also had good teachers who inspired me. Later I found myself wanting to contribute in a meaningful way to correcting what I saw to be misrepresentations of reality in the academic literature about people who live in ghettos."

Linda Liske Belgrave (article 45), who earned her Ph.D. from Case Western Reserve University, is Associate Professor of Sociology at the University of Miami. Using a qualitative approach, she has published in sociology journals, primarily on gerontology, health care, and collective behavior.

Belgrave took her first course in sociology because "the pickings were slim, and sociology happened to fit my schedule. I was an older student, with a family and a job, and sociology addressed important issues in a way that 'rang true.' Sociology opened new worlds, and it felt 'like coming home.' Before the quarter was over, I was hooked, and I immediately changed my major to sociology. Without ever having said, 'I want to be a sociologist,' I found that I became one." Belgrave, a political activist, is also a ballet student.

Peter L. Berger (article 1) received his Ph.D. in Sociology from the New School for Social Research. He is Professor of Sociology at Boston University and the author of numerous books, including *Business and Democracy: Cohabitation or Contradiction?* (with Ann Bernstein), *A Far Glory: The Quest for Faith in an Age of Credulity,* and *Invitation to Sociology,* from which his selection in this book is taken.

Berger says, "I was born in Austria and came to the United States with my parents after the war. You might say that I became a sociologist by accident. I took some courses in sociology and liked them. I have always been curious about what makes people tick, and that is what sociology is all about."

Mae A. Biggs (article 18) earned her M.A. in Sociology at Southern Illinois University Edwardsville and is an associate of the Masters-Johnson Institute (Biological Research Institute) in St. Louis, Missouri.

Theodore Caplow (article 10) earned his Ph.D. in Sociology at the University of Minnesota. He is Professor of Sociology at the University of Virginia. Among his books are *The Academic Marketplace* (with Reece McGee), *The First Measured Century: An Illustrated Guide to Trends in America 1900– 2000,* and *Middletown Families: Fifty Years of Change and Continuity* (with Howard Bahr, Bruce Chadwick, Reuben Hill, and Margaret Williamson).

Caplow says, "As an undergraduate at Columbia, I planned to become a historian. But a friend invited me to sit in on a course he was taking with Professor Robert Lynd, and I was captivated. Years later, I followed his footsteps to Middletown."

Napoleon A. Chagnon (article 8) earned his Ph.D. in Anthropology at the University of Michigan. He is Professor of Anthropology at the University of California at Santa Barbara and the author of *Yąnomamö: The Last Days of Eden; Yąnomamö Warfare, Social Organization and Marriage Alliances;* and the book from which his selection is taken, *Yąnomamö: The Fierce People.*

Daniel F. Chambliss (article 39), who received his Ph.D. from Yale University, is Sidney Wertimer Professor at Hamilton College. He has published *Champions: The Making of Olympic Swimmers* and *Beyond Caring: Hospitals, Nurses, and the Social Organization of Ethics,* the book from which his selection is adapted.

Chambliss, who does management consulting, also loves to coach competitive swimmers. He says, "Sociology was intellectually the freest discipline I encountered in college. You could study math or philosophy or psychology and apply them all in sociology. It is the broadest of the social sciences. There are no artificial limits."

William J. Chambliss (article 24) received his Ph.D in Sociology at Indiana University and is Professor of Sociology at George Washington University. His books include *On the Take: From Petty Crooks to Presidents, Law, Order and Power,* and *Power, Politics, and Crime.* Professor Chambliss is a past President of the American Society of Criminology (1987–88) and a past President of the Society for the Study of Social Problems (1992–93).

Chambliss says, "I became a sociologist out of an interest in doing something about crime. I remained a sociologist because it became clear to me that until we have a greater understanding of the political and economic conditions that lead some societies to have excessive amounts of crime we will never be able to do anything about the problem. Sociology is a beautiful discipline that affords an opportunity to investigate just about anything connected with human behavior and still claim an identity with a discipline. This is its strength, its promise, and why I find it thoroughly engaging, enjoyable, and fulfilling."

John R. Coleman (article 19) was the President of Haverford College from 1967 to 1977 and then President of the Edna McConnell Clark Foundation in New York City. He has decided to try his hand at business and now runs "The Inn at Long Last" in Chester, Vermont.

Kingsley Davis (article 12) received his Ph.D. in Sociology at Harvard University and is Distinguished Professor of Sociology at the University of Southern California and Senior Research Fellow at the Hoover Institution on War, Revolution and Peace at Stanford University. His books include *Human Society, The Population of India and Pakistan,* and *Below-Replacement Fertility in Industrial Societies: Causes, Consequences, Policy.*

Davis, who often travels to remote places on the globe, likes sociology because "first, sociology deals with all aspects of society, not just economic behavior or political matters; second, in regard to social change, sociology takes a longer view than most other social science fields. I became a sociologist because I wanted to write and decided that I had better learn something to write, so I elected to learn sociology. Also, I wanted to know how the social system works. We were in the Great Depression at the time, so a social science should be able to analyze and explain that terrible catastrophe."

Donna Eder (article 14), who earned her Ph.D. in Sociology at the University of Wisconsin, is Professor of Sociology at Indiana University. She has written *School Talk: Gender and Adolescent Culture,* the book from which her selection is taken.

Barbara Ehrenreich (article 33) is a freelance writer and political satirist who has published widely. Her books include *Debating P.C.: The Controversy over Political Correctness on College Campuses; Blood Rites: Origins and History of the Passions of War;* and *Fear of Falling: The Inner Life of the Middle Class.*

Kai Erikson (article 20) was awarded a Ph.D. in Sociology at the University of Chicago. He is Professor of Sociology at Yale University. Among his books are *Wayward Puritans, A New Species of Trouble: Explorations in Disaster, Trauma, and Community,* and *Everything in Its Path: The Destruction of Community in the Buffalo Creek Flood.*

Douglas E. Foley (article 35) received his Ph.D. in Anthropology of Education at Stanford University and is Professor of Anthropology at the University of Texas. He is the author of *From Peones to Politicos: Class and Ethnicity in a South Texas Town, 1900–1987, Learning Capitalist Culture: Deep in the Heart of Tejas,* and (with Aurolyn Luykx) *The Citizen Factory: Schooling and Cultural Production in Bolivia.*

Foley says that he likes to write cultural critiques of American society, with the hope of changing it, of helping to make it more egalitarian and humane.

Annette Fuentes (article 33) is the author (with Barbara Ehrenreich) of *Women in the Global Factory.*

Herbert J. Gans (article 30) received his Ph.D. in City Planning and Sociology from the University of Pennsylvania. He is Robert S. Lynd Professor of Sociology at Columbia University and has written such books as *The Urban Villagers; The War against the Poor: The Underclass and Antipoverty Policy;* and *Popular Culture and High Culture: An Analysis and Evaluation of Taste.* Professor Gans is a past President of the American Sociological Association (1987–88).

Gans "finds sociology more interesting than hobbies." He says: "When I was in high school, I thought I would become a journalist, but then when I got to college I discovered that the articles I enjoyed writing most were sociology. From then on I was pretty sure I would become a sociologist." He adds, "The deeper reason I became a sociologist is because I am a refugee from Nazi Germany, and ever since I came to the United States as a teenager in 1940, I have been trying to understand the country which took me in." Whenever possible—and his family agrees—Gans rents an apartment for a month in a European city or medieval town and "explores it, living in it fully."

Erving Goffman (article 11) earned his Ph.D. in Sociology at the University of Chicago and at the time of his death in 1982 was Director of the Center for Urban Ethnography at the University of Pennsylvania. His many books include

Stigma; Behavior in Public Places; and the book from which his selection is taken, *The Presentation of Self in Everyday Life.*

Harry L. Gracey (article 34) received his Ph.D. in Sociology at the New School for Social Research. He is in private practice in organizational development in Cambridge, Massachusetts, and has published *Curriculum or Craftsmanship?: The Dilemma of the Teacher in the Bureaucratic System* and *Readings in Introductory Sociology* (with Dennis H. Wrong).

Gracey says, "What led me to study sociology was a curiosity about how things work, which in my case got focused on the world of social life, rather than on the physical or biological world. Sociology, uniquely among the social sciences, I think, 'lifts the veil of ideology' on the working of society to see what is really going on—and who is doing it and how it is being done."

Edward T. Hall (article 9) was awarded his Ph.D. at Columbia University. He is Emeritus Professor of Anthropology at Northwestern University. His books include *The Silent Language, The Hidden Dimension,* and *The Dance of Life: The Other Dimension of Time.*

Mildred R. Hall (article 9) received her B.A. from Barnard College and (with Edward T. Hall) has written *The Fourth Dimension in Architecture; Hidden Differences: Doing Business with the Japenese;* and *Understanding Cultural Differences.*

V. Lee Hamilton (article 41), who received her Ph.D. in Social Psychology in the Department of Social Relations at Harvard University, is Professor of Sociology at the University of Maryland. She has published *Crimes of Obedience: Toward a Social Psychology of Authority and Responsibility* (with Herbert Kelman), *Everyday Justice: Responsibility and the Individual in Japan and the United States,* and *Social Psychological Approaches to Responsibility and Justice: The View Across Cultures.*

Hamilton says: "My undergraduate degree was in psychology, but my graduate program was interdisciplinary. After I completed the Ph.D., I could have gone into psychology or sociology, and I chose sociology because of its structural emphasis. I like sociology because it is a perspective—the way a person thinks—and I tend to think that way." Some of Hamilton's favorite activities are hiking and travel.

Marvin Harris (article 38) received his Ph.D. from Columbia University. He is Professor of Anthropology at the University of Florida. Following his primary interest, cultural anthropology, Harris searches for the practical reasons that underly customs that on the surface seem unreasonable or even bizarre. His numerous writings include *Cows, Pigs, Wars, and Witches: The Riddles of*

Culture; Cannibals and Kings: The Origins of Cultures; and *Theories of Culture in Postmodern Times.*

James M. Henslin (articles 2, 4, 13, 18, and 22) earned his Ph.D. in Sociology at Washington University in St. Louis. He is Professor Emeritus of Sociology at Southern Illinois University Edwardsville. His books include *Social Problems; Sociology: A Down-to-Earth Approach;* and *Essentials of Sociology: A Down-to-Earth Approach.*

Henslin says, "My early childhood was marked by poverty. I was born in a rented room in a minister's parsonage. Then my parents made a leap in their economic status—we moved into our own home, a converted garage, with no running water or indoor plumbing! My parents continued their climb in status, and when I was thirteen they built one of the nicest houses in town. These experiences helped make me keenly aware of the significance of 'place' and opportunity in social life." He adds, "I like sociology because of its tremendous breadth—from social class and international stratification to the self and internal conflicts. No matter how diverse your curiosities, you can follow them and they are still part of sociology. Everything that is part of the landscape of human behavior comes under the lens of sociology."

Stephen Higley (article 32) received his Ph.D. in Geography from the University of Illinois at Urbana-Champaign. He is Associate Professor of Geography at the University of Montevallo. Higley wrote *Privilege, Power, and Race: The Geography of the American Upper Class,* the book from which his selection is taken.

As an urban social geographer, Higley's approach to geography is close to sociology. He stresses the consequences of the stratification (or geographical structure) of U.S. metropolitan areas on school systems, public amenities, social services, and even for stereotyping people from different social classes. He says, "The upper class has the means and the influence to create a distinct style of life that minimizes their contact with other social classes. One of the most important vehicles for this separation is where they live and how they control it (of course, with the help of the upper middle class)."

Arlie Hochschild (article 37) received her Ph.D. in Sociology from the University of California, Berkeley, where she is now Professor of Sociology. She has published *The Managed Heart: Commercialization of Human Feeling; The Time Bind: When Work Becomes Home and Home Becomes Work;* and *The Second Shift: Inside the Two-Job Marriage;* the book from which her selection is taken.

Hochschild says, "I majored in international relations at Swarthmore College (a combination of history, economics, and political science) in the early sixties when my college had no sociology department. By chance I discovered David Riesman's *The Lonely Crowd,* his *Individualism Reconsidered,* and C. Wright Mills' *People, Politics and Power.* It was between the covers of these exciting books that I decided that there was a powerful lens through which to see the world—and I wanted to get on the other side of it."

Robert A. Hummer (article 28), who received his Ph.D. from Florida State University, is Assistant Professor in the Department of Sociology at the University of Texas, Austin. He has published (with Richard Rogers and Charles Nam) *Living and Dying in the U.S.A.: Behavioral, Health, and Social Differentials of Adult Mortality.*

Hummer says he became a sociologist because "sociology provides me a better way of understanding the complex world in which I live." He enjoys traveling with his wife and daughter, fishing, and watching the Detroit Tigers.

Jennifer Hunt (article 40) received her Ph.D. in Sociology from the City University of New York and is Associate Professor of Sociology at Montclair State University. She is also a research candidate in the clinical training program at the Psychoanalytic Institute at the New York University Medical Center.

Hunt has written *Psychoanalytic Aspects of Fieldwork.* She likes sociology because "it provides an unusual opportunity to explore other cultural worlds by doing in-depth fieldwork."

Sidney Katz (article 27), who earned a Bachelor in Social Sciences from Carleton University and a Master of Social Work at the University of Toronto, is a professional writer. He has published hundreds of articles and two books and has done considerable radio and TV broadcasting. He has been a columnist, a feature writer, and an editor at the *Toronto Star* and at *Maclean's Magazine.* He says, "I have retired several times, but it hasn't stuck."

Herbert Kelman (article 41), who received his Ph.D. in psychology from Yale University, is Richard Clarke Cabot Professor of Social Ethics at Harvard University. His books include *International Behavior: A Social-Psychological Analysis; A Time to Speak: On Human Values and Social Research;* and the book from which his selection is taken, *Crimes of Obedience: Toward a Social Psychology of Authority and Responsibility* (with V. Lee Hamilton).

Kelman says, "I was trained in psychology, but I was a social activist before I became a scholar. I like sociology because of the perspective it brings to issues in peace, justice, and social change. Outside of my work in civil rights, peace, and human rights, I like folk dancing. I also enjoy listening to ethnic music and music from the Middle Ages."

Jean Kilbourne (article 36) received her Ed.D. from Boston University, with a focus on Humanistic and Behavioral Studies. As a lecturer, media critic, filmmaker, and writer, she travels around the country giving lectures on college campuses and for conferences and organizations. She is the author of *Can't*

Buy My Love: How Advertising Changes the Way We Think and Feel (originally published as *Deadly Persuasion: Why Women and Girls Must Fight the Addictive Power of Advertising.*)

Kilbourne says that she "has always enjoyed sociology because it helps us to see how utterly similar and how completely unique human beings are. I've always been interested in understanding what makes us tick, individually and in communities and societies. I may have been the first person to examine the image of women in advertising and the advertising of alcohol and tobacco." Kilbourne, who is an avid reader of fiction, poetry, and mysteries, lives in Boston with her 13-year-old daughter. They enjoy bike-riding, rollerblading, skiing, and traveling.

Jonathan Kozol (article 31) received a B.A. at Harvard University. After teaching in the public schools for several years, he became a professional author. His books include *Death at an Early Age, Ordinary Resurrections,* and *Savage Inequalities: Children in America's Schools,* the book from which his selection is adapted.

He says that he is interested in exposing the injustices that affect children.

Helene M. Lawson (article 17) earned her Ph.D. at Loyola University. She is Associate Professor of Sociology at Brandeis University. She has written *Ladies on the Lot: Women, Car Sales, and the Pursuit of the American Dream,* the book from which her selection is taken.

Lawson says, "I decided to become a sociologist after getting a B.A. in Elementary Education and two M.A. degrees, one in Early Childhood and one in Gerontology. I was teaching people about human behavior, but I was not content with the explanations I gained from psychology, biology, or education. There was so much unhappiness. Sociology gave me a broader view of social institutions and the motivations for individual behavior, and, through its encompassing view of human institutions, even a vision of progress in which I find hope." Lawson's interests are broad, and, as she says, "My writings range from stories about gender equality in blue-collar families to what it's like to work on hair, and even the interactions of conservation officers with hunted animals." She is now doing research on the world of Internet courtship.

Zella Luria (article 15) received her Ph.D. in Psychology at Indiana University and is Professor of Psychology at Tufts University. She is the author of *The Psychology of Human Sexuality* (with Mitchel D. Rose) and *Human Sexuality* (with S. Friedman and Mitchel D. Rose).

Luria says, "What I appreciate about sociology is its exquisite attention to the group context for explanations of behavior."

Anne Machung (article 37), who works as an editor for a publishing firm, also does free-lance writing.

Joseph Marolla (article 5) earned his Ph.D. in Sociology at the University of Denver. He is Associate Professor of Sociology at Virginia Commonwealth University. He has published articles in social psychology, criminology, sociology of education, symbolic interaction, and self-esteem.

Marolla says, "I suppose, as much as anything else, I became a sociologist because my draft lottery number was 315 in the winter of 1969—which meant that I would not be going to Vietnam. At the time, I had given very little thought to life beyond the war. Once handed the option, school seemed the reasonable thing to do since I had been doing it for a while. I was an English major, and I moved to sociology because I thought it would broaden my creative writing. . . . What I most like about sociology is that it provides a broad picture and helps us see through the facade of life as we live it. This was appealing to me, and still is. Our research on rape is an example. Psychologists are convinced that rape is due to psychological dysfunction. We have demonstrated that rape is dramatically embedded in the culture."

Patricia Yancey Martin (article 28), who received her Ph.D. from Florida State University, is Professor of Sociology at Florida State University. Her books include *Feminist Organizations* (with Myra M. Ferree) and *The Social Environment* (with Gerald O'Connor).

Martin, whose favorite activity outside of teaching, gardening, and the arts, is traveling to Europe, says that she majored in English literature, but didn't like it enough to pursue it after the bachelor's degree. She thought she might be interested in sociology, and tried graduate school. "After I was in sociology a few years," she says, "I came to see the power of the sociological perspective." She adds, "I love trying to observe and explain the social world around me."

Philip Meyer (article 21) earned an M.A. in Political Science at the University of North Carolina, where he is now Professor of Journalism. His books include *The New Precision Journalism* and *Ethical Journalism: A Guide for Students, Practitioners, and Consumers,* and he has edited (with Edmund Tambeth and Esther Thorson) *Assessing Public Journalism.*

Laura L. Miller (article 44), who received her Ph.D. from Northwestern University, is Assistant Professor of Sociology at the University of California at Los Angeles. In addition to articles, she also has published *New Opportunities for Military Women: Effects Upon Readiness, Cohesion, and Morale* (with Margaret C. Harrell).

Miller, whose primary focus is human relations in the military, has done research on peacekeeping operations in Somalia, Macedonia, Haiti, and Bosnia. She also enjoys snowboarding, international travel, live music, and playing at the beach. She says, "In college I was interested in so many different subjects. Sociology was the answer for me, because as a sociologist I can study anything I want and never have to change jobs."

C. Wright Mills (article 3) received his Ph.D. in Sociology from the University of Wisconsin. His scathing criticisms of American society in such books as *White Collar, The Causes of World War III,* as well as the book from which his article is taken, *The Sociological Imagination,* made him one of the most controversial sociologists in the United States. At the time of his death in 1962, he was Professor of Sociology at Columbia University.

Horace Miner (article 7) earned his Ph.D. in Social Anthropology at the University of Chicago. He is Professor Emeritus of Anthropology at the University of Michigan. His books include *The Primitive City in Timbuctoo, St. Denis: A French Canadian Parish,* and *The City in Modern Africa.*

Miner says, "It was by accident that I became a sociologist. Having received my degree in social anthropology, it was easy to teach sociology when I received an offer. My courses were listed in both anthropology and sociology."

Clarence Page (article 29) is the editor of *A Foot in Each World: Essays and Articles* (with Leanita McClain), and the author of *Freedom's Champion: Elijah Lovejoy* (with Paul Simon) and *Showing My Color: Impolite Essays on Race and Identity,* the book from which his selection is taken.

Page says, "My interest in sociology dates back to my high school years. It is grounded in the same curiosity that informed my book of essays on race." He adds, "I like sociology because it tries to analyze and explain the group behaviors, attitudes, and relationships that raise the sort of questions I try to answer in my book."

George Ritzer (article 42), who received his Ph.D. from Cornell University, is Professor of Sociology at the University of Maryland. His books include *Expressing America: A Critique of the Global Credit Card Society; Sociological Theory,* and *The McDonaldization of Society: An Investigation into the Changing Character of Contemporary Life,* the book from which his selection is taken.

Ritzer says, "I became a sociologist because sociology offers me a variety of intellectual tools that allow me to better understand the wonderful complexity of social life." He especially enjoys the beach and long walks almost anywhere. Like many sociologists, his academic and personal lives blend into one another, making it difficult to know where one ends and the other begins.

David L. Rosenhan (article 26), who received his Ph.D. in Psychology from Columbia University, is Professor of Psychology and Law at Stanford University. His books include *Foundations of Abnormal Psychology* (with P. London), *Theory and Research in Abnormal Psychology,* and (with Martin Seligman and Elaine Walker) *Abnormal Psychology.*

Jerry Savells (article 43) received his Ph.D. in Sociology at Louisiana State University. He is Professor of Sociology at Wright State University. He has edited *The Changing Family: Making Way for Tomorrow* and *Marriage and the Family in a Changing Society* (both with Larry Cross).

Savells, whose favorite activity outside of teaching and doing sociology is fishing, earned his bachelor's degree in chemistry and biology at Murray State University. He says, "After working for a few years, I found the chemistry laboratory too confining. I decided that I wanted to move into an area where I could have more impact on people, and I returned to graduate school and studied sociology. I also served as an officer in the army, where I did some teaching, and thought that I would like to teach in an academic setting. I am fascinated with human behavior, with how people get together in social groups, and I have focused on families, especially on how families respond to social change."

Diana Scully (article 5) earned her Ph.D. in Sociology at the University of Illinois. She is Professor of Sociology and Coordinator of Women's Studies at Virginia Commonwealth University. She has written *Understanding Sexual Violence: A Study of Convicted Rapists* and *Men Who Control Women's Health: The Miseducation of Obstetrician Gynecologists.*

Scully says, "I changed my undergraduate major to sociology on the day that Martin Luther King was assassinated. I felt then and continue to believe that because of its focus on social structure sociology has a greater potential than other disciplines for understanding complex problems, such as racism and sexism, and therefore can be used as a tool for accomplishing change that is meaningful collectively and individually."

Kenneth J. Smith (article 45), who received his Ph.D. from Duke University, is Associate Professor of Sociology at the University of Miami. He has published articles in sociology on qualitative methods, mental illness, and collective behavior.

Smith says, "I was an undergraduate during the civil rights period and a graduate student during the Vietnam years. Sociology addressed the burning issues of the time. My 'left-Christian-peace-and-justice' background also influenced my decision to be a sociologist. Ultimately the purpose of sociology and the obligation of sociologists (as well as everyone else) is to improve the human condition. Becoming a sociologist is a decision I've never regretted." An active member in church and secular organizations devoted to human rights, Smith shares his sons' interests in sports cars and motorcycles.

Deborah Tannen (article 16) earned a Ph.D. in English literature at the University of California at Berkeley. After teaching English at several universities in the U.S. and Greece, she joined the Linguistics Department at Georgetown University, where she is University Professor. Her books include

Talking from 9 to 5; You Just Don't Understand: Women and Men in Conversation; and *The Argument Culture: Stopping America's War of Words.*

Barrie Thorne (article 15) earned her Ph.D. in Sociology at Brandeis University. She is Professor of Sociology and of Women's Studies at the University of California at Berkeley. Thorne is the author of *Gender Play: Girls and Boys in School,* and (with Barbara Laslett) the editor of *Feminist Sociology: Life Histories of a Movement,* and *Language, Gender and Society.*

William Foote Whyte (article 6), after earning his Ph.D. in sociology at the University of Chicago, taught at Cornell University, where he was Professor Emeritus of Industrial and Labor Relations at the time of his death in 2000. He published widely, with *Participant Observer: An Autobiography* and *Creative Problem Solving in the Field: Reflections on a Career* appearing shortly before his death. He is best known for *Street Corner Society,* the book from which his selection is taken.

Whyte said, "Sociology interested me as a way to advance my understanding of groups, organizations, and interorganization relations—and to see if I could find ways to contribute to social and economic development. Sociology has given me wide opportunities to engage in social exploration at home, in Canada, Latin America, and Spain. I have traveled extensively through Mexico and Central America, as well as brief visits to England, Switzerland, Italy, Israel, Japan, and China. I have spent two sabbatical years in Venezuela and Peru." Whyte added, "My favorite hobby up to age twenty-nine was playing tennis. An attack of polio ruled that out, but I have continued to travel until recently. Now, at age seventy-nine, my work and my hobby are the same: writing."

Philip G. Zimbardo (article 25) earned his Ph.D. in Social Psychology at Yale University and is Professor of Social Psychology at Stanford University. His books include *Psychology and Life* (with Shirley Radl), *The Shy Child: A Parent's Guide to Overcoming Shyness from Infancy to Adulthood,* and (with Michael R. Leippe) *The Psychology of Attitude Change.*

Zimbardo, who has taught in Italy and enjoys collecting and studying the arts and crafts of the Native Americans of the Northwest and Southwest, says that he likes sociology because of "the scope of the significant questions it raises about human behavior."

PART I   The Sociological Perspective

Sociology is an invitation to look behind the scenes of the social world—a passport, as it were, to a different way of viewing life.

I WOULD LIKE TO BEGIN this first introduction on a personal note. Since my early school days, reading has been one of my favorite pastimes. I used to read almost anything I could lay my hands on, but I was especially fascinated by books that explored people's lives—especially novels that described their life situations, thoughts, relationships, hopes and dreams, challenges and obstacles. Without knowing it, I was gaining an appreciation for understanding the social context in which people live out their lives—for seeing how important that context is in determining what people are like.

When I went to college, I discovered that there was a name for my interests: *sociology*. What an exciting revelation: I had found an entire academic discipline centered on understanding the general context in which people live and analyzing how their lives are influenced by it! I could not help wanting to read sociology, to take more courses, to immerse myself in it. I was hooked—so thoroughly, in fact, that eventually I decided to become a sociologist and spend my life in this fascinating endeavor.

The intention of this book is fourfold. First, I want to share some of the excitement and fascination of sociology. Then, through these readings, I want to make more visible the context of social life that affects us all. Third, if this is successful, you will gain a better understanding not only of people in general, but of your own self as well. Finally, I hope to whet your appetite for more sociology.

As Peter Berger says in the opening selection, the discovery of sociology can change your life. It can help you to understand the social forces you confront, the forces that constrain and free you as you go about living your life. This understanding offers a liberating potential: To gain insight into how these social forces influence your life allows you to stand somewhat apart from at

1

least some of them, and thereby to exert more creative control over your own life.

But just what is sociology? In my teaching I have found that introductory students often find this a vexing question. To provide a better grasp of what sociology is, then, in the second selection I compare sociology with the other social sciences. One of the main points of this article is that sociology casts an intellectual net that provides an unparalleled approach to understanding social life.

In the third and last article in this Part, C. Wright Mills turns again to this liberating potential that sociology offers. As he points out, this capacity centers on understanding three main issues: (1) the structure of society—that is, how the essential components of society are interrelated; (2) where one's society stands in human history and the changes that are occurring in it; and 3) what type of people prevail in one's society, how they are selected for prevalence, and what types are coming to prevail.

Thinking of life in these terms, says Mills, is a quality of mind that we should strive for. This "sociological imagination," to use his term for the sociological perspective, allows us to peer beyond our immediate confines, to seek out and understand the broader social and historical forces at work in our lives. One of the rewarding consequences of this perspective, he says, is that it enables us to see ourselves in a different light.

It is the goal of this first Part, then, to let you dip your feet in the sociological waters, to challenge you to venture into sociology, and, while venturing, to stimulate your sociological imagination.

1   Invitation to Sociology

PETER L. BERGER

Motivated by an intense desire to know what is "really happening," what goes on "behind the scenes," sociologists study almost every aspect of life in society. As Berger indicates, nothing is too sacred or too profane to be spared the sociologist's scrutiny. But when you penetrate the surface and peer behind the masks that individuals and organizations wear, you find a reality quite unlike the one that is so carefully devised and, just as carefully, put forward for public consumption.

This changed angle of vision, however, is dangerous, for once you have peered behind the scenes and viewed life in a new light, it is nearly impossible to revert to complacent assumptions. The old, familiar, and so very comfortable ways of looking at life become upset when your angle of vision changes. This potential of sociology, of course, is also part of its attraction.

THE SOCIOLOGIST (that is, the one we would really like to invite to our game) is a person intensively, endlessly, shamelessly interested in the doings of men. His* natural habitat is all the human gathering places of the world, wherever men come together. The sociologist may be interested in many other things. But his consuming interest remains in the world of men, their institutions, their history, their passions. And since he is interested in men, nothing that men do can be altogether tedious for him. He will naturally be interested in the events that engage men's ultimate beliefs, their moments of tragedy and grandeur and ecstasy. But he will also be fascinated by the commonplace, the everyday. He will know reverence, but this reverence will not prevent him from wanting to see and to understand. He may sometimes feel revulsion or contempt. But this also will not deter him from wanting to have his questions answered. The sociologist, in his quest for understanding, moves through the world of men without respect for the usual lines of demarcation. Nobility and degradation, power and obscurity, intelligence and folly—these are equally *interesting* to him, however unequal they may be in his personal values or tastes. Thus his questions may lead him to all possible levels of

---

*In this and a couple of other selections written before stylistic changes occurred in our language, "he," "his," "him," "himself," "man," "world of men," and so on, are generic, referring to both males and females. Although the linguistic style is outdated, the ideas are not.—Ed.

3

society, the best and the least known places, the most respected and the most despised. And, if he is a good sociologist, he will find himself in all these places because his own questions have so taken possession of him that he has little choice but to seek for answers.

It would be possible to say the same things in a lower key. We could say that the sociologist, but for the grace of his academic title, is the man who must listen to gossip despite himself, who is tempted to look through keyholes, to read other people's mail, to open cabinets. Before some otherwise unoccupied psychologist sets out now to construct an aptitude test for sociologists on the basis of sublimated voyeurism, let us quickly say that we are speaking merely by way of analogy. Perhaps some little boys consumed with curiosity to watch their maiden aunts in the bathroom later become inveterate sociologists. This is quite uninteresting. What interests us is the curiosity that grips any sociologist in front of a closed door behind which there are human voices. If he is a good sociologist he will want to open that door, to understand these voices. Behind each closed door he will anticipate some new facet of human life not yet perceived and understood.

The sociologist will occupy himself with matters that others regard as too sacred or as too distasteful for dispassionate investigation. He will find rewarding the company of priests or of prostitutes, depending not on his personal preferences but on the questions he happens to be asking at the moment. He will also concern himself with matters that others may find much too boring. He will be interested in the human interaction that goes with warfare or with great intellectual discoveries, but also in the relations between people employed in a restaurant or between a group of little girls playing with their dolls. His main focus of attention is not the ultimate significance of what men do, but the action in itself, as another example of the infinite richness of human conduct.

In these journeys through the world of men the sociologist will inevitably encounter other professional Peeping Toms. Sometimes these will resent his presence, feeling that he is poaching on their preserves. In some places the sociologist will meet up with the economist, in others with the political scientist, in yet others with the psychologist or the ethnologist. Yet chances are that the questions that have brought him to these places are different from the ones that propelled his fellow-trespassers. The sociologist's questions always remain essentially the same: "What are people doing with each other here?" "What are their relationships to each other?" "How are these relationships organized in institutions?" "What are the collective ideas that move men and institutions?" In trying to answer these questions in specific instances, the sociologist will, of course, have to deal with economic or political matters, but he will do so in a way rather different from that of the economist or the political scientist. The scene that he contemplates is the same human scene that these other scientists concern themselves with. But the sociologist's angle of vision is different. When this is understood, it becomes clear that it makes little sense to try to stake out a special enclave within which the sociologist will carry on business in his own right. Like Wesley the sociologist will have to confess that his parish is the world. But unlike some latter-day Wesleyans he will gladly share this parish with others. There is, however, one traveler whose path the sociologist will cross more often than anyone else's on his journeys. This is the historian. Indeed, as soon as the sociologist turns from the present to the past, his preoccupations are very hard indeed to distinguish from those of the historian. [T]he sociological journey will be much impoverished unless it is punctuated frequently by conversation with that other particular traveler.

Any intellectual activity derives excitement from the moment it becomes a trail of discovery. . . . The excitement of sociology is [not always to penetrate] into worlds that had previously been quite unknown . . . for instance, the world of crime, or the world of some bizarre religious sect, or the world fashioned by the exclusive concerns of some group such as medical specialists or military leaders or advertising executives. [M]uch of the time the sociologist moves in sectors of experience that are familiar to him and to most people in his society. He investigates communities, institutions, and activities that one can read about every day in the newspapers. Yet there is another excitement of discovery beckoning in his investigations. It is not the excitement of finding the familiar becoming transformed in its meaning. The fascination of sociology lies in the fact that its perspective makes us see in a new light the very world in which we have lived all of our lives. This also constitutes a transformation of consciousness. Moreover, this transformation is more relevant existentially than that of many other intellectual disciplines, because it is more difficult to segregate in some special compartment of the mind. The astronomer does not live in the remote galaxies, and the nuclear physicist can, outside his laboratory, eat and laugh and marry and vote without thinking about the insides of the atom. The geologist looks at rocks only at appropriate times, and the linguist speaks English with his wife. The sociologist lives in society, on the job and off it. His own life, inevitably, is part of his subject matter. Men being what they are, sociologists too manage to segregate their professional insights from their everyday affairs. But it is a rather difficult feat to perform in good faith.

The sociologist moves in the common world of men, close to what most of them would call real. The categories he employs in his analyses are only refinements of the categories by which other men live—power, class, status, race, ethnicity. As a result, there is a deceptive simplicity and obviousness about some sociological investigations. One reads them, nods at the familiar scene, remarks that one has heard all this before and don't people have better things to do than to waste their time on truisms—until one is suddenly brought up against an insight that radically questions everything one had previously assumed about this familiar scene. This is the point at which one begins to sense the excitement of sociology.

Let us take a specific example. Imagine a sociology class in a Southern college where almost all the students are white Southerners. Imagine a lecture on the subject of the racial system of the South. The lecturer is talking here of matters that have been familiar to his students from the time of their infancy. Indeed, it may be that they are much more familiar with the minutiae of this system than he is. They are quite bored as a result. It seems to them that he is only using more pretentious words to describe what they already know. Thus he may use the term "caste," one commonly used now by American sociologists to describe the Southern racial system. But in explaining the term he shifts to traditional Hindu society, to make it clearer. He then goes on to analyze the magical beliefs inherent in caste tabus, the social dynamics of commensalism and connubium, the economic interests concealed within the system, the way in which religious beliefs relate to the tabus, the effects of the caste system upon the industrial development of the society and vice versa—all in India. But suddenly India is not very far away at all. The lecture then goes back to its Southern theme. The familiar now seems not quite so familiar any more. Questions are raised that are new, perhaps raised angrily, but raised all the same. And at least some of the students have begun to understand that there are functions involved in this business of race that they have not read about in the newspapers (at least not those in their hometowns) and that their parents have not told them—partly, at least, because neither the newspapers nor the parents knew about them.

It can be said that the first wisdom of sociology is this—things are not what they seem. This too is a deceptively simple statement. It ceases to be simple after a while. Social reality turns out to have many layers of meaning. The discovery of each new layer changes the perception of the whole.

Anthropologists use the term "culture shock" to describe the impact of a totally new culture upon a newcomer. In an extreme instance such shock will be experienced by the Western explorer who is told, halfway through dinner, that he is eating the nice old lady he had been chatting with the previous day—a shock with predictable physiological if not moral consequences. Most explorers no longer encounter cannibalism in their travels today. However, the first encounters with polygamy or with puberty rites or even with the way some nations drive their automobiles can be quite a shock to an American visitor. With the shock may go not only disapproval or disgust but a sense of excitement that things can *really* be that different from what they are at home. To some extent, at least, this is the excitement of any first travel abroad. The experience of sociological discovery could be described as "culture shock" minus geographical displacement. In other words, the sociologist travels at home—with shocking results. He is unlikely to find that he is eating a nice old lady for dinner. But the discovery, for instance, that his own church has considerable money invested in the missile industry or that a few blocks from his home there are people who engage in cultic orgies may not be drastically different in emotional impact. Yet we would not want to imply that sociological discoveries are always or even usually outrageous to moral sentiment. Not at all. What they have in common with exploration in distant lands, however, is the sudden illumination of new and unsuspected facets of human existence in society. . . .

People who like to avoid shocking discoveries, who prefer to believe that society is just what they were taught in Sunday School, who like the safety of the rules and the maxims of what Alfred Schutz has called the "world-taken-for-granted," should stay away from sociology. People who feel no temptation before closed doors, who have no curiosity about human beings, who are content to admire scenery without wondering about the people who live in those houses on the other side of that river, should probably stay away from sociology. They will find it unpleasant or, at any rate, unrewarding. People who are interested in human beings only if they can change, convert, or reform them should also be warned, for they will find sociology much less useful than they hoped. And people whose interest is mainly in their own conceptual constructions will do just as well to turn to the study of little white mice. Sociology will be satisfying, in the long run, only to those who can think of nothing more entrancing than to watch men and to understand things human.

It may now be clear that we have, albeit deliberately, understated the case in the title of this chapter. [The chapter title from which this selection is taken is "Sociology as an Individual Pastime."] To be sure, sociology is an individual pastime in the sense that it interests some men and bores others. Some like to observe human beings, others to experiment with mice. The world is big enough to hold all kinds and there is no logical priority for one interest as against another. But the word "pastime" is weak in describing what we mean. Sociology is more like a passion. The sociological perspective is more like a demon that possesses one, that drives one compellingly, again and again, to the questions that are its own. An introduction to sociology is, therefore, an invitation to a very special kind of passion.

2 What Is Sociology? Comparing Sociology and the Social Sciences

JAMES M. HENSLIN

Introductory students often wrestle with the question of what sociology is. If you continue your sociological studies, however, that vagueness of definition—"Sociology is the study of society" or "Sociology is the study of social groups"—that frequently so bothers introductory students will come to be appreciated as one of sociology's strengths and one of its essential attractions. That sociology encompasses almost all human behavior is, indeed, precisely the appeal that draws many to sociology.

To help make clearer at the outset what sociology is, however, Henslin compares and contrasts sociology with the other social sciences. After examining similarities and differences in their approaches to understanding human behavior, he looks at how social scientists from these related academic disciplines would approach the study of juvenile delinquency.

Science and the Human Desire for Explanation

HUMAN BEINGS ARE FASCINATED with the world in which they live, and they aspire to develop ways to explain their experiences. People appear to have always felt this fascination—along with the intense desire to unravel the world's mysteries—for people in ancient times also attempted to explain their worlds. Despite the severe limitations that confronted them, the ancients explored the natural or physical world, constructing explanations that satisfied them. They also developed an understanding of their social world, the world of people with all their activities and myriad ways of dealing with one another. The ancients, however, mixed magic and superstition to explain their observations.

Today, we are no less fascinated with the world within which we live out our lives. We also investigate both the mundane and the esoteric. We cast a quizzical eye at the common rocks we find embedded in the earth, as well as at some rare variety of insect found only in an almost inaccessible region of remote Tibet. We subject our contemporary world to the constant probings of the instruments and machines we have developed to extend our senses. In our attempts to decipher our observations, we no longer are satisfied with traditional explanations of origins or of relationships. No longer do we unquestioningly accept explanations that earlier generations took for granted. Making observations with the aid of our new technology—such as electronic microscopes, satellites, and the latest generation of computers and software—we derive testable conclusions concerning the nature of our world.

As the ancients could only wish to do, we have been able to expand our objective study of the world beyond the confines of this planet. In our relentless pursuit after knowledge, we no longer are limited to speculation concerning the nature of the stars and planets. In the last couple of centuries the telescope has enabled us to make detailed and repetitive observations of the planets and other heavenly bodies. From these observations we have reached conclusions startlingly different from those which people traditionally drew concerning the relative place of the earth in our galaxy and the universe. In just the past few years, by means of space technology, we have been able to extend our senses, as it were, beyond anything we had before dreamed possible. We now are able to reach out by means of our spaceships, observational satellites, and space platforms to record data from other planets and—by means of computer-enhanced graphics—to gain a changing vision of our physical world. We have also been able to dig up and return to the earth samples of soil from the surface of the moon as well as to send probes to the radiation and magnetic belts of Jupiter, over a distance so great (or, we could say, with our technology still so limited) that they must travel eighteen months before they can send reports back to earth. Having discovered evidence of water and recent volcanic activity on Mars, we have begun to draw up plans to dig into its surface to find out if life exists on our "sister" planet.

A generation or so ago such feats existed only in the minds of "mad" scientists, who at that time seemed irrelevant to the public but whose ideas today are producing fascinating and frequently fearful consequences for our life on earth. Some of those scientists are giving serious thought to colonizing space, opening still another area of exciting exploration, but one whose consequences probably will be only inadequately anticipated. Others are drawing plans for real space wars, with potential outcomes so terrifying we can barely imagine them. For good and evil, science directly impinges on our contemporary life in society, leaving none of us unaffected.

The Natural and the Social Sciences

In satisfying our basic curiosities about the world, we have developed two parallel sets of sciences, each identified by its distinct subject matter. The first is called the *natural sciences*, the intellectual-academic endeavors designed to comprehend, explain, and predict the events in our *natural environment*. The endeavors of the natural scientists are divided into specialized fields of research and are given names on the basis of their particular subject matter—such as biology, geology, chemistry, and physics. These fields of knowledge are further subdivided into even more highly specialized areas, each with a further narrowing of content—biology into botany and zoology, geology into mineralogy and geomorphology, chemistry into its organic and inorganic branches, and physics into biophysics and quantum mechanics. Each of these divisions, in turn, is subdivided into further specialized areas. Each specialized area of investigation examines a particular "slice" of the natural world.

In their pursuit of a more adequate understanding of their world, people have not limited themselves to investigating nature. They have also developed a second primary area of science that focuses on the social world. These, the *social sciences,* examine human relationships. Just as the natural sciences are an attempt to understand objectively the world of nature, so the social sciences are an attempt to understand objectively the social world. Just as the world of nature contains ordered (or lawful) relationships that are not obvious but must be abstracted from nature through controlled observations, so the ordered relationships of the human or social world are not obvious but must be abstracted by means of controlled and repeated observations.

Like the natural sciences, the social sciences also are divided into specialized fields based on their subject matter. The usual or typical divisions of the social sciences are anthropology, economics, political science, psychology, and sociology, with history sometimes included in the enumeration, depending primarily on the preference of the person drawing the list. To be inclusive, I shall count history as a social science.

Like the natural sciences, the social sciences also are divided into further specialized fields, with these branches being named on the basis of their particular focus. Anthropology is divided into cultural and physical anthropology, economics into its macro and micro specialties, history into ancient and modern, political science into theoretical and applied, psychology into clinical and experimental, while sociology has its quantitative and qualitative branches. Except for sociology, we shall not be concerned with these finer divisions.

Sociology Contrasted with the Other Social Sciences

Since our focus is sociology, we shall take a brief look at each of the social sciences and contrast each with sociology. I should point out that the differences I shall elaborate are not always so clear in actual practice, for much that social scientists do as they practice their crafts greatly blurs the distinctions I am making.

Let's begin with *history,* the social science focusing on past events. Historians attempt to unearth the facts surrounding some event that they feel is of social significance. They attempt to establish the context, or social milieu, of the event—the important people, ideas, institutions, social movements, or preceding events that in some way appear to have influenced the outcome they desire to explain. From this context, which they reconstruct from records of the past, they abstract what they consider to be the most important elements, or *variables,* that caused the event. By means of those "causal" factors or variables, historians "explain" the past.

Political science focuses on politics or government. The political scientist studies the ways people govern themselves—the various forms of government, their structures, and their relationships to other institutions of society. The political scientist is especially interested in how people attain ruling positions in their society, how they maintain those positions once they secure them, and the consequences of the activities of rulers for those who are governed. In studying a government that has a constitutional electorate, such as ours, the political scientist is especially concerned with voting behavior.

Economics is another discipline in the social sciences that concentrates on a single social institution. Economists study the production, distribution, and allocation of the material goods and services of a society. They want to know what goods are being produced at what rate at what cost, and the variables that determine who gets what. They are also interested in the choices that underlie production—for example, why with limited resources a certain item is being produced instead of another. Some economists, but not nearly enough in my judgment, also are interested in the consequences for human life of the facts of production, distribution, and allocation of goods and services.

The traditional focus of *anthropology* has been on tribal and peasant peoples. Although there are other emphases, the primary concern of anthropologists is to understand *culture,* the total way of life of a group of people. Culture includes (1) the artifacts people produce, such as their tools, art, and weapons; (2) the group's structure, that is, the hierarchy and other group patterns that determine people's relationships to their fellow members; (3) ideas and values, especially the belief system of a people, and their effects on people's lives; and (4) their forms of communication, especially their language. The anthropologists' traditional focus on past societies and contemporary tribal peoples has widened, and some anthropologists study groups in industrialized settings. Anthropologists who focus on modern societies are practically indistinguishable from sociologists.

Psychology concentrates on processes occurring within the individual, within what they call the "skin-bound organism." The psychologist is primarily concerned with what is sometimes referred to as the "mind." Although still regularly used by the public, this term is used with reservation by some psychologists, probably, among other reasons, because no physical entity can be located that exactly corresponds to "mind." Psychologists typically study such phenomena as perception, attitudes, and values. They are also especially interested in personality, in mental aberration (or mental illness), and in how individuals cope with the problems they face.

Sociology is like history in that sociologists also attempt to establish the social contexts that influence people. Sociology is also similar to political science in that sociologists, too, study how people govern one another, especially the consequences for people's lives of various forms of government. Sociology is like economics in that sociologists also are highly interested in what happens to the goods and services of a society, especially the social consequences of production and distribution. Sociology is similar to anthropology in that sociologists also study culture and are particularly interested in the social consequences of material goods, group structure, and belief systems, as well as how people communicate with one another. Sociology is like psychology in that sociologists also study how people adjust to the problems and challenges they face in life.

With these overall similarities, then, where are the differences? Unlike historians, sociologists are primarily concerned with events in the present. Unlike political scientists and economists, sociologists do not concentrate on only a single social institution. Unlike anthropologists, sociologists primarily focus on industrialized societies. And unlike psychologists, to determine what influences people sociologists stress variables external to the individual.

The Example of Juvenile Delinquency

Because all the social sciences focus on human behavior, they differ from one another not so much in the content of what each studies but, rather, in what the social scientists look for when they conduct their studies. It is basically their approaches, their orientations, or their emphases that differentiate the social sciences. Accordingly, to make clearer the differences between them, it might be helpful to look at how different social scientists might approach the same topic. We shall use juvenile delinquency as our example.

Historians interested in juvenile delinquency would examine juvenile delinquency in some particular past setting, such as New York City in the 1920s or Los Angeles in the 1950s. The historian would try to interpret the delinquency by stressing the social context (or social milieu) of the period. For example, if delinquent gangs in New York City in the 1920s were the focus, historians might emphasize the social disruption caused by World War I; the problems of unassimilated, recently arrived ethnic groups; competition and rivalry for social standing among those ethnic groups; intergenerational conflict; the national, state, and local political and economic situation; and so on. The historian might also document the number of gangs, as well as their ethnic makeup. He or she would then produce a history of juvenile delinquency in New York City in the 1920s.

Political scientists are less likely to be interested in juvenile delinquency. But if they were, they would want to know how the existence of juvenile gangs is related to politics. For example, are the children of people who have less access to political decision making more likely to join gangs? Or political scientists might study the power structure within a particular gang by identifying its leaders and followers. They might then compare one gang with another, perhaps even drawing analogies with the political structure of some legitimate group.

Economists also are not likely to study delinquent gangs or juvenile delinquency. But if they did, they, of course, would emphasize the economic aspects of delinquency. They might determine how material goods, such as "loot," are allocated within a gang. But they would be more inclined to focus on delinquency in general, emphasizing the relationship of gangs to economic factors in the country. Economists might wish to examine the effects of economic conditions, such as booms and busts, on the formation of gangs or on the incidence or prevalence of delinquency. They might also wish to determine the cost of juvenile delinquency to the nation in terms of property stolen and destroyed and wages paid to police and social workers.

Anthropologists are likely to be highly interested in studying juvenile delinquency and the formation of juvenile gangs. If anthropologists were to study a particular gang, they might examine the implements of delinquency, such as tools used in car theft or in burglary. They would focus on the social organization of the gang, perhaps looking at its power structure. They would study the belief system of the group to see how it supports the group's delinquent activities. They would also concentrate on the ways in which group members communicate with one another, especially their *argot,* or special language. Anthropologists would stress the larger cultural context in order to see what it is about a culture, such as the ways in which it marks entry into manhood, that leads to the formation of such groups. They would compare their findings with what anthropologists have discovered about delinquency in other cultures. In making such a *cross-cultural comparison,* they probably would note that juvenile delinquency is not a universal phenomenon but is largely a characteristic of industrialized nations. They would point out that industrialized societies require many years of formal education for their youth. This postpones the age at which males are allowed to assume the role of manhood, and it is during this "in-between status," this literal "no-man's-land," that delinquency occurs. The emphasis given by anthropologists in such a study, then, would be true to their calling; that is, anthropologists would be focusing on culture.

Psychologists also have high interest in juvenile delinquency. When psychologists approach the subject, however, they tend to focus on what exists *within* the delinquent. They might test the assumption (or *hypothesis*) that, compared with their followers, gang leaders have more outgoing personality traits, or greater hostility and aggressiveness. Psychologists might also compare the personality traits of adolescent males who join gangs with boys from the same neighborhood or in the general population who do not become gang members. They might give a series of tests to determine whether gang members are more insecure, dominant, hostile, or aggressive than nonmembers.

Sociologists are also interested in most of the aspects emphasized by the other social scientists. Sociologists, however, ordinarily are not concerned with a particular gang from some past period, as historians might be, although they, too, try to identify the relevant social context. Sociologists focus on the power structure of gangs, as would political scientists, and they also are interested in certain aspects of property, as an economist might be. But sociologists would be more interested in the gang members' attitudes toward property, why delinquents feel it is legitimate to steal and vandalize, and how they divide up the property they steal.

Sociologists would also approach delinquency in a way quite similar to that of anthropologists and be interested in the same sorts of things. But sociologists would place strong emphasis on *social class* (which is based on occupation, income, and education). They would want to know if there is greater likelihood that a person will join a gang if his or her parents have little education, and how gang membership varies with income. If sociologists found that delinquency varies with education, age, sex, religion, income, or race–ethnicity, they would want to know the reasons for this. Do children of unskilled workers have a greater chance of becoming delinquent than the children of doctors and lawyers? If so, why?

The sociologists' emphases also separate them from psychologists. Sociologists are inclined to ignore personality, the primary focus of psychologists, and instead to stress the effects of social class on recruitment into delinquency. Sociologists also examine group structure and interaction. For example, both sociologists and psychologists would be interested in differences between a gang's leaders and followers. To discover these, however, sociologists are not likely to give paper-and-pencil tests. They are much more likely to observe *face-to-face interaction* among gang members (what they do in each other's presence). Sociologists would want to see if leaders and followers uphold the group's values differently; who suggests their activities; and who does what when they do them—whether the activity be simply some form of recreation or a criminal act. For example, do leaders maintain their leadership by committing more acts of daring and bravery than their followers?

Compared with other social scientists, sociologists are more likely to emphasize the routine activities of the police, the courts, and changing norms. The police approach their job with preconceived ideas about who is likely to commit crimes and who is not. Their ideas are based on what they have experienced "on the streets," as well as on stereotypes nurtured within their occupation. The police typically view some people (usually lower-class males living in some particular area of the city) to be more apt to commit crimes than males from other areas of the city, males from a higher social class, or females in general. How do the police develop their ideas? How are such stereotypes supported in their occupational subculture? What effects do they have on the police and on those whom they encounter? In other words, sociologists are deeply interested in finding out how the police define people and how those definitions help to determine whom the police arrest.

Sociologists are also interested in what occurs following an arrest.

Prosecutors wield much discretion. For the same act they can level a variety of charges. They can charge an individual with first degree burglary, second degree burglary, breaking and entering, or merely trespassing. Sociologists want to know how such decisions are made, as well as their effects on the lives of those charged with crimes. Sociologists also study what happens when an individual comes before a judge, especially the outcome of the trial by the type of offense and the sex, age, or race–ethnicity of the offender. They also focus on the effects of detention and incarceration, as well as how people adjust when they are released back into the community.

Norms, the behaviors that people expect of others, obviously change over time. What was considered proper behavior a generation ago is certainly not the same as what is considered proper today. Consequently, the law changes, and acts considered to be law violations at one time are not necessarily considered criminal at another time. Similarly, acts not now considered criminal may become law violations at a later date. For example, at one point in our history drinking alcohol in public at age sixteen was within the law in many communities, while today it would be an act of delinquency. In the same way, a person under sixteen who is on the streets after 10 P.M. unaccompanied by an adult is breaking the law in some communities. But if the law is changed or if the sixteen-year-old has a birthday or moves to a different community, the same act is not a violation of the law. With marijuana, the case is similar. Millions of Americans break the law when they smoke grass, but for several years Alaska allowed possession of marijuana for personal use, a legal right later revoked.

Perhaps more than any of the other social scientists, the sociologist maintains a critical interest in the effects of changing legal definitions in determining what people are arrested for and charged with. In effect, sociologists are interested in what juvenile delinquency is in the first place. They take the definition of delinquency not as obvious but as problematic, something to be studied in the context of lawmaking, lawbreaking, and the workaday world of the judicial system.

By means of this example of juvenile delinquency, it is easy to see that the social sciences greatly overlap one another. Sociology, however, is an *overarching* social science, because sociologists are, for the most part, interested in the same things that other social scientists are interested in. They are, however, not as limited in their scope or focus as are the others. Except for its traditional concerns with tribal societies, anthropology is similarly broad in its treatment of human behavior.

Types of Sociology: Structural and Interactional

As sociologists study human behavior, they focus on people's *patterned* relationships; that is, sociologists study the recurring aspects of human behavior. This leads them to focus on two principal aspects of life in society: (1) *group membership* (including the *institutions* of society, the customary arrangements by which humans attempt to solve their perennial problems, such as the need for social order or dealing with sickness and death) and (2) *face-to-face interaction,* that is, what people do when they are in one another's presence. These twin foci lead to two principal forms of sociology, the structural and the interactional.

In the first type of sociology, *structural,* the focus is placed on the *group.* Structural sociologists are interested in determining how membership in a group, such as a religion, influences people's behavior and attitudes, such as how they vote, or perhaps how education affects the stand they take on social issues. For example, are there voting differences among Roman Catholics, Lutherans, Jews, and Baptists? If so, on what issues? And within the same religion, do people's voting patterns differ according to their income and education?

Also of interest to sociologists who focus on group memberships would be how people's attitudes toward social issues (or their voting) differ according to their age, sex, occupation, race or ethnicity, or even geographical residence—both by region of the country and by urban or rural setting. As you probably have gathered, the term "group" is being used in an extended sense. People do not have to belong to an actual group to be counted; sociologists simply "group" together people who have similar characteristics, such as age, height, weight, education, or, if it is thought relevant, even those who take their vacations in the winter versus those who take them during the summer. These are known as *aggregates,* people grouped together for the purpose of social research because of characteristics they have in common.

Note that sociologists with this first orientation concentrate on how group memberships affect people's attitudes and behavior. Ordinarily they do not simply want to know the proportion of Roman Catholics who vote Democratic (or, in sociological jargon, "the correlation between religious-group membership and voting behavior") but may try to determine what difference being a Roman Catholic makes in people's dating practices, in premarital sex, in birth control, in abortion, in what they do for recreation, or in how they treat their spouses and rear their children.

In the second type of sociology, the *interactional,* greater emphasis is placed on individuals. Some sociologists with this orientation focus on what people do when they are in the presence of one another. They directly observe their behavior, recording the interaction by taking notes or by using tape, video, or film. Other sociologists tap people's attitudes and behaviors more indirectly by interviewing them. Still others examine social records—from diaries and letters to court transcripts, even memorabilia of pop culture from *Playboy* and *Playgirl* to science fiction and comic books. They may systematically observe soap operas, children's cartoons, police dramas, situation comedies, or MTV. Sociologists who focus on interaction develop ways of classifying the *data*—what they have observed, read, recorded, or been told. From their direct and indirect observations of people, they draw conclusions about their attitudes and what significantly affects their lives.

Types of Sociology: Qualitative and Quantitative

Another important division among sociologists is based on the *methods* they use to study people. Some sociologists are statistically oriented, attempting to determine *numbers* to represent people's patterns of behavior. They stress that proper measurement by the use of statistical techniques is necessary if one is to understand human behavior. Many refer to this emphasis as *quantitative* sociology.

A group of sociologists who strongly disagree with this position concentrate instead on the *meaning* of what is happening to people. They focus on how people construct their worlds, how they develop their ideas and attitudes, and how they communicate with one another. They attempt to determine how people's meanings (called symbols, mental constructs, ideas, and stereotypes) affect their ideas about the self and their relationships to one another. Many refer to this emphasis as *qualitative* sociology.

Conclusion

From chicken to sociology, there are many ways of dividing up anything in life. And just as those most familiar with chicken may disagree about the proper way of cutting up a chicken, so those most familiar with sociology will disagree about how to slice up sociology. From my experiences, however, the divisions I have presented here appear to reflect accurately what is taking place in sociology today. Inevitably, however, other sociologists would disagree with this classification and probably would present another way of looking at our discipline. Nonetheless, I think you will find this presentation helpful for visualizing sociology.

It is similarly the case when it comes to evaluating the divisions within sociology. These are *not* neutral matters for sociologists. For example, almost all sociologists *feel strongly* about whether a qualitative or quantitative approach is the *proper* way to study human behavior.

Certainly my own biases strongly favor qualitative sociology. For me, there simply is no contest. I see qualitative sociology as more accurately reflecting people's lives, as being more closely tied into the realities that people experience—how they make sense of their worlds, how they cope with their problems, and how they try to maintain some semblance of order in their lives. Because I find this approach fascinatingly worthwhile, the qualitative approach is stressed in this book. You should note, however, that many sociologists find the quantitative approach to be the most rewarding way to study social life.

Wherever and whenever people come into one another's presence, there are potential data for the sociologist. The street, the bar, the classroom, or even the bedroom—all provide material for sociologists to observe and analyze. Nothing is really taboo for them. Sociologists regularly raise questions about most aspects of social life. Simply overhearing an ordinary conversation—or catching a glimpse of some unusual happening—is enough to whet the curiosity of many sociologists. In following that curiosity, they can simply continue to "overhear" conversations, but this time purposely, or they can conduct an elaborate study with a scientifically selected random sample backed by huge fundings from some agency. What sociologists study can be as socially significant as an urban riot or as common but personally significant as two people greeting with a handshake or parting with a kiss.

In this sense, then, the world belongs to the sociologist—for to the sociologist everything is fair game. The all-inclusiveness of sociology, indeed, is what makes sociology so intrinsically fascinating for many: Sociology offers a framework that provides a penetrating perspective on almost everything that we do in life.

Some of you who are being introduced to sociology through this essay may find the sociological approach to understanding human life rewarding enough to take other courses in sociology and, after college, to be attracted to books of sociological content. A few, perhaps, may even make sociology your life's vocation and thus embark on a lifelong journey that takes you to the far corners of human endeavor, as well as to people's more familiar pursuits. Certainly some of us, already captivated by sociology's enchantment, have experienced an unfolding panorama of intellectual delight in the midst of an intriguing exploration of the social world. And, in this enticing process, we have the added pleasure of constantly discovering and rediscovering our changing selves.

3   The Promise

C. WRIGHT MILLS

The "sociological imagination" is seeing how the unique historical circumstances of a particular society affect people and, at the same time, seeing how people affect history. Every individual lives out his or her life in a particular society, with the historical circumstances of that society greatly influencing what that individual becomes. People thus shaped by their society contribute, in turn, to the formation of their society and to the course of its history.

It is this quality of mind (termed the "sociological imagination" by Mills and the "sociological perspective" by others) that is presented for exploration in the readings of this book. As this intersection of biography and history becomes more apparent to you, your own sociological imagination will grow, bringing you a deepened and broadened understanding of social life—and of your own place within it.

NOWADAYS, MEN* OFTEN FEEL that their private lives are a series of traps. They sense that, within their everyday worlds, they cannot overcome their troubles, and, in this feeling, they are quite correct: What ordinary men are directly aware of and what they try to do are bounded by the private orbits in which they live; their visions and their powers are limited to the close-up scenes of job, family, neighborhood; in other milieux, they move vicariously and remain spectators. And the more aware they become, however vaguely, of ambitions and of threats that transcend their immediate locales, the more trapped they seem to feel.

Underlying this sense of being trapped are seemingly impersonal changes in the very structure of continent-wide societies. The facts of contemporary history are also facts about the success and the failure of individual men and women. When a society is industrialized, a peasant becomes a worker; a feudal lord is liquidated or becomes a businessman. When classes rise or fall, a man is employed or unemployed; when the rate of investment goes up or down, a man takes new heart or goes broke. When wars happen, an insurance salesman becomes a rocket launcher; a store clerk, a radar man; a wife lives alone; a child grows up without a father. Neither the life of an individual nor the history of a society can be understood without understanding both.

Yet, men do not usually define the troubles they endure in terms of historical change and institutional contradiction. The well-being they enjoy, they

---

*Again, as in several classic articles in this book, "man" is used in its generic sense; that is, it refers to both males and females. This form of expression is outdated, but the ideas are not.

do not usually impute to the big ups and downs of the societies in which they live. Seldom aware of the intricate connection between the patterns of their own lives and the course of world history, ordinary men do not usually know what this connection means for the kinds of men they are becoming and for the kinds of history-making in which they might take part. They do not possess the quality of mind essential to grasp the interplay of man and society, of biography and history, of self and world. They cannot cope with their personal troubles in such ways as to control the structural transformations that usually lie behind them.

Surely, it is no wonder. In what period have so many men been so totally exposed at so fast a pace to such earthquakes of change? That Americans have not known such catastrophic changes as have the men and women of other societies is due to historical facts that are now quickly becoming "merely history." The history that now affects every man is world history. Within this scene and this period, in the course of a single generation, one-sixth of mankind is transformed from all that is feudal and backward into all that is modern, advanced, and fearful. Political colonies are freed; new and less visible forms of imperialism, installed. Revolutions occur; men feel the intimate grip of new kinds of authority. Totalitarian societies rise, and are smashed to bits—or succeed fabulously. . . . After two centuries of hope, even formal democracy is restricted to a quite small portion of mankind. Everywhere in the underdeveloped world, ancient ways of life are broken up and vague expectations become urgent demands. Everywhere in the overdeveloped world, the means of authority and of violence become total in scope and bureaucratic in form. . . .

The very shaping of history now outpaces the ability of men to orient themselves in accordance with cherished values. And which values? Even when they do not panic, men often sense that older ways of feeling and thinking have collapsed, and that newer beginnings are ambiguous to the point of moral stasis. Is it any wonder that ordinary men feel they cannot cope with the larger worlds with which they are so suddenly confronted? That they cannot understand the meaning of their epoch for their own lives? That—in defense of selfhood—they become morally insensible, trying to remain altogether private men? Is it any wonder that they come to be possessed by a sense of the trap?

It is not only information that they need—in this Age of Fact, information often dominates their attention and overwhelms their capacities to assimilate it. It is not only the skills of reason that they need—although their struggles to acquire these often exhaust their limited moral energy.

What they need, and what they feel they need, is a quality of mind that will help them to use information and to develop reason in order to achieve lucid summations of what is going on in the world and of what may be happening within themselves. It is this quality, I am going to contend, that journalists and scholars, artists and publics, scientists and editors are coming to expect of what may be called the sociological imagination.

The sociological imagination enables its possessor to understand the larger historical scene in terms of its meaning for the inner life and the external career of a variety of individuals. It enables him to take into account how individuals, in the welter of their daily experience, often become falsely conscious of their social positions. Within that welter, the framework of modern society is sought, and within that framework the psychologies of a variety of men and women are formulated. By such means, the personal uneasiness of individuals is focused upon explicit troubles, and the indifference of publics is transformed into involvement with public issues.

The first fruit of this imagination—and the first lesson of the social science that embodies it—is the idea that the individual can understand his own experience and gauge his own fate only by locating himself within his period, that he can know his own chances in life only by becoming aware of those of all individuals in his circumstances. In many ways, it is a terrible lesson; in many ways, a magnificent one. We do not know the limits of man's capacities for supreme effort or willing degradation, for agony or glee, for pleasurable brutality or the sweetness of reason. But in our time we have come to know that the limits of "human nature" are frighteningly broad. We have come to know that every individual lives, from one generation to the next, in some society; that he lives out a biography, and that he lives it out within some historical sequence. By the fact of his living he contributes, however minutely, to the shaping of this society and to the course of its history, even as he is made by society and by its historical push and shove.

The sociological imagination enables us to grasp history and biography and the relations between the two within society. That is its task and its promise. To recognize this task and this promise is the mark of the classic social analyst. It is characteristic of Herbert Spencer—turgid, polysyllabic, comprehensive; of E. A. Ross—graceful, muckraking, upright; of Auguste Comte and Emile Durkheim; of the intricate and subtle Karl Mannheim. It is the quality of all that is intellectually excellent in Karl Marx; it is the clue to Thorstein Veblen's brilliant and ironic insight, to Joseph Schumpeter's many-sided constructions of reality; it is the basis of the psychological sweep of W. E. H. Lecky no less than of the profundity and clarity of Max Weber. And it is the signal of what is best in contemporary studies of man and society.

No social study that does not come back to the problems of biography, of history, and of their intersections within a society has completed its intellectual journey. Whatever the specific problems of the classic social analysts, however limited or however broad the features of social reality they have examined, those who have been imaginatively aware of the promise of their work have consistently asked three sorts of questions:

1. What is the structure of this particular society as a whole? What are its

essential components, and how are they related to one another? How does it differ from other varieties of social order? Within it, what is the meaning of any particular feature for its continuance and for its change?

2. Where does this society stand in human history? What are the mechanics by which it is changing? What is its place within, and its meaning for, the development of humanity as a whole? How does any particular feature we are examining affect, and how is it affected by, the historical period in which it moves? And this period—what are its essential features? How does it differ from other periods? What are its characteristic ways of history-making?

3. What varieties of men and women now prevail in this society and in this period? And what varieties are coming to prevail? In what ways are they selected and formed, liberated and repressed, made sensitive and blunted? What kinds of "human nature" are revealed in the conduct and character we observe in this society in this period? And what is the meaning for "human nature" of each and every feature of the society we are examining?

Whether the point of interest is a great power state or a minor literary mood, a family, a prison, a creed—these are the kinds of questions the best social analysts have asked. They are the intellectual pivots of classic studies of man in society—and they are the questions inevitably raised by any mind possessing the sociological imagination. For that imagination is the capacity to shift from one perspective to another—from the political to the psychological; from examination of a single family to comparative assessment of the national budgets of the world; from the theological school to the military establishment; from considerations of an oil industry to studies of contemporary poetry. It is the capacity to range from the most impersonal and remote transformations to the most intimate features of the human self—and to see the relations between the two. Back of its use, there is always the urge to know the social and historical meaning of the individual in the society and in the period in which he has his quality and his being.

That, in brief, is why it is by means of the sociological imagination that men now hope to grasp what is going on in the world, and to understand what is happening in themselves as minute points of the intersections of biography and history within society. In large part, contemporary man's self-conscious view of himself as at least an outsider, if not a permanent stranger, rests upon an absorbed realization of social relativity and of the transformative power of history. The sociological imagination is the most fruitful form of this self-consciousness. By its use, men whose mentalities have swept only a series of limited orbits often come to feel as if suddenly awakened in a house with which they had only supposed themselves to be familiar. Correctly or incorrectly, they often come to feel that they can now provide themselves with adequate summations, cohesive assessments, comprehensive orientations. Older decisions that once appeared sound now seem to them products of a mind unaccountably dense. Their capacity for astonishment is made lively again. They acquire a new way of thinking; they experience a transvaluation of values. In a word, by their reflection and by their sensibility, they realize the cultural meaning of the social sciences.

Perhaps the most fruitful distinction with which the sociological imagination works is between the "personal troubles of milieu" and the "public issues of social structure." This distinction is an essential tool of the sociological imagination and a feature of all classic work in social science.

Troubles occur within the character of the individual and within the range of his immediate relations with others; they have to do with his self and with those limited areas of social life of which he is directly and personally aware. Accordingly, the statement and the resolution of troubles properly lie within the individual as a biographical entity and within the scope of his immediate milieu—the social setting that is directly open to his personal experience and, to some extent, his willful activity. A trouble is a private matter: Values cherished by an individual are felt by him to be threatened.

Issues have to do with matters that transcend these local environments of the individual and the range of his inner life. They have to do with the organization of many such milieux into the institutions of a historical society as a whole, with the ways in which various milieux overlap and interpenetrate to form the larger structure of social and historical life. An issue is a public matter: Some value cherished by publics is felt to be threatened. Often, there is a debate about what that value really is and about what it is that really threatens it. This debate is often without focus, if only because it is the very nature of an issue, unlike even widespread trouble, that it cannot very well be defined in terms of the immediate and everyday environments of ordinary men. An issue, in fact, often involves a crisis in institutional arrangements, and often, too, it involves what Marxists call "contradictions" or "antagonisms."

In these terms, consider unemployment. When, in a city of 100,000, only one man is unemployed, that is his personal trouble, and for its relief we properly look to the character of the man, his skills, and his immediate opportunities. But when, in a nation of 50 million employees, 15 million men are unemployed, that is an issue, and we may not hope to find its solution within the range of opportunities open to any one individual. The very structure of opportunities has collapsed. Both the correct statement of the problem and range of possible solutions require us to consider the economic and political institutions of the society, and not merely the personal situation and character of a scatter of individuals.

Consider war. The personal problem of war, when it occurs, may be how to survive it or how to die in it with honor; how to make money out of it; how to climb into the higher safety of the military apparatus; or how to contribute to the war's termination. In short, according to one's values, to find a set of milieux and within it to survive the war or make one's death in it meaningful. But the structural issues of war have to do with its causes; with what types of men its throws up into command; with its effects upon economic and political, family and religious institutions; with the unorganized irresponsibility of a world of nation-states.

Consider marriage. Inside a marriage, a man and a woman may experience personal troubles; but, when the divorce rate during the first four years of marriage is 250 out of every 1,000 attempts, this is an indication of a structural issue having to do with the institutions of marriage and the family and other institutions that bear upon them.

Or consider the metropolis—the horrible, beautiful, ugly, magnificent sprawl of the great city. For many upper-class people, the personal solution to the problem of the city is to have an apartment with private garage under it in the heart of the city, and forty miles out, a house by Henry Hill, garden by Garrett Eckbo, on a hundred acres of private land. In these two controlled environments—with a small staff at each end and a private helicopter connection—most people could solve many of the problems of personal milieux caused by the facts of the city. But all this, however splendid, does not solve the public issues that the structural fact of the city poses. What should be done with this wonderful monstrosity? Break it all up into scattered units, combining residence and work? Refurbish it as it stands? Or, after evacuation, dynamite it and build new cities according to new plans in new places? What should those plans be? And who is to decide and to accomplish whatever choice is made? These are structural issues; to confront them and to solve them requires us to consider political and economic issues that affect innumerable milieux.

Insofar as an economy is so arranged that slumps occur, the problem of unemployment becomes incapable of personal solution. Insofar as war is inherent in the nation-state system and in the uneven industrialization of the world, the ordinary individual in his restricted milieu will be powerless—with or without psychiatric aid—to solve the troubles this system or lack of system imposes upon him. Insofar as the family as an institution turns women into darling little slaves and men into their chief providers and unweaned dependents, the problem of a satisfactory marriage remains incapable of purely private solution. Insofar as the overdeveloped megalopolis and the overdeveloped automobile are built-in features of the overdeveloped society, the issues of urban living will not be solved by personal ingenuity and private wealth.

What we experience in various and specific milieux, I have noted, is often caused by structural changes. Accordingly, to understand the changes of many personal milieux, we are required to look beyond them. And the number and variety of such structural changes increase as the institutions within which we live become more embracing and more intricately connected with one another. To be aware of the idea of social structure and to use it with sensibility is to be capable of tracing such linkages among a great variety of milieux. To be able to do that is to possess the sociological imagination.

What are the major issues for publics and the key troubles of private individuals in our time? To formulate issues and troubles, we must ask what values are cherished yet threatened, and what values are cherished and supported, by the characterizing trends of our period. In the case both of threat and of support, we must ask what salient contradictions of structure may be involved.

When people cherish some set of values and do not feel any threat to them, they experience *well-being.* When they cherish values but *do* feel them to be threatened, they experience a crisis—either as a personal trouble or as a public issue. And, if all their values seem involved, they feel the total threat of panic.

But suppose people are neither aware of any cherished values nor experience any threat? That is the experience of *indifference,* which, if it seems to involve all their values, becomes apathy. Suppose, finally, they are unaware of any cherished values, but still are very much aware of a threat? That is the experience of *uneasiness,* of anxiety, which, if it is total enough, becomes a deadly, unspecified malaise.

Ours is a time of uneasiness and indifference—not yet formulated in such ways as to permit the work of reason and the play of sensibility. Instead of troubles—defined in terms of values and threats—there is often the misery of vague uneasiness; instead of explicit issues, there is often merely the beat feeling that all is somehow not right. Neither the values threatened nor whatever threatens them has been stated; in short, they have not been carried to the point of decision. Much less have they been formulated as problems of social science. . . .

We are frequently told that the problems of our decade, or even the crises of our period, have shifted from the external realm of economics and now have to do with the quality of individual life—in fact, with the question of whether there is soon going to be anything that can properly be called individual life. Not child labor but comic books, not poverty but mass leisure, are at the center of concern. Many great public issues as well as many private troubles are described in terms of "psychiatric"—often, it seems in a pathetic attempt to avoid the large issues and problems of modern society. Often, this statement seems to rest upon a provincial narrowing of interest to the Western societies, or even to the United States—thus ignoring two-thirds of mankind; often, too, it arbitrarily divorces the individual life from the larger institutions within which that life is enacted, and which on occasion bear upon it more grievously than do the intimate environments of childhood.

Problems of leisure, for example, cannot even be stated without considering problems of work. Family troubles over comic books cannot be formulated as problems without considering the plight of the contemporary family in its new relations with the newer institutions of the social structure. Neither leisure nor its debilitating uses can be understood as problems without recognition of the extent to which malaise and indifference now form the social and personal climate of contemporary American society. In this climate, no problems of the "private life" can be stated and solved without recognition of the crisis of ambition that is part of the very career of men at work in the incorporated economy.

It is true, as psychoanalysts continually point out, that people do often have the "increasing sense of being moved by obscure forces within themselves that they are unable to define." But it is *not* true, as Ernest Jones asserted, that "man's chief enemy and danger is his own unruly nature and the dark forces pent up within him." On the contrary: "Man's chief danger" today lies in the unruly forces of contemporary society itself, with its alienating methods of production, its enveloping techniques of political domination, its international anarchy—in a word, its pervasive transformations of the very "nature" of man and the conditions and aims of his life.

It is now the social scientist's foremost political and intellectual task—for here the two coincide—to make clear the elements of contemporary uneasiness and indifference. It is the central demand made upon him by other cultural workmen—by physical scientists and artists, by the intellectual community in general. It is because of this task and these demands, I believe, that the social sciences are becoming the common denominator of our cultural period, and the sociological imagination, our most needed quality of mind.

PART II Doing Sociological Research

IN THE INTRODUCTION TO PART I, you learned that sociologists are fascinated with the unknown—how we constantly want to peer behind locked doors to better understand social life. This second Part will show you how sociologists open those doors. I wrote the first selection in this Part to give you an overview of the research methods that sociologists use. Diana Scully and Joseph Marolla then follow with an article based on interviewing in a difficult situation. William Foote Whyte, who became a masterful researcher, then closes this Part with a review of his clumsy first attempts at field work.

As we begin to pry open some of the doors that people so carefully lock, you will be able to catch a glimpse of what goes on behind them. For example, from Scully's and Marolla's research, you will better understand why men rape. In and of itself, such an understanding is valuable, but the selections in this Part have an additional purpose—to introduce you to the two major activities of sociologists: (1) conducting empirical research and (2) constructing a theoretical base. Let's look at each of these activities.

When sociologists do their craft, these twin tasks merge. They are so joined to one another that neither is more important than the other—nor does one necessarily come before the other. For the sake of presentation, however, let's say that the *first* task of sociology is to conduct empirical research. *Empirical* means "based on objective observations." Sociologists cannot draw conclusions based on guesswork, hunches, custom, superstition, common sense, or how they would like the world to be. They must gather information that represents people's attitudes and behaviors accurately. Then they must report their observations openly, spelling out in detail how they conducted their studies so that others can test their conclusions.

Sociologists use a variety of methods to do their research, several of which are represented by articles in this book. To mention a few: an experiment (article 21, on compliance to authority), interviewing (article 44, on women in the military), and documents or secondary sources (article 12, the classic report on abused children, Anna and Isabelle). Article 13, on childhood, is even based on a method for which we have no standard name. We could make up a fancy term such as *post-event reflexivity*, or we could simply call it recall and analysis.

As sociologists do their research, they sometimes find that using just one method is not enough to accomplish their goals, and they combine methods. The study of how married couples split up housework (article 37), for example, is based on interviewing combined with participant observation. Most of the articles in this book, however, are based on participant observation, which you will read about in the selection that opens this Part (as well as a more detailed analysis in the opening to Part V).

Because no specific reading summarizes the *second* task of sociology, constructing a theoretical base, I shall provide an overview at this point.

The word *theory* sometimes scares students. It shouldn't, for *all of us are theorists.* To see what I mean by this, let's start with a basic point—how we make sense out of life. Facts never interpret themselves; yet we constantly want to know the meaning of the things that happen to us. To find this meaning, we place our experiences (our "facts") into a conceptual framework. That is, we take a "fact" (which can be someone's behavior, something we see on television—anything that happened to us) and compare it with what we know about "that kind of thing." We then use "what we know" to interpret that "fact."

Doing this gives us an understanding of what that event or "fact" of life means. Whether our understanding is right or wrong is not the point. The point is that we all do this as a regular part of our everyday lives. We feel a need to know how "events" are related to one another. By placing them into "frameworks" that we carry around in our heads, we arrive at that meaning. This process can be called "everyday theorizing." In essence, then, all of us are theorists all the time.

So why be scared of theory? We all know how to "do" theory. Now let's consider how sociologists "do" theory.

Like the events of everyday life, sociological "facts" (the observations, measurements, or research results of sociologists) do not come with built-in meanings. They, too, must be interpreted. To make sense of them, sociologists place their findings into conceptual frameworks that they have developed. These frameworks provide explanations of how pertinent "facts" are related to one another. The basic difference between sociological theory and everyday-life theory is that sociological theory is more rigorous. Sociologists constantly check to see how the "empirical" (the things observed) match a theory—and then refine the theory to match the real world.

A *theory,* then, is a conceptual framework that interprets "facts," that shows how they are related to one another. Because each theory provides a framework that interprets sociological observations, it offers a unique explanation of reality. This will become clearer as we examine the three dominant theories of sociology. You will see how each theory reveals a contrasting picture of social life.

The *first* theory is called *symbolic interactionism* (or *symbolic interaction*). It stresses what you already know quite well—that you live in a world filled with meaning. You are surrounded by *people* who mean something to you (from your parents to your friends), by *objects* that represent something special (your clothing, your pet, your car, your room), and by *events* that are filled with meaning (first kiss, first date, first job, birthdays, holidays, anniversaries). The term *symbol* refers to the meanings that such things have for us. And symbols are what *symbolic* interactionists focus on—how we construct meanings, how we use symbols to communicate with one another, and how symbols are the foundation of our social world.

Symbolic interactionism has three major themes: (1) human beings have a self; (2) people construct meanings, and act on the basis of those meanings; and (3) people take into account the possible reactions of others. Let's look at each of these points.

1. *Human beings have a self.* This means that we have the capacity to think, to talk about, and to reflect on our own actions (what we have done), future actions (what we plan to do), even our thoughts and feelings about our actions (such as what we regret having done). We are even able to tell others what was going on in our mind when we did something. That is, just as we can reflect on the actions and motives of others, so we can reflect on our own actions, analyze our own motives, and evaluate how we feel about what we did or what happened to us. This is called "making the self an object."

2. *People construct meanings, and act on the basis of those meanings.* We reflect on our experiences, and we interpret (or give meaning to) what happens to us. As we evaluate how others react to us and to events, we further refine those meanings. The significance of this human trait is that the meanings we give to our experiences (the objects, the important events—the "facts" of our life) become the basis for how we act.

   This sounds abstract and vague, but it is what we do all the time. For example, if someone makes physical contact with us, we want to know what it means. If we interpret the contact as an "accidental bump," it requires nothing but a mumbled apology—but if we interpret it as a "push" or a "stomp," our reactions are quite different. The actual act is the same in either case, but our *interpretation* determines what it means for us, as well as indicating what our "appropriate" reaction should be. Note that the basis for our "appropriate" reaction does not depend on the act, but on the symbols we apply—that is, how we interpret (or define) the act.

How we interpret (or "symbolize") life's events is actually a good deal more complicated than I have just sketched. While we all place our experiences into categories, the categories we use differ from individual to individual. Even an accidental bump, for example, has different meanings to people of different backgrounds. I am reminded of this by Kody Scott's fascinating book, *Monster*, in which an accidental bump can be an invitation to death.

3. *People take into account the possible reactions of others*. We are always aware of how others might react to something that we are thinking about doing, and we take those anticipated reactions into account as we make decisions about what to do. This is called *taking the role of others*, which simply means that we adjust our behavior to how we think people might react.

As is apparent, taking the role of others is a regular part of everyday life. We take the role of individuals ("specific others") and of groups of people ("the generalized other"). For example, if a Chicago Bulls player were tempted to accept a bribe, he might think, "What would my coach or mom [a specific other] think if I took this?" He probably would also think, "What would my team and the American public [a generalized other] think of me if they found out?"

In sum: Central to symbolic interactionism is the principle that to understand people's behavior we must understand their symbolic worlds. That is, we must understand how people think about life, how they mentally construct their worlds. Accordingly, sociologists study the meanings that people give to things, to events, and to other people, for symbols hold the key to understanding both our attitudes and our behavior.

The *second* theory is called *functionalism*. Functionalists stress that society is an integrated system made up of various parts. When working properly, each part contributes to the stability of society: that is, each part fulfills a function that helps keep society going. Sometimes, however, a part fails to work correctly; that is, it becomes *dysfunctional*. This creates problems for other parts of the system, for they were depending on it. In short, functionalists stress how the parts of society are interrelated, and how a change in one part of society affects its other parts.

To illustrate functionalism, let's consider why divorce is so prevalent in U.S. society. Functionalists first point out that the family performs important functions for the entire society. Over the millennia, the family's traditional functions have been economic production, the distribution of property, the socialization of children, reproduction, recreation, sexual control of its members, and taking care of its sick, injured, and aged. During the past couple of hundred years (especially the last hundred), as society industrialized profound changes occurred that have left no aspect of social life untouched.

The consequences for the family have been especially remarkable. Consider how industrialization has eroded the family's traditional functions. For example, medical personnel now take care of the family's sick and injured, often the family's elderly are placed in homes for the aged, and almost all economic production has moved from family to factories. As its basic functions have been at least partially taken over by other units of society, the family has weakened. Simply put, the "ties that bind" became fewer—and with fewer functions holding them together, husbands and wives became more prone to break up.

The *third* dominant theory in sociology is *conflict theory*. From this perspective, society is viewed as a system in which its various parts are in conflict. For their survival and to improve their relative position in society, each group competes for resources. There are not enough resources to satisfy each group; each group tends to want more power, more wealth, more prestige, and so on. Consequently, groups compete with one another for a larger share of these limited resources. Those groups that already have more than their share are not about to redistribute what they have willingly. Instead, they hold on to it for dear life, while trying to enlarge what they already have. Conflict is the inevitable result.

As a consequence, say conflict theorists, society is not like a smoothly running machine, as the functionalists picture it, with each part contributing to the well-being of the other parts. Rather, society is more like a machine running wildly out of kilter and ready to break apart. The results of this inherent conflict show up as racism, with one racial–ethnic group pitted against another; sexism, with men and women squared off in the struggle for dominance; social class conflict, with the exploitation of the powerless by a ruling elite; ageism, with a struggle for finances (Social Security) dividing the generations of workers; and so on.

Due to space limitations, I can provide only this brief sketch of these three theories that dominate sociology today. Among the many examples of *symbolic interactionism* in this book, you might look at selections by Goffman (11), Lawson (17), and Henslin and Biggs (18). The readings by Gans (30), Harris (38), and Savells (43) provide examples of *functionalism*, while the ones by Kozol (31) and Gracey (34) are examples of *conflict theory*. The dominant orientation of this book is symbolic interactionism.

This Part of the book, then, builds upon the first Part. I hope that it will help you to better appreciate how sociologists do their research and how they interpret what they find.

4 How Sociologists Do Research

JAMES M. HENSLIN

Guesswork does not go very far in helping us to understand our social world. Some of our guesses, hunches, and ideas that pass for common sense are correct. Others are not. And we seldom know the difference.

Sociologists must gather data in such a way that what they report is objective—presenting information that represents what is really "out there." To do so, they must use methods that other researchers can repeat (*replicate*) to check their findings. They also must tie their findings into what other researchers have already reported and into sociological theory. In this overview of *research methods,* Henslin outlines the procedures that sociologists use to gather data.

Renée had never felt fear before—at least not like this. It had begun as a vague feeling that something was out of place. Then she felt it creep up her spine, slowly tightening as it clawed its way upward. Now it was like a fist pounding inside her skull.

Renée never went anywhere with strangers. Hadn't her parents hammered that into her head since she was a child? And now, at 19, she wasn't about to start breaking *that* rule.

And yet here she was, in a car with a stranger. He seemed nice enough. And it wasn't as though he were some strange guy on the side of the road or anything. She had met George at Patricia's party, and. . . .

Renée had first been attracted by his dark eyes. They seemed to light up his entire face when he smiled. And when he asked her to dance, Renée felt flattered. He was a little older, a little more sure of himself than most of the guys she knew. Renée liked that: It was a sign of maturity.

As the evening wore on and he continued to be attentive to her, it seemed natural to accept his offer to take her home.

But then they passed the turn to her dorm. She didn't understand his mumbled reply about "getting something." And as he turned off on the country road, that clawing at the back of her neck had begun.

As he looked at her, his eyes almost pierced the darkness. "It's time to pay, Babe," he said, as he clawed at her blouse.

Renée won't talk about that night. She doesn't want to recall anything that happened then.

IN THIS PAPER we examine how sociologists do research. To better understand how they gather data, let's focus on this basic question: How can we gather reliable information on rape—which is to say on both rapists *and* their victims?

Sociology and Common Sense

Common sense will give us some information. From common sense (a kind of knowledge not based on formal investigation, but on ideas that we pick up from our groups, mixed with abstractions from our own experiences), we know that her rape was a significant event in Renée's life. And from common sense we know that rape has ongoing effects, that it can trigger fears and anxieties, and that it can make women distrust men.

It so happens that these ideas are true. But many other common-sense ideas, even though glaringly obvious to us, are *not* true, and so we need research to test the validity and accuracy of our ideas. For example, common sense also tells us that one reason men rape is the revealing clothing that some women wear. And common sense may tell us that men who rape are sexually deprived. These common-sense ideas, however, are not on target. Researchers have found that men who rape don't care what a woman is wearing. Most don't even care who the woman is. She is simply an object for their lust, drives for power and exploitation, and, sometimes, frustration and anger. Researchers have also found that rapists may or may not be sexually deprived—the same as with men who do not rape. For example, many rapists have wives or girl friends with whom they have an ongoing sexual relationship.

If it is neither provocative clothing nor sexual deprivation, then, what *does* cause rape? And what effects does rape have on victims? Phrasing the matter this way—instead of assuming that we know the answers—not only opens up our minds but also underscores the pressing need for sociological research. We need to search for empirical findings that will take us completely out of the realm of guesswork and well beyond common sense.

Let's see how sociologists do their research. We shall look first at a research model, and then at the research methods used in sociology.

A Research Model

As shown in Figure 4.1, eight basic steps are involved in social research. As you look at each of these steps, be aware that this is an ideal model. In some research these steps are collapsed, in others their order may be rearranged, while in still others one or more steps may be omitted.

1. SELECTING A TOPIC

The first step is to select a topic. What is it that you want to know more about? Many sociologists simply follow their curiosity, their drive to know. They become interested in a particular topic, and they pursue it. Sometimes sociologists choose a topic simply because funds are available. At other times, some social problem, such as rape, has become a pressing issue and the sociologist wants to gather data that will help people better understand—and perhaps help solve it.

2. DEFINING THE PROBLEM

The second step is to define the problem, to determine what you want to learn about the topic. To develop a researchable question, you need to focus on a specific area or problem. For example, you may want to determine the education and work experiences of rapists, or the average age of their victims.

Figure 4.1 The Research Model (*Modification of Fig. 2.2 in Schaefer and Lamm 1998.*)

3. REVIEWING THE LITERATURE

The third step is to review the literature. Nobody wants to rediscover the wheel. If the question has already been answered, you want to know that. In addition, a review of what has been written on the topic can stir your ideas, help sharpen your questions, and help you accomplish the next step.

4. FORMULATING A HYPOTHESIS

The fourth step is to formulate a *hypothesis,* a statement of what you expect to find based on a theory. A hypothesis predicts a relationship between or among *variables* (factors thought to be significant). For example, the statement "Men who are more socially isolated are more likely to rape than are men who are more socially integrated" is an example of a hypothesis. Hypotheses (the plural) need *operational definitions*—that is, precise ways to measure their concepts. In this example, you would need operational definitions for three concepts: social integration, social isolation, and rape.

5. CHOOSING A RESEARCH METHOD

The ways by which sociologists collect data are called *research methods.* You need to select a method that will answer the questions you have formulated. (In the next section, beginning on page 38, I go into detail concerning the six research methods used by sociologists.)

6. COLLECTING THE DATA

The next step is to gather the data. Great care needs to be taken to assure that the data are both valid and reliable. *Validity* means the extent to which the operational definitions measure what you intend to measure. In other words, do your definitions or measures of social isolation and integration *really* measure these concepts and not something else?

The concept of rape is not as simple to define (or operationalize) as it may seem. For example, there are various degrees of sexual assault. Look at Table 4.1, which depicts a variety of forced sexual activities. Deciding which of these constitute rape for the purposes of your research project is an example of the difficulties of developing operational definitions. Certainly not all of these acts are rape—and, therefore, not all of those who did them are rapists.

Reliability refers to the extent to which your measures and studies give consistent results. Inadequate operational definitions and sampling (covered later) will prevent reliability. For example, if other researchers want to replicate (repeat) your study but your measure of rape is inadequate, they will exclude acts that you included, and include acts that you excluded. In that case, how can you compare the results?

TABLE 4.1   Date Rape and Other Unwanted Sexual Activities Experienced by College Undergraduates

UNWANTED SEXUAL ACTIVITY	WOMEN WHO REPORTED THIS HAD HAPPENED TO THEM (%)	MEN WHO REPORTED THEY HAD DONE THIS (%)
He kissed without tongue contact	3.7	2.2
He kissed with tongue contact	12.3	0.7
He touched/kissed her breasts through her clothes	24.7	7.3
He touched/kissed her breasts under her clothes	22.6	13.1
He touched her genitals through her clothes	28.8	15.3
He touched her genitals under her clothes	28.4	13.9
He performed oral sex on her	9.9	8.8
He forced her to touch his genitals through his clothes	2.9	0.7
He forced her to touch his genitals under his clothes	5.8	2.2
He forced her to perform oral sex on him	2.5	4.4
He forced her to have sexual intercourse	20.6	15.3

These are the results of a survey of 380 women and 368 men enrolled in introductory psychology courses at Texas A&M University. Percentages add up to more than 100 because often more than one unwanted sexual activity occurred on the same date.

Source: Based on Muehlenhard and Linton 1987:190.

7. ANALYZING THE RESULTS

After the data are gathered, it is time to analyze them. Sociologists have specific techniques for doing this, each of which requires special training. They range from statistical tests (of which there are many, each with its own rules for application) to *content analysis* (examining the content of something in order to identify its themes—in this case perhaps magazine articles and television reports about rape, or even diaries kept by women who have been raped). If a hypothesis has been part of the research (and not all social research has hypotheses), it is during this step that it is tested.

8. SHARING THE RESULTS

Now it is time to wrap up the research. In this step you write a report that shares your findings with the scientific community. You relate your findings to the literature, to show how they are connected to what has previously been discovered. You explain your research procedures so others can *replicate* them—i.e., can repeat the study to test its findings. In this way science slowly builds, adding finding to finding.

Now let's look in greater detail at the fifth step to examine the research methods that sociologists use.

Six Research Methods

Sociologists use six *research methods* (also called research designs). These *procedures for gathering data* are surveys, secondary analysis, documents, experiments, unobtrusive measures, and participant observation.

SURVEYS

Let's suppose that you want to know how many women are raped each year. The *survey*—having people answer a series of questions—would be an appropriate method to use.

Before using this method, however, you have to decide whom you will survey. What is your *population;* that is, what is the target group that you want to learn about? Is it all females in the world? Only U.S. or Canadian females? The females in a particular state, county, or city? Only females above a certain age? Or only women on your college campus?

Let's suppose that your research interest is modest—that you want only to know the extent of rape on your campus. Ideally, you would survey all women students. But let's also suppose that your college enrollment is large, making this impractical. To get at the answer, then, you must select a smaller group, a *sample* of individuals, from whom you can generalize to the entire campus. How you choose your sample is crucial, for it will affect the results of your study. For example, you will get different results if you survey only freshmen or seniors—or only women taking introductory sociology or advanced physics classes.

What kind of sample will allow you to *generalize* to the entire campus? The best is a *random* sample. This does *not* mean that you stand on some campus corner and ask questions of whomever happens to walk by. *In a random sample everyone in the population has the same chance of being included in the study.* In this case, since the population is all women taking classes at your college, all such women must have the same chance of being included in your research—whether they are freshmen, sophomores, juniors, seniors, or graduate students. It also means that such factors (*variables*) as a woman's choice of major, her grade point average, or whether she is a day or evening student cannot affect her chances of being a part of your sample.

To obtain a random sample, you would need a list of all women currently enrolled in your college. To determine which students become part of the sample, you might assign a number to each name on the list and then use random numbers to determine which particular women become part of the sample. (Random numbers are available on tables in statistics books, and can be generated by computer.)

Because a random sample represents the population (in this case women students at your college), you can generalize your findings to all the women students on your campus, whether they were part of the sample or not.

In some surveys, *questionnaires*, a list of questions, are mailed to people. Although such *self-administered questionnaires* allow a large number of people to be sampled at a lower cost, control is lost. For example, under what conditions did people (*respondents*) fill them out? Who influenced their answers?

Other surveys use *interviews:* Respondents are asked questions directly. This is usually done on a face-to-face basis, although some interviews are conducted over the telephone. The advantage of this type of survey is that the researchers bring control to the situation. They know the conditions under which the interviews took place and that each question was asked in precisely the same way. Its disadvantages include not only the more limited number of questionnaires that can be completed, and the increased cost, but also *interviewer bias,* the effects that interviewers can have on respondents that lead to biased answers. For example, although respondents may be willing to write an anonymous answer, they may not want to express their opinions to another person directly. Some even try to make their answers match what they think the interviewer wants to hear.

Sociologists sometimes use *closed-ended questions,* called *structured interviews.* Each question is followed by a list of possible answers. The advantages are that these are faster to administer, and make it easier for the answers to be *coded* (categorized) so they can be fed into a computer for analysis. If you use closed-ended questions, you will have to be careful to make sure that they represent people's opinions. For example, if you were to ask "What do you think should be done to rapists?" and the only choices you provide are to castrate or kill them, you would not be taking accurate measurements of people's opinions. Similarly, if you begin a question with, "Don't you agree that" ("rapists should be locked up for life"—or whatever you want to add), you would tilt the results toward agreement with a particular position.

Questions, then, must be carefully worded so they do not slant answers—because biased findings are worthless. It takes a great deal of training to construct questions that are free of bias, and sociologists are extremely critical of both how questions are worded and how they are administered (given).

To better tap the depth and diversity of people's experiences and attitudes, you may wish to use *open-ended questions,* called *unstructured interviews,* that allow people to answer in their own words. The primary advantage of this type of interview is that it allows people to express their full range of opinions. The major disadvantage is that it is difficult to compare people's answers. For example, how would you compare these answers to the question "What do you think causes rape?"

"They haven't been raised right."
"I think they must have had problems with their mother."
"We ought to kill every one!"
"They're all sick."
"I don't want to talk about it."

The research topic we are considering also brings up another significant item. Let's suppose that you want to interview rape victims. Would they really give honest answers? Will a woman even admit to a stranger that she has been raped, much less talk about it? Wouldn't all your efforts be futile?

If you were to simply walk up to a stranger on the street and ask if she had ever been raped, you can guess the results—and they certainly would give little basis for placing confidence in your findings. Researchers must establish *rapport* (pronounced ruh–pour), a feeling of trust, with their respondents. When it comes to sensitive topics, areas about which people may feel embarrassment, shame, hostility, or other deep emotions, rapport is all the more important.

Once rapport is gained (often through building trust by explaining the significance of the research, assuring anonymity, and first asking nonsensitive questions), victims usually will talk about rape. For example, each year researchers conduct a national crime survey in which they interview a random sample of 49,000 households—about 90,000 Americans. They find that most rape victims will talk about their experiences. These national crime surveys show that rape is three times as high as the official statistics, and that most rape is committed by someone the victim knows (*Statistical Abstract of the United States* 1999: page 212).

SECONDARY ANALYSIS

In *secondary analysis*, the second research method we shall consider, the researcher analyzes data already collected by others. For example, if you were to examine the basic data gathered by the interviewers who did the national crime survey just mentioned, you would be doing secondary analysis.

Ordinarily, researchers prefer to gather their own data, but lack of resources, especially time and money, may make this preference impossible to fulfill. In addition, data already gathered may contain a wealth of information not pertinent to the purposes of those who did the original study. It simply lies there, waiting to be analyzed.

While this approach can solve problems of access, it also poses its own problems. Not having directly carried out the research, how can you be sure that the data were systematically gathered and accurately recorded, and biases avoided? That may not be an easy task, especially if the original data were gathered by numerous researchers, not all of whom were equally qualified.

DOCUMENTS

The use of *documents,* written sources, is a third research method employed by sociologists. To investigate social life, sociologists examine such diverse sources as books, newspapers, diaries, bank records, police reports, immigration records, household accounts, and records kept by schools, hospitals, and other organizations. (Although they are not commonly called documents, also included here are movies, television programs, videotapes, computer disks, and CD-ROMs.)

To apply this method to the study of rape, you might examine police reports. They may reveal what proportion of all arrests are for rape; how many of the men arrested go to trial; what proportion is convicted, put on probation, sent to prison; and so forth. If these are your questions, police statistics could be valuable.

But for other questions, police records would be useless. For example, if you want to know about the adjustment of rape victims, they would tell you nothing. Other documents, however, may lend themselves to this question. If your campus has a rape crisis center, for example, it might have records that would provide key information. Or you may obtain diaries kept by victims, and search them for clues to their reactions—especially how their orientations change over time. If you couldn't find such diaries, you might contact a sample of rape victims and ask them to keep diaries. Locating that sample is extremely difficult—but, again, the rape crisis center could be the key. Their personnel might ask victims to keep the diaries. (To my knowledge, however, no sociologist has yet studied rape in this way.)

I am writing, of course, about an ideal case, as though the rape crisis center is opening its arms to you. In actual fact it may not cooperate at all, refusing to ask victims to keep diaries and not even letting you near their records. Access, then, is another problem researchers constantly face. Simply put, you can't study something unless you can gain access to it.

EXPERIMENTS

A fourth research method is the *experiment.* This is the classic method of the natural sciences. Sociologists seldom use it, however, because they are more likely to be interested in broad features of society and social behavior, or in studying a social group in a natural setting, neither of which lends itself to an experiment.

The basic purpose of an experiment is to identify cause-and-effect relationships—to find out what causes what. Ordinarily, experiments are used to test a hypothesis. Experiments involve *independent variables* (those factors that cause a change in something) and *dependent variables* (those factors that are changed). Before the experiment, you must measure the dependent variable. Then, after introducing the independent variable, you again measure the dependent variable in order to see what change has occurred.

Let's assume, for example, that you want to test the hypothesis that pornography creates attitudes that favor rape. The independent variable would be pornography, the dependent variable attitudes toward rape. You can measure a group of men's attitudes toward rape and then use random numbers to divide the men into two subgroups. To one group, the *experimental group,* you introduce the independent variable (such as violent pornographic movies). The other group, the *control group,* is not exposed to the independent variable (that is, they are not shown these movies). You then measure the dependent variable in both groups. Changes in the dependent variable (in this case attitudes toward rape) are due to what only the experimental group received, the independent variable (in this case, the pornography).

Because there is always some chance that unknown third variables have not been evenly distributed among the groups, you would need to retest your results by repeating the experiment with other groups of men.

UNOBTRUSIVE MEASURES

The fifth method we shall consider is *unobtrusive measures:* observing people's behavior when they do not know they are being studied. For example, social researchers have studied the level of whiskey consumption in a "dry" town by counting empty bottles in trash cans; the degree of fear induced through telling ghost stories by measuring the shrinking diameter of a circle of seated children; and the popularity of exhibits at Chicago's Museum of Science and Industry by the wear upon tiles in front of the various displays (Webb et al. 1966).

Unobtrusive measures could also be used to study rape. For example, you could observe rapists in prison when they do not know they are being watched. You might arrange for the leader of a therapy group for rapists to be called out of the room. During his absence, you could use a one-way mirror to observe the men's interactions, and video cameras to preserve what they say and do. You might even have a stooge bring up a certain topic. Such an approach would probably tell you more about the men's real attitudes than most other techniques.

Professional ethics, however, might disallow such a study. And I know of no research that has applied this method to the study of rape.

PARTICIPANT OBSERVATION (FIELD WORK)

Let's turn to my favorite method, one that involves the researcher in the most direct way. In *participant observation* (or field work) the researcher *participates* in a research setting while *observing* what is happening in that setting.

How is it possible to study rape by participant observation? It would seem that this method would not apply. If one considers being present during rape, it certainly does not. But there are many other questions about rape that can be answered by participant observation, answers that cannot be gained as adequately by any other method.

Let's suppose that your interest is the adjustment of rape victims. You would like to learn how the rape has affected their behavior and their orientations to the world. For example, how has their victimization affected their hopes and goals, their dating patterns, their ideas about men and intimacy? Participant observation can provide detailed answers to such questions.

Let's go back to your campus again. Assume that your campus has a rape crisis intervention center. This setting lends itself to participant observation, for here you can observe rape victims from the time they first report the attack to their later participation in individual and group counseling. With good rapport, you can even spend time with victims outside this setting, observing how it affects other aspects of their lives.

Participant observation has the added benefit of allowing you to study whatever happens to occur while you are in the setting. In this instance, you would also be able to study the operation of the rape crisis center. As you observe counselors at work, you could also study *their* attitudes and behaviors.

As you may have noticed, in participant observation the personal characteristics of the researcher are important. Could a man, for example, conduct such research? Technically, the answer is yes. Properly introduced and with the right attitudes, men could do this research. But granted the topic, and especially the emotional states of females who have been brutally victimized by males, it may be more appropriate for women sociologists to conduct this research. Their chances of success are likely to be higher.

In conducting research, then, sociologists must be aware of such variables as the sex, age, race–ethnicity, personality, and even height and weight of the researcher (Henslin 1990). While important in all research methods (for example, in surveys men who are being interviewed may be more talkative to young, shapely women than to obese men), these variables are especially important in participant observation.

Participant observers face a problem with generalizability. Although they look for principles of human behavior, it is difficult to know the extent to which their findings apply beyond the setting in which they occur. Consequently, most participant observation is exploratory in nature: The findings document in detail what people in a particular setting are experiencing and how they are reacting to those experiences, suggesting that other people who face similar situations will react in similar ways.

I find participant observation the most exciting of the methods. It is the type of sociology that I like to do and the type I like to read about. From these studies, I gain a depth of understanding of settings that I want to know more about but for whatever reason am not able to study, and in some cases am not even able to enter. If I were a woman, for example, I might have volunteered for work in my campus's rape crisis center—a technique often used by sociologists to solve the problem of access.

Conclusion: A Note on Choosing Research Methods

As you have seen, a critical factor in choosing a research method is the questions you wish to answer. Each method lends itself much better to answering particular interests or questions than do other methods. You also have seen that access to subjects is crucial in deciding which research method to use. Two other factors are significant in this choice: the resources available to the researcher, and the researcher's background or training. For example, a researcher who prefers to conduct a survey may find that finances will not permit it, and instead turn to the study of documents. The researcher's background is similarly significant in this choice. Researchers who have been trained in *quantitative techniques* (an emphasis on precise measurement, numbers, statistics) are more likely to use surveys, while researchers who have been trained in *qualitative techniques* (generally, making direct observations of what people do and say) lean toward participant observation. The particular training that sociologists receive in graduate school, which sometimes depends on capricious events, orients them toward certain research methods. They feel comfortable with those, and tend to continue to use them throughout their careers.

References

Henslin, James M. (1990). "It's not a lovely place to visit, and I wouldn't want to live there." In Robert G. Burgess (ed.), *Studies in Qualitative Methodology II*: 51–76. Greenwich, CT: JAI Press.

Muehlenhard, Charlene L., and Melaney A. Linton (1987). "Date rape: Familiar strangers." *Journal of Counseling Psychology 34*: 186–96.

Schaefer, Richard T., and Robert P. Lamm (1998). *Sociology*. 6th ed. New York: McGraw-Hill.

Statistical Abstract of the United States. Washington, D.C.: U.S. Government Printing Office, 1999.

Webb, Eugene J., Donald T. Campbell, Richard D. Schwartz, and Lee Sechrest (1966). *Unobtrusive Measures: Nonreactive Research in the Social Sciences*. Chicago: Rand McNally.

5 "Riding the Bull at Gilley's": Convicted Rapists Describe the Rewards of Rape

DIANA SCULLY
JOSEPH MAROLLA

As we saw in the previous reading, sociologists can choose from a variety of research methods. Rape was used as the example to illustrate the various ways in which sociologists collect data. In this selection, you can see how two sociologists used the research method known as *unstructured interviewing* to gather data on rape. What prompted their research was a question that many people wonder about: "Just why do men rape?"

Scully and Marolla interviewed a sample of men who had been sent to prison for rape. In what was a difficult situation, they established enough *rapport* that the men felt free to talk about their motives. From this selection, you should gain an understanding of the reasons why men commit this violent act. To determine how widespread (representative) these motives are, we need more studies, preferably with both convicted and unconvicted rapists. Perhaps you, now a student reading this book in the introductory course, will become a sociologist who will build on this study.

OVER THE PAST SEVERAL DECADES, rape has become a "medicalized" social problem. That is to say, the theories used to explain rape are predicated on psychopathological models. They have been generated from clinical experiences with small samples of rapists, often the therapists' own clients. Although these psychiatric explanations are most appropriately applied to the atypical rapist, they have been generalized to all men who rape and have come to inform the public's view on the topic.

Two assumptions are at the core of the psychopathological model: that rape is the result of idiosyncratic mental disease and that it often includes an uncontrollable sexual impulse (Scully and Marolla, 1985). For example, the presumption of psychopathology is evident in the often cited work of Nicholas Groth (1979). While Groth emphasizes the nonsexual nature of rape (power, anger, sadism), he also concludes, "Rape is always a symptom of some psychological dysfunction, either temporary and transient or chronic and repetitive" (Groth, 1979:5). Thus, in the psychopathological view, rapists lack the ability to control their behavior; they are "sick" individuals from the "lunatic fringe" of society.

In contradiction to this model, empirical research has repeatedly failed to find a consistent pattern of personality type or character disorder that reliably discriminates rapists from other groups of men (Fisher and Rivlin, 1971; Hammer and Jacks, 1955; Rada, 1978). Indeed, other research has found that fewer than 5 percent of men were psychotic when they raped (Abel et al., 1980).

Evidence indicates that rape is not a behavior confined to a few "sick" men, but many men have the attitudes and beliefs necessary to commit a sexually aggressive act. In research conducted at a midwestern university, Koss and her coworkers reported that 85 percent of men defined as highly sexually aggressive had victimized women with whom they were romantically involved (Koss and Leonard, 1984). A survey quoted in *The Chronicle of Higher Education* estimates that more than 20 percent of college women are the victims of rape and attempted rape (Meyer, 1984). These findings mirror research published several decades earlier which also concluded that sexual aggression was commonplace in dating relationships (Kanin, 1957, 1965, 1967, 1969; Kirkpatrick and Kanin, 1957). In their study of 53 college males, Malamuth, Haber, and Feshback (1980) found that 51 percent indicated a likelihood that they, themselves, would rape if assured of not being punished.

In addition, the frequency of rape in the United States makes it unlikely that responsibility rests solely with a small lunatic fringe of psychopathic men. Johnson (1980), calculating the lifetime risk of rape to girls and women aged twelve and over, makes a similar observation. Using Law Enforcement Assistance Association and Bureau of Census Crime Victimization Studies, he calculated that, excluding sexual abuse in marriage and assuming equal risk to all women, 20 to 30 percent of girls now 12 years old will suffer a violent sexual attack during the remainder of their lives. Interestingly, the lack of empirical support for the psychopathological model has not resulted in the demedicalization of rape, nor does it appear to have diminished the belief that rapists are "sick" aberrations in their own culture. This is significant because of the implications and consequences of the model.

A central assumption in the psychopathological model is that male sexual aggression is unusual or strange. This assumption removes rape from the realm of the everyday or "normal" world and places it in the category of "special" or "sick" behavior. As a consequence, men who rape are cast in the role of outsider and a connection with normative male behavior is avoided. Since, in this view, the source of the behavior is thought to be within the psychology of the individual, attention is diverted away from culture or social structure as contributing factors. Thus, the psychopathological model ignores evidence which links sexual aggression to environmental variables and which suggests that rape, like all behavior, is learned.

Cultural Factors in Rape

Culture is a factor in rape, but the precise nature of the relationship between culture and sexual violence remains a topic of discussion. Ethnographic data from pre-industrial societies show the existence of rape-free cultures (Broude and Green, 1976; Sanday, 1979), although explanations for the phenomenon differ. Sanday (1979) relates sexual violence to contempt for female qualities and suggests that rape is part of a culture of violence and an expression of male dominance. In contrast, Blumberg (1979) argues that in pre-industrial societies women are more likely to lack important life options and to be physically and politically oppressed where they lack economic power relative to men. That is, in pre-industrial societies relative economic power enables women to win some immunity from men's use of force against them.

Among modern societies, the frequency of rape varies dramatically, and the United States is among the most rape-prone of all. In 1980, for example, the rate of reported rape and attempted rape for the United States was eighteen times higher than the corresponding rate for England and Wales (West, 1983). Spurred by the Women's Movement, feminists have generated an impressive body of theory regarding the cultural etiology of rape in the United States. Representative of the feminist view, Griffin (1971) called rape "The All American Crime."

The feminist perspective views rape as an act of violence and social control which functions to "keep women in their place" (Brownmiller, 1975; Kasinsky, 1975; Russell, 1975). Feminists see rape as an extension of normative male behavior, the result of conformity or overconformity to the values and prerogatives which define the traditional male sex role. That is, traditional socialization encourages males to associate power, dominance, strength, virility, and superiority with masculinity, and submissiveness, passivity, weakness, and inferiority with femininity. Furthermore, males are taught to have expectations about their level of sexual needs and expectations for corresponding female accessibility which function to justify forcing sexual access. The justification for forced sexual access is buttressed by legal, social, and religious definitions of women as male property and sex as an exchange of goods (Bart, 1979). Socialization prepares women to be "legitimate" victims and men to be potential offenders (Weis and Borges, 1973). Herman (1984) concludes that the United States is a rape culture because both genders are socialized to regard male aggression as a natural and normal part of sexual intercourse.

Feminists view pornography as an important element in a larger system of sexual violence; they see pornography as an expression of a rape-prone culture where women are seen as objects available for use by men (Morgan, 1980; Wheeler, 1985). Based on his content analysis of 428 "adults only" books, Smith (1976) makes a similar observation. He notes that, not only is rape presented as part of normal male/female sexual relations, but the woman, despite her terror, is always depicted as sexually aroused to the point of cooperation. In the end, she is ashamed but physically gratified. The message—women desire and enjoy rape—has more potential for damage than the image of the violence *per se.*

The fusion of these themes—sex as an impersonal act, the victim's uncontrollable orgasm, and the violent infliction of pain—is commonplace in the actual accounts of rapists. Scully and Marolla (1984) demonstrated that many convicted rapists denied their crime and attempted to justify their rapes by arguing that their victim enjoyed herself despite the use of a weapon and the infliction of serious injuries, or even death. In fact, many argued, they had been instrumental in making *her* fantasy come true.

The images projected in pornography contribute to a vocabulary of motive which trivializes and neutralizes rape and which might lessen the internal controls that otherwise would prevent sexually aggressive behavior. Men who rape use this culturally acquired vocabulary to justify their sexual violence.

Another consequence of the application of psychopathology to rape is that it leads one to view sexual violence as a special type of crime in which the motivations are subconscious and uncontrollable rather than overt and deliberate as with other criminal behavior. Black (1983) offers an approach to the analysis of criminal and/or violent behavior which, when applied to rape, avoids this bias. Black suggests that it is theoretically useful to ignore that crime is criminal in order to discover what such behavior has in common with other kinds of conduct. From his perspective, much of the crime in modern societies, as in pre-industrial societies, can be interpreted as a form of "self help" in which the actor is expressing a grievance through aggression and violence. From the actor's perspective, the victim is deviant and his own behavior is a form of social control in which the objective may be conflict management, punishment, or revenge. For example, in societies where women are considered the property of men, rape is sometimes used as a means of avenging the victim's husband or father (Black, 1983). In some cultures rape is used as a form of punishment. Such was the tradition among the puritanical, patriarchal Cheyenne, where men were valued for their ability as warriors. It was Cheyenne custom that a wife suspected of being unfaithful could be "put on the prairie" by her husband. Military confreres then were invited to "feast" on the prairie (Hoebel, 1954; Llewellyn and Hoebel, 1941). The ensuing mass rape was a husband's method of punishing his wife.

Black's (1983) approach is helpful in understanding rape because it forces one to examine the goals that some men have learned to achieve through sexually violent means. Thus, one approach to understanding why some men rape is to shift attention from individual psychopathology to the important question of what rapists gain from sexual aggression and violence in a culture seemingly prone to rape. In this paper, we address this question using data from interviews conducted with 114 convicted, incarcerated rapists.

Methods

SAMPLE

During 1980 and 1981 we interviewed 114 convicted rapists. All of the men had been convicted of the rape or attempted rape of an adult woman and subsequently incarcerated in a Virginia prison. Men convicted of other types of sexual offense were omitted from the sample.

In addition to their convictions for rape, 39 percent of the men also had convictions for burglary or robbery, 29 percent for abduction, 25 percent for sodomy, 11 percent for first or second degree murder, and 12 percent had been convicted of more than one rape. The majority of the men had previous criminal histories, but only 23 percent had a record of past sex offenses and only 26 percent had a history of emotional problems. Their sentences for rape and accompanying crimes ranged from ten years to seven life sentences plus 380 years for one man. Twenty-two percent of the rapists were serving at least one life sentence. Forty-six percent of the rapists were white, 54 percent black. In age, they ranged from 18 to 60 years, but the majority were between 18 and 35 years. Based on a statistical profile of felons in all Virginia prisons prepared by the Virginia Department of Corrections, it appears that this sample of rapists was disproportionately white and, at the time of the research, somewhat better educated and younger than the average inmate.

All participants in this research were volunteers. In constructing the sample, age, education, race, severity of current offense, and past criminal record were balanced within the limitations imposed by the characteristics of the volunteer pool. Obviously the sample was not random and thus may not be typical of all rapists, imprisoned or otherwise.

How Offenders View the Rewards of Rape

REVENGE AND PUNISHMENT

As noted earlier, Black's (1983) perspective suggests that a rapist might see his act as a legitimized form of revenge or punishment. Additionally, he asserts that the idea of "collective liability" accounts for much seemingly random violence. "Collective liability" suggests that all people in a particular category are held accountable for the conduct of each of their counterparts. Thus, the victim of a violent act may merely represent the category of individual being punished.

These factors—revenge, punishment, and the collective liability of women—can be used to explain a number of rapes in our research. Several cases will illustrate ways in which these factors combined in various types of rape. Revenge-rapes were among the most brutal and often included beatings, serious injuries, and even murder.

Typically, revenge-rapes included the element of collective liability. That is, from the rapist's perspective, the victim was a substitute for the woman on whom he wanted revenge. As explained elsewhere (Scully and Marolla, 1984), an upsetting event, involving a woman, preceded a significant number of rapes. When they raped, these men were angry because of a perceived indiscretion, typically related to a rigid, moralistic standard of sexual conduct, which they required from "their woman" but, in most cases, did not abide by themselves. Over and over these rapists talked about using rape "to get even" with their wives or some other significant woman. Typical is a young man who, prior to the rape, had a violent argument with his wife over what eventually proved to be her misdiagnosed case of venereal disease. She assumed the disease had been contracted through him, an accusation that infuriated him. After fighting with his wife, he explained that he drove around "thinking about hurting someone." He encountered his victim, a stranger, on the road where her car had broken down. It appears she accepted his offered ride because her car was out of commission. When she realized that rape was pending, she called him "a son of a bitch," and attempted to resist. He reported flying into a rage and beating her, and he confided,

> I have never felt that much anger before. If she had resisted, I would have killed her. . . . The rape was for revenge. I didn't have an orgasm. She was there to get my hostile feelings off on.

Although not the most common form of revenge-rape, sexual assault continues to be used in retaliation against the victim's male partner. In one such case, the offender, angry because the victim's husband owed him money, went to the victim's home to collect. He confided, "I was going to get it one way or another." Finding the victim alone, he explained, they started to argue about the money and,

> I grabbed her and started beating the hell out of her. Then I committed the act. I knew what I was doing. I was mad. I could have stopped, but I didn't. I did it to get even with her and her husband.

Griffin (1971) points out that when women are viewed as commodities, "In raping another man's woman, a man may aggrandize his own manhood and concurrently reduce that of the other man" (p. 33).

Revenge-rapes often contained an element of punishment. In some cases, while the victim was not the initial object of the revenge, the intent was to punish her because of something that transpired after the decision to rape had been made or during the course of the rape itself. This was the case with a young man whose wife had recently left him. Although they were in the process of reconciliation, he remained angry and upset over the separation. The night of the rape, he met the victim and her friend in a bar where he had gone to watch a fight on TV. The two women apparently accepted a ride from him, but after taking her friend home, he drove the victim to his apartment. At his apartment, he found a note from his wife indicating she had stopped by to watch the fight with him. This increased his anger because he preferred his wife's company. Inside his apartment, the victim allegedly remarked that she was sexually interested in his dog, which, he reported, put him in a rage. In the ensuing attack, he raped and pistol-whipped the victim. Then he forced a vacuum cleaner hose, switched on suction, into her vagina and bit her breast, severing the nipple. He stated:

> I hated at the time, but I don't know if it was her (the victim). (Who could it have been?) My wife? Even though we were getting back together. I still didn't trust her.

During his interview, it became clear that this offender, like many of the men, believed men have the right to discipline and punish women. In fact, he argued that most of the men he knew would also have beaten the victim because "that kind of thing (referring to the dog) is not acceptable among my friends."

Finally, in some rapes, both revenge and punishment were directed at victims because they represented women whom these offenders perceived as collectively responsible and liable for their problems. Rape was used "to put women in their place" and as a method of proving their "manhood" by displaying dominance over a female. For example, one multiple rapist believed his actions were related to the feeling that women thought they were better than he was.

> Rape was a feeling of total dominance. Before the rapes, I would always get a feeling of power and anger. I would degrade women so I could feel there was a person of less worth than me.

Another, especially brutal, case involved a young man from an upper middle class background, who spilled out his story in a seven-hour interview conducted in his solitary confinement cell. He described himself as tremendously angry, at the time, with his girlfriend, who he believed was involved with him in a "storybook romance," and from whom he expected complete fidelity. When she went away to college and became involved with another man, his revenge lasted eighteen months and involved the rape and murder of five women, all strangers who lived in his community. Explaining his rape-murders, he stated:

> I wanted to take my anger and frustration out on a stranger, to be in control, to do what I wanted to do. I wanted to use and abuse someone as I felt used and abused. I was killing my girl friend. During the rapes and murders, I would think

about my girl friend. I hated the victims because they probably messed men over. I hated women because they were deceitful and I was getting revenge for what happened to me.

AN ADDED BONUS

Burglary and robbery commonly accompany rape. Among our sample, 39 percent of the rapists had also been convicted of one or the other of these crimes committed in connection with rape. In some cases, the original intent was rape, and robbery was an afterthought. However, a number of men indicated that the reverse was true in their situation. That is, the decision to rape was made subsequent to their original intent, which was burglary or robbery.

This was the case with a young offender who stated that he originally intended only to rob the store in which the victim happened to be working. He explained that when he found the victim alone,

> I decided to rape her to prove I had guts. She was just there. It could have been anybody.

Similarly, another offender indicated that he initially broke into his victim's home to burglarize it. When he discovered the victim asleep, he decided to seize the opportunity "to satisfy an urge to go to bed with a white woman, to see if it was different." Indeed a number of men indicated that the decision to rape had been made after they realized they were in control of the situation. This was also true of an unemployed offender who confided that his practice was to steal whenever he needed money. On the day of the rape, he drove to a local supermarket and paced the parking lot, "staking out the situation." His pregnant victim was the first person to come along alone and "she was an easy target." Threatening her with a knife, he reported the victim as saying she would do anything if he didn't harm her. At that point, he decided to force her to drive to a deserted area, where he raped her. He explained:

> I wasn't thinking about sex. But when she said she would do anything not to get hurt, probably because she was pregnant, I thought, "why not?"

The attitude of these men toward rape was similar to their attitude toward burglary and robbery. Quite simply, if the situation is right, "why not?" From the perspective of these rapists, rape was just another part of the crime—an added bonus.

SEXUAL ACCESS

In an effort to change public attitudes that are damaging to the victims of rape and to reform laws seemingly premised on the assumption that women both ask for and enjoy rape, many writers emphasize the violent and aggressive character of rape. Often such arguments appear to discount the part that sex plays in the crime. The data clearly indicate that from the rapists' point of view, rape is in part sexually motivated. Indeed, it is the sexual aspect of rape that distinguishes it from other forms of assault.

Rape as a means of sexual access also shows the deliberate nature of this crime. When a woman is unwilling or seems unavailable for sex, the rapist can seize what isn't volunteered. In discussing his decision to rape, one man made this clear.

> . . . a real fox, beautiful shape. She was a beautiful woman and I wanted to see what she had.

The attitude that sex is a male entitlement suggests that when a woman says "no," rape is a suitable method of conquering the "offending" object. If, for example, a woman is picked up at a party or in a bar or while hitchhiking (behavior which a number of the rapists saw as a signal of sexual availability), and the woman later resists sexual advances, rape is presumed to be justified. The same justification operates in what is popularly called "date rape." The belief that sex was their just compensation compelled a number of rapists to insist they had not raped. Such was the case of an offender who raped and seriously beat his victim when, on their second date, she refused his sexual advances.

> I think I was really pissed off at her because it didn't go as planned. I could have been with someone else. She led me on but wouldn't deliver. . . . I have a male ego that must be fed.

The purpose of such rapes was conquest, to seize what was not offered.

Despite the cultural belief that young women are the most sexually desirable, several rapes involved the deliberate choice of a victim relatively older than the assailant. Since the rapists were themselves rather young (26 to 30 years of age on the average), they were expressing a preference for sexually experienced, rather than elderly, women. Men who chose victims older than themselves often said they did so because they believed that sexually experienced women were more desirable partners. They raped because they also believed that these women would not be sexually attracted to them.

Finally, sexual access emerged as a factor in the accounts of black men who consciously chose to rape white women. The majority of rapes in the United States are intraracial. However, for the past 20 years, according to national data based on reported rapes as well as victimization studies, which include unreported rapes, the rate of black on white (B/W) rape has significantly exceeded the rate of white on black (W/B) rape (La Free, 1982). Indeed, we may be experiencing a historical anomaly, since, as Brownmiller (1975) has documented, white men have freely raped women of color in the past. The current structure of interracial rape, however, reflects contemporary racism and race relations in several ways.

First, the status of black women in the United States today is relatively lower than the status of white women. Further, prejudice, segregation, and other factors continue to militate against interracial coupling. Thus, the desire for sexual access to higher status, unavailable women, an important function in B/W rape, does not motivate white men to rape black women. Equally important, demographic and geographic barriers interact to lower the incidence of W/B rape. Segregation as well as the poverty expected in black neighborhoods undoubtedly discourages many whites from choosing such areas as a target for housebreaking or robbery. Thus, the number of rapes that would occur in conjunction with these crimes is reduced.

Reflecting in part the standards of sexual desirability set by the dominant white society, a number of black rapists indicated they had been curious about white women. Blocked by racial barriers from legitimate sexual relations with white women, they raped to gain access to them. They described raping white women as "the ultimate experience" and "high status among my friends. It gave me a feeling of status, power, macho." For another man, raping a white woman had a special appeal because it violated a "known taboo," making it more dangerous, and thus more exciting to him, than raping a black woman.

IMPERSONAL SEX AND POWER

The idea that rape is an impersonal rather than an intimate or mutual experience appealed to a number of rapists, some of whom suggested it was their preferred form of sex. The fact that rape allowed them to control rather than care encouraged some to act on this preference. For example, one man explained,

> Rape gave me the power to do what I wanted to do without feeling I had to please a partner or respond to a partner. I felt in control, dominant. Rape was the ability to have sex without caring about the woman's response. I was totally dominant.

Another rapist commented:

> Seeing them laying there helpless gave me the confidence that I could do it. . . . With rape, I felt totally in charge. I'm bashful, timid. When a woman wanted to give in normal sex, I was intimidated. In the rapes, I was totally in command, she totally submissive.

During his interview, another rapist confided that he had been fantasizing about rape for several weeks before committing his offense. His belief was that it would be "an exciting experience—a new high." Most appealing to him was the idea that he could make his victim "do it all for him" and that he would be in control. He fantasized that she "would submit totally and that I could have anything I wanted." Eventually, he decided to act because his older brother told him, "forced sex is great, I wouldn't get caught and, besides, women love it." Though now he admits to his crime, he continues to believe his victim "enjoyed it." Perhaps we should note here that the appeal of impersonal sex is not limited to convicted rapists. The amount of male sexual activity that occurs in homosexual meeting places as well as the widespread use of prostitutes suggests that avoidance of intimacy appeals to a large segment of the male population. Through rape men can experience power and avoid the emotions related to intimacy and tenderness. Further, the popularity of violent pornography suggests that a wide variety of men in this culture have learned to be aroused by sex fused with violence (Smith, 1976). Consistent with this observation, experimental research conducted by Malamuth et al. (1980) demonstrates that men are aroused by images that depict women as orgasmic under conditions of violence and pain. They found that, for female students, arousal was high when the victim experienced an orgasm and *no* pain, whereas male students were highly aroused when the victim experienced an orgasm *and* pain. On the basis of their results, Malamuth et al. suggest that forcing a woman to climax despite her pain and abhorrence of the assailant makes the rapist feel powerful; he has gained control over the only source of power historically associated with women, their bodies. In the final analysis, dominance was the objective of most rapists.

RECREATION AND ADVENTURE

Among gang rapists, most of whom were in their late teens or early twenties when convicted, rape represented recreation and adventure, another form of delinquent activity. Part of rape's appeal was the sense of male camaraderie engendered by participating collectively in a dangerous activity. To prove one's self capable of "performing" under these circumstances was a substantial challenge and also a source of reward. One gang rapist articulated this feeling very clearly.

> We felt powerful; we were in control. I wanted sex, and there was peer pressure. She wasn't like a person, no personality, just domination on my part. Just to show I could do it—you know, macho.

Our research revealed several forms of gang rape. A common pattern was hitchhike-abduction for the purpose of having sex. Though the intent was rape, a number of men did not view it as such because they were convinced that women hitchhiked primarily to signal sexual availability and only secondarily as a form of transportation. In these cases, the unsuspecting victim was driven to a deserted area, raped, and in the majority of cases physically injured. Sometimes, the victim was not hitchhiking; she was abducted at knife or gun point from the street, usually at night. Some of these men did not view this type of attack as rape either, because they believed a woman walking alone at night to be a prostitute. In addition, they were often convinced "she enjoyed it."

"Gang date" rape was another popular variation. In this pattern, one member of the gang would make a date with the victim. Then, without her knowledge or consent, she would be driven to a predetermined location and forcibly raped by each member of the group. One young man revealed this practice was so much a part of his group's recreational routine, they had rented a house for the purpose. From his perspective, the rape was justified because "usually the girl had a bad reputation, or we knew it was what she liked."

During his interview, another offender confessed to participating in twenty or thirty such "gang date" rapes because his driver's license had been revoked, making it difficult for him to "get girls." Sixty percent of the time, he claimed, "they were girls known to do this kind of thing," but "frequently, the girls didn't want to have sex with all of us." In such cases, he said, "It might start out as rape, but, then, they (the women) would quiet down and none ever reported it to the police." He was convicted for a gang rape, which he described as "the ultimate thing I ever did," because unlike his other rapes, the victim, in this case, was a stranger whom the group abducted as she walked home from the library. He felt the group's past experience with "gang date" rape had prepared them for this crime in which the victim was blindfolded and driven to the mountains where, though it was winter, she was forced to remove her clothing. Lying on the snow, she was raped by each of the four men several times before being abandoned near a farm house. This young man continued to believe that if he had spent the night with her, rather than abandoning her, she would not have reported it to the police.

Solitary rapists also used terms like "exciting," "a challenge," "an adventure" to describe their feelings about rape. Like the gang rapists, these men found the element of danger made rape all the more exciting. Typifying this attitude was one man who described his rape as intentional. He reported:

> It was exciting to get away with it (rape), just being able to beat the system, not women. It was like doing something illegal and getting away with it.

Another rapist confided that for him "rape was just more exciting and compelling" than a normal sexual encounter because it involved forcing a stranger. A multiple rapist asserted, "It was the excitement and fear and the drama that made rape a big kick."

FEELING GOOD

When the men were asked to recall their feelings immediately following the rape, only eight percent indicated that guilt or feeling bad was part of their emotional response. The majority said they felt good, relieved, or simply nothing at all. Some indicated they had been afraid of being caught or felt sorry for themselves. Only two men out of 114 expressed any concern or feeling for the victim. Feeling good or nothing at all about raping women is not an aberration limited to men in prison. Smithyman (1978), in his study of "undetected rapists"—rapists outside of prison—found that raping women had no impact on their lives, nor did it have a negative effect on their self-image.

Significantly, a number of men volunteered the information that raping had a positive impact on their feelings. For some, the satisfaction was in revenge. For example, the man who had raped and murdered five women:

> It seems like so much bitterness and tension had built up, and this released it. I felt like I had just climbed a mountain and now I could look back.

Another offender characterized rape as habit forming: "Rape is like smoking. You can't stop once you start." Finally, one man expressed the sentiments of many rapists when he stated,

> After rape, I always felt like I had just conquered something, like I had just ridden the bull at Gilley's.

Conclusions

This paper has explored rape from the perspective of a group of convicted, incarcerated rapists. The purpose was to discover how these men viewed sexual violence and what they gained from their behavior.

We found that rape was frequently a means of revenge and punishment. Implicit in revenge-rapes was the notion that women were collectively liable for the rapists' problems. In some cases, victims were substitutes for significant women on whom the men desired to take revenge. In other cases, victims were thought to represent all women, and rape was used to punish, humiliate, and "put them in their place." In both cases women were seen as a class, a category, not as individuals. For some men, rape was almost an afterthought, a bonus added to burglary or robbery. Other men gained access to sexually unavailable or unwilling women through rape. For this group of men, rape was a fantasy come true, a particularly exciting form of impersonal sex which enabled them to dominate and control women, by exercising a singularly male form of power. These rapists talked of the pleasures of raping—how for them it was a challenge, an adventure, a dangerous and "ultimate" experience. Rape made them feel good and, in some cases, even elevated their self-image.

The pleasure these men derived from raping reveals the extreme to which they objectified women. Women were seen as sexual commodities to be used or conquered rather than as human beings with rights and feelings. One young man expressed the extreme of the contemptful view of women when he confided to the female researcher.

> Rape is a man's right. If a woman doesn't want to give it, the man should take it. Women have no right to say no. Women are made to have sex. It's all they are good for. Some women would rather take a beating, but they always give in; it's what they are for.

This man murdered his victim because she wouldn't "give in."

Undoubtedly, some rapes, like some of all crimes, are idiopathic. However, it is not necessary to resort to pathological motives to account for all rape or other acts of sexual violence. Indeed, we find that men who rape have something to teach us about the cultural roots of sexual aggression. They force us to acknowledge that rape is more than an idiosyncratic act committed by a few "sick" men. Rather, rape can be viewed as the end point in a continuum of sexually aggressive behaviors that reward men and victimize women. In the way that motives for committing any criminal act can be rationally determined, reasons for rape can also be determined. Our data demonstrate that some men rape because they have learned that in this culture, sexual violence is rewarding. Significantly, the overwhelming majority of these rapists indicated they never thought they would go to prison for what they did. Some did not fear imprisonment because they did not define their behavior as rape. Others knew that women frequently do not report rape and of those cases that are reported, conviction rates are low, and therefore they felt secure. These men perceived rape as a rewarding, low-risk act. Understanding that otherwise normal men can and do rape is critical to the development of strategies for prevention.

We are left with the fact that all men do not rape. In view of the apparent rewards and cultural supports for rape, it is important to ask why some men do not rape. Hirschi (1969) makes a similar observation about delinquency. He argues that the key question is not "Why do they do it?" but rather "Why don't we do it?" (p. 34). Likewise, we may be seeking an answer to the wrong question about sexual assault of women. Instead of asking men who rape "Why?" perhaps we should be asking men who don't "Why not?"

References

Abel, G., J. Becker, and L. Skinner (1980). "Aggressive behavior and sex." *Psychiatric Clinics of North America 3:* 133–51.

Bart, P. (1979). "Rape as a paradigm of sexism in society—victimization and its discontents." *Women's Studies International Quarterly 2:* 347–57.

Black, D. (1983). "Crime as social control." *American Sociological Review 48:* 34–45.

Blumberg, R. L. (1979). "A paradigm for predicting the position of women: Policy implications and problems." Pp. 113–42 in J. Lipman-Blumen and J. Bernard (eds.), *Sex Roles and Social Policy.* London: Sage Studies in International Sociology.

Broude, G., and S. Green (1976). "Cross-cultural codes on twenty sexual attitudes and practices." *Ethnology 15:* 409–28.

Brownmiller, S. (1975). *Against Our Will.* New York: Simon & Schuster.

Fisher, G., and E. Rivlin (1971). "Psychological needs of rapists." *British Journal of Criminology 11:* 182–85.

Griffin, S. (1971, September). "Rape: The all American crime." *Ramparts 10:* 26–35.

Groth, N. (1979). *Men Who Rape.* New York: Plenum Press.

Hammer, E., and I. Jacks (1955). "A study of Rorschach flexnor and extensor human movements." *Journal of Clinical Psychology 11:* 63–67.

Herman, D. (1984). "The rape culture." Pp. 20–39 in J. Freeman (ed.), *Women: A Feminist Perspective.* Palo Alto, CA: Mayfield.

Hirschi, T. (1969). *Causes of Delinquency.* Berkeley: University of California Press.

Hoebel, E. A. (1954). *The Law of Primitive Man.* Boston: Harvard University Press.

Johnson, A. G. (1980). "On the prevalence of rape in the United States." *Signs* 6: 136–46.

Kanin, E. (1957). "Male aggression in dating-courtship relations." *American Journal of Sociology* 63: 197–204.

____ (1965). "Male sex aggression and three psychiatric hypotheses." *Journal of Sex Research* 1: 227–29.

____ (1967). "Reference groups and sex conduct norm violation." *Sociological Quarterly* 8: 495–504.

____ (1969). "Selected dyadic aspects of male sex aggression." *Journal of Sex Research* 5: 12–28.

Kasinsky, R. (1975, September). "Rape: A normal act?" *Canadian Forum,* pp. 18–22.

Kirkpatrick, C., and E. Kanin (1957). "Male sex aggression on a university campus." *American Sociological Review* 22: 52–58.

Koss, M. P., and K. E. Leonard (1984). "Sexually aggressive men: Empirical findings and theoretical implications." Pp. 213–32 in N. M. Malamuth and E. Donnerstein (eds.), *Pornography and Sexual Aggression.* New York: Academic Press.

LaFree, G. (1980). "The effect of sexual stratification by race on official reactions to rape." *American Sociological Review* 45: 824–54.

____ (1982). "Male power and female victimization: Towards a theory of interracial rape." *American Journal of Sociology* 88: 311–28.

Llewellyn, K. N., and E. A. Hoebel (1941). *The Cheyenne Way: Conflict and Case Law in Primitive Jurisprudence.* Norman: University of Oklahoma Press.

Malamuth, N., S. Haber, and S. Feshback (1980). "Testing hypotheses regarding rape: Exposure to sexual violence, sex difference, and the 'normality' of rapists." *Journal of Research in Personality* 14: 121–37.

Malamuth, N., M. Heim, and S. Feshback (1980). "Sexual responsiveness of college students to rape depictions: Inhibitory and disinhibitory effects." *Social Psychology* 38: 399–408.

Meyer, T. J. (1984, December 5). " 'Date rape': A serious problem that few talk about." *Chronicle of Higher Education.*

Morgan, R. (1980). "Theory and practice: Pornography and rape." Pp. 134–40 in L. Lederer (ed.), *Take Back the Night: Women on Pornography.* New York: William Morrow.

Rada, R. (1978). *Clinical Aspects of Rape.* New York: Grune & Stratton.

Russell, D. (1975). *The Politics of Rape.* New York: Stein & Day.

Sanday, P. R. (1979). *The Socio-Cultural Context of Rape.* Washington, D.C.:U.S. Dept. of Commerce, National Technical Information Service.

Scully, D., and J. Marolla (1984). "Convicted rapists' vocabulary of motive: Excuses and justifications." *Social Problems* 31: 530–44.

____ (1985). "Rape and psychiatric vocabulary of motive: Alternative perspectives." Pp. 294–312 in A. W. Burgess (ed.), *Rape and Sexual Assault: A Research Handbook.* New York: Garland Publishing.

Smith, D. (1976). "The social context of pornography." *Journal of Communications* 26: 16–24.

Smithyman, S. (1978). *The Undetected Rapist.* Unpublished dissertation. Claremont Graduate School.

West, D. J. (1983). "Sex offenses and offending." Pp. 1–30 in M. Tonry and N. Morris (eds.), *Crime and Justice: An Annual Review of Research.* Chicago: University of Chicago Press.

Weis, K., and S. Borges (1973). "Victimology and rape: The case of the legitimate victim." *Issues in Criminology* 8: 71–115.

Wheeler, H. (1985). "Pornography and rape: A feminist perspective." Pp. 374–91 in A. W. Burgess (ed.), *Rape and Sexual Assault: A Research Handbook.* New York: Garland Publishing.

6   Street Corner Society

WILLIAM FOOTE WHYTE

Field work is fascinating both to do and to read about, as it unites the researcher with the data in a way that no other sociological method allows. It is the closeness of the researcher to the people being studied, the first-hand observations and even participation in their lives, that allows the reader to gain a sense of "being there."

So it is with this selection from one of the most well-known books in sociology. In this classic work, Whyte lays bare some of the essentials of doing field work. Here you can see him struggling to find an acceptable role in an unfamiliar setting. He lets you look over his shoulder as he tries to discover a vantage point from which he can participate in this unfamiliar group, and yet remain somewhat aloof in order to be analytical. In remarkable candor, Whyte even lets you see some of the mistakes he made in this struggle. As you join him, you may sense the excitement of discovery that has hooked many of us on sociology.

First Efforts

WHEN I BEGAN MY WORK, I had had no training in sociology or anthropology. I thought of myself as an economist and naturally looked first toward the matters that we had taken up in economics courses, such as economics of slum housing. At the time I was sitting in on a course in slums and housing in the Sociology Department at Harvard. As a term project I took on a study of one block in Cornerville. To legitimize this effort, I got in touch with a private agency that concerned itself in housing matters and offered to turn over to them the results of my survey. With that backing, I began knocking on doors, looking into flats, and talking to the tenants about the living conditions. This brought me into contact with Cornerville people, but it would be hard now to devise a more inappropriate way of beginning a study such as I was eventually to make. I felt ill at ease at this intrusion, and I am sure so did the people. I wound up the block study as rapidly as I could and wrote it off as a total loss as far as gaining a real entry into the district.

Shortly thereafter I made another false start—if so tentative an effort may even be called a start. At that time I was completely baffled at the problem of finding my way into the district. Cornerville was right before me and yet so far away. I could walk freely up and down its streets, and I had even made my way into some of the flats, and yet I was still a stranger in a world completely unknown to me.

At this time I met a young economics instructor at Harvard who impressed me with his self-assurance and his knowledge of Eastern City. He had once been attached to a settlement house, and he talked glibly about his associations with the tough young men and women of the district. He also described how he would occasionally drop in on some drinking place in the area and strike up an acquaintance with a girl, buy her a drink, and then encourage her to tell him her life-story. He claimed that the women so encountered were appreciative of this opportunity and that it involved no further obligation.

This approach seemed at least as plausible as anything I had been able to think of. I resolved to try it out. I picked on the Regal Hotel, which was on the edge of Cornerville. With some trepidation I climbed the stairs to the bar and entertainment area and looked around. There I encountered a situation for which my adviser had not prepared me. There were women present all right, but none of them was alone. Some were there in couples, and there were two or three pairs of women together. I pondered this situation briefly. I had little confidence in my skill at picking up one female, and it seemed inadvisable to tackle two at the same time. Still, I was determined not to admit defeat without a struggle. I looked around me again and now noticed a threesome: one man and two women. It occurred to me that here was a maldistribution of females which I might be able to rectify. I approached the group and opened with something like this: "Pardon me. Would you mind if I joined you?" There was a moment of silence while the man stared at me. He then offered to throw me downstairs. I assured him that this would not be necessary and demonstrated as much by walking right out of there without any assistance.

I subsequently learned that hardly anyone from Cornerville ever went into the Regal Hotel. If my efforts there had been crowned with success, they would no doubt have led somewhere but certainly not to Cornerville.

For my next effort I sought out the local settlement houses. They were open to the public, . . . [and they] proved the right place for me at this time, for it was here that I met Doc. I had talked to a number of the social workers about my plans and hopes to get acquainted with the people and study the district. [T]he head of girls' work in the Norton Street House understood what I needed. She began describing Doc to me. He was, she said, a very intelligent and talented person who had at one time been fairly active in the house but had dropped out, so that he hardly ever came in any more. Perhaps he could understand what I wanted, and he must have the contacts that I needed. . . .

In a sense, my study began on the evening of February 3, 1937, when the social worker called me in to meet Doc. She showed us into her office and then left so that we could talk. . . .

As I remember it, I said that I had been interested in congested city districts in my college study but had felt very remote from them. I hoped to study the problems in such a district. I felt I could do very little as an outsider. Only if I could get to know the people and learn their problems first hand would I be able to gain the understanding I needed.

Doc heard me out without any change of expression, so that I had no way of predicting his reaction. When I was finished, he asked: "Do you want to see the high life or the low life?"

"I want to see all that I can. I want to get as complete a picture of the community as possible."

"Well, any nights you want to see anything, I'll take you around. I can take you to the joints—gambling joints—I can take you around to the street corners. Just remember that you're my friend. That's all they need to know. I know these places, and, if I tell them that you're my friend, nobody will bother you. You just tell me what you want to see, and we'll arrange it."

The proposal was so perfect that I was at a loss for a moment as to how to respond to it. We talked a while longer, as I sought to get some pointers as to how I should behave in his company. He warned me that I might have to take the risk of getting arrested in a raid on a gambling joint but added that this was not serious. I only had to give a false name and then would get bailed out by the man that ran the place, paying only a five-dollar fine. I agreed to take this chance. I asked him whether I should gamble with the others in the gambling joints. He said it was unnecessary and, for a greenhorn like myself, very inadvisable.

At last I was able to express my appreciation. "You know, the first steps of getting to know a community are the hardest. I could see things going with you that I wouldn't see for years otherwise."

"That's right. You tell me what you want to see, and we'll arrange it. When you want some information, I'll ask for it, and you listen. When you want to find out their philosophy of life, I'll start an argument and get it for you. If there's something else you want to get, I'll stage an act for you. Not a scrap, you know, but just tell me what you want, and I'll get it for you."

"That's swell. I couldn't ask for anything better. Now I'm going to try to fit in all right, but, if at any time you see I'm getting off on the wrong foot, I want you to tell me about it."

"Now we're being too dramatic. You won't have any trouble. You come in as my friend. When you come in like that, at first everybody will treat you with respect. You can take a lot of liberties, and nobody will kick. After a while when they get to know you they will treat you like anybody else—you know, they say familiarity breeds contempt. But you'll never have any trouble. There's just one thing to watch out for. Don't spring [treat] people. Don't be too free with your money."

"You mean they'll think I'm a sucker?"

"Yes, and you don't want to buy your way in."

That was our beginning. At the time I found it hard to believe that I could move in as easily as Doc had said with his sponsorship. But that indeed was the way it turned out. . . .

Beginning with Doc

I can still remember my first outing with Doc. We met one evening at the Norton Street House and set out from there to a gambling place a couple of blocks away. I followed Doc anxiously down the long, dark hallway at the back of a tenement building. I was not worried about the possibility of a police raid. I was thinking about how I would fit in and be accepted. The door opened into a small kitchen almost bare of furnishings and with the paint peeling off the walls. As soon as we went in the door, I took off my hat and began looking around for a place to hang it. There was no place. I looked around, and here I learned my first lesson in participant observation in Cornerville: Don't take off your hat in the house—at least not when you are among men. It may be permissible, but certainly not required, to take your hat off when women are around.

Doc introduced me as "my friend Bill" to Chichi, who ran the place, and to Chichi's friends and customers. I stayed there with Doc part of the time in the kitchen, where several men would sit around and talk, and part of the time in the other room watching the crap game.

There was talk about gambling, horse races, sex, and other matters. Mostly I just listened and tried to act friendly and interested. We had wine and coffee with anisette in it, with the fellows chipping in to pay for the refreshments. (Doc would not let me pay my share on this first occasion.) As Doc had predicted, no one asked me about myself, but he told me later that, when I went to the toilet, there was an excited burst of conversation in Italian and that he had to assure them that I was not a G-man. He said he told them flatly that I was a friend of his, and they agreed to let it go at that.

We went several more times together to Chichi's gambling joint, and then the time came when I dared to go in alone. When I was greeted in a natural and friendly manner, I felt that I was now beginning to find a place for myself in Cornerville.

When Doc did not go off to the gambling joint, he spent his time hanging around Norton Street, and I began hanging with him. At first, Norton Street meant only a place to wait until I could go somewhere else. Gradually, as I got to know the men better, I found myself becoming one of the Norton Street gang.

Then the Italian Community Club was formed in the Norton Street Settlement, and Doc was invited to be a member. Doc maneuvered to get me into the club, and I was glad to join, as I could see that it represented something distinctly different from the corner gangs I was meeting.

As I began to meet the men of Cornerville, I also met a few of the girls. One girl I took to a church dance. The next morning the fellows on the street corner were asking me: "How your steady girl?" This brought me up short. I learned that going to the girl's house was something that you just did not do unless you hoped to marry her. Fortunately, the girl and her family knew that I did not know the local customs, so they did not assume that I was thus committed. However, this was a useful warning. After this time, even though I found some Cornerville girls exceedingly attractive, I never went out with them except on a group basis, and I did not make any more home visits either.

As I went along, I found that life in Cornerville was not nearly so interesting and pleasant for the girls as it was for the men. A young man had complete freedom to wander and hang around. The girls could not hang on street corners. They had to divide their time between their own homes, the homes of girl friends and relatives, and a job, if they had one. Many of them had a dream that went like this: some young man, from outside of Cornerville, with a little money, a good job, and a good education would come and woo them and take them out of the district. I could hardly afford to fill this role.

Training in Participant Observation

. . . As I began hanging about Cornerville, I found that I needed an explanation for myself and for my study. As long as I was with Doc and vouched for by him, no one asked me who I was or what I was doing. When I circulated in other groups or even among the Nortons without him, it was obvious that they were curious about me. . . . I soon found that people were developing their own explanation about me: I was writing a book about Cornerville. This might seem entirely too vague an explanation, and yet it sufficed. I found that my acceptance in the district depended on the personal relationships I developed far more than upon any explanations I might give. Whether it was a good thing to write a book about Cornerville depended entirely on people's opinions of me personally. If I was all right, then my project was all right; if I was no good, then no amount of explanation could convince them that the book was a good idea. . . .

I learned early in my Cornerville period the crucial importance of having the support of the key individuals in any groups or organizations I was studying. Instead of trying to explain myself to everyone, I found I was providing far more information about myself and my study to leaders such as Doc than I volunteered to the average corner boy. I always tried to give the impression that I was willing and eager to tell just as much about my study as anyone wished to know, but it was only with group leaders that I made a particular effort to provide really full information.

My relationship with Doc changed rapidly in this early Cornerville period. At first he was simply a key informant—and also my sponsor. As we spent more time together, I ceased to treat him as a passive informant. I discussed with him quite frankly what I was trying to do, what problems were puzzling me, and so on. Much of our time was spent in this discussion of ideas and observations, so that Doc became, in a very real sense, a collaborator in the research.

This full awareness of the nature of my study stimulated Doc to look for and point out to me the sorts of observations that I was interested in. Often when I picked him up at the flat where he lived with his sister and brother-in-law, he said to me: "Bill, you should have been around last night. You would have been interested in this." And then he would go on to tell me what had happened. Such accounts were always interesting and relevant to my study. . . .

In my interviewing methods I had been instructed not to argue with people or pass moral judgments upon them. This fell in with my own inclinations. I was glad to accept the people and to be accepted by them. However, this attitude did not come out so much in interviewing, for I did little formal interviewing. I sought to show this interested acceptance of the people and the community in my everyday participation.

I learned to take part in the street corner discussions on baseball and sex. This required no special training, since the topics seemed to be matters of almost universal interest. I was not able to participate so actively in discussions of horse-racing. I did begin to follow the races in a rather general and amateur way. I am sure it would have paid me to devote more study to the *Morning Telegraph* and other racing sheets, but my knowledge of baseball at least insured that I would not be left out of the street corner conversations.

While I avoided expressing opinions on sensitive topics, I found that arguing on some matters was simply part of the social pattern and that one could hardly participate without joining in the argument. I often found myself involved in heated but good-natured arguments about the relative merits of certain major-league ball players and managers. Whenever a girl or a group of girls would walk down the street, the fellows on the corner would make mental notes and later would discuss their evaluations of the females. These evaluations would run largely in terms of shape, and here I was glad to argue that Mary had a better "build" than Anna, or vice versa. Of course, if any of the men on the corner happened to be personally attached to Mary or Anna, no searching comments would be made, and I, too, would avoid this topic.

Sometimes I wondered whether just hanging on the street corner was an active enough process to be dignified by the term "research." Perhaps I should be asking these men questions. However, one has to learn when to question and when not to question as well as what questions to ask.

I learned this lesson one night in the early months when I was with Doc in Chichi's gambling joint. A man from another part of the city was regaling us with a tale of the organization of gambling activity. I had been told that he had once been a very big gambling operator, and he talked knowingly about many interesting matters. He did most of the talking, but the others asked questions and threw in comments, so at length I began to feel that I must say something in order to be part of the group. I said: "I suppose the cops were all paid off?"

The gambler's jaw dropped. He glared at me. Then he denied

vehemently that any policemen had been paid off and immediately switched the conversation to another subject. For the rest of that evening I felt very uncomfortable.

The next day Doc explained the lesson of the previous evening. "Go easy on that 'who,' 'what,' 'why,' 'when,' 'where' stuff, Bill. You ask those questions, and people will clam up on you. If people accept you, you can just hang around, and you'll learn the answers in the long run without even having to ask the questions."

I found that this was true. As I sat and listened, I learned the answers to questions that I would not even have had the sense to ask if I had been getting my information solely on an interviewing basis. I did not abandon questioning altogether, of course. I simply learned to judge the sensitiveness of the question and my relationship to the people so that I only asked a question in a sensitive area when I was sure that my relationship to the people involved was very solid.

When I had established my position on the street corner, the data simply came to me without very active efforts on my part. It was only now and then, when I was concerned with a particular problem and felt I needed more information from a certain individual, that I would seek an opportunity to get the man alone and carry on a more formal interview.

At first I concentrated upon fitting into Cornerville, but a little later I had to face the question of how far I was to immerse myself in the life of the district. I bumped into that problem one evening as I was walking down the street with the Nortons. Trying to enter into the spirit of the small talk, I cut loose with a string of obscenities and profanity. The walk came to a momentary halt as they all stopped to look at me in surprise. Doc shook his head and said: "Bill, you're not supposed to talk like that. That doesn't sound like you."

I tried to explain that I was only using terms that were common on the street corner. Doc insisted, however, that I was different and that they wanted me to be that way.

This lesson went far beyond the use of obscenity and profanity. I learned that people did not expect me to be just like them; in fact, they were interested and pleased to find me different, just so long as I took a friendly interest in them. Therefore, I abandoned my efforts at complete immersion. My behavior was nevertheless affected by street corner life. When John Howard first came down from Harvard to join me in the Cornerville study, he noticed at once that I talked in Cornerville in a manner far different from that which I used at Harvard. This was not a matter of the use of profanity or obscenity, nor did I affect the use of ungrammatical expressions. I talked in the way that seemed natural to me, but what was natural in Cornerville was different from what was natural at Harvard. In Cornerville, I found myself putting much more animation into my speech, dropping terminal *g*'s, and using gestures much more actively. (There was also, of course, the difference in the vocabulary that I used. When I was most deeply involved in Cornerville, I found myself rather tongue-tied in my visits to Harvard. I simply could not keep up with the discussions of international relations, of the nature of science, and so on, in which I had once been more or less at home.) . . .

My first spring in Cornerville served to establish for me a firm position in the life of the district. I had only been there several weeks when Doc said to me: "You're just as much of a fixture around this street corner as that lamp-post." Perhaps the greatest event signalizing my acceptance on Norton Street was the baseball game that Mike Giovanni organized against the group of Norton Street boys in their late teens. It was the old men who had won glorious victories in the past against the rising youngsters. Mike assigned me to a regular position on a team, not a key position perhaps (I was stationed in right field), but at least I was there. When it was my turn to bat in the last half of the ninth inning, the score was tied, there were two outs, and the bases were loaded. As I reached down to pick up my bat, I heard some of the fellows suggesting to Mike that he ought to put in a pinch-hitter. Mike answered them in a loud voice that must have been meant for me: "No, I've got confidence in Bill Whyte. He'll come through in the clutch." So, with Mike's confidence to buck me up, I went up there, missed two swings, and then banged a hard grounder through the hole between second and short. At least that is where they told me it went. I was so busy getting down to first base that I did not know afterward whether I had reached there on an error or a base hit.

That night, when we went down for coffee, Danny presented me with a ring for being a regular fellow and a pretty good ball player. I was particularly impressed by the ring, for it had been made by hand. Danny had started with a clear amber die discarded from his crap game and over long hours had used his lighted cigarette to burn a hole through it and to round the corners so that it came out a heart shape on top. I assured the fellows that I would always treasure the ring.

Perhaps I should add that my game-winning base hit made the score 18–17, so it is evident that I was not the only one who had been hitting the ball. Still, it was a wonderful feeling to come through when they were counting on me, and it made me feel still more that I belonged on Norton Street. . . .

Reflections on Field Research

. . . *Street Corner Society* is about particular people and situations and events. I wanted to write about Cornerville. I found that I could not write about Cornerville in general without discarding most of the data I had upon individuals and groups. It was a long time before I realized that I could explain Cornerville better through telling the stories of those individuals and groups than I could in any other way.

Instead of studying the general characteristics of classes of people, I was looking at Doc, Chick, Tony Cataldo, George Ravello, and others. Instead of getting a cross-sectional picture of the community at a particular point in time, I was dealing with a time sequence of interpersonal events.

Although I could not cover all Cornerville, I was building up the structure and functioning of the community through intensive examination of some of its parts—*in action*. I was relating the parts together through observing events between groups and between group leaders and the members of the larger institutional structures (of politics and the rackets). I was seeking to build a sociology based upon observed interpersonal events. That, to me, is the chief methodological and theoretical meaning of *Street Corner Society*.

The Cultural Context of Social Life

W HAT IS CULTURE? The concept is easier to grasp by description than by definition. For example, when we meet someone from a different culture, that person's culture is immediately evident to us. We see it in his or her clothing, jewelry, and gestures. We hear it when that person speaks a different language, or when, in speaking our language, the individual uses unfamiliar expressions or voices opinions unlike ours. We may even smell it in unfamiliar perfumes and body lotions. These characteristics, especially when they contrast sharply with our own, alert us to broad differences in the way that person was reared—to that person's culture.

Culture consists of *material* things, such as art, weapons, utensils, machines, clothing, and jewelry. Culture is also *nonmaterial*, consisting of the beliefs and patterns of behavior common to a group of people. Nonmaterial (or *symbolic*) culture is of primary interest to sociologists, for it provides the broad framework that people use to interpret life. Culture is the lens through which we see the world, the basis on which we construct reality and make our decisions.

Understanding how culture affects people's lives is essential to attaining a sociological imagination. But while we may become aware of culture's pervasive influence when we meet someone from a different culture, our perception of *our own* culture is quite another matter. We usually take *our* speech, *our* body language, *our* beliefs, and *our* ways of doing things for granted. We assume that these are normal or natural, and almost without exception we perform them without question. As Ralph Linton said, "The last thing a fish would ever notice would be water." So it is with us: Except for unusual circumstances, the effects of our own culture generally remain imperceptible to us.

Yet culture's significance is profound—not only for our behavior, but also

71

for our orientations to life, and, ultimately, for our very being. It would be difficult to identify any aspect of who and what we are that is untouched by culture. We came into this life without a language, without values, with no ideas about religion, education, war, money, jobs, friendship, love, truth, honesty, honor, humor, family relationships, and so on. At birth, we possessed no such fundamental orientations to social life—which are so essential in determining the type of people we are. Yet now we take them for granted. This, we might say, is culture *within* us.

These learned and shared ways of believing and of doing things (another way to define culture) penetrate our being at an early age. They become part of our basic assumptions about what normal is. They form the screen through which we perceive and evaluate our world. Seldom do we question these assumptions, because like water for a fish, they form our framework for viewing life but remain beyond our ordinary perception.

On occasion, however, some unusual event may challenge our background assumptions. This makes our assumptions more visible to us, and, if we are fortunate, it even makes us aware of how arbitrary they are. For example, when several Americans converge at a ticket booth they usually line up on the basis of time of arrival. The ticket seller, sharing the same culture, also assumes the normalcy of this behavior and expects to sell tickets on a "first come, first served" basis. To us, this seems the natural way of doing things, and we engage in this behavior routinely, and without thought.

But in northern Africa, where people's ideas of how to use space sharply contrast with ours, when several people want a ticket each pushes his or her way toward the ticket booth. With no idea similar to our "first come, first served" notion, the ticket seller first dispenses tickets to the noisiest, the pushiest, and (not incidentally) those with the longest arms.

When I traveled in northern Africa, I found this part of their culture most upsetting. It violated my basic expectations of how people *ought* to act—expectations that I did not even know I held until they were challenged so abruptly. At that point I experienced *culture shock*, the sudden inability to depend on the basic orientations to everyday life learned in childhood. That I was several inches taller than most Arabs, however, and was able to outreach almost everyone, helped me to adjust (partially) to this different way of doing things. I never did get used to the idea that pushing ahead of others was "right," though, and always felt guilty about using the accident of my height to receive preferential treatment.

It is to sensitize us to this aspect of life in society—to how cultural factors so fundamentally influence our lives—that the selections in this third Part are directed. Each reading introduces us to aspects of our social lives that ordinarily go unquestioned and unnoticed. Horace Miner helps make visible our basic assumptions about taking care of the body; Napoleon Chagnon exposes our taken-for-granted assumptions about sharing, making requests, and how to treat strangers and guests; Edward and Mildred Hall illustrate how culture influences our posture, gestures, eye contact, and use of space in face-to-face communication; Theodore Caplow uncovers the cultural rules, many hidden beneath our consciousness, that govern our giving of Christmas gifts; and Erving Goffman helps us to see how our nonverbal communications are intricate ways by which we attempt to manipulate people's opinions of us. These analyses of culture can serve as starting points from which we can begin to analyze other assumptions of reality that we unquestioningly hold, and thus gain a startlingly different perspective of social life—and of our own roles in it.

7 Body Ritual Among the Nacirema

HORACE MINER

As part of their culture, all peoples develop ideas about proper ways to care for their bodies. The Nacirema, however, have advanced these ideas to an extraordinary degree, and they spend a good deal of their time, energy, and income following the rituals prescribed by their culture. Taking care of the body in the prescribed manner is so important to these people that even a good part of their childrearing revolves around instructing their children in the precise manner of fulfilling their cultural rituals. With intense and prolonged training, accompanied by punishing children who fail to conform while shunning nonconforming adults, it is no wonder that almost all members of the Nacirema culture unquestioningly conform to their prescribed body rituals and dutifully pass them on to their own children.

A better understanding of the Nacirema culture might possibly shed some light on our own way of life.

THE ANTHROPOLOGIST HAS BECOME so familiar with the diversity of ways in which different peoples behave in similar situations that he is not apt to be surprised by even the most exotic customs. In fact, if all of the logically possible combinations of behavior have not been found somewhere in the world, he is apt to suspect that they must be present in some yet undescribed tribe. This point has, in fact, been expressed with respect to clan organization by Murdock. In this light, the magical beliefs and practices of the Nacirema present such unusual aspects that it seems desirable to describe them as an example of the extremes to which human behavior can go.

Professor Linton first brought the ritual of the Nacirema to the attention of anthropologists twenty years ago, but the culture of this people is still very poorly understood. They are a North American group living in the territory between the Canadian Cree, the Yaqui and Tarahumare of Mexico, and the Carib and Arawak of the Antilles. Little is known of their origin, although tradition states that they came from the east.

Nacirema culture is characterized by a highly developed market economy which has evolved in a rich natural habitat. While much of the people's time is devoted to economic pursuits, a large part of the fruits of these labors and a considerable portion of the day are spent in ritual activity. The focus of this activity is the human body, the appearance and health of which loom as a dominant concern in the ethos of the people. While such a concern is certainly not unusual, its ceremonial aspects and associated philosophy are unique.

The fundamental belief underlying the whole system appears to be that the human body is ugly and that its natural tendency is to debility and disease. Incarcerated in such a body, man's only hope is to avert these characteristics through the use of the powerful influences of ritual and ceremony. Every household has one or more shrines devoted to this purpose. The more powerful individuals in the society have several shrines in their houses and, in fact, the opulence of a house is often referred to in terms of the number of such ritual centers it possesses. Most houses are of wattle and daub construction, but the shrine rooms of the more wealthy are walled with stone. Poorer families imitate the rich by applying pottery plaques to their shrine walls.

While each family has at least one such shrine, the rituals associated with it are not family ceremonies but are private and secret. The rites are normally only discussed with children, and then only during the period when they are being initiated into these mysteries. I was able, however, to establish sufficient rapport with the natives to examine these shrines and to have the rituals described to me.

The focal point of the shrine is a box or chest which is built into the wall. In this chest are kept the many charms and magical potions without which no native believes he could live. These preparations are secured from a variety of specialized practitioners. The most powerful of these are the medicine men, whose assistance must be rewarded with substantial gifts. However, the medicine men do not provide the curative potions for their clients, but decide what the ingredients should be and then write them down in an ancient and secret language. This writing is understood only by the medicine men and by the herbalists who, for another gift, provide the required charm.

The charm is not disposed of after it has served its purpose, but is placed in the charm-box of the household shrine. As these magical materials are specific for certain ills, and the real or imagined maladies of the people are many, the charm-box is usually full to overflowing. The magical packets are so numerous that people forget what their purposes were and fear to use them again. While the natives are very vague on this point, we can only assume that the idea in retaining all the old magical materials is that their presence in the charm-box, before which the body rituals are conducted, will in some way protect the worshipper.

Beneath the charm-box is a small font. Each day every member of the family, in succession, enters the shrine room, bows his head before the charm-box, mingles different sorts of holy water in the font, and proceeds with a brief rite of ablution. The holy waters are secured from the Water Temple of the community, where the priests conduct elaborate ceremonies to make the liquid ritually pure.

In the hierarchy of magical practitioners, and below the medicine men in prestige, are specialists whose designation is best translated "holy-mouth-men." The Nacirema have an almost pathological horror of and fascination with the mouth, the condition of which is believed to have a supernatural influence on all social relationships. Were it not for the rituals of the mouth, they believe that their teeth would fall out, their gums bleed, their jaws shrink, their friends desert them, and their lovers reject them. They also believe that a strong relationship exists between oral and moral characteristics. For example, there is a ritual ablution of the mouth for children which is supposed to improve their moral fiber.

The daily body ritual performed by everyone includes a mouth-rite. Despite the fact that these people are so punctilious about care of the mouth, this rite involves a practice which strikes the uninitiated stranger as revolting. It was reported to me that the ritual consists of inserting a small bundle of hog hairs into the mouth, along with certain magical powders, and then moving the bundle in a highly formalized series of gestures.

In addition to the private mouth-rite, the people seek out a holy-mouth-man once or twice a year. These practitioners have an impressive set of paraphernalia, consisting of a variety of augers, awls, probes, and prods. The use of these objects in the exorcism of the evils of the mouth involves almost unbelievable ritual torture of the client. The holy-mouth-man opens the client's mouth and, using the above mentioned tools, enlarges any holes which decay may have created in the teeth. Magical materials are put into these holes. If there are no naturally occurring holes in the teeth, large sections of one or more teeth are gouged out so that the supernatural substance can be applied. In the client's view, the purpose of these ministrations is to arrest decay and draw friends. The extremely sacred and traditional character of the rite is evident in the fact that the natives return to the holy-mouth-men year after year, despite the fact that their teeth continue to decay.

It is to be hoped that, when a thorough study of the Nacirema is made, there will be careful inquiry into the personality structure of these people. One has but to watch the gleam in the eye of a holy-mouth-man, as he jabs an awl into an exposed nerve, to suspect that a certain amount of sadism is involved. If this can be established, a very interesting pattern emerges, for most of the population shows definite masochistic tendencies. It was to these that Professor Linton referred in discussing a distinctive part of the daily body ritual which is performed only by men. This part of the rite involves scraping and lacerating the surface of the face with a sharp instrument. Special women's rites are performed only four times during each lunar month, but what they lack in frequency is made up in barbarity. As part of this ceremony, women bake their heads in small ovens for about an hour. The theoretically interesting point is that what seems to be a preponderantly masochistic people have developed sadistic specialists.

The medicine men have an imposing temple, or *latipso,* in every community of any size. The more elaborate ceremonies required to treat very sick patients can only be performed at this temple. These ceremonies involve not only the thaumaturge but a permanent group of vestal maidens who move sedately about the temple chambers in distinctive costume and headdress.

The *latipso* ceremonies are so harsh that it is phenomenal that a fair proportion of the really sick natives who enter the temple ever recover. Small children whose indoctrination is still incomplete have been known to resist attempts to take them to the temple because "that is where you go to die." Despite this fact, sick adults are not only willing but eager to undergo the protracted ritual purification, if they can afford to do so. No matter how ill the supplicant or how grave the emergency, the guardians of many temples will not admit a client if he cannot give a rich gift to the custodian. Even after one has gained admission and survived the ceremonies, the guardians will not permit the neophyte to leave until he makes still another gift.

The supplicant entering the temple is first stripped of all his or her clothes. In everyday life the Nacirema avoids exposure of his body and its natural functions. Bathing and excretory acts are performed only in the secrecy of the household shrine, where they are ritualized as part of the body-rites. Psychological shock results from the fact that body secrecy is suddenly lost upon entry into the *latipso*. A man whose own wife has never seen him in an excretory act, suddenly finds himself naked and assisted by a vestal maiden while he performs his natural functions into a sacred vessel. This sort of ceremonial treatment is necessitated by the fact that the excreta are used by a diviner to ascertain the course and nature of the client's sickness. Female clients, on the other hand, find their naked bodies are subjected to the scrutiny, manipulation, and prodding of the medicine men.

Few supplicants in the temple are well enough to do anything but lie on their hard beds. The daily ceremonies, like the rites of the holy-mouth-men, involve discomfort and torture. With ritual precision, the vestals awaken their miserable charges each dawn and roll them about on their beds of pain while performing ablutions, in the formal movements of which the maidens are highly trained. At other times they insert magic wands in the supplicant's mouth or force him to eat substances which are supposed to be healing. From time to time the medicine men come to their clients and jab magically treated needles into their flesh. The fact that these temple ceremonies may not cure, and may even kill the neophyte, in no way decreases the people's faith in the medicine men.

There remains one other kind of practitioner, known as a "listener." This witchdoctor has the power to exorcise the devils that lodge in the heads of people who have been bewitched. The Nacirema believe that parents bewitch their own children. Mothers are particularly suspected of putting a curse on children while teaching them the secret body rituals. The counter-magic of the witchdoctor is unusual in its lack of ritual. The patient simply tells the "listener" all his troubles and fears, beginning with the earliest difficulties he can remember. The memory displayed by the Nacirema in these exorcism sessions is truly remarkable. It is not uncommon for the patient to bemoan the rejection he felt upon being weaned as a babe, and a few individuals even see their troubles going back to the traumatic effects of their own birth.

In conclusion, mention must be made of certain practices which have their base in native esthetics but which depend upon the pervasive aversion to the natural body and its functions. There are ritual fasts to make fat people thin and ceremonial feasts to make thin people fat. Still other rites are used to make women's breasts larger if they are small, and smaller if they are large. General dissatisfaction with breast shape is symbolized in the fact that the ideal form is virtually outside the range of human variation. A few women afflicted with almost inhuman hyper-mammary development are so idolized that they make a handsome living by simply going from village to village and permitting the natives to stare at them for a fee.

Reference has already been made to the fact that excretory functions are ritualized, routinized, and relegated to secrecy. Natural reproductive functions are similarly distorted. Intercourse is taboo as a topic and scheduled as an act. Efforts are made to avoid pregnancy by the use of magical materials or by limiting intercourse to certain phases of the moon. Conception is actually very infrequent. When pregnant, women dress so as to hide their condition. Parturition takes place in secret, without friends or relatives to assist, and the majority of women do not nurse their infants.

Our review of the ritual life of the Nacirema has certainly shown them to be a magic-ridden people. It is hard to understand how they have managed to exist so long under the burdens which they have imposed upon themselves. But even such exotic customs as these take on real meaning when they are viewed with the insight provided by Malinowski when he wrote:

> Looking from far and above, from our high places of safety in the developed civilization, it is easy to see all the crudity and irrelevance of magic. But without its power and guidance early man could not have mastered his practical difficulties as he has done, nor could man have advanced to the higher stages of civilization.

8 Doing Fieldwork Among the Yąnomamö

NAPOLEON A. CHAGNON

As stated in the second reading, the primary difference between sociology and anthropology is the choice of research setting. That is, sociologists usually study people living in industrialized societies, while anthropologists usually focus on tribal and peasant groups. The distinction does not always hold, however, as some anthropologists do research in urban settings, and occasionally a sociologist wanders into peasant society. Consequently, it makes little difference that the fieldwork reported here was done by an anthropologist, for if a sociologist had done participant observation among the Yąnomamö, he or she would have written a similar account of those experiences. (Sociologists, however, are considerably less interested in kinship and genealogy.)

Note how the culture of the Yąnomamö sets the stage for their behaviors. Although from our perspective their behaviors are strange, this is the way of life that the Yąnomamö take for granted. What they experience is as natural for them as our way of life is for us. But, as Chagnon discovered firsthand, for someone from our culture to experience Yąnomamö life is to encounter an alien world. Chagnon experienced *culture shock*—that is, the fundamentals of life that he had learned and lived with from childhood no longer applied, and he was most uncomfortable with what he confronted. How would you have felt in his place?

THE YĄNOMAMÖ INDIANS live in southern Venezuela and the adjacent portions of northern Brazil. Some 125 widely scattered villages have populations ranging from 40 to 250 inhabitants, with 75 to 80 people the most usual number. In total numbers their population probably approaches 10,000 people, but this is merely a guess. Many of the villages have not yet been contacted by outsiders, and nobody knows for sure exactly how many uncontacted villages there are, or how many people live in them. By comparison to African or Melanesian tribes, the Yąnomamö population is small. Still, they are one of the largest unacculturated tribes left in all of South America.

But they have a significance apart from tribal size and cultural purity: The Yąnomamö are still actively conducting warfare. It is in the nature of man to fight, according to one of their myths, because the blood of "Moon" spilled on this layer of the cosmos, causing men to become fierce. I describe the Yąno-mamö as "the fierce people" because that is the most accurate single phrase that describes them. That is how they conceive themselves to be, and that is how they would like others to think of them.

I spent nineteen months with the Yąnomamö, during which time I ac-quired some proficiency in their language and, up to a point, submerged my-self in their culture and way of life. The thing that impressed me most was the importance of aggression in their culture. I had the opportunity to witness a good many incidents that expressed individual vindictiveness on the one hand and collective bellicosity on the other. These ranged in seriousness from the ordinary incidents of wife beating and chest pounding to dueling and orga-nized raiding by parties that set out with the intention of ambushing and killing men from enemy villages. One of the villages was raided approximately twenty-five times while I conducted the fieldwork, six times by the group I lived among. . . .

This is not to state that primitive man everywhere is unpleasant. By way of contrast, I have also done limited fieldwork among the Yąnomamö's north-ern neighbors, the Carib-speaking Makiritare Indians. This group was very pleasant and charming, all of them anxious to help me and honor bound to show any visitor the numerous courtesies of their system of etiquette. In short, they approached the image of primitive man that I had conjured up, and it was sheer pleasure to work with them. . . .

My first day in the field illustrated to me what my teachers meant when they spoke of "culture shock." I had traveled in a small, aluminum rowboat propelled by a large outboard motor for two and a half days. This took me from the Territorial capital, a small town on the Orinoco River, deep into Yąnomamö country. On the morning of the third day we reached a small mis-sion settlement, the field "headquarters" of a group of Americans who were working in two Yąnomamö villages. The missionaries had come out of these villages to hold their annual conference on the progress of their mission work, and were conducting their meetings when I arrived. We picked up a passenger at the mission station, James P. Barker, the first non-Yąnomamö to make a sus-tained, permanent contact with the tribe (in 1950). He had just returned from a year's furlough in the United States, where I had earlier visited him before leaving for Venezuela. He agreed to accompany me to the village I had se-lected for my base of operations to introduce me to the Indians. This village was also his own home base, but he had not been there for over a year and did not plan to join me for another three months. Mr. Barker had been living with this particular group about five years.

We arrived at the village, Bisaasi-teri, about 2:00 P.M. and docked the boat along the muddy bank at the terminus of the path used by the Indians to fetch their drinking water. It was hot and muggy, and my clothing was soaked with perspiration. It clung uncomfortably to my body, as it did thereafter for the remainder of the work. The small, biting gnats were out in astronomical numbers, for it was the beginning of the dry season. My face and hands were swollen from the venom of their numerous stings. In just a few moments I was to meet my first Yąnomamö, my first primitive man. What would it be like? I had visions of entering the village and seeing 125 social facts running about calling each other kinship terms and sharing food, each waiting and anxious to have me collect his genealogy. I would wear them out in turn. Would they like me? This was important to me; I wanted them to be so fond of me that they would adopt me into their kinship system and way of life, because I had heard that successful anthropologists always get adopted by their people. I had learned during my seven years of anthropological training at the University of Michigan that kinship was equivalent to society in primitive tribes and that it was a moral way of life, "moral" being something "good" and "desirable." I was determined to work my way into their moral system of kinship and become a member of their society.

My heart began to pound as we approached the village and heard the buzz of activity within the circular compound. Mr. Barker commented that he was anxious to see if any changes had taken place while he was away and wondered how many of them had died during his absence. I felt into my back pocket to make sure that my notebook was there and felt personally more secure when I touched it. Otherwise, I would not have known what to do with my hands.

I looked up and gasped when I saw a dozen burly, naked, filthy, hideous men staring at us down the shafts of their drawn arrows! Immense wads of green tobacco were stuck between their lower teeth and lips making them look even more hideous, and strands of dark-green slime dripped or hung from their noses. We arrived at the village while the men were blowing a hallucinogenic drug up their noses. One of the side effects of the drug is a runny nose. The mucus is always saturated with the green powder and the Indians usually let it run freely from their nostrils. My next discovery was that there were a dozen or so vicious, underfed dogs snapping at my legs, circling me as if I were going to be their next meal. I just stood there holding my notebook, helpless and pathetic. Then the stench of the decaying vegetation and filth struck me and I almost got sick. I was horrified. What sort of a welcome was this for the person who came here to live with you and learn your way of life, to become friends with you? They put their weapons down when they recognized Barker and returned to their chanting, keeping a nervous eye on the village entrances.

We had arrived just after a serious fight. Seven women had been abducted the day before by a neighboring group, and the local men and their guests had just that morning recovered five of them in a brutal club fight that nearly ended in a shooting war. The abductors, angry because they lost five of the seven captives, vowed to raid the Bisaasi-teri. When we arrived and entered the village unexpectedly, the Indians feared that we were the raiders. On several occasions during the next two hours the men in the village jumped to their feet, armed themselves, and waited nervously for the noise outside the village to be identified. My enthusiasm for collecting ethnographic curiosities diminished in proportion to the number of times such an alarm was raised. In fact, I was relieved when Mr. Barker suggested that we sleep across the river for the evening. It would be safer over there.

As we walked down the path to the boat, I pondered the wisdom of having decided to spend a year and a half with this tribe before I had even seen what they were like. I am not ashamed to admit, either, that had there been a diplomatic way out, I would have ended my fieldwork then and there. I did not look forward to the next day when I would be left alone with the Indians; I did not speak a word of their language, and they were decidedly different from what I had imagined them to be. The whole situation was depressing, and I wondered why I ever decided to switch from civil engineering to anthropology in the first place. I had not eaten all day, I was soaking wet from perspiration, the gnats were biting me, and I was covered with red pigment, the result of a dozen or so complete examinations I had been given by as many burly Indians. These examinations capped an otherwise grim day. The Indians would blow their noses into their hands, flick as much of the mucus off that would separate in a snap of the wrist, wipe the residue into their hair, and then carefully examine my face, arms, legs, hair, and the contents of my pockets. I asked Mr. Barker how to say "Your hands are dirty"; my comments were met by the Indians in the following way: They would "clean" their hands by spitting a quantity of slimy tobacco juice into them, rub them together, and then proceed with the examination.

Mr. Barker and I crossed the river and slung our hammocks. When he pulled his hammock out of a rubber bag, a heavy, disagreeable odor of mildewed cotton came with it. "Even the missionaries are filthy," I thought to myself. Within two weeks everything I owned smelled the same way, and I lived with the odor for the remainder of the fieldwork. My own habits of personal cleanliness reached such levels that I didn't even mind being examined by the Indians, as I was not much cleaner than they were after I had adjusted to the circumstances.

So much for my discovery that primitive man is not the picture of nobility and sanitation I had conceived him to be. I soon discovered that it was an enormously time-consuming task to maintain my own body in the manner to which it had grown accustomed in the relatively antiseptic environment of the northern United States. Either I could be relatively well fed and relatively comfortable in a fresh change of clothes and do very little fieldwork, or, I could do considerably more fieldwork and be less well fed and less comfortable.

It is appalling how complicated it can be to make oatmeal in the jungle. First, I had to make two trips to the river to haul the water. Next, I had to prime my kerosene stove with alcohol and get it burning, a tricky procedure when you are trying to mix powdered milk and fill a coffee pot at the same time: the alcohol prime always burned out before I could turn the kerosene on, and I would have to start all over. Or, I would turn the kerosene on, hoping that the element was still hot enough to vaporize the fuel, and not start a small fire in my palm-thatched hut as the liquid kerosene squirted all over the table and walls and ignited. It was safer to start over with the alcohol. Then I had to boil the oatmeal and pick the bugs out of it. All my supplies, of course, were carefully stored in Indian-proof, ratproof, moisture-proof, and insect-proof containers, not one of which ever served its purpose adequately. Just taking things out of the multiplicity of containers and repacking them afterward was a minor project in itself. By the time I had hauled the water to cook with, unpacked my food, prepared the oatmeal, milk, and coffee, heated water for dishes, washed and dried the dishes, repacked the food in the containers, stored the containers in locked trunks and cleaned up my mess, the ceremony of preparing breakfast had brought me almost up to lunch time.

Eating three meals a day was out of the question. I solved the problem by eating a single meal that could be prepared in a single container, or, at most, in two containers, washed my dishes only when there were no clean ones left, using cold river water, and wore each change of clothing at least a week to cut down on my laundry problem, a courageous undertaking in the tropics. I was also less concerned about sharing my provisions with the rats, insects, Indians, and the elements, thereby eliminating the need for my complicated storage process. I was able to last most of the day on *café con leche,* heavily sugared espresso coffee diluted about five to one with hot milk. I would prepare this in the evening and store it in a thermos. Frequently, my single meal was no more complicated than a can of sardines and a package of crackers. But at least two or three times a week I would do something sophisticated, like make oatmeal or boil rice and add a can of tuna fish or tomato paste to it. I even saved time by devising a water system that obviated the trips to the river. I had a few sheets of zinc roofing brought in and made a rain-water trap. I caught the water on the zinc surface, funneled it into an empty gasoline drum, and then ran a plastic hose from the drum to my hut. When the drum was exhausted in the dry season, I hired the Indians to fill it with water from the river.

I ate much less when I traveled with the Indians to visit other villages. Most of the time my travel diet consisted of roasted or boiled green plantains that I obtained from the Indians, but I always carried a few cans of sardines with me in case I got lost or stayed away longer than I had planned. I found peanut butter and crackers a very nourishing food, and a simple one to prepare on trips. It was nutritious and portable, and only one tool was required to prepare the meal, a hunting knife that could be cleaned by wiping the blade on a leaf. More importantly, it was one of the few foods the Indians would let me eat in relative peace. It looked too much like animal feces to them to excite their appetites.

I once referred to the peanut butter as the dung of cattle. They found this quite repugnant. They did not know what "cattle" were, but were generally aware that I ate several canned products of such an animal. I perpetrated this myth, if for no other reason than to have some peace of mind while I ate. Fieldworkers develop strange defense mechanisms, and this was one of my own forms of adaptation. On another occasion I was eating a can of frankfurters and growing very weary of the demands of one of my guests for a share in my meal. When he asked me what I was eating, I replied: "Beef." He then asked, "What part of the animal are you eating?" to which I replied, "Guess!" He stopped asking for a share.

Meals were a problem in another way. Food sharing is important to the Yąnomamö in the context of displaying friendship. "I am hungry," is almost a form of greeting with them. I could not possibly have brought enough food with me to feed the entire village, yet they seemed not to understand this. All they could see was that I did not share my food with them at each and every meal. Nor could I enter into their system of reciprocities with respect to food; every time one of them gave me something "freely," he would dog me for months to pay him back, not with food, but with steel tools. Thus, if I accepted a plantain from someone in a different village while I was on a visit, he would most likely visit me in the future and demand a machete as payment for the time that he "fed" me. I usually reacted to these kinds of demands by giving a banana, the customary reciprocity in their culture—food for food—but this would be a disappointment for the individual who had visions of that single plantain growing into a machete over time.

Despite the fact that most of them knew I would not share my food with them at their request, some of them always showed up at my hut during mealtime. I gradually became accustomed to this and learned to ignore their persistent demands while I ate. Some of them would get angry because I failed to give in, but most of them accepted it as just a peculiarity of the subhuman foreigner. When I did give in, my hut quickly filled with Indians, each demanding a sample of the food that I had given one of them. If I did not give all a share, I was that much more despicable in their eyes.

A few of them went out of their way to make my meals unpleasant, to spite me for not sharing; for example, one man arrived and watched me eat a cracker with honey on it. He immediately recognized the honey, a particularly esteemed Yąnomamö food. He knew that I would not share my tiny bottle and that it would be futile to ask. Instead, he glared at me and queried icily, "Shaki![1] What kind of animal semen are you eating on that cracker?" His question had the desired effect, and my meal ended.

Finally, there was the problem of being lonely and separated from your own kind, especially your family. I tried to overcome this by seeking personal friendships among the Indians. This only complicated the matter because all my friends simply used my confidence to gain privileged access to my cache of steel tools and trade goods, and looted me. I would be bitterly disappointed that my "friend" thought no more of me than to finesse our relationship exclusively with the intention of getting at any locked up possessions, and my depression would hit new lows every time I discovered this. The loss of the possession bothered me much less than the shock that I was, as far as most of them were concerned, nothing more than a source of desirable items; no holds were barred in relieving me of these, since I was considered something subhuman, a non-Yąnomamö.

The thing that bothered me most was the incessant, passioned, and aggressive demands the Indians made. It would become so unbearable that I would have to lock myself in my mud hut every once in a while just to escape from it: Privacy is one of Western culture's greatest achievements. But I did not want privacy for its own sake; rather, I simply had to get away from the begging. Day and night for the entire time I lived with the Yąnomamö I was plagued by such demands as: "Give me a knife, I am poor!"; "If you don't take me with you on your next trip to Widokaiya-teri, I'll chop a hole in your canoe!"; "Don't point your camera at me or I'll hit you!"; "Share your food with me!"; "Take me across the river in your canoe and be quick about it!"; "Give me a cooking pot!"; "Loan me your flashlight so I can go hunting tonight!"; "Give me medicine . . . I itch all over!"; "Take us on a week-long hunting trip with your shotgun!"; and "Give me an axe, or I'll break into your hut when you are away visiting and steal one!" And so I was bombarded by such demands day after day, months on end, until I could not bear to see an Indian.

It was not as difficult to become calloused to the incessant begging as it was to ignore the sense of urgency, the impassioned tone of voice, or the intimidation and aggression with which the demands were made. It was likewise difficult to adjust to the fact that the Yąnomamö refused to accept "no" for an answer until or unless it seethed with passion and intimidation—which it did after six months. Giving in to a demand always established a new threshold; the next demand would be for a bigger item or favor, and the anger of the Indians even greater if the demand was not met. I soon learned that I had to become very much like the Yąnomamö to be able to get along with them on their terms: sly, aggressive, and intimidating.

Had I failed to adjust in this fashion I would have lost six months of supplies to them in a single day or would have spent most of my time ferrying them around in my canoe or hunting for them. As it was, I did spend a considerable amount of time doing these things and did succumb to their outrageous demands for axes and machetes, at least at first. More importantly, had I failed to demonstrate that I could not be pushed around beyond a certain point, I would have been the subject of far more ridicule, theft, and practical jokes than was the actual case. In short, I had to acquire a certain proficiency in their kind of interpersonal politics and to learn how to imply subtly that certain potentially undesirable consequences might follow if they did such and such to me. They do this to each other in order to establish precisely the point at which they cannot goad an individual any further without precipitating retaliation. As soon as I caught on to this and realized that much of their aggression was stimulated by their desire to discover my flash point, I got along much better with them and regained some lost ground. It was sort of like a political game that everyone played, but one in which each individual sooner or later had to display some sign that his bluffs and implied threats could be backed up. I suspect that the frequency of wife beating is a component of this syndrome, since men can display their ferocity and show others that they are capable of violence. Beating a wife with a club is considered to be an acceptable way of displaying ferocity and one that does not expose the male to much danger. The important thing is that the man has displayed his potential for violence and the implication is that other men better treat him with respect and caution.

After six months, the level of demand was tolerable in the village I used for my headquarters. The Indians and I adjusted to each other and knew what to expect with regard to demands on their part for goods, favors, and services. Had I confined my fieldwork to just that village alone, the field experience would have been far more enjoyable. But, as I was interested in the demographic pattern and social organization of a much larger area, I made regular trips to some dozen different villages in order to collect genealogies or to recheck those I already had. Hence, the intensity of begging and intimidation was fairly constant for the duration of the fieldwork. I had to establish my position in some sort of pecking order of ferocity at each and every village.

For the most part, my own "fierceness" took the form of shouting back at the Yąnomamö as loudly and as passionately as they shouted at me, especially at first, when I did not know much of their language. As I became more proficient in their language and learned more about their political tactics, I became more sophisticated in the art of bluffing. For example, I paid one young man a machete to cut palm trees and make boards from the wood. I used these to fashion a platform in the bottom of my dugout canoe to keep my possessions dry when I traveled by river. That afternoon I was doing informant work in the village; the long-awaited mission supply boat arrived, and most of the Indians ran out of the village to beg goods from the crew. I continued to work in the village for another hour or so and went down to the river to say "hello" to the men on the supply boat. I was angry when I discovered that the Indians had chopped up all my palm boards and used them to paddle their own canoes across the river. I knew that if I overlooked this incident I would have invited them to take even greater liberties with my goods in the future. I crossed the river, docked amidst their dugouts, and shouted for the Indians to come out and see me. A few of the culprits appeared, mischievous grins on their faces. I gave a spirited lecture about how hard I had worked to put those boards in my canoe, how I had paid a machete for the wood, and how angry I was that they destroyed my work in their haste to cross the river. I then pulled out my hunting knife and, while their grins disappeared, cut each of their canoes loose, set them into the current, and let them float away. I left without further ado and without looking back.

They managed to borrow another canoe and, after some effort, recovered their dugouts. The headman of the village later told me with an approving chuckle that I had done the correct thing. Everyone in the village, except, of course, the culprits, supported and defended my action. This raised my status.

Whenever I took such action and defended my rights, I got along much better with the Yąnomamö. A good deal of their behavior toward me was directed with the forethought of establishing the point at which I would react defensively. Many of them later reminisced about the early days of my work when I was "timid" and a little afraid of them, and they could bully me into giving goods away.

Theft was the most persistent situation that required me to take some sort of defensive action. I simply could not keep everything I owned locked in trunks, and the Indians came into my hut and left at will. I developed a very effective means for recovering almost all the stolen items. I would simply ask a child who took the item and then take that person's hammock when he was not around, giving a spirited lecture to the others as I marched away in a faked rage with the thief's hammock. Nobody ever attempted to stop me from doing this, and almost all of them told me that my technique for recovering my possessions was admirable. By nightfall the thief would either appear with the stolen object or send it along with someone else to make an exchange. The others would heckle him for getting caught and being forced to return the item.

With respect to collecting the data I sought, there was a very frustrating problem. Primitive social organization is kinship organization, and to understand the Yąnomamö way of life I had to collect extensive genealogies. I could not have deliberately picked a more difficult group to work with in this regard: They have very stringent name taboos. They attempt to name people in such a way that when the person dies and they can no longer use his name, the loss of the word in the language is not inconvenient. Hence, they name people for specific and minute parts of things, such as "toenail of some rodent," thereby being able to retain the words "toenail" and "(specific) rodent," but not being able to refer directly to the toenail of that rodent. The taboo is maintained even for the living: One mark of prestige is the courtesy others show you by not using your name. The sanctions behind the taboo seem to be an unusual combination of fear and respect.

I tried to use kinship terms to collect genealogies at first, but the kinship terms were so ambiguous that I ultimately had to resort to names. They were quick to grasp that I was bound to learn everybody's name and reacted, without my knowing it, by inventing false names for everybody in the village. After having spent several months collecting names and learning them, this came as a disappointment to me: I could not cross-check the genealogies with other informants from distant villages.

They enjoyed watching me learn these names. I assumed, wrongly, that I would get the truth to each question and that I would get the best information by working in public. This set the stage for converting a serious project into a farce. Each informant tried to outdo his peers by inventing a name even more ridiculous than what I had been given earlier, or by asserting that the individual about whom I inquired was married to his mother or daughter, and the like. I would have the informant whisper the name of the individual in my ear, noting that he was the father of such and such a child. Everybody would then insist that I repeat the name aloud, roaring in hysterics as I clumsily pronounced the name. I assumed that the laughter was in response to the violation of the name taboo or to my pronunciation. This was a reasonable interpretation, since the individual whose name I said aloud invariably became angry. After I learned what some of the names meant, I began to understand what the laughter was all about. A few of the more colorful examples are: "hairy vagina," "long penis," "feces of the harpy eagle," and "dirty rectum." No wonder the victims were angry.

I was forced to do my genealogy work in private because of the horseplay and nonsense. Once I did so, my informants began to agree with each other and I managed to learn a few new names, real names. I could then test any new informant by collecting a genealogy from him that I knew to be accurate. I was able to weed out the more mischievous informants this way. Little by little I extended the genealogies and learned the real names. Still, I was unable to get the names of the dead and extend the genealogies back in time, and even my best informants continued to deceive me about their own close relatives. Most of them gave me the name of a living man as the father of some individual in order to avoid mentioning that the actual father was dead.

The quality of a genealogy depends in part on the number of generations it embraces, and the name taboo prevented me from getting any substantial information about deceased ancestors. Without this information, I could not detect marriage patterns through time. I had to rely on older informants for this information, but these were the most reluctant of all. As I became more proficient in the language and more skilled at detecting lies, my informants became better at lying. One of them in particular was so cunning and persuasive that I was shocked to discover that he had been inventing his information. He specialized in making a ceremony out of telling me false names. He would look around to make sure nobody was listening outside my hut, enjoin me to never mention the name again, act very nervous and spooky, and then grab me by the head to whisper the name very softly into my ear. I was always elated after an informant session with him, because I had several generations of dead ancestors for the living people. The others refused to give me this information. To show my gratitude, I paid him quadruple the rate I had given the others. When word got around that I had increased the pay, volunteers began pouring in to give me genealogies.

I discovered that the old man was lying quite by accident. A club fight broke out in the village one day, the result of a dispute over the possession of a woman. She had been promised to Rerebawa, a particularly aggressive young man who had married into the village. Rerebawa had already been given her older sister and was enraged when the younger girl began having an affair with another man in the village, making no attempt to conceal it from him. He challenged the young man to a club fight, but was so abusive in his challenge that the opponent's father took offense and entered the village circle with his son, wielding a long club. Rerebawa swaggered out to the duel and hurled insults at both of them, trying to goad them into striking him on the head with their clubs. This would have given him the opportunity to strike them on the head. His opponents refused to hit him, and the fight ended. Rerebawa had won a moral victory because his opponents were afraid to hit him. Thereafter, he swaggered around and insulted the two men behind their backs. He was genuinely angry with them, to the point of calling the older man by the name of his dead father. I quickly seized on this as an opportunity to collect an accurate genealogy and pumped him about his adversary's ancestors. Rerebawa had been particularly nasty to me up to this point, but we became staunch allies: We were both outsiders in the local village. I then asked about other dead ancestors and got immediate replies. He was angry with the whole group and not afraid to tell me the names of the dead. When I compared his version of the genealogies to that of the old man, it was obvious that one of them was lying. I challenged his information, and he explained that everybody knew that the old man was deceiving me and bragging about it in the village. The names the old man had given me were the dead ancestors of the members of a village so far away that he thought I would never have occasion to inquire about them. As it turned out, Rerebawa knew most of the people in that village and recognized the names.

I then went over the complete genealogical records with Rerebawa, genealogies I had presumed to be in final form. I had to revise them all because of the numerous lies and falsifications they contained. Thus, after five months of almost constant work on the genealogies of just one group, I had to begin almost from scratch!

Discouraging as it was to start over, it was still the first real turning point in my fieldwork. Thereafter, I began taking advantage of local arguments and animosities in selecting my informants, and used more extensively individuals who had married into the group. I began traveling to other villages to check the genealogies, picking villages that were on strained terms with the people about whom I wanted information. I would then return to my base camp and check with local informants the accuracy of the new information. If the informants became angry when I mentioned the new names I acquired from the unfriendly group, I was almost certain that the information was accurate. For this kind of checking I had to use informants whose genealogies I knew rather well: They had to be distantly enough related to the dead person that they would not go into a rage when I mentioned the name, but not so remotely related that they would be uncertain of the accuracy of the information. Thus, I had to make a list of names that I dared not use in the presence of each and every informant. Despite the precautions, I occasionally hit a name that put the informant into a rage, such as that of a dead brother or sister that other informants had not reported. This always terminated the day's work with that informant, for he would be too touchy to continue any further, and I would be reluctant to take a chance on accidentally discovering another dead kinsman so soon after the first.

These were always unpleasant experiences, and occasionally dangerous ones, depending on the temperament of the informant. On one occasion I was planning to visit a village that had been raided about a week earlier. A woman whose name I had on my list had been killed by the raiders. I planned to check each individual on the list one by one to estimate ages, and I wanted to remove her name so that I would not say it aloud in the village. I knew that I would be in considerable difficulty if I said this name aloud so soon after her death. I called on my original informant and asked him to tell me the name of the woman who had been killed. He refused, explaining that she was a close relative of his. I then asked him if he would become angry if I read off all the names on the list. This way he did not have to say her name and could merely nod when I mentioned the right one. He was a fairly good friend of mine, and I thought I could predict his reaction. He assured me that this would be a good way of doing it. We were alone in my hut so that nobody could overhear us. I read the names softly, continuing to the next when he gave a negative reply. When I finally spoke the name of the dead woman he flew out of his chair, raised his arm to strike me, and shouted: "You son-of-a-bitch![2] If you ever say that name again, I'll kill you!" He was shaking with rage, but left my hut quietly. I shudder to think what might have happened if I had said the name unknowingly in the woman's village. I had other, similar experiences in different villages, but luckily the dead person had been dead for some time and was not closely related to the individual into whose ear I whispered the name. I was merely cautioned to desist from saying any more names, lest I get people angry with me.

I had been working on the genealogies for nearly a year when another individual came to my aid. It was Kaobawa, the headman of Upper Bisaasi-teri, the group in which I spent most of my time. He visited me one day after the others had left the hut and volunteered to help me on the genealogies. He was poor, he explained, and needed a machete. He would work only on the condition that I did not ask him about his own parents and other very close kinsmen who were dead. He also added that he would not lie to me as the others had done in the past. This was perhaps the most important single event in my fieldwork, for out of this meeting evolved a very warm friendship and a very profitable informant-fieldworker relationship.

Kaobawa's familiarity with his group's history and his candidness were remarkable. His knowledge of details was almost encyclopedic. More than that, he was enthusiastic and encouraged me to learn details that I might otherwise have ignored. If there were things he did not know intimately, he would advise me to wait until he could check things out with someone in the village. This he would do clandestinely, giving me a report the next day. As I was constrained by my part of the bargain to avoid discussing his close dead kinsmen, I had to rely on Rerebawa for this information. I got Rerebawa's genealogy from Kaobawa.

Once again I went over the genealogies with Kaobawa to recheck them, a considerable task by this time: they included about two thousand names, representing several generations of individuals from four different villages. Rerebawa's information was very accurate, and Kaobawa's contribution enabled me to trace the genealogies further back in time. Thus, after nearly a year of constant work on genealogies, Yanomamö demography and social organization began to fall into a pattern. Only then could I see how kin groups formed and exchanged women with each other over time, and only then did the fissioning of larger villages into smaller ones show a distinct pattern. At this point I was able to begin formulating more intelligent questions because there was now some sort of pattern to work with. Without the help of Rerebawa and Kaobawa, I could not have made very much sense of the plethora of details I had collected from dozens of other informants.

Kaobawa is about 40 years old. I say "about" because the Yanomamö numeration system has only three numbers: one, two, and more-than-two. He is the headman of Upper Bisaasi-teri. He has had five or six wives so far and temporary affairs with as many more women, one of which resulted in a child. At the present time he has just two wives, Bahimi and Koamashima. He has had a daughter and a son by Bahimi, his eldest and favorite wife. Koamashima, about 20 years old, recently had her first child, a boy. Kaobawa may give Koamashima to his youngest brother. Even now the brother shares in her sexual services. Kaobawa recently gave his third wife to another of his brothers because she was beshi: "horny." In fact, this girl had been married to two other men, both of whom discarded her because of her infidelity. Kaobawa had one daughter by her; she is being raised by his brother.

Kaobawa's eldest wife, Bahimi, is about thirty-five years old. She is his first cross-cousin. Bahimi was pregnant when I began my fieldwork, but she killed the new baby, a boy, at birth, explaining tearfully that it would have competed with Ariwari, her nursing son, for milk. Rather than expose Ariwari to the dangers and uncertainty of an early weaning, she killed the new child instead. By Yanomamö standards, she and Kaobawa have a very tranquil household. He only beats her once in a while, and never very hard. She never has affairs with other men.

Kaobawa is quiet, intense, wise, and unobtrusive. He leads more by example than by threats and coercion. He can afford to be this way as he established his reputation for being fierce long ago, and other men respect him. He also has five mature brothers who support him, and he has given a number of his sisters to other men in the village, thereby putting them under some obligation to him. In short, his "natural" following (kinsmen) is large, and he does not have to constantly display his ferocity. People already respect him and take his suggestions seriously.

Rerebawa is much younger, only about twenty-two years old. He has just one wife by whom he has had three children. He is from Karohi-teri, one of the villages to which Kaobawa's is allied. Rerebawa left his village to seek a wife in Kaobawa's group because there were no eligible women there for him to marry.

Rerebawa is perhaps more typical than Kaobawa in the sense that he is concerned about his reputation for ferocity and goes out of his way to act tough. He is, however, much braver than the other men his age and backs up his threats with action. Moreover, he is concerned about politics and knows the details of intervillage relationships over a large area. In this respect he shows all the attributes of a headman, although he is still too young and has too many competent older brothers in his own village to expect to move easily into the position of leadership there.

He does not intend to stay in Kaobawa's group and has not made a garden. He feels that he has adequately discharged his obligations to his wife's parents by providing them with fresh game for three years. They should let him take the wife and return to his own village with her, but they refuse and try to entice him to remain permanently in Bisaasi-teri to provide them with game when they are old. They have even promised to give him their second daughter if he will stay permanently.

Although he has displayed his ferocity in many ways, one incident in particular shows what his character is like. Before he left his own village to seek a wife, he had an affair with the wife of an older brother. When he was discovered, his brother attacked him with a club. Rerebawa was infuriated so he grabbed an axe and drove his brother out of the village after soundly beating him with the flat of the blade. The brother was so afraid that he did not return to the village for several days. I recently visited his village with him. He made a point to introduce me to this brother. Rerebawa dragged him out of his hammock by the arm and told me, "This is the brother whose wife I had an affair with," a deadly insult. His brother did nothing and slunk back into his hammock, shamed, but relieved to have Rerebawa release the vise-grip on his arm.

Despite the fact that he admires Kaobawa, he has a low opinion of the others in Bisaasi-teri. He admitted confidentially that he thought Bisaasi-teri was an abominable group: "This is a terrible neighborhood! All the young men are lazy and cowards and everybody is committing incest! I'll be glad to get back home." He also admired Kaobawa's brother, the headman of Monou-teri. This man was killed by raiders while I was doing my fieldwork. Rerebawa was disgusted that the others did not chase the raiders when they discovered the shooting: "He was the only fierce one in the whole group; he was my close friend. The cowardly Monou-teri hid like women in the jungle and didn't even chase the raiders!"

Even though Rerebawa is fierce and capable of being quite nasty, he has a good side as well. He has a very biting sense of humor and can entertain the group for hours on end with jokes and witty comments. And, he is one of few

Yąnomamö that I feel I can trust. When I returned to Bisaasi-teri after having been away for a year, Rerebawa was in his own village visiting his kinsmen. Word reached him that I had returned, and he immediately came to see me. He greeted me with an immense bear hug and exclaimed, "Shaki! Why did you stay away so long? Did you know that my will was so cold while you were gone that at times I could not eat for want of seeing you?" I had to admit that I missed him, too.

Of all the Yąnomamö I know, he is the most genuine and the most devoted to his culture's ways and values. I admire him for that, although I can't say that I subscribe to or endorse these same values. By contrast, Kaobawa is older and wiser. He sees his own culture in a different light and criticizes aspects of it he does not like. While many of his peers accept some of the superstitions and explanatory myths as truth and as the way things ought to be, Kaobawa questions them and privately pokes fun at some of them. Probably, more of the Yąnomamö are like Rerebawa, or at least try to be.

Notes

1. "Shaki," or, rather, "Shakiwa," is the name they gave me because they could not pronounce "Chagnon." They like to name people for some distinctive feature when possible. *Shaki* is the name of a species of noisome bees; they accumulate in large numbers around ripening bananas and make pests of themselves by eating into the fruit, showering the people below with the debris. They probably adopted this name for me because I was also a nuisance, continuously prying into their business, taking pictures of them, and, in general, being where they did not want me.

2. This is the closest English translation of his actual statement, the literal translation of which would be nonsensical in our language.

9 The Sounds of Silence

EDWARD T. HALL
MILDRED R. HALL

When we refer to communication, we generally think about words. People who are talking, however, use much more than words to communicate with one another. *How* they say things is just as important—sometimes more so—than *what* they say. Their inflections, tones, pauses, cadence, and volume also convey meanings. If people are speaking face-to-face, their gestures, expressions, mannerisms, and use of space also contain significant messages.

Nonverbal communication is especially significant in conveying feelings and attitudes. Through ways so subtle that they lie beyond even our own perception—and ways so obvious that no one can miss the message—we communicate feelings of comfort and discomfort, trust and distrust, pleasure or tension, suspicions, uncertainties, desires, and a host of other feelings and concerns.

Yet we seldom think about our nonverbal communications. Our body language, for example, usually seems to be "just doing what is natural." Researchers, however, have found little that is "natural" about it. Like our speech, our body language and other forms of nonverbal communication are acquired. Thus, the specific ways by which people communicate these messages vary from one group to another, as the Halls make evident in this selection.

BOB LEAVES HIS APARTMENT at 8:15 A.M. and stops at the corner drugstore for breakfast. Before he can speak, the counterman says, "The usual?" Bob nods yes. While he savors his Danish, a fat man pushes onto the adjoining stool and overflows into his space. Bob scowls, and the man pulls himself in as much as he can. Bob has sent two messages without speaking a syllable.

Henry has an appointment to meet Arthur at 11:00 A.M.; he arrives at 11:30. Their conversation is friendly, but Arthur retains a lingering hostility. Henry has unconsciously communicated that he doesn't think the appointment is very important or that Arthur is a person who needs to be treated with respect.

George is talking to Charley's wife at a party. Their conversation is entirely trivial, yet Charley glares at them suspiciously. Their physical proximity and the movements of their eyes reveal that they are powerfully attracted to each other.

José Ybarra and Sir Edmund Jones are at the same party, and it is important for them to establish a cordial relationship for business reasons. Each is trying to be warm and friendly, yet they will part with mutual distrust, and their business transaction will probably fall through. José, in Latin fashion, moves closer and closer to Sir Edmund as they speak, and this movement is being miscommunicated as pushiness to Sir Edmund, who keeps backing away from this intimacy, which in turn is being miscommunicated to José as coldness. The silent languages of Latin and English cultures are more difficult to learn than their spoken languages.

In each of these cases, we see the subtle power of nonverbal communication. The only language used throughout most of the history of humanity (in evolutionary terms, vocal communication is relatively recent), it is the first form of communication you learn. You use this preverbal language, consciously and unconsciously, every day to tell other people how you feel about yourself and them. This language includes your posture, gestures, facial expressions, costume, the way you walk, even your treatment of time and space and material things. All people communicate on several different levels at the same time but are usually aware of only the verbal dialogue and don't realize that they respond to nonverbal messages. But when a person says one thing and really believes something else, the discrepancy between the two can usually be sensed. Nonverbal communication systems are much less subject to the conscious deception that often occurs in verbal systems. When we find ourselves thinking, "I don't know what it is about him, but he doesn't seem sincere," it's usually this lack of congruity between a person's words and his behavior that makes us anxious and uncomfortable.

Few of us realize how much we all depend on body movement in our conversation or are aware of the hidden rules that govern listening behavior. But we know instantly whether or not the person we're talking to is "tuned in," and we're very sensitive to any breach in listening etiquette. In white middle-class American culture, when someone wants to show he is listening to someone else, he looks either at the other person's face or, specifically, at his eyes, shifting his gaze from one eye to the other.

If you observe a person conversing, you'll notice that he indicates he's listening by nodding his head. He also makes little "Hmm" noises. If he agrees with what's being said, he may give a vigorous nod. To show pleasure or affirmation, he smiles; if he has some reservations, he looks skeptical by raising an eyebrow or pulling down the corners of his mouth. If a participant wants to terminate the conversation, he may start shifting his body position, stretching his legs, crossing or uncrossing them, bobbing his foot, or diverting his gaze from the speaker. The more he fidgets, the more the speaker becomes aware that he has lost his audience. As a last measure, the listener may look at his watch to indicate the imminent end of the conversation.

Talking and listening are so intricately intertwined that a person cannot do one without the other. Even when one is alone and talking to oneself, there is part of the brain that speaks while another part listens. In all conversations, the listener is positively or negatively reinforcing the speaker all the time. He may even guide the conversation without knowing it, by laughing or frowning or dismissing the argument with a wave of his hand.

The language of the eyes—another age-old way of exchanging feelings—is both subtle and complex. Not only do men and women use their eyes differently, but there are class, generational, regional, ethnic, and national cultural differences. Americans often complain about the way foreigners stare at people or hold a glance too long. Most Americans look away from someone who is using his eyes in an unfamiliar way because it makes them self-conscious. If a man looks at another man's wife in a certain way, he's asking for trouble, as indicated earlier. But he might not be ill-mannered or seeking to challenge the husband. He might be a European in this country who hasn't learned our visual mores. Many American women visiting France or Italy are acutely embarrassed because, for the first time in their lives, men really look at them—their eyes, hair, nose, lips, breasts, hips, legs, thighs, knees, ankles, feet, clothes, hairdo, even their walk. These same women, once they have become used to being looked at, often return to the United States and are overcome with the feeling that "No one ever really looks at me anymore."

Analyzing the mass of data on the eyes, it is possible to sort out at least three ways in which the eyes are used to communicate: dominance vs. submission, involvement vs. detachment, and positive vs. negative attitude. In addition, there are three levels of consciousness and control, which can be categorized as follows: (1) conscious use of the eyes to communicate, such as the flirting blink and the intimate nosewrinkling squint; (2) the very extensive category of unconscious but learned behavior governing where the eyes are directed and when (this unwritten set of rules dictates how and under what circumstances the sexes, as well as people of all status categories, look at each other); and (3) the response of the eye itself, which is completely outside both awareness and control—changes in the cast (sparkle) of the eye and the pupillary reflex.

The eye is unlike any other organ of the body, for it is an extension of the brain. The unconscious pupillary reflex and the cast of the eye have been known by people of Middle Eastern origin for years—although most are unaware of their knowledge. Depending on the context, Arabs and others look directly at the eyes or deeply *into* the eyes of their interlocutor. We became aware of this in the Middle East several years ago while looking at jewelry. The merchant suddenly started to push a particular bracelet at a customer and said, "You buy this one." What interested us was that the bracelet was not the one that had been consciously selected by the purchaser. But the merchant, watching the pupils of the eyes, knew what the purchaser really wanted to buy. Whether he specifically knew *how* he knew is debatable.

A psychologist at the University of Chicago, Eckhard Hess, was the first to conduct systematic studies of the pupillary reflex. His wife remarked one evening, while watching him reading in bed, that he must be very interested in the text because his pupils were dilated. Following up on this, Hess slipped some pictures of nudes into a stack of photographs that he gave to his male assistant. Not looking at the photographs but watching his assistant's pupils, Hess was able to tell precisely when the assistant came to the nudes. In further experiments, Hess retouched the eyes in a photograph of a woman. In one print, he made the pupils small, in another, large; nothing else was changed. Subjects who were given the photographs found the woman with the dilated pupils much more attractive. Any man who has had the experience of seeing a woman look at him as her pupils widen with reflex speed knows that she's flashing him a message.

The eye-sparkle phenomenon frequently turns up in our interviews of couples in love. It's apparently one of the first reliable clues in the other person that love is genuine. To date, there is no scientific data to explain eye sparkle; no investigation of the pupil, the cornea, or even the white sclera of the eye shows how the sparkle originates. Yet we all know it when we see it.

One common situation for most people involves the use of the eyes in the street and in public. Although eye behavior follows a definite set of rules, the rules vary according to the place, the needs and feelings of the people, and their ethnic background. For urban whites, once they're within definite recognition distance (sixteen to thirty-two feet for people with average eyesight), there is mutual avoidance of eye contact—unless they want something specific: a pickup, a handout, or information of some kind. In the West and in small towns generally, however, people are much more likely to look and greet one another, even if they're strangers.

It's permissible to look at people if they're beyond recognition distance, but once inside this sacred zone, you can only steal a glance at strangers. You *must* greet friends, however; to fail to do so is insulting. Yet, to stare too fixedly even at them is considered rude and hostile. Of course, all of these rules are variable.

A great many blacks, for example, greet each other in public even if they don't know each other. To blacks, most eye behavior of whites has the effect of giving the impression that they aren't there, but this is due to white avoidance of eye contact with *anyone* in the street.

Another very basic difference between people of different ethnic backgrounds is their sense of territoriality and how they handle space. This is the silent communication, or miscommunication, that caused friction between Mr. Ybarra and Sir Edmund Jones in our earlier example. We know from the research that everyone has around himself an invisible bubble of space that contracts and expands depending on several factors: his emotional state, the activity he's performing at the time, and his cultural background. This bubble is a kind of mobile territory that he will defend against intrusion. If he is accustomed to close personal distance between himself and others, his bubble will be smaller than that of someone who's accustomed to greater personal distance. People of northern European heritage—English, Scandinavian, Swiss, and German—tend to avoid contact. Those whose heritage is Italian, French, Spanish, Russian, Latin American, or Middle Eastern like close personal contact.

People are very sensitive to any intrusion into their spatial bubble. If someone stands too close to you, your first instinct is to back up. If that's not possible, you lean away and pull yourself in, tensing your muscles. If the intruder doesn't respond to these body signals, you may then try to protect yourself, using a briefcase, umbrella, or raincoat. Women—especially when traveling alone—often plant their pocketbooks in such a way that no one can get very close to them. As a last resort, you may move to another spot and position yourself behind a desk or a chair that provides screening. Everyone tries to adjust the space around himself in a way that's comfortable for him; most often, he does this unconsciously.

Emotions also have a direct effect on the size of a person's territory. When you're angry or under stress, your bubble expands and you require more space. New York psychiatrist Augustus Kinzel found a difference in what he calls body-buffer zones between violent and nonviolent prison inmates. Dr. Kinzel conducted experiments in which each prisoner was placed in the center of a small room, and then Dr. Kinzel slowly walked toward him. Nonviolent prisoners allowed him to come quite close, while prisoners with a history of violent behavior couldn't tolerate his proximity and reacted with some vehemence.

Apparently, people under stress experience other people as looming larger and closer than they actually are. Studies of schizophrenic patients have indicated that they sometimes have a distorted perception of space, and several psychiatrists have reported patients who experience their body boundaries as filling up an entire room. For these patients, anyone who comes into the room is actually inside their body, and such an intrusion may trigger a violent outburst.

Unfortunately, there is little detailed information about normal people who live in highly congested urban areas. We do know, of course, that the noise, pollution, dirt, crowding, and confusion of our cities induce feelings of stress in most of us, and stress leads to a need for greater space. The man who's packed into a subway, jostled in the street, crowded into an elevator, and forced to work all day in a bull pen or in a small office without auditory or visual privacy is going to be very stressed at the end of his day. He needs places that provide relief from constant overstimulation of his nervous system. Stress from overcrowding is cumulative, and people can tolerate more crowding early in the day than later; note the increased bad temper during the evening rush hour as compared with the morning melee. Certainly one factor in people's desire to commute by car is the need for privacy and relief from crowding (except, often, from other cars); it may be the only time of the day when nobody can intrude.

In crowded public places, we tense our muscles and hold ourselves stiff, and thereby communicate to others our desire not to intrude on their space and, above all, not to touch them. We also avoid eye contact, and the total effect is that of someone who has "tuned out." Walking along the street, our bubble expands slightly as we move in a stream of strangers, taking care not to bump into them. In the office, at meetings, in restaurants, our bubble keeps changing as it adjusts to the activity at hand.

Most white middle-class Americans use four main distances in their business and social relations: intimate, personal, social, and public. Each of these distances has a near and a far phase and is accompanied by changes in the volume of the voice. Intimate distance varies from direct physical contact with another person to a distance of six to eighteen inches and is used for our most private activities—caressing another person or making love. At this distance, you are overwhelmed by sensory inputs from the skin, the fragrance of perfume, even the sound of breathing—all of which literally envelop you. Even at the far phase, you're still within easy touching distance. In general, the use of intimate distance in public between adults is frowned on. It's also much too close for strangers, except under conditions of extreme crowding.

In the second zone—personal distance—the close phase is one and a half to two and a half feet: it's at this distance that wives usually stand from their husbands in public. If another woman moves into this zone, the wife will most likely be disturbed. The far phase—two and a half to four feet—is the distance used to "keep someone at arm's length" and is the most common spacing used by people in conversation.

The third zone—social distance—is employed during business transactions or exchanges with a clerk or repairman. People who work together tend to use close social distance—four to seven feet. This is also the distance for conversation at social gatherings. To stand at this distance from someone who is seated has a dominating effect (e.g., teacher to pupil, boss to secretary). The far phase of the third zone—seven to twelve feet—is where people stand when someone says, "Stand back so I can look at you." This distance lends a formal tone to business or social discourse. In an executive office, the desk serves to keep people at this distance.

The fourth zone—public distance—is used by teachers in classrooms or speakers at public gatherings. At its farthest phase—twenty-five feet and beyond—it is used for important public figures. Violations of this distance can lead to serious complications. During his 1970 U.S. visit, the president of France, Georges Pompidou, was harassed by pickets in Chicago, who were permitted to get within touching distance. Since pickets in France are kept behind barricades a block or more away, the president was outraged by this insult to his person, and President Nixon was obliged to communicate his concern as well as offer his personal apologies.

It is interesting to note how American pitchmen and panhandlers exploit the unwritten, unspoken conventions of eye and distance. Both take advantage of the fact that once explicit eye contact is established, it is rude to look away, because to do so means to brusquely dismiss the other person and his needs. Once having caught the eye of his mark, the panhandler then locks on, not letting go until he moves through the public zone, the social zone, the personal zone and, finally, into the intimate sphere, where people are most vulnerable.

Touch also is an important part of the constant stream of communication that takes place between people. A light touch, a firm touch, a blow, a caress are all communications. In an effort to break down barriers among people, there's been a recent upsurge in group-encounter activities, in which strangers are encouraged to touch one another. In special situations such as these, the rules for not touching are broken with group approval, and people gradually lose some of their inhibitions.

Although most people don't realize it, space is perceived and distances are set not by vision alone but with all the senses. Auditory space is perceived with the ears, thermal space with the skin, kinesthetic space with muscles of the body, and olfactory space with the nose. And, once again, it's one's culture that determines how his senses are programmed—which sensory information ranks highest and lowest. The important thing to remember is that culture is very persistent. In this country, we've noted the existence of culture patterns that determine distance between people in the third and fourth generations of some families, despite their prolonged contact with people of very different cultural heritages.

Whenever there is great cultural distance between two people, there are bound to be problems arising from differences in behavior and expectations. An example is the American couple who consulted a psychiatrist about their marital problems. The husband was from New England and had been brought up by reserved parents who taught him to control his emotions and to respect the need for privacy. His wife was from an Italian family and had been brought up in close contact with all the members of her large family, who were extremely warm, volatile, and demonstrative.

When the husband came home after a hard day at the office, dragging his feet and longing for peace and quiet, his wife would rush to him and smother him. Clasping his hands, rubbing his brow, crooning over his weary head, she never left him alone. But when the wife was upset or anxious about her day, the husband's response was to withdraw completely and leave her alone. No comforting, no affectionate embrace, no attention—just solitude. The woman became convinced her husband didn't love her, and in desperation she consulted a psychiatrist. Their problem wasn't basically psychological but cultural.

Why has man developed all these different ways of communicating messages without words? One reason is that people don't like to spell out certain kinds of messages. We prefer to find other ways of showing our feelings. This is especially true in relationships as sensitive as courtship. Men don't like to be rejected, and most women don't want to turn a man down bluntly. Instead, we work out subtle ways of encouraging or discouraging each other that save face and avoid confrontations.

How a person handles space in dating others is an obvious and very sensitive indicator of how he or she feels about the other person. On a first date, if a woman sits or stands so close to a man that he is acutely conscious of her physical presence—inside the intimate-distance zone—the man usually construes it to mean that she is encouraging him. However, before the man starts moving in on the woman, he should be sure what message she's really sending; otherwise, he risks bruising his ego. What is close to someone of northern European background may be neutral or distant to someone of Italian heritage. Also, women sometimes use space as a way of misleading a man, and there are few things that put men off more than women who communicate contradictory messages, such as women who cuddle up and then act insulted when a man takes the next step.

How does a woman communicate interest in a man? In addition to such familiar gambits as smiling at him, she may glance shyly at him, blush, and then look away. Or she may give him a real come-on look and move in very close when he approaches. She may touch his arm and ask for a light. As she leans forward to light her cigarette, she may brush him lightly, enveloping him in her perfume. She'll probably continue to smile at him, and she may use what ethologists call preening gestures—touching the back of her hair, thrusting her breasts forward, tilting her hips at she stands, or crossing her legs if she's seated, perhaps even exposing one thigh or putting a hand on her thigh and stroking it. She may also stroke her wrists as she converses or show the palm of her hand as a way of gaining his attention. Her skin may be unusually flushed or quite pale, her eyes brighter, the pupils larger.

If a man sees a woman whom he wants to attract, he tries to present himself by his posture and stance as someone who is self-assured. He moves briskly and confidently. When he catches the eye of the woman, he may hold her glance a little longer than normal. If he gets an encouraging smile, he'll move in close and engage her in small talk. As they converse, his glance shifts over her face and body. He too, may make preening gestures—straightening his tie, smoothing his hair, or shooting his cuffs.

How do people learn body language? The same way they learn spoken language—by observing and imitating people around them as they're growing up. Little girls imitate their mothers or an older female. Little boys imitate their fathers or a respected uncle or a character on television. In this way, they learn the gender signals appropriate for their sex. Regional, class, and ethnic patterns of body behavior are also learned in childhood and persist throughout life. . . .

Nonverbal communications signal to members of your own group what kind of person you are, how you feel about others, how you'll fit into and work in a group, whether you're assured or anxious, the degree to which you feel comfortable with the standards of your own culture, as well as deeply significant feelings about the self, including the state of your own psyche. For most of us, it's difficult to accept the reality of another's behavioral system. And, of course, none of us will ever become fully knowledgeable of the importance of every nonverbal signal. But as long as each of us realizes the power of these signals, the society's diversity can be a source of great strength rather than a further—and subtly powerful—source of division.

10 The Rules for Giving Christmas Gifts

THEODORE CAPLOW

Our lives are bound by rules. I'm not referring to just the laws of the land or the official policies of your college. As important as these are, they pale into insignificance when we compare them with the rules of everyday life. From the time we wake up in the morning to the time we go to bed at night, our lives are governed by a complex system of norms or expectations. These rules govern not only what we do, including what we say and how we say it, but even the look on our face as we say it.

You might think that I'm being extreme in this statement, that as a sociologist I'm getting carried away with my subject matter. We seem to experience freedom, and we think that we think independent thoughts and have independent feelings—but do we? Consider the implications of this article. In his study of Middletown (Muncie, Indiana), Caplow and his research team found that the residents of this town followed highly detailed rules in their Christmas giving. These rules were so powerful that almost everyone followed them—yet people could not verbalize these rules. We, too, follow implicit rules in our everyday lives, not just in giving gifts, but in *everything* we do. As with the residents of Muncie, these background assumptions (or rules) are so embedded in our consciousness that we, too, would have a difficult time telling someone what they were. Yet we and others follow them, which allows interaction to flow and group life to exist. Such is the power of socialization into culture.

THE CELEBRATION OF CHRISTMAS, the high point of the [holiday cycle in Middletown], mobilizes almost the entire population for several weeks, accounts for about 4% of its total annual expenditures, and takes precedence over ordinary forms of work and leisure. In order to include this large phenomenon, we interviewed a random sample of 110 Middletown adults. . . . The survey included an inventory of all Christmas gifts given and received by these respondents. . . . The total number of gifts inventoried was 4,347, a mean of 39.5 per respondent.

How are the rules that appear to govern Christmas gift-giving in Middletown communicated and enforced? There are no enforcement agents and little indignation against violators. Nevertheless, the level of participation is very high. Here are some typical gift-giving rules that are enforced effectively in Middletown without visible means of enforcement and indeed without any widespread awareness of their existence:

The Tree Rule

> Married couples with children of any age should put up Christmas trees in their homes. Unmarried persons with no living children should not put up Christmas trees. Unmarried parents (widowed, divorced, or adoptive) may put up trees but are not required to do so.

Conformity with the Tree Rule in our survey sample may be fairly described as spectacular.

Nobody in Middletown seems to be consciously aware of the norm that requires married couples with children of any age to put up a Christmas tree, yet the obligation is so compelling that, of the 77 respondents in this category who were at home for Christmas, only one failed to so. Few of the written laws that agents of the state attempt to enforce with endless paperwork and threats of violence are so well obeyed as this unwritten rule that is promulgated by no identifiable authority and backed by no evident threat. Indeed, the existence of the rule goes unnoticed. People in Middletown think that putting up a Christmas tree is an entirely voluntary act. They know that it has some connection with children, but they do not understand that married couples with children of any age are effectively required to have trees and that childless unmarried people are somehow prevented from having them.

The Wrapping Rule

> Christmas gifts must be wrapped before they are presented.

A subsidiary rule requires that the wrapping be appropriate, that is, emblematic, and another subsidiary rule says that wrapped gifts are appropriately displayed as a set but that unwrapped gifts should not be so displayed. Conformity with these rules is exceedingly high. An unwrapped object is so clearly excluded as a Christmas gift that Middletown people who wish to give something at that season without defining it as a Christmas gift have only to leave the object unwrapped. Difficult-to-wrap Christmas gifts, like a pony or a piano, are wrapped symbolically by adding a ribbon or bow or card and are hidden until presentation.

In nearly every Middletown household, the wrapped presents are displayed under or around the Christmas tree as a glittering monument to the family's affluence and mutual affection. Picture taking at Christmas gatherings is clearly a part of the ritual; photographs were taken at 65% of the recorded gatherings. In nearly all instances, the pile of wrapped gifts was photographed; and individual participants were photographed opening a gift, ideally at the moment of "surprise."

The Decoration Rule

Any room where Christmas gifts are distributed should be decorated by affixing Christmas emblems to the walls, the ceiling, or the furniture. This is done even in nondomestic places, like offices or restaurant dining rooms, if gifts are to be distributed there. Conformity to this rule was perfect in our sample of 366 gatherings at which gifts were distributed, although, once again, the existence of the rule was not recognized by the people who obeyed it.

The same lack of recognition applies to the interesting subsidiary rule that a Christmas tree should not be put up in an undecorated place, although a decorated place need not have a tree. Unmarried, childless persons normally decorate their homes, although they have no trees, and decorations without a tree are common in public places, but a Christmas tree in an undecorated room would be unseemly.

The Gathering Rule

Christmas gifts should be distributed at gatherings where every person gives and receives gifts.

Compliance with this rule is very high. More than nine-tenths of the 1,378 gifts our respondents received, and of the 2,969 they gave, were distributed in gatherings, more than three-quarters of which were family gatherings. Most gifts mailed or shipped by friends and relatives living at a distance were double wrapped, so that the outer unceremonious wrappings could be removed and the inner packages could be placed with other gifts to be opened at a gathering. In the typical family gathering, a number of related persons assemble by prearrangement at the home of one of them where a feast is served; the adults engage in conversation; the children play; someone takes photographs; gifts are distributed, opened, and admired; and the company then disperses. The average Middletown adult fits more than three of these occasions into a 24–hour period beginning at Christmas Eve, often driving long distances and eating several large dinners during that time.

The Dinner Rule

> Family gatherings at which gifts are distributed include a "traditional Christmas dinner."

This is the rule that participants in Middletown's Christmas ritual may disregard if they wish, but it is no less interesting because compliance is only partial. Presumably, this rule acquired its elective character because the pattern of multiple gatherings described above requires many gatherings to be scheduled at odd hours when dinner either would be inappropriate or, if the dinner rule were inflexible, would require participants to overeat beyond the normal expectations of the season. However, 65% of the survey respondents had eaten at least one traditional Christmas dinner the previous year.

There appears to be a subsidiary rule that traditional Christmas dinners served in homes should be prepared exclusively by women. There was not a single reported instance in this survey of a traditional Christmas dinner prepared by a man.

The Gift Selection Rules

> A Christmas gift should (a) demonstrate the giver's familiarity with the receiver's preferences; (b) surprise the receiver, either by expressing more affection—measured by the aesthetic or practical value of the gift—than the receiver might reasonably anticipate or more knowledge than the giver might reasonably be expected to have; (c) be scaled in economic value to the emotional value of the relationship.

The economic values of any giver's gifts are supposed to be sufficiently scaled to the emotional values of relationships that, when they are opened in the bright glare of the family circle, the donor will not appear to have disregarded either the legitimate inequality of some relationships by, for example, giving a more valuable gift to a nephew than to a son, or the legitimate equality of other relationships by, for example, giving conspicuously unequal gifts to two sons.

Individuals participating in these rituals are not free to improvise their own scales of emotional value for relationships. The scale they are supposed to use, together with its permissible variations, is not written down anywhere but is thoroughly familiar to participants. From analysis of the gifts given and received by our survey respondents, we infer the following rules for scaling the emotional value of relationships.

The Scale

(a) A spousal relationship should be more valuable than any other for both husband and wife, but the husband may set a higher value on it than the wife.

(b) A parent-child relationship should be less valuable than a spousal relationship but more valuable than any other relationship. The parent may set a higher value on it than the child does.

(c) The spouse of a married close relative should be valued as much as the linking relative.

(d) Parents with several children should value them equally throughout their lives.

(e) Children with both parents still living, and still married to each other, may value them equally *or* may value their mothers somewhat more than their fathers. A married couple with two pairs of living, still-married parents should value each pair equally. Children of any age with divorced, separated, *or* re-married parents may value them unequally.

(f) Siblings should be valued equally in childhood but not later. Adult siblings who live close by and are part of one's active network should be equally valued, along with their respective spouses, but siblings who live farther away may be valued unequally.

(g) Friends of either sex, aside from sexual partners treated as quasi-spouses, may be valued as much as siblings but should not be valued as much as spouses, parents, or children.

(h) More distant relatives—like aunts *or* cousins—may be valued as much as siblings but should not be valued as much as spouses, parents, or children.

It is a formidable task to balance these ratios every year and to come up with a set of Christmas gifts that satisfies them. Small wonder that Middletown people complain that Christmas shopping is difficult, and fatiguing. But although they complain, they persist in it year after year without interruption. People who are away from home for Christmas arrange in advance to have their gifts distributed to the usual receivers and to open their own gifts ceremoniously. People confined by severe illness delegate others to do shopping and wrapping. Although our random sample of Middletown adults included several socially isolated persons, even the single most isolated respondent happened to have an old friend with whom he exchanged expensive gifts.

Given the complexity of the rules, errors and failures in gift selection can be expected to occur, and they frequently do. Indeed, the four or five shopping days immediately after Christmas are set aside in Middletown stores for return or exchange of badly selected gifts. A number of respondents described relatives who make a point of being impossible to please. The standard disappointing gift is an article of clothing in the wrong size. Women are particularly resentful of oversized items that seem to say the giver perceives them as "fat." Children are often insulted by inattentive relatives who give them toys that are too "young." The spouse's or lover's gift that is disliked by the receiver is a sign of alienation. Two of the five couples in our sample for whom such gifts were reported at Christmas 1978 had separated by the time of the interview several weeks later.

Fitness Rules

Rules about the fitness of gifts (e.g., women should not give cut flowers to men) are too numerous to specify, but one deserves passing attention. Money is an appropriate gift from senior to junior kin, but an inappropriate gift from junior to senior kin, regardless of the relative affluence of the parties. This is another rule which appears to be unknown to the people who obey it. Of 144 gifts of money given by persons in our sample to those in other generations, 94% went to junior kin, and of the 73 money gifts respondents received from persons in other generations, 93% were from senior kin. A gift certificate may be given to a parent or grandparent to whom an outright gift of money would be improper. . . .

The Reciprocity Rule

> Participants in this gift system should give (individually or jointly) at least one Christmas gift every year to their mothers, fathers, sons, daughters; to the current spouses of these persons; and to their own spouses.

By the operation of this rule, participants expect to receive at least one gift in return from each of these persons excepting infants. Conformity runs about 90% for each relationship separately and for the aggregate of all such relationships. Gifts to grandparents and grandchildren seem to be equally obligatory if these live in the same community or nearby, but not at greater distances.

The Reciprocity Rule does not require reciprocated gifts to be of equal value. Parents expect to give more valuable and more numerous gifts to their minor children and to their adult children living at home than they receive in return. This imbalance is central to the entire ritual. The iconography of Middletown's secular Christmas emphasizes unreciprocated giving to children by the emblematic figure of Santa Claus, and the theme of unreciprocated giving provides one of the few connections between the secular and religious iconography of the festival—the Three Wise Men coming from a distant land to bring unreciprocated gifts to a child.

Equivalence of value tends to be disregarded in gift-giving between husbands and wives and between parents and their adult children. Husbands often give more valuable gifts to wives than they receive from them. The gifts of parents to adult children are approximately balanced in the aggregate—about the same number of substantial gifts are given in each direction—but there is no insistence on equivalence in particular cases, and when we examine such relationships one by one, we discover many unbalanced exchanges, which seem to be taken for granted.

Only in the relationship between siblings and sibling couples do we find any active concern that the gifts exchanged be of approximately equal value, and even there it is more important to give gifts of approximately equal value to several siblings than to exchange gifts of equal value with each of them.

Empirically, the gift-giving between adults and children in our sample was highly unbalanced, in both quantity and value. Respondents gave 946 gifts to persons under 18 and received 145 in return; 89 of these were of substantial value and six of the return gifts were. In about one-third or these relationships, no gift was returned to the adult either by the child or in the child's name. In most of the remaining relationships, the child returned a single gift of token or modest value.

Discussion

Since the problem is to account for the uniformities of gift-giving behavior revealed by the data, speaking of rules begs the question to some extent. Although we infer from the uniformities observed in Middletown's Christmas gift-giving that, somewhere in the culture, there must be statements to which the observed behavior is a response, the crucial point is that we cannot find those statements in any explicit form. Indeed, they are not recognized by participants in the system. In effect, the rules of the game are unfamiliar to the players, even though they can be observed to play meticulously by the rules. Instructions for Christmas gift-giving are not found in administrative regulations or popular maxims or books of etiquette; they are not *promulgated*.

Gift exchange, in effect, is a language that employs objects instead of words as its lexical elements. In this perspective, every culture has a language of presentation [i.e., the obligatory exchange of objects] to express important interpersonal relationships on special occasions, just as it has a verbal language to create and manage meaning for other purposes. The language of presentation, like the verbal language, begins to be learned in early childhood and is used with increasing assurance as the individual matures and acquires social understanding. The problem of accounting for the enforcement of gift-giving rules without visible means is simplified if we take them to be linguistic rules, or at least as similar to them, because linguistic rules, for the most part, are enforced among native speakers of a language without visible means and without being recognized explicitly.

Visualizing Christmas gift-giving as a language or, more precisely, as a dialect or code, helps to explain, among other matters, the preference for the simultaneous exchange of gifts at family gatherings rather than in private.

In most cases such a gathering is composed of a parent-child unit containing one or two parents and one or more children together with other persons who are tied to that unit by shared membership in another parent-child unit, such as children's children, children's spouses, parents' siblings, or parents' parents. Although there is room at a family gathering for a friend or distant relative who otherwise might be solitary at Christmas, there is no convenient way of including any large number of persons to whom no gift messages are owed.

Under the Scaling Rules, gift messages are due from every person in a parent-child relationship to every other. The individual message says "I value you according to the degree of our relationship" and anticipates the response "I value you in the same way." But the compound message that emerges from the unwrapping of gifts in the presence of the whole gathering allows more subtle meanings to be conveyed. It permits the husband to say to the wife "I value you more than my parents" or the mother to say to the daughter-in-law "I value you as much as my son so long as you are married to him" or the brother to say to the brother "I value you more than our absent brothers, but less than our parents and much less than my children."

These statements, taken together, would define and sustain a social structure, if only because, by their gift messages, both parties to each dyadic relationship confirm that they have the same understanding of the relationship, and the bystanders, who are interested parties, endorse that understanding by tacit approval. The compound messages would have a powerful influence even if they were idiosyncratic and each parent-child unit had its own method of scaling relationships. In fact, there are some observable differences in scaling from one Middletown family to another and from one subcultural group to another, but the similarities are much more striking than the differences. We attribute this commonality to the shared dialect of Christmas gift-giving, hyper-developed in Middletown and elsewhere in the United States in response to commercial promotion, stresses in the family institution, and constant reiteration by the mass media. Once the dialect is known, these factors continue to enlarge its vocabulary and its domain.

Another circumstance facilitating the standardization of the dialect is that nearly every individual in this population belongs to more than one parent-child unit for Christmas gift-giving purposes. Because these units are linked and cross-linked to other units in a network that ultimately includes the larger part of the community, they would probably tend to develop a common set of understandings about appropriate kinship behavior, even without the reinforcement provided by domestic rituals.

The most powerful reinforcement remains to be mentioned. In the dialect of Christmas gift-giving, the absence of a gift is also a lexical sign, signifying either the absence of a close relationship, as in the Christmas contact of cousins, or the desire to terminate a close relationship, as when a husband gives no gift to his wife. People who have once learned the dialect cannot choose to forget it, nor can they pretend to ignore messages they understand. Thus, without any complicated normative machinery, Middletown people find themselves compelled to give Christmas gifts to their close relatives, lest they inadvertently send them messages of hostility. In this community, where most people depend on their relatives for emotional and social support, the consequences of accidentally sending them a hostile message are too serious to contemplate, and few are willing to run the risk.

In sum, we discover that the participants in this gift-giving system are themselves the agents who enforce its complex rules, although they do so unknowingly and without conscious reference to a system. The dialect, once learned, imposes itself by linguistic necessity, and the enforcement of its rules is the more effective for being unplanned.

11 The Presentation of Self in Everyday Life

ERVING GOFFMAN

All the world's a stage
And all the men and women merely players.
They have their exits and their entrances;
And one man in his time plays many parts. . . .
         William Shakespeare
         As You Like It, Act 2, Scene 7

This quotation from Shakespeare could well serve as the keynote for the following selection. Taking Shakespeare's statement seriously, Goffman presents a dramaturgical model of human life and uses it as the conceptual framework for understanding life-in-society. In this view, people in everyday life are actors on stage, the audience consists of those persons who observe what others are doing, the parts are the roles that people play (whether occupational, familial, friendship roles, or whatever), the dialogue consists of ritualized conversational exchanges ("Hi. How ya doin'?"; "Hey, bro', wha's hapnin'?"; "How's it goin'?"; the hellos, the goodbyes, and the in-betweens), while the costuming consists of whatever clothing happens to be in style.

Goffman's insightful analysis provides a framework from which we can gain a remarkably different perspective of what we do in life—at home, at school, with friends, while on a date, or while shopping. When understood properly, however, you may find this approach to understanding human behavior disturbing. For example, if we are all actors playing roles on the stage of life, where is the "real me"? Is all of life merely a "put-on," play acting, a masquerade of some sort? Does not this framework for understanding human interaction constitute an essentially cynical and manipulative approach to life, a sort of everyday Machiavellianism?

WHEN AN INDIVIDUAL ENTERS the presence of others, they commonly seek to acquire information about him or to bring into play information about him already possessed. They will be interested in his general socio-economic status, his conception of self, his attitude toward them, his competence, his trustworthiness, etc. Although some of this information seems to be sought almost as an end in itself, there are usually quite practical reasons for acquiring it. Information about the individual helps to define the situation, enabling others to know in advance what he will expect of them and what they may expect of him. Informed in these ways, the others will know how best to act in order to call forth a desired response from him.

For those present, many sources of information become accessible and many carriers (or "sign-vehicles") become available for conveying this information. If unacquainted with the individual, observers can glean clues from his conduct and appearance which allow them to apply their previous experience with individuals roughly similar to the one before them or, more important, to apply untested stereotypes to him. They can also assume from past experience that only individuals of a particular kind are likely to be found in a given social setting. They can rely on what the individual says about himself or on documentary evidence he provides as to who and what he is. If they know, or know of, the individual by virtue of experience prior to the interaction, they can rely on assumptions as to the persistence and generality of psychological traits as a means of predicting his present and future behavior.

However, during the period in which the individual is in the immediate presence of the others, few events may occur which directly provide the others with the conclusive information they will need if they are to direct wisely their own activity. Many crucial facts lie beyond the time and place of interaction or lie concealed within it. For example, the "true" or "real" attitudes, beliefs, and emotions of the individual can be ascertained only indirectly, through his avowals or through what appears to be involuntary expressive behavior. Similarly, if the individual offers the others a product or service, they will often find that during the interaction there will be no time and place immediately available for eating the pudding that the proof can be found in. They will be forced to accept some events as conventional or natural signs of something not directly available to the senses. In Ichheiser's terms,[1] the individual will have to act so that he intentionally or unintentionally *expresses* himself, and the others will in turn have to be *impressed* in some way by him.

The expressiveness of the individual (and therefore his capacity to give impressions) appears to involve two radically different kinds of sign activity: the expression that he *gives,* and the expression that he *gives off.* The first involves verbal symbols or their substitutes which he uses admittedly and solely to convey the information that he and the others are known to attach to these symbols. This is communication in the traditional and narrow sense. The second involves a wide range of action that others can treat as symptomatic of the actor, the expectation being that the action was performed for reasons other than the information conveyed in this way. As we shall have to see, this distinction has an only initial validity. The individual does of course intentionally convey misinformation by means of both of these types of communication, the first involving deceit, the second feigning.

Taking communication in both its narrow and broad sense, one finds that when the individual is in the immediate presence of others, his activity will have a promissory character. The others are likely to find that they must accept the individual on faith, offering him a just return while he is present before them in exchange for something whose true value will not be established until after he has left their presence. (Of course, the others also live by inference in their dealings with the physical world, but it is only in the world of social interaction that the objects about which they make inferences will purposely facilitate and hinder this inferential process.) The security that they justifiably feel in making inferences about the individual will vary, of course, depending on such factors as the amount of information they already possess about him, but no amount of such past evidence can entirely obviate the necessity of acting on the basis of inferences. As William I. Thomas suggested:

> It is also highly important for us to realize that we do not as a matter of fact lead our lives, make our decisions, and reach our goals into everyday life either statistically or scientifically. We live by inference. I am, let us say, your guest. You do not know, you cannot determine scientifically, that I will not steal your money or your spoons. But inferentially I will not, and inferentially you have me as a guest.[2]

Let us now turn from the others to the point of view of the individual who presents himself before them. He may wish them to think highly of him, or to think that he thinks highly of them, or to perceive how in fact he feels toward them, or to obtain no clearcut impression; he may wish to ensure sufficient harmony so that the interaction can be sustained, or to defraud, get rid of, confuse, mislead, antagonize, or insult them. Regardless of the particular objective which the individual has in mind and of his motive for having this objective, it will be in his interests to control the conduct of the others, especially their responsive treatment of him.[3] This control is achieved largely by influencing the definition of the situation which the others come to formulate, and he can influence this definition by expressing himself in such a way as to give them the kind of impression that will lead them to act voluntarily in accordance with his own plan. Thus, when an individual appears in the presence of others, there will usually be some reason for him to mobilize his activity so that it will convey an impression to others which it is in his interests to convey. Since a girl's dormitory mates will glean evidence of her popularity from the calls she receives on the phone, we can suspect that some girls will arrange for calls to be made, and Willard Waller's finding can be anticipated.

> It has been reported by many observers that a girl who is called to the telephone in the dormitories will often allow herself to be called several times, in order to give all the other girls ample opportunity to hear her paged.[4]

Of the two kinds of communication—expressions given and expressions given off—this report will be primarily concerned with the latter, with the more theatrical and contextual kind, the non-verbal, presumably unintentional kind, whether this communication be purposely engineered or not. As an example of what we must try to examine, I would like to cite at length a novelistic incident in which Preedy, a vacationing Englishman, makes his first appearance on the beach of his summer hotel in Spain:

> But in any case he took care to avoid catching anyone's eye. First of all, he had to make it clear to those potential companions of his holiday that they were of no concern to him whatsoever. He stared through them, round them, over them— eyes lost in space. The beach might have been empty. If by chance a ball was thrown his way, he looked surprised; then let a smile of amusement lighten his face (Kindly Preedy), looked round dazed to see that there *were* people on the beach, tossed it back with a smile to himself and not a smile *at* the people, and then resumed carelessly his nonchalant survey of space.
>
> But it was time to institute a little parade, the parade of the Ideal Preedy. By devious handlings he gave any one who wanted to look a chance to see the title of the book—a Spanish translation of Homer, classic thus, but not daring, cosmopolitan too—and then gathered together his beachwrap and bag into a neat sand-resistant pile (Methodical and Sensible Preedy), rose slowly to stretch at ease his huge frame (Big-Cat Preedy), and tossed aside his sandals (Carefree Preedy, after all).
>
> The marriage of Preedy and the sea! There were alternative rituals. The first involved the stroll that turns into a run and a dive straight into the water, thereafter smoothing into a strong splashless crawl towards the horizon. But of course not really to the horizon. Quite suddenly he would turn on to his back and thrash great white splashes with his legs, somehow thus showing that he could have swum further had he wanted to, and then would stand up a quarter out of water for all to see who it was.
>
> The alternative course was simpler; it avoided the cold-water shock, and it avoided the risk of appearing too high-spirited. The point was to appear to be so used to the sea, the Mediterranean, and this particular beach, that one might as well be in the sea as out of it. It involved a slow stroll down and into the edge of the water—not even noticing his toes were wet, land and water all the same to *him!*—with his eyes up at the sky gravely surveying portents, invisible to others, of the weather (Local Fisherman Preedy).[5]

The novelist means us to see that Preedy is improperly concerned with the extensive impressions he feels his sheer bodily action is giving off to those around him. We can malign Preedy further by assuming that he has acted merely in order to give a particular impression, that this is a false impression, and that the others present receive either no impression at all, or worse still, the impression that Preedy is affectedly trying to cause them to receive. But the important point for us here is that the kind of impression Preedy thinks he is making is in fact the kind of impression that others correctly and incorrectly glean from someone in their midst.

I have said that when an individual appears before others his actions will influence the definition of the situation which they come to have. Sometimes the individual will act in a thoroughly calculating manner, expressing himself in a given way solely in order to give the kind of impression to others that is likely to evoke from them a specific response he is concerned to obtain. Sometimes the individual will be calculating in his activity but be relatively unaware that this is the case. Sometimes he will intentionally and consciously express himself in a particular way, but chiefly because the traditions of his group or social status require this kind of expression and not because of any particular response (other than vague acceptance or approval) that is likely to be evoked from those impressed by the expression. Sometimes the traditions of an individual's role will lead him to give a well-designed impression of a particular kind and yet he may be neither consciously nor unconsciously disposed to create such an impression. The others, in their turn, may be suitably impressed by the individual's efforts to convey something, or may misunderstand the situation and come to conclusions that are warranted neither by the individual's intent nor by the facts. In any case, in so far as the others act *as if* the individual had conveyed a particular impression, we may take a functional or pragmatic view and say that the individual has "effectively" projected a given definition of the situation and "effectively" fostered the understanding that a given state of affairs obtains.

There is one aspect of the others' response that bears special comment here. Knowing that the individual is likely to present himself in a light that is favorable to him, the others may divide what they witness into two parts: a part that is relatively easy for the individual to manipulate at will, being chiefly his verbal assertions, and a part in regard to which he seems to have little concern or control, being chiefly derived from the expressions he gives off. The others may then use what are considered to be the ungovernable aspects of his expressive behavior as a check upon the validity of what is conveyed by the governable aspects. In this a fundamental asymmetry is demonstrated in the communication process, the individual presumably being aware of only one stream of his communication, the witness of this stream and one other. For example, in Shetland Isle one crofter's wife, in serving native dishes to a visitor from the mainland of Britain, would listen with a polite smile to his polite claims of liking what he was eating; at the same time she would take note of the rapidity with which the visitor lifted his fork or spoon to his mouth, the eagerness with which he passed food into his mouth, and the gusto expressed in chewing the food, using these signs as a check on the stated feelings of the eater. The same woman, in order to discover what one acquaintance (A) "actually" thought of another acquaintance (B), would wait until B was in the presence of A but engaged in conversation with still another person (C). She would then covertly examine the facial expressions of A as he regarded B in conversation with C. Not being in conversation with B, and not being directly observed by him, A would sometimes relax usual constraints and tactful deceptions, and freely express what he was "actually" feeling about B. This Shetlander, in short, would observe the unobserved observer.

Now given the fact that others are likely to check up on the more controllable aspects of behavior by means of the less controllable, one can expect that sometimes the individual will try to exploit this very possibility, guiding the impression he makes through behavior felt to be reliably informing.[6] For example, in gaining admission to a tight social circle, the participant observer may not only wear an accepting look while listening to an informant, but may also be careful to wear the same look when observing the informant talking to others; observers of the observer will then not as easily discover where he actually stands. A specific illustration may be cited from Shetland Isle. When a neighbor dropped in to have a cup of tea, he would ordinarily wear at least a hint of an expectant warm smile as he passed through the door into the cottage. Since lack of physical obstructions outside the cottage and lack of light within it usually made it possible to observe the visitor unobserved as he approached the house, islanders sometimes took pleasure in watching the visitor drop whatever expression he was manifesting and replace it with a sociable one just before reaching the door. However, some visitors, in appreciating that this examination was occurring, would blindly adopt a social face a long distance from the house, thus ensuring the projection of a constant image.

This kind of control upon the part of the individual reinstates the symmetry of the communication process, and sets the stage for a kind of information game—a potentially infinite cycle of concealment, discovery, false revelation, and rediscovery. It should be added that since the others are likely to be relatively unsuspicious of the presumably unguided aspect of the individual's conduct, he can gain much by controlling it. The others of course may sense that the individual is manipulating the presumably spontaneous aspects of his behavior, and seek in this very act of manipulation some shading of conduct that the individual has not managed to control. This again provides a check upon the individual's behavior, this time his presumably uncalculated behavior, thus re-establishing the asymmetry of the communication process. Here I would like only to add the suggestion that the arts of piercing an individual's effort at calculated unintentionality seem better developed than our capacity to manipulate our own behavior, so that regardless of how many steps have occurred in the information game, the witness is likely to have the advantage over the actor, and the initial asymmetry of the communication process is likely to be retained.

When we allow that the individual projects a definition of the situation when he appears before others, we must also see that the others, however passive their role may seem to be, will themselves effectively project a definition of the situation by virtue of their response to the individual and by virtue of any lines of action they initiate to him. Ordinarily the definitions of the situation projected by the several different participants are sufficiently attuned to one another so that open contradiction will not occur. I do not mean that there will be the kind of consensus that arises when each individual present candidly expresses what he really feels and honestly agrees with the expressed feelings of the others present. This kind of harmony is an optimistic ideal and in any case not necessary for the smooth working of society. Rather, each participant is expected to suppress his immediate heartfelt feelings, conveying a view of the situation which he feels the others will be able to find at least temporarily acceptable. The maintenance of this surface of agreement, this veneer of consensus, is facilitated by each participant concealing his own wants behind statements which assert values to which everyone present feels obliged to give lip service. Further, there is usually a kind of division of definitional labor. Each participant is allowed to establish the tentative official ruling regarding matters which are vital to him but not immediately important to others, e.g., the rationalizations and justifications by which he accounts for his past activity. In exchange for this courtesy he remains silent or noncommittal on matters important to others but not immediately important to him. We have then a kind of interactional *modus vivendi*. Together, the participants contribute to a single over-all definition of the situation which involves not so much a real agreement as to what exists but rather a real agreement as to whose claims concerning what issues will be temporarily honored. Real agreement will also exist concerning the desirability of avoiding an open conflict of definitions of the situation.[7] I will refer to this level of agreement as a "working consensus." It is to be understood that the working consensus established in one interaction setting will be quite different in content from the working consensus established in a different type of setting. Thus, between two friends at lunch, a reciprocal show of affection, respect, and concern for the other is maintained. In service occupations, on the other hand, the specialist often maintains an image of disinterested involvement in the problem of the client, while the client responds with a show of respect for the competence and integrity of the specialist. Regardless of such differences in content, however, the general form of these working arrangements is the same.

In noting the tendency for a participant to accept the definitional claims made by the others present, we can appreciate the crucial importance of the information that the individual *initially* possesses or acquires concerning his fellow participants, for it is on the basis of this initial information that the individual starts to define the situation and starts to build up lines of responsive action. The individual's initial projection commits him to what he is proposing to be and requires him to drop all pretenses of being other things. As the interaction among the participants progresses, additions and modifications in this initial informational state will of course occur, but it is essential that these later developments be related without contradiction to, and even built up from, the initial positions taken by the several participants. It would seem that an individual can more easily make a choice as to what line of treatment to demand from and extend to the others present at the beginning of an encounter than he can alter the line of treatment that is being pursued once the interaction is under way.

In everyday life, of course, there is a clear understanding that first impressions are important. Thus, the work adjustment of those in service occupations will often hinge upon a capacity to seize and hold the initiative in the service relation, a capacity that will require subtle aggressiveness on the part of the server when he is of lower socio-economic status than his client. W. F. Whyte suggests the waitress as an example:

> The first point that stands out is that the waitress who bears up under pressure does not simply respond to her customers. She acts with some skill to control their behavior. The first question to ask when we look at the customer relationship is, "Does the waitress get the jump on the customer, or does the customer get the jump on the waitress?" The skilled waitress realizes the crucial nature of this question. . . .
> The skilled waitress tackles the customer with confidence and without hesitation. For example, she may find that a new customer has seated himself before she could clear off the dirty dishes and change the cloth. He is now leaning on the table studying the menu. She greets him, says, "May I change the cover, please?" and, without waiting for an answer, takes his menu away from him so that he moves back from the table, and she goes about her work. The relationship is handled politely but firmly, and there is never any question as to who is in charge.[8]

When the interaction that is initiated by "first impressions" is itself merely the initial interaction in an extended series of interactions involving the same participants, we speak of "getting off on the right foot" and feel that it is crucial that we do so. Thus, one learns that some teachers take the following view:

> You can't ever let them get the upper hand on you or you're through. So I start out tough. The first day I get a new class in, I let them know who's boss. . . . You've got to start off tough; then you can ease up as you go along. If you start out easy-going, when you try to be tough, they'll just look at you and laugh.[9]

Similarly, attendants in mental institutions may feel that if the new patient is sharply put in his place the first day on the ward and made to see who is boss, much future difficulty will be prevented.[10]

Given the fact that the individual effectively projects a definition of the situation when he enters the presence of others, we can assume that events may occur within the interaction which contradict, discredit, or otherwise throw doubt upon this projection. When these disruptive events occur, the interaction itself may come to a confused and embarrassed halt. Some of the assumptions upon which the responses of the participants had been predicted become untenable, and the participants find themselves lodged in an interaction for which the situation has been wrongly defined and is now no longer defined. At such moments the individual whose presentation has been discredited may feel ashamed while the others present may feel hostile, and all the participants may come to feel ill at ease, nonplussed, out of countenance, embarrassed, experiencing the kind of anomy that is generated when the minute social system of face-to-face interaction breaks down.

In stressing the fact that the initial definition of the situation projected by an individual tends to provide a plan for the cooperative activity that follows— in stressing this action point of view—we must not overlook the crucial fact that any projected definition of the situation also has a distinctive moral character. It is this moral character of projections that will chiefly concern us in this report. Society is organized on the principle that any individual who possesses certain social characteristics has a moral right to expect that others will value and treat him in an appropriate way. Connected with this principle is a second, namely that an individual who implicitly or explicitly signifies that he has certain social characteristics ought in fact to be what he claims he is. In consequence, when an individual projects a definition of the situation and thereby makes an implicit or explicit claim to be a person of a particular kind, he automatically exerts a moral demand upon the others, obliging them to value and treat him in the manner that persons of his kind have a right to expect. He also implicitly forgoes all claims to be things he does not appear to be[11] and hence forgoes the treatment that would be appropriate for such individuals. The others find, then, that the individual has informed them as to what is and as to what they *ought* to see as the "is."

One cannot judge the importance of definitional disruptions by the frequency with which they occur, for apparently they would occur more frequently were not constant precautions taken. We find that preventive practices are constantly employed to avoid these embarrassments and that corrective practices are constantly employed to compensate for discrediting occurrences that have not been successfully avoided. When the individual employs these strategies and tactics to protect his own projections, we may refer to them as "defensive practices"; when a participant employs them to save the definition of the situation projected by another, we speak of "protective practices" or "tact." Together, defensive and protective practices comprise the techniques employed to safeguard the impression fostered by an individual during his presence before others. It should be added that while we may be ready to see that no fostered impression would survive if defensive practices were not employed, we are less ready perhaps to see that few impressions could survive if those who received the impression did not exert tact in their reception of it.

In addition to the fact that precautions are taken to prevent disruption of projected definitions, we may also note that an intense interest in these disruptions comes to play a significant role in the social life of the group. Practical jokes and social games are played in which embarrassments which are to be taken unseriously are purposely engineered.[12] Fantasies are created in which devastating exposures occur. Anecdotes from the past—real, embroidered, or fictitious—are told and retold, detailing disruptions which occurred, almost occurred, or occurred and were admirably resolved. There seems to be no grouping which does not have a ready supply of these games, reveries, and cautionary tales, to be used as a source of humor, a catharsis for anxieties, and a sanction for inducing individuals to be modest in their claims and reasonable in their projected expectations. The individual may tell himself through dreams of getting into impossible positions. Families tell of the time a guest got his dates mixed and arrived when neither the house nor anyone in it was ready for him. Journalists tell of times when an all-too-meaningful misprint occurred, and the paper's assumption of objectivity or decorum was humorously discredited. Public servants tell of times a client ridiculously misunderstood form instructions, giving answers which implied an unanticipated and bizarre definition of the situation.[13] Seamen, whose home away from home is rigorously he-man, tell stories of coming back home and inadvertently asking mother to "pass the fucking butter."[14] Diplomats tell of the time a near-sighted queen asked a republican ambassador about the health of his king.[15]

To summarize, then, I assume that when an individual appears before others he will have many motives for trying to control the impression they receive of the situation.

Notes

1. Gustav Ichheiser, "Misunderstandings in Human Relations," Supplement to *The American Journal of Sociology*, 55 (September, 1949):6–7.

2. Quoted in E. H. Volkart, editor, *Social Behavior and Personality, Contributions of W. I. Thomas to Theory and Social Research* (New York: Social Science Research Council, 1951), p. 5.

3. Here I owe much to an unpublished paper by Tom Burns of the University of Edinburgh. He presents the argument that in all interaction a basic underlying theme is the desire of each participant to guide and control the responses made by the others present. A similar argument has been advanced by Jay Haley in a recent unpublished paper, but in regard to a special kind of control, that having to do with defining the nature of the relationship of those involved in the interaction.

4. Willard Waller, "The Rating and Dating Complex," *American Sociological Review*, 2:730.

5. William Sansom, *A Contest of Ladies* (London: Hogarth, 1956), pp. 230–32.

6. The widely read and rather sound writings of Stephen Potter are concerned in part with signs that can be engineered to give a shrewd observer the apparently incidental cues he needs to discover concealed virtues the gamesman does not in fact possess.

7. An interaction can be purposely set up as a time and place for voicing differences in opinion, but in such cases participants must be careful to agree not to disagree on the proper tone of voice, vocabulary, and degree of seriousness in which all arguments are to be phrased, and upon the mutual respect which disagreeing participants must carefully continue to express toward one another. This debaters' or academic definition of the situation may also be invoked suddenly and judiciously as a way of translating a serious conflict of views into one that can be handled within a framework acceptable to all present.

8. W. F. Whyte, "When Workers and Customers Meet," Chap. VII, *Industry and Society*, ed. W. F. Whyte (New York: McGraw-Hill, 1946), pp. 132–33.

9. Teacher interview quoted by Howard S. Becker, "Social Class Variations in the Teacher-Pupil Relationship," *Journal of Educational Sociology*, 25:459.

10. Harold Taxel, "Authority Structure in a Mental Hospital Ward" (unpublished Master's thesis, Department of Sociology, University of Chicago, 1953).

11. This role of the witness in limiting what it is the individual can be has been stressed by Existentialists, who see it as a basic threat to individual freedom. See Jean-Paul Sartre, *Being and Nothingness,* trans. by Hazel E. Barnes (New York: Philosophical Library, 1956), pp. 365 ff.

12. Erving Goffman, "Communication Conduct in an Island Community" (unpublished Ph.D. dissertation, Department of Sociology, University of Chicago, 1953), pp. 319–27.

13. Peter Blau, *Dynamics of Bureaucracy: A Study of Interpersonal Relationships in Two Government Agencies,* 2nd ed. (Chicago: University of Chicago Press, 1963).

14. Walter M. Beattie, Jr., "The Merchant Seaman" (unpublished M. A. Report, Department of Sociology, University of Chicago, 1950), p. 35.

15. Sir Frederick Ponsonby, *Recollections of Three Reigns* (New York: Dutton, 1952), p. 46.

PART IV

Socialization and Gender

ESSENTIAL TO OUR SURVIVAL following birth is *sociali-zation*—learning to become full-fledged members of a human group. As we saw in Part III, this learning involves such fundamental, taken-for-granted aspects of group life as ideas about health and morality, and the many nuances of nonverbal communication. We saw that socialization involves learning rules (what we should and should not do under different circumstances) and values (what is considered good or bad, desirable or undesirable), as well as expectations about how we should present the self in different social settings.

The *agents of socialization* include our parents, brothers and sisters and other relatives, friends and neighbors, as well as clergy and schoolteachers. They also include people we do not know and never will know, such as clerks and shoppers who, by their very presence—and the expectations we know they have of us—influence our behavior in public settings, and thereby shape it for similar situations in the future. Through this process of socialization each of us develops a *personality*, the tendency to behave in particular ways, which distinguishes us from others.

Essential to our forming an identity is socialization into gender—that is, our learning how to be masculine or feminine. (The term *sex* refers to biological characteristics, while the term *gender* refers to what is expected of people because of those characteristics. We inherit our sex, but we learn our gender. Sex is male or female, while gender is masculinity or femininity.)

Although we come into this world with the biological equipment of a male or a female, these physical organs do not determine what we shall be like as a male or a female. Whether or not we defer to members of the opposite sex, for example, is not an automatic result of our particular sexual equipment but is due to what we learn is proper for us because of the particular biological equipment we possess. This learning process is called *gender* or *sex role social-ization*.

Our gender extends into almost every area of our lives, even into situations for which it may be quite irrelevant. For example, if we are grocery clerks, by means of our clothing, language, and gestures we communicate to others that we are *male* or *female* clerks. Because gender cuts across most aspects of social life, sociologists refer to gender as a *master trait*.

Challenged for generations (the women's movement was active before our grandparents were born), the expectations attached to the sexes have undergone substantial modification in recent years. One can no longer safely assume particular behavior on the part of another simply because of that person's sex. Despite such changes, however, most Americans follow rather traditional lines as they socialize their children. Changes in something as basic as gender take place slowly, and male dominance remains a fact of social life.

What would we humans be like if we were untouched by culture? Although there is much speculation, no one knows the answer to this question, for any behavior or attitude that we examine is embedded within cultural learning. The closest we can come to answering the question is to observe those children who have received the least introduction to their culture—as Kingsley Davis does in the opening selection. Even isolated children, such as Anna and Isabelle, however, have been exposed to a culture, even though minimally. One really cannot think of humanity apart from culture, then, for culture shapes humanity.

In the past, an occasional naked, wild-looking child was discovered living alone in the wilderness. They could not speak, walked and crawled on all fours, and pounced on small animals, devouring them raw while emitting guttural sounds. Such *feral* ("wild") *children* were thought to have been raised by animals and to be untouched by human culture. Although documented cases of feral children exist—one boy discovered in 1798 was even studied intensely by scientists—the presumption today is that feral children had been abandoned by their parents because they were mentally handicapped. If so, the study of feral children does not answer the question of what humans would be like if they were untouched by culture. If it did, the answer certainly would not be encouraging—granted their lack of language, pouncing on and devouring small animals, and so on.

It is through our association with other humans, then, that we learn what it means to be human. To provide a context for appreciating the implications of this fundamental aspect of life, this part opens with a classic article by Kingsley Davis, in which he relates the story of Anna. Essential to our becoming human is our socialization into gender, the primary focus of Part IV. Here we explore the question of how we learn gender, the sex roles we are socially destined to play. Memories of childhood may surface while reading my analysis of some of the processes by which males are socialized into social dominance. Focusing on childhood, I examine experiences that direct boys into a world distinct from the female world, that often lead boys and men to think of themselves as superior, and that later make it difficult for men and women to communicate in depth and to maintain "significant relationships" with each other. Donna Eder continues this focus on children's experiences. The interactions of the girls she observed in middle school reveal another emphasis on superficiality, how appearance (or attractiveness) becomes an essential orientation of the self. Barrie Thorne and Zella Luria continue to place the sociological spotlight on the world of children, examining how schoolchildren separate their activities and friendships on the basis of sex and engage in forms of play that help to maintain male dominance in society. Deborah Tannen closes this Part with an analysis of how men and women express themselves. She highlights communication styles that not only hinder communication between men and women but which also may reflect underlying gender differences in orientations to social life.

Taken together, these articles help us to better understand how gender pervades our lives. They ought to provide considerable insight into your own socialization into gender—how you became masculine or feminine—and, once propelled into that role, how your ongoing experiences in society continue to influence your attitudes and behaviors.

12 Extreme Isolation

KINGSLEY DAVIS

What could the editor possibly mean by this article's heading in the table of contents: "Learning to be human"? Isn't it obvious that we humans are born human? Certainly this is true concerning our *biological* characteristics, that is, our possession of arms, legs, head, and torso, as well as our internal organs.

But to act like other people, to think the way others think—and perhaps even the ability to think—are *learned* characteristics. These are the result of years of exposure to people living in groups, especially the acquisition of language.

Just how much does biology contribute to what we are, and how much is due to social life? (Or, in Davis' terms, what are the relative contributions of the biogenic and the sociogenic factors?) Although this question has intrigued many, no one has yet been able to unravel its mystery. According to the findings reported here, however, the contributions of the social group reach much farther and are of greater fundamental consequence than most of us imagine. Our speech, for example, helps shape our basic attitudes and orientations to life. As indicated in this article, however, the social group may even contribute characteristics that we ordinarily presume are biological, such as our ability to walk. Although this selection will not present any "final answers" to this age-old question, it should stir up your sociological imagination.

EARLY IN 1940 THERE APPEARED . . . an account of a girl called Anna.[1] She had been deprived of normal contact and had received a minimum of human care for almost the whole of her first six years of life. At this time observations were not complete and the report had a tentative character. Now, however, the girl is dead, and with more information available,[2] it is possible to give a fuller and more definitive description of the case from a sociological point of view.

Anna's death, caused by hemorrhagic jaundice, occurred on August 6, 1942. Having been born on March 1 or 6,[3] 1932, she was approximately ten and a half years of age when she died. The previous report covered her development up to the age of almost eight years; the present one recapitulates the earlier period on the basis of new evidence and then covers the last two and a half years of her life.

Early History

The first few days and weeks of Anna's life were complicated by frequent changes of domicile. It will be recalled that she was an illegitimate child, the second such child born to her mother, and that her grandfather, a widowed farmer in whose house her mother lived, strongly disapproved of this new evidence of the mother's indiscretion. This fact led to the baby's being shifted about.

Two weeks after being born in a nurse's private home, Anna was brought to the family farm, but the grandfather's antagonism was so great that she was shortly taken to the house of one of her mother's friends. At this time a local minister became interested in her and took her to his house with an idea of possible adoption. He decided against adoption, however, when he discovered that she had vaginitis. The infant was then taken to a children's home in the nearest large city. This agency found that at the age of only three weeks she was already in a miserable condition, being "terribly galled and otherwise in very bad shape." It did not regard her as a likely subject for adoption but took her in for a while anyway, hoping to benefit her. After Anna had spent nearly eight weeks in this place, the agency notified her mother to come and get her. The mother responded by sending a man and his wife to the children's home with a view to their adopting Anna, but they made such a poor impression on the agency that permission was refused. Later the mother came herself and took the child out of the home and then gave her to this couple. It was in the home of this pair that a social worker found the girl a short time thereafter. The social worker went to the mother's home and pleaded with Anna's grandfather to allow the mother to bring the child home. In spite of threats, he refused. The child, by then more than four months old, was next taken to another children's home in a near-by town. A medical examination at this time revealed that she had impetigo, vaginitis, umbilical hernia, and a skin rash.

Anna remained in this second children's home for nearly three weeks, at the end of which time she was transferred to a private foster-home. Since, however, the grandfather would not, and the mother could not, pay for the child's care, she was finally taken back as a last resort to the grandfather's house (at the age of five and a half months). There she remained, kept on the second floor in an attic-like room because her mother hesitated to incur the grandfather's wrath by bringing her downstairs.

The mother, a sturdy woman weighing about 180 pounds, did a man's work on the farm. She engaged in heavy work such as milking cows and tending hogs and had little time for her children. Sometimes she went out at night, in which case Anna was left entirely without attention. Ordinarily, it seems, Anna received only enough care to keep her barely alive. She appears to have been seldom moved from one position to another. Her clothing and bedding were filthy. She apparently had no instruction, no friendly attention.

It is little wonder that, when finally found and removed from the room in the grandfather's house at the age of nearly six years, the child could not talk, walk, or do anything that showed intelligence. She was in an extremely emaciated and undernourished condition, with skeletonlike legs and a bloated abdomen. She had been fed on virtually nothing except cow's milk during the years under her mother's care.

Anna's condition when found, and her subsequent improvement, have been described in the previous report. It now remains to say what happened to her after that.

Later History

In 1939, nearly two years after being discovered, Anna had progressed, as previously reported, to the point where she could walk, understand simple commands, feed herself, achieve some neatness, remember people, etc. But she still did not speak, and, though she was much more like a normal infant of something over one year of age in mentality, she was far from normal for her age.

On August 30, 1939, she was taken to a private home for retarded children, leaving the county home where she had been for more than a year and a half. In her new setting she made some further progress, but not a great deal. In a report of an examination made November 6 of the same year, the head of the institution pictured the child as follows:

> Anna walks about aimlessly, makes periodic rhythmic motions of her hands, and, at intervals, makes guttural and sucking noises. She regards her hands as if she had seen them for the first time. It was impossible to hold her attention for more than a few seconds at a time—not because of distraction due to external stimuli but because of her inability to concentrate. She ignored the task in hand to gaze vacantly about the room. Speech is entirely lacking. Numerous unsuccessful attempts have been made with her in the hope of developing initial sounds. I do not believe that this failure is due to negativism or deafness but that she is not sufficiently developed to accept speech at this time. . . . The prognosis is not favorable. . . .

More than five months later, on April 25, 1940, a clinical psychologist, the late Professor Francis N. Maxfield, examined Anna and reported the following: large for her age; hearing "entirely normal"; vision apparently normal; able to climb stairs; speech in the "babbling stage" and "promise for developing intelligible speech later seems to be good." He said further that "on the Merrill–Palmer scale she made a mental score of 19 months. On the Vineland social maturity scale she made a score of 23 months.[4]

Professor Maxfield very sensibly pointed out that prognosis is difficult in such cases of isolation. "It is very difficult to take scores on tests standardized under average conditions of environment and experience," he wrote, "and interpret them in a case where environment and experience have been so unusual." With this warning he gave it as his opinion at that time that Anna would eventually "attain an adult mental level of six or seven years."[5]

The school for retarded children, on July 1, 1941, reported that Anna had reached 46 inches in height and weighed 60 pounds. She could bounce and catch a ball and was said to conform to group socialization, though as a follower rather than a leader. Toilet habits were firmly established. Food habits were normal, except that she still used a spoon as her sole implement. She could dress herself except for fastening her clothes. Most remarkable of all, she had finally begun to develop speech. She was characterized as being at about the two-year level in this regard. She could call attendants by name and bring in one when she was asked to. She had a few complete sentences to express her wants. The report concluded that there was nothing peculiar about her, except that she was feebleminded—"probably congenital in type."[6]

A final report from the school made on June 22, 1942, and evidently the last report before the girl's death, pictured only a slight advance over that given above. It said that Anna could follow directions, string beads, identify a few colors, build with blocks, and differentiate between attractive and unattractive pictures. She had a good sense of rhythm and loved a doll. She talked mainly in phrases but would repeat words and try to carry on a conversation. She was clean about clothing. She habitually washed her hands and brushed her teeth. She would try to help other children. She walked well and could run fairly well, though clumsily. Although easily excited, she had a pleasant disposition.

Interpretation

Such was Anna's condition just before her death. It may seem as if she had not made much progress, but one must remember the condition in which she had been found. One must recall that she had no glimmering of speech, absolutely no ability to walk, no sense of gesture, not the least capacity to feed herself even when the food was put in front of her, and no comprehension of cleanliness. She was so apathetic that it was hard to tell whether or not she could hear. And all this at the age of nearly six years. Compared with this condition, her capacities at the time of her death seem striking indeed, though they do not amount to much more than a two-and-a-half-year mental level. One conclusion therefore seems safe, namely, that her isolation prevented a considerable amount of mental development that was undoubtedly part of her capacity. Just what her original capacity was, of course, is hard to say; but her development after her period of confinement (including the ability to walk and run, to play, dress, fit into a social situation, and, above all, to speak) shows that she had at least this capacity—capacity that never could have been realized in her original condition of isolation.

A further question is this: What would she have been like if she had received a normal upbringing from the moment of birth? A definitive answer would have been impossible in any case, but even an approximate answer is made difficult by her early death. If one assumes, as was tentatively surmised in the previous report, that it is "almost impossible for any child to learn to speak, think, and act like a normal person after a long period of early isolation," it seems likely that Anna might have had a normal or near-normal capacity, genetically speaking. On the other hand, it was pointed out that Anna represented "a marginal case, [because] she was discovered before she had reached six years of age," an age "young enough to allow for some plasticity."[7] While admitting, then, that Anna's isolation *may* have been the major cause (and was certainly a minor cause) of her lack of rapid mental progress during the four and a half years following her rescue from neglect, it is necessary to entertain the hypothesis that she was congenitally deficient.

In connection with this hypothesis, one suggestive though by no means conclusive circumstance needs consideration, namely, the mentality of Anna's forebears. Information on this subject is easier to obtain, as one might guess, on the mother's than on the father's side. Anna's maternal grandmother, for example, is said to have been college educated and wished to have her children receive a good education, but her husband, Anna's stern grandfather, apparently a shrewd, hard-driving, calculating farmowner, was so penurious that her ambitions in this direction were thwarted. Under the circumstances her daughter (Anna's mother) managed, despite having to do hard work on the farm, to complete the eighth grade in a country school. Even so, however, the daughter was evidently not very smart. "A schoolmate of [Anna's mother] stated that she was retarded in school work; was very gullible at this age; and that her morals even at this time were discussed by other students." Two tests administered to her on March 4, 1938, when she was thirty-two years of age, showed that she was mentally deficient. On the Standard Revision of the Binet–Simon Scale her performance was equivalent to that of a child of eight years, giving her an I.Q. of 50 and indicating mental deficiency of "middle-grade moron type."[8]

As to the identity of Anna's father, the most persistent theory holds that he was an old man about seventy-four years of age at the time of the girl's birth. If he was the one, there is no indication of mental or other biological deficiency, whatever one may think of his morals. However, someone else may actually have been the father.

To sum up: Anna's heredity is the kind that *might* have given rise to innate mental deficiency, though not necessarily.

Comparison with Another Case

Perhaps more to the point than speculations about Anna's ancestry would be a case for comparison. If a child could be discovered who had been isolated about the same length of time as Anna but had achieved a much quicker recovery and a greater mental development, it would be a stronger indication that Anna was deficient to start with.

Such a case does exist. It is the case of a girl found at about the same time as Anna and under strikingly similar circumstances. A full description of the details of this case has not been published, but in addition to newspaper reports, an excellent preliminary account by a speech specialist, Dr. Marie K. Mason, who played an important role in the handling of the child, has appeared.[9] Also the late Dr. Francis N. Maxfield, clinical psychologist at Ohio State University, as was Dr. Mason, has written an as yet unpublished but penetrating analysis of the case.[10] Some of his observations have been included in Professor Zingg's book on feral man.[11] The following discussion is drawn mainly from these enlightening materials. The writer, through the kindness of Professors Mason and Maxfield, did have a chance to observe the girl in April, 1940, and to discuss the features of her case with them.

Born apparently one month later than Anna, the girl in question, who has been given the pseudonym Isabelle, was discovered in November, 1938, nine months after the discovery of Anna. At the time she was found she was approximately six and a half years of age. Like Anna, she was an illegitimate child and had been kept in seclusion for that reason. Her mother was a deaf-mute, having become so at the age of two, and it appears that she and Isabelle had spent most of their time together in a dark room shut off from the rest of the mother's family. As a result Isabelle had no chance to develop speech; when she communicated with her mother, it was by means of gestures. Lack of sunshine and inadequacy of diet had caused Isabelle to become rachitic. Her legs in particular were affected; they "were so bowed that as she stood erect the soles of her shoes came nearly flat together, and she got about with a skittering gait."[12] Her behavior toward strangers, especially men, was almost that of a wild animal, manifesting much fear and hostility. In lieu of speech she made only a strong croaking sound. In many ways she acted like an infant. "She was apparently utterly unaware of relationships of any kind. When presented with a ball for the first time, she held it in the palm of her hand, then reached out and stroked my face with it. Such behavior is comparable to that of a child of six months."[13] At first it was even hard to tell whether or not she could hear, so unused were her senses. Many of her actions resembled those of deaf children.

It is small wonder that, once it was established that she could hear, specialists working with her believed her to be feeble-minded. Even on nonverbal tests her performance was so low as to promise little for the future. Her first score on the Stanford–Binet was 19 months, practically at the zero point of the scale. On the Vineland social maturity scale her first score was 39, representing an age level of two and a half years.[14] "The general impression was that she was wholly uneducable and that any attempt to teach her to speak, after so long a period of silence, would meet with failure."[15]

In spite of this interpretation, the individuals in charge of Isabelle launched a systematic and skillful program of training. It seemed hopeless at first. The approach had to be through pantomime and dramatization, suitable to an infant. It required one week of intensive effort before she even made her first attempt at vocalization. Gradually she began to respond, however, and, after the first hurdles had at last been overcome, a curious thing happened. She went through the usual stages of learning characteristic of the years from one to six not only in proper succession but far more rapidly than normal. In a little over two months after her first vocalization she was putting sentences together. Nine months after that she could identify words and sentences on the printed page, could write well, could add to ten, and could retell a story after hearing it. Seven months beyond this point she had a vocabulary of 1,500–2,000 words and was asking complicated questions. Starting from an educational level of between one and three years (depending on what aspect one considers), she had reached a normal level by the time she was eight and a half years old. In short, she covered in two years the stages of learning that ordinarily require six.[16] Or, to put it another way, her I.Q. trebled in a year and a half.[17] The speed with which she reached the normal level of mental development seems analogous to the recovery of body weight in a growing child after an illness, the recovery being achieved by an extra fast rate of growth for a period after the illness until normal weight for the given age is again attained.

When the writer saw Isabelle a year and a half after her discovery, she gave him the impression of being a very bright, cheerful, energetic little girl. She spoke well, walked and ran without trouble, and sang with gusto and accuracy. Today she is over fourteen years old and has passed the sixth grade in a public school. Her teachers say that she participates in all school activities as normally as other children. Though older than her classmates, she has fortunately not physically matured too far beyond their level.[18]

Clearly the history of Isabelle's development is different from that of Anna's. In both cases there was exceedingly low, or rather blank, intellectual level to begin with. In both cases it seemed that the girl might be congenitally feeble-minded. In both a considerably higher level was reached later on. But the Ohio girl achieved a normal mentality within two years, whereas Anna was still markedly inadequate at the end of four and half years. This difference in achievement may suggest that Anna had less initial capacity. But an alternative hypothesis is possible.

One should remember that Anna never received the prolonged and expert attention that Isabelle received. The result of such attention, in the case of the Ohio girl, was to give her speech at an early stage, and her subsequent rapid development seems to have been a consequence of that. "Until Isabelle's speech and language development, she had all the characteristics of a feeble-minded child." Had Anna, who, from the standpoint of psychometric tests and early history, closely resembled this girl at the start, been given a mastery of speech at an earlier point by intensive training, her subsequent development might have been much more rapid.[19]

The hypothesis that Anna began with a sharply inferior mental capacity is therefore not established. Even if she were deficient to start with, we have no way of knowing how much so. Under ordinary conditions she might have been a dull normal or, like her mother, a moron. Even after the blight of her isolation, if she had lived to maturity, she might have finally reached virtually the full level of her capacity, whatever it may have been. That her isolation did have a profound effect upon her mentality, there can be no doubt. This is proved by the substantial degree of change during the four and a half years following her rescue.

Consideration of Isabelle's case serves to show, as Anna's case does not clearly show, that isolation up to the age of six, with failure to acquire any form of speech and hence failure to grasp nearly the whole world of cultural meaning, does not preclude the subsequent acquisition of these. Indeed, there seems to be a process of accelerated recovery in which the child goes through the mental stages at a more rapid rate than would be the case in normal development. Just what would be the maximum age at which a person could remain isolated and still retain the capacity for full cultural acquisition is hard to say. Almost certainly it would not be as high as age fifteen; it might possibly be as low as age ten. Undoubtedly various individuals would differ considerably as to the exact age.

Anna's is not an ideal case for showing the effects of extreme isolation, partly because she was possibly deficient to begin with, partly because she did not receive the best training available, and partly because she did not live long enough. Nevertheless, her case is instructive when placed in the record with numerous other cases of extreme isolation. This and the previous article about her are meant to place her in the record. It is to be hoped that other cases will be described in the scientific literature as they are discovered (as unfortunately they will be), for only in these rare cases of extreme isolation is it possible "to observe *concretely separated* two factors in the development of human personality which are always otherwise only analytically separated, the biogenic and the sociogenic factors."[20]

Notes

1. Kingsley Davis, "Extreme Social Isolation of a Child," *American Journal of Sociology,* XLV (January, 1940), 554–65.
2. Sincere appreciation is due to the officials in the Department of Welfare, Commonwealth of Pennsylvania, for the kind cooperation in making available the records concerning Anna and discussing the case frankly with the writer. Helen C. Hubbell, Florentine Hackbusch, and Eleanor Mecklenburg were particularly helpful, as was Fanny L. Matchette. Without their aid neither of the reports on Anna could have been written.
3. The records are not clear as to which day.

4. Letter to one of the state officials in charge of the case.

5. *Ibid.*

6. Progress report of the school.

7. Davis, *op. cit.,* p. 564.

8. The facts set forth here as to Anna's ancestry are taken chiefly from a report of mental tests administered to Anna's mother by psychologists at a state hospital where she was taken for this purpose after the discovery of Anna's seclusion. This excellent report was not available to the writer when the previous paper on Anna was published.

9. Marie K. Mason, "Learning to Speak after Six and One-Half Years of Silence," *Journal of Speech Disorders,* VII (1942), 295–304.

10. Francis N. Maxfield, "What Happens When the Social Environment of a Child Approaches Zero." The writer is greatly indebted to Mrs. Maxfield and to Professor Horace B. English, a colleague of Professor Maxfield, for the privilege of seeing this manuscript and other materials collected on isolated and feral individuals.

11. J. A. L. Singh and Robert M. Zingg, *Wolf-Children and Feral Man* (New York: Harper & Bros., 1941), pp. 248–51.

12. Maxfield, unpublished manuscript cited above.

13. Mason, *op. cit.,* p. 299.

14. Maxfield, unpublished manuscript.

15. Mason, *op. cit.,* p. 299.

16. *Ibid.,* pp. 300–304.

17. Maxfield, unpublished manuscript.

18. Based on a personal letter from Dr. Mason to the writer, May 13, 1946.

19. This point is suggested in a personal letter from Dr. Mason to the writer, October 22, 1946.

20. Singh and Zingg, *op. cit.,* pp. xxi–xxii, in a foreword by the writer.

13 On Becoming Male: Reflections of a Sociologist on Childhood and Early Socialization

JAMES M. HENSLIN

Although relations between men and women are enveloped in social change, men still dominate the social institutions of the Western world: law, politics, business, religion, education, the military, medicine, science, sports, and in many ways, even marriage and family. Despite far-reaching social change, women often find themselves in the more backstage, nurturing, and supportive roles—and those roles generally are supportive of the more dominant roles men play.

Why? Is this a consequence of genetic heritage—males and females being born with different predispositions? Or is it due to culture, because males are socialized into dominance? While there is considerable debate among academics on this matter, sociologists side almost unanimously with the proponents of socialization. In this article, Henslin analyzes some of the socialization experiences that place males in a distinctive social world and prepare them for dominance. This selection is an attempt to penetrate the taken-for-granted, behind-the-scenes aspects of socialization into masculine sexuality. Whether male or female, you might find it useful to contrast your experiences in growing up with those the author describes.

ACCORDING TO THE PREVAILING sociological perspective, our masculinity or femininity is not biologically determined. Although our biological or genetic inheritance gives each of us the sex organs of a male or female, how our "maleness" or "femaleness" is expressed depends on what we learn. Our masculinity or femininity, that is, what we are like as sexual beings—our orientations and how we behave as a male or a female—does not depend on biology but on social learning. It can be said that while our gender is part of our biological inheritance, our sexuality (or masculinity or femininity) is part of our social inheritance.

If this sociological position is correct—that culture, not anatomy, is our destiny—how do we become the "way we are"?[1] What factors shape or influence us into becoming masculine or feminine? If our behaviors do not come from our biology, how do we end up having behaviors that are typically associated with our gender? If they *are* learned, how do our behaviors, attitudes, and other basic orientations come to be felt by us as natural and essential to our identity? (And they are indeed essential to our identity.) In what ways is the process of "becoming" related to the social structure of society?

Not only would it take volumes to answer these questions fully, but it would also be impossible, since the answers are only now slowly being unraveled by researchers. In this short and rather informal article, I will be able to indicate only some of the basics underlying this foundational learning. I will focus exclusively on being socialized into masculinity, and will do this by reflecting on (1) my own experience in "becoming"; (2) my observations as a sociologist of the experiences of others; and (3) what others have shared with me concerning their own experiences. The reader should keep in mind that this article is meant to be neither definitive nor exhaustive, but is designed to depict general areas of male socialization and thereby to provide insight into the acquisition of masculinity in our culture.

In the Beginning . . .

Except for a few rare instances,[2] each of us arrives in this world with a clearly definable physical characteristic that sets us apart from about half the rest of the world. This characteristic makes a literal world of difference. Our parents become excited about whether we have been born with a penis or a vagina. They are usually either happy or disappointed about which organ we possess, seldom feeling neutral about the matter. They announce it to friends, relatives, and sometimes to complete strangers ("It's a boy!" "It's a girl!"). Regardless of how they feel about it, on the basis of our possessing a particular physical organ they purposely, but both consciously and subconsciously, separate us into two worlds. Wittingly and unwittingly, they thereby launch us onto a career that will encompass almost every aspect of our lives—and will remain with us until death.

Colors, Clothing, and Toys

While it is not inherently more masculine or feminine than red, yellow, purple, orange, white, or black, the color blue has become associated arbitrarily with *infantile masculinity*. After what is usually a proud realization that the neonate possesses a penis (which marks him as a member of the overlords of the universe), the inheritor of dominance is wrapped in blue. This color is merely an arbitrary choice, as originally any other would have done as well. But now that the association is made, no other will do. The announcing colors maintain their meaning for only a fairly short period, gradually becoming sexually neutralized.[3] Pink, however, retains at least part of its meaning of sexuality, for even adult males tend to shy away from it.

Our parents gently and sometimes not so gently push us onto a predetermined course. First they provide clothing designated appropriate to our masculine status. Even as infants our clothing displays sexual significance, and our parents are extremely careful that we never are clothed in either dresses or ruffles. For example, while our plastic panties are designed to keep mothers, fathers, and their furniture and friends dry, our parents make absolutely certain that ours are never pink with white ruffles. Even if our Mom had run out of all other plastic panties, she would rather stay home than take us out in public wearing ruffled pinkies. Mom would probably feel a twinge of guilt over such cross-dressing even in private.[4]

So both Mom and Dad are extremely cautious about our clothing. Generally plain, often simple, and usually sturdy, our clothing is designed to take the greater "rough and tumble" that they know boys are going to give it. They also choose clothing that will help groom us into future adult roles; depending on the style of the period, they dress us in little sailor suits, miniature jogging togs, or two-piece suits with matching ties. Although at this early age we could care less about such things, and their significance appears irrelevant to us, our parents' concern is always present. If during a supermarket expedition even a stranger mistakes our sexual identity, this agitates our parents, challenging their sacred responsibility to maintain the reality-ordering structure of the sex worlds. Such mistaken identification forces them to rethink their activities in proper sex typing, their deep obligation to make certain that their offspring is receiving the right start in life. They will either ascribe the mistake to the stupidity of the stranger or immediately forswear some particular piece of clothing.

Our parents' "gentle nudging" into masculinity does not overlook our toys. These represent both current activities thought sexually appropriate and those symbolic of our future masculinity of courage, competition, daring—and of violence. We are given trucks, tanks, and guns. Although our mother might caution us about breaking them, it is readily apparent by her tone and facial expressions that she does not mean what she says. We can continue to bang them together roughly, and she merely looks at us—sometimes quite uncomprehendingly, and occasionally muttering something to the effect that boys will be boys. We somehow perceive her sense of confirmation and we bang them all the more, laughing gleefully at the approval we know it is bringing.

Play and the Sexual Boundaries of Tolerance

We can make all sorts of expressive sounds as we play. We can shout, grunt, and groan on the kitchen floor or roll around in the sandbox. As she shoves us out the door, Mom always cautions us not to get dirty, but when we come in filthy her verbal and gestural disapproval is only mild. From holistic perception, of which by now we have become young masters, we have learned that no matter what Mom's words say, they do not represent the entirety of her feelings.

When we are "all dressed up" before going somewhere, or before company comes, Mom acts differently. We learn that at those times she means what she says about not getting dirty. If we do not want "fire in our pants," we'd better remain clean—at least for a while, for we also learn that after company has come and has had a glimpse of the neat and clean little boy (or, as they say, "the nice little gentleman" or the "fine young man"), we can go about our rough and tumble ways. Pushing, shouting, running, climbing, and other expressions of competition, glee, and freedom then become permissible. We learn that the appearance required at the beginning of a visit is quite unlike that which is passable at the end of the visit.

Our more boisterous and rougher play continues to help us learn the limits of our parents' tolerance. As we continuously test those limits, somewhat to our dismay we occasionally find that we unwittingly have crossed beyond them. Through what is at times painful trial and error, we learn both the limits and how they vary with changed circumstance. We eventually learn those edges extremely well and know, for example, precisely how much more we can "get away with" when company comes than when only the immediate family is present, when Mom and Dad are tired or when they are arguing.

As highly rational beings, who are seldom adequately credited by adults for our keen cunning, we learn to calculate those boundaries exceedingly carefully. We eventually come to the point where we know precisely where the brink is—that one more word of back talk, one more quarrel with our brother, sister, or friend, even a small one, or even one more whine will move our parents from words to deeds, and their wrath will fall abruptly upon us with full force. Depending on our parents' orientation to childrearing (or often simply upon their predilection of the moment, for at these times theory tends to fly out the window), this will result in either excruciating humiliation in front of our friends accompanied by horrible (though momentary) physical pain, or excruciating humiliation in front of our friends accompanied by the horrifying (and longer) deprivation of a privilege (which of course we know is really a "right" and is being unjustifiably withheld from us).

On Freedom and Being

As we calculate those boundaries of tolerance (or in the vernacular used by our parents and well understood by us, find out how much they can "stand"), we also learn something about our world vis-à-vis that of those strange female creatures who coinhabit our space. We learn that we can get dirtier, play rougher, speak louder, act more crudely, wander farther from home, stay away longer, and talk back more.

We see that girls live in a world foreign to ours. Theirs is quieter, neater, daintier, and in general more subdued. Sometimes our worlds touch, but then only momentarily. We learn, for example, that while little sisters might be all right to spend an occasional hour with on a rainy afternoon, they are, after all, "only girls." They cannot really enter our world, and we certainly do not want to become part of theirs, with its greater restrictions and fewer challenges. Occasionally, we even find ourselves delighting in this distinction as we taunt them about not being able to do something because it is "not for girls."

If we sometimes wonder about the reason for the differences between our worlds, our curiosity quickly runs its course, for we know deep down that these distinctions are proper. They are *girls,* and, as our parents have told us repeatedly, we are NOT girls. We have internalized the appropriateness of our worlds; some things are right for us, others for them. Seldom are we sorry for the tighter reins placed on girls. We are just glad that we are not one of "them." We stick with "our own kind" and immensely enjoy our greater freedom. Rather than lose ourselves in philosophical reflections about the inequalities of this world (greatly beyond our mental capacities at this point anyway), we lose ourselves in exultation over our greater freedom and the good fortune that made us boys instead of girls.

That greater freedom becomes the most prized aspect of our existence. Before we are old enough to go to school (and later, during summer or weekends and any other nonschool days), when we awaken in the morning we can hardly wait to get our clothes on. Awaiting us is a world of adventure. If we are up before Mom, we can go outside and play in the yard. Before venturing beyond voice distance, however, we have to eat our "wholesome" breakfast, one that somehow is always in the process of "making a man" out of us. After this man-producing breakfast, which might well consist of little more than cereal, we are free to roam, to discover, to experience. There are no dishes to do, no dusting, sweeping, or cleaning. Those things are for sisters, mothers, and other females.

Certainly we have spatial and associational restrictions placed on us, but they are much more generous than those imposed on girls of our age. We know how many blocks we can wander and whom we are allowed to see. But just as significant, we know how to go beyond that distance without getting caught and how to play with the "bad boys" and the "too big boys" without

Mom ever being the wiser. So long as we are home within a certain time limit, despite verbal restrictions we really are free to come and go.

We do learn to accept limited responsibility in order to guard our freedom, and we are always pestering other mothers for the time or, when we are able, arranging for them to tell us when it is "just about noon" so we can make our brief appearance for lunch—and then quickly move back into the exciting world of boy activities. But we also learn to lie a lot, finding out that it is better to say anything plausible rather than to admit that we violated the boundaries and be "grounded," practically the worst form of punishment we can receive. Consequently, we learn to deny, to avoid, to deceive, to tell half-truths, and to involve ourselves in other sorts of subterfuge rather than to admit violations that might restrict our freedom of movement.

Our freedom is infinitely precious to us, for whether it is cops and robbers or space bandits, the Lone Ranger or Darth Vader, ours is an imaginary world filled with daring and danger. Whether it is six-shooters with bullets or space missiles with laser disintegrators, we are always shooting or getting shot. There are always the good guys and the bad guys. Always there is a moral victory to be won. We are continuously running, shouting, hiding, and discovering. The world is filled with danger, with the inopportune and unexpected lurking just around the corner. As the enemy stalks us, the potential of sudden discovery and the sweet joys of being undetected are unsurpassable. Nothing in adulthood, despite its great allure, its challenges and victories yet to be experienced, will ever be greater than this intense bliss of innocence—and part of the joy of this period lies in being entirely unaware of that savage fact of life.

. . . And the Twain Shall Never Meet

Seldom do we think about being masculine. Usually we are just being. The radical social differences that separate us from girls have not gone unnoticed, of course. Rather, these essential differences in life-orientations not only have penetrated our consciousness but also have saturated our very beings. Our initial indifference to things male and female has turned to violent taste and distaste. We have learned our lessons so well that we sometimes end up teaching our own mothers lessons in gender. For example, we would rather be caught dead than to wear sissy clothing, and our tantrums will not cease until our mothers come to their senses and relent concerning putting something on us that we consider sissified.

We know there are two worlds, and we are grateful for the one we are in. Ours is superior. The evidence continually bombards us, and we exult in masculine privilege. We also protect our sexual boundaries from encroachment and erosion. The encroachment comes from tomboys who strive to become part of our world. We tolerate them—up to a point. But by excluding them from some activities, we let them know that there are irrevocable differences that forever separate us.

The erosion comes from sissies. Although we are not yet aware that we are reacting to a threat to our developing masculine identity, we do know that sissies make us uncomfortable. We come to dislike them intensely. To be a sissy is to be a traitor to one's very being. It is to be "like a girl," that which we are not—and that which we definitely never will be.

Sissies are to be either pitied or hated. While they are not girls, neither are they real boys. They look like us, but they bring shame on us because they do not represent anything we are. We are everything they are not. Consequently, we separate ourselves from them in the most direct manner possible. While we may be brutal, this breach is necessary, for we must define clearly the boundaries of our own existence—and one way that we know who we are is by knowing what we are not.

So we shame sissies. We make fun of anyone who is not the way he "ought" to be. If he hangs around the teacher or girls during recess instead of playing our rough and tumble games, if he will not play sports because he is afraid of getting dirty or being hurt, if he backs off from a fight, if he cries or whines, or even if he gets too many A's, we humiliate and ridicule him. We gather around him in a circle. We call him a sissy. We say, "Shame! Shame!" We call him gay, fag, and queer. We tell him he is a girl and not fit for us.

And as far as we are concerned, he never will be fit for us. He belongs to some strange status, not quite a girl and not quite a boy. Whatever he is, he certainly is not one of us. WE don't cry when we are punished or hurt. WE don't hang around girls. WE are proud of our average grades. WE play rough games. WE are not afraid of getting hurt. (Or if we are, we would never let it show.) WE are not afraid of sassing the teacher—or at least of calling the teacher names when his or her back is turned. We know who we are. We are boys.

The Puberty Shock

We never know, of course, how precarious our sexual identity is. From birth we have been set apart from females, and during childhood we have severely separated ourselves both from females and from those who do not match our standards of masculinity. Our existence is well defined, our world solid. By the end of grade school the pecking order is clear. For good or ill, each of us has been locked into a system of well-honed, peer-determined distinctions, our destiny determined by a heavily defended social order. Our masculine world seems secure, with distinct boundaries that clearly define "us" from "them." We know who we are, and we are cocky about it.

But then comes puberty, and overnight the world undergoes radical metamorphosis. Girls suddenly change. Right before our eyes the flat chests we have always taken for granted begin to protrude. Two little bumps magically appear, and while we are off playing our games, once in a while we cast quizzical glances in the direction of the girls. Witnessing a confusing, haunting change, we shrug off the dilemma and go back to our games.

Then the change hits us. We feel something happening within our own bodies. At first the feeling is vague, undefined. There is no form to it. We just know that something is different. Then we begin to feel strange stirrings within us. These stirrings come on abruptly, and that abruptness begins to shake everything loose in our secure world. Until this time our penis has never given us any particular trouble. It has just "been there," appended like a finger or toenail. It has been a fact of life, something that "we" had and "they" didn't. But now it literally springs to life, taking on an existence of its own and doing things that we once could not even imagine would ever take place. This sometimes creates embarrassment, and there are even times when, called to the blackboard to work out some problem, we must play dumb because of the bulge that we never willed.

It is a new game. The girls in our class are different. We are different. And we never will be the same.

We are forced into new concepts of masculinity. We find this upsetting, but fortunately we do not have to begin from scratch. We can build on our experiences, for mostly the change involves just one area of our lives, girls, and we are able to keep the rest intact. We can still swagger, curse, sweat, get dirty, and bloody ourselves in our games. While the girls still watch us admiringly from the sidelines as we "do our manly thing," we also now watch them more closely as they "do their womanly thing" and strut before us in tight sweaters.

While the girls still admire our toughness, a change is now demanded. At times we must show gentleness. We must be cleaner and watch our language more than before. We must even show consideration. Those shifting requirements are not easy to master, but we have the older, more experienced boys to count on—and they are more than willing to initiate us into this new world and, while doing so, to demonstrate their (always) greater knowledge and skills in traversing the social world.

The Transition into Artificiality

It is with difficulty that we make the transition. A new sexuality is really required, and such radical change could be easy for no one. We already have been fundamentally formed, and what we really learn at this point is to be more adept role-players. We behave one way when we are with the guys. This is the "natural" way, the way we feel. It is relaxed and easy. And we learn to act a different way while we are around girls. This form of presentation we find more contrived and artificial, for it requires greater politeness, consideration, and gentleness. In other words, it is contrary to what we have learned previously, to what we have become.

Consequently we hone our acting skills, the ability to put on expected performances. We always have been actors; it is just that we learned our earlier role at a more formative period, and, *having formed us,* this role now provides greater fit. And acting differently while we are around females is nothing new. We have been practicing that since we were at our mother's knee. But now the female expectations are more pressing as our worlds more frequently intersect. Although we become fairly skilled at meeting these expectations, they never become part of our being. Always they consist of superficial behaviors added onto what is truly and, by this time, "naturally" us.

This lesson in artificiality reinforces our many exercises in manipulation. We learn that to get what we want, whether that be an approving smile, a caress, a kiss, or more, we must meet the expectations of the one from whom we desire something. We are no strangers to this foundational fact of life, of course, but the masks we must wear in these more novel situations, our uncomfortable gestures and the requisite phrasing, make us awkward strangers to ourselves. We wonder why we are forced into situations that require such constant posing and posturing.

But awkward or not (and as we become more proficient at the game, much of the initial discomfort leaves), we always come back for more. By now sports and games with the fellows are no longer enough. Females seemingly hold the key to our happiness. They can withhold or grant as they see fit. And for favors to be granted, this demanding intersexual game must be played.

The Continuing Masculine World—and Marriage

Eventually we become highly adept players in this intersexual game. We even come to savor our maturing manipulative abilities as the game offers highly stimulating physical payoffs. Our growing skills let us determine if a particular encounter will result in conquest, and thus calculate if it is worth the pursuit. To meet the challenge successfully provides yet another boost to our masculinity.

The hypocrisies and deceits the game requires sometimes disturb us. We really want to be more honest than the game allows. But we do not know how to bring that about—and still succeed at the game *and* our masculinity.

Discomforts arising from the game, especially the intimate presence of the female world, must be relieved. Manly activities provide us refuge from this irritant, endeavors in which we men can truly understand one another, where we share a world of aspiration, conflict, and competition. Here we can laugh at the same things and talk the way we really feel with much less concern about the words we choose. We know that among men our interests, activities, and desires form an essential part of a shared, self-encapsulating world.

To continue to receive the rewards offered by females, on occasion we must leave our secure world of manliness momentarily to penetrate the conjoint world occupied by our feminine counterparts. But such leave-takings remain temporary, never a "real" part of us. Always waiting for us are the "real" conversations that reflect the "real" world, that exciting realm whose challenging creativity, competition, and conflict help make life worth living.

And we are fortunate in having at our fingertips a socially constructed semi-imaginary masculine world, one we can summon at will to retreat into its beckoning confines. This world of televised football, baseball, basketball, wrestling, boxing, hockey, soccer, and car racing is part of the domain of men. At least here is a world, manly and comfortable, that offers us refuge from that threatening feminine world, allowing us to withdraw from its suffocating demands of sharing and intimacy. This semi-imaginary world offers continual appeal because it summons up subconscious feelings from our childhood, adolescence, and, eventually as we grow older, early manhood.

Many of us would not deny that the characteristics we males learn or, if you prefer, the persons we tend to become, fail to provide an adequate basis for developing fulfilling intersexual relationships. But those characteristics, while underlying what is often the shallowness of our relationships with women, are indeed us. They are the logical consequence of our years of learning our culture. We have become what we painstakingly have been shaped to become. Although willing participants in our social destiny, we are heirs of a culture that preceded our arrival on the social scene.

Some of us, only with great difficulty, have overcome our masculine socialization into intersexual superficiality and have developed relationships with wives and girlfriends that transcend the confines of those cultural dictates. But such relearning, painfully difficult, comes at a price, leaving in its wake much hurt and brokenness.

Hardly any aspect of this process of becoming a man in our society augurs well for marriage. The separateness of the world that we join at birth signals our journey into an intricate process whereby we become a specific type of being. Our world diverges in almost all respects from the world of females. Not only do we look different, not only do we talk differently and act differently, but our fundamental thinking and orientations to life sharply contrast with theirs. This basic divergence is difficult for women to grasp and, when grasped, is often accompanied by a shudder of disbelief and distaste at the revelatory insight into such dissimilar reality. Yet we are expected to unite permanently with someone from this contradispositional world and, despite our essential differences, not only to share a life space but also to join our goals, hopes, dreams, and aspirations.

Is it any wonder, then, that in the typical case men remain strangers to women, and women to men, with marriage a crucible of struggle?

Notes

1. The diversity of opinion among sociologists regarding the nature/nurture causes of behavioral differences of males and females is illustrated in *Society* magazine (September/October 1986:4–39). The connection between ideology and theoretical interpretation of data is especially apparent in this heated exchange. I also discuss this topic in my introductory textbooks, *Sociology: A Down-to-Earth Approach* and *Essentials of Sociology: A Down-to-Earth Approach,* both published by Allyn & Bacon of Boston, and both in many editions.

2. Of about one in every 30,000 births, the sex of a baby is unclear. A genetic disorder called congenital adrenal hyperplasis results in the newborn having parts of both male and female genitals (*St. Louis Globe-Democrat,* March 10–11, 1979, p. 3D).

3. When people (almost exclusively women) are invited to a baby shower and the expectant mother has not yet given birth (or if they wish to take advantage of a sale and buy a gift in advance of the delivery), they find themselves in a quandary. The standard solution to this problem of not knowing the sex of the child (at least in the Midwest) is to purchase either clothing of yellow color or a "sex neutral" item. With ultrasound and other technology that can determine the sex of fetuses, the surprise factor has been eliminated for many parents—as well as for their friends.

4. Duly noted, of course, are the historical arbitrariness and relativity of the gender designation of clothing, with the meaning of ruffles and other stylistic variations depending on the historical period.

14 On Becoming Female: Lessons Learned in School

DONNA EDER

In the previous article, we focused on how socialization puts boys on a distinct road in life. We saw how boys' experiences give them distinct orientations to the world, including what they feel they can reasonably expect out of life—and how those orientations become a divisive factor in marriage and other male–female relationships. In this article, we turn the focus on girls' experiences in peer groups. We examine further how peer groups vitally influence our orientations, even how we view the self.

The author of this article headed a team that explored the social world of girls in middle school. This is a vital age, for at this point in life girls are becoming more aware of their sexual identity. Eder watched and listened as the girls interacted with one another, and as they interacted with boys, about whom they were ambivalent. Their statements, which disclose inner feelings, conflicts, rivalries, and jealousies, also reveal the ongoing formation of a self. Note especially the role that peers play in the developing identity of the girls—and how the peer interactions focus on the superficialities of appearance. How do you think this emphasis on appearance and attractiveness becomes part of women's orientations to life and influences their interactions?

ATTRACTIVENESS has long been part of the construction of femininity. . . . Preoccupation [with appearance] among American women prevents them from focusing on more constructive aspects of themselves, such as who they are or what they are capable of accomplishing. It is becoming more and more clear that this is one of the main areas in which women are hindered by stereotypical notions of femininity.

At Woodview [Middle School], concerns about attractiveness were promoted primarily through the high-status activity of cheerleading. This focus was most evident during the cheerleading tryouts. The teacher who organized the tryouts told the judges to keep [appearance] in mind as they selected the candidates.

149

> She also told them to pay attention to the person's weight, saying, "If you don't like the way they look, you wouldn't like them to stand in front of you."

This message conveys the essence of cheerleaders as adornments to a team as well as promoters of team enthusiasm and support. The fact that cheerleaders are seen as team representatives makes their appearance salient in the context of a culture that places a high value on female beauty. To be the best representatives, they should be highly attractive as well as capable of promoting school spirit.

Officially, appearance was included in the judging of cheerleaders under the category of "sparkle." Ten of the fifty total points a candidate could obtain were allotted to this category, as the cheerleading coach explained to the candidates during one of the practice sessions prior to the tryouts.

> At one point, Mrs. Tolson started to tell them what they were going to be judged on, saying they would get ten points for sparkle, which was their smile, personality, bubbliness, appearance, attractiveness—not that all cheerleaders had to be attractive, but it was important to have a clean appearance, not to be sloppy, have messy or greasy hair, because that doesn't look like a cheerleader.

Throughout the practice sessions girls were reminded to wear a clean, neat outfit for tryouts and to have clean, neatly combed hair. This emphasis on neatness continued despite the physical nature of this activity, which includes cartwheels and backflips. It was important to have the skills to do these gymnastic routines, but it was equally important to find ways to maintain a neat, feminine appearance throughout the performance. This again conveys the message to girls that how they look is as important as what they do.

Another way in which cheerleading candidates were encouraged to enhance their looks was by remembering to smile. Smiling was considered an important part of the cheerleading role—something that made you "look like a cheerleader." Girls were encouraged to smile to cover up feelings that might accompany their efforts, such as pain and concentration.

> When they were doing a stunt, she [the coach] said she wanted them to smile through the pain. Later on, when they were practicing the stunts in front of the eighth-graders, Karla [an eighth-grade cheerleader] continually reminded them to smile as they were working on their jumps. The way Karla put it was, "Smile the whole time."

The judges themselves evaluated the candidates' appearance during the decision-making process. Both neatness and cuteness were mentioned, as were the quality of their smiles. For example, one judge noted that the girl they were discussing had a cute smile. Another judge disagreed, indicating through imitation that the girl's smile was forced. This judge rated her more negatively than did the first one. Although weight was taken into account, one year some girls who were considered overweight were selected. The judges suggested that they be put on diets, preserving the idea that thinness is an important aspect of cheerleaders' appearance.

The high profile given to cheerleading means that traits that are valued in cheerleaders also have a greater impact on the school's informal peer culture.

Boys' Focus on Girls' Appearance in Peer Interaction

Many Woodview boys focused their evaluation of girls on their attractiveness. In fact, male interest in their bodies as being sexual and appealing could arouse the deepest level of appearance anxiety in girls. For example, one day a group of eighth-grade girls discussed a male ranking of female peers.

> Penny said that she had seen a list some boys had made which rated girls in the class. Karla was at the top, then Sara, then Peggy or Darlene. They said that they had told these guys, "Thanks a lot" for not including them on the list. Bonnie said, "Did you notice that all of those girls are early figure people?" indicating that the reason she thought they were rated highly was because they have a figure already. Then they pointed to Sara and said, "There she is. She's the one with the big hips. You can't miss her."

Informal rankings such as this remind girls that they are being evaluated on a daily basis, even when they haven't entered formal beauty contests or cheerleading tryouts.

Boys frequently referred to the physical appearance of girls they knew, both in their presence and when the girls were absent. For example, one day a boy announced at lunch, "Any girl who thinks she's beautiful, stand up." The appearance of someone's girlfriend was a typical topic of conversation, usually implying that some feature of hers was unattractive or that she was ugly in general. Even some of the prettiest girls in the school, cheerleaders and other high-status-group members, were criticized by boys for having ugly faces or deficient bodies.

The Role of Girls' Gossip

Even when girls are by themselves, their conversations are often dominated by cultural standards and male perspectives that highlight the importance of good looks. Girls themselves contribute to this, especially through gossip about the looks and dress of other girls. When we first told students we were interested in finding out what they did during their free time, some girls told us that mainly they talked about other girls. Given the frequency of this activity, many girls were constantly confronted with the topic of female appearance.

It was evident from the girls' comments that the continual focus on other girls' looks further added to their anxieties about their own appearance.

> There was an interesting discussion between Peggy and Lisa about the girl that Bob is taking to the dance. They talked about whether she was cute or not and ended up agreeing that she was a stack of bones. That generated some discussion about weight and Lisa said that she [Lisa] was fat. Peggy said that she wasn't. Then Wendy wondered if she was a stack of bones and Lisa told her that no, she was just right—that she wasn't skinny and she wasn't fat either. [Stephanie's notes]

While these girls got reassurance from their friends that they were neither too fat nor too thin, in most cases girls did not openly reveal their concerns and thus did not receive such assurance. Instead, many girls were likely to remain self-conscious and insecure about their body type and weight. Girls from lower-working-class backgrounds often couldn't afford to buy name-brand clothes and shoes, and their attire was often subject to criticism by girls who could afford nicer clothes. Comments about people's clothes were often made loudly enough for the targets to hear.

> As Lynn walked by they jeered at her and made fun of her. . . . One of these girls was going, "Oooh, look at those pants! Ohh, how could you wear those?" [Stephanie's notes]

At other times people were directly ridiculed.

> She also said that the cheerleaders made fun of people if they didn't wear Nike or Adidas shoes. They'd look at her and say, "Oh, where did you get your shoes?" She said that she just wears plain old tennis shoes. [Cathy's notes]

Besides being appraised on the basis of their attire, girls were also evaluated for their body weight and type. Girls who were particularly overweight were frequent targets of gossip, as in this extensive discussion of an isolate by several sixth-graders.

> A large part of what these girls did today was make fun of one girl, Gloria. One girl would say, "Here is the airplane; the pilot says, 'Will somebody please come up front,' and all of a sudden somebody walks up front," showing with her hands how the plane dives. Then somebody else says, "Or here's the plane flying," and she shows it flying lopsided with her hands. "Then Gloria walks over to the other side and it flips the other way." Or, "Here's the airplane and there's a weak spot in the middle, and Gloria walks down the aisle and she falls through." [Stephanie's notes]

This episode continued with other jokes about Gloria, including using her as a trampoline in gym class and how she could serve as a windblock for all of them at once.

It was not just overweight girls who were made fun of and evaluated, however. Girls who were too skinny were also criticized, as were girls who had large hips or large breasts. Girls have no control over most of these physical characteristics. Perhaps because of the extensive nature of this type of gossip, girls often try to increase their control over their weight by dieting, which leads, in more severe cases, to eating disorders such as anorexia and bulimia. Although this focus on body weight may seem obsessive, it makes sense in light of the frequency of body critiques in girls' evaluative talk and in the media.

Given the importance of good looks for gaining status among peers and avoiding negative evaluations, it is not surprising that girls devote so much attention to their appearance. Ironically, another relatively frequent theme of gossip was negatively judging others for putting too much emphasis on their looks. Girls seemed particularly critical of girls who tried to stand out in some manner, either by dressing in a unique fashion or by making themselves "too attractive" or "too sexy."

A group of sixth-graders spent much of one lunch period making fun of a popular girl for wearing a particularly unusual outfit to school.

> There was a long discussion throughout lunch about Jane, who I have been told before is the most popular girl in the sixth grade. Today she was wearing a khaki outfit, matching pants and a shirt—sort of a safari look. The first thing that got the conversation going was that Ilene started talking about a girl that had a "jungle suit" on. And Nicki, Jesse, and Kristy all sort of joined in with this conversation, and even Andrea played along with it for a while. They started out by saying that they'd seen her in the hall, given her the Tarzan yell, and she'd turned around and looked at them and they'd said, "Where'd you get the jungle outfit?" And they wondered if she was going to give the Tarzan yell back. They started talking about it as though she was Tarzan's monkey, Cheetah, and then the conversation sort of strayed from clothes and went to how she won the dog contest—how she's the number one dog of the school, which is the exact opposite since she's so popular. She does look older. She had her hair up, and had quite a bit of makeup on. [Stephanie's notes]

In another case, a group of eighth-grade girls was critical of a local beauty pageant contestant of high school age who visited the school to collect money for her campaign. In this case, they claimed that she used makeup to give a false image of beauty, and that underneath she was really ugly.

Eighth-Grade
PENNY: I'm not giving it to her.
CINDY: The only thing that makes her look anything is all the makeup and [unclear]

PENNY: She had a picture and she's standing there like this, she's going [Poses with one hand on her hip and one by her head]

CINDY: Her face is probably this skinny but it looks that big cuz of all the makeup she has on it.

PENNY: She's *ugly*, ugly, ugly! [In a low voice]

BONNIE: She looks like a cow.

This girl was criticized for her attempts to be "too attractive" and "too sexy." In her case, a flirtatious pose in one of her photographs was seen as evidence of trying to be too sexy.

These different themes of gossip add to the already confusing message girls receive about their appearance. On the one hand they are continually faced with media messages that emphasize the importance of using makeup and fashionable attire to enhance their attractiveness and their sexuality. If they do succeed in looking, acting, or dressing like the models they see in the media, however, they are likely to be accused of portraying false images or wanton sexuality. Furthermore, this practice of criticizing the objects of sexual gaze deflects criticism away from boys and men for viewing girls in this limited manner. Thus, girls blame each other for drawing sexual attention to themselves rather than criticizing the social practices that promote a view of girls and women as sexual objects.

Attractiveness as an Increasing Concern for Girls

Appearance is already a salient concern among these students, and it is likely to increase in importance for many as they get older. The number of school-sponsored contests that emphasize attractiveness increases in high school as girls are selected for pompon teams, cheerleading, baton twirlers in marching bands, and so on. In most of these cases, girls choose to enter these contests, although sometimes this "choice" may be the result of maternal pressure. A more powerful form of school-sponsored competition is the selection of prom queens, homecoming queens, and attendants in which girls are annually evaluated on their attractiveness, often without ever volunteering to enter such competitions. Generally, school officials assume that every girl in the school wants to enter, which implies that all girls wish to be judged on the basis of their appearance. At the same time, diverse subcultures often develop within large high schools, some of which places less emphasis on stereotypical gender concerns such as appearance.

[Conclusion]

[These experiences] send girls a strong message that what they do and who they are is less important then how they look. Even girls in achievement roles, such as basketball team members, continue to receive messages about the importance of appearance. Such an emphasis prepares girls for adult careers and occupations where appearance continues to be an explicit or implicit basis for hiring and retaining employees. . . .

Girls and women continue to be viewed as sexual objects within the media as well as other arenas from cheerleading and pompon teams to swimsuit competitions. Increasingly, adult female models are portrayed as innocent and childlike in their sexual allure, while young girls are depicted as erotic and seductive. Since girls are cast as sexual objects at such an early age, they often internalize this image as a central aspect of their identity. It then becomes extraordinarily difficult for them to move beyond this self-image to develop a greater sense of their own erotic potential as well as their general creative life force. This denial contributes to such largely female maladies as anorexia and bulimia as well as a growing obsession with plastic surgery among adolescent girls.

Through objectification, women are denied their sense of totality. To be viewed primarily as a physical and sexual object is to experience denial of self as a whole person with thoughts, feelings, and actions. Women must struggle to overcome a perception of self as object rather than subject before they can begin the process of self-definition as total and complete human beings. Only then can they develop their unique interests and have a real impact on the world around them.

15 Sexuality and Gender in Children's Daily Worlds

BARRIE THORNE
ZELLA LURIA

In this selection, the researchers focus on children's play, examining its implications for relations between men and women. Their observations are likely to bring back many memories of your own childhood. You will also become aware that children's play is not simply play, but has serious sociological meaning—in this instance, the fierce maintenance of social boundaries between males and females.

To gather their data, Thorne and Luria studied fourth- and fifth-graders in four schools within three states. They found that the children usually are very careful to separate their friendships and activities on the basis of sex. Girls of this age are more concerned about "being nice," while the interests of boys center on sports and testing the limits of rules. The larger groups into which they band provide each boy a degree of protection and anonymity. The sociological significance of children's play is that both boys and girls are helping to socialize one another into primary adult gender roles, girls being more concerned with intimacy, emotionality, and romance, and boys with independence and sexuality. They are writing the "scripts" that they will follow as adults.

THE AMBIGUITIES OF "SEX"—a word used to refer to biological sex, to cultural gender, and also to sexuality—contain a series of complicated questions. Although our cultural understandings often merge these three domains, they can be separated analytically; their interrelationships lie at the core of the social organization of sex and gender. In this paper we focus on the domains of gender and sexuality as they are organized and experienced among elementary school children, especially nine- to eleven-year-olds. This analysis helps illuminate age-based variations and transitions in the organization of sexuality and gender.

We use "gender" to refer to cultural and social phenomena—divisions of labor, activity, and identity which are associated with but not fully determined

156

by biological sex. The core of sexuality, as we use it here, is desire and arousal. Desire and arousal are shaped by and associated with socially learned activities and meanings which Gagnon and Simon (1973) call "sexual scripts." Sexual scripts—defining who does what, with whom, when, how, and what it means—are related to the adult society's view of gender (Miller and Simon, 1981). Nine- to eleven-year-old children are beginning the transition from the gender system of childhood to that of adolescence. They are largely defined (and define themselves) as children, but they are on the verge of sexual maturity, cultural adolescence, and a gender system organized around the institution of heterosexuality. Their experiences help illuminate complex and shifting relationships between sexuality and gender.

First we explore the segregated gender arrangements of middle childhood as contexts for learning adolescent and adult sexual scripts. We then turn from their separate worlds to relations *between* boys and girls, and examine how fourth- and fifth-grade children use sexual idioms to mark gender boundaries. Separate gender groups and ritualized, asymmetric relations between girls and boys lay the groundwork for the more overtly sexual scripts of adolescence.

The Daily Separation of Girls and Boys

Gender segregation—the separation of girls and boys in friendships and casual encounters—is central to daily life in elementary schools. A series of snapshots taken in varied school settings would reveal extensive spatial separation between girls and boys. When they choose seats, select companions for work or play, or arrange themselves in line, elementary school children frequently cluster into same-sex groups. At lunchtime, boys and girls often sit separately and talk matter-of-factly about "girls' tables" and "boys' tables." Playgrounds have gendered spaces: boys control some areas and activities, such as large playing fields and basketball courts; and girls control smaller enclaves like jungle-gym areas and concrete spaces for hopscotch or jump-rope. Extensive gender segregation in everyday encounters and in friendships has been found in many other studies of elementary- and middle-school children. Gender segregation in elementary and middle schools has been found to account for more segregation than race (Schofield, 1982).

Gender segregation is not total. Snapshots of school settings would also reveal some groups with a fairly even mix of boys and girls, especially in games like kickball, dodgeball, and handball, and in classroom and playground activities organized by adults. Some girls frequently play with boys, integrating their groups in a token way, and a few boys, especially in the lower grades, play with groups of girls. In general, there is more gender segregation when children are freer to construct their own activities.

Most of the research on gender and children's social relations emphasizes patterns of separation, contrasting the social organization and cultures of girls' groups with those of boys. In brief summary: Boys tend to interact in larger and more publicly visible groups; they more often play outdoors, and their activities take up more space than those of girls. Boys engage in more physically aggressive play and fighting; their social relations tend to be overtly hierarchical and competitive. Organized sports are both a central activity and a major metaphor among boys; they use a language of "teams" and "captains" even when not engaged in sports.

Girls more often interact in smaller groups or friendship pairs, organized in shifting alliances. Compared with boys, they more often engage in turn-taking activities like jump-rope and doing tricks on the bars, and they less often play organized sports. While boys use a rhetoric of contests and teams, girls describe their relations using language which stresses cooperation and "being nice." But the rhetorics of either group should not be taken for the full reality. Girls *do* engage in conflict, although it tends to take more indirect forms than the direct insults and challenges more often found in interactions among boys, and between girls and boys.

Interaction Among Boys

In daily patterns of talk and play, boys in all-male groups often build towards heightened and intense moments, moments one can describe in terms of group arousal with excited emotions. This especially happens when boys violate rules.

Dirty words are a focus of rules, and rule breaking, in elementary schools. Both girls and boys know dirty words, but flaunting of the words and risking punishment for their use was more frequent in boys' than in girls' groups in all the schools we studied. In the middle-class Massachusetts public school, both male and female teachers punished ballplayers for [their dirty words]. But teachers were not present after lunch and before school, when most group-directed play took place. A female paraprofessional, who alone managed almost 150 children on the playground, never intervened to stop bad language in play; the male gym teacher who occasionally appeared on the field at after-lunch recess always did. Boys resumed dirty talk immediately after he passed them. Dirty talk is a staple part of the repertoire of the boys' groups (also see Fine, 1980). Such talk defines their groups as, at least in part, outside the reach of the school's discipline.

Some of the dirty talk may be explicitly sexual, as it was in the Massachusetts public school when a group of five fifth-grade boys played a game called "Mad Lib" (also described in Luria, 1983). The game consisted of a paragraph (in this case, a section of a textbook discussing the U.S. Constitution) with key words deleted, to be filled in by the players. Making the paragraph absurd and violating rules to create excitement seemed to be the goal of the game. The boys clearly knew that their intentions were "dirty": They requested the field observer not to watch the game.

Sports, dirty words, and testing the limits are part of what boys teach boys how to do. The assumption seems to be: Dirty words, sports interest and knowledge, and transgression of politeness are closely connected.

RULE TRANSGRESSION: COMPARING GIRLS' AND BOYS' GROUPS

Rule transgression in *public* is exciting to boys in their groups. Boys' groups are attentive to potential consequences of transgression, but, compared with girls, groups of boys appear to be greater risk-takers. Adults tending and teaching children do not often undertake discipline of an entire boys' group; the adults might lose out and they cannot risk that. Girls are more likely to affirm the reasonableness of rules, and, when it occurs, rule-breaking by girls is smaller scale. This may be related to the smaller size of girls' groups and to adults' readiness to use rules on girls who seem to believe in them. It is dubious if an isolated pair of boys (a pair is the model size of girls' groups) could get away with the rule-breaking that characterizes the larger male group. A boy may not have power, but a boys' *group* does. Teachers avoid disciplining whole groups of boys, partly for fear of seeming unfair. Boys rarely identify those who proposed direct transgressions and, when confronted, they claim (singly), "I didn't start it; why should I be punished?"

Boys are visibly excited when they break rules together—they are flushed as they play, they wipe their hands on their jeans, some of them look guilty. The Mad Lib game described above not only violates rules, it also evokes sexual meanings within an all-male group. Arousal is not purely individual; in this case, it is shared by the group. . . . The audience for the excitement is the gender-segregated peer group, where each boy increases the excitement by adding still a "worse" word. All of this takes place in a game ("rules") context, and hence with anonymity despite the close-up contact of the game.

While we never observed girls playing a Mad Lib game of this sort, some of our female students recall playing the game in grade school but giving it up after being caught by teachers, or out of fear of being caught. Both boys and girls may acquire knowledge of the game, but boys repeatedly perform it because their gender groups give support for transgression.

These instances all suggest that boys experience a shared, arousing context for transgression, with sustained gender group support for rule-breaking. Girls' groups may engage in rule-breaking, but the gender group's support for repeated public transgression is far less certain. The smaller size of girls' gender groupings in comparison with those of boys, and girls' greater susceptibility to rules and social control by teachers, make girls' groups easier to control. Boys' larger groups give each transgressor a degree of anonymity. Anonymity—which means less probability of detection and punishment—enhances the contagious excitement of rule-breaking.

The higher rates of contagious excitement, transgression, and limit-testing in boys' groups means that when they are excited, boys are often "playing" to male audiences. The public nature of such excitement forges bonds among boys. This kind of bonding is also evident when boys play team sports, and when they act aggressively toward marginal or isolated boys. Such aggression is both physical and verbal (taunts like "sissy," "fag," or "mental"). Sharing a target of aggression may be another source of arousal for groups of boys.

THE TIE TO SEXUALITY IN MALES

When Gagnon and Simon (1973) argued that there are gender-differentiated sexual scripts in adolescence, they implied what our observations suggest: the gender arrangements and subcultures of middle childhood prepare the way for the sexual scripts of adolescence. Fifth- and sixth-grade boys share pornography, in the form of soft-core magazines like *Playboy* and *Penthouse,* with great care to avoid confiscation. Like the Mad Lib games with their forbidden content, soft-core magazines are also shared in all-male contexts, providing explicit knowledge about what is considered sexually arousing and about attitudes and fantasies. Since pornography is typically forbidden for children in both schools and families, this secret sharing occurs in a context of rule-breaking.

While many theorists since Freud have stressed the importance of boys loosening ties and identification with females (as mother surrogates), few theorists have questioned why "communally aroused" males do not uniformly bond sexually to other males. If the male groups of fifth and sixth grade are the forerunners of the "frankly" heterosexual gender groups of the junior and high school years, what keeps these early groups from open homosexual expression? Scripting in same-gender peer groups may, in fact, be more about gender than about sexual orientation. Boys, who will later view themselves as having homosexual or heterosexual preferences, are learning patterns of masculinity. The answer may also lie in the teaching of homophobia.

By the fourth grade, children, especially boys, have begun to use homophobic labels—"fag," "faggot," "queer"—as terms of insult, especially for marginal boys. They draw upon sexual allusions (often not fully understood, except for their negative and contaminating import) to reaffirm male hierarchies and patterns of exclusion. As "fag" talk increases, relaxed and cuddling patterns of touch decrease among boys. Kindergarten and first-grade boys touch one another frequently and with ease, with arms around shoulders, hugs, and holding hands. By fifth grade, touch among boys becomes more constrained, gradually shifting to mock violence and the use of poking, shoving, and ritual gestures like "give five" (flat hand slaps) to express bonding. The tough surface of boys' friendships is no longer like the gentle touching of girls in friendship.

Interaction Among Girls

In contrast with the larger, hierarchical organization of groups of boys, fourth- and fifth-grade girls more often organize themselves in pairs of "best friends" linked in shifting coalitions. These pairs are not "marriages"; the pattern is more one of dyads moving into triads, since girls often participate in two or more pairs at one time. This may result in quite complex social networks. Girls often talk about who is friends with or "likes" whom; they continually negotiate the parameters of friendships.

For example, in the California school, Chris, a fifth-grade girl, frequently said that Kathryn was her "best friend." Kathryn didn't proclaim the friendship as often; she also played and talked a lot with Judy. After watching Kathryn talk to Judy during a transition period in the classroom, Chris went over, took Kathryn aside, and said with an accusing tone, "You talk to Judy more than me." Kathryn responded defensively, "I talk to you as much as I talk to Judy."

In talking about their relationships with one another, girls use a language of "friends," "nice," and "mean." They talk about who is most and least "liked," which anticipates the concern about "popularity" found among junior high and high school girls (Eder, 1985). Since relationships sometimes break off, girls hedge bets by structuring networks of potential friends. The activity of constructing and breaking dyads is often carried out through talk with third parties. Some of these processes are evident in a sequence recorded in a Massachusetts school:

> The fifth-grade girls, Flo and Pauline, spoke of themselves as "best friends," while Flo said she was "sort of friends" with Doris. When a lengthy illness kept Pauline out of school, Flo spent more time with Doris. One day Doris abruptly broke off her friendship with Flo and began criticizing her to other girls. Flo, who felt very badly, went around asking others in their network, "What did I do? Why is Doris being so mean? Why is she telling everyone not to play with me?"

On school playgrounds girls are less likely than boys to organize themselves into team sports. They more often engage in small-scale, turn-taking kinds of play. When they jump rope or play on the bars, they take turns performing and watching others perform in stylized movements which may involve considerable skill. Sometimes girls work out group choreographies, counting and jumping rope in unison, or swinging around the bars. In other synchronized body rituals, clusters of fifth- and sixth-grade girls practice cheerleading routines or dance steps. In interactions with one another, girls often use relaxed gestures of physical intimacy, moving bodies in harmony, coming close in space, and reciprocating cuddly touches. We should add that girls also poke and grab, pin one another from behind, and use hand-slap rituals like "giving five," although less frequently than boys.

In other gestures of intimacy, which one rarely sees among boys, girls stroke or comb their friends' hair. They notice and comment on one another's physical appearance such as haircuts or clothes. Best friends monitor one another's emotions. They share secrets and become mutually vulnerable through self-disclosure, with an implicit demand that the expression of one's inadequacy will induce the friend to disclose a related inadequacy. In contrast, disclosure of weakness among boys is far more likely to be exposed to others through joking or horsing around.

IMPLICATIONS FOR SEXUALITY

Compared with boys, girls are more focused on constructing intimacy and talking about one-to-one relationships. Their smaller and more personal groups provide less protective anonymity than the larger groups of boys. Bonding through mutual self-disclosure, especially through disclosure of vulnerability, and breaking off friendships by "acting mean," teach the creation, sustaining, and ending of emotionally intimate relations. Girls' preoccupation with who is friends with whom, and their monitoring of cues of "nice" and "mean," liking and disliking, teach them strategies for forming and leaving personal relationships. In their interactions girls show knowledge of motivational rules for dyads and insight into both outer and inner realities of social relationships. Occasionally, girls indicate that they see boys as lacking such "obvious" knowledge.

Girls' greater interest in verbally sorting out relationships was evident during an incident in the Massachusetts public school. The fifth-grade boys often insulted John, a socially isolated boy who was not good at sports. On one such occasion during gym class, Bill, a high status boy, angrily yelled "creep" and "mental" when John fumbled the ball. The teacher stopped the game and asked the class to discuss the incident. Both boys and girls vigorously talked about "words that kill," with Bill saying he was sorry for what he said, that he had lost control in the excitement of the game. The girls kept asking, "How could anyone do that?" The boys kept returning to, "When you get excited, you do things you don't mean." Both girls and boys understood and verbalized the dilemma, but after the group discussion the boys dropped the topic. The girls continued to converse, with one repeatedly asking, "How could Bill be so stupid? Didn't he know how he'd make John feel?"

When talking with one another, girls use dirty words much less often than boys do. The shared arousal and bonding among boys which we think occurs around public rule-breaking has as its counterpart the far less frequent giggling sessions of girls, usually in groups larger than three. The giggling often centers on carefully guarded topics, sometimes, although not always, about boys.

The sexually related discourse of girls focuses less on dirty words than on themes of romance. In the Michigan school, first- and second-grade girls often jumped rope to rhymes about romance. A favorite was, "Down in the Valley Where the Green Grass Grows," a saga of heterosexual romance which, with the name of the jumper and a boy of her choice filled in, concludes: " . . . along came Jason, and kissed her on the cheek . . . first comes love, then comes marriage, then along comes Cindy with a baby carriage." In the Michigan and California schools, fourth- and fifth-grade girls talked privately about crushes and about which boys were "cute," as shown in the following incident recorded in the lunchroom of the Michigan school:

The girls and boys from one of the fourth-grade classes sat at separate tables. Three of the girls talked as they peered at a nearby table of fifth-grade boys, "Look behind you," one said. "Ooh," said the other two. "That boy's named Todd." "I know where my favorite guy is . . . there," another gestured with her head while her friends looked.

In the Massachusetts private school, fifth-grade girls plotted about how to get particular boy–girl pairs together.

As Gagnon and Simon (1973) have suggested, two strands of sexuality are differently emphasized among adolescent girls and boys. Girls emphasize and learn about the emotional and romantic before the explicitly sexual. The sequence for boys is the reverse; commitment to sexual acts precedes commitment to emotion-laden, intimate relationships and the rhetoric of romantic love. Dating and courtship, Gagnon suggests, are processes in which each sex teaches the other what each wants and expects. The exchange, as they point out, does not always go smoothly. Indeed, in heterosexual relationships among older adults, tension often persists between the scripts (and felt needs) of women and of men.

Children's Sexual Meanings and the Construction of Gender Arrangements

Girls and boys, who spend considerable time in gender-separate groups, learn different patterns of interaction which, we have argued, lay the groundwork for the sexual scripts of adolescence and adulthood. However, sexuality is not simply delayed until adolescence. Children engage in sexual practices—kissing, erotic forms of touch, masturbation, and sometimes intercourse. As school-based observers, we saw only a few overt sexual activities among children, mostly incidents of public, cross-gender kissing, surrounded by teasing, chasing, and laughter.

HETEROSEXUAL TEASING AND THE IMPORTANCE OF THIRD PARTIES

The special loading of sexual words and gestures makes them useful for accomplishing non-sexual purposes. Sexual idioms provide a major resource which children draw upon as they construct and maintain gender segregation. Through the years of elementary school, children use with increasing frequency heterosexual idioms—claims that a particular girl or boy "likes," "has a crush on," or is "goin' with" someone from the other gender group.

Children's language for heterosexual relationships consists of a very few, often repeated, and sticky words. In a context of teasing, the charge that a particular boy "likes" a particular girl (or vice versa) may be hurled like an insult. The difficulty children have in countering such accusations was evident in a conversation between the observer and a group of third-grade girls in the lunchroom at the Michigan school:

> Susan asked me what I was doing, and I said I was observing the things children do and play. Nicole volunteered, "I like running when boys chase all the girls. See Tim over there? Judy chases him all around the school. She likes him." Judy, sitting across the table, quickly responded, "I hate him. I like him for a friend." "Tim loves Judy," Nicole said in a loud, sing-song voice.

Sexual and romantic teasing marks social hierarchies. The most popular children and the pariahs—the lowest status, excluded children—are most frequently mentioned as targets of "liking." Linking someone with a pariah suggests shared contamination and is an especially vicious tease.

When a girl or boy publicly says that she or he "likes" someone or has a boyfriend or girlfriend, that person defines the romantic situation and is less susceptible to teasing than those targeted by someone else. Crushes may be secretly revealed to friends, a mark of intimacy, especially among girls. The entrusted may then go public with the secret ("Wendy likes John"), which may be experienced as betrayal, but which also may be a way of testing the romantic waters. Such leaks, like those of government officials, can be denied or acted upon by the original source of information.

Third parties—witnesses and kibbitzers—are central to the structure of heterosexual teasing. The teasing constructs dyads (very few of them actively "couples"), but within the control of larger gender groups. Several of the white fifth-graders in the Michigan and California schools and some of the black students in the Massachusetts schools occasionally went on dates, which were much discussed around the schools. Same-gender groups provide launching pads, staging grounds, and retreats for heterosexual couples, both real and imagined. Messengers and emissaries go between groups, indicating who likes whom and checking out romantic interest. By the time "couples" actually get together (if they do at all), the groups and their messengers have provided a network of constructed meanings, a kind of agenda for the pair. As we have argued, gender-divided peer groups sustain different meanings of the sexual. They also regulate heterosexual behavior by helping to define the emerging sexual scripts of adolescence (who "likes" whom, who might "go with" whom, what it means to be a couple).

HETEROSEXUALLY CHARGED RITUALS

Boundaries between boys and girls are also emphasized and maintained by heterosexually charged rituals like cross-sex chasing. Formal games of tag and informal episodes of chasing punctuate life on playgrounds. The informal episodes usually open with a provocation—taunts like "You can't get me!" or "Slobber monster!"; bodily pokes; or the grabbing of possessions like a hat or scarf. The person who is provoked may ignore the taunt or poke, handle it verbally ("Leave me alone!"), or respond by chasing. After a chasing sequence, which may end after a short run or a pummeling, the chaser and chased may switch roles.

Chasing has a gendered structure. When boys chase one another, they often end up wrestling or in mock fights. When girls chase girls, they less often wrestle one another to the ground. Unless organized as a formal game like "freeze tag," same-gender chasing goes unnamed and usually undiscussed. But children set apart cross-gender chasing with special names—"girls chase the boys," "boys chase the girls"; "the chase"; "chasers"; "chase and kiss"; "kiss-chase"; "kissers and chasers"; "kiss or kill"—and with animated talk about the activity. The names vary by region and school, but inevitably contain both gender and sexual meanings.

When boys and girls chase one another, they become, by definition, separate teams. Gender terms override individual identities, especially for the other team: "Help, a girl's chasin' me!"; "C'mon Sarah, let's get that boy"; "Tony, help save me from the girls." Individuals may call for help from, or offer help to, others of their gender. In acts of treason they may also grab someone of their gender and turn them over to the opposing team, as when, in the Michigan school, Ryan grabbed Billy from behind, wrestled him to the ground, and then called, "Hey girls, get 'im."

Names like "chase and kiss" mark the sexual meanings of cross-gender chasing. The threat of kissing—most often girls threatening to kiss boys—is a ritualized form of provocation. Teachers and aides are often amused by this form of play among children in the lower grades. They are more perturbed by cross-gender chasing among fifth- and sixth-graders, perhaps because at those ages some girls "have their development" (breasts make sexual meanings seem more consequential), and because of the more elaborate patterns of touch and touch avoidance in chasing rituals among older children. The principal of one Michigan school forbade the sixth-graders from playing "pom-pom," a complicated chasing game, because it entailed "inappropriate touch."

Cross-gender chasing is sometimes structured around rituals of pollution, such as "cooties," where individuals or groups are treated as contaminating or "carrying germs." Children have rituals for transferring cooties (usually touching someone else and shouting "You've got cooties!"), for immunization (e.g., writing "CV" for "cootie vaccination" on their arms), and for eliminating cooties (e.g., saying "no gives" or using "cootie catchers" made of folded paper). Boys may transmit cooties, but cooties usually originate with girls. One version of cooties played in Michigan is called "girl stain." Although cooties is framed as play, the import may be serious. Female pariahs—the ultimate school untouchables by virtue of gender and some added stigma such as being overweight or from a very poor family—are sometimes called "cootie queens" or "cootie girls." Conversely, we have never heard or read about "cootie kings" or "cootie boys."

In these cross-gender rituals girls are defined as sexual. Boys sometimes threaten to kiss girls, but it is girls' kisses and touch which are deemed especially contaminating. Girls more often use the threat of kissing to tease boys and to make them run away, as in this example recorded among fourth-graders on the playground of the California school:

> Smiling and laughing, Lisa and Jill pulled a fourth-grade boy along by his hands, while a group of girls sitting on the jungle-gym called out, "Kiss him, kiss him." Grabbing at his hair, Lisa said to Jill, "Wanna kiss Jonathan?" Jonathan got away, and the girls chased after him. "Jill's gonna kiss your hair," Lisa yelled.

The use of kisses as a threat is double-edged, since the power comes from the threat of pollution. A girl who frequently uses this threat may be stigmatized as a "kisser."

Gender-marked rituals of teasing, chasing, and pollution heighten the boundaries between boys and girls. They also convey assumptions which get worked into later sexual scripts: (1) that girls and boys are members of distinctive, opposing, and sometimes antagonistic groups; (2) that cross-gender contact is potentially sexual and contaminating, fraught with both pleasure and danger; and (3) that girls are more sexually defined (and polluting) than boys.

Conclusion

Social scientists have often viewed the heterosexual dating rituals of adolescence—when girls and boys "finally" get together—as the concluding stage after the separate, presumably non-sexual, boys' and girls' groups that are so prevalent in childhood. We urge a closer look at the organization of sexuality and of gender in middle and late childhood. The gender-divided social worlds of children are not totally asexual. And same-gender groups have continuing import in the more overtly sexual scripts of adolescence and adulthood.

From an early age "the sexual" is prescriptively heterosexual and male homophobic. Children draw on sexual meanings to maintain gender segregation—to make cross-gender interaction risky and to mark and ritualize boundaries between "the boys" and "the girls." In their separate gender groups, girls and boys learn somewhat different patterns of bonding—boys sharing the arousal of group rule-breaking; girls emphasizing the construction of intimacy, and themes of romance. Coming to adolescent sexual intimacy from different and asymmetric gender subcultures, girls and boys bring somewhat different needs, capacities, and types of knowledge.

References

Eder, Dona (1985). "The cycle of popularity: interpersonal relations among female adolescents." *Sociology of Education* 58: 154–65.

Fine, Gary Alan (1980). "The natural history of preadolescent male friendship groups." Pp. 293–320 in Hugh C. Foot, Antony J. Chapman, and Jean R. Smith (eds.), *Friendship and Social Relations in Children*. New York: Wiley.

Gagnon, John H., and William Simon (1973). *Sexual Conduct*. Chicago: Aldine.

Luria, Zella (1983). "Sexual fantasy and pornography: two cases of girls brought up with pornography." *Archives of Sexual Behavior* 11: 395–404.

Miller, Patricia Y., and William Simon (1981). "The development of sexuality in adolescence." Pp. 383–407 in Joseph Adelson (ed.), *Handbook of Adolescent Psychology*. New York: Wiley.

Schofield, Janet (1982). *Black and White in School*. New York: Praeger.

16 But What Do You Mean? Women and Men in Conversation

DEBORAH TANNEN

We seldom realize how precarious social interaction is between men and women. For the most part, we manage to get our ideas across to one another with little difficulty. Sometimes, however, communication across gender lines leaves us headshakingly confused that "the other" could have said that, thought that, done that—giving us a glimmer that our worlds really are different. Sociologically, men and women represent distinct worlds of socialization—with all the differences this implies, from ideas about sex and love to the best ways to get ahead in life.

Are there really major differences in male/female communications? Or are these statements exaggerations? You be the judge, as you read Tannen's summary of how women and men communicate. See how her analysis compares with your own experiences. You might also consider the implications of this analysis for problems experienced by couples "going together," as well as for difficulties between husbands and wives.

CONVERSATION IS A RITUAL. We say things that seem obviously the thing to say, without thinking of the literal meaning of our words, any more than we expect the question "How are you?" to call forth a detailed account of aches and pains.

Unfortunately, women and men often have different ideas about what's appropriate, different ways of speaking. Many of the conversational rituals common among women are designed to take the other person's feelings into account, while many of the conversational rituals common among men are designed to maintain the one-up position, or at least avoid appearing one-down. As a result, when men and women interact—especially at work—it's often women who are at the disadvantage. Because women are not trying to avoid the one-down position, that is unfortunately where they may end up.

Here, the biggest areas of miscommunication.

1. Apologies

Women are often told they apologize too much. The reason they're told to stop doing it is that, to many men, apologizing seems synonymous with putting oneself down. But there are many times when "I'm sorry" isn't self-deprecating, or even an apology; it's an automatic way of keeping both speakers on an equal footing. For example, a well-known columnist once interviewed me and gave me her phone number in case I needed to call her back. I misplaced the number and had to go through the newspaper's main switchboard. When our conversation was winding down and we'd both made ending-type remarks, I added "Oh, I almost forgot—I lost your direct number, can I get it again?" "Oh, I'm sorry," she came back instantly, even though she had done nothing wrong and *I* was the one who'd lost the number. But I understood she wasn't really apologizing; she was just automatically reassuring me she had no intention of denying me her number.

Even when "I'm sorry" *is* an apology, women often assume it will be the first step in a two-step ritual: I say "I'm sorry" and take half the blame, then you take the other half. At work, it might go something like this:

A. When you typed this letter, you missed this phrase I inserted.
B. Oh, I'm sorry. I'll fix it.
A. Well, I wrote it so small it was easy to miss.

When both parties share blame, it's a mutual face-saving device. But if one person, usually the woman, utters frequent apologies and the other doesn't, she ends up looking as if she's taking the blame for mishaps that aren't her fault. When she's only partially to blame, she looks entirely in the wrong.

I recently sat in on a meeting at an insurance company where the sole woman, Helen, said "I'm sorry" or "I apologize" repeatedly. At one point she said, "I'm thinking out loud. I apologize." Yet the meeting was intended to be an informal brain-storming session, and *everyone* was thinking out loud.

The reason Helen's apologies stood out was that she was the only person in the room making so many. And the reason I was concerned was that Helen felt the annual bonus she had received was unfair. When I interviewed her colleagues, they said that Helen was one of the best and most productive workers—yet she got one of the smallest bonuses. Although the problem might have been outright sexism, I suspect her speech style, which differs from that of her male colleagues, masks her competence.

Unfortunately, not apologizing can have its price too. Since so many women use ritual apologies, those who don't may be seen as hard-edged. What's important is to be aware of how often you say you're sorry (and why), and to monitor your speech based on the reaction you get.

2. Criticism

A woman who cowrote a report with a male colleague was hurt when she read a rough draft to him and he leapt into a critical response—"Oh, that's too dry! You have to make it snappier!" She herself would have been more likely to say, "That's a really good start. Of course, you'll want to make it a little snappier when you revise."

Whether criticism is given straight or softened is a matter of convention. In general, women use more softeners. I noticed this difference when talking to an editor about an essay I'd written. While going over changes she wanted to make, she said, "There's one more thing. I know you may not agree with me. The reason I noticed the problem is that your other points are so lucid and elegant." She went on hedging for several more sentences until I put her out of her misery: "Do you want to cut that part?" I asked—and of course she did. But I appreciated her tentativeness. In contrast, another editor (a man) I once called summarily rejected my idea for an article by barking, "Call me when you have something new to say."

Those who are used to ways of talking that soften the impact of criticism may find it hard to deal with the right-between-the-eyes style. It has its own logic, however, and neither style is intrinsically better. People who prefer criticism given straight are operating on an assumption that feelings aren't involved. "Here's the dope. I know you're good; you can take it."

3. Thank-Yous

A woman manager I know starts meetings by thanking everyone for coming, even though it's clearly their job to do so. Her "thank-you" is simply a ritual.

A novelist received a fax from an assistant in her publisher's office; it contained suggested catalogue copy for her book. She immediately faxed him her suggested changes and said, "Thanks for running this by me," even though her contract gave her the right to approve all copy. When she thanked the assistant, she fully expected him to reciprocate: "Thanks for giving me such a quick response." Instead, he said, "You're welcome." Suddenly, rather than an equal exchange of pleasantries, she found herself positioned as the recipient of a favor. This made her feel like responding, "Thanks for nothing!"

Many women use "thanks" as an automatic conversation starter and closer; there's nothing literally to thank you for. Like many rituals typical of women's conversation, it depends on the goodwill of the other to restore the balance. When the other speaker doesn't reciprocate, a woman may feel like someone on a seesaw whose partner abandoned his end. Instead of balancing in the air, she has plopped to the ground, wondering how she got there.

4. Fighting

Many men expect the discussion of ideas to be a ritual fight—explored through verbal opposition. They state their ideas in the strongest possible terms, thinking that if there are weaknesses someone will point them out, and by trying to argue against those objections, they will see how well their ideas hold up.

Those who expect their own ideas to be challenged will respond to another's ideas by trying to poke holes and find weak links—as a way of *helping*. The logic is that when you are challenged you will rise to the occasion: Adrenaline makes your mind sharper, you get ideas and insights you would not have thought of without the spur of battle.

But many women take this approach as a personal attack. Worse, they find it impossible to do their best work in such a contentious environment. If you're not used to ritual fighting, you begin to hear criticism of your ideas as soon as they are formed. Rather than making you think more clearly, it makes you doubt what you know. When you state your ideas, you hedge in order to fend off potential attacks. Ironically, this is more likely to *invite* attack because it makes you look weak.

Although you may never enjoy verbal sparring, some women find it helpful to learn how to do it. An engineer who was the only woman among four men in a small company found that as soon as she learned to argue, she was accepted and taken seriously. A doctor attending a hospital staff meeting made a similar discovery. She was becoming more and more angry with a male colleague who'd loudly disagreed with a point she'd made. Her better judgment told her to hold her tongue, to avoid making an enemy of this powerful senior colleague. But finally she couldn't hold it any longer, and she rose to her feet and delivered an impassioned attack on his position. She sat down in a panic, certain she had permanently damaged her relationship with him. To her amazement, he came up to her afterward and said, "That was a great rebuttal. I'm really impressed. Let's go out for a beer after work and hash out our approaches to this problem."

5. Praise

A manager I'll call Lester had been on his new job six months when he heard that the women reporting to him were deeply dissatisfied. When he talked to them about it, their feelings erupted; two said they were on the verge of quitting because he didn't appreciate their work, and they didn't want to wait to be fired. Lester was dumbfounded: He believed they were doing a fine job. Surely, he thought, he had said nothing to give them the impression he didn't like their work. And indeed he hadn't. That was the problem. He had said *nothing*—and the women assumed he was following the adage "If you can't say something nice, don't say anything." He thought he was showing confidence in them by leaving them alone.

Men and women have different habits in regard to giving praise. For example, Deidre and her colleague William both gave presentations at a conference. Afterward, Deidre told William, "That was a great talk." He thanked her. Then she asked, "What did you think of mine?" and he gave her a lengthy and detailed critique. She found it uncomfortable to listen to his comments. But she assured herself that he meant well, and that his honesty was a signal that she, too, should be honest when he asked for a critique of his performance. As a matter of fact, she had noticed quite a few ways in which he could have improved his presentation. But she never got a chance to tell him because he never asked—and she felt put down. The worst part was that it seemed she had only herself to blame, since she *had* asked what he thought of her talk.

But had she really asked for his critique? The truth is, when she asked for his opinion, she was expecting a compliment, which she felt was more or less required following anyone's talk. When he responded with criticism, she figured, Oh, he's playing "Let's critique each other"—not a game she'd initiated, but one which she was willing to play. Had she realized he was going to criticize her and not ask her to reciprocate, she would never have asked in the first place.

It would be easy to assume that Deidre was insecure, whether she was fishing for a compliment or soliciting a critique. But she was simply talking automatically, performing one of the many conversational rituals that allow us to get through the day. William may have sincerely misunderstood Deidre's intention—or may have been unable to pass up a chance to one-up her when given the opportunity.

6. Complaints

"Troubles talk" can be a way to establish rapport with a colleague. You complain about a problem (which shows that you are just folks) and the other person responds with a similar problem (which puts you on equal footing). But while such commiserating is common among women, men are likely to hear it as a request to *solve* the problem.

One woman told me she would frequently initiate what she thought would be pleasant complaint-airing sessions at work. She'd just talk about situations that bothered her just to talk about them, maybe to understand them better. But her male office mate would quickly tell her how she could improve the situation. This left her feeling condescended to and frustrated. She was delighted to see this very impasse in a section in my book *You Just Don't Understand,* and showed it to him. "Oh," he said, "I see the problem. How can we solve it?" Then they both laughed, because it had happened again: He short-circuited the detailed discussion she'd hoped for and cut to the chase of finding a solution.

Sometimes the consequences of complaining are more serious: A man might take a woman's lighthearted griping literally, and she can get a reputation as a chronic malcontent. Furthermore, she may be seen as not up to solving the problems that arise on the job.

7. Jokes

I heard a man call in to a talk show and say, "I've worked for two women and neither one had a sense of humor. You know, when you work with men, there's a lot of joking and teasing." The show's host and the guest (both women) took his comment at face value and assumed the women this man worked for were humorless. The guest said, "Isn't it sad that women don't feel comfortable enough with authority to see the humor?" The host said, "Maybe when more women are in authority roles, they'll be more comfortable with power." But although the women this man worked for *may* have taken themselves too seriously, it's just as likely that they each had a terrific sense of humor, but maybe the humor wasn't the type he was used to. They may have been like the woman who wrote to me: "When I'm with men, my wit or cleverness seems inappropriate (or lost!) so I don't bother. When I'm with my women friends, however, there's no hold on puns or cracks and my humor is fully appreciated."

The types of humor women and men tend to prefer differ. Research has shown that the most common form of humor among men is razzing, teasing, and mock-hostile attacks, while among women it's self-mocking. Women often mistake men's teasing as genuinely hostile. Men often mistake women's mock self-deprecation as truly putting themselves down.

Women have told me they were taken more seriously when they learned to joke the way the guys did. For example, a teacher who went to a national conference with seven other teachers (mostly women) and a group of administrators (mostly men) was annoyed that the administrators always found reasons to leave boring seminars, while the teachers felt they had to stay and take notes. One evening, when the group met at a bar in the hotel, the principal asked her how one such seminar had turned out. She retorted, "As soon as you left, it got much better." He laughed out loud at her response. The playful insult appealed to the men—but there was a trade-off. The women seemed to back off from her after this. (Perhaps they were put off by her using joking to align herself with the bosses.)

There is no "right" way to talk. When problems arise, the culprit may be style differences—and *all* styles will at times fail with others who don't share or understand them, just as English won't do you much good if you try to speak to someone who knows only French. If you want to get your message across, it's not a question of being "right"; it's a question of using language that's shared—or at least understood.

PART V   Social Groups and Social Structure

N<small>O ONE IS ONLY A MEMBER</small> of humanity in general; each of us is also a member of particular social groups. We live in a certain country and in a particular neighborhood. We belong to a family and are members of a gender and a racial–ethnic group. We have certain peers with whom we identify. Most of us work at a job and have friends, and many of us go to school or belong to churches, clubs, or other social organizations. The articles in this Part are meant to sensitize us to how social groups and social structure have far-reaching effects on our lives. Let's see what some of those effects are.

No fact of social life is more important than group membership. *To belong to a group is to yield to others the right to make certain decisions about our behavior, while assuming obligations to act according to the expectations of those others.* This is illustrated by a parent saying to a teenage daughter or son, "As long as you are living under my roof, you had better be home by midnight." In this instance, the parents are saying that as long as the daughter or son wants to remain a member of the social group known as the household, her or his behavior must conform to their expectations. So it is with *all* the groups to which we belong: By our membership and participation in them, we relinquish to others at least some control over our own lives.

Those groups that come with our birth are called *involuntary memberships* or *associations*. These include our family and our sexual, ethnic, and racial groups. In contrast, those groups which we choose to join are called *voluntary memberships* or *associations*. The Boy and Girl Scouts, professional associations, church groups, clubs, friendship cliques, and work groups are examples. In certain instances we willingly, sometimes even gladly, conform to their rules and expectations in order to become members. In all groups, we

175

must modify some of our behaviors in order to remain members in good standing.

Not all memberships in voluntary associations involve the same degree of willingness to yield to others a measure of control over our lives. There even are groups, as in some jobs, where we can hardly bear to remain a member but feel that, under the circumstances, we cannot quit. Sociologists still use the term *voluntary association* to refer to such memberships. *Both* voluntary and involuntary memberships have deep effects on our lives, for our participation in a group, whether it is willing or unwilling, shapes not only our behaviors but also our ideas about life.

It is easy to see that social groups have far-reaching effects on our lives— for, as stressed in Part IV, we would not even be "human" without group membership. But what about the second term in the title of this Part? What does *social structure* mean? By this term, sociologists mean that the various social groups that make up our lives are not simply a random collection of components; rather, they are interrelated and form a significant unit that surrounds us.

I know that if any term in sociology sounds vague and irrelevant, it is "social structure." This term, however, also refers to highly significant matters— for *the social organization that underlies your life determines your relationships with others*. To better see what this term means, we can note that "social structure" encompasses five "levels." As I summarize them, I shall go from the broadest to the narrowest level.

The first two levels are *inter*societal; that is, they refer to international relationships. *First*, on the broadest level, social structure refers to relationship among blocs (or groups) of nations. Examples are the West's dependence on the Mideast for much of its oil, and the domination of the poor, Least Industrialized Nations by the wealthy, Most Industrialized Nations. The *second* level, the next broadest, refers to relationships between particular nations, such as the extensive role that the United States plays in the Canadian economy. These first two levels—the international dimensions of social structure— sensitize us to relationships based on historical events as well as current balances of power and resources among nations.

The next three levels are *intra*societal; that is, they refer to relationships *within* a society. The *first* level is quite broad. It refers to how the social institutions within a society are related to one another. This level sensitizes us to how political decisions affect the military, how economic booms and busts affect families, and the like. The *second*, a narrower level, refers to patterns between social groups, such as the relationship between McDonald's and other firms in the fast-food business. The *third*, the narrowest level, deals with such matters as how people are organized within a particular group—such as an individual's role as leader or follower, or the parents' authority over their young children that empowers them to determine what the children eat, where they live, what schools they attend, and how they are to be disciplined.

This Part opens with an unusual focus, that of car selling. Helene Lawson, who interviewed men and women who sell cars, details how the socialization we stressed in Part IV shows up in distinct sales styles. (Another way of phrasing this is that gender is part of the social structure of the automobile industry—just as it is part of our own experience of social life, whatever corner of society we find ourselves in.) In the next article, Mae Biggs and I look at how vaginal examinations are organized. We use Erving Goffman's dramaturgical model to uncover the means by which nonsexuality is sustained during pelvic examinations. John Coleman then focuses on city life, pinpointing the debilitating isolation of the urban homeless. In the final selection, Kai Erikson examines what happens when social structure breaks down. His analysis of the flood at Buffalo Creek reveals how social structure is essential to our social and psychological well-being.

A DIGRESSION ON PARTICIPANT OBSERVATION

Because several articles in this Part—and many in the book itself—are based on participant observation, it is useful to take a closer look at this research method. Lawson observed car salespeople at work (and also interviewed them). For years, before Biggs went to graduate school, she worked as a gynecological nurse. Coleman, who became concerned about homeless people, slept in their shelters and wandered the streets of New York City. As these researchers *participated* in the lives of the people they were studying, they systematically *observed* what was happening; hence the term *participant observation*.

To gather their data, participant observers sometimes place greater emphasis on observing people, at other times on participating in their lives. In an earlier article (number 6), you saw how Whyte moved into an ethnic neighborhood with the express purpose of analyzing it. Lawson's focus was observation of the car salespeople, and she did little participation. In contrast, because Biggs didn't go to graduate school until after many years of work as a gynecological nurse, her emphasis was almost solely on participation. This is also the basis of Coleman's study of the homeless. Regardless of whether participation or observation receives the greater emphasis, when a researcher reports on personal observations of a social setting, the term *participant observation* is used to describe this method of studying social life. (The terms *field research*, *fieldwork*, *ethnographic research*, and *qualitative research* are also used to refer to this technique of studying people.)

Participant observation allows researchers to provide rich, detailed descriptions that, by retaining some of the "flavor" of the settings, bring the reader close to the events that occurred. Thus, in the article on the homeless you can sense the crushing despair of people living on the streets. Although participant observation lends itself to such rich, insightful descriptions, it is not the method, of course, but the author who does the communicating. We depend on an author's skills for learning what life is like in some group, even for gaining a sense of being there. Consequently, in article 21, the account of the experiment on conformity, although it is far from participant observation, you will feel the dilemma faced by the experimenter's victims.

As I stressed in my article on research methods in Part II, a chief concern of sociologists is to gather accurate information about the people they study. To do this, sociologists try to be objective, to leave their biases behind both when they gather data and as they interpret those data for books, articles, and other reports they write. A primary distinction between research methods is whether they are *quantitative* or *qualitative*. Participant observation is an example of a qualitative method, and is exploratory or descriptive. Quantitative methods place the emphasis on measuring precise differences between individuals and groups.

Through their training and experience, sociologists come to prefer some particular method of gathering data. They also associate with one another, both on the basis of the subject matter they are interested in *and* on the basis of the research methods they employ. Consequently, the qualitative and quantitative approaches to social research have become major identifiers among sociologists. Although sociologists have their preferences, and sometimes feel strongly that one approach is vastly superior, both qualitative and quantitative methods are valid means with which to gather data about social life.

In this book, the emphasis is on studies based on the qualitative approach. These selections impart the meanings and experiences of the groups being studied, sometimes even the "flavor" of being a member of these groups. As I see it, this approach best imparts the excitement of sociological discovery.

17 Attacking Nicely: Women Selling Cars

HELENE M. LAWSON

The articles in the preceding Part stressed how boys and girls experience childhood differently. These differences are not a superficial matter, something that has little or no consequence for later life. We don't simply fold childhood away, shutting it up in some drawer as we would a discarded toy. Rather, we carry these experiences with us for the rest of our lives. Our distinct socialization as boys or girls equips us with specific sets of attitudes, behaviors, and orientations. These become an essential part of how we approach the world, helping to set us on different roads in life's journey

The result is not that all women act one way and all men another. Sociologists don't make such a claim. Rather, they say that because of our socialization, women and men tend to show distinct approaches to life's tasks. These differences are often subtle, but they show up in almost everything we do. As Lawson analyzes people who sell cars, some of these distinctions become apparent. None of these characteristics is inevitable, the unvarying consequence of biology, or socialization, or a combination thereof. As socialization changes, then, we can expect to see these behaviors—and even feelings—similarly change.

IN OUR SOCIETY car sales work goes against the norms of trust in human relations. Customers are aware that salespersons are trained in impression management techniques based on empathy to win confidence or on aggressive intimidation to overcome resistance to high prices (Oda 1983; Prus 1989). In addition, the car business is unstable; salesman and customers will probably never see each other again. This makes for transient relationships and an environment where the building of trust is problematic. In fact, throughout the whole social structure of sales interactions, there is little trust.

Researchers find that persons who enter this occupation cope with dishonesty, distrust and immoral dealings in various ways. One way is to concentrate on monetary goals as a measure of success and status (Leidner 1991). A second way is to suppress reflections on the unethical tasks they perform (Oakes 1990). A third way is to claim innocence through apparent unawareness of illicit doings. A fourth way is to claim one was merely following orders. And lastly, workers blame the recipients or victims of their services for negative interactions (Hughes 1962).

Working under these conditions is especially problematic for women who have been socialized as mothers and care takers to be concerned with the needs of others and to maintain honesty in relations (Dinnerstein 1976; Mead 1934; Chodorow 1978; Gilligan 1982). Although few articles have been written about women's experience in the field of high commission sales, there is research on women in other high pressure, male-dominated fields such as management (Kanter 1977) and the military (Rustad 1984). These studies find that women take on stereotypical male or female roles to adapt to a structure in which they experience inherent role conflict (Turner 1990).

My research examines how women handle the conflict between their socialized roles and their adopted role of car salesperson. I will describe both how the women themselves change and how they are also changing the interactions within the workplace, shaping new definitions of what it is to be a car salesperson. This study, therefore, analyzes modes of personal adaption as well as modes of social change. To provide a framework for understanding these changes, I have identified a concept—adapting to an incompatible status through role making—as well as five categories of this concept, "Innocents," "Ladies," "Tough Guys," "Reformers," and "Retreaters." I use these categories to describe how women deal with co-workers and customers when they enter the field, and the changes that emerge as they progress along their career paths, from selling their first cars to becoming experienced salespersons. In an effort to explore the ways in which gender roles operate in the bartering and negotiations endemic to selling cars, the article focuses on saleswomen's initial values and attitudes toward co-workers and customers, the adaptations they make as they become more experienced, and finally, the ways in which some women change the dealership itself.

Data Collection and Sample

I collected the data for this study from in-depth interviews with and observations with 35 car saleswomen and 15 car salesmen at car agencies and restaurants in the Chicago metropolitan area, over a period of three years from 1987 to 1991. The informants were recontacted at intervals in order to follow their career paths. In two instances, I became a customer out of necessity because I needed a car, buying automobiles from women who did not know I was doing research until after the purchases were completed. An additional male informant was a personal friend who began selling on a commission basis about the same time I started to do my research and who spoke with me about his progress on a daily basis.

How Women Come In

An examination of the work women did before beginning car sales shows that most had traditional women's careers, such as teaching, waitressing, social work, retail sales and secretarial jobs. These occupations primarily involved service to others and paid low wages. Although ex-teachers complained that students were discipline problems, "little monsters" and "heathens," and ex-sales clerks and beauticians said customers were "pains in the ass," because they returned used merchandise or couldn't make up their minds about how they wanted their hair done, the women basically liked what they did in these jobs, especially the supportive relationships they had with co-workers. However, these women found it difficult to make a living and support families. Such women, with no previous sales experience, were usually encouraged to try car sales by male friends or family members who stressed the possibility of better pay. When they entered car sales, many assumed they would be able to make friends and establish good co-worker relations as they had done at their previous work. Nina commented:

> I used to cashier at a discount drug store, The pay was bad, but I got a real break on formula for the baby and make-up and stuff like that. Mostly, I stayed because the other saleswomen were terrific. We laughed a lot. . . . told each other our problems. When the store closed, I decided to try car sales. I figured, "What the hell. People like me. I shouldn't have a problem." And I was excited to work for commission.

The hours are very long in car sales and salesmen, for the most part, socialize during slow times, telling each other how well they are doing, commiserating over losses, telling jokes or "kibitzing." To further cement friendships, many salesmen go drinking together after work. Most had been in car sales before so they knew others in the field. But even male novices to car sales said they were accepted by one clique or another. Newcomer women also attempted to befriend salesmen and socialize during slow times. They want to talk about a customer who gave them a hard time, family life, or even the weather. But when they approached the men, the women were usually rejected or harassed. Nina related:

> When I would try to make conversation with other salesman they were very gross. They swear. They pat you on the butt like this. If I did well, the guys would say, "What do you need to sell a car, a bra?" If I was five minutes late, the boss would send me home. The guys would laugh. They made me an example.

Women who attempted to go to bars with salesmen after working hours developed a bad reputation. Evelyn observed:

> You have to be careful. Women learn quick around here. You don't party. You don't hang out with the guys after work. Those who do are called "sluts" or "whores."

Co-worker relations between men and women were strained, and since there were usually only one or two saleswomen at most dealerships, women could not form their own cliques. Interactions between the two sexes remained an area of conflict, and probably will continue as such until there is a more equal balance between women and men car salespersons.

There are, however, more important areas than co-worker relations on which women must concentrate. If they are to succeed, saleswomen must interact well with customers. Yet, all 35 saleswomen remembered many initial contact experiences with male customers as upsetting and negative. These women agreed that most "older" men reacted in a rude, insulting manner when approached. Some openly refused to deal with women. Sara said these men "did not want to answer questions about their income or credit rating, or even discuss cars with a woman." Arlene said some "older men used foul language," or were so abrasive that saleswomen ended up "turning them over to a salesman." Because new saleswomen generally began work with no car sales experience, this rejection added to their self doubt and caused them to feel they needed to learn more about cars in order to sell them.

The car has traditionally been identified with men, and most saleswomen said they knew "little" about automobiles. They did not grow up fixing cars, talking about them with friends, or understanding how they operate. Therefore, at the beginning, many of the women said they thought it was most important to become technically knowledgeable about cars. Joyce had been in car sales for two months:

> I think it is important to be able to talk to a customer about the vehicle—to understand how the engine works and what benefits the make has over others. I watch videos. I listen to other salesmen. I read all the pamphlets. I want to learn as much as I can.

To make maters more difficult, salespersons were not given much training. Newcomers were usually "thrown out on the floor" and had to figure out what to do on their own. Newcomers, men or women, had a hard time closing their first sales, because they lacked experience. Novices were generally hired by the type of dealership salespersons called "green pea stores." This is an agency which usually hires inexperienced salespersons and has managers close sales in the final stages of bargaining. Larry, a general manager, explained the social arrangements of these types of sales which function to shelter newcomers from the guilt and pressure of customer relations:

They [management] try to keep new salespeople in the dark as far as gross cost on cars. They think it makes them more believable to customers. If the manager tells you, "no, you can't sell that car for this amount," for whatever reason, "this is the price you got to sell it for," you have to go out there, and that is what you do.

Ann, whose father owned a car dealership, said that even more experienced salespersons only got to see the front page of an invoice:

There's an invoice that they [the dealership] can show you [the salesperson] and a customer can buy the car, usually for $100 over the invoice. But, you [the salesperson] will never see the back page which is all their profit. When they [the dealership] sell a car for invoice there is like about $1,200 usually in that figure. If you're talking Cadillac, it's more like $5,000.

Once newcomers in green pea stores had been at work a month or so, management expected them to begin to close on their own. Although salespersons were told by management at the beginning of their careers that making money for the dealership was paramount, the first steps most salespersons, men or women, took was to try to sell the customer a car close to the amount he or she wanted to pay. Generally this was lower than management would like, and meant a smaller commission for the salesperson. However, most women said pleasing the customer through a cheap price made them feel good because they felt they were helping someone.

At the beginning I believed I didn't need to be greedy because there was a price I could sell at that would make everybody happy—the customer, my manager and myself. If you sell enough cars, you are going to make money anyway.

How Women Change

Yet, what women said about first sales in which they made high commissions show how their values were affected by their work. Fran discussed her new attitude:

I'll tell you about my first big sale because that one I remember very well. I was working for about a couple [of] weeks, and it was right after the auto show, and a young dentist came in with his wife, and he had his hands in his pockets jingling his money, and he goes, "I want to buy a Spider [Alfa Romeo]." I found out what the list price was and I wrote it down. I got a $5,000 deposit from him and he took his credit out and I knew nothing. I went into the boss and he almost died. So he goes, "Don't lose this one!" I sold that car way over cost and I didn't even know I was doing it. It was the most exciting thing I had ever done. When he [the customer] came in to pick up the car, he said, "I wanted that car so bad, and I guess I really got screwed." At the beginning I believed it was wrong to ask for too much money—that it was greedy. After that, I started going for the buck.

This sale was exciting for many reasons. It was unexpected, the manager was pleased, and the saleswoman made a large commission. But most of all, selling seemed so easy, as though it were done through luck or magic. Therefore, the saleswoman did not need to blame herself for "screwing" the customer. Events like this became a turning point in women's careers, when attitudes and values toward making lots of money at others' expense became fun.

And in order to sell themselves, women developed roles. They made tools of their personalities and gender traits in order to coerce customers into buying cars, distancing themselves from their potential disloyalty to the other in the relationship.

Innocents

Probably because the first high commission sale made by most newcomers was painless and negotiated in ignorance, many women continued on in the role of the Innocent. Innocents did not use crude language or insider argot. They employed dress and demeanor to portray their particular role. Denise, a younger woman, played school girl:

> I've got a baby face and I do not pose a threat to anybody who walks in—young, old, seasoned buyer, first timer. I put people at ease. I don't scare anybody. I've sold many campers wearing sweats with sorority letters on the bottom. I have a face that will show people I'm honest.

Innocents continued to view their success as "luck" or "magic," both factors out of their control. They said that most customers would sell themselves a car if they [the saleswomen] said little. Innocents adapted through avoidance. They wore blinders so they did not see the dubious dealings going on around them and could deny being a party to the transactions. The woman who sold me my most recent car exemplified this orientation. She originally described the car as having been a manufacturer representative's car, a "brass hat." A week after I purchased the car, I dropped my pen and was feeling around underneath the front seat, when I felt a small plastic object. This turned out to be a key chain from a car rental agency in Florida. It had my car's identification number on it.

I called the rental agency and they verified that the car had indeed been theirs but they had recently sold it to Mazda. I do not think I would have bought this car if I had known it was previously used as a rental car. When I confronted Phyllis with the key chain, she replied:

Is that true? I never asked too many questions. I know I saw literature on the car. . . . that it came from an auction. I know they buy when Mazda is having auctions. I thought is was a manufacturer rep's car.

Other experienced Innocents in my study told me when sales are slow they "dummy up" [use ignorance to sell cars], because customers believed that newcomers did not possess the ability to devise ways of cheating them. The greater trust in the saleswoman made the customers less resistant to her pitches.

Ladies

Women who wished to remain in the field, but were uncomfortable with the Innocent role, had several options. One was to become Ladies, taking on exaggerated feminine characteristics. Ladies said customers were more easily manipulated through forms of stereotypical feminine behavior than through aggressive "pushy" tactics. They cajoled and nurtured male customers in order to deter sexual harassment and to sell cars. Their work relationships became patterned to fit relationships men have experienced in families. Ann, a 52-year-old grandmother, described how she used the goodness of her maternal role to gain trust and respect from her customers: "I tell them, 'Look at these pictures on my desk. I am a mother. I am a grandmother. I wouldn't hurt you, now would I?'"

Ladies helped customers feel comfortable, served them coffee, listened with apparent interest to their problems and generally treated them with familial warmth and hospitality. Rita labeled this method of sales "attacking nicely":

You have to be nice and talk to the [customers] and make them feel at home before you can sell them a car. It is usually easier to sell a car if you establish rapport. This guy and I got to talking, and he said something about playing the accordion and we established a great rapport because I play the accordion. He still drops in to see me every now and then.

Ladies also attempted to manipulate male management and co-workers through these stereotypical feminine traits. I watched saleswomen sew buttons on managers' and co-workers' shirts, bring them home cooked food, and do clerical chores such as locating cars, or assisting with paperwork. These Ladies were still seen as outsiders, different from the group, and less than equal; but they had become non-threatening, like older sisters or mothers, and they were respected. Mary played big sister:

Salesmen come to me for advice with their love life. They don't treat me like I'm one of the guys. They watch their mouths. They are very careful about talking dirty or swearing or anything like that. They treat me like a lady.

Tough Guys

Some women went directly from Innocents to Tough Guys, where they attempted to adapt the aggressive, competitive male model of sales. Generally these women said they took on this role because they were told to "toughen up or get out." To toughen up means to block feelings. To Tough Guys this was interpreted as being able to handle verbal abuse in order to become "one of the boys." Once Sheila became insensitive toward the use of profanity and sexual innuendos, she was allowed to join the men:

At first I used to break down and cry and show them I was scared or frightened of them. Then they just kept on more. They teased me, called me a 'bimbo' and asked me if it was that time of the month when I got depressed. At home, we never swore; we showed respect. I had to toughen up. Me, I'm just like one of the guys. They use profanity; I do too.

This woman not only accepted harassment; she had been socialized to use it against others. Most Tough Guys worked at high-volume dealerships they labeled "Revolving Door," "Beat 'Em up," and "Slam Dunk 'Em" stores. Generally, women at these agencies had to make enough sales to meet a high quota and were continually worried about being fired. Therefore, they learned to "fight for the door" [grab persons who walk in the door before other salespersons got to them], and pushed hard on these would-be customers, often intimidating them in order to make quick sales. This style of selling resulted in many negative interactions which Tough Guys blamed on customers.

Innocents and Ladies labeled customers too, but Tough Guys were more extreme in their antagonism. Innocents viewed customers as "knowledgeable about cars," but "rude" or "disrespectful." Tough Guys put customers in an "out-group" as "enemies" who needed to be conquered. Respondents described what they did using argot that depicted a wrestling match between themselves and the customer where they "pinned customers down." Tough Guy language became progressively more violent and warlike. Women claimed to "put customers away," and "do 'em in." Carol blamed the customer for causing the dishonesty and animosity in car sales:

Some customers really want our vehicle, but they come here to see if they can rip you off, and they will. They lie about the condition of their trade-ins. They bring a car that they just brought to the repair shop and the mechanic said it was going to cost $700 to fix the damage. That's why they want to trade it in. They lie about their credit ratings, and they say they can get cars at other dealerships for less. The people who come in here can afford bucks. Probably, the more money they have, the harder it is to get it away from them.

Tough Guys valued most what the customer gave them, not what they could do for the customer. Gina defined a "good" customer as one who gave her lots of money, and a " bad" customer as one who tried to bargain:

We have wonderful people like Mr. Smith. What a wonderful guy. He brought his wife with him. She picked out the car. They added every accessory on it imaginable. The first price that I gave him he bought the car at. So the dealership made millions of dollars on it, and I made millions of dollars on it. But other people are always trying to chew you down. They're whiners, complainers. They deserve nothing and wouldn't be happy under any circumstance.

Yet, even when Tough Guys sold at high volume dealerships, blamed the customer for dishonesty in the business, sold more aggressively, and distanced themselves from concern for customer needs, male co-workers felt female Tough Guys were not equal to salesmen in their competitive attitudes. Frank, a manager, said:

The women, they're more laid back. They don't have what it takes, the "killer instinct." People will buy under pressure. They feel intimidated. I have the killer instinct. My first four months I was here every day, 12 hours a day, because I didn't want to miss anything. I wanted to have the most numbers. I just wanted to win. I wanted to be on top, to get every walk-in. Competitiveness. Just about every guy here now has it. They hate to lose.

I found that more than a few of the women informants—Innocents, Ladies, Reformers as well as Tough Guys, had to change their family and social life drastically in order to fit into the male work world and make a living wage. Married and single women had to curtail their social activities. Younger women even lived at home with their parents because they could not find the time to keep up an apartment. Not unexpectedly, divorced women like Fran, who were responsible for the care of young children, had the hardest time dividing their loyalties between work and family:

Before, when I was married, I worked part-time at home doing typing. I was there when Billy came home from school and we did lots of things together. Now, I can only spend Sunday and Wednesday with him. I have no time for myself, and it's hard. I need to help him with homework, do chores like grocery shop and laundry, go to the dentist—things like that. It is very hard.

Yet Tough Guys, even those who found car sales hard work, did not fight for change. They continued to try and fit into the male model of work.

Reformers

Reformers believed that women were intrinsically better at selling than men. They generally began as Ladies who were motivated to change the way work was structured because of how they felt about what they did, and the conflict this brought them. Most Reformers were in conflict over the imposed priorities and resultant interactions between themselves and their customers. They wanted to be more client centered. Many wanted a life style that did not divide work from home so drastically.

Ladies who turned to Reform usually began by distancing themselves from male co-workers. They stopped mothering and nurturing them. Reformers usually continued to relate to customers through the role of Lady. Betty felt that most salesmen were crass, ignorant, and dishonest, and therefore, befriending them was dangerous:

> I am not like salesmen. We [women] are not even in the same business as they are. I am an educated professional. I smile, and am polite to them [male co-workers], but it is best to tell them nothing. They try to steal your customers. They lie to management about you.

Reformers who led Reform were very concerned with building trust. For this reason they were willing to risk effort and time in interactions that might not result in a sale. They spent more time with customers who were not easily sold, might need more time to consider their purchase, or wanted to "kick the tires," leave and perhaps return later. Reformers like Evelyn said patience and understanding bring in referrals because previous customers remember you:

> I come on very soft, and I spend a lot of time with people. If I'm not going to be able to make money, I still treat people nice and spend time with them, because down the road, I might get some business.

Lorber (1984) and Lunneborg (1990) found similar patterns in their studies. Medical women scheduled longer appointments with fewer patients in order to devote more time and energy to answering questions and listening to concerns. And, women stockbrokers spent more time learning about client's particular needs rather than attempting to push them into pre-arranged high-profit packages.

In addition to spending time developing trust, Reformers, more than any other category of saleswomen, fought for the stability needed to develop a work environment which encouraged trust. This was in opposition to the male sales model which defined success as a move to a higher volume and more lucrative dealership or a dealership that sold more expensive cars. Most salesmen moved from dealership to dealership, depending on where the "grass was greener," i.e., what cars were hotter sellers that season, where they thought they could make higher commissions, or where they were promised a contract for salary plus commission. In contrast, Nina managed to remain at her dealership for six years, and defined success in terms of stability, trust, and ongoing customer relationships as well as money gained:

> I have been here six years. Right now I'm not making as much money because the business is slow and the cars aren't selling as well as in the past, but I have repeaters and referrals and I still make a good living. If I move to another place, that place may not do so well in the long run. My boss trusts me, and it is a good place to work.

The concept of "trust" between management and salespersons was seldom found in this field, where upper management sometimes replaced complete sales forces overnight. When Reformers managed to be more stable, distrust was minimized for customers. Clients could expect to get to know their car salespersons and form ongoing trusting relationships concerning service or future dealings, as they do with doctors, dentists, or other tradepersons.

Some Reformers were willing to make less money to find time for family. A few women even fought for and achieved part-time status. Ann was ecstatic:

> After 12 years, I finally got management to let me work part-time. Now I have time for my grandchildren; I can go shopping with my daughter, and see some friends. I have missed doing these things. I have been put on salary so I make less, but I'm doing okay. The owner knows my capabilities, and I have lots of steadies. They're willing to come in when I'm there.

Although Ann became a part-timer in 1990, she was fired six months later. Her boss complained she "did not fit with the team any longer" and had "lost her love for the work." She felt the real story was that "the car business is in a recession," and she was "fully vested" in a retirement program which was costing the dealership too much to keep her. Ann seemed very confused by the owner's singular disloyalty to her after 13 years because she made "good money" for the dealer over a long period of time, and her part-time pay was a relatively small salary of $100 a day. Yet, the mere fact that Reformers were continuing to demand and receive shorter hours, a concession rarely heard of in this field, changed the structure of the workplace and set important precedents.

Retreaters

Early on, many newcomers became disenchanted with car sales because they could find no role that allowed them to adapt to the changes they had to undergo to make a living at this work. Most Retreaters left the field because they felt the customer deserved better treatment—more honesty, lower prices, and less pressure to buy something he or she did not need. Retreaters could not distance themselves from their feelings, and did not "feel good" about what they had to do to build a career in car sales. Leah quit after a year:

> I told my manager I wanted to sell a lot of cars cheaper, and he screamed at me. I would say, "I'll sell a whole bunch for you, but I'm not going to make a whole lot of money on any one of them because I just couldn't do that, because I've got to shop with these people and live with them."

Mary, in the business for six months, was also leaving:

> I don't like the selling aspect of car sales. If you do well and you make your boss happy, you feel sick inside. I have a conscience. I am not the kind of individual who can gain your confidence and respect during the initial transaction of purchasing a car and then when it comes down to the dollars and cents, treat you like I never met you, which is to make the highest profit off of you. 90% of the men in this business have no conscience. When you purchase a car and come back, they'll start hiding. They pretend they don't know you for fear you're coming back to make a complaint, to address something that was not dealt with properly in the first place. I don't like approaching people and having that look come over their faces and having to overcome that objection of, "No, I'm not a crook," and "Yes, I'll sell you a car cheap," knowing I can't because if you sell a car cheap the boss will say, "What are you doing, giving my cars away? Do you want to work here long?"

The sales culture's firmly established response to these self-recriminations was to encourage the salesperson's estrangement from a higher conscience (Prus 1989; Oakes 1990). Saleswomen were told to "toughen up or get out." They were expected to confine their emotions to feeling good about making a lot of money. If women complained to their bosses about their guilty consciences, they suffered negative sanctions. Complaints about having to overcharge or pressure customers resulted in ridicule, taunts, or they were sent home for the day. Such women were told they were weak and could not "make it" in car sales. On the other hand, saleswomen were praised and rewarded for how much over-invoice they could sell a car. A really big sale was talked about throughout the area dealerships and the salesperson became a celebrity. This resulted in a lack of introspection on the part of many salespersons. They stopped reflecting about what they were doing and reasoned that this was the way things should be done in order to keep the dealer in business and to keep their jobs.

Male Roles Compared

Males also take on the Innocent, Tough Guy, Retreater, and even a "Mr. Nice Guy" role, which is comparable to that of the Lady, but my principal observation is that all men who remained in the field eventually became Tough Guys. For these men, this role was not as much of an act as it appeared to be for the women. It is a role representing the behavior expected of salesmen by their peers. It seems to be a natural consequence, in the heat of the sales arena, for men eventually to become hard boiled. Men said that they wanted to be tough.

When men or women enter the field, they are forced into the role of the Innocent. However, none of the men interviewed in this study were without previous sales experience. So the Innocent role for men appears to be transient. Unlike women, who would cultivate the role of innocence, men wanted to shed any such appellation as soon as possible.

The Tough Guy role for men seemed to be something that became part of their personality over time. In contrast, the roles for women often appeared to be masks to hide their true identities and feelings—feelings which were often quite disparate from those they chose to express.

The Retreater men and the Retreater women were quite similar when interviewed. They were people who were unable to feel comfortable meeting management's expectations. One of the men who left car sales went into consumer electronic sales at a bargain center, where the prices were fixed and haggling was absent. He, as did the women, wanted more respect in his sales interactions.

Discussion

Interactions between salespersons and customers are becoming more positive through the moderating effect of women in the sales force. Their continued introspection and gendered values have exerted a subtle but significant influence. Car saleswomen's definition of success seemed to include more factors than mere profit. Quality of life, both at work and in the home, [was] more important to them than mere gain. Reformers defined success to include a stable work environment where trust could be built, and a home life which could include a family. These gendered values, reflected in the classification scheme used in my work, show that sales tactics based on these ethics help women to remain reflective, as well as to build success. The linking between the Reformer and the Lady categories is an argument in favor of the idea that the expression of even stereotypical female behavior may exert a positive influence in improving relations in the workplace.

However, changes that did take place depended upon the strategies adopted by the women, and the philosophy of the dealership where they worked. Often changes were not permanent. Yet, the fact that Reformers were usually top-volume sellers made them enviable examples to men they worked with. They showed men that profit need not be sacrificed in order to obtain other rewards such as job stability, trustful relations with customers, and shorter work hours to accommodate family life. These rewards, often thought to be unobtainable, may lure men to emulate women's examples. Because women are increasingly entering male fields where humaneness in relations has been devalued, their ability to construct role models combining profit-making with concern for others needs future study.

References

Chodorow, Nancy. 1978. *The Reproduction of Mothering.* Berkeley: The University of California Press.

Dinnerstein, Dorothy. 1976. *The Mermaid and the Minotaur: Sexual Arrangements and Human Malaise.* New York: Harper Colophon.

Gilligan, Carol. 1982. *In a Different Voice.* Cambridge: Harvard University Press.

Hughes, Everett C. 1962. "Good People and Dirty Work." *Social Problems* 10:3–11.

Kanter, Rosabeth. 1977. *Men and Women of the Corporation.* New York: Basic Books.

Leidner, Robin. 1991. "Serving Hamburgers and Selling Insurance: Gender, Work, and Identity in Interactive Service Jobs." *Gender and Society* 5:154–177.

Lorber, Judith. 1984. *Women as Physicians: Careers, Status and Power.* New York: Tavistock.

Lunneborg, Patricia. 1990. *Women Changing Work.* New York: Bergin & Garvey.

Mead, George Herbert. 1934. *Mind, Self and Society.* Chicago: University of Chicago Press.

Oakes, Guy. 1990. *The Soul of the Salesman.* New Jersey: Humanities Press International.

Oda, Massami. 1983. "Predicting Sales Performance of Car Salesmen by Personality Traits." *Japanese Journal of Psychology* 54:73–80.

Prus, Robert. 1989. *Pursuing Customers: An Ethnography of Market Activities.* California: Sage.

Rustad, Michael L. 1984. "Female Tokenism in the Volunteer Army." In F. Fisher and C. Sirianni (eds), *Critical Studies in Organization and Bureaucracy.* Philadelphia: Temple University Press.

Turner, R.H. 1990. "Role Change." *Annual Review of Sociology* 16:87–110.

18 Behavior in Pubic Places: The Sociology of the Vaginal Examination

JAMES M. HENSLIN
MAE A. BIGGS

All of us depend on others for the successful completion of the roles we play. In many ways, this makes cooperation the essence of social life (with due apologies to my conflict-theorist friends). Without teamwork, performances fall apart, people become disillusioned, jobs don't get done—and, ultimately, society is threatened. Accordingly, much of our socialization centers on learning to be good team players.

The work setting lends itself well to examining cooperative interaction and to seeing how people develop ways of handling differences—"working arrangements" that defuse threats to fragile social patterns. For example, instructors often accept from students excuses that they know do not match reality. For their part, students often publicly accept what instructors teach, even though they privately disagree with those interpretations. Not only is confrontation unpleasant, and therefore preferable to avoid, but it also is a threat to the continuity of interaction. Thus both instructors and students generally allow one another enough leeway to "get on with business" (which some might say is education, while others—more cynical—might say is the one earning a living and the other a degree).

One can gain much insight into the nature of society by trying to identify the implicit understandings that guide our interactions in everyday life. In this selection, Henslin and Biggs draw on Goffman's dramaturgical framework as they focus on the vaginal examination. Note how much teamwork is required to make the definition stick that nothing sexual is occurring.

GENITAL BEHAVIOR IS PROBLEMATIC for most of us. We are socialized at a very early age into society's dictates concerning the situations, circumstances, and purposes of allowable and unallowable genital exposure.

Our thanks to Erving Goffman for commenting on this paper while it was in manuscript form and for suggesting the title, a play on his book, *Behavior in Public Places*. Because the physicians in this study are men, the pronoun "he" is used.

After a U.S. female has been socialized into her society's expectations regarding the covering and privacy of specified areas of her body, especially her vagina, exposure of her pubic area becomes something that is problematic for her. Even for a woman who has overcome feelings of modesty and perhaps of shame at genital exposure in the presence of her sexual partner, the problem frequently recurs during the vaginal examination. Although her exposure is supposed to be nonsexual, the vaginal examination can be so threatening that for many women it not only punctures their feelings of modesty but it also threatens their self, their feelings of who they are.

Because emotions become associated with the genital area through the learning of meanings and taboos, the vaginal examination is an especially interesting process; it is an elaborately ritualized form of social interaction designed to desexualize the sexual organs. From a sociological point of view, what happens during such interaction? Since a (if not *the*) primary concern of the persons involved is that all the interaction be defined as nonsexual, with even the hint of sexuality to be avoided, what structural restraints on behavior operate? How does the patient cooperate in maintaining this definition of nonsexuality? In what ways are the roles of doctor, nurse, and patient performed such that each contributes to this definition?

This analysis is based on a sample of 12,000 to 14,000 vaginal examinations. Biggs served as an obstetrical nurse in hospital settings and as an office nurse for general practitioners for fourteen years, giving us access to this area of human behavior which ordinarily is not sociologically accessible. Based on these observations, we have divided the interaction of the vaginal examination into five major scenes. Let's examine what occurs as each of these scenes unfolds.

The setting for the vaginal examination may be divided into two areas (see Figure 18.1). Although there are no physical boundaries that demarcate the two areas, highly specific and ritualized interaction occurs in each. Area 1, where Scenes I and V are played, includes that portion of the "office-examination" room which is furnished with a desk and three chairs. Area 2, where Scenes II, III, and IV take place, contains an examination table, a swivel stool, a gooseneck lamp, a table for instruments, and a sink with a mirror above it.

Scene I: The Personalized Stage: The Patient as Person

The interaction flow of Scene I is as follows: (a) the doctor enters the "office-examination" room; (b) greets the patient; (c) sits down; (d) asks the patient why she is there; (e) questions her on specifics; (f) decides on a course of action, specifically whether a pelvic examination is needed or not; (g) if he thinks a pelvic is needed, he signals the nurse on the intercom and says, "I want a pelvic in room (X)"; (h) he gets up, and (i) leaves the room.

During this scene, the patient is treated as a full person; that is, the

AREA 1
Patient as Person
(Scenes I and V)

AREA 2
Patient as Pelvic
Transitional Area of Depersonalization and
Repersonalization (Scenes II, III, IV)

Figure 18.1   The Doctor's Office—Examination Room

courtesies of middle-class conversation are followed, and, in addition to gathering medical information, if the doctor knows the patient well he may intersperse his medical queries with questions about her personal life. The following interaction that occurred during Scene I demonstrates the doctor's treatment of his patient as a full person:

> DOCTOR (upon entering the room): Hello, Joyce, I hear you're going to Southern Illinois University.
>
> PATIENT: Yes, I am. I've been accepted, and I have to have my health record completed.

The doctor then seated himself at his desk and began filling out the health record that the patient gave him. He interspersed his questions concerning the record form with questions about the patient's teaching, about the area of study she was pursuing, about her children, their health and their schooling. He then said, "Well, we have to do this right. We'll do a pelvic on you." He then announced via the intercom, "I want to do a pelvic on Joyce in room 1." At that point he left the room.

This interaction sequence is typical of the interaction that occurs in Scene I between a doctor and a patient he knows well. When the doctor does not know the patient well, he does not include his patient's name, either her first or last name, in his announcement to the nurse that she should come into the room. In such a case, he simply says, "I want to do a pelvic in room 1," or, "Pelvic in room 1." The doctor then leaves the room, marking the end of the scene.

Scene II: The Depersonalized Stage: Transition from Person to Pelvic

When at the close of Scene I the doctor says, "Pelvic in room (X)," he is in effect announcing the transition of the person to a pelvic. It is a sort of advance announcement, however, of a coming event, because the transition has not yet been effected. The doctor's signal for the nurse to come in is, in fact, a signal that the nurse should now help the patient make the transition from a person to a pelvic. Additionally, it also serves as an announcement to the patient that she is about to undergo this metamorphosis.

The interaction flow which accomplishes the transition from person to pelvic is as follows: Upon entering the room, the nurse, without preliminaries, tells the patient, "The doctor wants to do a vaginal examination on you. Will you please remove your panties?" While the patient is undressing, the nurse prepares the props. She positions the stirrups of the examination table and arranges the glove, the lubricant, and the speculum (the instrument which, when inserted into the vagina, allows visual examination of the vaginal tract). She then removes the drape sheet from a drawer and directs the patient onto the table, covers the patient with the drape sheet, assists her in placing her feet into the stirrups, and positions her hips, putting her into the lithotomy position (lying on her back with knees flexed and out).

MEANING OF THE DOCTOR'S ABSENCE

The doctor's exiting just before this scene means that the patient will be undressing in his absence. This is not accidental. In many cases, the doctor may leave because another patient is waiting, but even if there are no waiting patients, the doctor always exits at the end of Scene I. His leaving means that he will not witness the patient undressing, thereby successfully removing any suggestion that a striptease is being performed, or that he is acting as a voyeur. From the patient's point of view, this greatly reduces embarrassment and other problems that would occur if she were to undress in front of the doctor. When the doctor returns, only a particularized portion of the woman's body will be exposed for the ensuing interaction. As we shall see, at that point the doctor is no longer dealing with a person, but he is, rather, confronted by a "pelvic."

THE PROBLEM OF UNDERCLOTHING

Undressing and nudity are problematic for the patient since she has been socialized into not undressing before strangers.[1] Almost without exception, when the woman undresses in Scene II, she turns away from the nurse and the door, even though the door is closed. She removes only her panties in the typical case, but a small number of patients also remove their shoes.

After the patient has removed her panties and/or girdle, she faces the problem of what to do with them. Panties and girdles do not have the same meaning as other items of clothing, such as a sweater, that can be casually draped around the body or strewn on furniture. Clothing is considered to be an extension of the self (Gross and Stone 1964), and clothing often comes to represent the particular part of the body that it covers. In this case, this means that panties represent to women their "private area." Comments made by patients that illustrate the problematics of panty exposure include: "The doctor doesn't want to look at these," "I want to get rid of these before he comes in," and, "I don't want the doctor to see these old things."

Some patients seem to be at a loss in solving this problem and turn to the nurse for guidance, asking her directly what they should do with their underclothing. Most patients, however, do not ask for directions, but hide their panties in some way. The favorite hiding or covering seems to be in or under the purse.[2] Other women put their panties in the pocket of their coat or in the folds of a coat or sweater, some cover them with a magazine, and some cover them with their own body on the examination table. It is rare that a woman leaves her panties exposed somewhere in the room.[3]

THE DRAPE SHEET

Another problematic area in the vaginal examination is what being undressed can signify. Disrobing for others frequently indicates preparation for sexual relations. Since sexuality is the very thing that this scene is oriented toward removing, a mechanism is put into effect to eliminate sexuality—the drape sheet. After the patient is seated on the table, the nurse places a drape sheet from just below her breasts (she still has her blouse on) to over her legs. Although the patient is draped by the sheet, when she is positioned on the table with her legs in the stirrups, her pubic region is exposed. Usually it is not necessary for the doctor even to raise a fold in the sheet in order to examine her genitals.

Since the drape sheet does not cover the genital area, but, rather, leaves it exposed, what is its purpose? The drape sheet depersonalizes the patient. It sets the pubic area apart, letting the doctor view the pubic area in isolation, separating the pubic area from the person. The pubic area or female genitalia becomes an object isolated from the rest of the body. Because of the drape sheet, the doctor, in his position on the low stool, does not see the patient's face. He no longer sees or needs to deal with a person, just the exposed genitalia marked off by the drape sheet. Yet, from the patient's point of view in her supine position, her genitals are covered! When *she* looks down at her body, she does not see exposed genitalia. The drape sheet effectively hides her pubic area *from herself* while exposing it to the doctor.

THIGH BEHAVIOR

U.S. girls are given early and continued socialization in "limb discipline," being taught at a very early age to keep their legs close together while they are sitting or while they are retrieving articles from the ground. They receive such instructions from their mothers as, "Keep your dress down," "Put your legs together," and "Nice girls don't let their panties show." Evidence of socialization into "acceptable" thigh behavior shows up in the vaginal examination while the women are positioned on the examination table and waiting for the doctor to arrive. They do not let their thighs fall outwards in a relaxed position, but they try to hold their upper or mid-thighs together until the doctor arrives. They do this even in cases where it is very difficult for them to do so, such as when the patient is in her late months of pregnancy.

Although the scene has been carefully orchestrated to desexualize the ensuing interaction, and although the patient is being depersonalized such that when the doctor returns he primarily has a pelvic to deal with and not a person, at this point in the interaction sequence the patient's "proper" thigh behavior shows that she is still holding onto her sexuality and "personality." Only later, when the doctor reenters the scene, will she fully consent to the desexualized and depersonalized role and let her thighs fall outwards.

After the props are ready and the patient is positioned, the nurse announces to the doctor via intercom that the stage is set for the third scene, saying, "We're ready in room (X)."

Scene III: The Depersonalized Stage: The Person as Pelvic

FACE-TO-PUBIC INTERACTION

The interaction to this point, as well as the use of props, has been structured to project a singular definition of the situation—that of legitimate doctor–patient interaction and, specifically, the nonsexual examination of a woman's vaginal region by a man. To support this definition, team performance is vital (Goffman 1959: 104). Although the previous interaction has been part of an ongoing team performance, it has been sequential, leading to the peak of the performance, the vaginal examination itself. At this time, the team goes into a tandem cooperative act, utilizing its resources to maintain the legitimation of the examination. The combined performance reinforces the specific role of each team member. The doctor, while standing, places a plastic glove on his right hand, again symbolizing the depersonalized nature of the action: By using the glove, he is saying that he will not himself be actually touching the "private area," that the glove will serve as an insulator.[4] It is at this point that he directs related questions to the patient regarding such things as her bowels or bladder. Then, while he is still in this standing position, the nurse in synchronization actively joins the performance by squeezing a lubricant onto his outstretched gloved fingers, and the doctor inserts the index and middle fingers of his right hand into the patient's vagina while externally palpating (feeling) the uterus. He then withdraws his fingers from the vagina, seats himself on the stool, inserts a speculum, and while the nurse positions the gooseneck lamp behind him, he visually examines the cervix.

Prior to this third scene, the interaction has been dyadic only, consisting of nurse and patient in Scene II and doctor and patient in Scene I. In this scene, however, the interaction becomes triadic, with the doctor, nurse, and patient simultaneously involved in the performance. The term triadic, however, does not even come close to accurately describing the role-playing of this scene. Since the patient has essentially undergone a metamorphosis from a person to an object—having been objectified or depersonalized—the focus of the interaction is now on a specific part of her body. The positioning of her legs, the use of the drape sheet, the shining of the light, and the doctor's location on the stool have made the patient's pubic region the focus of interaction. This location of actors and arrangement and use of props also blocks out the "talklines" between the doctor and patient, physically obstructing their exchange of glances (Goffman 1963: 161). Interaction between the doctor and the patient is no longer "face-to-face," being perhaps now more accurately described as "face-to-pubic" interaction.

BREASTS AS NONSEXUAL OBJECTS

To project and maintain the definition of nonsexuality in the vaginal examination also requires the desexualization of other parts of the body that are attributed to have sexual meaning in our culture, specifically the breasts. When the breasts are to be examined in conjunction with a vaginal examination, a rather interesting ritual is employed. The goal of this ritual—like that of the vaginal ritual—is to objectify the breasts by isolating them from the rest of the body, permitting the doctor to see the breasts apart from the person. In this ritual, after the patient has removed her upper clothing, a towel is placed across her breasts, and the drape sheet is then placed on top of the towel. Since the towel in and of itself more than sufficiently covers the breasts, we can only conclude that the purpose of the drape sheet is to enhance the definition of nonsexual interaction. Additionally, the doctor first removes the sheet from the breasts and exposes the towel. He then lifts the towel from *one* breast, makes his examination, and *replaces* the towel over that breast. He then examines the other breast in exactly the same way, again replacing the towel after the examination.

THE NURSE AS CHAPERONE

That the interaction in Scene III is triadic is not accidental, nor is it instrumentally necessary. It is, rather, designed to help desexualize the vaginal examination. Instrumentally, the nurse functions merely to lubricate the doctor's fingers and to hand him the speculum. He obviously could do these things himself. It becomes apparent, then, that doing these things is not the purpose of the nurse's presence, that she plays an entirely different role in this scene. That role is chaperone, the person assigned to be present when an umarried man and woman come together in order to give assurance to interested persons that no sexual acts take place. Although the patient has been depersonalized, or at least this is the definition that the team has been attempting to project and maintain, the possibility exists that the vaginal examination can erupt into a sexual scene. Because of this possibility (or the potential accusation that sexual behavior has taken place), the nurse is always present.[5] Interestingly, with contemporary sexual mores so vastly different from those of a century ago, this medical setting is one of the few remaining examples of the chaperone in our society. It is a significant role, for it helps the performance to be initiated and to continue smoothly to its logical conclusion.

THE PATIENT AS A NONPERSON TEAM MEMBER

With this definition of objectification and desexualization, the patient represents a vagina disassociated from a person. She has been dramaturgically transformed for the duration of this scene into a nonperson (Goffman 1959:152).[6] This means that while he is seated and performing the vaginal examination, the doctor need not interact with the patient as a person; he no longer needs to carry on a conversation nor to maintain eye contact with her. Furthermore, this means that he now is permitted to carry on a "side conversation" with the person with whom he does maintain eye contact, his nurse. For example, during one examination the doctor looked up at the nurse and said: "Hank and I really caught some good-sized fish while we were on vacation. He really enjoyed himself." He then looked at his "work" and announced, "Cervix looks good; no inflammation—everything appears fine down here." Ordinarily, for middle-class interactions such ignoring of the presence of a third person would constitute a breach of etiquette, but *in this case there really isn't a third person present.* The patient has been "depersonalized," to such an extent that the rules of conversation have changed, and no breach of etiquette has taken place.[7]

Although she has been defined as an object, the patient is actually the third member of the team. Her assignment is to "play the role of an object"; that is, she contributes to the flow of the interaction by acting as an object and not as a person. Through studied alienation from the interaction, she demonstrates what is known as dramaturgical discipline (Goffman 1959:216–18). She studiously gazes at the ceiling or wall, only occasionally allowing herself the luxury (or is it the danger?) of fleeting eye contact with the nurse. Eye contact with the doctor, of course, is prevented by the position of her legs and the drape sheet.

After the doctor tells the patient to get dressed, he leaves the room, and the fourth scene is ready to unfold.

Scene IV: The Repersonalizing Stage: The Transition from Pelvic to Person

During this stage of the interaction the patient undergoes a demetamorphosis, dramaturgically changing from vaginal object to person. Immediately after the doctor leaves, the nurse assists the patient into a sitting position, and she gets off the table. The nurse then asks the patient if she would like to use a towel to cleanse her genital area, and about 80 percent of the patients accept the offer. In this scene, it is not uncommon for patients to make some statement concerning their relief that the examination is over. Statements such as "I'm glad that's over with" seem to indicate the patient's overt recognition of the changing scene, to acknowledge that she is now entering a different phase of the drama.

During this repersonalizing stage, the patient is concerned with regrooming and recostuming. Patients frequently ask if they look all right, and the common question "My dress isn't too wrinkled, is it?" appears to indicate the patient's awareness of and desire to be ready for the resumption of roles other than vaginal object. Her dress isn't too wrinkled for what? It must be that she is asking whether it is too wrinkled for (1) her resumption of the role of (patient as) person and (2) her resumption of nonpatient roles.

Modesty continues to operate during this scene, and it is interesting that patients who have just had their genital area thoroughly examined both visually and tactually by the doctor are concerned that this same man will see their underclothing. ("He won't be in before I get my underwear on, will he?") They are now desiring and preparing for the return to the feminine role. They apparently fear that the doctor will reenter the room as they literally have one foot in and one foot out of their panties. They want to have their personal front reestablished to their own satisfaction before the return of this man and the onset of the next scene. For this, they strive for the poise and composure that they deem fitting the person role for which they are now preparing, frequently using either their own pocket-mirror or the mirror above the sink to check their personal front.

During this transitional role, patients indicate by their comments to the nurse that they are to again be treated as persons. While they are dressing, they frequently speak about their medical problems, their aches and pains, their fight against gaining weight, or feelings about their pregnancy. In such ways they are reasserting the self and are indicating that they are again entering "personhood."

The patient who best illustrates awareness that she had undergone a process of repersonalization is the woman who, after putting on her panties, said, "There! Just like new again." She had indeed moved out of her temporary and uncomfortable role as object, and her reappearance as person matched her self-concept.

After the patient has recostumed and regroomed, the nurse directs the patient to a chair alongside the doctor's desk. She then announces via intercom to the doctor, "The patient is dressed," or, "The patient is waiting." It is significant that at this point the woman is referred to as "patient" in the announcement to the doctor and not as "pelvic" as she was at the end of the second scene. Sometimes the patient is also referred to by name in this announcement. The patient has completed her demetamorphosis at this point, and the nurse, by the way she refers to her, is officially announcing the transition.

The nurse then leaves the room, and her interaction with the patient ceases.

Scene V: The Repersonalized Stage: The Patient as Person Once Again

When the doctor makes his third entrance, the patient has again resumed the role of person and is interacted with on this basis. The doctor makes eye contact with her, speaks to her, and listens to her. During this fifth scene, the patient's whole personal front is visible. The doctor informs the patient of the results of her examination, he may prescribe medications, and, wherever indicated, he suggests further care. He also tells the patient whether or not she need see him again.

For us, the significance of the interaction of Scene V is that the patient is again allowed to interact *as a person within the role of patient*. The doctor allows room for questions that the patient might have about the results of the examination, and he also gives her the opportunity to ask about other medical problems that she might be experiencing.

Interaction between the doctor and patient terminates as the doctor gets up from his chair and moves toward the door.

Conclusion: Desexualization of the Sacred

In concluding this analysis, we shall briefly indicate that conceptualizing the vagina as a sacred object yields a perspective that appears to be of value in analyzing the vaginal examination. Sacred objects are surrounded by rules protecting the object from being profaned, rules governing who may approach the "sacred," under what circumstances it may be approached, and what may and may not be done during such an approach (Durkheim 1965:51–59). If these rules are followed, the "sacred" will lose none of its "sacredness," but if they are violated, the sacred will be profaned.

Apart from the husband and significant others,[8] except in a medical setting and by the actors about whom we are speaking, no one else may approach the vagina other than the self and still have it retain its sacred character.[9] Because of this, the medical profession has taken great pains to establish a dramaturgical ritual that will ensure the continued sacredness of the vaginas of its female patients, one that will avoid even the imputation of taboo violation. Accordingly, as we have herein analyzed, by dramaturgically desexualizing the vagina by dissociating it from the person, and by elaborately defining it as just another organ of the body, this ritual of the vaginal examination allows the doctor to approach the sacred without profaning it or violating taboos. The vaginal examination is a fascinating example of how reality is socially constructed, in this instance of how physicians are able to handle a woman's vagina and yet maintain a definition of nonsexuality.

Notes

1. With a society that is as clothing and bodily conscious as is ours, undressing and nudity are problematic for many, but perhaps more for females than for males since males are more likely to experience structured situations in which they undress and are nude before others, such as showering after high school physical education classes, while females in the same situation are often afforded a greater degree of privacy with, for example, private shower stalls in place of the mass showers of the males. This is not always the case, however, and Theresa France (private communication) reports that in her classes the girls also had communal showers.

2. From a psychiatric orientation this association of the panties with the purse is fascinating, given the Freudian interpretation that the purse signifies the female genitalia.

3. In some examination rooms, the problem of where to put the undergarments is solved by the provision of a special drawer for them located beneath the examination table.

4. It is true, of course, that the glove also serves instrumental purposes, such as protecting the physician from diseases that might be transmitted by means of digital–vaginal contact—and patients from diseases the physician might transmit from one patient to another.

5. It is interesting to note that even the corpse of a female is defined as being in need of such chaperonage. Erving Goffman, on reading this paper in manuscript form, commented that hospital etiquette dictates that "when a male attendant moves a female stiff from the room to the morgue he be accompanied by a female nurse."

6. Compare what Goffman (1959:104) has to say about secrets shared by team members. Remember that the patient in this interaction is not simply a member of the audience. She is also a team member, vitally interested in projecting and maintaining the definition of nonsexuality. Another reader of this paper, who wishes to remain anonymous, reports that during one of her pregnancies she had a handsome, young, and unmarried Hungarian doctor and that during vaginal examinations with him she would "concentrate on the instruments being used and the uncomfortableness of the situation" so as not to become sexually aroused.

7. While "playing the role" of an object, the patient is still able to hear verbal exchange, of course, and she could enter the interaction if she so desired. As such, side comments between doctor and nurse must be limited. In certain other doctor-patient situations, however, the patient completely leaves the "person role," such as when the patient is anesthetized, which allows much freer banter among medical personnel. In delivery rooms of hospitals, for example, it is not uncommon for the obstetrician to comment while stitching the episiotomy, "She's like a new bride now," or, when putting in the final stitch, to say, "This is for the old man." Additionally, while medical students are stitching their first episiotomy, instructing doctors have been known to say, "It's not tight enough. Put one more in for the husband."

8. While consensual approaches by boyfriends certainly run less risk of violating the sacred than at earlier periods in our history, this depends a good deal on the individual's religion and age.

9. It is perhaps for this reason that prostitutes ordinarily lack respect: They have profaned the sacred. And in doing so, not only have they failed to limit vaginal access to culturally prescribed individuals, but they have added further violation by allowing vaginal access on a monetary basis. They have, in effect, sold the sacred.

References

Durkheim, Emile (1965). *The Elementary Forms of the Religious Life.* New York: The Free Press (1915 copyright by George Allen & Unwin Ltd.).

Goffman, Erving (1959). *The Presentation of Self in Everyday Life.* Garden City, NY: Doubleday Anchor Books.

Goffman, Erving (1963). *Behavior in Public Places: Notes on the Social Organization of Gatherings.* New York: The Free Press.

Gross, Edward, and Gregory Stone (1964). "Embarrassment and the Analysis of Role Requirements," *American Journal of Sociology* 70: 1–15.

19 Diary of a Homeless Man

JOHN R. COLEMAN

Can you imagine yourself being without a home? Think of what it must be like not to have a house or apartment, not to have your own room or even one you must share with a sibling. No living room with television, no kitchen with a refrigerator you can "raid" whenever you want. Night falls, and you don't know where you'll sleep. Day breaks, and you have no place to go, nothing to do—and no one who cares.

Such is life for some people in our society—the discards of the advanced technological society, those who have been left behind in our culturally mandated frantic pursuit after material wealth. Like others, Coleman, the president of a small, private college, had seen these strange people on the streets of the city. Like others, he wondered what their life was like. But unlike most others, he decided to find out first hand—by directly experiencing their world. He left his comfortable, upper–middle-class home and joined the street people. This is his engrossing account of that experience.

Wednesday, 1/19

SOMEHOW, 12 DEGREES at 6 A.M. was colder than I had counted on. I think of myself as relatively immune to cold, but standing on a deserted sidewalk outside Penn Station with the thought of ten days ahead of me as a homeless man, the immunity vanished. When I pulled my collar closer and my watch cap lower, it wasn't to look the part of a street person; it was to keep the wind out.

My wardrobe wasn't much help. I had bought my "new" clothes—flannel shirt, baggy sweater, torn trousers, the cap and the coat—the day before on Houston Street for $19. "You don't need to buy shoes," the shop-keeper had said. "The ones you have on will pass for a bum's." I was hurt; they were shoes I often wore to the office.

Having changed out of my normal clothes in the Penn Station men's room and stowed them in a locker, I was ready for the street. Or thought so.

Was I imagining it, or were people looking at me in a completely different way? I felt that men, especially the successful-looking ones in their forties and over, saw me and wondered. For the rest, I wasn't there.

At Seventh Avenue and 35th Street, I went into a coffee shop. The counterman looked me over carefully. When I ordered the breakfast special—99 cents plus tax—he told me I'd have to pay in advance. I did (I'd brought $40 to see me through the ten days), but I noticed that the other customers were given checks, and paid only when they left.

By 9:30, I had read a copy of the *Times* retrieved from a trash basket; I had walked most of the streets around the station; I had watched the construction at the new convention center. There was little else to do.

Later, I sat and watched the drug sales going on in Union Square. Then I went into the Income Maintenance Center on 14th Street and watched the people moving through the welfare lines. I counted the trucks on Houston Street.

I vaguely remembered a quote to the effect that "idleness is only enjoyable when you have a lot to do." It would help to be warm, too.

There was ample time and incentive to stare at the other homeless folk on the street. For the most part, they weren't more interesting than the typical faces on Wall Street or upper Madison Avenue. But the extreme cases caught and held the eye. On Ninth Avenue, there was a man on the sidewalk directing an imaginary (to me) flow of traffic. And another, two blocks away, tracing the flight of planes or birds—or spirits—in the winter sky. And there was a woman with gloves tied to her otherwise bare feet.

Standing outside the Port Authority Bus Terminal was a man named Howard. He was perhaps my age, but the seasons had left deeper marks on his face. "Come summertime, it's all going to be different," he told me. "I'm going to have a car to go to the beach. And I'm going to get six lemons and make me a jug of ice-cold lemonade to go with the car.

"This whole country's gone too far with the idea of one person being at the top. It starts with birthday parties. Who gets to blow out the candle? One person. And it takes off from there. If we're ever going to make things better, we gotta start with those candles."

Was there any chance of people like us finding work?

"Jobs are still out there for the young guys who want them," Howard said. "But there's nothing for us. Never again. No, I stopped dreaming about jobs a long time ago. Now I dream about cars. And lemonade."

Drugs and alcohol are common among the homeless. The damage done by them was evident in almost every street person I saw. But which was cause, and which was effect? Does it matter, once this much harm has been done?

My wanderings were all aimless. There was no plan, no goal, no reason to be anywhere at any time. Only hours into this role, I felt a useless part of the city streets. I wasn't even sure why I was doing this. . . .

A weathered drifter told me about a hideaway down in the bowels of the station, where it was warm and quiet. I found my way there and lay down on some old newspapers to sleep.

How long did I sleep? It didn't seem long at all. I was awakened by a flashlight shining in my eyes, and a voice, not an unkind one, saying, "You can't sleep here. Sorry, but you have to go outside."

I hadn't expected to hear that word "sorry." It was touching.

I left and walked up to 47th Street, between Fifth and Madison Avenues, where I knew there was a warm grate in the sidewalk. (I've been passing it every morning for over five years on my way to work.) One man was asleep there already. But there was room for two, and he moved over.

Thursday, 1/20

When you're spending the night on the street, you learn to know morning is coming by the kinds of trucks that roll by. As soon as there are other than garbage trucks—say, milk or bread trucks—you know the night will soon be over.

I went back to Penn Station to clean up in the washroom. The care with which some of the other men with me bathed themselves at the basins would have impressed any public-health officer. And I couldn't guess from the appearance of their clothes who would be the most fastidious.

I bought coffee and settled back to enjoy it out of the main traffic paths in the station. No luck. A cop found me and told me to take it to the street.

After breakfast ($1.31 at Blimpie), I walked around to keep warm until the public library opened. I saw in a salvaged copy of the *Times* that we had just had our coldest night of the year, well below zero with the windchill factor, and that a record 4,635 people had sought shelter in the city's hostels.

The library was a joy. The people there treated me the same as they might have had I been wearing my business suit. To pass the time, I got out the city's welfare reports for 50 years ago. In the winter of 1933, the city had 4,524 beds available for the homeless, and all were said to be filled every night. The parallel to 1983 was uncanny. But, according to the reports, the man in charge of the homeless program in 1933, one Joseph A. Manning, wasn't worried about the future. True, the country was in the midst of a depression. But there had been a slight downturn in the numbers served in the shelters in the two months immediately preceding his report. This meant, wrote Manning, that "the depression, in the parlance of the ring, is K.O.'d."

Already, I notice changes in me. I walk much more slowly. I no longer see a need to beat a traffic light or to be the first through a revolving door. Force of habit still makes me look at my wrist every once in a while. But there's no watch there, and it wouldn't make any difference if there were. The thermometer has become much more important to me now than any timepiece could be. . . .

The temperature rose during the day. Just as the newspaper headlines seem to change more slowly when you're on the streets all day long, so the temperature seems to change more rapidly and tellingly.

At about 9 P.M., I went back to the heated grate on 47th Street. The man who had been there last night was already in place. He made it clear that there was again room for me.

I asked him how long he had been on the streets.

"Eleven years, going on twelve," he said.

"This is only my second night."

"You may not stick it out. This isn't for every man."

"Do you ever go into the shelters?"

"I couldn't take that. I prefer this anytime."

Friday, 1/21

When I left my grate mate—long before dawn—he wished me a good day. I returned the gesture. He meant his, and I meant mine.

In Manhattan's earliest hours, you get the feeling that the manufacture and removal of garbage is the city's main industry. So far, I haven't been lucky or observant enough to rescue much of use from the mounds of trash waiting for the trucks and crews. The best find was a canvas bag that will fit nicely over my feet at night.

I'm slipping into a routine: Washing up at the station. Coffee on the street. Breakfast at Blimpie. A search for the *Times* in the trash baskets. And then a leisurely stretch of reading in the park.

Some days bring more luck than others. Today I found 20 cents in a pay-phone slot and heard a young flutist playing the music of C.P.E. Bach on Sixth Avenue between 9th and 10th streets. A lot of people ignored her, even stepped over her flute case as if it were litter on the sidewalk. More often than not, those who put money in the case looked embarrassed. They seemed to be saying, "Don't let anyone see me being appreciative."

By nightfall, the streets were cruelly cold once again. . . .

I headed for the 47th Street grate again but found my mate gone. There was no heat coming up through it. Do they turn it off on Friday nights? Don't we homeless have any rights?

On the northwest corner of Eighth Avenue and 33rd Street, there was a blocked-off subway entrance undergoing repair. I curled up against the wall there under some cardboard sheets. Rain began to fall, but I stayed reasonably dry and was able to get to sleep.

At some point, I was awakened by a man who had pulled back the upper piece of cardboard.

"You see my partner here. You need to give us some money."

I was still half-asleep. "I don't have any."

"You must have something, man."

"Would I be sleeping here in the rain if I did?"

His partner intervened. "C'mon. Leave the old bastard alone. He's not worth it."

"He's got something. Get up and give it to us."

I climbed to my feet and began fumbling in my pocket. Both men were on my left side. That was my chance. Suddenly I took off and ran along 33rd Street toward Ninth Avenue. They gave no chase. And a good thing, too, because I was too stiff with cold to run a good race.

Saturday, 1/22

A man I squatted next to in a doorway on 29th Street said it all: "The onliest thing is to have a warm place to sleep. That and having somebody care about you. That'd be even onlier."

He had what appeared to be rolls of paper toweling wrapped around one leg and tied with red ribbon. But the paper, wet with rain by now, didn't seem to serve any purpose.

I slept little. The forecast was for more rain tomorrow, so why wish the night away?

The morning paper carried news of Mayor Koch's increased concern about the homeless.

But what can he do? He must worry that the more New York does to help, the greater the numbers will grow. At the moment he's berating the synagogues for not doing anything to take street people in.

Watching people come and go at the Volvo tennis tournament at Madison Square Garden, I sensed how uncomfortable they were at the presence of the homeless. Easy to love in the abstract, not so easy face to face.

It's no wonder that the railway police are under orders to chase us out of sight.

Perhaps a saving factor is that we're not individuals. We're not people anybody knows. So far I've had eye contact with only three people who know me in my other life. None showed a hint of recognition. One was the senior auditor at Arthur Andersen & Company, the accounting firm that handles the Clark Foundation, my employer. One was a fellow lieutenant in the Auxiliary Police Force, a man with whom I had trained for many weeks. And one was an owner in the cooperative apartment where I live. . . .

Early in the evening I fell asleep on the Seventh Avenue steps outside the Garden. Three Amtrak cops shook me awake to ask if two rather good-looking suitcases on the steps were mine. I said that I had never seen them.

One cop insisted that I was lying, but then a black man appeared and said they belonged to a friend of his. The rapid-fire questioning from two of the cops soon made that alibi rather unlikely. The third cop was going through the cases and spreading a few of the joints he found inside on the ground.

As suddenly as it had begun, the incident was over. The cops walked away, and the man retrieved the bags. I fell back to sleep. Some hours later when I woke up again, the black man was still there, selling.

Sunday, 1/23

A new discovery of a warm and dry, even scenic, place to sit on a rainy day: the Staten Island Ferry.

For one 25-cent fare, I had four crossings of the harbor, read all I wanted of the copy of the Sunday *Times* I'd found, and finished the crossword puzzle.

When I got back to the Garden, where the tennis tournament was in its last hours, I found the police were being extra diligent in clearing us away from the departing crowds. One older woman was particularly incensed at being moved. "You're ruining my sex life," she shouted. "That's what you're doing. My sex life. Do you hear?"

A younger woman approached me to ask if I was looking for love. "No, ma'am. I'm just trying to stay out of the rain." . . .

So, back to the unused subway entrance, because there was still no heat across town on the 47th Street grate.

The night was very cold. Parts of me ached as I tried to sleep. Turning over was a chore, not only because the partially wet cardboard had to be re-arranged with such care, but also because the stiffer parts of my body seemed to belong to someone else. Whatever magic there was in those lights cutting down through the fog was gone by now. All I wanted was to be warm and dry once more. Magic could wait.

Monday, 1/24

Early this morning I went to the warren of employment agencies on 14th Street to see if I could get a day's work. There was very little action at most of these last-ditch offices, where minimum wages and sub-minimum conditions are the rule.

But I did get one interview and thought I had a dishwashing job lined up. I'd forgotten one thing. I had no identification with me. No identification, no job.

There was an ageless, shaggy woman in Bryant Park this morning who delivered one of the more interesting monologues I've heard. For a full ten minutes, with no interruption from me beyond an occasional "Uh huh," she analyzed society's ills without missing a beat.

Beginning with a complaint about the women's and men's toilets in the park being locked ("What's a poor body to do?"), she launched into the strengths of the Irish, who, though strong, still need toilets more than others, and the weaknesses of the English and the Jews, the advantages of raising turkeys over other fowl, and the wickedness of Eleanor Roosevelt in letting the now Queen Mother and that stuttering king of hers rave so much about the hot dogs served at Hyde Park that we had no alternative but to enter World War II on their side. The faulty Russian satellite that fell into the Indian Ocean this morning was another example of shenanigans, she said. It turns out the Russians and Lady Diana, "that so-called Princess of Wales," are in cahoots to keep us so alarmed about such things far away from home that we don't get anything done about prayer in schools or the rest of it. But after all, what would those poor Protestant ministers do for a living if the children got some real religion in school, like the kind we got from the nuns, God bless them?

That at least was the gist of what she said. I know I've missed some of the finer points.

At 3:30 P.M., with more cold ahead, I sought out the Men's Shelter at 8 East 3rd Street. This is the principal entry point for men seeking the city's help. It provides meals for 1,300 or so people every day and beds for some few of those. I had been told that while there was no likelihood of getting a bed in this building I'd be given a meal here and a bed in some other shelter.

I've seen plenty of drawings of London's workhouses and asylums in the times of Charles Dickens. Now I've seen the real thing, in the last years of the twentieth century in the world's greatest city.

The lobby and the adjacent "sitting room" were jammed with men standing, sitting, or stretched out in various positions on the floor. It was as lost a collection of souls as I could have imagined. Old and young, scarred and smooth, stinking and clean, crippled and hale, drunk and sober, ranting and still, parts of another world and parts of this one. The city promises to take in anyone who asks. Those rejected everywhere else find their way to East 3rd Street.

The air was heavy with the odors of Thunderbird wine, urine, sweat, and, above all, nicotine and marijuana. Three or four Human Resources Administration police officers seemed to be keeping the violence down to tolerable levels, but barely so.

After a long delay, I got a meal ticket for dinner and was told to come back later for a lodging ticket.

It was time to get in line to eat. This meant crowding into what I can only compare to a cattle chute in a stockyard. It ran along two walls of the sitting room and was already jammed. A man with a bullhorn kept yelling at us to stand up and stay in line. One very old and decrepit (or drunk?) man couldn't stay on his feet. He was helped to a chair, from which he promptly fell onto the floor. The bullhorn man had some choice obscenities for him, but they didn't seem to have any effect. The old man just lay there; and we turned our thoughts back to the evening meal.

I made a quick, and probably grossly unfair, assessment of the hundreds of men I could see in the room. Judging them solely by appearance, alertness, and body movements, I decided that one-quarter of them were perfectly able to work; they, more likely than not, were among the warriors who helped us win the battle against inflation by the selfless act of joining the jobless ranks. Another quarter might be brought back in time into job-readiness by some counseling and some caring for them as individuals. But the other half seemed so ravaged by illness, addiction, and sheer neglect that I couldn't imagine them being anything but society's wards from here on out to—one hopes—a peaceful end.

At the appointed hour, we were released in groups of twenty or thirty to descend the dark, filthy steps to the basement eating area. The man with the bullhorn was there again, clearly in charge and clearly relishing the extra power given to his voice by electric amplification. He insulted us collectively and separately without pause, but because his vocabulary was limited it tended to be the same four-letter words over and over.

His loudest attack on me came when I didn't move fast enough to pick up my meal from the counter. His analysis of certain flaws in my white ancestry wasn't hard to follow, even for a man in as much of a daze as I was.

The shouting and the obscenities didn't stop once we had our food. Again and again we were told to finish and get out. Eating took perhaps six minutes, but those minutes removed any shred of dignity a man might have brought in with him from the street.

Back upstairs, the people in charge were organizing the people who were to go to a shelter in Brooklyn. Few had volunteered, so there was more haranguing.

In the line next to the one where I was waiting for my lodging ticket a fight suddenly broke out. One man pulled a long knife from his overcoat pocket. The other man ran for cover, and a police officer soon appeared to re-move the man with the knife from the scene. The issue, it seems, was one of proper places in the line.

There still weren't enough Brooklyn volunteers to suit the management, so they brought in their big gun: Mr. Bullhorn. "Now, listen up," he barked. "There aren't any buses going to Ft. Washington [another shelter] until 11:30, so if you want to get some sleep, go to Brooklyn. Don't ask me any questions. Just shut up and listen. It's because you don't listen up that you end up in a place like this."

I decided to ask a question anyway, about whether there would still be a chance for me to go to Brooklyn once I got my lodging ticket. He turned on me and let me have the full force of the horn: "Don't ask questions, I said. You're not nobody."

The delays at the ticket-issuing window went on and on. Three staff members there seemed reasonably polite and even efficient. The fourth and heaviest one—I have no idea whether it was a man or woman—could not have moved more slowly without coming to a dead halt. The voice of someone who was apparently a supervisor came over the public-address system from time to time to apologize for the delay in going to the Ft. Washington shelter, which was in an armory, but any good he did from behind the scenes was undone by the staff out front and a "see-no-work, hear-no-work, do-no-work" attendant in the office.

As 11:30 approached, we crowded back into the sitting room to get ready to board the buses. A new martinet had appeared on the scene. He got as much attention through his voice, cane, and heavy body as Mr. Bullhorn had with his amplifying equipment. But this new man was more openly vile and excitable; he loved the power that went with bunching us all up close together and then ordering us to stretch out again in a thinner line. We practiced that routine several times. . . .

Long after the scheduled departure, the lines moved. We sped by school buses to the armory at Ft. Washington Avenue and 168th Street. There we were met, just before 2:30 A.M., by military police, social workers, and private guards. They marched us into showers (very welcome), gave us clean underwear, and sent us upstairs to comfortable cots arranged in long rows in a room as big as a football field.

There were 530 of us there for the night, and we were soon quiet.

Tuesday, 1/25

We were awakened at 6 A.M. by whistles and shouting, and ordered to get back onto the buses for the return trip to lower Manhattan as soon as possible.

Back at 8 East 3rd Street, the worst of the martinets were off duty. So I thought breakfast might be a bit quieter than dinner had been. Still, by eight, I had seen three incidents a bit out of the ordinary for me.

A man waiting for breakfast immediately ahead of me in the cattle chute suddenly grabbed a chair from the adjoining area and prepared to break it over his neighbor's head. In my haste to get out of the way, I fell over an older man sleeping against the wall. After some shouts about turf, things cooled off between the fighters, and the old man forgave me.

In the stairwell leading down to the eating area, a young man made a sexual advance to me. When I withdrew from him and stupidly reached for my coat pocket, he thought I was going for a weapon. He at once pinned me against the wall and searched my pockets; there was nothing there.

As I came out of the building onto East 3rd Street, two black Human Resources Administration policemen were bringing two young blacks into the building. One officer had his man by the neck. The other officer had his man's hands cuffed behind his back and repeatedly kicked him hard in the buttocks.

My wanderings were still more aimless today. I couldn't get East 3rd Street out of my mind. What could possibly justify some of that conduct? If I were a staff member there, would I become part of the worst in that pattern? Or would I simply do as little, and think as little, as possible?

At day's end I can't recall much of where I went or why I went there.

Only isolated moments remain with me. Like . . . staring at the elegant crystal and silver in the shops just north of Madison Square Park and wondering what these windows say to the people I'd spent the night with.

Much too soon it was time to go back to the shelter for dinner and another night. At first I thought I didn't have the guts to do it again. Does one have to do *this* to learn who the needy are? I wanted to say, "Enough! There's only so much I need to see."

But I went back to the shelter anyway, probably because it took more guts to quit than it did to go ahead.

A man beside me in the tense dinner line drove one truth of this place home to me. "I never knew hell came in this color," he said.

I was luckier in my assignment for the night. I drew the Keener Building, on Wards Island, a facility with a capacity of 416 men. The building was old and neglected, and the atmosphere of a mental hospital, which it once was, still hung over it. But the staff was polite, the rooms weren't too crowded (there were only twelve beds in Room 326), the single sheet on each bed was clean, and there was toilet paper in the bathroom.

There were limits and guards and deprivations, but there was also an orderliness about the place. Here, at least, I didn't feel I had surrendered all of my dignity at the door.

Wednesday, 1/26

. . . Back to the shelter on East 3rd Street for dinner.

There is simply no other situation I've seen that is so devoid of any graces at all, so tense at every moment, or so empty of hope. The food isn't bad, and the building is heated; that's all it has going for it.

The only cutlery provided is a frail plastic spoon. With practice you can spread hard oleo onto your bread with the back of one. If there's liver or ham, you don't have to cut it; just put it between the two pieces of bread that go with each meal. Everything else—peas, collard greens, apple pudding, plums—can be managed with the spoon. And talk over dinner or sipping, rather than gulping, coffee isn't all that important.

What is hardest to accept is the inevitable jungle scene during the hour you stand in line waiting to eat. Every minute seems to be one that invites an explosion. You know instinctively that men can't come this often to the brink without someone going over. One person too many is going to try to jump ahead in line. One particular set of toes is going to be stepped on by mistake. And the lid is going to blow.

The most frightening people here are the many young, intensely angry blacks. Hatred pours out in all of their speech and some of their actions. I could spend a lot of time imagining how and why they became so completely angry—but if I were the major, the counselor, or the man with the bullhorn, I wouldn't know how to divert them from that anger any more. Hundreds and hundreds of men here have been destroyed by alcohol or drugs. A smaller, but for me more poignant, number are being destroyed by hate.

Their loudest message—and because their voices are so strong it is very loud indeed—is "Respect me, man." The constant theme is that someone or some group is putting them down, stepping on them, asking them to conform to a code they don't accept, getting in their way, writing them off.

So most of the fights begin over turf. A place in line. A corner to control. The have-nots scrapping with the have-nots. . . .

Tonight, I chose the Brooklyn shelter because I thought the buses going there would leave soonest. The shelter, a converted school, is on Williams Avenue and has about 400 beds.

We left in fairly good time but learned when we got to the shelter that no new beds would be assigned until after 11 P.M. We were to sit in the auditorium until then.

At about ten, a man herded as many of us newcomers as would listen to him into a corner of the auditorium. There he delivered an abusive diatribe outlining the horror that lay ahead for our possessions and our bodies during the night to come. It made the ranting at East 3rd Street seem tame.

It's illustrative of what the experience of homelessness and helplessness does to people that all of us—regardless of age, race, background, or health—listened so passively.

Only at midnight, when some other officials arrived, did we learn that this man had no standing whatsoever. He was just an underling who strutted for his time on the stage before any audience cowed enough to take what he dished out. . . .

Thursday, 1/27

Back on the street this morning, I became conscious of how little time I had left to live this way. There seemed so much still to do, and so little time in which to do it.

One part of me tells me I have been fully a part of this. I know I walk with slower steps and bent shoulders. . . . I know I worry a lot more about keeping clean.

But then I recall how foolish that is, I'm acting. This will end tomorrow night. I can quit any time I want to. And unlike my mate from 47th Street, I haven't the slightest idea of what eleven years of sleeping on a grate amount to.

Early this afternoon, I went again to the Pavilion restaurant, where I had eaten five times before. I didn't recognize the man at the cash register.

"Get out," he said.

"But I have money."

"You heard me. Get out." His voice was stronger.

"That man knows me," I said, looking toward the owner in the back of the restaurant.

The owner nodded, and the man at the register said, "Okay, but sit in the back."

If this life in the streets had been real, I'd have gone out the door at the first "Get out." And the assessment of me as not worthy would have been self-fulfilling; I'd have lost so much respect for myself that I wouldn't have been worthy of being served the next time. The downward spiral would have begun.

Until now I haven't understood the extent of nicotine addiction. Dependencies on drugs and alcohol have been around me for a long time, but I thought before that smoking was a bad habit rather easy to overcome.

How many times have I, a nonsmoker, been begged for a cigarette in these days? Surely hundreds. Cigarettes are central. A few folks give them away, a small number sell them for up to 8 cents apiece, and almost all give that last pathetic end of a butt to the first man who asks for what little bit is left. I know addiction now as I didn't before.

Tonight, after a repeat of the totally degrading dinner-line scene at East 3rd Street, I signed up for Keener once again. No more Brooklyn for me.

Sitting upstairs with the other Keener-bound men, I carelessly put my left foot on the rung of the chair in front of me, occupied by a young black.

"Get your foot off, yo."

("Yo" means "Hey, there," "Watch yourself," "Move along," and much more.)

I took it off. "Sorry," I said.

But it was too late. I had broken a cardinal rule. I had violated the man's turf. As we stood in the stairwell waiting for the buses, he told a much bigger, much louder, much angrier friend what I had done.

That man turned on me.

"Wait till we get you tonight, whitey. You stink. Bad. The worst I've ever smelled. And when you put your foot on that chair, you spread your stink around. You better get yourself a shower as soon as we get there, but it won't save you later on. . . . And don't sit near me or him on the bus. You hear, whitey?"

I didn't reply.

The bombardment went on as we mounted the bus. No one spoke up in my defense. Three people waved me away when I tried to sit next to them. The next person, black and close to my age, made no objection when I sat beside him.

The big man continued to tirade for a while, but he soon got interested in finding out from the driver how to go about getting a bus-driver's license. Perhaps he had come down from a high.

I admit I was scared. I wrote my name, address, and office telephone number on a piece of paper and slipped it into my pocket. At least someone would know where to call if the threats were real. I knew I couldn't and wouldn't defend myself in this setting.

While we stood in line on Wards Island waiting for our bed assignments, there were plenty of gripes about the man who was after me. But no one said anything directly to him. Somehow it didn't seem that this was the night when the meek would inherit the earth.

I slept fitfully. I don't like lying with the sheet hiding my face.

Friday, 1/28

I was up and out of Keener as early as possible. That meant using some of my little remaining money for a city-bus ride back to Manhattan, but it was worth it to get out of there.

After breakfast on East 3rd Street, I was finished with the public shelters. That was an easy break for me to make, because I had choices and could run.

The day was cold and, for the early hours, clear. I washed the memory of the big man at 3rd Street out of my mind by wandering through the Fulton Fish Market. I walked across the Brooklyn Bridge and even sang as I realized how free I was to relax and enjoy its beauty.

With a cup of coffee and the *Times,* I sat on a cinder block by the river and read. In time, I wandered through the Wall Street district and almost learned the lay of some of the streets.

I walked up to the Quaker Meeting House at Rutherford Place and 15th Street. Standing on the porch outside, I tried hard to think how the doctrine that "there is that of God in every person" applied to that man last night and to some of the others I had encountered in these ten days. I still think it applies, but it isn't always easy to see how. . . .

Darkness came. I got kicked out of both the bus terminal and Grand Central. I got my normal clothes out of the locker at Penn Station, changed in the men's room, and rode the AA train home.

My apartment was warm, and the bed was clean.

That's the onliest thing.

20 Disaster at Buffalo Creek

KAI ERIKSON

Social structure is a vague concept. It is difficult to attach an image to it. Disaster, for example, is a concept, but it is easy to learn because we attach to it vivid, emotionally laden events. Social structure, in contrast, refers to how the things around us are organized. If we say that most people have friends of their same sex, age, and social class, we are referring to social structure, in this case that of friendship. If we note that the graduates of Ivy League colleges have a much better chance of being hired by the top law and business firms, we are again referring to social structure—in this case how education and economics are linked, and how this affects our chances in life. If we observe that women are much more likely to become nurses, librarians, and homemakers, again we are referring to social structure, in this instance to how gender affects what happens to us in life.

Social structure, then, is how things in life are organized or related to one another. Social structure, though ordinarily invisible to us, plays a vital role in our lives. It provides part of the background assumptions on which we base our decisions. We depend on its familiar rhythms to know where we fit in, and, ultimately, who we are. What would happen, then, if our social structure were suddenly yanked out from under us? In this article, Erikson examines that very situation as he analyzes how people's lives were changed when a flood destroyed their social structure.

SOME 615 SURVIVORS of the Buffalo Creek flood were examined by psychiatrists one and one-half years after the event, and 570 of them, a grim 93 percent, were found to be suffering from an identifiable emotional disturbance. A skeptical neighbor from another of the behavioral sciences may want to make allowance for the fact that psychiatrists looking for mental disorder are more than apt to find it; but even so, the sheer volume of pathology is horrifying.

The medical names for the conditions observed are depression, anxiety, phobia, emotional liability, hypochondria, apathy; and the broader syndrome into which these various symptoms naturally fall is post-traumatic neurosis, or, in a few cases, post-traumatic psychosis. But the nearest expressions in everyday English would be something like confusion, despair, and hopelessness.

Most of the survivors responded to the disaster with a deep sense of loss—a nameless feeling that something had gone grotesquely awry in the order of things, that their minds and spirits had been bruised beyond repair, that they would never again be able to find coherence, that the world as they knew it had come to an end. Now these feelings, of course, were experienced as a generalized, pervading sense of gloom, and the men and women of the hollow did not try to catalog the various strains that contributed to it. But there are recognizable themes in the stories they tell that give us some idea of what the sources of their pain might be.

On Being Numbed

Almost everybody who survived the disaster did so by the thinnest of margins; and the closeness of their escapes, combined with the relentless savagery of the water, left them feeling numbed and depleted—almost as if the mad rush to safety had consumed most of their energy and the ferocity of the waves passing below them had somehow drawn off what reserves were left.

No sooner had they escaped, however, than people began to feel that they were unable to move, caught in a sluggish bank of fog, held back—as in a dream—by forces that slackened the muscles and paralyzed the will. A number of people remember having gone limp or having lost control of their limbs. Quite a few others compared their reactions to a dream state. And some simply went blank in mind as well as limp in body, as if yielding to the enormity of what was happening.

This process of retreating into a limp slump has been noted again and again in disaster research. But on Buffalo Creek, the process appears to have been somewhat exaggerated by the extraordinary power of the flood and by the helpless state in which it left its victims. To be drained of energy, to be emptied of motive and self, is to be on the verge of death itself—and that is how many of the survivors viewed their own condition later.

Faces of Death

Virtually everyone on Buffalo Creek had a very close encounter with death, either because they felt doomed themselves or because they lost relatives and friends or because they came into contact with dead bodies. . . . So death seemed to be everywhere, overhead, underfoot, crouched in every pile of wreckage, waiting to be recognized. . . .

Survival and Guilt

Where one finds death on so large a scale, one also finds guilt. It is one of the ironies of human life that individuals are likely to regret their own survival when others around them are killed in what seems like a meaningless and capricious way, in part because they cannot understand by what logic they came to be spared. People who sense the hand of God in it have many hard questions to ponder, and none of them are very comforting. . . .

The Furniture of Self

. . . It is important to remember that the people of the creek had invested a great deal of time and money and pride in the process of converting the old company shacks into comfortable new dwellings. The flood cleaned out some ragged housing as it made its way down the hollow—more than the residents like to remember—but the average home had been renovated in a hundred ways. A refurbished house on Buffalo Creek served as the emblem of one's rise out of poverty. It was a measure of security, an extension of self, a source of identity. It was not only the outer shell in which one lived out one's life, but a major feature of that life.

Moreover, people lost possessions of considerable meaning to them—not only trucks and cars and appliances with an established trade-in value but mementos of no measurable worth that were highly cherished. Objects such as family Bibles or photographs, a father's favorite gun or a mother's proudest embroidery had a place in the household almost like holy relics, and their loss was deeply mourned. They were a link with the past, and they were a link with the future.

Loss of Faith in Order

The disaster on Buffalo Creek had the effect of reducing people's already brittle confidence in the natural and especially in the social order. . . .

The Buffalo Creek survivors, without saying so directly, have quite clearly lost much of their confidence in the workings of nature. They are troubled about the condition of the mountains, now scraped out inside and slashed with strip mine benches; they are troubled about the water poised over their heads in other dams both real and imaginary; they are troubled about tornadoes and avalanches, floods and rock slides, earthquakes and explosions; and they are troubled about the natural capacity of their bodies and spirits to handle all the emergencies of life.

Moreover, the people of Buffalo Creek have lost their confidence in the coal company responsible for the dam. This point may be difficult to explain, because most readers will have no difficulty at all understanding why they might resent the company. But it was part of the life of the creek. It employed hundreds of people and was represented locally by officials who lived in the area, were known by first names, and were merged into the community as individual persons. The residents knew that the company was a giant corporation with headquarters in New York, but they continued to visualize it as a kind of manorial presence at the head of the hollow that was implicated somehow in the affairs of the community. It was a proprietor, a patron—and it had obligations to fulfill.

The company violated those obligations, first by building an unworthy dam, and second by reacting to the disaster in the manner of a remote bureaucracy with holdings to protect rather than in the manner of a concerned patron with constituents to care for. The heart of the company turned out to be located a thousand miles away, and its first reflex was to treat the survivors—many of them employees with decades of loyal service—as potential adversaries in a court action.

. . . So the prevailing feeling is one of bitterness, a bitterness so sharp that it seems to speak of betrayal as well as of personal injury.

Uniqueness of Buffalo Creek

So these were some of the effects of the individual trauma—that first numbing moment of pain and shock and helplessness. A few paragraphs of description can scarcely begin to convey what the tragedy must have felt like to the survivors or how it has influenced their lives, but the themes noted here correspond closely to ones noted in reports of other disasters; to that extent at least, what happened on Buffalo Creek is similar to all those other floods and bombings and hurricanes and earthquakes that interrupt the flow of human life so often.

But there are differences, too. Two years after the flood, Buffalo Creek was almost as desolate as it had been the day following—the grief as intense, the fear as strong, the anxiety as sharp, the despair as dark. People still looked out at the world with vacant eyes and drifted from one place to another with dulled and tentative movements. They rarely smiled and rarely played. They were not sure how to relate to one another. They were unsettled and deeply hurt.

Under normal circumstances, one would expect the survivors of such a disaster to convalesce gradually as the passage of time acted to dim old memories and generate new hopes. It is a standard article of psychiatric wisdom that the symptoms of trauma ought to disappear over time, and when they do not—as was generally the case on Buffalo Creek—a peculiar strain of logic is likely to follow. If one has not recovered from the effects of trauma within a reasonable span of time, or so the theory goes, it follows that the symptoms themselves must have been the result of a mental disorder predating the event itself.

Unless we are ready to entertain the possibility that virtually all the people on Buffalo Creek suffered from a palpable emotional disorder on the morning of February 26, 1972, we will have to look elsewhere for a way to explain their distress; and my argument is that a second trauma, a *collective trauma,* followed closely on the first, immobilizing recovery efforts and bringing a number of other problems into focus.

Loss of Communality

The people of Buffalo Creek were wrenched out of their communities and torn away from the very human surround in which they had been so deeply enmeshed. Much of the drama is drained away when we begin to talk of such things, partly because the loss of communality seems a step removed from the vivid terror of the disaster itself and partly because the people of the hollow, so richly articulate when describing the flood and their reaction to it, do not really know how to express what their separation from the familiar tissues of home has meant to them. The closeness of communal ties is experienced on Buffalo Creek as a part of the natural order of things, and residents are no more aware of that presence than fish are aware of the water they swim in. It is simply there, the envelope in which they live, and it is taken entirely for granted.

Communality on Buffalo Creek can best be described as a state of mind shared among a particular gathering of people; and this state of mind, by definition, does not lend itself to sociological abstraction. It does not have a name or a cluster of distinguishing properties. It is a quiet set of understandings that become absorbed into the atmosphere and are thus a part of the natural order. And the key to that network of understanding is a constant readiness to look after one's neighbors—or rather, to know without being asked what needs to be done.

The difficulty is that people invest so much of themselves in that kind of social arrangement that they become absorbed by it, almost captive to it, and the larger collectivity around you becomes an extension of your own personality, an extension of your own flesh. This pattern not only means that you are diminished as a person when that surrounding tissue is stripped away, but that you are no longer able to reclaim as your own the emotional resources invested in it. To "be neighborly" is not a quality you can carry with you into a new situation like negotiable emotional currency: The old community was your niche in the classical ecological sense, and your ability to relate to that niche meaningfully is not a skill easily transferred to another setting. This situation is true whether you move into another community, or whether a new set of neighbors moves in around your old home. . . .

In places like Buffalo Creek, the community in general can be described as the locus for activities that are normally regarded as the exclusive property of individuals. It is the *community* that cushions pain, the *community* that provides a context for intimacy, the *community* that represents morality and serves as the repository for old tradition.

Most of the traumatic symptoms experienced by the Buffalo Creek survivors are a reaction to the loss of communality as well as a reaction to the disaster itself: The fear, apathy, and demoralization one encounters along the entire length of the hollow are derived from the shock of being ripped out of a meaningful community setting as well as the shock of meeting that cruel black water. The line between the two phenomena is difficult to draw. But it seems clear that much of the agony experienced on Buffalo Creek is related to the fact that the hollow is quiet, devastated, without much in the way of a nourishing community life.

Morale and Morality

The Buffalo Creek survivors must face the post-disaster world in a state of severe demoralization, both in the sense that they have lost much of their individual morale and in the sense that they have lost (or fear they have lost) many of their moral anchors. The lack of morale is reflected in a weary apathy, a feeling that the world has more or less come to an end and that there are no longer any compelling reasons for doing anything. People are drained of energy and conviction in part because the activities that once sustained them on an everyday basis—working, caring, playing—seem to have lost their direction and purpose in the absence of a larger communal setting. They feel that the ground has gone out from under them.

The clinical name for this state of mind, of course, is *depression;* and one can hardly escape the impression that it is, at least in part, a reaction to the ambiguities of post-disaster life in the hollow. Most of the survivors never realized the extent to which they relied on the rest of the community to reflect back a sense of meaning to them, never understood the extent to which they depended on others to supply them with a point of reference. When survivors say they feel "adrift," "displaced," "uprooted," "lost," they mean that they do not seem to belong to anything and that there are no longer any familiar social landmarks to help them fix their position in time and space. They are depressed, yes, but it is a depression born of the feeling that they are suspended pointlessly in the middle of nowhere.

This failure of personal morale is accompanied by a deep suspicion that moral standards are beginning to collapse all over the hollow; and in some ways, at least, it would appear that they are. As so frequently happens in human life, the forms of misbehavior people find cropping up in their midst are exactly those about which they are most sensitive. The use of alcohol, always problematic in mountain society, has evidently increased, and there are rumors spreading throughout the trailer camps that drugs have found their way to the creek. The theft rate has risen too, and this rise has always been viewed in Appalachia as a sure index of social disorganization.

The cruelest cut of all, however, is that once close and devoted families are having trouble staying within the pale they formerly observed so carefully. Adolescent boys and girls appear to be slipping away from parental control and are becoming involved in nameless delinquencies, and there are reports from several of the trailer camps that younger wives and husbands are meeting one another in circumstances that violate all the local codes. A home is a moral sphere as well as a physical dwelling, of course, and it would seem that the boundaries of moral space began to splinter as the walls of physical space were washed down the creek.

Yet the seeming collapse of morality on Buffalo Creek differs in several important respects from the kinds of anomie sociologists think they see elsewhere in modern America. For one thing, those persons who seem to be deviating most emphatically from prevailing community norms are usually the first to judge their own behavior as unacceptable and even obnoxious. Adolescents are eager to admit that they sometimes get into trouble, and those of their elders who drink more than the rules of the hollow normally permit are likely to call themselves "alcoholics" under circumstances that seem remarkably premature to jaded strangers from the urban North. To that extent, the consensus has held: local standards as to what qualifies as deviation remain largely intact, even though a number of people see themselves as drifting away from that norm.

Moreover, there is an interesting incongruity in the reports of immorality one hears throughout the hollow. It would seem that virtually everyone in the trailer camps is now living next to persons of lower moral stature than was the case formerly, and this situation, of and by itself, is a logistical marvel. Where did all those sordid people come from? How could a community of decent souls suddenly generate so much iniquity?

It probably makes sense to suppose that quite a few of the survivors are acting more coarsely now than they did before the disaster. But something else may be going on here, too. The relative strangers who move next door and bring their old life-styles with them may be acting improperly by some objective measure or they may not but they are always acting in a unfamiliar way— and the fact of the matter may very well be that strangers, even if they come from the same general community, are almost by definition less "moral" than neighbors. They do not fall within the pale of local clemency and so do not qualify for the allowances neighbors make for one another on the grounds that they know the motives involved.

The old community had niches for some forms of deviation, like the role of the town drunk, and ways to absorb others into the larger tissue of communal life. But the disaster washed away the packing around those niches, leaving the occupants exposed to the frowning glances of new neighbors. So the problem has two dimensions. On the one hand, people who had not engaged in any kind of misbehavior before are now, by their own admission, doing so. On the other hand, the unfamiliar manners of a stranger seem to hint darkly of sin all by themselves, and personal habits that once passed as mild eccentricities in the old neighborhood now begin to look like brazen vices in the harsher light of the new. . . .

Loss of Connection

It would be stretching a point to imply that the communities strung out along Buffalo Creek were secure nests in which people had found a full measure of satisfaction and warmth, but it is wholly reasonable to insist that they were like the air people breathed—sometimes harsh, sometimes chilly, but always a basic fact of life. For better or worse, the people of the hollow were deeply enmeshed in the fabric of their community; they drew their very being from it. And when the fabric was torn away by the disaster, people found themselves exposed and alone, suddenly dependent on their own personal resources.

And the cruel fact of the matter is that many survivors, when left on their own mettle, proved to have but few resources—not because they lacked the heart or the competence, certainly, but because they had always put their abilities in the service of the larger society and did not know how to recall them for their own purposes. A good part of their personal strength turned out to be the reflected strength of the collective—on loan, as it were, from the communal store—and they discovered to their great discomfort that they were not good at making decisions, not good at getting along with others, not good at maintaining themselves as separate persons in the absence of a supportive surround.

Many survivors fear that they are beginning to suffer the kind of stunned disorientation and even madness that can result from prolonged stretches of isolation. One result of this fear is that people tend to draw further and further into themselves and to become even more isolated. This behavior is that of wounded animals who crawl off somewhere to nurse their hurts. It is also the behavior of people who string rough coils of barbed wire around their lonely outposts because they feel they have nothing to offer those who draw near.

So the lonesomeness increases and is reinforced. People have heavy loads of grief to deal with, strong feelings of inadequacy to overcome, blighted lives to restore—and they must do all these things without much in the way of personal resources or self-confidence. Solving problems and making decisions—those are the hard part.

The inability of people to come to terms with their own isolated selves is counterpointed by an inability to relate to others on an interpersonal, one-to-one basis. Human relations along Buffalo Creek took their shape from the expectations pressing in on them from all sides like a firm but invisible mold: They were governed by the customs of the neighborhood, the traditions of the family, the ways of the community. And when the mold was stripped away by the disaster, something began to happen to those relationships. . . .

In places like Buffalo Creek, where attachments between people are seen as a part of the natural scheme of things—inherited by birth or acquired by proximity—the idea of "forming" friendships or "building" relationships seems a little odd. These attachments are not engineered; they simply happen when the communal tone is right. So people are not sure what to do.

One result of these problems is that what remains of the community seems to have lost its most significant quality—the power it generated in people to care for each other in times of need, to console each other in times of distress, to protect each other in times of danger. Looking back, then, it does seem that the general community was stronger than the sum of its parts. When the people of the hollow were sheltered together in the embrace of a secure community, they were capable of extraordinary acts of generosity; but when they tried to relate to one another as individuals, as separate entities, they found that they could no longer mobilize whatever resources are required for caring and nurturing.

Behind this inability to care is a wholly new emotional tone on the creek—a deep distrust even of old neighbors, a fear, in fact, of those very persons on whom one once staked one's life. A disaster like the one that hammered Buffalo Creek makes everything in the world seem unreliable, even other survivors, and that base is a very fragile one on which to build a new community.

PART VI Deviance and Social Control

FOR SOCIETY TO EXIST, people must be able to know what to expect of others. If they couldn't do this, the world would be in chaos. Because the behavior of humans is not controlled by instincts, people develop *norms* (rules and expectations) to provide regularity, or patterns, to social life. Norms provide a high degree of certainty in what, without them, would be a hopelessly disoriented world. If everyone followed his or her own inclinations and no one knew what to expect of others, we would have chaos.

The confidence we can place in others is only relative, however, because not everyone follows all the rules all the time. In fact *deviance*, the violation of rules and expectations, is universal. All members of society violate some of the expectations that others have of them. In this sense, all of us are deviants.

Because the word *deviant* in common usage is equivalent to perverted, dirty, twisted, and nasty, to say that all of us are deviants may strike you as strange. It is important to stress that as the word is used in sociology, *deviance is not a term of negative judgment,* as it is when used by nonsociologists. To sociologists, the term simply refers to activities that violate the expectations of others. Unlike common usage, in sociology this term is neutral, passing judgment neither on the merit of the rules nor on those who violate them.

The norms that people develop to control one another cover a fascinating variety of human behavior. They include rules and expectations concerning our appearance, manner, and conduct.

1. *Appearance* (what we look like): the norms concerning clothing, make-up, hairstyle, and other such presentational aspects of our body, including its cleanliness and odors. These rules also cover the *social extensions of the person*, those objects thought to represent the individual in some way, such as the person's home, car, and, often, even the individual's pet.

2. *Manner* (our style of doing things): people's expectations about how we will express ourselves, such as our facial expressions, gestures, and other body language. Manner includes *personal style* (gruff and direct-to-the-point; pleasant and charming), the expectations others have of us because of how we acted in the past. Manner also includes *group style*, expectations attached to us because of our membership in a social group (race, ethnic, gender, occupation, age, and so on—"the way they are").

3. *Conduct* (what we say, what we do): rules covering the rest of human behavior, specifying what we can and cannot do or say, as well as the circumstances that require or forbid that we say or do something. These include rules of *authority* (who has the right to give which order to whom), rules of *obligation* (who has the responsibility to do what for whom), and rules of *account giving* (what we are expected to say when we are asked for an explanation). Account-giving rules even specify the degree to which we are expected to be honest, to go into detail, or to avoid implicating others.

These everyday rules of appearance, manner, and conduct are sliced very fine. They specify the circumstances that apply, how we must phrase what we say, such as with how much respect or informality, even our facial expressions and eye contact when we do or say it. In other words, hardly a single aspect of our lives goes untouched by rules made by others—most of whom are long ago dead. None of us is a free agent, able to do as we please. Rather, *social control* is a basic fact of social life, enveloping all of us in its pervasive net of expectations.

Norms also follow social status. That is, they differ according to the social positions we occupy, especially those watershed identities of age, gender, occupation, and social class. For example, as you know, the rules of conduct, appearance, and manner differ for convicts, CEO's, students, children, old people, men and women. Looking at this list, you can see that expectations (or rules) depend on reputation, prestige, wealth, occupation, age, and gender. In some instances, they also vary according to race or ethnicity.

The rules also change as we switch audiences. For example, as teenagers know so well, their parents' expectations usually aren't even close to what their friends expect of them. Similarly, we are expected to act one way when we are with members of our own age, gender, or racial–ethnic group, but differently when we are with others. Our everyday norms even dictate distinct clothing for different audiences (or as we are more likely to phrase it, for different occasions)—for a college classroom, for a formal dance, for the beach, and so on. In short, to change physical locations is to transform stages and audiences, bringing distinct expectations of how we are to present the self.

These complex expectations define *in* and define *out*: Those who conform to the norms are accorded the status of members-in-good-standing, while those who deviate from them are usually defined as outsiders of some sort. Often objects of suspicion, sometimes of derision and hostility, deviants are reacted to in a number of ways. They may be given more attention in order to bring them back into line, or they may be ostracized or kicked out of the group. For mild deviations, they may simply be stared at. People may also gossip about them, joke about them, divorce them, strike their names from guest lists, or demote or fire them. In more extreme cases of rule violations, the offender may be shunned or physically attacked. In the most extreme cases, they are tried and imprisoned—or even put to death.

This list of some of the social reactions to deviance indicates that people are extremely concerned with rule-following and rule-breaking behaviors. Challenging fundamental expectations about how social life is run, deviants are often seen as a threat to people's welfare. With such a stake in the conformity of others, then, people react to deviants—sharply and negatively if they consider the deviance threatening, but tolerantly and perhaps even with amusement if they believe it to be mild.

In this Part, we examine both deviance and social control. The opening selection is a forceful reminder of the situational grounding of our morality. As Philip Meyer recounts Stanley Milgram's classic experiment, we come face to face with the power of social groups—they are so potent they can get us to participate in acts we know are evil. In the next selection, I tell the story of an airplane crash in the Andes—looking at how social control operated among the survivors, who ate their deceased friends and relatives. Then Elijah Anderson examines the structural features that make crack dealing a common event in U.S. ghettos. William Chambliss turns the focus on how community reactions to delinquents have far-reaching effects on their adult lives. Philip Zimbardo then describes his intriguing experiment, in which he uncovered structural bases for the hostile relationships between prisoners and prison guards. David Rosenhan closes this Part by asking the intriguing question of whether or not we can tell the sane from the insane.

21 If Hitler Asked You to Electrocute a Stranger, Would You? Probably

PHILIP MEYER

Let's take the title of this selection seriously for a moment. Suppose that Hitler did ask you to electrocute a stranger, would you? "Of course, I wouldn't" is our immediate response. "*I* wouldn't even *hurt* a stranger just because someone asked me, much less electrocute the person."

Such an answer certainly seems reasonable, but unfortunately it may not be true. Consider two aspects of the power of groups over our lives. First, we all do things that we prefer not to—from going to work and taking tests when we really want to stay in bed to mowing the grass or doing the dishes when we want to watch television. Our roles and relationships require that we do them, and our own preferences become less important than fulfilling the expectations of others. Second, at least on occasion, most of us feel social pressures so strongly that we do things that conflict with our morals. Both these types of behavior are fascinating to sociologists, for they indicate how *social structure*—the way society is organized—shapes our lives.

But electrocute someone? Isn't that carrying the point a little too far? One would certainly think so. The experiments described by Meyer, however, indicate that people's positions in groups are so significant that even "nice, ordinary" people will harm strangers upon request. You may find the implications of authority and roles arising from these experiments disturbing. Many of us do.

IN THE BEGINNING, Stanley Milgram was worried about the Nazi problem. He doesn't worry much about the Nazis anymore. He worries about you and me, and perhaps, himself a little bit too.

Stanley Milgram is a social psychologist, and when he began his career at Yale University in 1960 he had a plan to prove, scientifically, that Germans are different. The Germans-are-different hypothesis had been used by historians, such as William L. Shirer, to explain the systematic destruction of the Jews by the Third Reich. One madman could decide to destroy the Jews and even create a master plan for getting it done. But to implement it on the scale that

Hitler did meant that thousands of other people had to go along with the scheme and help to do the work. The Shirer thesis, which Milgram set out to test, is that Germans have a basic character flaw which explains the whole thing, and this flaw is a readiness to obey authority without question, no matter what outrageous acts the authority commands.

The appealing thing about this theory is that it makes those of us who are not Germans feel better about the whole business. Obviously, you and I are not Hitler, and it seems equally obvious that we would never do Hitler's dirty work for him. But now, because of Stanley Milgram, we are compelled to wonder. Milgram developed a laboratory experiment which provided a systematic way to measure obedience. His plan was to try it out in New Haven on Americans and then go to Germany and try it out on Germans. He was strongly motivated by scientific curiosity, but there was also some moral content in his decision to pursue this line of research, which was in turn colored by his own Jewish background. If he could show that Germans are more obedient than Americans, he could then vary the conditions of the experiment and try to find out just what it is that makes some people more obedient than others. With this understanding, the world might, conceivably, be just a little bit better.

But he never took his experiment to Germany. He never took it any farther than Bridgeport. The first finding, also the most unexpected and disturbing finding, was that we Americans are an obedient people: not blindly obedient, and not blissfully obedient, just obedient. "I found so much obedience," says Milgram softly, a little sadly, "I hardly saw the need for taking the experiment to Germany."

There is something of the theater director in Milgram, and his technique, which he learned from one of the old masters in experimental psychology, Solomon Asch, is to stage a play with every line rehearsed, every prop carefully selected, and everybody an actor except one person. That one person is the subject of the experiment. The subject, of course, does not know he is in a play. He thinks he is in real life. The value of this technique is that the experimenter, as though he were God, can change a prop here, vary a line there, and see how the subject responds. Milgram eventually had to change a lot of the script just to get people to stop obeying. They were obeying so much, the experiment wasn't working—it was like trying to measure oven temperature with a freezer thermometer.

The experiment worked like this: If you were an innocent subject in Milgram's melodrama, you read an ad in the newspaper or received one in the mail asking for volunteers for an educational experiment. The job would take about an hour and pay $4.50. So you make an appointment and go to an old Romanesque stone structure on High Street with the imposing name of The Yale Interaction Laboratory. It looks something like a broadcasting studio. Inside, you meet a young, crew-cut man in a laboratory coat who says he is Jack Williams, the experimenter. There is another citizen, fiftyish, Irish face, an accountant, a little overweight, and very mild and harmless looking. This other citizen seems nervous and plays with his hat while the two of you sit in chairs side by side and are told that the $4.50 checks are yours no matter what happens. Then you listen to Jack Williams explain the experiment.

It is about learning, says Jack Williams in a quiet, knowledgeable way. Science does not know much about the conditions under which people learn and this experiment is to find out about negative reinforcement. Negative reinforcement is getting punished when you do something wrong, as opposed to positive reinforcement which is getting rewarded when you do something right. The negative reinforcement in this case is electric shock. You notice a book on the table, titled, *The Teaching-Learning Process,* and you assume that this has something to do with the experiment.

Then Jack Williams takes two pieces of paper, puts them in a hat, and shakes them up. One piece of paper is supposed to say, "Teacher," and the other, "Learner." Draw one and you will see which you will be. The mild-looking accountant draws one, holds it close to his vest like a poker player, looks at it, and says, "Learner." You look at yours. It says, "Teacher." You do not know that the drawing is rigged, and both slips say "Teacher." The experimenter beckons to the mild-mannered "learner."

"Want to step right in here and have a seat, please?" he says. "You can leave your coat on the back of that chair . . . roll up your right sleeve, please. Now what I want to do is strap down your arms to avoid excessive movement on your part during the experiment. This electrode is connected to the shock generator in the next room.

"And this electrode paste," he says, squeezing some stuff out of a plastic bottle and putting it on the man's arm, "is to provide a good contact and to avoid a blister or burn. Are there any questions now before we go into the next room?"

You don't have any, but the strapped-in "learner" does.

"I do think I should say this," says the learner. "About two years ago, I was in the veterans' hospital . . . they detected a heart condition. Nothing serious, but as long as I'm having these shocks, how strong are they—how dangerous are they?"

Williams, the experimenter, shakes his head casually. "Oh, no," he says. "Although they may be painful, they're not dangerous. Anything else?"

Nothing else. And so you play the game. The game is for you to read a series of word pairs: for example, blue-girl, nice-day, fat-neck. When you finish the list, you read just the first word in each pair and then a multiple-choice list of four other words, including the second word of the pair. The learner, from his remote, strapped-in position, pushes one of four switches to indicate which of the four answers he thinks is the right one. If he gets it right, nothing happens and you go on to the next one. If he gets it wrong, you push a switch that buzzes and gives him an electric shock. And then you go on to the next word. You start with 15 volts and increase the number of volts by 15 for each wrong answer. The control board goes from 15 volts on one end to 450 volts on the other. So that you know what you are doing, you get a test-shock yourself, at 45 volts. It hurts. To further keep you aware of what you are doing to that man in there, the board has verbal descriptions of the shock levels, ranging from "Slight Shock" at the left-hand side, through "Intense Shock" in the middle, to "Danger: Severe Shock" toward the far right. Finally, at the very end, under 435- and 450-volt switches, there are three ambiguous X's. If, at any point, you hesitate, Mr. Williams calmly tells you to go on. If you still hesitate, he tells you again.

Except for some terrifying details, which will be explained in a moment, this is the experiment. The object is to find the shock level at which you disobey the experimenter and refuse to pull the switch.

When Stanley Milgram first wrote this script, he took it to 14 Yale psychology majors and asked them what they thought would happen. He put it this way: Out of one hundred persons in the teacher's predicament, how would their break-off points be distributed along the 15- to 450-volt scale? They thought a few would break off very early, most would quit someplace in the middle, and a few would go all the way to the end. The highest estimate of the number out of 100 who would go all the way to the end was three. Milgram then informally polled some of his fellow scholars in the psychology department. They agreed that very few would go to the end. Milgram thought so too.

"I'll tell you quite frankly," he says, "before I began this experiment, before any shock generator was built, I thought that most people would break off at 'Strong Shock' or 'Very Strong Shock.' You would get only a very, very small proportion of people going out to the end of the shock generator, and they would constitute a pathological fringe."

In his pilot experiments, Milgram used Yale students as subjects. Each of them pushed the shock switches, one by one, all the way to the end of the board.

So he rewrote the script to include some protests from the learner. At first, they were mild, gentlemanly, Yalie protests, but "it didn't seem to have as much effect as I thought it would or should," Milgram recalls. "So we had more violent protestation on the part of the person getting the shock. All of the time, of course, what we were trying to do was not to create a macabre situation, but simply to generate disobedience. And that was one of the first findings. This was not only a technical deficiency of the experiment, that we didn't get disobedience. It really was the first finding: that obedience would be much greater than we had assumed it would be and disobedience would be much more difficult than we had assumed."

As it turned out, the situation did become rather macabre. The only meaningful way to generate disobedience was to have the victim protest with great anguish, noise, and vehemence. The protests were tape-recorded so that all the teachers ordinarily would hear the same sounds and nuances, and they started with a grunt at 75 volts, proceeded through a "Hey, that really hurts," at 125 volts, got desperate with, "I can't stand the pain—don't do that," at 180 volts, reached complaints of heart trouble at 195, an agonized scream at 285, a refusal to answer at 315, and only heartrending, ominous silence after that.

Still, 65 percent of the subjects, 20- to 50-year-old American males, everyday, ordinary people, like you and me, obediently kept pushing those levers in the belief that they were shocking the mild-mannered learner, whose name was Mr. Wallace, and who was chosen for the role because of his innocent appearance, all the way up to 450 volts.

Milgram was not getting enough disobedience so that he had something he could measure. The next step was to vary the circumstances to see what would encourage or discourage obedience. There seemed very little left in the way of discouragement. The victim was already screaming at the top of his lungs and feigning a heart attack. So whatever new impediment to obedience reached the brain of the subject had to travel by some route other than the ear. Milgram thought of one.

He put the learner in the same room with the teacher. He stopped strapping the learner's hand down. He rewrote the script so that at 150 volts the learner took his hand off the shock plate and declared that he wanted out of experiment. He rewrote the script some more so that the experimenter then told the teacher to grasp the learner's hand and physically force it down on the plate to give Mr. Wallace his unwanted electric shock.

"I had the feeling that very few people would go on at that point, if any," Milgram says. "I thought that would be the limit of obedience that you would find in the laboratory."

It wasn't.

Although [years have] gone by, Milgram still remembers the first person to walk into the laboratory in the newly rewritten script. He was a construction worker, a very short man. "He was so small," says Milgram, "that when he sat on the chair in front of the shock generator, his feet didn't reach the floor. When the experimenter told him to push the victim's hand down and give the shock, he turned to the experimenter, and he turned to the victim, his elbow went up, he fell down on the hand of the victim, his feet kind of tugged to one side, and he said, 'Like this, boss?' Zzumph!"

The experiment was played out to its bitter end. Milgram tried it with 40 different subjects. And 30 percent of them obeyed the experimenter and kept on obeying.

"The protests of the victim were strong and vehement, he was screaming his guts out, he refused to participate, and you had to physically struggle with him in order to get his hand down on the shock generator," Milgram remembers. But 12 out of 40 did it.

Milgram took his experiment out of New Haven. Not to Germany, just 20 miles down the road to Bridgeport. Maybe, he reasoned, the people obeyed because of the prestigious setting of Yale University. If they couldn't trust a learning center that had been there for two centuries, whom could they trust? So he moved the experiment to an untrustworthy setting.

The new setting was a suite of three rooms in a run-down office building in Bridgeport. The only identification was a sign with a fictitious name: "Research Associates of Bridgeport." Questions about professional connections got only vague answers about "research for industry."

Obedience was less in Bridgeport. Forty-eight percent of the subjects stayed for the maximum shock, compared to 65 percent at Yale. But this was enough to prove that far more than Yale's prestige was behind the obedient behavior.

[Since the experiments] Stanley Milgram has been trying to figure out what makes ordinary American citizens so obedient. The most obvious answer—that people are mean, nasty, brutish, and sadistic—won't do. The subjects who gave the shocks to Mr. Wallace to the end of the board did not enjoy it. They groaned, protested, fidgeted, argued, and in some cases, were seized by fits of nervous, agitated giggling.

"They even try to get out of it," says Milgram, "but they are somehow engaged in something from which they cannot liberate themselves. They are locked into a structure, and they do not have the skills or inner resources to disengage themselves. . . ."

"The results, as seen and felt in the laboratory," he has written, "are disturbing. They raise the possibility that human nature, or more specifically the kind of character produced in American democratic society, cannot be counted on to insulate its citizens from brutality and inhumane treatment at the direction of malevolent authority. A substantial proportion of people do what they are told to do, irrespective of the content of the act and without limitation of conscience, so long as they perceive that the command comes from a legitimate authority. If, in this study, an anonymous experimenter can successfully command adults to subdue a 50-year-old man and force on him painful electric shocks against his protest, one can only wonder what government, with its vastly greater authority and prestige, can command of its subjects. . . ."

Stanley Milgram has his problems, too. He believes that in the laboratory situation, he would not have shocked Mr. Wallace. His professional critics reply that in his real-life situation he has done the equivalent. He has placed innocent and naive subjects under great emotional strain and pressure in selfish obedience to his quest for knowledge. When you raise this issue with Milgram, he has an answer ready. There is, he explains patiently, a critical difference between his naive subjects and the man in the electric chair. The man in the electric chair (in the mind of the naive subject) is helpless, strapped in. But the naive subject is free to go at any time.

Immediately after he offers this distinction, Milgram anticipates the objection.

"It's quite true," he says. "that this is almost a philosophic position, because we have learned that some people are psychologically incapable of disengaging themselves. But that doesn't relieve them of the moral responsibility."

The parallel is exquisite. "The tension problem was unexpected," says Milgram in his defense. But he went on anyway. The naive subjects didn't expect the screaming protests from the strapped-in learner. But they went on.

"I had to make a judgment," says Milgram. "I had to ask myself, was this harming the person or not? My judgment is that it was not. Even in the extreme cases, I wouldn't say that permanent damage results."

Sound familiar? "The shocks may be painful," the experimenter kept saying, "but they're not dangerous."

After the series of experiments was completed, Milgram sent a report of the results to his subjects and a questionnaire, asking whether they were glad or sorry to have been in the experiment. Eighty-three and seven-tenths percent said they were glad and only 1.3 percent were sorry; 15 percent were neither sorry nor glad. However, Milgram could not be sure at the time of the experiment that only 1.3 percent would be sorry.

Kurt Vonnegut, Jr., put one paragraph in the preface to *Mother Night,* in 1966, which pretty much says it for the people with their fingers on the shock-generator switches, for you and me, and maybe even for Milgram. "If I'd been born in Germany," Vonnegut said, "I suppose I would have *been* a Nazi, bopping Jews and gypsies and Poles around, leaving boots sticking out of snow-banks, warming myself with my sweetly virtuous insides. So it goes."

Just so. One thing that happened to Milgram back in New Haven during the days of the experiment was that he kept running into people he'd watched from behind the one-way glass. It gave him a funny feeling, seeing those people going about their everyday business in New Haven and knowing what they would do to Mr. Wallace if ordered to. Now that his research results are in and you've thought about it, you can get this funny feeling too. You don't need one-way glass. A glance in your own mirror may serve just as well.

22 The Survivors of the F-227

JAMES M. HENSLIN

A theme running through our previous readings is that each culture provides guidelines for how to view the world, even for how we determine right and wrong. The perspective we learn envelops us much as a fish is immersed in water. Almost all the world's cultures uphold the idea that it is wrong to eat human flesh. (Some exceptions do apply, such as warriors who used to eat the heart or kidneys of slain enemies in an attempt to acquire the source of their strength or courage.) Thus it is safe to say that nowhere in the world is there a culture whose members regularly consume people as food. Yet, in the unusual situation recounted here, that is precisely what these people did.

Note how, even in the midst of reluctantly committing acts they themselves found extremely repugnant—and ones they fully knew that the world condemns—this group developed norms to govern their behavior. This was crucial for these survivors, because group support, along with its attendant norms, is critical in maintaining a sense of a "good" self. At the conclusion of the article, Henslin shows how this event is more than simply an interesting story—that it represents the essence of social life.

LOCATED BETWEEN BRAZIL AND ARGENTINA, near Buenos Aires, is tiny Uruguay. On October 12, 1972, a propeller-driven Fairchild F-227 left Uruguay's capital, Montevideo, bound for Santiago, Chile—a distance of about 900 miles. On board were 15 members of an amateur rugby team from Uruguay, along with 25 of their relatives and friends. The pilots, from the Uruguayan Air Force, soon became concerned about turbulence over the Andes Mountains. Winds blowing in from the Pacific were colliding with air currents coming from the opposite direction, creating a turbulence that could toss a plane around like a scrap of paper in a wind storm.

Since the threat was so great, the pilots decided to land in Mendoza, Argentina, where everyone spent the night. The next day, with the weather only slightly improved, the crew debated about turning back. Several of the rugby players taunted them, saying they were cowards. When the captain of a plane which had just flown over the Andes reported that the F-227 should be able to fly over the turbulence, the Fairchild's pilots decided to continue the trip. Once again airborne, the young passengers laughed about its being Friday the 13th as some threw a rugby ball around and others played cards. Many of them still in their teens, and all of them from Uruguay's upper class (two were nephews of the president of Uruguay), they were in high spirits.

Over the Andes the plane flew into a thick cloud, and the pilots had to fly by instrument. Amid the turbulence they hit an "air pocket," and the plane suddenly plunged 3,000 feet. When the passengers abruptly found themselves below the cloud, one young man turned to another and said, "Is it normal to fly so close?" He was referring to the mountainside just 10 feet off the right wing.

With a deafening roar, the right wing sheared off as it hit the side of the mountain. The wing whipped over the plane and knocked off the tail. The steward, the navigator, and three of the rugby players still strapped in their seats were blown out of the gaping hole. Then the left wing broke off and, like a toboggan going 200 miles an hour, the fuselage slid on its belly into a steep, snow-covered valley.

As night fell, the survivors huddled in the wreckage. At 12,000 feet the cold, especially at night, was brutal. There was little fuel, because not much wood is used in the construction of airplanes. They had almost no food—basically some chocolate that the passengers had bought on their overnight stay in Mendoza. There were a few bottles of wine, and the many cartons of cigarettes they had purchased at a duty-free shop.

The twenty-seven who survived the crash expected to be rescued quickly. At most, they thought, they would have to spend the night on the mountain top. Seventy days later, only sixteen remained alive.

The chocolate and wine didn't go very far, and provided little nourishment. The plane, off course by a hundred miles or so and painted white, was not only difficult to track, but virtually invisible against the valley's deep layer of snow: Search planes were unable to locate the wreckage.

As the days went by, the survivors' spirits seemed to be sucked into a hopeless pit. Hunger and starvation began to bear down on them. They felt cold all the time. They became weaker and had difficulty keeping their balance. Their skin became wrinkled, like that of old people. Although no one mentioned it, several of the young men began to realize that their only chance to survive was to eat the bodies of those who died in the crash. The corpses lay strewn in the snow around the plane, perfectly preserved by the bitter cold.

The thought of cutting into the flesh of their friends was too ghastly a prospect to put into words. Finally, however, Canessa, a medical student, brought up the matter with his friends. He asserted that the bodies were no longer people. The soul was gone, he said, and the body was simply meat— and essential to their survival. They were growing weaker, and they could not survive without food. And what food was there besides the corpses? "They are no more human beings than the dead flesh of the cattle we eat at home," he said.

Days later, the topic moved from furtive discussion in a small group to open deliberation among all the survivors. Inside the plane, arguing the matter, Canessa reiterated his position. His three closest friends supported him, adding, "We have a duty to survive. If we don't eat the bodies, it is a sin. We must do this not just for our own sakes but also for our families. In fact," they continued, "God wants us to survive, and He has provided these bodies so we can live." Some, however, just shook their heads, the thought too disturbing to even contemplate.

Serbino pushed the point. He said, "If I die, I want you to eat my body. I want you to use it." Some nodded in agreement. In an attempt to bring a little humor to the black discussion, he added, "If you don't, I'll come back and give you a swift kick in the butt." Some said that while they did not think it would be wrong to eat the bodies, they themselves could never do it. The arguments continued for hours.

Four of the young men went outside. Near the plane, the buttocks of a body protruded from the snow. No one spoke as they stared at it. Wordlessly, Canessa knelt and began to cut with the only instrument he had found, a piece of broken glass. The flesh was frozen solid, and he could cut only slivers the size of matchsticks. Canessa laid the pieces on the roof of the plane, and the young men went back inside. They said that the meat was drying in the sun. The others looked mutely at one another. No one made a move to leave the plane.

Canessa decided that he would have to be the first. Going outside, he picked up a sliver of meat. Staring at it, almost transfixed, he became as though paralyzed. He simply couldn't make his hand move to his mouth. Summoning every ounce of courage, he forced his hand upwards. While his stomach recoiled, he pushed the meat inside his mouth and forced himself to swallow. Later, Serbino took a piece. He tried to swallow, but the sliver hung halfway down his throat. Quickly grabbing some snow, he managed to wash it down. Canessa and Serbino were joined by others, who also ate.

The next morning, on the transistor radio they had struggled so hard to get working, their hearts plunged when they heard that the air force had called off the search. The survivors knew that this announcement almost sealed their fate. The only way out, if there was one, was on their own. They held a meeting and decided that the fittest should try to seek help—even though no one knew where to seek it. But none was strong enough to try. With the snow's crust breaking under every step, even to walk was exhausting. There was only one way to regain strength, and, without giving the thought words, everyone knew what it was.

Canessa and Strauch went outside. The corpse was in the same position as before. They took a deep breath and began to hack meat off the bone. They laid the strips on the plane to thaw in the sun. The knowledge that no rescuers were looking for them encouraged others to join in eating the human flesh. They forced themselves to swallow—their consciences, seconded by their stomachs, accusing them of extreme wrongdoing. Still, they forced the flesh down, telling themselves over and over that there was no other way to survive.

Some, however, could not. Javier and Liliana Methol, husband and wife, though they longed to return to their children, could not eat human flesh. They said that the others could do as they liked, but perhaps God wanted them to choose to die.

The survivors began to organize. Canessa took charge of cutting up the bodies, while a group of the younger ones had the job of preventing the corpses from rotting by keeping them covered with snow. Another group had the task of seeing that the plane was kept in order. Even the weakest had a job to do: They were able to hold pieces of aluminum in the sun to melt snow for drinking water.

The first corpses they ate were those of the crew, strangers to them.

One day, when it was too cold to melt snow, they burned wooden Coca-Cola crates that they had found in the luggage compartment. After they had water, they roasted some meat over the embers. There was only enough heat to brown the pieces, but they found the flavor better—tasting, as they said, like beef, but softer. Canessa said they should never do this again, for heat destroys proteins. "You have to eat it raw to get its full value," he argued. Rejecting his advice, the survivors cooked the meat when they had the chance, about once or twice a week. Daily, the recurring question was, "Are we cooking today?"

Liliana told Javier that after they got back home she wanted to have another baby. He agreed. As they looked at one another, though, they saw eyes sunken into their sockets and bones protruding from their cheeks. They knew there was no hope, unless. . . . Liliana and Javier shuddered as they picked up a piece of meat.

Some never could eat. Although the others argued with them, they never could overcome their feelings of revulsion. They continued to refuse, and so day by day grew weaker. Others, however, grew accustomed to what they were doing. They became able to cut meat from a body before everyone's eyes. They could even eat larger pieces, which they had to chew and taste.

As time went on, they developed a set of rules. They would not eat the women's bodies. No one *had* to eat. The meat would be rationed, and no one could eat more than his or her share. The three who were going to leave in search of help could eat more than the others. One corpse would always be finished before another would be started. (It was overlooked when those who had the disagreeable job of cutting the corpses ate a little as they cut.)

They refused to eat certain parts of the body—the lungs, the skin, the head, and the genitals.

There were some things they never could get used to, such as cutting up a close friend. When they dug a corpse out of the snow, it was preserved just as it had been at the moment of death. If the eyes had been open when the friend died, they were still open, now staring back at them. Everyone understood that no one had to eat a friend or relative.

Survival work became more organized. Those who could stomach it would cut large chunks from a body and pass them to another team, who would slice them with razor blades into smaller pieces. This was not as disagreeable a task, for, separated from the body, the meat was easier to deal with.

The sheets of fat from a body lay outside the rules. They were dried in the sun until a crust formed. Anyone could eat as much as they wished. But the fat wasn't as popular as the meat.

Also outside the rationing system were the pieces of the first carcasses they had cut up, before they developed the rules. Those pieces lay about the snow, and anyone who wanted could scavenge them. Some could never stomach the liver, others the heart or kidneys, and many could not eat the intestines of the dead. Three young men refused the red meat of the muscles.

The dead became part of their lives. One night, Inciarte reached up to get something from the hat rack and was startled when an icy hand brushed against his cheek. Apparently someone had sneaked it in as a late snack.

Constipation was an unexpected complication of their diet. As day after day went by without defecation, they began to worry that their insides would burst. Eventually they developed a sort of contest, wondering who would be the last hold-out. After 28 days, only two had not defecated. At 32, only one. Finally, on the 34th day, Bobby François joined the others.

The three who had been selected to go in search of rescuers had to solve the problem of preventing their feet from freezing. The skin of the dead provided the solution. By cutting an arm just above and below the elbow, and slowly pulling, the skin came away with its subcutaneous layers of fat. Sewing up the lower end made an insulated pair of socks.

Their bland diet became boring. As their bodies and minds cried out for variety, they began to seek new tastes. After eating the meat from a bone, they would crack it open and scoop out the marrow. Everyone liked the marrow. Some sought out the blood clots from around the heart. Others even ate parts of bodies that had started to rot. Many were revolted by this, but, as time went on, more of the survivors did the same.

Canessa, Parrado, and Vizintin were selected to go in search of help. Before they left, Parrado took aside a couple of friends and said that they might run short of food before help could arrive. "I prefer you don't," he whispered, "but I'll understand if you eat my mother and sister."

Ten days after the expeditionaries set out, they stumbled into a shepherd's hut. The news of their survival, long after they had been given up for dead, came as a shock to their friends and relatives. Those still waiting on the mountain were rescued by helicopter—just four days before Christmas.

Although the survivors felt a compulsive need to talk about what they had done, at first physicians and government officials kept the cannibalism a secret. When the news leaked out, however, it made headlines around the world. One survivor explained, "It was like a heart transplant. The dead sustained the living." Another said, "It was like holy communion. God gives us the body and blood of Christ in holy communion. God gave us these bodies and blood to eat."

All were Roman Catholics, and they asked forgiveness. The priests replied that they did not need forgiveness, for they had done nothing wrong. There was no soul in the bodies, the priests explained, and in extreme conditions, if there is no other way to survive, it is permissible to eat the dead. After consultation with relatives, it was decided to bury what was left of the dead at the crash site.

The young men, rejoining their families, became celebrities. They shunned the spotlight, however, banded together, and thought of themselves as special people. As persons who had survived the impossible, they felt that they had a unique purpose in life.

The world's reaction to the events in the Andes was shock and horror—mixed with fascination. As one Chilean paper asked in its headlines, "What would *you* have done?"

The Social Construction of Reality

I was going to let the story stop here, but I was told by a person very influential in my life that I really ought to make the sociology explicit. So let's see what sociological lessons we can derive from this tragedy in the Andes.

First, the main lesson, one from which the other points follow, comes from the symbolic interactionists, who stress that *our world is socially constructed.* By this, they mean that nothing contains built-in meanings. In other words, whatever meaning something has is arbitrary: We humans have given it a particular meaning, but we could just as well have given it a different meaning. *Second,* it is through a social process that we determine meanings; that is, people jointly decide on the meanings to assign events and objects. *Third,* because meanings (or what things symbolize to people) are arbitrary, people can change them. I am aware that these statements may sound extremely vague, but they should become clear as we look at how these survivors constructed their reality.

We might begin by asking what the meaning of a human body is. As with other aspects of life, a group can assign to a body any meaning that it wishes, for, by itself, a body has no meaning. These survivors did not begin to develop their definitions from scratch, however, for they brought to the Andes meanings that they had learned in their culture—basically that a body, while not a person, is still human, and must be treated with respect. A related meaning they had learned is that a human body is "not food." Such an understanding may seem natural to us because it matches our own cultural definitions—which obscures the arbitrary nature of the definition.

Fourth, when circumstances change, definitions can become outmoded—even definitions about fundamental aspects of life. *Fifth,* even though definitions no longer "work," changes in basic orientations do not come easily. *Sixth,* anyone who suggests such changes is likely to be seen as a threatening deviant. Shock, horror, or ridicule may be the reactions, and—for persons who persist on a disorienting course—shunning, ostracism, and violence may result. *Seventh,* the source of radical new ideas is extremely significant in determining whether or not they gain acceptance. *Eighth,* if an individual can drum up group support, then there exists a *social* basis for the new, competing definition. *Ninth,* if the group that offers the new definition can get enough others to accept it, then the common definition of reality will change. *Tenth,* changed circumstances make people more open to accepting new definitions of reality.

In this case, Canessa did not want to appear as a deviant, so he furtively proposed a new definition—entrusting it at first to only a few close friends. Even there, however, since it violated basic definitions acquired in early socialization, it was initially met with resistance. But the friends had high respect for Canessa, who had completed a year of medical school, and they were won over. This small group then proposed their new definition of human bodies to the larger group. Eventually, in the growing realization that death was imminent, this definition won out.

Eleventh, behavior follows definitions. That is, definitions of reality are not just abstract ideas; they also indicate the boundaries of what is allowable. We tend to do what our definitions allow. In this case, when the definition of human bodies changed, so did the survivors' behavior: The changed definition allowed them to eat human corpses.

Twelfth, definitions also follow behavior. That is, as people engage in an activity, they tend to develop ideas that lend support to what they are doing. In this instance, the eating of human flesh—especially since it was a group activity—reinforced the initial definition that had been only tentatively held, that the flesh was no longer human. Eventually; at least for many, the flesh indeed became meat—so much so that some people were even able to take a human hand to bed for a late-night snack.

Thirteenth, for their very survival, all groups must have norms. By allowing people to know what to expect in a given situation, norms provide a basic structure for people's relationships with one another. Without norms, anarchy and chaos would reign.

This principle also applies to groups that make deviance part of their activities. Although a superficial view from the outside may make such groups appear disorganized and without rules, they are in fact very normative. Groups of outlaw motorcyclists, for example, share an elaborate set of rules about what they expect from one another, most of which, like those of other groups, are not in written form. In short, norms cover even deviant activities, for, without them, how can group members know what to expect of one another?

The Andes survivors developed a basic set of norms to provide order to their deviant activity. Some of those norms were:

1. No one had to violate his or her conscience. If someone did not wish to eat human flesh, no one would force them.
2. Some bodies were "off limits."
3. Meat was rationed, with a specified amount for each person:
   a. Fat was outside the rationing system, and
   b. Leftover parts from the first bodies were outside the rationing system.
4. Meat was distributed according to an orderly system, namely:
   a. Everyone who wished to could eat, and
   b. Designated parts of the body could be "wasted."

Fourteenth, human groups tend to stratify, that is, to sort themselves out on a basis of inequality, with some getting more of a group's resources, some less. A norm concerning eating human flesh that I did not mention above illustrates this principle: Those persons deemed most valuable to the group were allowed to eat more. These were persons who were going in search of rescue and those who performed the disagreeable task of cutting up the bodies. This unequal division of resources represents the formation of a basic system of social stratification.

Fifteenth, human groups tend to organize themselves. In this instance, the survivors did not just randomly cut away at the bodies, but specific tasks were assigned. Teamwork developed to coordinate tasks, with some individuals performing specialized jobs in making the meat edible. Even the weakest had a part to play. The incipient social stratification just mentioned is another example of organization, one that sociologists call the division of labor. *Sixteenth,* an essential part of the human tendency to organize is the emergence of leadership—to direct and coordinate the activities of others. In this case, Canessa stands out.

Seventeenth, people attempt to maintain a respectable sense of self. These survivors were conforming individuals in that they had accepted the norms of their society and were striving for a respectable place within it. They wanted to continue to think of themselves as good people. Yet, they had to make a decision about doing an activity that went beyond the bounds of what they looked at as normal—one they even knew that "everyone" defined as wrong.

Eighteenth, it is possible to maintain a "good" self-image and still engage in deviant activities. Because the essence of human society is the social construction of reality, so the key to the self also lies in how reality is defined. If you can redefine an activity to make it "not deviant," then it does not threaten your sense of a "good" self. In this present instance, the Andes survivors looked on eating human flesh as part of their "duty to survive." To do a duty is a good thing, and, accordingly, the acts required by it cannot be "bad." In fact, they must be "good." (The most infamous example of the use of this basic principle was Hitler's SS, who looked on killing Jews as necessary for the survival of the "Aryan" race and culture. They even termed the slaughter a "good" act and their participation in it as patriotic and self-sacrificing.)

This principle helps many people get through what otherwise would be excruciatingly painful nights—for they would toss sleeplessly owing to a gnawing conscience. Redefinition, by keeping one's sense of self intact, allows people to participate in a variety of acts condemned by society—even those disapproved by the self. For most people, redefinition involves much less dramatic acts than eating human flesh, such as a college student cheating on a test or a boss firing a worker.

Nineteenth, some people participate in deviant acts even though they remain unconvinced about such redefinitions. (Some do not even attempt to redefine them.) They may do so from a variety of motives—from what they consider "sheer necessity" to the desire to reach a future goal. Liliana and Javier, who decided that they wanted a baby, are an example. Such persons have greater difficulty adjusting to their acts than those who redefine them as "good." (Even the latter may have difficulty, for redefinitions may be only partial, especially in the face of competing definitions.)

Twentieth, people feel they must justify their actions to others. This process of justifying the self involves clothing definitions of reality in forms thought to be acceptable to others. In order for definitions to be accepted, they must be made to fit into the others' already-existing definitional framework. In this case, the survivors first justified their proposed actions by redefining the bodies as meat and by saying that they had a duty to survive. After their rescue—speaking to a Roman Catholic audience—they used the analogy of holy communion to justify their act.

Twenty-first, to gain institutional support is to secure a broad, solid base for one's definitions of reality. Then one no longer stands alone, which is to invite insanity, nor is one a member of a small group, which is to invite ridicule and may require cutting off oneself from the larger group. In this case, institutional support was provided by the Roman Catholic Church, which, while not accepting the survivors' analogy of cannibalism as communion, allowed them to avoid the label of sin by defining their actions as allowable under the circumstances.

Finally, note that these principles are fundamental to human life. They do not simply apply to the Andes survivors—or to deviants in general—but they underlie human society. For all of us, reality is socially constructed, and the story of the Andes survivors contains the essence of human society.

23 Selling Crack

ELIJAH ANDERSON

A primary focus in Part V was social structure, how the things that make up social life are organized. We saw how social structure vitally affects our welfare, even our social and mental well-being. Another aspect of social structure is that it pushes us toward or away from deviance. Rule breaking is not random. Rather, the way society is laid out (another way to say social structure) makes some groups more or less likely to participate in certain forms of deviance.

Anderson lives in Philadelphia, the city that is the focus of this research. Over a period of years, he observed, talked to, and interacted with crack dealers, their clients, friends, and families. As you read this article, try to determine the structural features of society that make crack dealing a regular part of ghetto life today. You should be able to see why you were more likely to become a college student and less likely to become a crack dealer than these residents of inner-city Philadelphia. Such is the powerful effect of social structure on our lives.

The Cultural Economic Connection

ANYONE WHO WANTS TO UNDERSTAND the widespread social dislocation in the inner-city poor community must approach these problems—along with other urban ills—from a structural as well as a cultural standpoint. Liberals and conservatives alike today tend to stress values like individual responsibility when considering such issues as drugs, violence, teen pregnancy, family formation, and the work ethic. Some commentators readily blame "welfare" for poverty and find it hard to see how anyone, even the poor, would deliberately deviate from the norms of the mainstream culture. But the profound changes our society is currently undergoing in the way it organizes work have enormous cultural implications for the ability of the populations most severely affected by these developments to function in accordance with mainstream norms.

The United States has for some time been moving from manufacturing to a service and high-tech economy in which the well-being of workers, particularly those with low skills and little education, is subordinated to the bottom line. In cities like Philadelphia certain neighborhoods have been devastated by the effects of deindustrialization. Many jobs have become automated, been transferred to developing countries, or moved to nearby cities like King of Prussia. For those who cannot afford a car, travel requires two hours on public transportation from the old city neighborhoods where concentrations of black people, Hispanics, and working-class whites live.

With widespread joblessness, many inner-city people become stressed and their communities become distressed. Poor people adapt to these circumstances in the ways they know, meeting the exigencies of their situation as best they can. The kinds of problems that trigger moral outrage begin to emerge: teen pregnancy, welfare dependency, and the underground economy. Its cottage industries of drugs, prostitution, welfare scams, and other rackets are there to pick up the economic slack. Quasi-legal hustling is part of it; people do odd jobs under the table and teach young people to follow their lead. Some people have a regular second or third job entirely off the books.

The drug trade is certainly illegal, but it is the most lucrative and most accessible element of the underground economy and has become a way of life in numerous inner-city communities. Many youngsters dream of leading the drug dealer's life, or at least their highly glamorized conceptions of this life. Of course, drugs have been around for a long time, but they have become deeply rooted in the inner-city black community, a situation largely tolerated by civic authorities and the police. As law-abiding residents witness this situation, they become ever more cynical and alienated.

Here it is important to underscore the connections between jobs, drugs, and alienation. Many of the young blacks who have difficulty obtaining a job feel victimized by prejudice and discrimination. Such feelings of victimization may lead to a greater understanding, if not tolerance, of those who resort to dealing drugs to "survive." In these circumstances the drug trade, so dangerous and problematic for local communities and for society, becomes normal happenstance. In destitute inner-city communities, it is in fact becoming increasingly difficult to distinguish poverty from drug involvement. For example, many welfare mothers have become intimately connected with the drug trade, either as users or as what might be called support personnel, by allowing drug-dealing boyfriends or male relatives to use their homes as crack houses or drug depots in exchange for money or favors.

In addition, the young man who sells drugs is often encouraged and motivated to create new markets, sometimes recruiting his own family members into the drug culture, thus at times leading to their drug dependency. Why? Because he has come to covet the material things he sees dangled before him, things that become important not simply as practical items but as status symbols among his peers. A particular brand of eyeglasses or shoes or pants can indicate a person's social standing, bestowing on him a certain amount of self-esteem. Timberland boots, for example, which support a roughneck or macho image, are now being worn by many drug dealers and have come to be considered hip. The owner of such items, through his exhibitions and displays, is thus able to gain deference from and status among his peers. Media images—television, movies, the consumer mentality—fuel these desires as well. And when the regular economy cannot provide the means for satisfying them, some of the most desperate people turn to the underground economy.

See But Don't See

People residing in the drug-infested, depressed inner-city community may understand the economic need for the drug trade. Many residents become demoralized yet often try to coexist with it, rationalizing that the boys who deal drugs are not necessarily bad boys but are simply doing what they think they need to do to make money. They themselves, however, don't want to be victimized by the trade, nor do they want their friends and loved ones to be harmed. Many have come to believe that the police and the public officials don't care about their communities, and this belief encourages them to give up any hope of doing something about the drug trade. As a result, they may condemn the dealing but also tolerate it. They become inured to it. They also understand that some local people rely on it for financial support. The Robin Hood phenomenon helps the justification process. As was mentioned above, some dealers try to assist their community by surreptitiously donating money to various organizations and helping to support their families and friends with drug profits. One drug dealer told me he paid for his aunt's surgery as well as for all his mother's bills, and he was very proud of having done that. He was proud of having taken his girlfriend out to fancy restaurants, proud of everything he had become. He knew drug dealing was wrong, but he accepted his role in it. Of course, not everybody in the community is so accepting of the drug trade. Most people have very, very negative feelings about dealing, feelings that are most obviously on display when violence occurs. That is an important point—some people object only when violence erupts.

Another reason for seeing and yet not seeing drug transactions is that as people walk the streets of the community, they cannot help seeing what's going on, but are afraid to get involved. Concerned for their own safety, they don't even want people to notice them witnessing what is going on. After an incident like a shooting or a gang war, people tend to clam up for fear of retribution, especially where the authorities are concerned. If a bust occurs, anyone who is considered to have been paying too much attention to the drug activity might be suspected of having told the police about it. The way people deal with this fear and the need to protect themselves is by seeing but not seeing.

Many parents see but don't see for another reason: they realize that their own son is probably involved in the trade. They disapprove of it, but they also benefit from it. A mother who receives money, sometimes even large sums of money, from her son may not ask too many questions about its source. She just accepts the fact that the money is there somehow. Since it is sorely needed, there is a strong incentive not to interrupt the flow. Some people are so torn over what they are tolerating that they pray and ask forgiveness from the Lord for their de facto approval. Yet they cannot bring themselves to intervene.

The economic unraveling in so many of these communities puts people up against the wall and encourages them to do things that they would otherwise be morally reluctant to do. A boy who can't get a job in the regular economy becomes a drug dealer not all at once but by increments. These boys make a whole set of choices and decisions based in part on what they are able to do successfully. A boy who grows up on the streets thoroughly invested in the code of the street is also closer to the underground economy. Once mastered, the savoir faire of the street world—knowing how to deal coolly with people, how to move, look, act, dress—is a form of capital, not a form middle-class people would respect, but capital that can nonetheless be cashed in.

Since the code of the street is sanctioned primarily by violence and the threat of violent retribution (an eye for an eye and a tooth for a tooth), the more inner-city youths choose this route in life, the more normative the code of the street becomes in the neighborhood. Neighbors are encouraged to choose between an abstract code of justice that is disparaged by the most dangerous people on the streets and a practical code that is geared toward survival in the public spaces of their community.

Children growing up in these circumstances learn early in life that this is the way things are and that the lessons of those who might teach them otherwise become less and less relevant. Surrounded by violence and by indifference to the innocent victims of drug dealers and users alike, the decent people are finding it harder and harder to maintain a sense of community. Thus violence comes to regulate life in the drug-infested neighborhoods and the putative neighborhood leaders are increasingly the people who control the violence.

The ramifications of this state of affairs reach far beyond inner-city communities. A startling study by the Sentencing Project revealed that 33 percent of young black men in their twenties are under the supervision of the criminal justice system—in jail, in prison, on probation, or on parole. This astounding figure must be considered partly responsible for the widespread perception of young black men as dangerous and not to be trusted. This kind of demonization affects all young blacks—those of the middle class, those of the dwindling working class, as well as the street element.

Clocking: The Drug Trade as a Living

The introduction of crack has exacerbated the problem. Because it is cheap and readily available, it can support many dealers. Boys can acquire the needed skills—"street knowledge" and the ability to act on it—just by growing up in the impoverished innner-city neighborhood. Whatever a boy's home life is like, growing up in the 'hood means learning to some degree the code of the streets, the prescriptions and proscriptions of public behavior. He must be able to handle himself in public, and his parents, no matter how decent they are, may strongly encourage him to learn the rules. And because of various barriers he can often parlay that experience into a place in the drug trade much more easily than into a reasonable job. The relative ease of that transition speaks volumes about the life circumstances of inner-city adolescents.

For many impoverished young black men of the inner city, the opportunity for dealing drugs is literally just outside the door. By selling drugs, they have a chance to put more money into their pockets than they could get by legal means, and they can present themselves to peers as hip, in sharp contrast to the square image of those who work in places like McDonald's and wear silly uniforms. In fact, the oppositional culture has dubbed opting to sell drugs "getting legal." Martin, [a] decent, law-abiding young man, was often accosted by his drug-dealing peers as he stepped outside his door and headed for his regular job with the remark "Hey, Martin. When you gon' get legal?" He would simply reply, "Later for that. Later for that." When one needs money, which is always, this way of making it can seem like a godsend, and other boys encourage him to sell.

A common way of getting into the drug trade is to be part of a neighborhood peer group that begins to sell. A boy's social group can be easily transformed from a play group or a group that hangs around the corner listening to rap music or playing basketball—relatively innocuous activities—to a drug gang. The change requires a drug organizer to approach the group and consult the leader or "main man." The leader then begins to distribute opportunities to deal drugs—which is a kind of power—to various of his friends, his "boys." In time the small neighborhood group becomes a force to be reckoned with in the community, while taking an ever sharper interest in issues of turf and territory. The group then works to confuse concerns having to do with money and with protecting turf. The leader can paint an enticing picture for these boys, and he has an incentive to do so because the deed enhances his power. With "top dogs," "middle dogs," and "low dogs," the system resembles a pyramid scheme.

Youths who have strong family grounding—very decent folks, churchgoing families with a nuclear or quasi-nuclear structure and with love and concern for the younger people—are often the most resistant. But those who are drawn by the group, who get caught up with the responsibilities of breadwinning, with little opportunity to do so in the regular economy, sometimes resolve the tension by joining the drug trade. In turn, as they become serious dealers, these boys will often sell drugs to anybody who will buy them, including their own relatives; money and group loyalty become paramount issues. In this connection they may develop not only an excuse but a whole rap, a way of cajoling people to try crack just to get them hooked, because they know how quickly one can become addicted. For instance, they may approach someone as a friend and invite him or her to share some of their own supply, saying things like "It's not going to hurt you, it's not bad, you can handle it.

Strikingly, they may even become customers themselves—it is easy enough to become hooked by trying it once. Through the posturing required to prevail in the street life, many young people come to feel invincible, or they develop a profound need to show others they feel this way. And the power that accrues to dealers compounds the sense that they can control anything, even a crack cocaine high. In these circumstances they become "the man." Sometimes such a dealer does manage on crack off and on for a couple of years. Getting high now and then, he feels he is handling it, but, as the wiser dealers say, there is a fine line between handling it and having it handle you. At some inopportune moment he may be suddenly overcome with an insatiable need for the drug. Such a person is said to be "jonesing" for it; he is filled with such an intense desire for a high that he loses control of his actions. The predator becomes the prey—a common occurrence.

Like any marketing enterprise, the drug trade requires production and distribution networks. Another requirement is social control. Among drug dealers that requirement is satisfied by the use and threat of violence. Violence is not always intended, but it occurs easily as a result of both the intense competition for customers and the general disorganization that marks the lives of so many young dealers. Misunderstandings easily arise, such as "messing up" somebody's money—not paying for drugs that one has been advanced, thus squandering the dealer's investment. The older and established dealers are obligated to "do in" the people who have messed up their money, because otherwise they would lose credibility and status on the streets. Attempted takeovers of the business of rival dealers are also common. Though there is room in the system for more people now than there was before crack, competition remains fierce, especially as the belief that anyone can get rich dealing drugs becomes increasingly prevalent. The push to get in on the drug trade can in this sense be likened to the gold rush.

It is understood on the streets that the drug trade itself is unforgiving. To make a misstep is to risk getting roughed up, shot, or killed. When a seemingly senseless killing occurs, people in the community immediately assume it is drug-related. Those who get into the trade realize they are playing with fire but, given the presumed financial stakes, may feel they have no choice or are up to the challenge. Often the people who get hurt "deserved it," in terms of the code of the drug trade: they "crossed somebody big," or they "thought they were slick." People in the community understand this rationale, and it seems that the police acknowledge it too. Once a crime is drug-related, there often seems to be little interest and accountability in bringing the people who perpetrated it to justice.

Arguments over "business" are frequently settled on the spot, typically on the basis of arbitrary considerations, unfounded assumptions, or outright lies. There is also an ongoing fight for turf because of the large number of dealers, some connected with an organization, others freelancing. When a gang is set up in a particular area, its members know the streets and control the turf. As the trade becomes profitable, however, would-be dealers from outside the gang may want to do business in the same area or even take it over. A person who tries to muscle in, however, is threatening not just the current dealer's economic well-being but that part of the community as well. The connections of many of these boys go deep in the community through extended families, who may rely on the money. If a dealer is pushed out, he and a portion of the community can face financial disaster. As a result, some dealers are ready to fight to keep their turf, and people often get wounded or killed in the process.

There are major and minor turf wars. A major turf war often spawns smaller ones. In a major fight—whether the weapons are words, fists, or guns, but especially if they are guns—the dispute gets settled, at least for the time being. But everyone has an interpretation of what happened. The interpretations are exchanged in the various neighborhood institutions, including barbershops, taverns, and street corners, where people gather and talk, and an understanding of the original fight is negotiated. Since at least some of the people involved know the principal participants personally, they may take sides, becoming emotionally invested in having their version of the event prevail, and the discussions themselves can become heated and lead to violence.

Some boys simply crave the status associated with being a dealer. They want to wear a beeper, to be seen to be "clocking," to be associated with something hip and lucrative, even though it is an underground enterprise. Drug dealers are living the fast life; they are living on the edge. Older people will give young dealers advice, telling them that they are "living too fast." But everyone knows that once a person gets into that world, it is very hard to get out. The dealer can get hooked on the money and the material things it can buy, just as someone can get hooked on the drug; the adventure, the thrill of danger, and the respect people give him are also addictive. Furthermore, his associates in the trade may not let him out, because he knows too much and might pass information on to the wrong people, or they may want to make him an example. Much of his ability to maneuver depends on his identity and connections (his cousins, brothers, uncles, his other associates in the trade, his gang members, his boys) and on his status. Often the higher his status, the more leeway and independence he has—the more "juice" he has. The truly independent people, those who have achieved a high level of respect, may be able to get out in ways other people cannot, because they have established that they can be trusted. But often the only sure way of getting out is to get out of town.

Violent Fallout

Drug users also engage in violence. Many users start out as victims—when family members or boyfriends who deal drugs actively get them hooked in order to expand their markets—but they then become victimizers, robbing others to support their habits. Although some of the violence is focused and some is not, the result is a constant sense of uncertainty, a belief that anything can happen at any time. The successful dealer must be ever vigilant, but of course this makes him jittery and prone to react violently at the slightest perceived provocation. Furthermore, under the influence of drugs people's behavior may become unpredictable or truly dangerous. In these situations innocent bystanders, sometimes small children, can be shot or killed. Since drug trafficking permeates so much of the inner-city community, all its residents, whether involved with drugs or not, are at risk of finding themselves the unintended target of a stray bullet. The awareness of this constant danger fosters anxiety and skittishness even among the decent people, who therefore become more likely themselves to overreact in an uncertain encounter; these people may move, if they can.

Also fueling the violence that attends the drug trade is the proliferation of guns, which have become for many people easily accessible. Guns were in the community in the past, but mostly in the hands of adults. Today, kids fourteen and younger have guns, or they know how and where to get them. In the inner-city community, one can often hear gunshots in the distance but no sirens afterward. The likelihood is that the shots are being fired by young boys playing with guns, at times just shooting them off for the fun of it, usually in the middle of the night. Guns can have personality and status attached to them; they even have records. The price of a used gun indicates its history. A gun that "has a body on it" (was used to kill someone) is cheap because the person who is ultimately caught with it might be held responsible for murder. Moreover, in a society where so much economic inequality exists, for the severely alienated and desperate a gun can become like a bank card—an equalizer. Such a boy—or, increasingly, girl—who desperately needs money may use a gun to stick somebody up without a second thought. In a peculiar way, however, the prevalence of and ready access to guns may keep certain strangers honest and more careful in how they approach others. In these circumstances a kind of Wild West mentality obtains in some of the more dangerous neighborhoods, in which the fear of getting shot can constrain people from violating others.

As a result of the general atmosphere of danger, even people with a nonviolent orientation buy guns for protection. In Philadelphia not long ago, a blacks minister and resident of an inner-city community shot and killed an intruder. The incident sparked a good deal of discussion, but the general reaction of his black neighbors was, "Well, he did what he had to do." In fact, such incidents do not occur just in the inner city. In the gentrified neighborhood adjacent to the minister's, a white doctor going to bed one night heard a rumbling downstairs. He came down with his gun and in the darkness announced, "I have a gun." The rumbling continued, so he fired, killing an intruder in his kitchen with a bullet to the back of the head. He and his wife went to the police station, returned home at two in the morning, and cleaned up the blood.

It turned out that the intruder was apparently trying to steal the small kitchen television set to sell on the street, which could have brought a few dollars for crack. But this white doctor was so disturbed at having killed a young black man in those circumstances that he immediately moved out of his house and left the community. Thus the casualties of violence include people who simply get caught up in it—not just those who get shot but sometimes those who perpetrate the violence as well.

The Crack Culture: Rationale and Consequences

It must be continually underscored that much of this violence and drug activity is a reflection of the dislocations brought about by economic transformations, shifts that are occurring in the context of the new global economy. As was indicated above, where the wider economy is not receptive to these dislocated people, the underground economy is. That does not mean that anyone without a job is suddenly going to become a drug dealer; the process is not that simple. But the facts of race relations, unemployment, dislocation, and destitution create alienation, and alienation allows for a certain receptivity to overtures made by people seeking youthful new recruits for the drug trade.

Numerous inner-city black people continue to be locked out of many working-class occupations. Lack of education and training are often at issue, but, as Du Bois noted long ago, so is the problem of employers' racial preferences and social connections with prospective co-workers. For example, the building trades—plumbing, carpentry, roofing, and so forth—are often organized around family connections: fathers and uncles bring in their sons and nephews. To get a certificate to work in these trades, a young man requires a mentor, who not only teaches him skills but legitimizes him as a member of the trade. So the system perpetuates the dominance of ethnic groups that have been organized a long time. Now, the inner-city drug trade is composed of uncles and nephews too. From this perspective working-class Italians and Irish and others have their niche, and many severely alienated and desperate young blacks, at least those who are enterprising, can be said to have their niche too—in the drug trade. As Du Bois would have appreciated, such behavior, while not to be condoned, is understandable as a manifestatioin of racism and persistent poverty.

In the inner-city community, drug dealing thus becomes recognized as work, though it is an occupation that overwhelming numbers of residents surely despise. Yet there are Robin Hood types among the drug dealers, who distribute some of their profits in the community, buying things for people, financially helping out their friends and relatives, as well as complete strangers. One drug dealer told me how bad he felt when he found out that a woman who had bought crack from one of his underlings had kids and had used all her welfare money for the drugs. He sought the woman out and gave her half her money back. His rationale was that business is business but that the kids shouldn't go hungry.

Crack's addictive quality has led to the rapid establishment of a crack culture and makes it easy to maintain a clientele. The belief in the community is that crack addiction is immediate and permanent. Once you try crack, it is said, you're always "chasing the ghost"—the high that you get the first time is so intense that you can never achieve it again, but the desire to do so is strong enough that you keep pursuing it. One drug dealer told me that he has never seen anybody walk away from crack permanently; even if a user gets off it for two years, he said, the right drug dealer can easily hook him again by talking to him in the right way. I said to this dealer, "Knowing this, why do you sell crack? Isn't this like killing people, annihilating your own people?" He replied nonchalantly, "Well, if I wasn't doing it, somebody else would." To many inner-city residents, crack has become a seemingly permanent fixture of life, and dealing is a way to earn a living—even, for a few, to become rich.

24 The Saints and the Roughnecks

WILLIAM J. CHAMBLISS

When people deviate from what is expected of them, other people react. But on what do their reactions depend? Do they depend simply on the nature of the deviance itself, or is more involved? If so, what sorts of things?

It is these fascinating questions that Chambliss examines in this study of two groups of delinquents in the same high school. He found that although both groups were involved in serious and repetitive delinquent acts, one was perceived as a group of saints, the other was viewed as a bunch of roughnecks. After analyzing what influenced people's perceptions, and hence their reactions to the boys, Chambliss examines the far-reaching effects of those reactions. He indicates that in the case of the roughnecks, people's reactions helped lock the boys into behaviors that continued after high school, eventually leading to prison or to low-paying jobs. In contrast, social reactions to the saints set them on a life-course that not only meant staying out of prison but also entering well-paying positions of prestige.

EIGHT PROMISING YOUNG MEN—children of good, stable, white upper-middle-class families, active in school affairs, good pre-college students—were some of the most delinquent boys at Hanibal High School. While community residents knew that these boys occasionally sowed a few wild oats, they were totally unaware that sowing wild oats completely occupied the daily routine of these young men. The Saints were constantly occupied with truancy, drinking, wild driving, petty theft, and vandalism. Yet no one was officially arrested for any misdeed during the two years I observed them.

This record was particularly surprising in light of my observations during the same two years of another gang of Hanibal High School students, six lower-class white boys known as the Roughnecks. The Roughnecks were constantly in trouble with police and community even though their rate of delinquency was about equal with that of the Saints. What was the cause of this disparity? the result? The following consideration of the activities, social class, and community perceptions of both gangs may provide some answers.

The Saints from Monday to Friday

The Saints' principal daily concern was with getting out of school as early as possible. The boys managed to get out of school with minimum danger that they would be accused of playing hookey through an elaborate procedure for obtaining "legitimate" release from class. The most common procedure was for one boy to obtain the release of another by fabricating a meeting of some committee, program, or recognized club. Charles might raise his hand in his 9:00 chemistry class and ask to be excused—a euphemism for going to the bathroom. Charles would go to Ed's math class and inform the teacher that Ed was needed for a 9:30 rehearsal of the drama club play. The math teacher would recognize Ed and Charles as "good students" involved in numerous school activities and would permit Ed to leave at 9:30. Charles would return to his class, and Ed would go to Tom's English class to obtain his release. Tom would engineer Charles's escape. The strategy would continue until as many of the Saints as possible were freed. After a stealthy trip to the car (which had been parked in a strategic spot), the boys were off for a day of fun.

Over the two years I observed the Saints, this pattern was repeated nearly every day. There were variations on the theme, but in one form or another, the boys used this procedure for getting out of class and then off the school grounds. Rarely did all eight of the Saints manage to leave school at the same time. The average number avoiding school on the days I observed them was five.

Having escaped from the concrete corridors the boys usually went either to a pool hall on the other (lower-class) side of town or to a café in the suburbs. Both places were out of the way of people the boys were likely to know (family or school officials), and both provided a source of entertainment. The pool hall entertainment was the generally rough atmosphere, the occasional hustler, the sometimes drunk proprietor and, of course, the game of pool. The café's entertainment was provided by the owner. The boys would "accidentally" knock a glass on the floor or spill cola on the counter—not all the time, but enough to be sporting. They would also bend spoons, put salt in sugar bowls and generally tease whoever was working in the café. The owner had opened the café recently and was dependent on the boys' business which was, in fact, substantial since between the horsing around and the teasing they bought food and drinks.

The Saints on Weekends

On weekends the automobile was even more critical than during the week, for on weekends the Saints went to Big Town—a large city with a population of over a million 25 miles from Hanibal. Every Friday and Saturday night most of the Saints would meet between 8:00 and 8:30 and would go into Big Town. Big

Town activities included drinking heavily in taverns or nightclubs, driving drunkenly through the streets, and committing acts of vandalism and playing pranks.

By midnight on Fridays and Saturdays the Saints were usually thoroughly high, and one or two of them were often so drunk they had to be carried to the cars. Then the boys drove around town, calling obscenities to women and girls; occasionally trying (unsuccessfully so far as I could tell) to pick girls up; and driving recklessly through red lights and at high speeds with their lights out. Occasionally they played "chicken." One boy would climb out the back window of the car and across the roof to the driver's side of the car while the car was moving at high speed (between 40 and 50 miles an hour); then the driver would move over and the boy who had just crawled across the car roof would take the driver's seat.

Searching for "fair game" for a prank was the boys' principal activity after they left the tavern. The boys would drive alongside a foot patrolman and ask directions to some street. If the policeman leaned on the car in the course of answering the question, the driver would speed away, causing him to lose his balance. The Saints were careful to play this prank only in an area where they were not going to spend much time and where they could quickly disappear around a corner to avoid having their license plate number taken.

Construction sites and road repair areas were the special province of the Saints' mischief. A soon-to-be-repaired hole in the road inevitably invited the Saints to remove lanterns and wooden barricades and put them in the car, leaving the hole unprotected. The boys would find a safe vantage point and wait for an unsuspecting motorist to drive into the hole. Often, though not always, the boys would go up to the motorist and commiserate with him about the dreadful way the city protected its citizenry.

Leaving the scene of the open hole and the motorist, the boys would then go searching for an appropriate place to erect the stolen barricade. An "appropriate place" was often a spot on a highway near a curve in the road where the barricade would not be seen by an oncoming motorist. The boys would wait to watch an unsuspecting motorist attempt to stop and (usually) crash into the wooden barricade. With saintly bearing the boys might offer help and understanding.

A stolen lantern might well find its way onto the back of a police car or hang from a street lamp. Once a lantern served as a prop for a reenactment of the "midnight ride of Paul Revere" until the "play," which was taking place at 2:00 A.M. in the center of a main street of Big Town, was interrupted by a police car several blocks away. The boys ran, leaving the lanterns on the street, and managed to avoid being apprehended.

Abandoned houses, especially if they were located in out-of-the-way places, were fair game for destruction and spontaneous vandalism. The boys would break windows, remove furniture to the yard and tear it apart, urinate on the walls, and scrawl obscenities inside.

Through all the pranks, drinking, and reckless driving the boys managed miraculously to avoid being stopped by police. Only twice in two years was I aware that they had been stopped by a Big Town policeman. Once was for speeding (which they did every time they drove whether they were drunk or sober), and the driver managed to convince the policeman that it was simply an error. The second time they were stopped they had just left a nightclub and were walking through an alley. Aaron stopped to urinate and the boys began making obscene remarks. A foot patrolman came into the alley, lectured the boys and sent them home. Before the boys got to the car one began talking in a loud voice again. The policeman, who had followed them down the alley, arrested this boy for disturbing the peace and took him to the police station where the other Saints gathered. After paying a $5.00 fine, and with the assurance that there would be no permanent record of the arrest, the boy was released.

The boys had a spirit of frivolity and fun about their escapades. They did not view what they were engaged in as "delinquency," though it surely was by any reasonable definition of that word. They simply viewed themselves as having a little fun and who, they would ask, was really hurt by it? The answer had to be no one, although this fact remains one of the most difficult things to explain about the gang's behavior. Unlikely though it seems, in two years of drinking, driving, carousing, and vandalism no one was seriously injured as a result of the Saints' activities.

The Saints in School

The Saints were highly successful in school. The average grade for the group was "B," with two of the boys having close to a straight "A" average. Almost all of the boys were popular and many of them held offices in the school. One of the boys was vice president of the student body one year. Six of the boys played on athletic teams.

At the end of their senior year, the student body selected ten seniors for special recognition as the "school wheels"; four of the ten were Saints. Teachers and school officials saw no problem with any of these boys and anticipated that they would all "make something of themselves."

How the boys managed to maintain this impression is surprising in view of their actual behavior in school. Their technique for covering truancy was so successful that teachers did not even realize that the boys were absent from school much of the time. Occasionally, of course, the system would backfire and then the boy was on his own. A boy who was caught would be most contrite, would plead guilty and ask for mercy. He inevitably got the mercy he sought.

Cheating on examinations was rampant, even to the point of orally communicating answers to exams as well as looking at one another's papers. Since none of the group studied, and since they were primarily dependent on one another for help, it is surprising that grades were so high. Teachers contributed to the deception in their admitted inclination to give these boys (and presumably others like them) the benefit of the doubt. When asked how the boys did in school, and when pressed on specific examinations, teachers might admit that they were disappointed in John's performance, but would quickly add that they "knew that he was capable of doing better," so John was given a higher grade than he had actually earned. How often this happened is impossible to know. During the time that I observed the group, I never saw any of the boys take homework home. Teachers may have been "understanding" very regularly.

One exception to the gang's generally good performance was Jerry, who had a "C" average in his junior year, experienced disaster the next year, and failed to graduate. Jerry had always been a little more nonchalant than the others about the liberties he took in school. Rather than wait for someone to come get him from class, he would offer his own excuse and leave. Although he probably did not miss any more class than most of the others in the group, he did not take the requisite pains to cover his absences. Jerry was the only Saint whom I ever heard talk back to a teacher. Although teachers often called him a "cut up" or a "smart kid," they never referred to him as a troublemaker or as a kid headed for trouble. It seems likely, then, that Jerry's failure his senior year and his mediocre performance his junior year were consequences of his not playing the game the proper way (possibly because he was disturbed by his parents' divorce). His teachers regarded him as "immature" and not quite ready to get out of high school.

The Police and the Saints

The local police saw the Saints as good boys who were among the leaders of the youth in the community. Rarely, the boys might be stopped in town for speeding or for running a stop sign. When this happened the boys were always polite, contrite, and pled for mercy. As in school, they received the mercy they asked for. None ever received a ticket or was taken into the precinct by the local police.

The situation in Big Town, where the boys engaged in most of their delinquency, was only slightly different. The police there did not know the boys at all, although occasionally the boys were stopped by a patrolman. Once they were caught taking a lantern from a construction site. Another time they were stopped for running a stop sign, and on several occasions they were stopped for speeding. Their behavior was as before: contrite, polite, and penitent. The urban police, like the local police, accepted their demeanor as sincere. More important, the urban police were convinced that these were good boys just out for a lark.

The Roughnecks

Hanibal townspeople never perceived the Saints' high level of delinquency. The Saints were good boys who just went in for an occasional prank. After all, they were well dressed, well mannered, and had nice cars. The Roughnecks were a different story. Although the two gangs of boys were the same age, and both groups engaged in an equal amount of wild-oat sowing, everyone agreed that the not-so-well-dressed, not-so-well-mannered, not-so-rich boys were heading for trouble. Townspeople would say, "You can see the gang members at the drugstore, night after night, leaning against the storefront (sometimes drunk) or slouching around inside buying cokes, reading magazines, and probably stealing old Mr. Wall blind. When they are outside and girls walk by, even respectable girls, these boys make suggestive remarks. Sometimes their remarks are downright lewd."

From the community's viewpoint, the real indication that these kids were in trouble was that they were constantly involved with the police. Some of them had been picked up for stealing, mostly small stuff, of course, "but still it's stealing small stuff that leads to big time crimes." "Too bad," people said. "Too bad that these boys couldn't behave like the other kids in town; stay out of trouble, be polite to adults, and look to their future."

The community's impression of the degrees to which this group of six boys (ranging in age from 16 to 19) engaged in delinquency was somewhat distorted. In some ways the gang was more delinquent than the community thought; in other ways they were less.

The fighting activities of the group were fairly readily and accurately perceived by almost everyone. At least once a month, the boys would get into some sort of fight, although most fights were scraps between members of the group or involved only one member of the group and some peripheral hanger-on. Only three times in the period of observation did the group fight together: once against a gang from across town, once against two blacks, and once against a group of boys from another school. For the first two fights the group went out "looking for trouble"—and they found it both times. The third fight followed a football game and began spontaneously with an argument on the football field between one of the Roughnecks and a member of the opposition's football team.

Jack has a particular propensity for fighting and was involved in most of the brawls. He was a prime mover of the escalation of arguments into fights.

More serious than fighting, had the community been aware of it, was theft. Although almost everyone was aware that the boys occasionally stole things, they did not realize the extent of the activity. Petty stealing was a frequent event for the Roughnecks. Sometimes they stole as a group and coordinated their efforts; other times they stole in pairs. Rarely did they steal alone.

The thefts ranged from very small things like paperback books, comics, and ballpoint pens to expensive items like watches. The nature of the thefts

varied from time to time. The gang would go through a period of systematically lifting items from automobiles or school lockers. Types of thievery varied
with the whim of the gang. Some forms of thievery were more profitable than
others, but all thefts were for profit, not just thrills.

Roughnecks siphoned gasoline from cars as often as they had access to an
automobile, which was not very often. Unlike the Saints, who owned their own
cars, the Roughnecks would have to borrow their parents' cars, an event which
occurred only eight or nine times a year. The boys claimed to have stolen cars
for joy rides from time to time.

Ron committed the most serious of the group's offenses. With an uniden-
tified associate the boy attempted to burglarize a gasoline station. Although
this station had been robbed twice previously in the same month, Ron denied
any involvement in either of the other thefts. When Ron and his accomplice
approached the station, the owner was hiding in the bushes beside the station.
He fired both barrels of a double-barreled shotgun at the boys. Ron was severely injured; the other boy ran away and was never caught. Though he remained in critical condition for several months, Ron finally recovered and
served six months of the following year in reform school. Upon release from
reform school, Ron was put back a grade in school, and began running around
with a different gang of boys. The Roughnecks considered the new gang less
delinquent than themselves, and during the following year Ron had no more
trouble with the police.

The Roughnecks, then, engaged mainly in three types of delinquency:
theft, drinking, and fighting. Although community members perceived that
this gang of kids was delinquent, they mistakenly believed that their illegal activities were primarily drinking, fighting, and being a nuisance to passersby.
Drinking was limited among the gang members, although it did occur, and
theft was much more prevalent than anyone realized.

Drinking would doubtless have been more prevalent had the boys had
ready access to liquor. Since they rarely had automobiles at their disposal, they
could not travel very far, and the bars in town would not serve them. Most of the
boys had little money, and this, too, inhibited their purchase of alcohol. Their
major source of liquor was a local drunk who would buy them a fifth if they
would give him enough extra to buy himself a pint of whiskey or a bottle of wine.

The community's perception of drinking as prevalent stemmed from the
fact that it was the most obvious delinquency the boys engaged in. When one
of the boys had been drinking, even a casual observer seeing him on the corner would suspect that he was high.

There was a high level of mutual distrust and dislike between the
Roughnecks and the police. The boys felt very strongly that the police were
unfair and corrupt. Some evidence existed that the boys were correct in their
perception.

The main source of the boys' dislike for the police undoubtedly stemmed
from the fact that the police would sporadically harass the group. From the

standpoint of the boys, these acts of occasional enforcement of the law were whimsical and uncalled for. It made no sense to them, for example, that the police would come to the corner occasionally and threaten them with arrest for loitering when the night before the boys had been out siphoning gasoline from cars and the police had been nowhere in sight. To the boys, the police were stupid on the one hand, for not being where they should have been and catching the boys in a serious offense, and unfair on the other hand, for trumping up "loitering" charges against them.

From the viewpoint of the police, the situation was quite different. They knew, with all the confidence necessary to be a policeman, that these boys were engaged in criminal activities. They knew this partly from occasionally catching them, mostly from circumstantial evidence ("the boys were around when those tires were slashed"), and partly because the police shared the view of the community in general that this was a bad bunch of boys. The best the police could hope to do was to be sensitive to the fact that these boys were engaged in illegal acts and arrest them whenever there was some evidence that they had been involved. Whether or not the boys had in fact committed a particular act in a particular way was not especially important. The police had a broader view: their job was to stamp out these kids' crimes; the tactics were not as important as the end result.

Over the period that the group was under observation, each member was arrested at least once. Several of the boys were arrested a number of times and spent at least one night in jail. While most were never taken to court, two of the boys were sentenced to six months' incarceration in boys' schools.

The Roughnecks in School

The Roughnecks' behavior in school was not particularly disruptive. During school hours they did not all hang around together, but tended instead to spend most of their time with one or two other members of the gang who were their special buddies. Although every member of the gang attempted to avoid school as much as possible, they were not particularly successful and most of them attended school with surprising regularity. They considered school a burden—something to be gotten through with a minimum of conflict. If they were "bugged" by a particular teacher, it could lead to trouble. One of the boys, Al, once threatened to beat up a teacher and, according to the other boys, the teacher hid under a desk to escape him.

Teachers saw the boys the way the general community did, as heading for trouble, as being uninterested in making something of themselves. Some were also seen as being incapable of meeting the academic standards of the school. Most of the teachers expressed concern for this group of boys and were willing to pass them despite poor performance, in the belief that failing them would only aggravate the problem.

The group of boys had a grade point average just slightly above "C." No one in the group failed either grade, and no one had better than a "C" average. They were very consistent in their achievement or, at least, the teachers were consistent in their perception of the boys' achievement.

Two of the boys were good football players. Herb was acknowledged to be the best player in the school, and Jack was almost as good. Both boys were criticized for their failure to abide by training rules, for refusing to come to practice as often as they should, and for not playing their best during practice. What they lacked in sportsmanship they made up for in skill, apparently, and played every game no matter how poorly they had performed in practice or how many practice sessions they had missed.

Two Questions

Why did the community, the school, and the police react to the Saints as though they were good, upstanding, nondelinquent youths with bright futures but to the Roughnecks as though they were tough, young criminals who were headed for trouble? Why did the Roughnecks and the Saints in fact have quite different careers after high school—careers which, by and large, lived up to the expectations of the community?

The most obvious explanation for the differences in the community's and law enforcement agencies' reactions to the two gangs is that one group of boys was "more delinquent" than the other. Which group was more delinquent? The answer to this question will determine in part how we explain the differential responses to these groups by the members of the community and, particularly, by law enforcement and school officials.

In sheer number of illegal acts, the Saints were the more delinquent. They were truant from school for at least part of the day almost every day of the week. In addition, their drinking and vandalism occurred with surprising regularity. The Roughnecks, in contrast, engaged sporadically in delinquent episodes. While these episodes were frequent, they certainly did not occur on a daily or even a weekly basis.

The difference in frequency of offenses was probably caused by the Roughnecks' inability to obtain liquor and to manipulate legitimate excuses from school. Since the Roughnecks had less money than the Saints, and teachers carefully supervised their school activities, the Roughnecks' hearts may have been as black as the Saints', but their misdeeds were not nearly as frequent.

There are really no clear-cut criteria by which to measure qualitative differences in antisocial behavior. The most important dimension is generally referred to as the "seriousness" of the offenses.

If seriousness encompasses the relative economic costs of delinquent acts, then some assessment can be made. The Roughnecks probably stole an average of about $5.00 worth of goods a week. Some weeks the figure was considerably higher, but these times must be balanced against long periods when almost nothing was stolen.

The Saints were more continuously engaged in delinquency, but their acts were not for the most part costly to property. Only their vandalism and occasional theft of gasoline would so qualify. Perhaps once or twice a month they would siphon a tankful of gas. The other costly items were street signs, construction lanterns, and the like. All of these acts combined probably did not quite average $5.00 a week, partly because much of the stolen equipment was abandoned and presumably could be recovered. The difference in cost of stolen property between the two groups was trivial, but the Roughnecks probably had a slightly more expensive set of activities than did the Saints.

Another meaning of seriousness is the potential threat of physical harm to members of the community and to the boys themselves. The Roughnecks were more prone to physical violence; they not only welcomed an opportunity to fight; they went seeking it. In addition, they fought among themselves frequently. Although the fighting never included deadly weapons, it was still a menace, however minor, to the physical safety of those involved.

The Saints never fought. They avoided physical conflict both inside and outside the group. At the same time, though, the Saints frequently endangered their own and other people's lives. They did so almost every time they drove a car, especially if they had been drinking. Sober, their driving was risky; under the influence of alcohol it was horrendous. In addition, the Saints endangered the lives of others with their pranks. Street excavations left unmarked were a very serious hazard.

Evaluating the relative seriousness of the two gangs' activities is difficult. The community reacted as though the behavior of the Roughnecks was a problem, and they reacted as though the behavior of the Saints was not. But the members of the community were ignorant of the array of delinquent acts that characterized the Saints' behavior. Although concerned citizens were unaware of much of the Roughnecks' behavior as well, they were much better informed about the Roughnecks' involvement in delinquency than they were about the Saints'.

Visibility

Differential treatment of the two gangs resulted in part because one gang was infinitely more visible than the other. This differential visibility was a direct function of the economic standing of the families. The Saints had access to automobiles and were able to remove themselves from the sight of the community. In as routine a decision as to where to go to have a milkshake after school, the Saints stayed away from the mainstream of community life. Lacking transportation, the Roughnecks could not make it to the edge of town. The center of town was the only practical place for them to meet since their homes were scattered throughout the town and any noncentral meeting place put an undue hardship on some members. Through necessity the Roughnecks congregated in a crowded area where everyone in the community passed frequently, including teachers and law enforcement officers. They could easily see the Roughnecks hanging around the drugstore.

The Roughnecks, of course, made themselves even more visible by making remarks to passersby and by occasionally getting into fights on the corner. Meanwhile, just as regularly, the Saints were either at the café on one edge of town or in the pool hall at the other edge of town. Without any particular realization that they were making themselves inconspicuous, the Saints were able to hide their time-wasting. Not only were they removed from the mainstream of traffic, but they were almost always inside a building.

On their escapades the Saints were also relatively invisible, since they left Hanibal and traveled to Big Town. Here, too, they were mobile, roaming the city, rarely going to the same area twice.

Demeanor

To the notion of visibility must be added the difference in the responses of group members to outside intervention with their activities. If one of the Saints was confronted with an accusing policeman, even if he felt he was truly innocent of a wrongdoing, his demeanor was apologetic and penitent. A Roughneck's attitude was almost the polar opposite. When confronted with a threatening adult authority, even one who tried to be pleasant, the Roughneck's hostility and disdain were clearly observable. Sometimes he might attempt to put up a veneer of respect, but it was thin and was not accepted as sincere by the authority.

School was no different from the community at large. The Saints could manipulate the system by feigning compliance with the school norms. The availability of cars at school meant that once free from the immediate sight of the teacher, the boys could disappear rapidly. And this escape was well enough planned that no administrator or teacher was nearby when the boys left. A Roughneck who wished to escape for a few hours was in a bind. If it were possible to get free from class, downtown was still a mile away, and even if he arrived there, he was still very visible. Truancy for the Roughnecks meant almost certain detection, while the Saints enjoyed almost complete immunity from sanctions.

Bias

Community members were not aware of the transgressions of the Saints. Even if the Saints had been less discreet, their favorite delinquencies would have been perceived as less serious than those of the Roughnecks.

In the eyes of the police and school officials, a boy who drinks in an alley and stands intoxicated on the street corner is committing a more serious offense than is a boy who drinks to inebriation in a nightclub or a tavern and drives around afterwards in a car. Similarly, a boy who steals a wallet from a store will be viewed as having committed a more serious offense than a boy who steals a lantern from a construction site.

Perceptual bias also operates with respect to the demeanor of the boys in the two groups when they are confronted by adults. It is not simply that adults dislike the posture affected by boys of the Roughneck ilk; more important is the conviction that the posture adopted by the Roughnecks is an indication of their devotion and commitment to deviance as a way of life. The posture becomes a cue, just as the type of the offense is a cue, to the degree to which the known transgressions are indicators of the youths' potential for other problems.

Visibility, demeanor, and bias are surface variables which explain the day-to-day operations of the police. Why do these surface variables operate as they do? Why did the police choose to disregard the Saints' delinquencies while breathing down the backs of the Roughnecks?

The answer lies in the class structure of American society and the control of legal institutions by those at the top of the class structure. Obviously, no representative of the upper class drew up the operational chart for the police which led them to look in the ghettos and on street corners—which led them to see the demeanor of lower-class youth as troublesome and that of upper-middle-class youth as tolerable. Rather, the procedures simply developed from experience—experience with irate and influential upper-middle-class parents insisting that their son's vandalism was simply a prank and his drunkenness only a momentary "sowing of wild oats"—experience with cooperative or indifferent, powerless, lower-class parents who acquiesced to the law's definition of their son's behavior.

Adult Careers of the Saints and the Roughnecks

The community's confidence in the potential of the Saints and the Roughnecks apparently was justified. If anything, the community members underestimated the degree to which these youngsters would turn out "good" or "bad."

Seven of the eight members of the Saints went on to college immediately after high school. Five of the boys graduated from college in four years. The sixth one finished college after two years in the army, and the seventh spent four years in the air force before returning to college and receiving a B.A. degree. Of these seven college graduates, three went on for advanced degrees. One finished law school and is now active in state politics, one finished medical school and is practicing near Hanibal, and one boy is now working for a

Ph.D. The other four college graduates entered submanagerial, managerial, or executive training positions with larger firms.

The only Saint who did not complete college was Jerry. Jerry had failed to graduate from high school with the other Saints. During his second senior year, after the other Saints had gone on to college, Jerry began to hang around with what several teachers described as a "rough crowd"—the gang that was heir apparent to the Roughnecks. At the end of his second senior year, when he did graduate from high school, Jerry took a job as a used-car salesman, got married, and quickly had a child. Although he made several abortive attempts to go to college by attending night school, when I last saw him (ten years after high school) Jerry was unemployed and had been living on unemployment for almost a year. His wife worked as a waitress.

Some of the Roughnecks have lived up to community expectations. A number of them were headed for trouble. A few were not.

Jack and Herb were the athletes among the Roughnecks, and their athletic prowess paid off handsomely. Both boys received unsolicited athletic scholarships to college. After Herb received his scholarship (near the end of his senior year), he apparently did an about-face. His demeanor became very similar to that of the Saints. Although he remained a member in good standing of the Roughnecks, he stopped participating in most activities and did not hang out on the corner as often.

Jack did not change. If anything, he became more prone to fighting. He even made excuses for accepting the scholarship. He told the other gang members that the school had guaranteed him a "C" average if he would come to play football—an idea that seems far-fetched, even in this day of highly competitive recruiting.

During the summer after graduation from high school, Jack attempted suicide by jumping from a tall building. The jump would certainly have killed most people trying it, but Jack survived. He entered college in the fall and played four years of football. He and Herb graduated in four years, and both are teaching and coaching in high schools. They are married and have stable families. If anything, Jack appears to have a more prestigious position in the community than does Herb, though both are well respected and secure in their positions.

Two of the boys never finished high school. Tommy left at the end of his junior year and went to another state. That summer he was arrested and placed on probation on a manslaughter charge. Three years later he was arrested for murder; he pleaded guilty to second degree murder and is serving a 30-year sentence in the state penitentiary.

Al, the other boy who did not finish high school, also left the state in his senior year. He is serving a life sentence in a state penitentiary for first degree murder.

Wes is a small-time gambler. He finished high school and "bummed around." After several years he made contact with a bookmaker who employed him as a runner. Later he acquired his own area and has been working it ever since. His position among the bookmakers is almost identical to the position he had in the gang; he is always around, but no one is really aware of him. He makes no trouble, and he does not get into any. Steady, reliable, capable of keeping his mouth closed, he plays the game by the rules, even though the game is an illegal one.

That leaves only Ron. Some of his former friends reported that they had heard he was "driving a truck up north," but no one could provide any concrete information.

Reinforcement

The community responded to the Roughnecks as boys in trouble, and the boys agreed with that perception. Their pattern of deviancy was reinforced, and breaking away from it became increasingly unlikely. Once the boys acquired an image of themselves as deviants, they selected new friends who affirmed that self-image. As that self-conception became more firmly entrenched, they also became willing to try new and more extreme deviances. With their growing alienation came freer expression of disrespect and hostility for representatives of the legitimate society. This disrespect increased the community's negativism, perpetuating the entire process of commitment to deviance. Lack of a commitment to deviance works the same way. In either case, the process will perpetuate itself unless some event (like a scholarship to college or a sudden failure) external to the established relationship intervenes. For two of the Roughnecks (Herb and Jack), receiving college athletic scholarships created new relations and culminated in a break with the established pattern of deviance. In the case of one of the Saints (Jerry), his parents' divorce and his failing to graduate from high school changed some of his other relations. Being held back in school for a year and losing his place among the Saints had sufficient impact on Jerry to alter his self-image and virtually to assure that he would not go on to college as his peers did. Although the experiments of life can rarely be reversed, it seems likely in view of the behavior of the other boys who did not enjoy this special treatment by the school that Jerry, too, would have "become something" had he graduated as anticipated. For Herb and Jack outside intervention worked to their advantage; for Jerry it was his undoing.

Selective perception and labeling—finding, processing, and punishing some kinds of criminality and not others—means that visible, poor, nonmobile, outspoken, undiplomatic "tough" kids will be noticed, whether their actions are seriously delinquent or not. Other kids, who have established a reputation for being bright (even though underachieving), disciplined, and involved in respectable activities, who are mobile and monied, will be invisible when they deviate from sanctioned activities. They'll sow their wild oats—

perhaps even wider and thicker than their lower-class cohorts—but they won't be noticed. When it's time to leave adolescence most will follow the expected path, settling into the ways of the middle class, remembering fondly the delinquent but unnoticed fling of their youth. The Roughnecks and others like them may turn around, too. It is more likely that their noticeable deviance will have been so reinforced by police and community that their lives will be effectively channeled into careers consistent with their adolescent background.

25 The Pathology of Imprisonment

PHILIP G. ZIMBARDO

Why are our prisons such powder kegs? To most people, this is not a difficult question and the answer is obvious—because of the kind of people who are locked up in prisons: They are criminals, antisocial, and disposed to violence. If not that, then they hate the guards, the food, or the restrictions of prison life (which is what they deserved in the first place!). Similarly, people have little difficulty explaining why prison guards are brutal: It is either the type of people with whom the guards must deal ("animals") or the type of people who are attracted to being prison guards in the first place ("sadistic types"). Such reasons are commonly cited to explain prison violence, but it turns out that much more fundamental social processes are involved. As Zimbardo's remarkable experiment uncovered, the structuring of relationships within the prison lays a firm foundation for prison brutality and violence.

While reading this fascinating account, you may begin to think about how prisons could be improved in order to minimize violence. To reach such a goal, what changes would you suggest that we make in the social structure of prisons?

I was recently released from solitary confinement after being held therein for 37 months [months!]. A silent system was imposed upon me and to even whisper to the man in the next cell resulted in being beaten by guards, sprayed with chemical mace, blackjacked, stomped and thrown into a strip-cell naked to sleep on a concrete floor without bedding, covering, wash basin or even a toilet. The floor served as toilet and bed, and even there the silent system was enforced. To let a moan escape your lips because of the pain and discomfort . . . resulted in another beating. I spent not days, but months there during my 37 months in solitary. . . . I have filed every writ possible against the administrative acts of brutality. The state courts have all denied the petitions. Because of my refusal to let the things die down and forget all that happened during my 37 months in solitary . . . I am the most hated prisoner in [this] penitentiary, and called a "hard-core incorrigible."

Maybe I am an incorrigible, but if true, it's because I would rather die than to accept being treated as less than a human being. I have never complained of my prison sentence as being unjustified except through legal means of appeals. I have never put a knife on a guard's throat and demanded my release. I know that thieves must be punished and I don't justify stealing, even though I am a thief myself. but now I don't think I will be a thief when I am released. No, I'm not re-habilitated. It's just that I no longer think of becoming wealthy by stealing. I now only think of killing—killing those who have beaten me and treated me as if I were a dog. I hope and pray for the sake of my own soul and future life of free-dom that I am able to overcome the bitterness and hatred which eats daily at my soul, but I know to overcome it will not be easy.

THIS ELOQUENT PLEA FOR PRISON REFORM—for humane treatment of human beings, for the basic dignity that is the right of every American—came to me secretly in a letter from a prisoner who cannot be identified because he is still in a state correctional institution. He sent it to me because he read of an experiment I recently conducted at Stanford University. In an attempt to understand just what it means psychologically to be a pris-oner or a prison guard, Craig Haney, Curt Banks, Dave Jaffe, and I created our own prison. We carefully screened over 70 volunteers who answered an ad in a Palo Alto city newspaper and ended up with about two dozen young men who were selected to be part of this study. They were mature, emotionally sta-ble, normal, intelligent college students from middle-class homes throughout the United States and Canada. They appeared to represent the cream of the crop of this generation. None had any criminal record and all were relatively homogeneous on many dimensions initially.

Half were arbitrarily designated as prisoners by a flip of a coin, the others as guards. These were the roles they were to play in our simulated prison. The guards were made aware of the potential seriousness and danger of the situa-tion and their own vulnerability. They made up their own formal rules for maintaining law, order, and respect, and were generally free to improvise new ones during their eight-hour, three-man shifts. The prisoners were unexpect-edly picked up at their homes by a city policeman in a squad car, searched, handcuffed, fingerprinted, booked at the Palo Alto station house, and taken blindfolded to our jail. There they were stripped, deloused, put into a uniform, given a number, and put into a cell with two other prisoners where they ex-pected to live for the next two weeks. The pay was good ($15 a day), and their motivation was to make money.

We observed and recorded on videotape the events that occurred in the prison, and we interviewed and tested the prisoners and guards at various points throughout the study. Some of the videotapes of the actual encounters between the prisoners and guards were seen on the NBC News feature "Chronolog" on November 26, 1971.

At the end of only six days we had to close down our mock prison because what we saw was frightening. It was no longer apparent to most of the subjects (or to us) where reality ended and their roles began. The majority had indeed become prisoners or guards, no longer able to clearly differentiate between role playing and self. There were dramatic changes in virtually every aspect of their behavior, thinking, and feeling. In less than a week the experience of imprisonment undid (temporarily) a lifetime of learning; human values were suspended, self-concepts were challenged, and the ugliest, most base, pathological side of human nature surfaced. We were horrified because we saw some boys (guards) treat others as if they were despicable animals, taking pleasure in cruelty, while other boys (prisoners) became servile, dehumanized robots who thought only of escape, of their own individual survival, and of their mounting hatred for the guards.

We had to release three prisoners in the first four days because they had such acute situational traumatic reactions as hysterical crying, confusion in thinking, and severe depression. Others begged to be paroled, and all but three were willing to forfeit all the money they had earned if they could be paroled. By then (the fifth day) they had been so programmed to think of themselves as prisoners that when their request for parole was denied, they returned docilely to their cells. Now, had they been thinking as college students acting in an oppressive experiment, they would have quit once they no longer wanted the $15 a day we used as our only incentive. However, the reality was not quitting an experiment but "being paroled by the parole board from the Stanford County Jail." By the last days, the earlier solidarity among the prisoners (systematically broken by the guards) dissolved into "each man for himself." Finally, when one of their fellows was put into solitary confinement (a small closet) for refusing to eat, the prisoners were given a choice by one of the guards: give up their blankets and the incorrigible prisoner would be let out, or keep their blankets and he would be kept in all night. They voted to keep their blankets and to abandon their brother.

About a third of the guards became tyrannical in their arbitrary use of power, in enjoying their control over other people. They were corrupted by the power of their roles and became quite inventive in their techniques of breaking the spirit of the prisoners and making them feel they were worthless. Some of the guards merely did their jobs as tough but fair correctional officers, and several were good guards from the prisoners' point of view since they did them small favors and were friendly. However, no good guards ever interfered with a command by any of the bad guards; they never intervened on the side of the prisoners, they never told the others to ease off because it was only an experiment, and they never even came to me as prison superintendent or experimenter in charge to complain. In part, they were good because the others were bad; they needed the others to help establish their own egos in a positive light. In a sense, the good guards perpetuated the prison more than the other guards because their own need to be liked prevented them from disobeying or violating the implicit guards' code. At the same time, the act of befriending the prisoners created a social reality which made the prisoners less likely to rebel.

By the end of the week the experiment had become a reality, as if it were a Pirandello play directed by Kafka that just keeps going after the audience has left. The consultant for our prison, Carlo Prescott, an exconvict with 16 years of imprisonment in California's jails, would get so depressed and furious each time he visited our prison, because of its psychological similarity to his experiences, that he would have to leave. A Catholic priest who was a former prison chaplain in Washington, D.C., talked to our prisoners after four days and said they were just like the other first-timers he had seen.

But in the end, I called off the experiment not because of the horror I saw out there in the prison yard, but because of the horror of realizing that *I* could have easily traded places with the most brutal guard or become the weakest prisoner full of hatred at being so powerless that I could not eat, sleep, or go to the toilet without permission of the authorities. *I* could have become Calley at My Lai, George Jackson at San Quentin, one of the men at Attica, or the prisoner quoted at the beginning of this article.

Individual behavior is largely under the control of social forces and environmental contingencies rather than personality traits, character, will power, or other empirically unvalidated constructs. Thus we create an illusion of freedom by attributing more internal control to ourselves, to the individual, than actually exists. We thus underestimate the power and pervasiveness of situational controls over behavior because: (a) they are often nonobvious and subtle, (b) we can often avoid entering situations where we might be so controlled, (c) we label as "weak" or "deviant" people in those situations who do behave differently from how we believed we would.

Each of us carries around in our heads a favorable self-image in which we are essentially just, fair, humane, and understanding. For example, we could not imagine inflicting pain on others without much provocation or hurting people who had done nothing to us, who in fact were even liked by us. However, there is a growing body of social psychological research which underscores the conclusion derived from this prison study. Many people, perhaps the majority, can be made to do almost anything when put into psychologically compelling situations—regardless of their morals, ethics, values, attitudes, beliefs, or personal convictions. My colleague, Stanley Milgram, has shown that more than 60 percent of the population will deliver what they think is a series of painful electric shocks to another person even after the victim cries for mercy, begs them to stop, and then apparently passes out. The subjects complained that they did not want to inflict more pain but blindly obeyed the command of the authority figure (the experimenter) who said that they must go on. In my own research on violence, I have seen mild-mannered co-eds repeatedly give shocks (which they thought were causing pain) to another girl, a stranger whom they had rated very favorably, simply by being made to feel anonymous and put in a situation where they were expected to engage in this activity.

Observers of these and similar experimental situations never predict their outcomes and estimate that it is unlikely that they themselves would behave similarly. They can be so confident only when they are outside the situation. However, since the majority of people in these studies do act in nonrational, nonobvious ways, it follows that the majority of observers would also succumb to the social psychological forces in the situation.

With regard to prisons, we can state that the mere act of assigning labels to people and putting them into a situation where those labels acquire validity and meaning is sufficient to elicit pathological behavior. This pathology is not predictable from any available diagnostic indicators we have in the social sciences, and is extreme enough to modify in very significant ways fundamental attitudes and behavior. The prison situation, as presently arranged, is guaranteed to generate severe enough pathological reactions in both guards and prisoners as to debase their humanity, lower their feelings of self-worth, and make it difficult for them to be part of a society outside of their prison.

For years our national leaders have been pointing to the enemies of freedom, to the fascist or communist threat to the American way of life. In so doing they have overlooked the threat of social anarchy that is building within our own country without any outside agitation. As soon as a person comes to the realization that he is being imprisoned by his society or individuals in it, then, in the best American tradition, he demands liberty and rebels, accepting death as an alternative. The third alternative, however, is to allow oneself to become a good prisoner—docile, cooperative, uncomplaining, conforming in thought, and complying in deed.

Our prison authorities now point to the militant agitators who are still vaguely referred to as part of some communist plot, as the irresponsible, incorrigible troublemakers. They imply that there would be no trouble, riots, hostages, or deaths if it weren't for this small band of bad prisoners. In other words, then, everything would return to "normal" again in the life of our nation's prisons if they could break these men.

The riots in prison are coming from within—from within every man and woman who refuses to let the system turn them into an object, a number, a thing, or a no-thing. It is not communist-inspired, but inspired by the spirit of American freedom. No man wants to be enslaved. To be powerless, to be subject to the arbitrary exercise of power, to not be recognized as a human being is to be a slave.

To be a militant prisoner is to become aware that the physical jails are but more blatant extensions of the forms of social and psychological oppression experienced daily in the nation's ghettos. They are trying to awaken the conscience of the nation to the ways in which the American ideals are being perverted, apparently in the name of justice but actually under the banner of apathy, fear, and hatred. If we do not listen to the pleas of the prisoners at Attica to be treated like human beings, then we have all become brutalized by our priorities for property rights over human rights. The consequence will not only be more prison riots but a loss of all those ideals on which this country was founded.

The public should be aware that they own the prisons and that their business is failing. The 70 percent recidivism rate and the escalation in severity of crimes committed by graduates of our prisons are evidence that current prisons fail to rehabilitate the inmates in any positive way. Rather, they are breeding grounds for hatred of the establishment, a hatred that makes every citizen a target of violent assault. Prisons are a bad investment for us taxpayers. Until now we have not cared; we have turned over to wardens and prison authorities the unpleasant job of keeping people who threaten us out of our sight. Now we are shocked to learn that their management practices have failed to improve the product and instead turn petty thieves into murderers. We must insist upon new management or improved operating procedures.

The cloak of secrecy should be removed from the prisons. Prisoners claim they are brutalized by the guards; guards say it is a lie. Where is the impartial test of the truth in such a situation? Prison officials have forgotten that they work for us, that they are only public servants whose salaries are paid by our taxes. They act as if it is their prison, like a child with a toy he won't share. Neither lawyers, judges, the legislature, nor the public is allowed into prisons to ascertain the truth unless the visit is sanctioned by authorities and until all is prepared for their visit. I was shocked to learn that my request to join a congressional investigating committee's tour of San Quentin and Soledad was refused, as was that of the news media.

There should be an ombudsman in every prison, not under the pay or control of the prison authority, and responsible only to the courts, the state legislature, and the public. Such a person could report on violations of constitutional and human rights.

Guards must be given better training than they now receive for the difficult job society imposes upon them. To be a prison guard as now constituted is to be put in a situation of constant threat from within the prison, with no social recognition from the society at large. As was shown graphically at Attica, prison guards are also prisoners of the system who can be sacrificed to the demands of the public to be punitive and the needs of politicians to preserve an image. Social scientists and business administrators should be called upon to design and help carry out this training.

The relationship between the individual (who is sentenced by the courts to a prison term) and his community must be maintained. How can a prisoner return to a dynamically changing society that most of us cannot cope with after being out of it for a number of years? There should be more community involvement in these rehabilitation centers, more ties encouraged and promoted between the trainees and family and friends, more educational opportunities to prepare them for returning to their communities as more valuable members of it than they were before they left.

Finally, the main ingredient necessary to effect any change at all in prison reform, in the rehabilitation of a single prisoner, or even in the optimal development of a child is caring. Reform must start with people—especially people with power—caring about the well-being of others. Underneath the toughest, society-hating convict, rebel, or anarchist is a human being who wants his existence to be recognized by his fellows and who wants someone else to care about whether he lives or dies and to grieve if he lives imprisoned rather than lives free.

26 On Being Sane in Insane Places

DAVID L. ROSENHAN

On the one hand, it is not uncommon for people who violate *explicit* rules written into law to find themselves enmeshed in a formal system that involves passing judgment on their fitness to remain in society. As we have just seen with the preceding selection, removing people's freedom can thrust them into a highly volatile situation. On the other hand, people who violate *implicit* rules (the assumptions about what characterizes "normal" people) also can find themselves caught up in a formal system that involves passing judgment on their fitness to remain in society. "If found guilty of insanity," they, too, are institutionalized—placed in the care of keepers who oversee almost all aspects of their lives.

The taken-for-granted assumption in institutionalizing people who violate implicit rules is that we are able to tell the sane from the insane. If we cannot do so, the practice itself would be insane! In that case, we would have to explicitly question contemporary psychiatry as a mechanism of social control. But what kind of question is this? Even most of us non-psychiatrists are certain that we can tell the difference between who is sane and who is not. However, in a fascinating experiment, Rosenhan put to the test whether or not even psychiatrists can differentiate between the sane and the insane. As detailed in this account, the results contain a few surprises.

IF SANITY AND INSANITY EXIST . . . how shall we know them? The question is neither capricious nor itself insane. However much we may be personally convinced that we can tell the normal from the abnormal, the evidence is simply not compelling. It is commonplace, for example, to read about murder trials wherein eminent psychiatrists for the defense are contradicted by equally eminent psychiatrists for the prosecution on the matter of the defendant's sanity. More generally, there are a great deal of conflicting data on the reliability, utility, and meaning of such terms as "sanity," "insanity," "mental illness," and "schizophrenia."[1] Finally, as early as 1934, Benedict suggested that normality and abnormality are not universal.[2] What is viewed as normal in one culture may be seen as quite aberrant in another. Thus, notions of normality and abnormality may not be quite as accurate as people believe they are.

To raise questions regarding normality and abnormality is in no way to question the fact that some behaviors are deviant or odd. Murder is deviant. So, too, are hallucinations. Nor does raising such questions deny the existence of the personal anguish that is often associated with "mental illness." Anxiety and depression exist. Psychological suffering exists. But normality and abnormality, sanity and insanity, and the diagnoses that flow from them may be less substantive than many believe them to be.

At its heart, the question of whether the sane can be distinguished from the insane (and whether degrees of insanity can be distinguished from each other) is a simple matter: Do the salient characteristics that lead to diagnoses reside in the patients themselves or in the environments and contexts in which observers find them? From Bleuler, through Kretschmer, through the formulators of the recently revised *Diagnostic and Statistical Manual* of the American Psychiatric Association, the belief has been strong that patients present symptoms, that those symptoms can be categorized, and, implicitly, that the sane are distinguishable from the insane. More recently, however, this belief has been questioned. Based in part on theoretical and anthropological considerations, but also on philosophical, legal, and therapeutic ones, the view has grown that psychological categorization of mental illness is useless at best and downright harmful, misleading, and pejorative at worst. Psychiatric diagnoses, in this view, are in the minds of the observers and are not valid summaries of characteristics displayed by the observed.[3,4,5]

Gains can be made in deciding which of these is more nearly accurate by getting normal people (that is, people who do not have, and have never suffered, symptoms of serious psychiatric disorders) admitted to psychiatric hospitals and then determining whether they were discovered to be sane and, if so, how. If the sanity of such pseudopatients were always detected, there would be *prima facie* evidence that a sane individual can be distinguished from the insane context in which he is found. Normality (and presumably abnormality) is distinct enough that it can be recognized wherever it occurs, for it is carried within the person. If, on the other hand, the sanity of the pseudopatients were never discovered, serious difficulties would arise for those who support traditional modes of psychiatric diagnosis. Given that the hospital staff was not incompetent, that the pseudopatient had been behaving as sanely as he had been outside of the hospital, and that it had never been previously suggested that he belonged in a psychiatric hospital, such an unlikely outcome would support the view that psychiatric diagnosis betrays little about the patient but much about the environment in which an observer finds him.

This article describes such an experiment. Eight sane people gained secret admission to twelve different hospitals.[6] Their diagnostic experiences constitute the data of the first part of this article; the remainder is devoted to a description of their experiences in psychiatric institutions. Too few psychiatrists and psychologists, even those who have worked in such hospitals, know what the experience is like. They rarely talk about it with former patients, perhaps because they distrust information coming from the previously insane. Those who have worked in psychiatric hospitals are likely to have adapted so thoroughly to the settings that they are insensitive to the impact of that experience. And while there have been occasional reports of researchers who submitted themselves to psychiatric hospitalization,[7] these researchers have commonly remained in the hospitals for short periods of time, often with the knowledge of the hospital staff. It is difficult to know the extent to which they were treated like patients or like research colleagues. Nevertheless, their reports about the inside of the psychiatric hospital have been valuable. This article extends those efforts.

Pseudopatients and Their Settings

The eight pseudopatients were a varied group. One was a psychology graduate student in his twenties. The remaining seven were older and "established." Among them were three psychologists, a pediatrician, a psychiatrist, a painter, and a housewife. Three pseudopatients were women, five were men. All of them employed pseudonyms, lest their alleged diagnoses embarrass them later. Those who were in mental health professions alleged another occupation in order to avoid the special attentions that might be accorded by staff, as a matter of courtesy or caution, to ailing colleagues.[8] With the exception of myself (I was the first pseudopatient and my presence was known to the hospital administrator and chief psychologist and, so far as I can tell, to them alone), the presence of pseudopatients and the nature of the research program were not known to the hospital staffs.[9]

The settings were similarly varied. In order to generalize the findings, admission into a variety of hospitals was sought. The twelve hospitals in the sample were located in five different states on the East and West coasts. Some were old and shabby; some were quite new. Some were research-oriented, others not. Some had good staff-patient ratios; others were quite understaffed. Only one was a strictly private hospital. All of the others were supported by state or federal funds, or in one instance, by university funds.

After calling the hospital for an appointment, the pseudopatient arrived at the admissions office complaining that he had been hearing voices. Asked what the voices said, he replied that they were often unclear, but as far as he could tell they said "empty," "hollow," and "thud." The voices were unfamiliar and were of the same sex as the pseudopatient. The choice of these symptoms was occasioned by their apparent similarity to existential symptoms. Such symptoms are alleged to arise from painful concerns about the perceived meaninglessness of one's life. It is as if the hallucinating person were saying, "My life is empty and hollow." The choice of these symptoms was also determined by the *absence* of a single report of existential psychoses in the literature.

Beyond alleging the symptoms and falsifying name, vocation, and employment, no further alterations of person, history, or circumstances were made. The significant events of the pseudopatient's life history were presented as they had actually occurred. Relationships with parents and siblings, with spouse and children, with people at work and in school, consistent with the aforementioned exceptions, were described as they were or had been. Frustrations and upsets were described along with joys and satisfactions. These facts are important to remember. If anything, they strongly biased the subsequent results in favor of detecting sanity, since none of their histories or current behaviors were seriously pathological in any way.

Immediately upon admission to the psychiatric ward, the pseudopatient ceased simulating *any* symptoms of abnormality. In some cases, there was a brief period of mild nervousness and anxiety, since none of the pseudopatients really believed that they would be admitted so easily. Indeed, their shared fear was that they would be immediately exposed as frauds and greatly embarrassed. Moreover, many of them had never visited a psychiatric ward; even those who had, nevertheless had some genuine fears about what might happen to them. Their nervousness, then, was quite appropriate to the novelty of the hospital setting, and it abated rapidly.

Apart from that short-lived nervousness, the pseudopatient behaved on the ward as he "normally" behaved. The pseudopatient spoke to patients and staff as he might ordinarily. Because there is uncommonly little to do on a psychiatric ward, he attempted to engage others in conversation. When asked by staff how he was feeling, he indicated that he was fine, that he no longer experienced symptoms. He responded to instructions from attendants, to calls for medication (which was not swallowed), and to dining-hall instructions. Beyond such activities as were available to him on the admissions ward, he spent his time writing down his observations about the ward, its patients, and the staff. Initially these notes were written "secretly," but as it soon became clear that no one much cared, they were subsequently written on standard tablets of paper in such public places as the dayroom. No secret was made of these activities.

The pseudopatient, very much as a true psychiatric patient, entered a hospital with no foreknowledge of when he would be discharged. Each was told that he would have to get out by his own devices, essentially by convincing the staff that he was sane. The psychological stresses associated with hospitalization were considerable, and all but one of the pseudopatients desired to be discharged almost immediately after being admitted. They were, therefore, motivated not only to behave sanely, but to be paragons of cooperation. That their behavior was in no way disruptive is confirmed by nursing reports, which have been obtained on most of the patients. These reports uniformly indicate that the patients were "friendly," "cooperative," and "exhibited no abnormal indications."

The Normal Are Not Detectably Sane

Despite their public "show" of sanity, the pseudopatients were never detected. Admitted, except in one case, with a diagnosis of schizophrenia,[10] each was discharged with a diagnosis of schizophrenia "in remission." The label "in remission" should in no way be dismissed as a formality, for at no time during any hospitalization had any question been raised about any pseudopatient's simulation. Nor are there any indications in the hospital records that the pseudopatient's status was suspect. Rather, the evidence is strong that, once labeled schizophrenic, the pseudopatient was stuck with that label. If the pseudopatient was to be discharged, he must naturally be "in remission"; but he was not sane, nor, in the institution's view, had he ever been sane.

The uniform failure to recognize sanity cannot be attributed to the quality of the hospitals, for, although there were considerable variations among them, several are considered excellent. Nor can it be alleged that there was simply not enough time to observe the pseudopatients. Length of hospitalization ranged from seven to fifty-two days, with an average of nineteen days. The pseudopatients were not, in fact, carefully observed, but this failure clearly speaks more to traditions within psychiatric hospitals than to lack of opportunity.

Finally, it cannot be said that the failure to recognize the pseudopatients' sanity was due to the fact that they were not behaving sanely. While there was clearly some tension present in all of them, their daily visitors could detect no serious behavioral consequences—nor, indeed, could other patients. It was quite common for the patients to "detect" the pseudopatients' sanity. During the first three hospitalizations, when accurate counts were kept, 35 of a total of 118 patients on the admissions ward voiced their suspicions, some vigorously. "You're not crazy. You're a journalist, or a professor [referring to the continual note-taking]. You're checking up on the hospital." While most of the patients were reassured by the pseudopatient's insistence that he had been sick before he came in but was fine now, some continued to believe that the pseudopatient was sane throughout his hospitalization.[11] The fact that the patients often recognized normality when staff did not raises important questions.

Failure to detect sanity during the course of hospitalization may be due to the fact that physicians operate with a strong bias toward what statisticians call the type 2 error.[5] This is to say that physicians are more inclined to call a healthy person sick (a false positive, type 2) than a sick person healthy (a false negative, type 1). The reasons for this are not hard to find: It is clearly more dangerous to misdiagnose illness than health. Better to err on the side of caution, to suspect illness even among the healthy.

But what holds for medicine does not hold equally well for psychiatry. Medical illnesses, while unfortunate, are not commonly pejorative. Psychiatric diagnoses, on the contrary, carry with them personal, legal, and social stigmas.[12] It was therefore important to see whether the tendency toward diagnosing the sane insane could be reversed. The following experiment was arranged at a research and teaching hospital whose staff had heard these findings but doubted that such an error could occur in their hospital. The staff was informed that at some time during the following three months, one or more pseudopatients would attempt to be admitted into the psychiatric hospital. Each staff member was asked to rate each patient who presented himself at admissions or on the ward according to the likelihood that the patient was a pseudopatient. A 10-point scale was used, with a 1 and 2 reflecting high confidence that the patient was a pseudopatient.

Judgments were obtained on 193 patients who were admitted for psychiatric treatment. All staff who had had sustained contact with or primary responsibility for the patient—attendants, nurses, psychiatrists, physicians, and psychologists—were asked to make judgments. Forty-one patients were alleged, with high confidence, to be pseudopatients by at least one member of the staff. Twenty-three were considered suspect by at least one psychiatrist. Nineteen were suspected by one psychiatrist and one other staff member. Actually, no genuine pseudopatient (at least from my group) presented himself during this period.

The experiment is instructive. It indicates that the tendency to designate sane people as insane can be reversed when the stakes (in this case, prestige and diagnostic acumen) are high. But what can be said of the nineteen people who were suspected of being "sane" by one psychiatrist and another staff member? Were these people truly "sane," or was it rather the case that in the course of avoiding the type 2 error the staff tended to make more errors of the first sort—calling the crazy "sane"? There is no way of knowing. But one thing is certain: Any diagnostic process that lends itself so readily to massive errors of this sort cannot be a very reliable one.

The Stickiness of Psychodiagnostic Labels

Beyond the tendency to call the healthy sick—a tendency that accounts better for diagnostic behavior on admission than it does for such behavior after a lengthy period of exposure—the data speak to the massive role of labeling in psychiatric assessment. Having once been labeled schizophrenic, there is nothing the pseudopatient can do to overcome the tag. The tag profoundly colors others' perceptions of him and his behavior.

From one viewpoint, these data are hardly surprising, for it has long been known that elements are given meaning by the context in which they occur. Gestalt psychology made this point vigorously, and Asch[13] demonstrated that there are "central" personality traits (such as "warm" versus "cold") which are so powerful that they markedly color the meaning of other information in forming an impression of a given personality.[14] "Insane," "schizophrenic," "manic-depressive," and "crazy" are probably among the most powerful of such central traits. Once a person is designated abnormal, all of his other behaviors and characteristics are colored by that label. Indeed, that label is so powerful that many of the pseudopatients' normal behaviors were overlooked entirely or profoundly misinterpreted. Some examples may clarify this issue.

Earlier I indicated that there were no changes in the pseudopatient's personal history and current status behond those of name, employment, and, where necessary, vocation. Otherwise, a veridical description of personal history and circumstances was offered. Those circumstances were not psychotic. How were they made consonant with the diagnosis of psychosis? Or were those diagnoses modified in such a way as to bring them into accord with the circumstances of the pseudopatient's life, as described by him?

As far as I can determine, diagnoses were in no way affected by the relative health of the circumstances of a pseudopatient's life. Rather, the reverse occurred: The perception of his circumstances was shaped entirely by the diagnosis. A clear example of such translation is found in the case of a pseudopatient who had had a close relationship with his mother but was rather remote from his father during his early childhood. During adolescence and beyond, however, his father became a close friend, while his relationship with his mother cooled. His present relationship with his wife was characteristically close and warm. Apart from occasional angry exchanges, friction was minimal. The children had rarely been spanked. Surely there is nothing especially pathological about such a history. Indeed, many readers may see a similar pattern in their own experiences, with no markedly deleterious consequences. Observe, however, how such a history was translated in the psychopathological context, this from the case summary prepared after the patient was discharged.

> This white 39-year-old male . . . manifests a long history of considerable ambivalence in close relationships, which begins in early childhood. A warm relationship with his mother cools during adolescence. A distant relationship to his father is described as becoming very intense. Affective stability is absent. His attempts to control emotionality with his wife and children are punctuated by angry outbursts and, in the case of the children, spankings. And while he says that he has several good friends, one senses considerable ambivalence embedded in those relationships also. . . .

The facts of the case were unintentionally distorted by the staff to achieve consistency with a popular theory of the dynamics of schizophrenic reaction.[15] Nothing of an ambivalent nature had been described in relations with parents, spouse, or friends. To the extent that ambivalence could be inferred, it was probably not greater than is found in all human relationships. It is true the pseudopatient's relationships with his parents changed over time, but in the ordinary context that would hardly be remarkable—indeed, it might very well be expected. Clearly, the meaning ascribed to his verbalizations (that is, ambivalence, affective instability) was determined by the diagnosis: schizophrenia.

An entirely different meaning would have been ascribed if it were known that the man was "normal."

All pseudopatients took extensive notes publicly. Under ordinary circumstances, such behavior would have raised questions in the minds of observers, as, in fact, it did among patients. Indeed, it seemed so certain that the notes would elicit suspicion that elaborate precautions were taken to remove them from the ward each day. But the precautions proved needless. The closest any staff member came to questioning these notes occurred when one pseudopatient asked his physician what kind of medication he was receiving and began to write down the response. "You needn't write it," he was told gently. "If you have trouble remembering, just ask me again."

If no questions were asked of the pseudopatients, how was their writing interpreted? Nursing records for three patients indicate that the writing was seen as an aspect of their pathological behavior. "Patient engages in writing behavior" was the daily nursing comment on one of the pseudopatients who was never questioned about his writing. Given that the patient is in the hospital, he must be psychologically disturbed. And given that he is disturbed, continuous writing must be a behavioral manifestation of that disturbance, perhaps a subset of the compulsive behaviors that are sometimes correlated with schizophrenia.

One tacit characteristic of psychiatric diagnosis is that it locates the sources of aberration within the individual and only rarely within the complex of stimuli that surrounds him. Consequently, behaviors that are stimulated by the environment are commonly misattributed to the patient's disorder. For example, one kindly nurse found a pseudopatient pacing the long hospital corridors. "Nervous, Mr. X?" she asked. "No, bored," he said.

The notes kept by pseudopatients are full of patient behaviors that were misinterpreted by well-intentioned staff. Often enough, a patient would go "berserk" because he had, wittingly or unwittingly, been mistreated by, say, an attendant. A nurse coming upon the scene would rarely inquire even cursorily into the environmental stimuli of the patient's behavior. Rather, she assumed that his upset derived from his pathology, not from his present interactions with other staff members. Occasionally, the staff might assume that the patient's family (especially when they had recently visited) or other patients had stimulated the outburst. But never were the staff found to assume that one of themselves or the structure of the hospital had anything to do with a patient's behavior. One psychiatrist pointed to a group of patients who were sitting outside the cafeteria entrance half an hour before lunchtime. To a group of young residents, he indicated that such behavior was characteristic of the oral-acquisitive nature of the syndrome. It seemed not to occur to him that there were very few things to anticipate in the psychiatric hospital besides eating.

A psychiatric label has a life and an influence of its own. Once the impression has been formed that the patient is schizophrenic, the expectation is that he will continue to be schizophrenic. When a sufficient amount of time has passed, during which the patient has done nothing bizarre, he is considered to be in remission and available for discharge. But the label endures beyond discharge, with the unconfirmed expectation that he will behave as a schizophrenic again. Such labels, conferred by mental health professionals, are as influential on the patient as they are on his relatives and friends, and it should not surprise anyone that the diagnosis acts on all of them as a self-fulfilling prophecy. Eventually, the patient himself accepts the diagnosis, with all of its surplus meanings and expectations, and behaves accordingly.[15]

The inferences to be made from these matters are quite simple. Much as Zigler and Phillips have demonstrated that there is enormous overlap in the symptoms presented by patients who have been variously diagnosed,[16] so there is enormous overlap in the behaviors of the sane and the insane. The sane are not "sane" all of the time. We lose our tempers "for no good reason." We are occasionally depressed or anxious, again for no good reason. And we may find it difficult to get along with one or another person—again for no reason that we can specify. Similarly, the insane are not always insane. Indeed, it was the impression of the pseudopatients while living with them that they were sane for long periods of time—that the bizarre behaviors upon which their diagnoses were allegedly predicated constituted only a small fraction of their total behavior. If it makes no sense to label ourselves permanently depressed on the basis of an occasional depression, then it takes better evidence than is presently available to label all patients insane or schizophrenic on the basis of bizarre behaviors or cognitions. It seems more useful, as Mischel[17] has pointed out, to limit our discussions to *behaviors*, the stimuli that provoke them, and their correlates.

It is not known why powerful impressions of personality traits, such as "crazy" or "insane," arise. Conceivably, when the origins of and stimuli that give rise to a behavior are remote or unknown, or when the behavior strikes us as immutable, trait labels regarding the *behavior* arise. When, on the other hand, the origins and stimuli are known and available, discourse is limited to the behavior itself. Thus, I may hallucinate because I am sleeping, or I may hallucinate because I have ingested a peculiar drug. These are termed sleep-induced hallucinations, or dreams, and drug-induced hallucinations, respectively. But when the stimuli to my hallucinations are unknown, that is called craziness, or schizophrenia—as if that inference were somehow as illuminating as the others. . . .

The Consequences of Labeling and Depersonalization

Whenever the ratio of what is known to what needs to be known approaches zero, we tend to invent "knowledge" and assume that we understand more than we actually do. We seem unable to acknowledge that we simply don't know. The needs for diagnosis and remediation of behavioral and emotional problems are enormous. But rather than acknowledge that we are just embarking on understanding, we continue to label patients "schizophrenic," "manic-depressive," and "insane," as if in those words we had captured the essence of understanding. The facts of the matter are that we have known for a long time that diagnoses are often not useful or reliable, but we have nevertheless continued to use them. We now know that we cannot distinguish insanity from sanity. It is depressing to consider how that information will be used.

Not merely depressing, but frightening. How many people, one wonders, are sane but not recognized as such in our psychiatric institutions? How many have been needlessly stripped of their privileges of citizenship, from the right to vote and drive to that of handling their own accounts? How many have feigned insanity in order to avoid the criminal consequences of their behavior, and, conversely, how many would rather stand trial than live interminably in a psychiatric hospital—but are wrongly thought to be mentally ill? How many have been stigmatized by well-intentioned, but nevertheless erroneous, diagnoses? On the last point, recall again that a "type 2 error" in psychiatric diagnosis does not have the same consequences it does in medical diagnosis. A diagnosis of cancer that has been found to be in error is cause for celebration. But psychiatric diagnoses are rarely found to be in error. The label sticks, a mark of inadequacy forever.

Notes

1. P. Ash, *J. Abnorm. Soc. Psychol. 44*, 272 (1949); A. T. Beck, *Amer. J. Psychiat. 119*, 210 (1962); A. T. Boisen, *Psychiatry 2*, 233 (1938); N. Kreitman, *J. Ment. Sci. 107*, 876 (1961); N. Kreitman, P. Sainsbury, J. Morrisey, J. Towers, J. Scrivener, *ibid.*, p. 887; H. O. Schmitt and C. P. Fonda, *J. Abnorm. Soc. Psychol. 52*, 262 (1956); W. Seeman, *J. Nerv. Ment. Dis. 118*, 541 (1953). For an analysis of these artifacts and summaries of the disputes, see J. Zubin, *Annu. Rev. Psychol. 18*, 373 (1967); L. Phillips and J. G. Draguns, *ibid. 22*, 447 (1971).

2. R. Benedict. *J. Gen. Psychol. 10*, 59 (1934).

3. See in this regard H. Becker, *Outsiders: Studies in the Sociology of Deviance* (New York: Free Press, 1963); B. M. Braginsky, D. D. Braginsky, K. Ring, *Methods of Madness: The Mental Hospital as a Last Resort* (New York: Holt, Rinehart & Winston, 1969); G. M. Crocetti and P. V. Lemkau, *Amer. Sociol. Rev. 30*, 577 (1965); E. Goffman, *Behavior in Public Places* (New York: Free Press, 1964); R. D. Laing, *The Divided Self: A Study of Sanity and Madness* (Chicago: Quadrangle, 1960); D. L. Phillips, *Amer. Sociol. Rev. 28*, 963 (1963); T. R. Sarbin, *Psychol. Today 6*, 18 (1972); E. Schur, *Amer J. Sociol. 75*, 309 (1969); T. Szasz, *Law, Liberty and Psychiatry* (New York: Macmillan, 1963); *The Myth of Mental Illness: Foundations of a Theory of Mental Illness* (New York: Hoeber Harper, 1963). For a critique of some of these views, see W. R. Gove, *Amer. Sociol. Rev. 35*, 873 (1970).

4. E. Goffman. *Asylums* (Garden City, NY: Doubleday, 1961).

5. T. J. Scheff, *Being Mentally Ill: A Sociological Theory* (Chicago: Aldine, 1966).

6. Data from a ninth pseudopatient are not incorporated in this report because, although his sanity went undetected, he falsified aspects of his personal history, including his marital status and parental relationships. His experimental behaviors therefore were not identical to those of the other pseudopatients.

7. A. Barry, *Bellevue Is a State of Mind* (New York: Harcourt Brace Jovanovich, 1971); I. Belknap, *Human Problems of a State Mental Hospital* (New York: McGraw-Hill, 1956); W. Caudill, F. C. Redlich, H. R. Gilmore, E. B. Brody, *Amer J. Orthopsychiat. 22,* 314 (1952); A. R. Goldman, R. H. Bohr, T. A. Steinberg, *Prof. Psychol. 1,* 427 (1970); unauthored, *Roche Report 1* (No. 13), 8 (1971).

8. Beyond the personal difficulties that the pseudopatient is likely to experience in the hospital, there are legal and social ones that, combined, require considerable attention before entry. For example, once admitted to a psychiatric institution, it is difficult, if not impossible, to be discharged on short notice, state law to the contrary notwithstanding. I was not sensitive to these difficulties at the outset of the project, nor to the personal and situational emergencies that can arise, but later a writ of habeas corpus was prepared for each of the entering pseudopatients and an attorney was kept "on call" during every hospitalization. I am grateful to John Kaplan and Robert Bartels for legal advice and assistance in these matters.

9. However distasteful such concealment is, it was a necessary first step to examining these questions. Without concealment, there would have been no way to know how valid these experiences were; nor was there any way of knowing whether whatever detections occurred were a tribute to the diagnostic acumen of the staff or to the hospital's rumor network. Obviously, since my concerns are general ones that cut across individual hospitals and staffs, I have respected their anonymity and have eliminated clues that might lead to their identification.

10. Interestingly, of the twelve admissions, eleven were diagnosed as schizophrenic and one, with the identical symptomatology, as manic-depressive psychosis. This diagnosis has a more favorable prognosis, and it was given by the only private hospital in our sample. On the relations between social class and psychiatric diagnosis, see A. B. Hollingshead and F. C. Redlich, *Social Class and Mental Illness: A Community Study* (New York: Wiley, 1958).

11. It is possible, of course, that patients have quite broad latitudes in diagnosis and therefore are inclined to call many people sane, even those whose behavior is patently aberrant. However, although we have no hard data on this matter, it was our distinct impression that this was not the case. In many instances, patients not only singled us out for attention, but came to imitate our behaviors and styles.

12. J. Cumming and E. Cumming, *Community Ment. Health 1,* 135 (1965); A. Farina and K. Ring. *J. Abnorm. Psychol. 70,* 47 (1965); H. E. Freeman and O. G. Simmons, *The Mental Patient Comes Home* (New York: Wiley, 1963); W. J. Johannsen, *Mental Hygiene 53,* 218 (1969); A. S. Linsky, *Soc. Psychiat. 5,* 166 (1970).

13. S. E. Asch, *J. Abnorm. Soc. Psychol. 41,* 258 (1946); *Social Psychology* (New York: Prentice-Hall, 1952).

14. See also, I. N. Mensh and J. Wishner, *J. Personality 16,* 188 (1947); J. Wishner, *Psychol. Rev. 67,* 96 (1960); J. S. Bruner and R. Tagiuri, in *Handbook of Social Psychology,* G. Lindzey, ed. (Cambridge, MA: Addison-Wesley, 1954), vol. 2, pp. 634–54; J. S. Bruner, D. Shapiro, R. Tagiuri, in *Person Perception and Interpersonal Behavior,* R. Tagiuri and L. Petrullo, eds. (Stanford, CA: Stanford Univ. Press, 1958), pp. 277–88.

15. For an example of a similar self-fulfilling prophecy, in this instance dealing with the "central" trait of intelligence, see R. Rosenthal and L. Jacobson, *Pygmalion in the Classroom* (New York: Holt, Rinehart & Winston, 1968).

16. E. Zigler and L. Phillips, *J. Abnorm. Soc. Psychol.* 63, 69 (1961). See also R. K. Freudenberg and J. P. Robertson, *A.M.A. Arch. Neurol. Psychiatr.* 76, 14 (1956).

17. W. Mischel, *Personality and Assessment* (New York: Wiley, 1968).

PART VII Social Inequality

ALL SOCIETIES, PAST AND PRESENT, are marked by inequalities of some sort. Some people are stronger, learn more quickly, are swifter, shoot weapons more accurately, or have more of *whatever is considered important in that particular society*. Other inequalities, whatever form they take, may appear more contrived—such as distinctions of social rank based on wealth. But whether based on biological characteristics, social skills, or money, no system of dividing people into different groups is inevitable. Rather, each is arbitrary. Yet all societies rank their members, and whatever arbitrary criteria they use appear quite reasonable to them.

The primary social division in small, tribal groups is drawn along the line of gender. Sorted into highly distinctive groupings, men and women in these societies engage in separate activities—ones deemed "appropriate" for each sex. Indeed, in these small groups gender usually represents a cleavage that cuts across most of social life. These peoples also draw finer distinctions along much more individualistic lines of personality, skills, and reputation. Of all human groups, hunting and gathering societies—where most activities revolve around subsistence and there is little or no material surplus—appear to have the least stratification. These societies apparently also have the least *gender typing*, or division of activities by sex.

Perhaps the primary significance of a group's hierarchies and statuses—no matter what form they may take in a particular society—is that they surround the individual with *boundaries*. Setting limits and circumscribing one's possibilities in life, these social divisions establish the framework of socialization. They launch the individual onto the social scene by presenting to him or her an already existing picture of what he or she ought to expect from life.

None of us escapes this fundamental fact of social life, which sociologists call *social inequality* and *social stratification*. No matter into which society we are born, then, each of us inherits some system of social stratification. The boundaries and limits that come with social inequality have extensive consequences, for they envelop almost all aspects of our lives—our relationships with others, our behaviors, beliefs, and attitudes, our goals and aspirations, even our perception of the social world and of the self.

In analyzing the social inequality of contemporary society, sociologists focus on very large groupings of people. They call these groups *social classes*, which are determined by people's rankings on income, education, and occupation. The more income and education one has and the higher the prestige accorded one's work, the higher one's social class. Conversely, the lower one's income, education, and prestige of occupation, the lower one's social class.

On the basis of income, education, and occupation, one can divide Americans into three principle social classes: upper, middle, and lower. The *upper* are the very rich (a million dollars wouldn't even begin to buy your way in); the *middle*—primarily professionals, managers, executives, and other business people—is heavily rewarded with the material goods our society has to offer; and the *lower*, to understate the matter, receives the least.

Some sociologists add an upper and a lower to each of these divisions and say there are *six* social classes in the United States: an upper-upper and lower-upper, an upper-middle and lower-middle, and an upper-lower and lower-lower.

Membership in the *upper-upper* class is the most exclusive of all, accorded not only on the basis of huge wealth but also according to how long that money has been in the family—the longer the better. Somehow or other, it is difficult to make many millions of dollars while remaining scrupulously honest in business dealings. It appears that many people who have entered the monied classes have cut moral corners, at least here and there. This "taint" to the money disappears with time, however, and the later generations of Vanderbilts, Rockefellers, Mellons, DuPonts, Chryslers, Kennedys, Morgans, Nashes, and so on are considered to have "clean" money simply by virtue of the passage of time. They can be philanthropic as well as rich. They have attended the best private schools and universities, the male heirs probably have entered law, and they protect their vast fortunes and economic empires with far-flung political connections and contributions.

And the *lower-upper* class? These people have money, but it is new, and therefore suspect. They lack "breeding" and proper social background. They have not gone to the right schools and cannot be depended on for adequate in-group loyalty. Unable themselves to make the leap into the upper-upper class, their hope for social supremacy lies in their children: If their children go to the right schools *and* marry into the upper-upper class, what has been denied the parents will be granted the children.

The *upper-middle* class consists primarily of people who have entered the professions or higher levels of management. They are doctors, professors, lawyers, dentists, pharmacists, and clergy. They are bank presidents and successful contractors and other business people. Their education is high, their income adequate for most of their needs.

The *lower-middle* class consists largely of lower-level managers, white-collar workers in the service industries, and the more highly paid and skilled blue-collar workers. Their education and income, as well as the prestige of their work, are correspondingly lower than those of their upper-middle class counterparts.

The *upper-lower* class is also known as the working class. (Americans find this term much more agreeable than the term "lower," as "lower" brings negative things to mind, while "working" elicits more positive images.) This class consists primarily of blue-collar workers who work regularly, not seasonally, at their jobs. Their education is limited, and little prestige is attached to their work. With the changes in wages and lifestyles of recent years, however, it often is difficult to distinguish this class from the lower-middle class.

At the bottom of the ladder of social inequality is the *lower-lower* class. This is the social class that gets the worst of everything society has to offer. Its members have the least education and the least income, and often their work is disdained, because, as with sharecropping and other menial labor, it usually requires few skills, is "dirty," and is the type of work that most people try to avoid. The main difference between the lower-lower and the upper-lower classes is that the upper-lower class works the year round while the lower-lower class doesn't. Members of the lower-lower class live on welfare, handouts, and occasional work. They generally are considered the ne'er-do-wells of society.

To illustrate social class membership in U.S. society, let's look at the automotive industry. The Fords, for example, own and control an international manufacturing and financial empire whose net worth is truly staggering. Their vast accumulation of wealth, like their accrued power, is now several generations old. Their children attend elite schools, know how to spend money in the "right" way, and can be trusted to make their family and class interests paramount in life. They are without question members of the upper-upper class.

Next in line come top Ford executives, those who, with stock options and bonuses, earn several million dollars annually. Because they are new to wealth and power, they remain on the rung below, and are considered members of the lower-upper class.

A husband and wife who own a successful Ford agency are members of the upper-middle class. Their income clearly sets them apart from the majority of Americans, and they have an enviable reputation in the community. More than likely they also exert greater-than-average influence in community affairs, but find their capacity to wield power highly limited.

The sales staff, as well as those who work in the office, are members of the lower-middle class. Their income is less, their education is likely to be less, and people assign less prestige to their work than to that of the owners of the agency.

Mechanics who repair customers' cars would ordinarily be considered members of the upper-lower class. High union wages, however, have blurred this distinction, and they might more properly be classified as members of the lower-middle class. People who "detail" used cars (making them appear newer by washing and polishing them, painting their tires and floor mats, and so on) earn only minimum wage and are members of the upper-lower class.

Window washers and janitors who are hired to clean the agency only during the busy season and then are laid off when business slacks off are members of the lower-lower class. (If they are year-round employees of the agency, they are members of the upper-lower class.) Their income is the least, as is their education, while the prestige accorded their work is also minimal.

It is significant to note that children are assigned the social class of their parents. For this reason, sociologists say we are born into a social class. Sociologists call this *ascribed membership* (compared with membership one earns or gains, which is called *achieved membership*). If a child of someone who "details" used cars for a living goes to college, works as a salesperson in the agency part-time and during vacations, and then eventually buys the agency, he or she experiences *upward social mobility*. The individual's new social class is said to be achieved membership. Conversely, if a child of the agency's owner becomes an alcoholic, fails to get through college, and takes a lower-status job, that person experiences *downward social mobility*. The resulting change in social class is also called *achieved membership*. (As you can see, "achieved" does not equal "achievement.")

You should note that this division into six social classes is not the only way that sociologists look at our social class system. In fact, sociologists have arrived at no single, standard, agreed-upon overview of the U.S. class system. Like others, this outline of classes is both arbitrary and useful, but it does not do justice to the nuances and complexities of our class system.

One view within sociology (called *conflict* or *Marxist*) holds that to understand social inequality we need focus only on income. What is the *source* of a person's income? Know this, and you know the person's social class. There are those with money and those without money. The monied class owns the means of production—the factories and machinery and buildings—and lives off their investments. The other class exchanges its labor to produce more money for the wealthy owners. In short, the monied class (the *capitalists*, or owners) is in the controlling sector of society, while those who sell their labor (the *workers*) are controlled by them. With society divided into the haves and the have-nots, insist conflict theorists, it is misleading to pay attention to the fine distinctions among those with or without money.

Be that as it may (and this debate continues among sociologists), society certainly is stratified. And the sociological (and personal) significance of social inequality is that it determines our *life chances*, the probabilities as to the fate we may expect in life. It is obvious that not everyone has the same chances in life, and the single most significant factor in determining a person's life chances in our society is money. Simply put, if you have money, you can do a lot of things you can't do if you do not have it. And the more money you have, the more control over life you have, and the more likely you are to find life pleasant.

Beyond this obvious point, however, lies a connection between social inequality and life chances that is not so readily evident. It involves such things as one's chances of dying during infancy; being killed by accident, fire, or homicide; becoming a drug addict; getting arrested; ending up in prison; dropping out of school; getting divorced; becoming disabled; or, in old age, having a meager life, plagued by illness and supported only by Social Security. All vary inversely with social class; that is, the lower people's social class, the higher the chances that these things will happen to them. Conversely, the higher their social class, the smaller the risk of these events taking place.

As we examine social inequality in this Part, we consider some of its major dimensions and emphasize its severe and lifelong effects. Our opening article on physical appearance may seem to hit only a light note, but Sidney Katz points to implications that, ordinarily lying beyond our perception, have deep consequences for our lives. The next article by Patricia Martin and Robert Hummer on fraternities and rape at first blush may seem strikingly out of place. Its implications go far beyond the specific setting and events, however, for its focus is gender inequality, the broadest and largest-scale social inequality of all. We then turn our focus on race–ethnicity, an aspect of inequality in U.S. society that pervades so much of social life. The experiences recounted by Clarence Page give us insight not only into the process of developing a racial identity but also into the consequences of that identity. From here, we turn the focus on poverty. We first consider Herbert Gans' claim that poverty is so functional for society that it can never be eliminated. Then, through Jonathan Kozol's description of U.S. schools, we gain understanding of how education helps to maintain (or reproduce) the U.S. class system. Stephen Higley concludes this Part with a focus on an understudied group, the wealthy and powerful upper class, or as it is often called in sociology, the ruling class.

27 The Importance of Being Beautiful

SIDNEY KATZ

A chief characteristic of all societies is *social stratification,* a term that refers to a group's system of ranking. All of us find ourselves ranked according to a variety of dimensions, from our parents' social class when we are young to our own achievements, or lack thereof, when we grow older. Where we go to high school, if we attend college, and if so, where—make a difference in people's eyes. People rank us by our speech, by our walk, and even by things we own or display, from the car we drive to the clothing we wear.

Central to much of the ranking done on a face-to-face level is attractiveness. Because of appearance, we judge others—and are judged by them. This type of ranking is ordinarily thought to have little consequence beyond such temporary, individual matters as whether or not we can get a date this weekend—personally significant and intense, yes, but probably of little long-term consequence. As Katz points out, however, rankings based on attractiveness have significant consequences for our lives.

UNLIKE MANY PEOPLE, I was neither shocked nor surprised when the national Israeli TV network fired a competent female broadcaster because she was not beautiful. I received the news with aplomb because I had just finished extensive research into "person perception," an esoteric branch of psychology that examines the many ways in which physical attractiveness—or the lack of it—affects all aspects of your life.

Unless you're a 10—or close to it—most of you will respond to my findings with at least some feelings of frustration or perhaps disbelief. In a nutshell, you can't overestimate the importance of being beautiful. If you're beautiful, without effort you attract hordes of friends and lovers. You are given higher school grades than your smarter—but less appealing—classmates. You compete successfully for jobs against men or women who are better qualified but less alluring. Promotions and pay raises come your way more easily. You are able to go into a bank or store and cash a cheque with far less hassle than a plain Jane or John. And these are only a few of the many advantages enjoyed by those with a ravishing face and body.

"We were surprised to find that beauty had such powerful effects," confessed Karen Dion, a University of Toronto social psychologist who does person perception research. "Our findings also go against the cultural grain.

People like to think that success depends on talent, intelligence, and hard work." But the scientific evidence is undeniable.

In large part, the beautiful person can attribute his or her idyllic life to a puzzling phenomenon that social scientists have dubbed the "halo effect." It defies human reason, but if you resemble Jane Fonda or Paul Newman it's assumed that you're more generous, trustworthy, sociable, modest, sensitive, interesting, and sexually responsive than the rest of us. Conversely, if you're somewhat physically unattractive, because of the "horns effect" you're stigmatized as being mean, sneaky, dishonest, antisocial, and a poor sport to boot.

The existence of the halo/horns effect has been established by several studies. One, by Dion, looked at perceptions of misbehavior in children.

Dion provided 243 female university students with identical detailed accounts of the misbehavior of a seven-year-old school child. She described how the youngster had pelted a sleeping dog with sharp stones until its leg bled. As the animal limped away, yelping in pain, the child continued the barrage of stones. The 243 women were asked to assess the seriousness of the child's offence and to give their impression of the child's normal behavior. Clipped to half of the reports were photos of seven-year-old boys or girls who had been rated "high" in physical attractiveness; the other half contained photos of youngsters of "low" attractiveness. "We found," said Dion, "that the opinions of the adults were markedly influenced by the appearance of the children."

One evaluator described the stone thrower, who in her report happened to be an angelic-looking little girl, in these glowing terms: "She appears to be a perfectly charming little girl, well mannered and basically unselfish. She plays well with everyone, but, like everyone else, a bad day may occur. . . . Her cruelty need not be taken too seriously." For the same offence, a homely girl evoked this comment from another evaluator: "I think this child would be quite bratty and would be a problem to teachers. She'd probably try to pick a fight with other children. . . . She would be a brat at home. All in all, she would be a real problem." The tendency throughout the 243 adult responses was to judge beautiful children as ordinarily well behaved and unlikely to engage in wanton cruelty in the future; the unbeautiful were viewed as being chronically antisocial, untrustworthy, and likely to commit similar transgressions again.

Dion found the implications of this study mind boggling. Every kid who was homely would be highly vulnerable in the classroom and elsewhere. Prejudged by his or her appearance, a vicious cycle is set in motion. The teacher views the child as having negative traits and treats him accordingly; the child responds by conforming to the teacher's expectations. Dion thinks that adults must realize to what extent their opinion of a child can be biased by the child's appearance: "When there's a question of who started a classroom disturbance, who broke the vase—adults are more likely to identify the unattractive child as the culprit."

The same standards apply in judging adults. The beautiful are assumed innocent. John Jurens, a colorful private investigator, was once consulted by a small Toronto firm which employed 40 people. Ten thousand dollars' worth of merchandise had disappeared, and it was definitely an inside job. After an intensive investigation, which included the use of a lie detector, Jurens was certain he had caught the thief. She was 24 years old and gorgeous—a lithe princess with high cheekbones, green eyes and shining, long black hair. The employer dismissed Jurens's proof with the comment, "You've made a mistake. It just can't be her." Jurens commented sadly, "A lot of people refuse to believe that beautiful can be bad."

David Humphrey, a prominent Ontario criminal lawyer, observed, "If a beautiful woman is on trial, you practically have to show the judge and jury a movie of her committing the crime in order to get a conviction." Another experienced lawyer, Aubrey Golden, has found it difficult defending a man charged with assault or wife-beating if he's a brutish-looking hulk. By the same token, a rape victim who happens to be stocky is a less credible witness than a slender, good-looking woman.

The halo and horns effect often plays an important role in sentencing by courts. After spending 17 days observing cases heard in an Ontario traffic court, Joan Finegan, a graduate psychology student at the University of Western Ontario, concluded that pleasant and neat-looking defendants were fined an average of $6.31 less than those who were "messy." The same probeauty bias was found by a British investigator in a series of simulated court cases. Physically appealing defendants were given prison terms almost three years less than those meted out to unattractive ones for precisely the same offence.

Beauty—or the lack of it—influences a person's entire life. The halo and horns effect comes into play beginning with birth and continues throughout the various stages of life.

Early Life

The flawless, seraphlike infant is irresistible. It receives an inordinate amount of attention and love. The child is constantly picked up, cuddled, and cooed to. In contrast, the unattractive baby may suffer neglect and rejection, which can have enduring effects on its personality and mental health. "When a child is unappealing because he's been born with a visible physical defect," said Dr. Ian Munro, a specialist in reconstructive facial surgery at the Hospital for Sick Children in Toronto, "parents are sometimes reluctant to touch, fondle, or give their child the normal displays of affection."

Later, when the baby attends nursery school, the halo and horns effect is even more potent. "Nursery school teachers," observed Dr. Ellen Berscheid, a psychologist who has conducted extensive person perception research at the University of Minnesota, "often insist that all children are beautiful, yet they can, when they're asked, rank their pupils by appearance." Even more note-worthy, the children themselves, despite their tender years, "behave in accordance with the adult ranking."

One nursery school study by Berscheid and Dion revealed that unattractive kids were not as well liked by their peers as the attractive ones. They were accused of "fighting a lot," "hitting other students," and "yelling at the teacher." Furthermore, other students labeled them "fraidy cats." They needed help to complete their work. When asked to name the person in class who scared them the most, the children usually nominated an unattractive classmate.

At School

It's sad but true that grade school teachers tend to judge their pupils largely on the basis of their looks. Consider the provocative study conducted by two American psychologists, Elaine Walster and Margaret Clifford: Four hundred grade five teachers were asked to examine identical report cards. They itemized the student's grades in various subjects, his or her work habits, attendance record, and attitudes. There was only one difference. Half of the report cards had the photo of an attractive boy or girl attached to the upper right-hand corner; half, the photo of a less attractive child. The teachers were then asked a number of specific questions based on the information provided. They concluded that the beautiful children had higher IQs, were more likely to go to college, and had parents who were more interested in education.

Parents should be concerned about these results. Because of an inflated opinion of the beautiful child, the teacher can be expected to give him more than his share of friendliness, encouragement, and time. And, consequently, the beautiful one will blossom—at the expense of his not-so-beautiful classmates.

The College Years

The beautiful person reaps an even richer harvest when he or she attends college. In one test, 60 male undergraduates were handed a 700-word essay on the effects of televised violence on the behavior of children. The authors, they were told, were freshmen coeds, and the undergrads were asked to assign a grade to the essay and to give their impression of the writer's abilities. Half of the students received an essay that was excellently written; the other half were given an essay that was a mishmash of clichés, grammatical errors, and sloppy writing. One-third of the papers had attached to them the photo of the alleged author—a young woman of striking beauty. Another third contained the likeness of an unappealing woman, while the remaining third were submitted without a photograph. When the evaluations were tallied, it was found that the beautiful person was consistently awarded a higher mark for her essay than the unattractive one. The essays without photos attached were usually given average marks. The investigators, David Landy and Harold Sigall, psychologists at the University of Rochester at the time of the study, concluded, "If you are ugly, you are not discriminated against as long as your performance is impressive. However, should performance be below par, attractiveness matters: you may be able to get away with inferior work if you are beautiful."

Not surprisingly, college students also preferred beauty when grading the desirability of a date. In interviews 376 young men and 376 young women assured investigators that it was "vulgar" to judge people by their appearance. They then proceeded to list the human qualities that they really valued; intelligence, friendliness, sincerity, "soul," and warmth. Yet when these same people were interviewed after going out on a blind date that was arranged by a computer, it became apparent that they were blind to everything *but* the physical appearance of their partners. The more beautiful the partner, the more he or she was liked. Features such as exceptional personality, high intelligence, and shared interests hardly seemed to count at all. "We were surprised to find that a *man's* physical attractiveness was the largest determinant of how well he was liked by a woman," observed Elaine Walster, one of the psychologists who conducted the study.

In addition to giving top marks to their beautiful classmates as dates, college students also predict glittering futures for them. In one study by Dion, Berscheid, and Walster, the opinion was almost unanimous that the physically appealing would contract better marriages, make better husbands and wives, and lead more fulfilling social and career lives. This finding is all the more impressive, Dion explained, because "the unattractive people in our sample were by no means at the extremes of unattractiveness—they possessed only a minor flaw to their beauty."

Marriage

It's logical that a beautiful person's marriage should be idyllic. An alluring woman, say, might have a busier social life than her less appealing sisters and therefore have a better chance of meeting a compatible mate. She's also apt to be more sexually responsive. Good-looking women fall in love more often and have more sexual experiences than others. "And," observed Berscheid, "since in almost all areas of human endeavor practice makes perfect, it may well be that beautiful women are indeed sexually warmer simply because of experience."

One thing is certain: the power of beauty is such that the status of even a homely man skyrockets if he marries a dazzling woman. People discover positive qualities in him they never before noticed: self-confidence, likability, friendliness. Sigall and Landy refer to this phenomenon as "a generalized halo effect" and offer this explanation: "People viewing individuals who are romantically linked to an attractive person try to make sense of the association. In effect, they may ask themselves, 'Why is *she,* desirable as she appears to be, involved with him?' The observers may answer the question by attributing favorable qualities to him."

Careers

If you're a good-looking male over six feet tall, don't worry about succeeding at your career.

A study of university graduates by the *Wall Street Journal* revealed that well proportioned wage earners who were six-foot-two or taller earned 12 percent more than men under six feet. "For some reason," explained Ronald Burke, a York University psychologist and industrial consultant, "tall men are assumed to be dynamic, decisive, and powerful. In other words, born leaders." A Toronto consultant for Drake Personnel, one of the largest employment agencies in Canada, recalled trying to find a sales manager for an industrial firm. He sent four highly qualified candidates, only to have them all turned down. "The fifth guy I sent over was different," said the consultant. "He stood six-foot-four. He was promptly hired."

The well favored woman also has a distinct edge when it comes to getting a job she's after. "We send out three prospects to be interviewed, and it's almost always the most glamorous one that's hired," said Edith Geddes of the Personnel Centre, a Toronto agency that specializes in female placements. "We sometimes feel bad because the best qualified person is not chosen." Dr. Pam Ennis, a consultant to several large corporations, observed, "Look at the photos announcing promotions in the *Globe and Mail* business section. It's no accident that so many of the women happen to be attractive and sexy-looking." Ennis, an elegant woman herself, attributes at least part of her career success to good looks. Her photograph appears on the brochures she mails out to companies soliciting new clients. "About eight out of 10 company presidents give me an appointment," she said. "I'm sure that many of them are curious to see me in person. Beauty makes it easier to establish rapport."

In an experiment designed to test the effect of stating or not stating an intent to change the listener's point of view, it was discovered that an attractive woman was more persuasive than an unattractive woman. In one session, an attractive woman disguised her good looks. Her dress was ill-fitting, she wore no makeup on her oily skin, her hair was a tattered mess, and the trace of a moustache was etched on her upper lip. She attempted to persuade a classroom of men that a general education was superior to a specialized one. Her arguments, in large part, failed to change their points of view.

The same woman then made herself as alluring as possible. She wore chic, tight-fitting clothes and tasteful makeup, and sported a fashionable coiffeur. Using the identical argument, she had little difficulty in persuading a second group of men to share her enthusiasm for a general education.

Every ugly duckling who has transformed herself into a Cinderella knows about the persuasive powers of beauty. Eleanor Fulcher, who runs a model and charm school in Toronto, says, "A woman can make things happen by improving her appearance. I've seen it hundreds of times."

Old Age

An elderly person's attractiveness influences the way in which he or she is treated in nursing homes and hospitals. Doctors and nurses give better care to the beautiful ones.

Lena Nordholm, an Australian behavioral scientist, presented 289 doctors, nurses, social workers, speech therapists, and physiotherapists with photos of eight attractive and unattractive men and women. They were asked to speculate about what kind of patients they would be. The good-lookers were judged to be more cooperative, better motivated, and more likely to improve than their less attractive counterparts. Pam Ennis, the consultant, commented, "Because the doctor feels that beautiful patients are more likely to respond to his treatment, he'll give them more time and attention."

In the myths that shape modern civilization, beauty is equated with success. It has been that way since time began. In most of literature, the heroines are beautiful. Leo Tolstoy wrote, "It is amazing how complete is the delusion that beauty is goodness."

We like to think we have moved beyond the era when the most desirable woman was the beauty queen, but we haven't. Every day we make assumptions about the personality of the bank teller, the delivery man, or the waitress by their looks. The way in which we attribute good and bad characteristics still has very little to do with fact. People seldom look beyond a pleasing facade, a superficial attractiveness. But the professors of person perception are not discouraged by this. They want to educate us. Perhaps by arming us with the knowledge and awareness of why we discriminate against the unattractive, we'll learn how to prevent this unwitting bigotry. Just maybe, we can change human nature.

28 Fraternities and Rape on Campus

PATRICIA YANCEY MARTIN
ROBERT A. HUMMER

College certainly is a varied experience: challenging, with its many assignments, higher academic standards, and new vocabularies; frustrating, when concepts don't seem to sink in and instructors demand too much; fulfilling, with the satisfactions that come from forming new friendships and a sense of accomplishment as courses are passed and new ideas mastered; and, at the end, threatening, when the world of work and careers looms and, by comparison, college life suddenly appears so comfortable, almost serene.

On many campuses, fraternities are part of college life, a welcome respite from onerous classroom demands. They provide friendships, fun, diversion, sometimes even a test or paper to help pass a particularly grueling course. In some cases, bonds are formed that become significant for successful careers. There is a darker side to fraternities, however, a stress on hypermasculinity and calculated exploitation that destroys people. It is this dark side of fraternities that Martin and Hummer explore.

MANY RAPES, FAR MORE THAN COME to the public's attention, occur in fraternity houses on college and university campuses. . . .

The study reported here examined dynamics associated with the social construction of fraternity life, with a focus on processes that foster the use of coercion, including rape, in fraternity men's relations with women. We make no claims that all fraternities are "bad" or that all fraternity men are rapists. Our observations indicated, however, that rape is especially probable in fraternities because of the kinds of organizations they are, the kinds of members they have, the practices their members engage in, and a virtual absence of university or community oversight. . . . We conclude that unless fraternities change in fundamental ways, little improvement can be expected.

Methodology

We developed a conceptual framework from an initial case study of an alleged gang rape at Florida State University that involved four fraternity men and an eighteen-year-old coed. The group rape took place on the third floor of a fraternity house and ended with the "dumping" of the woman in the hallway of a neighboring fraternity house. According to newspaper accounts, the victim's blood-alcohol concentration, when she was discovered, was .349 percent, more than three times the legal limit for automobile driving and an almost lethal amount. One law enforcement officer reported that sexual intercourse occurred during the time the victim was unconscious. When the victim was found, she was comatose and had suffered multiple scratches and abrasions. Crude words and a fraternity symbol had been written on her thighs. When law enforcement officials tried to investigate the case, fraternity members refused to cooperate. This led, eventually, to a five-year ban of the fraternity from campus by the university and by the fraternity's national organization.

In trying to understand how such an event could have occurred, and how a group of over 150 members (exact figures are unknown because the fraternity refused to provide a membership roster) could hold rank, deny knowledge of the event, and allegedly lie to a grand jury, we analyzed newspaper articles about the case and conducted open-ended interviews with a variety of respondents about the case and about the fraternities, rapes, alcohol use, gender relations, and sexual activities on campus. Our data included over 100 newspaper articles on the initial gang rape case; open-ended interviews with Greek (social fraternity and sorority) and non-Greek (independent) students (N = 20); university administrators (N = 8, five men, three women); and alumni advisers to Greek organizations (N = 6). Open-ended interviews were held also with judges, public and private defense attorneys, victim advocates, and state prosecutors regarding the processing of sexual assault cases. . . .

Fraternities and the Social Construction of Men and Masculinity

Our research indicated that fraternities are vitally concerned—more than with anything else—with masculinity. They work hard to create a macho image and context and try to avoid any suggestion of "wimpishness," effeminacy, and homosexuality. Valued members display, or are willing to go along with, a narrow conception of masculinity that stresses competition, athleticism, dominance, winning, conflict, wealth, material possessions, willingness to drink alcohol, and sexual prowess vis-à-vis women.

VALUED QUALITIES OF MEMBERS

When fraternity members talked about the kind of pledges they prefer, a litany of stereotypical and narrowly masculine attributes and behaviors was recited and feminine or woman-associated qualities and behaviors were expressly denounced. Fraternities seek men who are "athletic," "big guys," good in intramural competition, "who can talk college sports." Males "who are willing to drink alcohol," "who drink socially," or "who can hold their liquor" are sought. Alcohol and activities associated with the recreational use of alcohol are cornerstones of fraternity social life. Non-drinkers are viewed with skepticism and rarely selected for membership.

Fraternities try to avoid "geeks," nerds, and men said to give the fraternity a "wimpy" or "gay" reputation. Art, music, and humanities majors, majors in traditional women's fields (nursing, home economics, social work, education), men with long hair, and those whose appearance or dress violate current norms are rejected. Clean-cut, handsome men who dress well (are clean, neat, conforming, fashionable) are preferred. . . .

One fraternity man, a senior, said his fraternity recruited "some big guys, very athletic" over a two-year period to help overcome its image of wimpiness. His fraternity had won the interfraternity competition for highest grade-point average several years running but was looked down on as "wimpy, dancy, even gay." With their bigger, more athletic recruits, "our reputation improved; we're a much more recognized fraternity now." Thus a fraternity's reputation and status depend on members' possession of stereotypically masculine traits. Good grades, campus leadership, and community service are "nice" but masculinity dominance—for example, in athletic events, physical size of members, athleticism of members—counts most.

One fraternity man, a junior, said: "We watch a guy [a potential pledge] talk to women . . . we want guys who can relate to girls." Assessing a pledge's ability to talk to women is, in part, a preoccupation with homosexuality and a conscious avoidance of men who seem to have effeminate manners or qualities. If a member is suspected of being gay, he is ostracized and informally drummed out of the fraternity. A fraternity with a reputation as wimpy or tolerant of gays is ridiculed and shunned by other fraternities. . . .

THE STATUS AND NORMS OF PLEDGESHIP

A pledge (sometimes called an associate member) is a new recruit who occupies a trial membership status for a specific period of time. The pledge period (typically ranging from ten to fifteen weeks) gives fraternity brothers an opportunity to assess and socialize new recruits. Pledges evaluate the fraternity also and decide if they want to become brothers. The socialization experience is structured partly through assignment of a Big Brother to each pledge. Big Brothers are expected to teach pledges how to become a brother and to support them as they progress through the trial membership period. Some pledges are repelled by the pledging experience, which can entail physical abuse; harsh discipline; and demands to be subordinate, follow orders, and engage in demeaning routines and activities, similar to those used by the military to "make men out of boys" during boot camp.

. . . One fraternity pledge who quit the fraternity he had pledged described an experience during pledgeship as follows:

> This one guy was always picking on me. No matter what I did, I was wrong. One night after dinner, he and two other guys called me and two other pledges into the chapter room. He said, "Here, X, hold this twenty-five-pound bag of ice at arm's length 'til I tell you to stop." I did it even though my arms and hands were killing me. When I asked if I could stop, he grabbed me around the throat and lifted me off the floor. I thought he would choke me to death. He cussed me and called me all kinds of names. He took one of my fingers and twisted it until it nearly broke. . . . I stayed in the fraternity for a few more days, but then I decided to quit. I hated it. Those guys are sick. They like seeing you suffer.

Fraternities' emphasis on toughness, withstanding pain and humiliation, obedience to superiors, and using physical force to obtain compliance contributes to an interpersonal style that de-emphasizes caring and sensitivity but fosters intragroup trust and loyalty. If the least macho or most critical pledges drop out, those who remain may be more receptive to, and influenced by, masculinist values and practices that encourage the use of force in sexual relations with women and the covering up of such behavior.

NORMS AND DYNAMICS OF BROTHERHOOD

Brother is the status occupied by fraternity men to indicate their relations to each other and their membership in a particular fraternity organization or group. Brother is a male-specific status; only males can become brothers, although women can become "Little Sisters," a form of pseudomembership. "Becoming a brother" is a rite of passage that follows the consistent and often lengthy display by pledges of appropriately masculine qualities and behaviors. Brothers have a quasi-familial relationship with each other, are normatively said to share bonds of closeness and support, and are sharply set off from non-members. Brotherhood is a loosely defined term used to represent the bonds that develop among fraternity members and the obligations and expectations incumbent upon them. . . .

Some of our respondents talked about brotherhood in almost reverential terms, viewing it as the most valuable benefit of fraternity membership. One senior, a business-school major who had been affiliated with a fairly high-status fraternity throughout four years on campus, said:

> Brotherhood spurs friendship for life, which I consider its best aspect, although I didn't see it that way when I joined. Brotherhood bonds and unites. It instills

values of caring about one another, caring about community, caring about ourselves. The values and bonds [of brotherhood] continually develop over the four
years [in college] while normal friendships come and go.

Despite this idealization, most aspects of fraternity practice and conception are more mundane. Brotherhood often plays itself out as an overriding
concern with masculinity and, by extension, femininity. As a consequence, fraternities comprise collectivities of highly masculinized men with attitudinal
qualities and behavioral norms that predispose them to sexual coercion of
women. The norms of masculinity are complemented by conceptions of
women and femininity that are equally distorted and stereotyped and that may
enhance the probability of women's exploitation.

PRACTICES OF BROTHERHOOD

Practices associated with fraternity brotherhood that contribute to the sexual
coercion of women include a preoccupation with loyalty, group protection and
secrecy, use of alcohol as a weapon, and involvement in violence and physical
force. . . .

Loyalty, Group Protection, and Secrecy. Loyalty is a fraternity preoccupation. Members are reminded constantly to be loyal to the fraternity and to
their brothers. Among other ways, loyalty is played out in the practices of
group protection and secrecy. The fraternity must be shielded from criticism.
Members are admonished to avoid getting the fraternity in trouble and to
bring all problems "to the chapter" (local branch of a national social fraternity)
rather than to outsiders. Fraternities try to protect themselves from close
scrutiny and criticism by the Interfraternity Council (a quasi-governing body
composed of representatives from all social fraternities on campus), their fraternity's national office, university officials, law enforcement, the media, and
the public. Protection of the fraternity often takes precedence over what is
procedurally, ethically, or legally correct. Numerous examples were related to
us of fraternity brothers' lying to outsiders to "protect the fraternity."

Group protection was observed in the alleged gang rape case with which
we began our study. Except for one brother, a rapist who turned state's evidence, the entire remaining fraternity membership was accused by university
and criminal justice officials of lying to protect the fraternity. Members consistently failed to cooperate even though the alleged crimes were felonies, involved only four men (two of whom were not even members of the local
chapter), and the victim of the crime nearly died. According to a grand jury's
findings, fraternity officers repeatedly broke appointments with law enforcement officials, refused to provide police with a list of members, and refused to
cooperate with police and prosecutors investigating the case.

Secrecy, a priority value and practice in fraternities . . . is a boundary-maintaining mechanism, demarcating in-group from out-group, us from them. Secret rituals, handshakes, and mottos are revealed to pledge brothers as they are initiated into full brotherhood. Since only brothers are supposed to know a fraternity's secrets, such knowledge affirms membership in the fraternity and separates a brother from others. Extending secrecy tactics from protection of private knowledge to protection of the fraternity from criticism is a predictable development. Our interviews indicated that individual members knew the difference between right and wrong, but fraternity norms that emphasize loyalty, group protection, and secrecy often overrode standards of ethical correctness.

Alcohol as Weapon. Alcohol use by fraternity men is normative. They use it on weekdays to relax after class and on weekends to "get drunk," "get crazy," and "get laid." The use of alcohol to obtain sex from women is pervasive—in other words, it is used as a weapon against sexual reluctance. According to several fraternity men whom we interviewed, alcohol is the major tool used to gain sexual mastery over women. . . . One fraternity man, a twenty-one-year-old senior, [said:] " . . . You have to buy them drinks or find out if she's drunk enough. . . . "

A similar strategy is used collectively. A fraternity man said that at parties with Little Sisters: "We provide them with 'hunch punch' and things get wild. We get them drunk and most of the guys end up with one." "Hunch punch" he said, "is a girls' drink made up of overproof alcohol and powdered Kool-Aid, no water or anything, just ice. It's very strong. Two cups will do a number on a female." He had plans in the next academic term to surreptitiously give hunch punch to women in a "prim and proper" sorority because "having sex with prim and proper sorority girls is definitely a goal." These women are a challenge because they "won't openly consume alcohol and won't get openly drunk as hell." Their sororities have "standards committees" that forbid heavy drinking and easy sex.

In the gang rape case, our sources said that many fraternity men on campus believed the victim had a drinking problem and was thus an "easy make." According to newspaper accounts, she had been drinking alcohol on the evening she was raped; the lead assailant is alleged to have given her a bottle of wine after she arrived at his fraternity house. Portions of the rape occurred in a shower, and the victim was reportedly so drunk that her assailants had difficulty holding her in a standing position. While raping her, her assailants repeatedly told her they were members of another fraternity under the apparent belief that she was too drunk to know the difference. Of course, if she was too drunk to know who they were, she was too drunk to consent to sex.

One respondent told us that gang rapes are wrong and can get one expelled, but he seemed to see nothing wrong in sexual coercion one-on-one. He seemed unaware that the use of alcohol to obtain sex from a woman is grounds for a claim that a rape occurred. Few women on campus (who also may not know these grounds) report date rapes, however; so the odds of detection and punishment are slim for fraternity men who use alcohol for "seduction" purposes.

Violence and Physical Force.   Fraternity men have a history of violence. Their record of hazing, fighting, property destruction, and rape has caused them problems with insurance companies. Two university officials told us that fraternities "are the third riskiest property to insure behind toxic waste dumps and amusement parks." . . .

Fraternities' Commodification of Women

In claiming that women are treated by fraternities as commodities, we mean that fraternities knowingly, and intentionally, *use* women for their benefit. Fraternities use women as bait for new members, as servers of brothers' needs, and as sexual prey.

Women as Bait.   Fashionably attractive women help a fraternity attract new members. As one fraternity man, a junior, said, "They are good bait." Beautiful, sociable women are believed to impress the right kind of pledges and give the impression that the fraternity can deliver this type of woman to its members. Photographs of shapely, attractive coeds are printed in fraternity brochures and videotapes that are distributed and shown to potential pledges. The women pictured are often dressed in bikinis, at the beach, and are pictured hugging the brothers of the fraternity. One university official says such recruitment materials give the message: "Hey, they're here for you, you can have whatever you want," and, "we have the best-looking women. Join us and you can have them, too." Another commented: "Something's wrong when males join an all-male organization as the best place to meet women. It's so illogical."

Fraternities compete in promising access to beautiful women. One fraternity man, a senior, commented that "the attraction of girls [i.e., a fraternity's success in attracting women] is a big status symbol for fraternities." One university official commented that the use of women as a recruiting tool is so well entrenched that fraternities that might be willing to forgo it say they cannot afford to unless other fraternities do so as well. One fraternity man said, "Look, if we don't have Little Sisters, the fraternities that do will get all the good pledges." Another said, "We won't have as good a rush [the period during which new members are assessed and selected] if we don't have these women around."

In displaying good-looking, attractive, skimpily dressed, nubile women to potential members, fraternities implicitly, and sometimes explicitly, promise sexual access to women. One fraternity man commented that "part of what being in a fraternity is all about is the sex" and explained how his fraternity uses Little Sisters to recruit new members:

> We'll tell the sweetheart [the fraternity's term for Little Sister], "You're gorgeous; you can get him." We'll tell her to fake a scam and she'll go hang all over him during a rush party, kiss him, and he thinks he's done wonderful and wants to join. The girls think it's great too. It's flattering for them.

Women as Servers.   The use of women as servers is exemplified in the Little Sister program. Little Sisters are undergraduate women who are rushed and selected in a manner parallel to the recruitment of fraternity men. They are affiliated with the fraternity in a formal but unofficial way and are able, indeed required, to wear the fraternity's Greek letters. Little Sisters are not full-fledged fraternity members, however, and fraternity national offices and most universities do not register or regulate them. Each fraternity has an officer called Little Sister Chairman who oversees their organization and activities. The Little Sisters elect officers among themselves, pay monthly dues to the fraternity, and have well-defined roles. Their dues are used to pay for the fraternity's social events, and Little Sisters are expected to attend and hostess fraternity parties and hang around the house to make it a "nice place to be." One fraternity man, a senior, described Little Sisters this way: "They are very social girls, willing to join in, be affiliated with the group, devoted to the fraternity." Another member, a sophomore, said: "Their sole purpose is social—attend parties, attract new members, and 'take care' of the guys." . . .

Women as Sexual Prey.   Little Sisters are a sexual utility. Many Little Sisters do not belong to sororities and lack peer support for refraining from unwanted sexual relations. One fraternity man (whose fraternity has 65 members and 85 Little Sisters) told us they had recruited "wholesale" in the prior year to "get lots of new women." The structural access to women that the Little Sister program provides and the absence of normative supports for refusing fraternity members' sexual advances may make women in this program particularly susceptible to coerced sexual encounters with fraternity men.

Access to women for sexual gratification is a presumed benefit of fraternity membership, promised in recruitment materials and strategies, and through brothers' conversations with new recruits. One fraternity man said: "We always tell the guys that you get sex all the time, there's always new girls. . . . After I became a Greek, I found out I could be with females at will." A university official told us that, based on his observations, "no one [i.e., fraternity men] on this campus wants to have 'relationships.' They just want to have fun [i.e., sex]." Fraternity men plan and execute strategies aimed at obtaining sexual gratification, and this occurs at both individual and collective levels.

Individual strategies include getting a woman drunk and spending a great deal of money on her. As for collective strategies, most of our undergraduate inteviewees agreed that fraternity parties often culminate in sex and that this outcome is planned. One fraternity man said fraternity parties often involve sex and nudity and can "turn into orgies." Orgies may be planned in advance, such as the Bowery Ball party held by one fraternity. A former fraternity member said of this party:

> The entire idea behind this is sex. Both men and women come to the party wearing little or nothing. There are pornographic pinups on the walls and usually porno movies playing on the TV. The music carries sexual overtones. . . . They just get schnockered [drunk] and, in most cases, they also get laid.

When asked about the women who come to such a party, he said: "Some Little Sisters just won't go. . . . The girls who do are looking for a good time, girls who don't know what it is, things like that."

Other respondents denied that fraternity parties are orgies but said that sex is always talked about among the brothers and they all know "who each other is doing it with." One member said that most of the time, guys have sex with their girlfriends "but with socials, girlfriends aren't allowed to come and it's their [members'] big chance [to have sex with other women]." The use of alcohol to help them get women into bed is a routine strategy at fraternity parties.

Conclusion

In general, our research indicated that the organization and membership of fraternities contribute heavily to coercive and often violent sex. Fraternity houses are occupied by same-sex (all men) and same-age (late teens, early twenties) peers whose maturity and judgment are often less than ideal. Yet fraternity houses are private dwellings that are mostly off-limits to, and away from scrutiny of, university and community representatives, with the result that fraternity house events seldom come to the attention of outsiders. Practices associated with the social construction of fraternity brotherhood emphasize a macho conception of men and masculinity, a narrow, stereotyped conception of women and femininity, and the treatment of women as commodities. Other practices contributing to coercive sexual relations and the cover-up of rapes include excessive alcohol use, competitiveness, and normative support for deviance and secrecy.

Some fraternity practices exacerbate others. Brotherhood norms require "sticking together" regardless of right or wrong; thus rape episodes are unlikely to be stopped or reported to outsiders, even when witnesses disapprove. The ability to use alcohol without scrutiny by authorities and alcohol's frequent association with violence, including sexual coercion, facilitate rape in fraternity houses. Fraternity norms that emphasize the value of maleness and masculinity over femaleness and femininity and that elevate the status of men and lower the status of women in members' eyes undermine perceptions and treatment of women as persons who deserve consideration and care. . . .

Our research led us to conclude that fraternity norms and practices influence members to view the sexual coercion of women, which is a felony crime, as sport, a contest, or a game. This sport is played not between men and women but between men and men. Women are the pawns or prey in the interfraternity rivalry game; they prove that a fraternity is successful or prestigious. The use of women in this way encourages fraternity men to see women as objects and sexual coercion as sport. Today's societal norms support young women's right to engage in sex at their discretion, and coercion is unnecessary in a mutually desired encounter. However, nubile young women say they prefer to be "in a relationship" to have sex while young men say they prefer to "get laid" without a commitment. In a fraternity context, getting sex without giving emotionally demonstrates "cool" masculinity. More important, it poses no threat to the bonding and loyalty of the fraternity brotherhood.

Unless fraternities' composition, goals, structures, and practices change in fundamental ways, women on campus will continue to be sexual prey for fraternity men. As all-male enclaves dedicated to opposing faculty and administration and to cementing in-group ties (i.e., fraternity members eschew any hint of homosexuality), their version of masculinity transforms women, and men with womanly characteristics, into the out-group. "Womanly men" are ostracized; feminine women are used to demonstrate members' masculinity. A case for or against fraternities cannot be made by studying individual members. The fraternity qua group and organization is at issue. Located on campus along with many vulnerable women, embedded in a sexist society, and caught up in masculinist goals, practices, and values, fraternities' violation of women—including forcible rape—should come as no surprise.

29 Showing My Color

CLARENCE PAGE

As you know, the circumstances we inherit at birth (sometimes called *social capital*) affect what happens to us in life. Some of us are born poor, others rich, and most of us in between. Some of us are born to single mothers, others to married parents; some to parents who are college graduates, others to parents who have not finished high school. Even our geography (South, West, rural, urban) sets up background factors that play a significant role in our orientations to life. Sociologists use the term *life chances* to refer to how the background factors that surround our birth affect our fate in life.

In the United States, race–ethnicity is a major divide. It opens and closes doors of opportunity and privilege. It is a primary source of identity, uniting us with some people, while separating us from others. Although race–ethnicity becomes a vital part of our identity, as with other concepts, we are not born with an awareness of our race or ethnicity. This we learn from others around us, which can be a jarring experience. In this selection, Page, a journalist, recounts how he learned that he was a black in a white society. He also shares examples of what this has meant for his life.

RACE HAS LONG HAD A RUDE PRESENCE in my life. While visiting relatives in Alabama as a child in the 1950s, I first saw water fountains marked "white" and "colored." I vaguely recall being excited. I rushed over to the one marked "colored" and turned it on, only to find, to my deep disappointment, that the water came out clear, just like the water back home in Ohio.

"Segregation," my dad said. I'd never heard the word before. My southern-born parents explained that it was something the white folks "down home" practiced. Some "home." Yet unpleasant experiences in the North already had taught me a more genteel, yet no less limiting, version.

"There are places white people don't want colored to go," my elders told me in their soft southern accents, "and white people make the rules."

We had plenty of segregation like that in the North. We just didn't have the signs, which made it cheaper and easier to deny. We could look out of my schoolhouse window to see a public swimming pool closed to nonwhites. We had to go across town to the separate-but-equal "pool for colored." The steel mill that was our town's biggest employer held separate picnics for colored and white employees, which seemed to be just fine with the employees.

Everyone had a good time, separately and unequally. I think the colored folks, who today would be called the "black community," were just happy to have something to call their own.

When I was about six years old, I saw a television commercial for an amusement park near the southern Ohio factory town where I grew up.

I chose to go. I told my parents. They looked at each other sadly and informed me that "little colored kids can't go there." I was crushed.

"I wish I was white," I told my parents.

"No, you don't!" Mom snapped. She gave me a look terrible enough to persuade me instantly that no, I didn't.

"Well, maybe for a few minutes, anyway?" I asked. "Just long enough for me to get past the front gate?" Then I could show them, I thought. I remember I wanted to show them what a terrific kid I was. I felt sorry for the little white children who would be deprived of getting to know me.

Throughout our childhood years, my friendships with white schoolchildren (and with Pancho from the only Latino family in the neighborhood) proceeded without interruption. Except for the occasional tiff over some injudicious use of the N-word or some other slur we had picked up from our elders, we played in each other's backyards as congenially as Spanky, Buckwheat, and the rest of the gang on the old Hal Roach *Our Gang* comedies we used to watch on television.

Yet it quickly became apparent to me that my white friends were growing up in a different reality from the one to which I was accustomed. I could tell from the way one white friend happily discussed his weekend at LeSourdesville Lake that he did not have a clue of my reality.

"Have you been?" he asked.

"Colored can't go there," I said, somewhat astonished that he had not noticed.

"Oh, that can't be," he said.

For a moment, I perked up, wondering if the park's policy had changed. "Have you seen any colored people there?" I asked.

My white friend thought for a moment, then realized that he had not. He expressed surprise. I was surprised that he was surprised.

By the time I reached high school in the early 1960s, LeSourdesville Lake would relax its racial prohibitions. But the lessons of it stuck with me. It taught me how easily white people could ignore the segregation problem because, from their vantage point, it was not necessarily a problem. It was not necessarily an advantage to them, either, although some undoubtedly thought so. White people of low income, high insecurity, or fragile ego could always say that, no matter how badly off they felt, at least they were not black. Segregation helped them uphold and maintain this illusion of superiority. Even those white people who considered themselves to have a well-developed sense of social conscience could easily rationalize segregation as something that was good for both races. We played unwittingly into this illusion, I thought, when my friends and I began junior high school and, suddenly thrust into the edgy, high hormonal world of adolescence, quickly gravitated into social cliques according to tastes and race.

It became even more apparent to me that my white friends and I were growing up in *parallel realities,* not unlike the parallel universes described in the science fiction novels and comic books I adored—or the "parallel realities" experienced by Serbs, Bosnians, and Croatians as described years later by feminist writer Slavenka Drakulic in *The Balkan Express.* Even as the evil walls of legal segregation were tumbling down, thanks to the hard-fought struggles of the civil rights movement, it occurred to me that my reality might never be quite the same as that experienced by my white friends. We were doomed, I felt, to dwell in our parallel realities. Separated by thick walls of prejudice, we would view each other through windows of stained-glass perceptions, colored by our personal experiences. My parents had taught me well.

"Don't be showin' yo' color," my parents would admonish me in my youth, before we would go out in public, especially among white folks. The phrase had special meaning in Negro conversations. Imbued with many subtle meanings and nuances, the showing of one's "color" could be an expression of chastisement or warning, admonishment or adulation, satire or self-hatred, anger or celebration. It could mean acting out or showing anger in a loud and uncivilized way.

Its cultural origins could be traced to the Africa-rooted tradition of "signifying," a form of witty, deliberately provocative, occasionally combative word play. The thrill of the game comes from taking one's opponent close to the edge of tolerable insult. Few subjects—except perhaps sex itself—could be a more sensitive matter between black people than talk about someone else's "color." The showing of one's "color" then, connoted the display of the very worst stereotypes anyone ever dreamed up about how black people behaved. "White people are not really white," James Baldwin wrote in 1961, "but colored people can sometimes be extremely colored."

Sometimes you can still hear black people say in the heat of frustration, "I almost showed my color today," which is a way of saying they almost lost their "cool," "dropped the mask," or "went off." Losing one's cool can be a capital offense by black standards, for it shows weakness in a world in which spiritual rigor is one of the few things we can call our own. Those who keep their cool repress their "color." It is cool, in other words, to be colorless.

Showing My Color (the title of the book from which this reading is taken) emerged from my fuming discontent with the current fashions of *racial denial,* steadfast repudiations of the difference race continues to make in American life. Old liberals, particularly white liberals who have become new conservatives, charge that racial pride and color consciousness threaten to "Balkanize" American life, as if it ever was a model of unity. Many demand that we "get past race." But denials of a cancer, no matter how vigorous they may be, will not make the malignancy go away.

No less august a voice than the Supreme Court's conservative majority has taken to arguing in the 1990s for a "color-blind" approach to civil rights law, the area of American society in which color and gender consciousness have made the most dramatic improvement in equalizing opportunities.

The words of the Reverend Martin Luther King, Jr., have been perverted to support this view. Most frequently quoted is his oft-stated dream of the day when everyone would "not be judged by the color of their skin but by the content of their character." I would argue that King never intended for us to forget *all* about color. Even in his historic "I Have a Dream" speech, from which this line most often is lifted, he also pressed the less-often quoted but piquantly salient point about "the promissory note" America gave freed slaves, which, when they presented it, was returned to them marked "insufficient funds."

● ● ●

I would argue that too much has been made of the virtue of "color blindness." I don't want Americans to be blind to my color as long as color continues to make a profound difference in determining life chances and opportunities. Nor do I wish to see so significant a part of my identity denied. "Ethnic differences are the very essence of cultural diversity and national creativity," black social critic Albert Murray wrote in *The Omni-Americans* (1970). "The problem is not the existence of ethnic differences, as is so often assumed, but the intrusion of such differences into areas where they do not belong."

Where, then *do* they belong? Diversity is enriching, but race intrudes rudely on the individual's attempts to define his or her own identity. I used to be "colored." Then I was "Negro." Then I became "black." Then I became "African-American." Today I am a "person of color." In three decades, I have been transformed from a "colored person" to a "person of color." Are you keeping up with me?

Changes in what we black people call ourselves are quite annoying to some white people, which is its own reward to some black people. But if white people are confused, so are quite a few black people. There is no one way to be black. We are a diverse people amid a nation of diverse people. Some black people are nationalists who don't want anything to do with white people. Some black people are assimilationists who don't want anything to do with other black people. Some black people are integrationists who move in and out of various groups with remarkable ease. Some of us can be any of the three at any given time, depending on when you happen to run into us.

Growing up as part of a minority can expose the individual to horrible bouts of identity confusion. I used to think of myself as something of a *transracial man,* a figure no less frustrated than a transsexual who feels trapped in the body of something unfamiliar and inappropriate to his or her inner self.

These bouts were most torturous during adolescence, the period of life when, trembling with the shock of nascent independence from the ways of one's elders, the budding individual stitches together the fragile garments of an identity to be worn into adulthood. Stuttering and uncooperative motor skills left me severely challenged in dancing, basket shooting, and various social applications; I felt woefully inadequate to the task of being "popular" in the hot centers of black social activity at my integrated high school and college. "Are you black?" an arbiter of campus militancy demanded one day, when he "caught" me dining too many times with white friends. I had the skin pass, sure enough, but my inclinations fell well short of his standards. But I was not satisfied with the standards of his counterparts in the white world, either. If I was not "black" enough to please some blacks, I would never be "white" enough to please all whites.

Times have changed. Choices abound for black people, if we can afford them. Black people can now go anywhere they choose, as long as they can pay the bill when they get there. If anyone tries to stop them or any other minorities just because of their color, the full weight of the federal government will step in on the side of the minorities. I thank God and the hard-won gains of the civil rights revolution for my ability to have more choices. But the old rules of race have been replaced in many ways by new ones.

• • •

Today, I live a well-integrated life in the suburbs [of Montgomery County, Maryland, outside Washington, D.C.]. Black folks still tell me how to be "black" when I stray from the racial party lines, while white folks tell me how to be "color-blind." I still feel as frustrated in my attempts to transcend race as a reluctant lemming must feel while being rushed over the brink by its herd. But I find I have plenty of company in my frustration. Integration has not been a simple task for upwardly mobile African-Americans, especially for those of us who happen also to be parents.

A few years ago, after talking to black friends who were raising teenage boys, I realized that I was about to face dilemmas not unlike those my parents faced. My son was turning three years old. Everyone was telling me that he was quite cute, and because he was the spitting image of his dad, I was the last to argue.

But it occurred to me that in another decade he would be not three but thirteen. If all goes well, somewhere along the way he is going to turn almost overnight from someone who is perceived as cute and innocent into someone who is perceived as a menace, the most feared creature on America's urban streets today, a *young black male*. Before he, like me when I was barred from a childhood amusement park, would have a chance to let others get to know him, he would be judged not by the content of his character, but by the color of his skin. . . .

• • •

My mom is gone now, after helping set me up with the sort of education that has freed me to make choices. I have chosen to move my father to a nice, predominantly white, antiseptically tidy retirement village near me in Maryland with large golf courses and swimming pools. It is the sort of place he might have scrubbed floors in but certainly not have lived in back in the old days. It has taken him a while to get used to having so many well-off white people behaving so nicely and neighborly to him, but he has made the adjustment well.

Still the ugly specter of racism does not easily vanish. He and the other hundred or so African-American residents decided to form a social club like the other ethnically or religiously based social clubs in the village. One night during their meeting in the main social room, someone scrawled *KKK* on little sheets of paper and slipped them under the windshields of some of their cars in the parking lot. "We think maybe some of the white people wanted the blacks to socialize with the whites, not in a separate group," one lady of the club told me. If so, they showed an unusual method for extending the arms of brotherhood.

I live in a community that worships diversity like a state religion, although individuals sometimes get tripped up by it. The excellent Spanish "immersion" program that one of the county's "magnet" schools installed to encourage middle-class parents to stay put has itself become a cover for "white flight" by disgruntled white parents. Many of them, despite a lack of empirical evidence, perceive the school's regular English program as inferior, simply because it is 90 percent minority and mostly composed of children who come from a less-fortunate socioeconomic background. So the Spanish immersion classes designed to encourage diversity have become almost exclusively white and Asian America, while the English classes have become almost exclusively—irony of ironies—black and Latino, with many of the children learning English as a second language. Statistically, the school is "diverse" and "integrated." In reality, its student body is divided by an indelible wall, separate but supposedly equal. . . .

Despite all these color-conscious efforts to educate the country's children in a color-blind ideal of racial equality, many of our children seem to be catching on to race codes anyway, although with a twist suitable to the hip-hop generation. One local junior high school teacher, when he heard his black students referring to themselves as "bad," had the facts of racial life explained to him like this: They were not talking about the "bad means good" slang popularized by Michael Jackson's *Bad* album. They meant "bad" in the sense of misbehaving and poorly motivated. The black kids are "bad," the students explained, and the white kids are "good." The Asian kids are "like white," and the Latino kids "try to be bad, like the blacks." Anyone who tried to break out of those stereotypes was trying to break the code, meaning that a black or Latino who tried to make good grades was "trying to be white."

It is enough, as Marvin Gaye famously sang, to make you want to holler and throw up both your hands. Yet my neighbors and I hate to complain too loudly because, unlike other critics you may read or hear about, we happen to be a liberal community that not only believes in the dream of integration and true diversity, but actually is trying to live it. . . .

We see icons of black success—Colin Powell, Douglas Wilder, Bill Cosby, Oprah Winfrey, Bryant Gumbel, the two Michaels: Jordan and Jackson—not only accepted but adored by whites in ways far removed from the arm's-length way white America regarded Jackie Robinson, Willie Mays, Lena Horne, and Marian Anderson.

Yet, although the media show happy images of blacks, whites, Asians, and Hispanics getting along, amicably consuming the good life, a fog of false contentment conceals menacing fissures cracking the national racial landscape.

Despite the growth of the black middle class, most blacks and whites live largely separate lives. School integration actually peaked in 1967, according to a Harvard study, and has declined ever since. Economic segregation has proceeded without interruption, distancing poor blacks not only from whites but also from upwardly mobile blacks, making the isolation and misery of poor blacks worse. One out of every two black children lives below the poverty line, compared to one out of every seven white children. Black infants in America die at twice the rate of white infants. A record-setting million inmates crowd the nation's prisons, half of them black. The black out-of-wedlock birth rate has grown from about 25 percent in 1965 to more than 60 percent (more than 90 percent in the South Bronx and other areas of concentrated black poverty). . . .

The decline of industrial America, along with low-skill, high-pay jobs, has left much of black America split in two along lines of class, culture, opportunity and hope. The "prepared" join the new black middle class, which grew rapidly in the 1970s and early 1980s. The unprepared populate a new culture, directly opposed not only to the predominantly white mainstream, but also to any blacks who aspire to practice the values of hard work, good English, and family loyalty that would help them to join the white mainstream. The results of this spiritual decline, along with economic decline, have been devastating. Although more black women go to college than ever before, it has become a commonplace to refer to young black males as an endangered species. New anti-black stereotypes replace the old. Prosperous, well-dressed African Americans still complain of suffering indignities when they try to hail a taxicab. The fact that the taxi that just passed them by was driven by a black cabby, native born or immigrant, makes no difference. . . .

Behind our questions of race lurk larger questions of identity, our sense of who we are, where we belong, and where we are going. Our sense of place and peoplehood within groups is a perpetual challenge in some lives, particularly lives in America, a land where identity bubbles quite often out of nothing more than a weird alchemy of history and choice. "When I discover who I am, I'll be free," Ralph Ellison once wrote.

I reject the melting pot metaphor. People don't melt. Americans prove it on their ethnic holidays, in the ways they dance, in the ways they sing, in the culturally connected ways they worship. Displaced people long to celebrate their ethnic roots many generations and intermarriages after their ancestors arrived in their new land. Irish-American celebrations of St. Patrick's Day in Boston, Chicago, and New York City are far more lavish than anything seen on that day in Dublin or Belfast. Mexican-American celebrations of Cinco de Mayo, the Fifth of May, are far more lavish in Los Angeles and San Antonio than anything seen that day in Mexico City. It is as if holidays give us permission to expose our former selves as we imagine them to be. Americans of European descent love to show their ethnic cultural backgrounds. Why do they get nervous only when black people show their love for theirs? Is it that black people on such occasions suddenly remind white people of vulnerabilities black people feel quite routinely as a minority in a majority white society? Is it that white people, by and large, do not like this feeling, that they want nothing more than to cleanse themselves of it and make sure that it does not come bubbling up again? Attempts by Americans to claim some ephemeral, all-inclusive "all-American" identity reminds me of Samuel Johnson's observation: "Sir, a man may be so much of everything, that he is nothing of anything."

Instead of the melting pot metaphor, I prefer the mulligan stew, a concoction my parents tell me they used to fix during the Great Depression, when there was not a lot of food around the house and they "made do" with whatever meats, vegetables, and spices they had on hand. Everything went into the pot and was stirred up, but the pieces didn't melt. Peas were easily distinguished from carrots or potatoes. Each maintained its distinctive character. Yet each loaned its special flavor to the whole, and each absorbed some of the flavor from the others. That flavor, always unique, always changing, is the beauty of America to me, even when the pot occasionally boils over. . . .

African Americans are as diverse as other Americans. Some become nationalistic and ethnocentric. Others become pluralistic or multicultural, fitting their black identity into a comfortable niche among other aspects of themselves and their daily lives. Whichever they choose, a comfortable identity serves to provide not only a sense of belonging and protection for the individual against the abuses of racism, but also, ultimately, a sturdy foundation from which the individual can interact effectively with other people, cultures, and situations beyond the world of blackness.

"Identity would seem to be the garment with which one covers the nakedness of the self," James Baldwin wrote in *The Devil Finds Work,* "in which case, it is best that the garment be loose, a little like the robes of the desert, through which one's nakedness can always be felt, and, sometimes, discerned. This trust in one's nakedness is all that gives one the power to change one's robes."

The cloak of proud black identity has provided a therapeutical warmth for my naked self after the chilly cocoon of inferiority imposed early in my life by a white-exalting society. But it is best worn loosely, lest it become as constricting and isolating for the famished individual soul as the garment it replaced.

The ancestral desire of my ethnic people to be "just American" resonates in me. But I cannot forget how persistently the rudeness of race continues to intrude between me and that dream. I can defy it, but I cannot deny it. . . .

30 The Uses of Poverty: The Poor Pay All

HERBERT J. GANS

Some people think that poverty simply means having to tighten your belt, but the meaning of poverty is much more profound. Sociologists have documented that the poor confront social conditions so damaging that their marriages are more likely to break up, they are sicker than others, their children are more likely to drop out of school and get in trouble with the law, they are more likely to be victimized by crime, and, on average, they die younger than most. It is difficult to romanticize poverty when one knows what its true conditions are.

In this selection, Gans does not document the degradation of the poor (although this is intrinsically present in his analysis), nor their failing health or troubled lives. Nor is his article a plea for social reform. Rather, from the observation that the poor are always present in society he concludes that this is because they perform vital services (functions) for society. (An essential assumption of *functionalism,* one of the theoretical schools in sociology, is that conditions persist in society only if they benefit—perform functions for—society or some of its parts.) In this selection, then, Gans tries to identify those functions.

Do you think the author has overlooked any "functions" of the poor? If his analysis, which many find startling, is not correct, what alternative explanation could you propose?

SOME YEARS AGO ROBERT K. MERTON applied the notion of functional analysis to explain the continuing though maligned existence of the urban political machine: If it continued to exist, perhaps it fulfilled latent—unintended or unrecognized—positive functions. Clearly it did. Merton pointed out how the political machine provided central authority to get things done when a decentralized local government could not act, humanized the services of the impersonal bureaucracy for fearful citizens, offered concrete help (rather than abstract law or justice) to the poor, and otherwise performed services needed or demanded by many people but considered unconventional or even illegal by formal public agencies.

Today, poverty is more maligned than the political machine ever was; yet it, too, is a persistent social phenomenon. Consequently, there may be some merit in applying functional analysis to poverty, in asking whether it also has positive functions that explain its persistence.

Merton defined functions as "those observed consequences [of a phenomenon] which make for the adaptation or adjustment of a given [social] system." I shall use a slightly different definition; instead of identifying functions for an entire social system, I shall identify them for the interest groups, socio-economic classes, and other population aggregates with shared values that "inhabit" a social system. I suspect that in a modern heterogeneous society, few phenomena are functional or dysfunctional for the society as a whole, and that most result in benefits to some groups and costs to others. Nor are any phenomena indispensable; in most instances, one can suggest what Merton calls "functional alternatives" or equivalents for them, i.e., other social patterns or policies that achieve the same positive functions but avoid the dysfunction. (In the following discussion, positive functions will be abbreviated as functions and negative functions as dysfunctions. Functions and dysfunctions, in the planner's terminology, will be described as benefits and costs.)

Associating poverty with positive functions seems at first glance to be unimaginable. Of course, the slumlord and the loan shark are commonly known to profit from the existence of poverty, but they are viewed as evil men, so their activities are classified among the dysfunctions of poverty. However, what is less often recognized, at least by the conventional wisdom, is that poverty also makes possible the existence or expansion of respectable professions and occupations, for example, penology, criminology, social work, and public health. More recently, the poor have provided jobs for professional and para-professional "poverty warriors," and for journalists and social scientists, this author included, who have supplied the information demanded by the revival of public interest in poverty.

Clearly, then, poverty and the poor may well satisfy a number of positive functions for many nonpoor groups in American society. I shall describe 13 such functions—economic, social, and political—that seem to me most significant.

The Functions of Poverty

First, the existence of poverty ensures that society's "dirty work" will be done. Every society has such work: physically dirty or dangerous, temporary, dead-end and underpaid, undignified, and menial jobs. Society can fill these jobs by paying higher wages than for "clean" work, or it can force people who have no other choice to do the dirty work—and at low wages. In America, poverty functions to provide a low-wage labor pool that is willing—or, rather, unable to be *un*willing—to perform dirty work at low cost. Indeed, this function of the poor is so important that in some Southern states, welfare payments have been cut off during the summer months when the poor are needed to work in the fields. Moreover, much of the debate about the Negative Income Tax and the Family Assistance Plan has concerned their impact on the work incentive, by which is actually meant the incentive of the poor to do the needed dirty work if the wages therefrom are no larger than the income grant. Many economic activities that involve dirty work depend on the poor for their existence: restaurants, hospitals, parts of the garment industry, and "truck farming," among others, could not persist in their present form without the poor.

Second, because the poor are required to work at low wages, they subsidize a variety of economic activities that benefit the affluent. For example, domestics subsidize the upper-middle and upper classes, making life easier for their employers and freeing affluent women for a variety of professional, cultural, civic, and partying activities. Similarly, because the poor pay a higher proportion of their income in property and sales taxes, among others, they subsidize many state and local governmental services that benefit more affluent groups. In addition, the poor support innovation in medical practice as patients in teaching and research hospitals and as guinea pigs in medical experiments.

Third, poverty creates jobs for a number of occupations and professions that serve or "service" the poor, or protect the rest of society from them. As already noted, penology would be minuscule without the poor, as would the police. Other activities and groups that flourish because of the existence of poverty are the numbers game, the sale of heroin and cheap wines and liquors, pentecostal ministers, faith healers, prostitutes, pawn shops, and the peacetime army, which recruits its enlisted men mainly from among the poor.

Fourth, the poor buy goods others do not want and thus prolong the economic usefulness of such goods—day-old bread, fruit and vegetables that would otherwise have to be thrown out, secondhand clothes, and deteriorating automobiles and buildings. They also provide incomes for doctors, lawyers, teachers, and others who are too old, poorly trained, or incompetent to attract more affluent clients.

In addition to economic functions, the poor perform a number of social functions.

Fifth, the poor can be identified and punished as alleged or real deviants in order to uphold the legitimacy of conventional norms. To justify the desirability of hard work, thrift, honesty, and monogamy, for example, the defenders of these norms must be able to find people who can be accused of being lazy, spendthrift, dishonest, and promiscuous. Although there is some evidence that the poor are about as moral and law-abiding as anyone else, they are more likely than middle-class transgressors to be caught and punished when they participate in deviant acts. Moreover, they lack the political and cultural power to correct the stereotypes that other people hold of them and thus continue to be thought of as lazy, spendthrift, etc., by those who need living proof that moral deviance does not pay.

Sixth, and conversely, the poor offer vicarious participation to the rest of the population in the uninhibited sexual, alcoholic, and narcotic behavior in which they are alleged to participate and which, being freed from the constraints of affluence, they are often thought to enjoy more than the middle classes. Thus many people, some social scientists included, believe that the poor not only are more given to uninhibited behavior (which may be true, although it is often motivated by despair more than by lack of inhibition) but derive more pleasure from it than affluent people (which research by Lee Rainwater, Walter Miller, and others shows to be patently untrue). However, whether the poor actually have more sex and enjoy it more is irrelevant; so long as middle-class people believe this to be true, they can participate in it vicariously when instances are reported in factual or fictional form.

Seventh, the poor also serve a direct cultural function when culture created by or for them is adopted by the more affluent. The rich often collect artifacts from extinct folk cultures of poor people; and almost all Americans listen to the blues, Negro spirituals, and country music, which originated among the Southern poor. Recently they have enjoyed the rock styles that were born, like the Beatles, in the slums; and in the last year, poetry written by ghetto children has become popular in literary circles. The poor also serve as culture heroes, particularly, of course, to the left; but the hobo, the cowboy, the hipster, and the mythical prostitute with a heart of gold have performed this function for a variety of groups.

Eighth, poverty helps to guarantee the status of those who are not poor. In every hierarchical society someone has to be at the bottom; but in American society, in which social mobility is an important goal for many and people need to know where they stand, the poor function as a reliable and relatively permanent measuring rod for status comparisons. This is particularly true for the working class, whose politics is influenced by the need to maintain status distinctions between themselves and the poor, much as the aristocracy must find ways of distinguishing itself from the *nouveaux riches.*

Ninth, the poor also aid the upward mobility of groups just above them in the class hierarchy. Thus a goodly number of Americans have entered the middle class through the profits earned from the provision of goods and services in the slums, including illegal or nonrespectable ones that upper-class and upper-middle-class businessmen shun because of their low prestige. As a result, members of almost every immigrant group have financed their upward mobility by providing slum housing, entertainment, gambling, narcotics, etc., to later arrivals—most recently to blacks and Puerto Ricans.

Tenth, the poor help to keep the aristocracy busy, thus justifying its continued existence. "Society" uses the poor as clients of settlement houses and beneficiaries of charity affairs; indeed, the aristocracy must have the poor to demonstrate its superiority over other elites who devote themselves to earning money.

Eleventh, the poor, being powerless, can be made to absorb the costs of change and growth in American society. During the nineteenth century, they did the backbreaking work that built the cities; today, they are pushed out of their neighborhoods to make room for "progress." Urban renewal projects to hold middle-class taxpayers in the city and expressways to enable suburbanites to commute downtown have typically been located in poor neighborhoods, since no other group will allow itself to be displaced. For the same reason, universities, hospitals, and civic centers also expand into land occupied by the poor. The major costs of the industrialization of agriculture have been borne by the poor, who are pushed off the land without recompense; and they have paid a large share of the human cost of the growth of American power overseas, for they have provided many of the foot soldiers for Vietnam and other wars.

Twelfth, the poor facilitate and stabilize the American political process. Because they vote and participate in politics less than other groups, the political system is often free to ignore them. Moreover, since they can rarely support Republicans, they often provide the Democrats with a captive constituency that has no other place to go. As a result, the Democrats can count on their votes, and be more responsive to voters—for example, the white working class—who might otherwise switch to the Republicans.

Thirteenth, the role of the poor in upholding conventional norms (see the *fifth* point, above) also has a significant political function. An economy based on the ideology of laissez-faire requires a deprived population that is allegedly unwilling to work or that can be considered inferior because it must accept charity or welfare in order to survive. Not only does the alleged moral deviancy of the poor reduce the moral pressure on the present political economy to eliminate poverty, but socialist alternatives can be made to look quite unattractive if those who will benefit most from them can be described as lazy, spendthrift, dishonest, and promiscuous.

The Alternatives

I have described 13 of the more important functions that poverty and the poor satisfy in American society, enough to support the functionalist thesis that poverty, like any other social phenomenon, survives in part because it is useful to society or some of its parts. This analysis is not intended to suggest that because it is often functional, poverty *should* exist, or that it *must* exist. For one thing, poverty has many more dysfunctions than functions; for another, it is possible to suggest functional alternatives.

For example, society's dirty work could be done without poverty, either by automation or by paying "dirty workers" decent wages. Nor is it necessary for the poor to subsidize the many activities they support through their low-wage jobs. This would, however, drive up the costs of these activities, which would result in higher prices to their customers and clients. Similarly, many of the professionals who flourish because of the poor could be given other roles. Social workers could provide counseling to the affluent, as they prefer to do anyway; and the police could devote themselves to traffic and organized crime.

Other roles would have to be found for badly trained or incompetent professionals now relegated to serving the poor, and someone else would have to pay their salaries. Fewer penologists would be employable, however. And pentecostal religion could probably not survive without the poor—nor would parts of the second- and third-hand-goods market. And in many cities, "used" housing that no one else wants would then have to be torn down at public expense.

Alternatives for the cultural functions of the poor could be found more easily and cheaply. Indeed, entertainers and adolescents are already serving as the deviants needed to uphold traditional morality and as devotees of orgies to "staff" the fantasies of vicarious participation.

The status functions of the poor are another matter. In a hierarchical society, some people must be defined as inferior to everyone else with respect to a variety of attributes, but they need not be poor in the absolute sense. One could conceive of a society in which the "lower class," though last in the pecking order, received 75 percent of the median income, rather than 15–40 percent, as is now the case. Needless to say, this would require considerable income redistribution.

The contribution the poor make to the upward mobility of the groups that provide them with goods and services could also be maintained without the poor's having such low incomes. However, it is true that if the poor were more affluent, they would have access to enough capital to take over the provider role, thus competing with, and perhaps rejecting, the "outsiders." (Indeed, owing in part to antipoverty programs, this is already happening in a number of ghettos, where white storeowners are being replaced by blacks.) Similarly, if the poor were more affluent, they would make less willing clients for upper-class philanthropy, although some would still use settlement houses to achieve upward mobility, as they do now. Thus "Society" could continue to run its philanthropic activities.

The political functions of the poor would be more difficult to replace. With increased affluence the poor would probably obtain more political power and be more active politically. With higher incomes and more political power, the poor would be likely to resist paying the costs of growth and change. Of course, it is possible to imagine urban renewal and highway projects that properly reimbursed the displaced people, but such projects would then become considerably more expensive, and many might never be built. This, in turn, would reduce the comfort and convenience of those who now benefit from urban renewal and expressways.

In sum, then, many of the functions served by the poor could be replaced if poverty were eliminated, but almost always at higher costs to others, particularly more affluent others. Consequently, a functional analysis must conclude that poverty persists not only because it fulfills a number of positive functions but also because many of the functional alternatives to poverty would be quite dysfunctional for the affluent members of society. A functional analysis thus ultimately arrives at much the same conclusion as radical sociology, except that radical thinkers treat as manifest what I describe as latent: that social phenomena that are functional for affluent or powerful groups and dysfunctional for poor or powerless ones persist; that when the elimination of such phenomena through functional alternatives would generate dysfunctions for the affluent or powerful, they will continue to persist; and that phenomena like poverty can be eliminated only when they become dysfunctional for the affluent or powerful, or when the powerless can obtain enough power to change society.

Postscript

Over the years, this article has been interpreted as either a direct attack on functionalism or a tongue-in-cheek satirical comment on it. Neither interpretation is true. I wrote the article for two reasons. First and foremost, I wanted to point out that there are, unfortunately, positive functions of poverty which have to be dealt with by antipoverty policy. Second, I was trying to show that functionalism is not the inherently conservative approach for which it has often been criticized, but that it can be employed in liberal and radical analyses.

31 Savage Inequalities

JONATHAN KOZOL

Social inequality so pervades our society that it leaves no area of life untouched. Consequently, because we are immersed in it, we usually take social inequality for granted. When social inequality does become visible to us, its *social* origins often disappear from sight. We tend to see social inequality as part of the *natural* ordering of life, often explaining it on the basis of people's individual characteristics. ("They" are lazier, dumber, less moral—or whatever—than others. That's the reason they have less than we do.) This selection, however, makes the *social* base of social inequality especially vivid.

To examine the U.S. educational system, Kozol traveled around the country and observed schools in poor, middle-class, and rich communities. Because schools are financed largely by local property taxes, wealthier communities are able to offer higher salaries and attract more qualified teachers, offer more specialized and advanced courses, purchase newer texts and equipment, and thereby provide their children better education. The extent of the disparities, however, is much greater than most people realize. As you read about the two schools contrasted in this selection, try to project yourself into each situation. How do you think that living in these communities and being a student in these schools would likely affect you—not only what you learn, but also your views on life, as well as your entire future?

"EAST OF ANYWHERE," writes a reporter for the *St. Louis Post-Dispatch,* "often evokes the other side of the tracks. But, for a first-time visitor suddenly deposited on its eerily empty streets, East St. Louis might suggest another world." The city, which is 98 percent black, has no obstetric services, no regular trash collection, and few jobs. Nearly a third of its families live on less than $7,500 a year; 75 percent of its population lives on welfare of some form. The U.S. Department of Housing and Urban Development describes it as "the most distressed small city in America."

Only three of the 13 buildings on Missouri Avenue, one of the city's major thoroughfares, are occupied. A 13-story office building, tallest in the city, has been boarded up. Outside, on the sidewalk, a pile of garbage fills a ten-foot crater.

The city, which by night and day is clouded by the fumes that pour from vents and smokestacks at the Pfizer and Monsanto chemical plants, has one of the highest rates of child asthma in America.

It is, according to a teacher at Southern Illinois University, "a repository for a nonwhite population that is now regarded as expendable." The *Post-Dispatch* describes it as "America's Soweto."

Fiscal shortages have forced the layoff of 1,170 of the city's 1,400 employees in the past 12 years. The city, which is often unable to buy heating fuel or toilet paper for the city hall, recently announced that it might have to cashier all but 10 percent of the remaining work force of 230. The mayor announced that he might need to sell the city hall and all six fire stations to raise needed cash. Last year the plan had to be scrapped after the city lost its city hall in a court judgment to a creditor. East St. Louis is mortgaged into the next century but has the highest property-tax rate in the state. . . .

The dangers of exposure to raw sewage, which backs up repeatedly into the homes of residents in East St. Louis, were first noticed at a public housing project, Villa Griffin. Raw sewage, says the *Post-Dispatch,* overflowed into a playground just behind the housing project, which is home to 187 children, "forming an oozing lake of . . . tainted water." . . . A St. Louis health official voices her dismay that children live with waste in their backyards. "The development of working sewage systems made cities livable a hundred years ago," she notes. "Sewage systems separate us from the Third World." . . .

The sewage, which is flowing from collapsed pipes and dysfunctional pumping stations, has also flooded basements all over the city. The city's vacuum truck, which uses water and suction to unclog the city's sewers, cannot be used because it needs $5,000 in repairs. Even when it works, it sometimes can't be used because there isn't money to hire drivers. A single engineer now does the work that 14 others did before they were laid off. By April the pool of overflow behind the Villa Griffin project has expanded into a lagoon of sewage. Two million gallons of raw sewage lie outside the children's homes. . . .

. . . Sister Julia Huiskamp meets me on King Boulevard and drives me to the Griffin homes.

As we ride past blocks and blocks of skeletal structures, some of which are still inhabited, she slows the car repeatedly at railroad crossings. A seemingly endless railroad train rolls past us to the right. On the left: a blackened lot where garbage has been burning. Next to the burning garbage is a row of 12 white cabins, charred by fire. Next: a lot that holds a heap of auto tires and a mountain of tin cans. More burnt houses. More trash fires. The train moves almost imperceptibly across the flatness of the land.

Fifty years old, and wearing a blue suit, white blouse, and blue head-cover, Sister Julia points to the nicest house in sight. The sign on the front reads MOTEL. "It's a whorehouse," Sister Julia says.

When she slows the car beside a group of teen-age boys, one of them steps out toward the car, then backs away as she is recognized.

The 99 units of the Villa Griffin homes—two-story structures, brick on the first floor, yellow wood above—form one border of a recessed park and playground that were filled with fecal matter last year when the sewage mains exploded. The sewage is gone now and the grass is very green and looks inviting. When nine-year-old Serena and her seven-year-old brother take me for a walk, however, I discover that our shoes sink into what is still a sewage marsh. An inch-deep residue of fouled water still remains.

Serena's brother is a handsome, joyous little boy, but troublingly thin. Three other children join us as we walk along the marsh: Smokey, who is nine years old but cannot yet tell time; Mickey, who is seven; and a tiny child with a ponytail and big brown eyes who talks a constant stream of words that I can't always understand.

"Hush, Little Sister," says Serena. I ask for her name, but "Little Sister" is the only name the children seem to know.

"There go my cousins," Smokey says, pointing to two teen-age girls above us on the hill.

The day is warm, although we're only in the second week of March; several dogs and cats are playing by the edges of the marsh. "It's a lot of squirrels here," says Smokey. "There go one!"

"This here squirrel is a friend of mine," says Little Sister.

None of the children can tell me the approximate time that school begins. One says five o'clock. One says six. Another says that school begins at noon.

When I ask what song they sing after the flag pledge, one says, "Jingle Bells."

Smokey cannot decide if he is in the second or third grade.

Seven-year-old Mickey sucks his thumb during the walk.

The children regale me with a chilling story as we stand beside the marsh. Smokey says his sister was raped and murdered and then dumped behind his school. Other children add more details: Smokey's sister was 11 years old. She was beaten with a brick until she died. The murder was committed by a man who knew her mother.

The narrative begins when, without warning, Smokey says, "My sister has got killed."

"She was my best friend," Serena says.

"They had beat her in the head and raped her," Smokey says.

"She was hollering out loud," says Little Sister.

I ask them when it happened. Smokey says, "Last year." Serena then corrects him and she says, "Last week."

"It scared me because I had to cry," says Little Sister.

"The police arrested one man but they didn't catch the other," Smokey says.

Serena says, "He was some kin to her."

But Smokey objects, "He weren't no kin to me. He was my momma's friend."

"Her face was busted," Little Sister says.

Serena describes this sequence of events: "They told her go behind the school. They'll give her a quarter if she do. Then they knock her down and told her not to tell what they had did."

I ask, "Why did they kill her?"

"They was scared that she would tell," Serena says.

"One is in jail," says Smokey. "They cain't find the other."

"Instead of raping little bitty children, they should find themselves a wife," says Little Sister.

"I hope," Serena says, "her spirit will come back and get that man."

"And *kill* that man," says Little Sister.

"Give her another chance to live," Serena says.

"My teacher came to the funeral," says Smokey.

"When a little child dies, my momma say a star go straight to Heaven," says Serena.

"My grandma was murdered," Mickey says out of the blue. "Somebody shot two bullets in her head."

I ask him, "Is she really dead?"

"She dead all right," says Mickey. "She was layin' there, just dead."

"I love my friends," Serena says. "I don't care if they no kin to me. I *care* for them. I hope his mother have another baby. Name her for my friend that's dead."

"I have a cat with three legs," Smokey says.

"Snakes hate rabbits," Mickey says, again for no apparent reason.

"Cats hate fishes," Little Sister says.

"It's a lot of hate," says Smokey.

Later, at the mission, Sister Julia tells me this: "The Jefferson School, which they attend, is a decrepit hulk. Next to it is a modern school, erected two years ago, which was to have replaced the one that they attend. But the construction was not done correctly. The roof is too heavy for the walls, and the entire structure has begun to sink. It can't be occupied. Smokey's sister was raped and murdered and dumped between the old school and the new one." . . .

The problems of the streets in urban areas, as teachers often note, frequently spill over into public schools. In the public schools of East St. Louis this is literally the case.

"Martin Luther King Junior High School," notes the *Post-Dispatch* in a story published in the early spring of 1989, "was evacuated Friday afternoon after sewage flowed into the kitchen. . . . The kitchen was closed and students were sent home." On Monday, the paper continues, "East St. Louis Senior High School was awash in sewage for the second time this year." The school had to be shut because of "fumes and backed-up toilets." Sewage flowed into the basement, through the floor, then up into the kitchen and the students' bathrooms. The backup, we read, "occurred in the food preparation areas."

School is resumed the following morning at the high school, but a few days later the overflow recurs. This time the entire system is affected, since the meals distributed to every student in the city are prepared in the two schools that have been flooded. School is called off for all 16,500 students in the district. The sewage backup, caused by the failure of two pumping stations, forces officials at the high school to shut down the furnaces.

At Martin Luther King, the parking lot and gym are also flooded. "It's a disaster," says a legislator. "The streets are under water; gaseous fumes are being emitted from the pipes under the schools," she says, "making people ill."

In the same week, the schools announce the layoff of 280 teachers, 166 cooks and cafeteria workers, 25 teacher aides, 16 custodians and 18 painters, electricians, engineers and plumbers. The president of the teachers' union says the cuts, which will bring the size of kindergarten and primary classes up to 30 students, and the size of fourth to twelfth grade classes up to 35, will have "an unimaginable impact" on the students. "If you have a high school teacher with five classes each day and between 150 and 175 students . . . , it's going to have a devastating effect." The school system, it is also noted, has been using more than 70 "permanent substitute teachers," who are paid only $10,000 yearly, as a way of saving money. . . .

East St. Louis, says the chairman of the state board, "is simply the worst possible place I can imagine to have a child brought up. . . . The community is in desperate circumstances." Sports and music, he observes, are, for many children here, "the only avenues of success." Sadly enough, no matter how it ratifies the stereotype, this is the truth; and there is a poignant aspect to the fact that, even with class size soaring and one quarter of the system's teachers being given their dismissal, the state board of education demonstrates its genuine but skewed compassion by attempting to leave sports and music untouched by the overall austerity.

Even sports facilities, however, are degrading by comparison with those found and expected at most high schools in America. The football field at East St. Louis High is missing almost everything—including goalposts. There are a couple of metal pipes—no crossbar, just the pipes. Bob Shannon, the football coach, who has to use his personal funds to purchase footballs and has had to cut and rake the football field himself, has dreams of having goalposts someday. He'd also like to let his students have new uniforms. The ones they wear are nine years old and held together somehow by a patchwork of repairs. Keeping them clean is a problem, too. The school cannot afford a washing machine. The uniforms are carted to a corner laundromat with fifteen dollars' worth of quarters. . . .

In the wing of the school that holds vocational classes, a damp, unpleasant odor fills the halls. The school has a machine shop, which cannot be used for lack of staff, and a woodworking shop. The only shop that's occupied this morning is the auto-body class. A man with long blond hair and wearing a white sweat suit swings a paddle to get children in their chairs. "What we need the most is new equipment," he reports. "I have equipment for alignment, for example, but we don't have money to install it. We also need a better form of egress. We bring the cars in through two other classes." Computerized equipment used in most repair shops, he reports, is far beyond the high school's budget. It looks like a very old gas station in an isolated rural town. . . .

The science labs at East St. Louis High are 30 to 50 years outdated. John McMillan, a soft-spoken man, teaches physics at the school. He shows me his lab. The six lab stations in the room have empty holes where pipes were once attached. "It would be great if we had water," says McMillan. . . .

Leaving the chemistry labs, I pass a double-sized classroom in which roughly 60 kids are sitting fairly still but doing nothing. "This is supervised study hall," a teacher tells me in the corridor. But when we step inside, he finds there is no teacher. "The teacher must be out today," he says.

Irl Solomon's history classes, which I visit next, have been described by journalists who cover East St. Louis as the highlight of the school. Solomon, a man of 54 whose reddish hair is turning white, has taught in urban schools for almost 30 years. A graduate of Brandeis University, he entered law school but was drawn away by a concern with civil rights. "After one semester, I decided that the law was not for me. I said, 'Go and find the toughest place there is to teach. See if you like it.' I'm still here. . . .

"I have four girls right now in my senior home room who are pregnant or have just had babies. When I ask them why this happens, I am told, 'Well, there's no reason not to have a baby. There's not much for me in public school.' The truth is, that's a pretty honest answer. A diploma from a ghetto high school doesn't count for much in the United States today. So, if this is really the last education that a person's going to get, she's probably perceptive in that statement. Ah, there's so much bitterness—unfairness—there, you know. Most of these pregnant girls are not the ones who have much self-esteem. . . .

"Very little education in the school would be considered academic in the suburbs. Maybe 10 to 15 percent of students are in truly academic programs. Of the 55 percent who graduate, 20 percent may go to four-year colleges: something like 10 percent of any entering class. Another 10 to 20 percent may get some other kind of higher education. An equal number join the military. . . .

"I don't go to physics class, because my lab has no equipment," says one student. "The typewriters in my typing class don't work. The women's toilets . . . " She makes a sour face. "I'll be honest," she says. "I just don't use the toilets. If I do, I come back into class and I feel dirty."

"I wanted to study Latin," says another student. "But we don't have Latin in this school."

"We lost our only Latin teacher," Solomon says.

A girl in a white jersey with the message DO THE RIGHT THING on the front raises her hand. "You visit other schools," she says. "Do you think the children in this school are getting what we'd get in a nice section of St. Louis?"

I note that we are in a different state and city.

"Are we citizens of East St. Louis or America?" she asks. . . .

In a seventh grade social studies class, the . . . teacher invites me to ask the class some questions. Uncertain where to start, I ask the students what they've learned about the civil rights campaigns of recent decades.

A 14-year-old girl with short black curly hair says this: "Every year in February we are told to read the same old speech of Martin Luther King. We read it every year. 'I have a dream. . . . ' It does begin to seem—what is the word?" She hesitates and then she finds the word: "perfunctory."

I ask her what she means.

"We have a school in East St. Louis named for Dr. King," she says. "The school is full of sewer water and the doors are locked with chains. Every student in that school is black. It's like a terrible joke on history."

It startles me to hear her words, but I am startled even more to think how seldom any press reporter has observed the irony of naming segregated schools for Martin Luther King. Children reach the heart of these hypocrisies much quicker than the grown-ups and the experts do. . . .

• • •

The train ride from Grand Central Station to suburban Rye, New York, takes 35 to 40 minutes. The high school is a short ride from the station. Built of handsome gray stone and set in a landscaped campus, it resembles a New England prep school. I enter the school and am directed by a student to the office.

The principal, a relaxed, unhurried man who, unlike many urban principals, seems gratified to have me visit in his school, takes me in to see the auditorium, which, he says, was recently restored with private charitable funds ($400,000) raised by parents. The crenellated ceiling, which is white and spotless, and the polished dark-wood paneling contrast with the collapsing structure of the auditorium at [another school I visited]. The principal strikes his fist against the balcony: "They made this place extremely solid." Through a window, one can see the spreading branches of a beech tree in the central courtyard of the school.

In a student lounge, a dozen seniors are relaxing on a carpeted floor that is constructed with a number of tiers so that, as the principal explains, "they can stretch out and be comfortable while reading."

The library is wood-paneled, like the auditorium. Students, all of whom are white, are seated at private carrels, of which there are approximately 40. Some are doing homework; others are looking through the *New York Times*. Every student that I see during my visit to the school is white or Asian, though I later learn there are a number of Hispanic students and that 1 or 2 percent of students in the school are black.

The typical student, the principal says, studies a foreign language for four or five years, beginning in the junior high school, and a second foreign language (Latin is available) for two years. Of 140 seniors, 92 are now enrolled in AP [advanced placement] classes. Maximum teacher salary will soon reach $70,000. Per-pupil funding is above $12,000 at the time I visit.

The students I meet include eleventh and twelfth graders. The teacher tells me that the class is reading Robert Coles, Studs Terkel, Alice Walker. He tells me I will find them more than willing to engage me in debate, and this turns out to be correct. Primed for my visit, it appears, they narrow in directly on the dual questions of equality and race.

Three general positions soon emerge and seem to be accepted widely. The first is that the fiscal inequalities "do matter very much" in shaping what a school can offer ("That is obvious," one student says) and that any loss of funds in Rye, as a potential consequence of future equalizing, would be damaging to many things the town regards as quite essential.

The second position is that racial integration—for example, by the busing of black children from the city or a nonwhite suburb to this school—would meet with strong resistance, and the reason would not simply be the fear that certain standards might decline. The reason, several students say straightforwardly, is "racial" or, as others say it, "out-and-out racism" on the part of adults.

The third position voiced by many students, but not all, is that equity is basically a goal to be desired and should be pursued for moral reasons, but "will probably make no major difference" since poor children "still would lack the motivation" and "would probably fail in any case because of other problems."

At this point, I ask if they can truly say "it wouldn't make a difference" since it's never been attempted. Several students then seem to rethink their views and say that "it might work, but it would have to start with preschool and the elementary grades" and "it might be 20 years before we'd see a difference."

At this stage in the discussion, several students speak with some real feeling of the present inequalities, which, they say, are "obviously unfair," and one student goes a little further and proposes that "we need to change a lot more than the schools." Another says she'd favor racial integration "by whatever means—including busing—even if the parents disapprove." But a contradictory opinion also is expressed with a good deal of fervor and is stated by one student in a rather biting voice: "I don't see why we should do it. How could it be of benefit to us?"

Throughout the discussion, whatever the views the children voice, there is a degree of unreality about the whole exchange. The children are lucid and their language is well chosen and their arguments well made, but there is a sense that they are dealing with an issue that does not feel very vivid, and that nothing that we say about it to each other really matters since it's "just a theoretical discussion." To a certain degree, the skillfulness and cleverness that they display seem to derive precisely from this sense of unreality. Questions of unfairness feel more like a geometric problem than a matter of humanity or conscience. A few of the students do break through the note of unreality, but, when they do, they cease to be so agile in their use of words and speak more awkwardly. Ethical challenges seem to threaten their effectiveness. There is the sense that they were skating over ice and that the issues we addressed were safely frozen underneath. When they stop to look beneath the ice they start to stumble. The verbal competence they have acquired here may have been gained by building walls around some regions of the heart.

"I don't think that busing students from their ghetto to a different school would do much good," one student says. "You can take them out of the environment, but you can't take the environment out of *them*. If someone grows up in the South Bronx, he's not going to be prone to learn." His name is Max and he has short black hair and speaks with confidence. "Busing didn't work when it was tried," he says. I ask him how he knows this and he says he saw a television movie about Boston.

"I agree that it's unfair the way it is," another student says. "We have AP [Advanced Placement] courses and they don't. Our classes are much smaller." But, she says, "putting them in schools like ours is not the answer. Why not put some AP classes into *their* school? Fix the roof and paint the halls so it will not be so depressing."

The students know the term "separate but equal," but seem unaware of its historical associations. "Keep them where they are but make it equal," says a girl in the front row.

A student named Jennifer, whose manner of speech is somewhat less refined and polished than that of the others, tells me that her parents came here from New York. "My family is originally from the Bronx. Schools are hell there. That's one reason that we moved. I don't think it's our responsibility to pay our taxes to provide for *them*. I mean, my parents used to live there and they wanted to get out. There's no point in coming to a place like this, where schools are good, and then your taxes go back to the place where you began."

I bait her a bit: "Do you mean that, now that you are not in hell, you have no feeling for the people that you left behind?"

"It has to be the people in the area who want an education. If your parents just don't care, it won't do any good to spend a lot of money. Someone else can't want a good life for you. You have got to want it for yourself." Then she adds, however, "I agree that everyone should have a chance at taking the same courses. . . ."

I ask her if she'd think it fair to pay more taxes so that this was possible.

"I don't see how that benefits me," she says.

32 The U.S. Upper Class

STEPHEN HIGLEY

Social inequality is a fact of life in all societies. Some people receive
more of their society's goods and services, others far less. This is the
way it has been in every known society of the past, is now, and—people's hopes to the contrary notwithstanding—likely always will be.

As much as many of us would wish it different, our own society is
no exception. We, too, are marked by vast divisions, especially of
wealth and power. Because the poor are the most accessible, research
on social inequality usually focuses on the poor. (Note the immediately
preceding three selections.) In this selection, in contrast, Higley examines the life situation of the rich. You might ask yourself in what ways
your life would be different if you had been born into one of the families on which this article focuses. Obviously, your material circumstances would be different, but the distinction of wealth and power
goes far beyond this obvious matter. It vitally affects our ideas of the
world—and of our place in it.

FROM A CLASS PERSPECTIVE, the American upper class exhibits
a class solidarity derived from the group awareness that they share a common
fate. They consider one another equals, and their voting behavior in support of
the Republican Party and their charitable efforts are the most obvious mani-
festations of their ability for joint action in the pursuit of common interests.

Those who are listed in the *Social Register* are chosen primarily for the
style of life (and, implicitly, the system of values) they exhibit. The main purpose of the *Social Register* is to restrict social intercourse for the members by
acting as a ready reference as to who is "in" and who is "out" of proper society.
Although it is hard to confirm (because of the *Social Register's* policy of not
responding to inquiries), the *Social Register* strives to "confine normal marriage to within the status circle" by requiring members who marry outside the
Register to resubmit themselves and their bride or groom for membership.
And the *Social Register* is but one element of the upper class's complete system of socialization. The American upper class has attempted to separate itself
socially from the *hoi polloi* literally from birth to death—from favored mater-
nity hospitals and attending physicians to specific retirement homes such as
Dunwoody Village in Newtown Square, Pennsylvania, and Cathedral Village
in Washington, D.C. . . . Between birth and retirement is a full array of

socializing institutions: prep schools, Ivy League schools, debutante balls, and metropolitan clubs, to name a few.

The upper-class families listed in the *Social Register* are direct descendants of the men who made great fortunes during the Gilded Age (1870–1910). . . . The short-term and long-term economic success of the upper class is fundamentally important to maintaining the style of life that differentiates the upper class from the other classes in society. Once a family no longer has the economic resources to give its members the advantages that money can buy in the United States, the fall from social grace is swift and sure. The family that is reduced to "shabby gentility" is an often-used literary device that underlines the importance of liquid assets to continued good standing in American society.

The men and women who defined late-nineteenth- and early-twentieth-century American upper-class society were overwhelmingly white, Anglo-Saxon, and Protestant. As the personal, ethnic, and religious characteristics were unofficially codified, social and generational seasoning became equally important for acceptance into upper-class society. No amount of improperly socialized new money could buy its way into "proper" upper-class society. . . .

If one subscribes to the Weberian theory that status is ultimately dependent on economic control and wealth, there are clear implications that the influence of white, Anglo-Saxon Protestants will inevitably decline in the twenty-first century. Although "WASP" and "upper class" have been synonymous in the past, it is apparent that the ethnic definition of upper class will be transformed and redefined in the future.

The transformation, or de-WASPing, of the upper class that is now taking place in the United States is not easily evident to the casual observer. The status order will eventually reflect the economic order, although there are a multitude of cultural bulwarks that make the change slower and more subtle than [some] anticipate. There is a powerful WASP cultural inertia in the United States, and it will take decades to effect changes in the way Americans define themselves culturally. WASP culture is essentially derivative of the English nobility, and to this day, Anglophilia continues to pervade the American upper class. Because the upper class provides a value and consumptive role model for the American upper-middle class, upper-class values are in turn transmitted to the rest of American society—the upper-middle class being relatively large and visible to the rest of society. . . .

The Elements of Upper-Class Cohesion

The American upper class has a large number of institutions and associational arrangement that have made it possible for members to pass through life with very little significant contact with other social classes. This section reviews the most important of these institutions: private boarding schools (prep schools), colleges, metropolitan and country clubs, and the Episcopal and Presbyterian churches. The role of debutante balls, service organizations, and charitable organizations as contributing factors in maintaining upper-class cohesion will also be explored. Finally, an in-depth look at the *Social Register* will examine the role of neighborhood and community in upper-class cohesiveness.

PRIVATE PREPARATORY SCHOOLS

Of all of the institutions that inculcate upper-class values, private preparatory schools may have the greatest role (Cookson and Persell 1985, 13–30). The role of private education begins with upper-class day schools. Baltzell, in his examination of the role of education, termed the local institutions *provincial family surrogates* in that their outlooks were local in nature (Baltzell 1958, 292–300). Baltzell chronicles the changing role and fortunes of the Protestant Episcopal Academy, the first educator of large numbers of Philadelphia's young male upper class. The Episcopal Academy was founded in 1785 and began catering consciously to the upper class in 1846. The institution's move in 1921 to the suburban Main Line in pursuit of its clientele maintained its primacy in Philadelphia. The Episcopal Academy was not without competitors, however; other day schools were Haverford, Penn Charter, and Chestnut Hill. There were also day schools (such as Springside, Shipley, and Agnes Irwin) for upper-class girls in Philadelphia that served the same socializing functions as the boys' schools (Baltzell 1958, 300–301).

The day schools' popularity began to wane in the second half of the nineteenth century as boarding schools became the preferred method of educating young upper-class men and women. Boarding schools made it possible to completely control the social and educational environment of the students (Cookson and Persell 1985, 31–48). Parents could be assured that their child would be raised away from the distractions of the large cities and their hordes of newly arrived aliens. The prep schools were staffed with teachers who could be relied on to transmit the values of the upper class. The WASP ethic of civility, honesty, principle, and service was imparted within a totally structured environment. The schools, particularly the Episcopalian schools, were modeled after the public schools of England, complete with "forms" for grades and "headmasters" for principals.

The day schools increasingly turned to the nouveau riche to fill the slots left by the defections of some of their constituency. In his 1980 article, "The Rise of American Boarding Schools and the Development of a National Upper Class," Levine writes that the original purpose of the schools was to protect the "old guard" of the upper class from the arrivistes, [the "newly arrived"—people who only recently became rich] with their newly minted family fortunes created during the last quarter of the nineteenth century. He theorizes that New England led the way in the creation of boarding schools as the

Boston Brahmins reacted to their imminent social eclipse by the much larger fortunes the Gilded Age was producing. The elites of cities such as New York and Philadelphia were able to participate in the industrialization of America, whereas the Boston Brahmins, whose fortunes were grounded largely in the trade from the Far East, were not as effective in gaining a share of the new wealth. The boarding schools were but one of a series of institutions founded during this era to create social distance between old money and new money. Country clubs and metropolitan clubs were other examples. It was also during this time that books such as the *Social Register* and various blue books were published to provide a scorecard as to who was in and who was out of proper society.

More important than the social distancing function prep schools provide is the common socializing force they exert on young men and women of the upper class. C. Wright Mills felt that prep schools were an essential element in the calculus of preserving privilege. He wrote:

> As a selection and training place of the upper classes, both old and new, the private school is a unifying influence, a force for the nationalization of the upper classes. The less important the pedigreed family becomes in the careful transmission of moral and cultural traits, the more important the private school—rather than the upper-class family—as the most important agency for transmitting the traditions of the upper social classes and regulating the new admission of wealth and talent. It is the characterizing point in the upper-class experience. (Mills 1956, 64–65)

Although upper-class schools were originally conceived to buffer the old guard from the nouveau riche, the need to infuse the upper class with new talent and money and the need to socialize the parvenus into the minutiae of upper-class culture led to the acceptance of some newly moneyed families. As sociologist Randall Collins notes, "Schools primarily teach vocabulary and inflection, styles of dress, aesthetic tastes, values and manners" (Collins 1971, 101). Levine's 1980 study found that, in general, it took one generation to socialize upper-class fortunes. The sons of fathers who acquired large fortunes in the early twentieth century often placed their children in the most prestigious boarding schools. The fathers were not above building a new library or classroom building to ensure their son's entrance. In most cases, the sons went on to Ivy League schools and became members of the upper-class secret societies and eating clubs. They were also likely to be listed in the Social Register. Gaining membership in upper-class secret societies and eating clubs would not present a problem because sponsorship would come easily from former schoolmates who were already members of the clubs.

Although there were literally hundreds of schools founded in the Gilded Age, a hierarchy of preferred schools quickly developed. At the top of the list in terms of prestige are the five Episcopalian boarding schools known collectively as St. Grottlesex (St. Paul's, St. Mark's, St. George's, Groton, and

Middlesex). St. Paul's is often held up as the quintessential upper-class school (Domhoff 1983). Located in Concord, New Hampshire, it has a campus of eighty buildings (for six hundred students) and is situated on two thousand acres of woods and open land. In 1981, the student-faculty ratio was 6.3 to 1 and the average class size was twelve.

The second group of prestigious prep schools is represented by Choate, Hotchkiss, and Kent—nondenominational schools that were founded specifically to cater to the burgeoning market for private, exclusive education at the turn of the century.

The two oldest schools are usually put in a class by themselves. The Phillips Academy (commonly called Andover) and the Phillips Exeter Academy were founded originally to provide secondary education for a large array of students before the advent of the public school system. With the growth of the public school systems, Andover and Exeter became oriented strictly to preparing students for college. Both schools are larger and less aristocratic and have higher academic standards than the other boarding schools mentioned (Cookson and Persell 1985, 38).

In summary, boarding schools offered a place where the upper class could rest assured that class-supportive values would be instilled in their young. Their children would be exposed to only those nouveau riche children who were "acceptable" and to none of the perceived evils of the city. They would make valuable social and business friendships that would be nourished in college and in the world of private clubs during their adult lives.

AN UPPER-CLASS COLLEGE EDUCATION

Just as there are preferred upper-class boarding schools to attend, there are preferred universities for young men and women of the upper class. The three universities that are considered most desirable by upper class parents are Harvard, Yale, and Princeton. These three are followed by any other schools in the Ivy League (Brown University has become increasingly popular among students) or any number of small prestigious schools located primarily in New England (for example, Williams, Amherst, or Trinity). If an upper-class family lives in a state with an academically prestigious public university, such as Wisconsin, Michigan, or California, it is increasingly considered appropriate to attend those universities. In addition, there are selected private regional universities that are considered acceptable as one's first choice. Examples of these schools are Duke, Stanford, and Northwestern.

FRATERNITIES AND EATING CLUBS

Once a young man has been accepted at Harvard, Princeton, or Yale, he is confronted with a large university that is dominated in numbers, if not tone, by members of other social classes. The solution to the problem of having to mix with the upper-middle class (or worse) is a system of private clubs similar to the fraternities and sororities found on many American campuses. The system of private clubs is best described in the words of Baltzell:

> An intricate system of exclusive clubs, like the fraternities on less rarefied American campuses, serve to insulate the members of the upper class from the rest of the students at Harvard, Princeton, and Yale. There are virtually "two nations" at Harvard. The private-school boys, with their accents, final clubs, and Boston debutante parties—about one-fifth of the student body—stand aloof and apart from the ambitious, talented, and less polished boys who come to Cambridge each year from public schools over the nation. (Baltzell 1958, 329–330)

The private eating clubs of Princeton were formed in the years following Woodrow Wilson's 1906 ban on fraternities. Juniors and Seniors joined eating clubs that had a "pecking order" based on social status. Upper-class young men usually joined the Ivy Club or the Cottage Club. The exclusivity of the eating clubs ended in the 1960s when the university compelled the clubs to accept all who had applied but had not been accepted.

At Harvard, Porcellian is the club of the most prestigious boarding schools such as St. Paul's and Groton. Other social clubs that are notable but of slightly less status are A.D., Fly, Spee, Delphic, and Owl. Porcellian's counterpart at Yale is the Fence Club. As at Harvard, there are a host of slightly prestigious clubs to join. Perhaps the senior societies are even more important than the social clubs at Yale. The two most important are the elite and meritorious Skull and Bones Club (of which former President George Bush is a member) and the more socially exclusive Scroll and Key Club. The purpose of these clubs is to build class solidarity and personal alliances that will be translated into lifetime friendships and business relationships at graduation (Baltzell 1958, 330–334).

At each critical juncture of a young person's life, the upper class has developed a series of supporting institutions to link individuals with a shared outlook and value system. By carefully molding young upper-class people into the established value system, the upper class assures its own continuity.

THE UPPER-CLASS WORLD OF PRIVATE CLUBS

On graduation, young men and women begin their careers with yet another array of private clubs that will act as an extended class-oriented family. One can differentiate between two types of private clubs, the metropolitan dining clubs and the more familiar suburban country clubs. Baltzell maintains that the metropolitan clubs are much more important than country clubs in terms of the social ascription of status.

Unlike the American middle classes, and resembling the lower classes, in fact, the Philadelphia upper class is largely male dominated and patriarchal.

The social standing of the male family head, the best index of which is his metropolitan club affiliation, usually determines the social position of the family as a whole (Baltzell 1958, 336).

The first American metropolitan club, following the British experience with such clubs, grew out of an informal gathering of the leading citizens to discuss daily affairs over coffee. In the days before reliable newspapers, it was a way to pass on news and keep informed of current events. The first club formed in the United States was the Philadelphia Club in 1835. It was closely followed by the Union Club of New York City, which was founded in 1836 (Baltzell 1958, 335–363). The metropolitan club subculture, with its distinctive mores and value rituals, was perceptively outlined by Wecter:

> The social club in America has done a great deal to keep alive the gentleman in the courtly sense. Here is a peculiar asylum from the Pandemonium of commerce, the bumptiousness of democracy, and the feminism of his own household. Here he is technically invisible from the critical female eye—a state of bliss reflected in the convention that a gentleman never bows to a lady from a club window and does not, according to best form, discuss ladies there. The club is the Great Good Place with its comfortable and slightly shabby leather chairs, the pleasant malt-like effluvium of its bar, the newspaper room with a club servant to repair quickly the symptoms of disarray, the catholicity of magazines from highbrows to La Vie Parisienne which in less stately company would seem a trifle sophomoric, the abundant newspaper, the good cigars and hearty carnivorous menus. . . .
>
> With what Henry James called "a certain light of fine old gentlemenly prejudice to guide it," the preeminently social club welcomes the serious frivolity of horses, hounds, foxes, and boats, but not the effeminate frivolity of aestheticism. Pedantry is also frowned upon; except for the Social Register, the World Almanac, and Lloyd's Register of American Yachts, not a volume in the club library has been taken down since the cross-word puzzle craze. It is comforting to think that one's sons and grandsons will sit in these same chairs, and firelight will flicker on the same steel engravings and oil portraits of past presidents—and though the stars may wheel in their courses and crowned heads totter to the guillotine, this little world will remain, so long as first mortgages and government bonds endure. (Wecter 1937, 253–255)

This evocative description of metropolitan clubs was written in 1937 and is dated in some details but still accurate in its main thrust.

There have been several recent legal challenges to the all-male membership policies of metropolitan clubs. The Supreme Court has ruled against the males-only policies of the clubs. The main argument made by female complainants was that women are excluded from important business transactions that are discussed in the clubs. Aldrich maintains that the women's victory will be mainly Pyrrhic because it is considered extremely bad form to discuss business in metropolitan clubs (Aldrich 1988, 122–123). However, Aldrich does not address the valuable alliances made in leisure that lead to business deals later, outside the confines of the club.

The suburban country club is less important than the metropolitan club, but it is significant in that the entire family are members and there are facilities and activities for all. The first American country club was established in 1882 in Brookline, Massachusetts; it is simply called The Country Club. These clubs are most frequently associated with golf, but they may include facilities for swimming, tennis, and, in some cases, polo. Americans are familiar with suburban country clubs, which have been enthusiastically established by the upper-middle class throughout the country.

As in the case of the metropolitan clubs, there is a status hierarchy among the country clubs. Because of the relatively small number of upper-class families, upper-class country clubs make up only a small portion of the private equity country clubs in the United States.

Yacht clubs are also an integral part of upper-class social life. Again, only a select few of the yacht clubs in America are favored by the American upper class. Similarly, there are a large number of historically oriented clubs, such as the well-known Daughters of the American Revolution and more obscure clubs such as the American Association of the Sovereign Military Order of Malta.

RELIGION AND THE UPPER CLASS

Observers of the American scene have long commented on the status differentiation of Protestant denominations. The upper class has had a long association with the Protestant Episcopal Church and to a lesser degree with the Presbyterian Church. The Episcopalian connection is a logical extension of the Anglophilia of the American upper class because the church has a number of characteristics that make it attractive to upper-class men and women. The richness of the church's ritual, the classic traditionalism of most Episcopalian architecture, and the sophisticated, urbane, and intellectual nature of its leaders have great appeal to the upper class (Cookson and Persell 1985, 44–48). The Episcopalian Church was very close to an established church for some parts of colonial America and was, in fact, the established church of the state of Virginia until 1786. Although the church suffered during and immediately following the Revolutionary War because of its close association with England and her Loyalists, it quickly recovered its status as a church of the educated elite in the postwar period.

Baltzell confirmed the alliance statistically by analyzing the church membership of those people in the upper class who were in both the 1940 edition of *Who's Who in America* and the 1940 Philadelphia *Social Register. Who's*

Who's listing of church membership enabled Baltzell to determine religious affiliation for 226 upper-class heads of households. Although 35 percent did not acknowledge a church membership, 42 percent were affiliated with the Episcopalian Church (compared with 1.0 percent of the total U.S. population). An additional 13 percent of those in *Who's Who* listed the Presbyterian Church as their place of worship (compared to 1.2 percent of the general population). Because of the general privacy of religious information, it is difficult to verify Baltzell's findings. However, it is fair to say that the subjective information on the relationship is indeed overwhelming. Of course, not all Episcopalians are upper class. The actual number of upper-class families within the church is small compared to the total membership of Episcopalian churches; however, the church carries the distinctive imprint of upper-class support, philanthropy, and values.

DEBUTANTE BALLS

The debutante season consists of a series of parties, teas, and dances held by upper-class families to formally announce the arrival and availability of their daughters for suitable matrimonial partners. Each major city holds a grand ball that is the highlight of the season. Debutante "coming-out" parties are yet another means of reinforcing class solidarity because the young women and men who participate are carefully screened to ensure upper-class exclusivity. Because upper-class endogamy is highly valued, the debutante season is a formal process, the sole purpose of which is to encourage and create upper-class familial unions. Although there is often a philanthropic cause behind the tens of thousands of dollars spent for each coming out, none of the participants are under any illusion as to the real purpose behind the festivities. The debutante season strengthens the bonds of intermetropolitan upper-class social relationships just as shared summer resort holidays strengthen intermetropolitan alliances.

THE SOCIAL REGISTER

Before the Civil War, "society" in most large American cities, including New York City, was small enough that members of the upper class knew each other informally. Invitations to balls and other "serious" social events were handled either by personal secretaries or by the hostess herself. There were also self-appointed social arbiters whose dictates could help the unsure hostess in determining who was "in" and who was "out" of society.

The role of individual society kingmakers would soon be eclipsed with the appearance of the first *Social Register* in 1886. Hundreds of new fortunes were being made (and lost) during the last two decades of the nineteenth century, and a book was needed to take the place of personal knowledge as to a family's acceptability in polite society.

The first edition of the *Social Register* was a listing of society in Newport, Rhode Island. The next year, 1887, saw the first appearance of the New York City edition. It has been published continuously ever since that date. The *Social Register* was not the first of its kind; there were many books that purported to list society in the 1880s. The secret of success for the founder, Louis Keller, was the quality of his list and his refusal to clutter the book with advertisements for wine merchants, dressmakers, and the like.

Another component of Keller's success was a strict code of secrecy that has been conscientiously maintained to the present. The all-enveloping veil of secrecy has given the book a mystique that has made it all the more alluring to those who aspire to join. The aura of exclusivity is enhanced by the *Social Register's* policy of rarely speaking to the press or publicly commenting on itself in any way.

Keller incorporated his idea as the Social Register Association; new editions quickly followed the New York City volume in Philadelphia and Boston (1890), Baltimore (1892), Chicago (1893), Washington, D.C. (1903), St. Louis and Buffalo (1903), Pittsburgh (1904), San Francisco (1906), and Cleveland and Cincinnati-Dayton (1910). At its height in the 1920s, there were 24 volumes. Many of these editions failed during the Great Depression because of the lack of a large and sophisticated industrial elite and/or insufficient interest on the part of the local population. This would explain the absence of a large number of *Social Register* families from Detroit, a city that made its fortune in the 1920s, and the three post–World War II growth centers of Dallas, Houston, and Los Angeles. The families that dominate the *Social Register* were created during the Gilded Age, and the sunbelt families would have to wait for their generational acculturation into upper-class mores.

The *Social Register* has remained the only social listing for the thirteen cities listed above since 1939. In 1977, the twelve editions were combined into one large book—a reflection of the national solidarity of the upper class and also of cost considerations (Birmingham 1978). The *Social Register* has subsequently become an address and telephone book for the American upper class. Along with this basic information, the *Register* also lists which boarding school and which university members attended, the year in which he or she graduated, and their club memberships. Members may also list their children and the schools they are attending or their current addresses. It has several useful appendices: "Married Maidens," a listing of the maiden names of the wives (very helpful in a divorce-prone culture), and "Dilatory Domiciles," for those who are late in returning their annual questionnaires. There is also a separate volume published each summer called the *Summer Social Register*. The summer edition lists summer homes and also has a yacht registry that lists the home port, tonnage, and year built for each yacht. As the upper class has added winter homes in the post–World War II period, they have tended to list those addresses in the main *Social Register*.

Getting into the *Social Register* and being dropped from the book have been subjects of endless speculation among the upper class and among gossip columnists. The best term to describe the process is *idiosyncratic*. There are three methods for obtaining membership. The most likely way to get in is to be born into it. The second is to marry into a listed family. However, a new bride or groom who is not in the *Register* must submit a new application to be accepted or rejected (without comment) by the "advisory committee." (The makeup of the committee has been the subject of much speculation, and some have questioned if there really is one.) The third way to gain a listing in the *Social Register* is to apply for membership. The prospective member fills out an application and if it passes initial review, he or she must then supply the committee with four or five recommendations from current listees. The application then goes to the advisory committee and the applicant is either accepted or rejected without comment. It is believed that the number that gain membership through this process is extremely limited (Winfrey 1980).

Even the ownership of the *Social Register* is veiled in mystery. When Keller died in 1924, he left the Association to several heirs. It was purchased by Malcolm Forbes in 1977 and remained in his family after his death in 1989, but who actually owns it is not known.

The reasons why members are dropped from the *Social Register* has also been the subject of much musing. Perhaps the surest way to guarantee elimination is to publicly disparage the *Social Register* or to be publicly disgraced. As long as one's personal foibles do not become public knowledge, one seems to be immune from being dropped. Another way to be banished is to marry an entertainer—one of the many groups of people who are *personae non gratae* in the *Social Register*.

The largest groups that are systematically excluded from the *Social Register* are Jews, African Americans, and Asian Americans. Although there are one known Black and several Jewish members, the *Social Register* remains a compendium that is overwhelming white, Anglo-Saxon, and Protestant American (*Newsday*, December 12, 1984, 10–11). A small percentage of the listees have French and Dutch surnames, but it is a challenge to find German, Scandinavian, or southern European surnames anywhere in the *Social Register*.

There are members of the upper class who have asked to have their names removed from the *Social Register* because of the *Register*'s discriminatory practices. Alfred Gwynne Vanderbilt and "Jock" Whitney were among the notable society people who asked to be deleted. It is politically astute for politicians to request that their names be deleted. George Bush had his name deleted before he received his complimentary listings as vice president and president. Former presidents and the chief justice of the Supreme Court are also given complimentary listings. There are many retired senators who are listed once it is "safe" to be associated with an organization that is so blatant in its discrimination.

[Summary]

The upper class has a distinct set of institutions that provide social and physical separation from the rest of society, and these institutions inculcate an intricate set of values and beliefs in both young and old. They affirm cultural and group solidarity within the upper class and clearly delineate class boundaries.

References

Aldrich, N. W., Jr. 1988. *Old Money: the Mythology of America's Upper Class.* New York: Knopf.

Baltzell, E. D. 1958. *Philadelphia Gentlemen: The Making of a National Upper Class.* New York: Free Press.

Birmingham, N. 1978. "Ask Me No Secrets." *Town and Country* vol. 132, October, 181.

Collins, R. 1971. "Functional and Conflict Theories of Educational Stratification." *American Sociological Review* 36: no.6, December 1,002–1,019.

Cookson, P. W., 3rd, and C. H. Persell, 1985. *Preparing for Power.* New York: Basic.

Domhoff, G. W. 1983. *Who Rules America Now?* New York: Touchstone.

Levine, S. B. 1980. "The Rise of American Boarding Schools and the Development of a National Upper Class." *Social Problems* 28, no.1: 63–94.

Mills, C. W. 1956. *The Power Elite.* London: Oxford University Press.

Social Register Association. 1986. *Social Register 1887, Facsimile Edition.* New York: Social Register Association.

Social Register Association. 1987. *Social Register 1988,* Vol. CII. New York: Social Register Association.

Social Register Association. 1987. *Social Register, Summer 1988,* Vol. CII. New York: Social Register Association.

Wecter, D. 1937. *The Saga of American Society.* New York: Charles Scribner's Sons.

Winfrey, C. 1980. "Society's 'In' Book: Does It Still Matter?," *New York Times,* 2 February.

PART VIII Social Institutions

AT FIRST GLANCE, the term *social institutions* appears far removed from everyday life. But in fact this term refers to concrete and highly relevant realities that profoundly affect our lives. Parents and their children, the basic family unit, constitute a social institution. So does the church, with its sacred books, clergy, and worship; and the law, with its police, lawyers, judges, courts, and prisons. Social institutions also means politics—running the full gamut of the U.S political process, from campaign lies told with a straight face to the official acts of Congress, the president, and his cabinet. Too, social institutions means the economic order, with new plants opening and old ones closing, working for a living, or drawing unemployment or welfare or a pension. Schools, colleges, and universities—places where people are socialized (as sociologists phrase the matter) or where they go to learn (as most other people put it)—also are examples of a social institution. This term also refers to science, with its test tubes and experiments, interviewers and questionnaires. It means doctors and nurses and hospitals, as well as the patients they treat, and the Medicare and Blue Cross and Blue Shield that people struggle to pay for in order to keep the U.S. medical enterprise from destroying their present and future finances. And social institutions means the military, with its generals and privates and tanks and planes, and the whole war game that at times threatens to become too real. Far from being removed from life, then, social institutions means all these vital aspects of life in society—and more.

To understand social life, it is necessary to understand the institutions of a society. It is not enough to understand what people do when they are in one another's presence. This certainly is significant, but it is only part of the

351

picture. The sociological (and personal) significance of social institutions is that *they provide the structure within which we live our lives.*

The characteristics of a society's institutions, in fact, dictate much of our interaction in everyday life. For example, because of the way our economic order is arranged, a common pattern is to work 8 hours a day, to be off 16, and to repeat this pattern five days a week. There is nothing natural about this pattern. Its regularity is but an arbitrarily imposed temporal arrangement for work, leisure, and personal concerns. Yet this one aspect of a single social institution has far-reaching effects on how we deal with our family and friends, how we meet our personal needs and nonwork obligations, and indeed on how we view time and even life itself.

Each social institution has similarly far-reaching effects on our lives and viewpoints. By shaping our society as a whole and establishing the context in which we live, these institutions give form to almost everything that is of concern to us. We can say, in fact, that if the social institutions of our society were different, we would be different people. We certainly could not be the same, for our ideas and attitudes and other orientations to the physical and social worlds would be changed.

Sociologists classify social institutions as primary and secondary. The *primary* U.S. social institutions are the economy, the political system, and the military establishment. According to conflict theory, these three social institutions dominate our society. Their top leaders make the major decisions that have the greatest impact on our society, and thereby on our own lives. With the dominant position of the United States in world affairs, these three social institutions are far-reaching, not only for our society but also for the rest of the world.

The *secondary* social institutions are the others: family, education, religion, sports, medicine, law, and the mass media. As the name implies, they are secondary in power, and, as conflict theorists stress, these secondary social institutions exist to serve the primary ones. According to conflict theory, the family produces workers (for the economy), voters and taxpayers (for the political system), and soldiers (for the military); the religious institution instills patriotism and acceptance of the current arrangement of power; sports take people's minds off social issues so they remain compliant workers; the medical institution produces wealth for capitalists and patches workers up so they can continue to work; the law keeps the poor under its yoke so they don't rebel and upset current power arrangements; and the mass media create desire for products so the capitalist class can become even wealthier.

To lead off this Part, Barbara Ehrenreich and Annette Fuentes place the focus once again on gender inequality, adding both a global dimension and a conflict perspective. Harry Gracey continues the conflict perspective as he analyzes kindergarten, viewing it as the means by which children learn to become conformists so they can take a "proper" place in life. In his analysis of football in a Texas high school, Douglas Foley shows how sports are related to the reproduction of gender, race, and social class. Jean Kilbourne then examines some of the far-reaching effects of the mass media, how they influence even our body images and sexual attitudes.

In the final four articles, we look at four more social institutions. Focusing on the family, Arlie Hochschild and Anne Machung examine the ongoing struggle of husbands and wives over housework. Marvin Harris then places the focus on the religious institution, using a functionalist lens to analyze the role of sacred cows in India. Daniel Chambliss gives us a behind-the-scenes view of the medical institution, while Jennifer Hunt's inside report of police violence allows us to peer behind the scenes of the legal institution. The final article in this Part, which focuses on the military, allows us to continue to look behind closed doors. As Herbert Kelman and Lee Hamilton analyze the My Lai massacre in Vietnam, they reveal not just the brutal, merciless slaughter but also the dynamics that led to this tragic event in U.S. history.

33 Life on the Global Assembly Line

BARBARA EHRENREICH
ANNETTE FUENTES

One of the world's most significant changes is the *globalization of capitalism*. Capitalism has won the cold war, and socialism is vanquished (at least for the time being). Victorious, capitalism is expanding rapidly into every nook and cranny of the planet. The so-called undeveloped nations ("undeveloped" only in a chauvinistic, ethnocentric sense of Western economic dominance, for they all have fully developed, intricate cultures) are part of this process. Eyeing the material wealth of the industrialized West, and mindful of its cultural dominance, like a separated lover these nations long to embrace capitalism. For their part, the capitalist nations view them as vast sources of cheap resources and expanding consumer potential.

Downsizing, a fancy way of saying that a company is firing workers, is part of globalization. In their pursuit of the bottom line, U.S. firms, followed more reluctantly by the Europeans and the Japanese, have laid off millions of workers. From the point of view of profit—which is capitalism's bottom line—this only makes sense, for in the Least Industrialized Nations millions of workers eagerly await the crumbs of the industrialized world. This is a capitalist's dream: workers willing to accept peanuts for wages, and glad to get them. As Ehrenreich and Fuentes point out, the most needy of these workers—and thus the most willing to work for the cheapest wages—are women.

In Ciudad Juárez, Mexico, Anna M. rises at 5 A.M. to feed her son before starting on the two-hour bus trip to the maquiladora (factory). He will spend the day along with four other children in a neighbor's one-room home. Anna's husband, frustrated by being unable to find work for himself, left for the United States six months ago. She wonders, as she carefully applies her new lip gloss, whether she ought to consider herself still married. It might be good to take a night course, become a secretary. But she seldom gets home before eight *at night, and the factory, where she stitches brassieres that will be sold in the United States through J.C. Penney, pays only $48 a week.*

In Penang, Malaysia, Julie K. is up before the three other young women with whom she shares a room, and starts heating the leftover rice from last night's supper. She looks good in the company's green-trimmed uniform, and she's proud to work in a modern, American-owned factory. Only not quite so proud as when she started working three years ago—she thinks as she squints out the door at a passing group of women. Her job involves peering all day through a microscope, bonding hair-thin gold wires to a silicon chip destined to end up inside a pocket calculator, and at twenty-one, she is afraid she can no longer see very clearly.

EVERY MORNING, BETWEEN FOUR and seven, thousands of women like Anna and Julie head out for the day shift. In Ciudad Juárez, they crowd into *ruteras* (rundown vans) for the trip from the slum neighborhoods to the industrial parks on the outskirts of the city. In Penang they squeeze, sixty or more at a time, into buses for the trip from the village to the low, modern factory buildings of the Bayan Lepas free-trade zone. In Taiwan, they walk from the dormitories—where the night shift is already asleep in the still-warm beds—through the checkpoints in the high fence surrounding the factory zone.

This is the world's new industrial proletariat: young, female, Third World. Viewed from the "first world," they are still faceless, genderless "cheap labor," signaling their existence only through a label or tiny imprint—"made in Hong Kong," or Taiwan, Korea, the Dominican Republic, Mexico, the Philippines. . . . Anyone whose image of Third World women features picturesque peasants with babies slung on their backs should be prepared to update it. Just in the last decade, Third World women have become a critical element in the global economy and a key "resource" for expanding multinational corporations.

It doesn't take more than second-grade arithmetic to understand what's happening. In many Third World countries, a woman will earn $3 to $5 a *day*. The logic of the situation is compelling: why pay someone in Massachusetts $5 an hour to do what someone in Manila will do for $2.50 a day? Or, as a corollary, why pay a male worker anywhere to do what a female worker will do for 40 to 60 percent less?

And so, almost everything that can be packed up is being moved out to the Third World, not heavy industry, but just about anything light enough to travel—garment manufacture, textiles, toys, footwear, pharmaceuticals, wigs, appliance parts, tape decks, computer components, plastic goods. . . . But what's going on is much more than a matter of runaway shops. Economists are talking about a "new international division of labor," in which the process of production is broken down and the fragments are dispersed to different parts of the world. In general, the low-skilled jobs are farmed out to the Third World, where labor costs are minuscule, while control over the overall process and technology remains safely at company headquarters in "first world" countries like the United States and Japan. . . .

So much any economist could tell you. What is less often noted is the *gender* breakdown of the emerging international division of labor. Eighty to ninety percent of the low-skilled assembly jobs that go to the Third World are performed by women—in a remarkable switch from earlier patterns of foreign-dominated industrialization. Until now, "development" under the aegis of foreign corporations has usually meant more jobs for men and—compared to traditional agricultural society—a diminished economic status for women. But multinational corporations and Third World governments alike consider assembly-line work—whether the product is Barbie dolls or missile parts—to be "women's work."

One reason is that women can, in many countries, still be legally paid less than men. But the sheer tedium of the jobs adds to the multinationals' preference for women workers—a preference made clear, for example, by this ad from a Mexican newspaper: *We need female workers, older than 17, younger than 30, single and without children: minimum education primary school, maximum education one year of preparatory school [high school]; available for all shifts.*

It's an article of faith with management that only women can do, or will do, the monotonous, painstaking work that American business is exporting to the Third World. Bill Mitchell, whose job is to attract United States businesses to the Bermudez Industrial Park in Ciudad Juárez, told us with a certain macho pride: "A man just won't stay in this tedious kind of work. He'd walk out in a couple of hours." The personnel manager of a light assembly plant in Taiwan told anthropologist Linda Gail Arrigo: "Young male workers are too restless and impatient to do monotonous work with no career value. If displeased, they sabotage the machines and even threaten the foreman. But girls? At most, they cry a little."

In fact, the American businessmen we talked to claimed that Third World women genuinely enjoy doing the very things that would drive a man to assault and sabotage. "You should watch these kids going into work," Bill Mitchell told us. "You don't have any sullenness here. They smile." A top-level management consultant who specializes in advising American companies on where to relocate their factories gave us this global generalization: "The [factory] girls genuinely enjoy themselves. They're away from their families. They have spending money. They can buy motorbikes, whatever. Of course, it's a regulated experience too—with dormitories to live in—so it's healthful experience."

What is the real experience of the women in the emerging Third World industrial work force? The conventional Western stereotypes leap to mind: You can't really compare, the standards are so different. . . . Everything's easier in warm countries. . . . They really don't have any alternatives. . . . Commenting on the low wages his company pays its women workers in Singapore, a Hewlett-Packard vice president said: "They live much differently here than we do. . . . " But the differences are ultimately very simple. To start with, they have less money.

The great majority of women in the new Third World work force live at or near the subsistence level for one person, whether they work for a multinational corporation or a locally owned factory. In the Philippines, for example, starting wages in U.S.-owned electronics plants are between $34 and $46 a month, compared to a cost of living of $37 a month; in Indonesia the starting wages are actually about $7 a month less than the cost of living. "Living," in these cases, should be interpreted minimally: a diet of rice, dried fish, and water—a Coke might cost a half-day's wages—and lodging in a room occupied by four or more other people. Rachael Grossman, a researcher with the Southeast Asia Resource Center, found women employees of U.S. multinational firms in Malaysia and the Philippines living four to eight in a room in boardinghouses, or squeezing into tiny extensions built onto squatter huts near the factory. Where companies do provide dormitories for their employees, they are not of the "healthful," collegiate variety implied by our corporate informant. Staff from the American Friends Service Committee report that dormitory space is likely to be crowded, with bed rotation paralleling shift rotation—while one shift works, another sleeps, as many as twenty to a room. In one case in Thailand, they found the dormitory "filthy," with workers forced to find their own place to sleep among "splintered floorboards, rusting sheets of metal, and scraps of dirty cloth." . . .

But wages on a par with what an eleven-year-old American could earn on a paper route, and living conditions resembling what Engels found in nineteenth-century Manchester are only part of the story. The rest begins at the factory gate. The work that multinational corporations export to the Third World is not only the most tedious, but often the most hazardous part of the production process. The countries they go to are, for the most part, those that will guarantee no interference from health and safety inspectors, trade unions, or even freelance reformers. As a result, most Third World factory women work under conditions that already have broken or will break their health—or their nerves—within a few years, and often before they've worked long enough to earn any more than a subsistence wage.

Consider first the electronics industry, which is generally thought to be the safest and cleanest of the exported industries. The factory buildings are low and modern, like those one might find in a suburban American industrial park. Inside, rows of young women, neatly dressed in the company uniform or T-shirt, work quietly at their stations. . . . In many plants toxic chemicals and solvents sit in open containers, filling the work area with fumes that can literally knock you out. "We have been told of cases where ten to twelve women passed out at once," an AFSC field worker in northern Mexico told us, "and the newspapers report this as 'mass hysteria.'"

In one stage of the electronics assembly process, the workers have to dip the circuits into open vats of acid. According to Irene Johnson and Carol Bragg, who toured the National Semiconductor plant in Penang, Malaysia, the women who do the dipping "wear rubber gloves and boots, but these sometimes leak, and burns are common." Occasionally, whole fingers are lost. More commonly, what electronics workers lose is the 20/20 vision they are required to have when they are hired. Most electronics workers spend seven to nine hours a day peering through microscopes, straining to meet their quota.

One study in South Korea found that most electronics assembly workers developed severe eye problems after only one year of employment; 88 percent had chronic conjunctivitis; 44 percent became near-sighted; and 19 percent developed astigmatism. A manager for Hewlett-Packard's Malaysia plant, in an interview with Rachael Grossman, denied that there were any eye problems: "These girls are used to working with 'scopes.' We've found no eye problems. But it sure makes me dizzy to look through those things."

Electronics, recall, is the "cleanest" of the exported industries. Conditions in the garment and textile industry rival those of any nineteenth-century sweatshops. The firms, generally local subcontractors to large American chains such as J.C. Penney and Sears, as well as smaller manufacturers, are usually even more indifferent to the health of their employees than the multinationals. Some of the worst conditions have been documented in South Korea, where the garment and textile industries have helped spark that country's "economic miracle." Workers are packed into poorly lit rooms, where summer temperatures rise above 100 degrees. Textile dust, which can cause permanent lung damage, fills the air. When there are rush orders, management may require forced overtime of as much as 48 hours at a stretch, and if that seems to go beyond the limits of human endurance, pep pills and amphetamine injections are thoughtfully provided. In her diary (ori-ginally published in a magazine now banned by the South Korean government), Min Chong Suk, thirty, a sewing-maching operator, wrote of working from 7 A.M. to 11:30 P.M. in a garment factory: "When [the apprentices] shake the waste threads from the clothes, the whole room fills with dust, and it is hard to breathe. Since we've been working in such dusty air, there have been increasing numbers of people getting tuberculosis, bronchitis, and eye diseases. Since we are women, it makes us so sad when we have pale, unhealthy, wrinkled faces like dried-up spinach. . . . It seems to me that no one knows our blood dissolves into the threads and seams, with sighs and sorrow."

In all the exported industries, the most invidious, inescapable health hazard is stress. On their home ground United States corporations are not likely to sacrifice human comfort for productivity. On someone else's home ground, however, anything goes. Lunch breaks may be barely long enough for a woman to stand in line at the canteen or hawkers' stalls. Visits to the bathroom are treated as a privilege; in some cases, workers must raise their hands for permission to use the toilet, and waits up to a half hour are common. Rotating shifts—the day shift one week, the night shift the next—wreak havoc with sleep patterns. Because inaccuracies or failure to meet production quotas can mean substantial pay losses, the pressures are quickly internalized; stomach ailments and nervous problems are not unusual in the multinationals' Third World female work force. . . .

As if poor health and the stress of factory life weren't enough to drive women into early retirement, management actually encourages a high turnover in many industries. "As you know, when seniority rises, wages rise," the management consultant in U.S. multinationals told us. He explained that it's cheaper to train a fresh supply of teenagers than to pay experienced women higher wages. "Older" women, aged twenty-three or twenty-four, are likely to be laid off and not rehired.

We estimate, based on fragmentary data from several sources, that the multinational corporations may already have used up (cast off) as many as 6 million Third World workers—women who are too ill, too old (thirty is over the hill in most industries), or too exhausted to be useful any more. Few "retire" with any transferable skills or savings. The lucky ones find husbands.

The unlucky ones find themselves at the margins of society—as bar girls, "hostesses," or prostitutes.

At 21, Julie's greatest fear is that she will never be able to find a husband. She knows that just being a "factory girl" is enough to give anyone a bad reputation. When she first started working at the electronics company, her father refused to speak to her for three months. Now every time she leaves Penang to go back to visit her home village she has to put up with a lecture on morality from her older brother—not to mention a barrage of lewd remarks from men outside her family. If they knew that she had actually gone out on a few dates, that she had been to a discotheque, that she had once kissed a young man who said he was a student . . . Julie's stomach tightens as she imagines her family's reaction. She tries to concentrate on the kind of man she would like to marry: an engineer or technician of some sort, someone who had been to California, where the company headquarters are located and where even the grandmothers wear tight pants and lipstick—someone who had a good attitude about women. But if she ends up having to wear glasses, like her cousin who worked three years at the "scopes," she might as well forget about finding anyone to marry her.

One of the most serious occupational hazards that Julie and millions of women like her may face is the lifelong stigma of having been a "factory girl." Most of the cultures favored by multinational corporations in their search for cheap labor are patriarchal in the grand old style: any young woman who is not under the wing of a father, husband, or older brother must be "loose." High levels of unemployment among men, as in Mexico, contribute to male resentment of working women. Add to all this the fact that certain companies— American electronics firms are in the lead—actively promote Western-style sexual objectification as a means of ensuring employee loyalty: there are company-sponsored cosmetics classes, "guess whose legs these are" contests, and swimsuit-style beauty contests where the prize might be a free night *for two* in a fancy hotel. Corporate-promoted Westernization only heightens the hostility many men feel toward any independent working women—having a job is bad enough, wearing jeans and mascara to work is going too far.

Anthropologist Patricia Fernandez, who has worked in a *maquiladora* herself, believes that the stigmatization of working women serves, indirectly, to keep them in line. "You have to think of the kind of socialization that girls experience in a very Catholic—or, for that matter, Muslim—society. The fear of having a 'reputation' is enough to make a lot of women bend over backward to be 'respectable' and ladylike, which is just what management wants." She points out that in northern Mexico, the tabloids delight in playing up stories of alleged vice in the *maquiladoras*—indiscriminate sex on the job, epidemics of venereal disease, fetuses found in factory rest rooms. "I worry about this because there are those who treat you differently as soon as they know you have a job at the *maquiladora*," one woman told Fernandez. "Maybe they think that if you have to work, there is a chance you're a whore."

And there is always the chance you'll wind up as one. Probably only a small minority of Third World factory workers turn to prostitution when their working days come to an end. But it is, as for women everywhere, the employment of last resort, the only thing to do when the factories don't need you and traditional society won't—or, for economic reasons, can't—take you back. In the Philippines, the brothel business is expanding as fast as the factory system. If they can't use you one way, they can use you another.

There has been no international protest about the exploitation of Third World women by multinational corporations—no thundering denunciations from the floor of the United Nations General Assembly, no angry resolutions from the Conference of the Non-Aligned Countries. Sociologist Robert Snow, who has been tracing the multinationals on their way south and eastward for years, explained why: "The Third World governments *want* the multinationals to move in. There's cutthroat competition to attract the corporations."

The governments themselves gain little revenue from this kind of investment, though—especially since most offer tax holidays and freedom from export duties in order to attract the multinationals in the first place. Nor do the people as a whole benefit, according to a highly placed Third World woman within the UN. "The multinationals like to say they're contributing to development," she told us, "but they come into our countries for one thing—cheap labor. If the labor stops being so cheap, they can move on. So how can you call that development? It depends on the people being poor and staying poor." But there are important groups that do stand to gain when the multinationals set up shop in their countries: local entrepreneurs who subcontract to the multinationals; Harvard- or Berkeley-educated "technocrats" who become local management; and government officials who specialize in cutting red tape for an "agent's fee" or an outright bribe.

In the competition for multinational investment, local governments advertise their women shamelessly, and an investment brochure issued by the

Malaysian government informs multinational executives that: "The manual dexterity of the Oriental female is famous the world over. Her hands are small, and she works fast with extreme care. Who, therefore, could be better qualified by nature and inheritance, to contribute to the efficiency of a bench-assembly production line than the Oriental girl?"

The Royal Thai Embassy sends American businesses a brochure guaranteeing that in Thailand, "the relationship between the employer and the employee is like that of a guardian and ward. It is easy to win and maintain the loyalty of workers as long as they are treated with kindness and courtesy." The facing page offers a highly selective photo-study of Thai womanhood: giggling shyly, bowing submissively, and working cheerfully on an assembly line. . . .

The governments advertise their women, sell them, and keep them in line for the multinational "johns." But there are other parties to the growing international traffic in women—such as the United Nations Industrial Development Organization (UNIDO), the World Bank, and the United States government itself.

UNIDO, for example, has been a major promoter of "free trade zones." These are enclaves within nations that offer multinational corporations a range of creature comforts, including: freedom from paying taxes and export duties; low-cost water, power, and buildings; exemption from whatever labor laws may apply in the country as a whole; and, in some cases, such security features as barbed wire, guarded checkpoints, and government-paid police.

Then there is the World Bank, which over the past decade has lent several billion dollars to finance the roads, airports, power plants, and even the first-class hotels that multinational corporations need in order to set up business in Third World countries. The Sri Lankan garment industry, which like other Third World garment industries survives by subcontracting to major Western firms, was set up on the advice of the World Bank and with a $20 million World Bank loan. This particular experiment in "development" offers young women jobs at a global low of $5 for a six-day week. Gloria Scott, the head of the World Bank's Women and Development Program, sounded distinctly uncomfortable when we asked her about the bank's role in promoting the exploitation of Third World women. "Our job is to help eliminate poverty. It is not our responsibility if the multinationals come in and offer such low wages. It's the responsibility of the governments." . . .

But the most powerful promoter of exploitative conditions for Third World women is the United States government itself. For example, the notoriously repressive Korean textile industry was developed with the help of $400 million in aid from the U.S. State Department. Malaysia became a low-wage haven for the electronics industry, thanks to technical assistance financed by AID, and to U.S. money (funneled through the Asian Development Bank) to help set up free trade zones. Taiwan's status as a "showcase for the free world" and a comfortable berth for multinationals is the result of three decades of financial transfusions from the United States. . . .

But the most obvious form of United States involvement, according to Lenny Siegel, the director of the Pacific Studies Center, is through "our consistent record of military aid to Third World governments that are capitalist, politically repressive, and are not striving for economic independence." Ironically, says Siegel, there are "cases where the United States made a big investment to make sure that any unions that formed would be pretty tame. Then we put in even more money to support some dictator who doesn't allow unions at all." . . .

What does our government have to say for itself? It's hard to get a straight answer—the few parts of the bureaucracy that deal with women and development seem to have little connection with those that are concerned with larger foreign policy issues. A spokesman for the Department of State told us that if multinationals offer poor working conditions (which he questioned), this was not their fault: "There are just different standards in different countries." Offering further evidence of a sheltered life, he told us that "corporations today are generally more socially responsible than even ten years ago. . . . We can expect them to treat their employees in the best way they can." But he conceded in response to a barrage of unpleasant examples, "Of course, you're going to have problems wherever you have human beings doing things." Our next stop was the Women's Division within AID. Staffer Emmy Simmons was aware of the criticisms of the quality of employment multinationals offer, but cautioned that "we can get hung up in the idea that it's exploitation without really looking at the alternatives for women." AID's concern, she said, was with the fact that population is outgrowing the agricultural capacity of many Third World countries, dislocating millions of people. From her point of view, multinationals at least provide some sort of alternative: "These people have to go somewhere."

34 Learning the Student Role: Kindergarten as Academic Boot Camp

HARRY L. GRACEY

As we have seen in the preceding Parts, each society (and each group) maintains a vital interest in making its members conform to expectations. A major social institution for which conformity is a primary goal is education. Educators want to graduate people who are acceptable to the community, not only in terms of marketable skills but also in terms of their ideas, attitudes, and behaviors. Whether it be grade school, high school, or college, educational administrators want instructors to teach standard ideas and facts, to steer clear of radical politics, and to not stir up trouble in the school or community. *Then* the social institution can go about its business—and that business, when you probe beneath official utterances and uncover the *"hidden curriculum,"* is producing conformists who fit well in society.

Although Gracey's focus is kindergarten, this article was chosen to represent the educational institution because it focuses on this essential nature of education, training in conformity. The primary goal of kindergarten is to teach children to be students—so they can participate in conformity. If this is what education really is about, where are intellectual stimulation, the excitement of discovery, and creativity—long associated in the public mind with education? The answer is that they may occur so long as they are noncontroversial. In other words they, too, are expected to reflect the conformist nature of the educational institution.

Based on your own extensive experiences with education, how do you react to the idea that the essence of the educational institution is training into conformity?

EDUCATION MUST BE CONSIDERED one of the major institutions of social life today. Along with the family and organized religion, however, it is a "secondary institution," one in which people are prepared for life in society as it is presently organized. The main dimensions of modern life, that is, the nature of society as a whole, are determined principally by the "primary institutions," which today are the economy, the political system, and the military establishment. Education has been defined by sociologists, classical and contemporary, as an institution which serves society by socializing people into it through a formalized, standardized procedure. At the beginning of the last century Emile Durkheim told student teachers at the University of Paris that education "consists of a methodical socialization of the younger generation." He went on to add:

It is the influence exercised by adult generations on those that are not ready for social life. Its object is to arouse and to develop in the child a certain number of physical, intellectual, and moral states that are demanded of him by the political society as a whole and by the special milieu for which he is specifically destined. . . . To the egotistic and asocial being that has just been born, [society] must, as rapidly as possible, add another, capable of leading a moral and social life. Such is the work of education.[1]

The education process, Durkheim said, "is above all the means by which society perpetually recreates the conditions of its very existence."[2] The contemporary educational sociologist Wilbur Brookover offers a similar formulation in his recent textbook definition of education:

Actually, therefore, in the broadest sense education is synonymous with socialization. It includes any social behavior that assists in the induction of the child into membership in the society or any behavior by which the society perpetuates itself through the next generation.[3]

The educational institution is, then, one of the ways in which society is perpetuated through the systematic socialization of the young, while the nature of the society which is being perpetuated—its organization and operation, its values, beliefs, and ways of living—are determined by the primary institutions. The educational system, like other secondary institutions, *serves* the society which is *created* by the operation of the economy, the political system, and the military establishment.

Schools, the social organizations of the educational institution, are today for the most part large bureaucracies run by specially trained and certified people. There are few places left in modern societies where formal teaching and learning are carried on in small, isolated groups, like the rural, one-room schoolhouses of [the 1800s]. Schools are large, formal organizations which tend to be parts of larger organizations, local community School Districts. These School Districts are bureaucratically organized and their operations are supervised by state and local governments. In this context, as Brookover says:

The term education is used . . . to refer to a system of schools, in which specifically designated persons are expected to teach children and youth certain types of acceptable behavior. The school system becomes a . . . unit in the total social structure and is recognized by the members of the society as a separate social institution. Within this structure a portion of the total socialization process occurs.[4]

Education is the part of the socialization process which takes place in the schools; and these are, more and more today, bureaucracies within bureaucracies.

Kindergarten is generally conceived by educators as a year of preparation for school. It is thought of as a year in which small children, five or six years old, are prepared socially and emotionally for the academic learning which will take place over the next twelve years. It is expected that a foundation of behavior and attitudes will be laid in kindergarten on which the children can acquire the skills and knowledge they will be taught in the grades. A booklet prepared for parents by the staff of a suburban New York school system says that the kindergarten experience will stimulate the child's desire to learn and cultivate the skills he will need for learning in the rest of his school career. It claims that the child will find opportunities for physical growth, for satisfying his "need for self-expression," acquire some knowledge, and provide opportunities for creative activity. It concludes, "The most important benefit that your five-year-old will receive from kindergarten is the opportunity to live and grow happily and purposefully with others in a small society." The kindergarten teachers in one of the elementary schools in this community, one we shall call the Wilbur Wright School, said their goals were to see that the children "grew" in all ways: physically, of course, emotionally, socially, and academically. They said they wanted children to like school as a result of their kindergarten experiences and that they wanted them to learn to get along with others.

None of these goals, however, is unique to kindergarten; each of them is held to some extent by teachers in the other six grades at Wright School. And growth would occur, but differently, even if the child did not attend school. The children already know how to get along with others, in their families and their play groups. The unique job of the kindergarten in the educational division of labor seems rather to be teaching children the student role. The student role is the repertoire of behavior and attitudes regarded by educators as appropriate to children in school. Observation in the kindergartens of the Wilbur Wright School revealed a great variety of activities through which children are shown and then drilled in the behavior and attitudes defined as appropriate for school and thereby induced to learn the role of student. Observations of the kindergartens and interviews with the teachers both pointed to the teaching and learning of classroom routines as the main element of the student role. The teachers expended most of their efforts, for the first half of the year at least, in training the children to follow the routines which teachers created. The children were, in a very real sense, *drilled* in tasks and activities created by the teachers for their own purposes and beginning and ending quite arbitrarily (from the child's point of view) at the command of the teacher. One teacher remarked that she hated September, because during the first month "everything has to be done rigidly, and repeatedly, until they know exactly what they're supposed to do." However, "by January," she said, "they know exactly what to do [during the day] and I don't have to be after them all the time." Classroom routines were introduced gradually from the beginning of the year in all the kindergartens, and the children were drilled in them as long as was necessary to achieve regular compliance. By the end of the school year, the successful kindergarten teacher has a well-organized group of children. They follow classroom routines automatically, having learned all the command signals and the expected responses to them. They have, in our terms, learned the student role. The following observation shows one such classroom operating at optimum organization on an afternoon late in May. It is the class of an experienced and respected kindergarten teacher.

An Afternoon in Kindergarten

At about 12:20 in the afternoon on a day in the last week of May, Edith Kerr leaves the teachers' room where she has been having lunch and walks to her classroom at the far end of the primary wing of Wright School. A group of five- and six-year-olds peers at her through the glass doors leading from the hall cloakroom to the play area outside. Entering her room, she straightens some material in the "book corner" of the room, arranges music on the piano, takes colored paper from her closet and places it on one of the shelves under the window. Her room is divided into a number of activity areas through the arrangement of furniture and play equipment. Two easels and a paint table near the door create a kind of passageway inside the room. A wedge-shaped area just inside the front door is made into a teacher's area by the placing of "her" things there: her desk, file, and piano. To the left is the book corner, marked off from the rest of the room by a puppet stage and a movable chalk-board. In it are a display rack of picture books, a record player, and a stack of children's records. To the right of the entrance are the sink and clean-up area. Four large round tables with six chairs at each for the children are placed near the walls about halfway down the length of the room, two on each side, leaving a large open area in the center for group games, block building, and toy truck driving. Windows stretch down the length of both walls, starting about three feet from the floor and extending almost to the high ceilings. Under the windows are long shelves on which are kept all the toys, games, blocks, paper, paints, and other equipment of the kindergarten. The left rear corner of the room is a play store with shelves, merchandise, and cash register; the right rear corner is a play kitchen with stove, sink, ironing board, and bassinette with baby dolls in it. This area is partly shielded from the rest of the room by a large standing display rack for posters and children's art work. A sandbox is found against the back wall between these two areas. The room is light, brightly colored, and filled with things adults feel five- and six-year-olds will find interesting and pleasing.

At 12:25 Edith opens the outside door and admits the waiting children. They hang their sweaters on hooks outside the door and then go to the center of the room and arrange themselves in a semi-circle on the floor, facing the teacher's chair, which she has placed in the center of the floor. Edith follows them in and sits in her chair checking attendance while waiting for the bell to ring. When she has finished attendance, which she takes by sight, she asks the children what the date is, what day and month it is, how many children are enrolled in the class, how many are present, and how many are absent.

The bell rings at 12:30 and the teacher puts away her attendance book. She introduces a visitor, who is sitting against the wall taking notes, as someone who wants to learn about schools and children. She then goes to the back of the room and takes down a large chart labeled "Helping Hands." Bringing it to the center of the room, she tells the children it is time to change jobs. Each child is assigned some task on the chart by placing his name, lettered on a paper "hand," next to a picture signifying the task—e.g., a broom, a blackboard, a milk bottle, a flag, and a Bible. She asks the children who wants each of the jobs and rearranges their "hands" accordingly. Returning to her chair, Edith announces, "One person should tell us what happened to Mark." A girl raises her hand, and when called on says, "Mark fell and hit his head and had to go to the hospital." The teacher adds that Mark's mother had written saying he was in the hospital.

During this time the children have been interacting among themselves, in their semi-circle. Children have whispered to their neighbors, poked one another, made general comments to the group, waved to friends on the other side of the circle. None of this has been disruptive, and the teacher has ignored it for the most part. The children seem to know just how much of each kind of interaction is permitted—they may greet in a soft voice someone who sits next to them, for example, but may not shout greetings to a friend who sits across the circle, so they confine themselves to waving and remain well within understood limits.

At 12:35 two children arrive. Edith asks them why they are late and then sends them to join the circle on the floor. The other children vie with each other to tell the newcomers what happened to Mark. When this leads to a general disorder Edith asks, "Who has serious time?" The children become quiet and a girl raises her hand. Edith nods and the child gets a Bible and hands it to Edith. She reads the Twenty-third Psalm while the children sit quietly. Edith helps the child in charge begin reciting the Lord's Prayer; the other children follow along for the first unit of sounds, and then trail off as Edith finishes for them. Everyone stands and faces the American flag hung to the right of the door. Edith leads the pledge to the flag, with the children again following the familiar sounds as far as they remember them. Edith then asks the girl in charge what song she wants and the child replies, "My Country." Edith goes to the piano and plays "America," singing as the children follow her words.

Edith returns to her chair in the center of the room and the children sit again in the semi-circle on the floor. It is 12:40 when she tells the children, "Let's have boys' sharing time first." She calls the name of the first boy sitting on the end of the circle, and he comes up to her with a toy helicopter. He turns and holds it up for the other children to see. He says, "It's a helicopter." Edith asks, "What is it used for?" and he replies, "For the army. Carry men.

For the war." Other children join in, "For shooting submarines." "To bring back men from space when they are in the ocean." Edith sends the boy back to the circle and asks the next boy if he has something. He replies "No" and she passes on to the next. He says "Yes" and brings a bird's nest to her. He holds it for the class to see, and the teacher asks, "What kind of bird made the nest?" The boy replies, "My friend says a rain bird made it." Edith asks what the nest is made of and different children reply, "mud," "leaves," and "sticks." There is also a bit of moss woven into the nest, and Edith tries to describe it to the children. They, however, are more interested in seeing if anything is inside it, and Edith lets the boy carry it around the semi-circle showing the children its insides. Edith tells the children of some baby robins in a nest in her yard, and some of the children tell about baby birds they have seen. Some children are asking about a small object in the nest which they say looks like an egg, but all have seen the nest now and Edith calls on the next boy. A number of children say, "I know what Michael has, but I'm not telling." Michael brings a book to the teacher and then goes back to his place in the circle of children. Edith reads the last page of the book to the class. Some children tell of books which they have at home. Edith calls the next boy, and three children call out, "I know what David has." "He always has the same thing." "It's a bang-bang." David goes to his table and gets a box which he brings to Edith. He opens it and shows the teacher a scale-model of an old-fashioned dueling pistol. When David does not turn around to the class, Edith tells him, "Show it to the children" and he does. One child says, "Mr. Johnson [the principal] said no guns." Edith replies, "Yes, how many of you know that?" Most of the children in the circle raise their hands. She continues, "That you aren't supposed to bring guns to school?" She calls the next boy on the circle and he brings two large toy soldiers to her which the children enthusiastically identify as being from "Babes in Toyland." The next boy brings an American flag to Edith and shows it to the class. She asks him what the stars and stripes stand for and admonishes him to treat it carefully. "Why should you treat it carefully?" she asks the boy. "Because it's our flag," he replies. She congratulates him, saying, "That's right."

"Show and Tell" lasted twenty minutes and during the last ten one girl in particular announced that she knew what each child called upon had to show. Edith asked her to be quiet each time she spoke out, but she was not content, continuing to offer her comment at each "show." Four children from other classes had come into the room to bring something from another teacher or to ask for something from Edith. Those with requests were asked to return later if the item wasn't readily available.

Edith now asks if any of the children told their mothers about their trip to the local zoo the previous day. Many children raise their hands. As Edith calls on them, they tell what they liked in the zoo. Some children cannot wait to be called on, and they call out things to the teacher, who asks them to be quiet. After a few of the animals are mentioned, one child says, "I liked the spooky house," and the others chime in to agree with him, some pantomiming fear and horror. Edith is puzzled, and asks what this was. When half the children try to tell her at once, she raises her hand for quiet, then calls on individual children. One says, "The house with nobody in it"; another, "The dark little house." Edith asks where it was in the zoo, but the children cannot describe its location in any way which she can understand. Edith makes some jokes but they involve adult abstractions which the children cannot grasp. The children have become quite noisy now, speaking out to make both relevant and irrelevant comments, and three little girls have become particularly assertive.

Edith gets up from her seat at 1:10 and goes to the book corner, where she puts a record on the player. As it begins a story about the trip to the zoo, she returns to the circle and asks the children to go sit at the tables. She divides them among the tables in such a way as to indicate that they don't have regular seats. When the children are all seated at the four tables, five or six to a table, the teacher asks, "Who wants to be the first one?" One of the noisy girls comes to the center of the room. The voice on the record is giving directions for imitating an ostrich and the girl follows them, walking around the center of the room holding her ankles with her hands. Edith replays the record, and all the children, table by table, imitate ostriches down the center of the room and back. Edith removes her shoes and shows that she can be an ostrich too. This is apparently a familiar game, for a number of children are calling out, "Can we have the crab?" Edith asks one of the children to do a crab "so we can all remember how," and then plays the part of the record with music for imitating crabs by. The children from the first table line up across the room, hands and feet on the floor and faces pointing toward the ceiling. After they have "walked" down the room and back in this posture they sit at their table and the children of the next table play "crab." The children love this; they run from their tables, dance about on the floor waiting for their turns, and are generally exuberant. Children ask for the "inch worm," and the game is played again with the children squirming down the floor. As a conclusion Edith shows them a new animal imitation, the "lame dog." The children all hobble down the floor on three "legs," table by table to the accompaniment of the record.

At 1:30 Edith has the children line up in the center of the room: she says, "Table one, line up in front of me," and children ask, "What are we going to do?" Then she moves a few steps to the side and says, "Table two over here; line up next to table one," and more children ask, "What for?" She does this for table three and table four, and each time the children ask, "Why, what are we going to do?" When the children are lined up in four lines of five each, spaced so that they are not touching one another, Edith puts on a new record and leads the class in calisthenics, to the accompaniment of the record. The children just jump around every which way in their places instead of doing the exercises, and by the time the record is finished, Edith, the only one following it, seems exhausted. She is apparently adopting the President's new "Physical Fitness" program for her classroom.

At 1:35 Edith pulls her chair to the easels and calls the children to sit on the floor in front of her, table by table. When they are all seated she asks,

"What are you going to do for worktime today?" Different children raise their hands and tell Edith what they are going to draw. Most are going to make pictures of animals they saw in the zoo. Edith asks if they want to make pictures to send to Mark in the hospital, and the children agree to this. Edith gives drawing paper to the children, calling them to her one by one. After getting a piece of paper, the children go to the crayon box on the righthand shelves, select a number of colors, and go to the tables, where they begin drawing. Edith is again trying to quiet the perpetually talking girls. She keeps two of them standing by her so they won't disrupt the others. She asks them, "Why do you feel you have to talk all the time?" and then scolds them for not listening to her. Then she sends them to their tables to draw.

Most of the children are drawing at their tables, sitting or kneeling in their chairs. They are all working very industriously and, engrossed in their work, very quietly. Three girls have chosen to paint at the easels, and having donned their smocks, they are busily mixing colors and intently applying them to their pictures. If the children at the tables are primitives and neo-realists in their animal depictions, these girls at the easels are the class abstract-expressionists, with their broad-stroked, colorful paintings.

Edith asks of the children generally, "What color should I make the cover of Mark's book?" Brown and green are suggested by some children "because Mark likes them." The other children are puzzled as to just what is going on and ask, "What book?" or "What does she mean?" Edith explains what she thought was clear to them already, that they are all going to put their pictures together in a "book" to be sent to Mark. She goes to a small table in the play-kitchen corner and tells the children to bring her their pictures when they are finished and she will write their message for Mark on them.

By 1:50 most children have finished their pictures and given them to Edith. She talks with some of them as she ties the bundle of pictures together—answering questions, listening, carrying on conversations. The children are playing in various parts of the room with toys, games, and blocks which they have taken off the shelves. They also move from table to table examining each other's pictures, offering compliments and suggestions. Three girls at a table are cutting up colored paper for a collage. Another girl is walking about the room in a pair of high heels with a woman's purse over her arm. Three boys are playing in the center of the room with the large block set, with which they are building walk-ways and walking on them. Edith is very much concerned about their safety and comes over a number of times to fuss over them. Two or three other boys are pushing trucks around the center of the room, and mild altercations occur when they drive through the block constructions. Some boys and girls are playing at the toy store, two girls are serving "tea" in the play kitchen, and one is washing a doll baby. Two boys have elected to clean the room, and with large sponges they wash the movable blackboard, the puppet stage, and then begin on the tables. They run into resistance from the children who are working with construction toys on the tables and do not want to dismantle their structures. The class is like a room full of bees, each intent on pursuing some activity, occasionally bumping into one another, but just veering off in another direction without serious altercation. At 2:05 the custodian arrives pushing a cart loaded with half-pint milk containers. He places a tray of cartons on the counter next to the sink, then leaves. His coming and going is unnoticed in the room (as, incidentally, is the presence of the observer, who is completely ignored by the children for the entire afternoon).

At 2:15 Edith walks to the entrance of the room, switches off the lights, and sits at the piano and plays. The children begin spontaneously singing the song, which is "Clean up, clean up. Everybody clean up." Edith walks around the room supervising the clean-up. Some children put their toys, the blocks, puzzles, games, and so on back on their shelves under the windows. The children making a collage keep right on working. A child from another class comes in to borrow the 45-rpm adaptor for the record player. At more urging from Edith the rest of the children shelve their toys and work. The children are sitting around their tables now, and Edith asks, "What record would you like to hear while you have your milk?" There is some confusion and no general consensus, so Edith drops the subject and begins to call the children, table by table, to come get their milk. "Table one," she says, and the five children come to the sink, wash their hands and dry them, pick up a carton of milk and a straw, and take it back to their table. Two talking girls wander about the room interfering with the children getting their milk and Edith calls out to them to "settle down." As the children sit, many of them call out to Edith the name of the record they want to hear. When all the children are seated at tables with milk, Edith plays one of these records called "Bozo and the Birds" and shows the children pictures in a book which go with the record. The record recites, and the book shows the adventures of a clown, Bozo, as he walks through a woods meeting many different kinds of birds who, of course, display the characteristics of many kinds of people or, more accurately, different stereotypes. As children finish their milk, they take blankets or pads from the shelves under the windows and lie on them in the center of the room, where Edith sits on her chair showing the pictures. By 2:30 half the class is lying on the floor on their blankets, the record is still playing, and the teacher is turning the pages of the book. The child who came in previously returns the 45-rpm adaptor, and one of the kindergartners tells Edith what the boy's name is and where he lives.

The record ends at 2:40. Edith says, "Children, down on your blankets." All the class is lying on blankets now. Edith refuses to answer the various questions individual children put to her because, she tells them, "it's rest time now." Instead she talks very softly about what they will do tomorrow. They are going to work with clay, she says. The children lie quietly and listen. One of the boys raises his hand and when called on tells Edith, "The animals in the zoo looked so hungry yesterday." Edith asks the children what they think about this and a number try to volunteer opinions, but Edith accepts only those offered in a "rest-time tone," that is, softly and quietly. After a brief discussion of animal feeding, Edith calls the names of the two children on milk detail and has them collect empty milk cartons from the tables and return them to the tray. She asks the two children on clean-up detail to clean up the room. Then she gets up from her chair and goes to the door to turn on the lights. At this signal, the children all get up from the floor and return their blankets and pads to the shelf. It is raining (the reason for no outside play this afternoon) and cars driven by mothers clog the school drive and line up along the street. One of the talkative little girls comes over to Edith and pointing out the window says, "Mrs. Kerr, see my mother in the new Cadillac?"

At 2:50 Edith sits at the piano and plays. The children sit on the floor in the center of the room and sing. They have a repertoire of songs about animals, including one in which each child sings a refrain alone. They know these by heart and sing along through the ringing of the 2:55 bell. When the song is finished, Edith gets up and coming to the group says, "Okay, rhyming words to get your coats today." The children raise their hands and as Edith calls on them, they tell her two rhyming words, after which they are allowed to go into the hall to get their coats and sweaters. They return to the room with these and sit at their tables. At 2:59 Edith says, "When you have your coats on, you may line up at the door." Half of the children go to the door and stand in a long line. When the three o'clock bell rings, Edith returns to the piano and plays. The children sing a song called "Goodbye," after which Edith sends them out.

Training for Learning and for Life

The day in kindergarten at Wright School illustrates both the content of the student role as it has been learned by these children and the processes by which the teacher has brought about this learning, or, "taught" them the student role. The children have learned to go through routines and to follow orders with unquestioning obedience, even when these make no sense to them. They have been disciplined to do as they are told by an authoritative person without significant protest. Edith has developed this discipline in the children by creating and enforcing a rigid social structure in the classroom through which she effectively controls the behavior of most of the children for most of the school day. The "living with others in a small society" which the school pamphlet tells parents is the most important thing the children will learn in kindergarten can be seen now in its operational meaning, which is learning to live by the routines imposed by the school. This learning appears to be the principal content of the student role.

Children who submit to school-imposed discipline and come to identify with it, so that being a "good student" comes to be an important part of their developing identities, *become* the good students by the school's definitions. Those who submit to the routines of the school but do not come to identify with them will be adequate students who find the more important part of their identities elsewhere, such as in the play group outside school. Children who refuse to submit to the school routines are rebels, who become known as "bad students" and often "problem children" in the school, for they do not learn the academic curriculum and their behavior is often disruptive in the classroom. Today schools engage clinical psychologists in part to help teachers deal with such children.

In looking at Edith's kindergarten at Wright School, it is interesting to ask how the children learn this role of student—come to accept school-imposed routines—and what, exactly, it involves in terms of behavior and attitudes. The most prominent features of the classroom are its physical and social structures. The room is carefully furnished and arranged in ways adults feel will interest children. The play store and play kitchen in the back of the room, for example, imply that children are interested in mimicking these activities of the adult world. The only space left for the children to create something of their own is the empty center of the room, and the materials at their disposal are the blocks, whose use causes anxiety on the part of the teacher. The room, being carefully organized physically by the adults, leaves little room for the creation of physical organization on the part of the children.

The social structure created by Edith is a far more powerful and subtle force for fitting the children to the student role. This structure is established by the very rigid and tightly controlled set of rituals and routines through which the children are put during the day. There is first the rigid "locating procedure" in which the children are asked to find themselves in terms of the month, date, day of the week, and the number of the class who are present and absent. This puts them solidly in the real world as defined by adults. The day is then divided into six periods whose activities are for the most part determined by the teacher. In Edith's kindergarten the children went through Serious Time, which opens the school day, Sharing Time, Play Time (which in clear weather would be spent outside), Work Time, Clean-up Time, after which they have their milk, and Rest Time, after which they go home. The teacher has programmed activities for each of these Times.

Occasionally the class is allowed limited discretion to choose between proffered activities, such as stories or records, but original ideas for activities are never solicited from them. Opportunity for free individual action is open only once in the day, during the part of Work Time left after the general class assignment has been completed (on the day reported the class assignment was drawing animal pictures for the absent Mark). Spontaneous interests or observations from the children are never developed by the teacher. It seems that her schedule just does not allow room for developing such unplanned events. During Sharing Time, for example, the child who brought a bird's nest told Edith, in reply to her question of what kind of bird made it, "My friend says it's a rain bird." Edith does not think to ask about this bird, probably because the answer is "childish," that is, not given in accepted adult categories of birds. The children then express great interest in an object in the nest, but the teacher ignores this interest, probably because the object is uninteresting to her. The soldiers from "Babes in Toyland" strike a responsive note in the children, but this is not used for a discussion of any kind. The soldiers are treated in the same way as objects which bring little interest from the children. Finally, at the end of Sharing Time the child-world of perception literally erupts in the class with the recollection of "the spooky house" at the zoo. Apparently this made more of an impression on the children than did any of the animals, but Edith is unable to make any sense of it for herself. The tightly imposed order of the class begins to break down as the children discover a universe of discourse of their own and begin talking excitedly with one another. The teacher is effectively excluded from this child's world of perception and for a moment she fails to dominate the classroom situation. She reasserts control, however, by taking the children to the next activity she has planned for the day. It seems never to have occurred to Edith that there might be a meaningful learning experience for the children in re-creating the "spooky house" in the classroom. It seems fair to say that this would have offered an exercise in spontaneous self-expression and an opportunity for real creativity on the part of the children. Instead, they are taken through a canned animal imitation procedure, an activity which they apparently enjoy, but which is also imposed upon them rather than created by them.

While children's perceptions of the world and opportunities for genuine spontaneity and creativity are being systematically eliminated from the kindergarten, unquestioned obedience to authority and rote learning of meaningless material are being encouraged. When the children are called to line up in the center of the room they ask "Why?" and "What for?" as they are in the very process of complying. They have learned to go smoothly through a programmed day, regardless of whether parts of the program make any sense to them or not. Here the student role involves what might be called "doing what you're told and never mind why." Activities which might "make sense" to the children are effectively ruled out, and they are forced or induced to participate in activities which may be "senseless," such as calisthenics.

At the same time the children are being taught by rote meaningless sounds in the ritual oaths and songs, such as the Lord's Prayer, the Pledge to the Flag, and "America." As they go through the grades children learn more and more of the sounds of these ritual oaths, but the fact that they have often learned meaningless sounds rather than meaningful statements is shown when they are asked to write these out in the sixth grade; they write them as groups of sounds rather than as a series of words, according to the sixth grade teachers at Wright School. Probably much learning in the elementary grades is of this character, that is, having no intrinsic meaning to the children, but rather being tasks inexplicably required of them by authoritative adults. Listening to sixth grade children read social studies reports, for example, in which they have copied material from encyclopedias about a particular country, an observer often gets the feeling that he is watching an activity which has no intrinsic meaning for the child. The child who reads, "Switzerland grows wheat and cows and grass and makes a lot of cheese" knows the dictionary meaning of each of these words but may very well have no conception at all of this "thing" called Switzerland. He is simply carrying out a task assigned by the teacher *because* it is assigned, and this may be its only "meaning" for him.

Another type of learning which takes place in kindergarten is seen in children who take advantage of the "holes" in the adult social structure to create activities of their own, during Work Time or out-of-doors during Play Time. Here the children are learning to carve out a small world of their own within the world created by adults. They very quickly learn that if they keep within permissible limits of noise and action they can play much as they please. Small groups of children formed during the year in Edith's kindergarten who played together at these times, developing semi-independent little groups in which they created their own worlds in the interstices of the adult-imposed physical and social world. These groups remind the sociological observer very much of the so-called "informal groups" which adults develop in factories and offices of large bureaucracies.[5] Here, too, within authoritatively imposed social organizations people find "holes" to create little subworlds which support informal, friendly, unofficial behavior. Forming and participating in such groups seems to be as much part of the student role as it is of the role of bureaucrat.

The kindergarten has been conceived of here as the year in which children are prepared for their schooling by learning the role of student. In the classrooms of the rest of the school grades, the children will be asked to submit to systems and routines imposed by the teachers and the curriculum. The days will be much like those of kindergarten, except that academic subjects will be substituted for the activities of the kindergarten. Once out of the school system, young adults will more than likely find themselves working in large-scale bureaucratic organizations, perhaps on the assembly line in the factory, perhaps in the paper routines of the white collar occupations, where they will be required to submit to rigid routines imposed by "the company" which may make little sense to them. Those who can operate well in this situation will be successful bureaucratic functionaries. Kindergarten, therefore, can be seen as preparing children not only for participation in the bureaucratic organization of large modern school systems, but also for the large-scale occupational bureaucracies of modern society.

Notes

1. Emile Durkheim, *Sociology and Education* (New York: The Free Press, 1956), pp. 71–72.

2. *Ibid.*, p. 123.

3. Wilbur Brookover, *The Sociology of Education* (New York: American Book Company, 1957), p. 4.

4. *Ibid.*, p. 6.

5. See, for example, Peter M. Blau, *Bureaucracy in Modern Society* (New York: Random House, 1956), Chapter 3.

35 The Great American Football Ritual

DOUGLAS E. FOLEY

Any visitor to the United States soon notices how important sports are to Americans. Baseball, football, basketball, hockey, softball, soccer, tennis, golf, swimming, gymnastics, track and field, auto racing, bowling, polo, horseshoes, bass fishing, skateboarding, and sky diving do not begin to exhaust the list. Some sports are taken more seriously than others, and a few have even become almost national obsessions—notably baseball, football, golf, basketball, and hockey. Although most sports are played "for fun," professional sports have become part of big business—yielding vast profits for players, managers, owners, and the companies that use them to sell a wide variety of products.

It would not take much of a trained sociological eye for a visitor to the United States to notice that some professional sports open with the singing of the national anthem, and to conclude from this that sports are vitally linked to patriotism. Besides this vital function of engendering national, regional, and local loyalties, sociologists have also analyzed how sports reproduce social class, gender, and race–ethnicity. As analyzed in this article, high school football serves as a means by which the adult generation reproduces its version of society—its status hierarchy, or customary divisions, of gender, race–ethnicity, and social classes. Following the "first wisdom" of sociology—that things are not what they seem, that there is a deeper layer of reality than appearances would indicate—sociologists conclude that high school football is much more than a game, that it is one of the ways of perpetuating social inequalities across the generations.

. . . THE SETTING OF THIS FIELD STUDY was "North Town," a small (8,000 population) South Texas farming/ranching community with limited industry, considerable local poverty, and a population that was 80% Mexican-American. "North Town High" had an enrollment of 600 students, and its sports teams played at the Triple-A level in a five-level state ranking system.

During the football season described here, I attended a number of practices, rode on the players' bus, and hung out with the coaches at the fieldhouse and with players during extensive classroom and lunchtime observations. I also participated in basketball and tennis practices and interviewed students extensively about student status groups, friendship, dating, and race relations. The participant observation and interviewing in the sports scene involved hundreds of hours of fieldwork over a 12-month period. . . .

The Weekly Pep Rally

Shortly after arriving in North Town I attended my first pep rally. Students, whether they liked football or not, looked forward to Friday afternoons. Regular 7th-period classes were let out early to hold a mass pep rally to support the team. Most students attended these events but a few used it to slip away from school early. During the day of this pep rally I overheard a number of students planning their trip to the game. Those in the school marching band (80) and in the pep club (50) were the most enthusiastic. . . .

The Friday afternoon pep rally was age-graded. The older, most prominent students took the center seats, thus signaling their status and loyalty. Younger first- and second-year students sat next to the leaders of the school activities if they were protégés of those leaders. In sharp contrast, knots and clusters of the more socially marginal students, the "druggers" and the "punks and greasers," usually claimed the seats nearest the exits, thus signaling their indifference to all the rah-rah speeches they had to endure. The "nobodies" or "nerds," those dutiful, conforming students who were followers, tended to sit in the back of the center regions. Irrespective of the general territory, students usually sat with friends from their age group. Teachers strategically placed themselves at the margins and down in front to assist in crowd control.

The pep rally itself was dominated by the coaches and players, who were introduced to the audience to reflect upon the coming contest. In this particular pep rally the team captains led the team onto the stage. All the Anglo players entered first, followed by all the Mexicano players. Coach Trujillo started out with the classic pep talk that introduced the team captains, who in turn stepped forward and spoke in an awkward and self-effacing manner, thus enacting the ideal of a sportsman—a man of deeds, not words. They all stuttered through several "uhs" and "ers," then quickly said, "I hope y'all come support us. Thanks." Generally students expected their jocks to be inarticulate and, as the cliché goes, strong but silent types. . . .

The Marching Band

The quality of the marching band was as carefully scrutinized as the football team by some community members. The band director, Dante Aguila, was keenly aware of maintaining an excellent winning band. Like sport teams, marching bands competed in local, district, and statewide contests and won rankings. The ultimate goal was winning a top rating at the state level. In addition, each band sent its best players of various instruments to district contests to compete for individual rankings. Individual band members could also achieve top rankings at the state level.

A certain segment of the student body began training for the high school marching band during their grade school years. Band members had a much more positive view of their participation in band than the players did. The band was filled with students who tended to have better grades and came from the more affluent families. The more marginal, deviant students perceived band members as "goodie goodies," "richies," and "brains." This characterization was not entirely true because the band boosters club did make an effort to raise money to help low-income students join the band. Not all band students were top students, but many were in the advanced or academic tracks. Band members were generally the students with school spirit who were proud to promote loyalty to the school and community. The marching band was also a major symbolic expression of the community's unity and its future generation of good citizens and leaders.

The view that band members were the cream of the crop was not widely shared by the football players. Many female band members were socially prominent and "cool," but some were also studious homebodies. On the other hand, "real men" supposedly did not sign up for the North Town band. According to the football players, the physically weaker, more effeminate males tended to be in the band. Males in the band were called "band fags." The only exceptions were "cool guys" who did drugs, or had their own rock and roll band, or came from musical families and planned to become professional musicians. . . .

The main masculinity test for "band fags" was to punch their biceps as hard as possible. If the victim returned this aggression with a defiant smile or smirk, he was a real man; if he winced and whined, he was a wimp or a fag. The other variations on punching biceps were pinching the forearm and rapping the knuckles. North Town boys generally punched and pinched each other, but this kind of male play toward those considered fags was a daily ritual degradation. These were moments when physically dominant males picked on allegedly more effeminate males and reaffirmed their place in the male pecking order. Ironically, however, the players themselves rarely picked on those they called "band fags." Males who emulated jocks and hoped to hang out with them were usually the hit men. The jocks signalled their real power and prestige by showing restraint toward obviously weaker males.

Cheerleaders and Pep Squads

As in most pep rallies, on the Friday I am describing, the cheerleaders were in front of the crowd on the gym floor doing dance and jumping routines in unison and shouting patriotic cheers to whip up enthusiasm for the team. The cheerleaders were acknowledged as some of the prettiest young women in the school and they aroused the envy of nobodies and nerds. Male students incessantly gossiped and fantasized about these young women and their reputations. . . . Students invariably had their favorites to adore and/or ridicule. Yet they told contradictory stories about the cheerleaders. When privately reflecting on their physical attributes and social status, males saw going with a cheerleader as guaranteeing their coolness and masculinity. Particularly the less attractive males plotted the seduction of these young women and reveled in the idea of having them as girlfriends. When expressing their views of these young women to other males, however, they often accused the cheerleaders of being stuck-up or sluts.

This sharp contradiction in males' discourse about cheerleaders makes perfect sense, however, when seen as males talking about females as objects to possess and dominate and through which to gain status. Conversations among males about cheerleaders were rhetorical performances that bonded males together and established their rank in the patriarchal order. In public conversations, males often expressed bravado about conquest of these "easy lays." In private conversations with intimate friends, they expressed their unabashed longing for, hence vulnerable emotional need for, these fantasized sexual objects. Hence, cheerleaders as highly prized females were dangerous, status-confirming creatures who were easier to relate to in rhetorical performances than in real life. Only those males with very high social status could actually risk relating to and being rejected by a cheerleader. The rest of the stories the young men told were simply male talk and fantasy.

Many young women were not athletic or attractive enough to be cheerleaders; nevertheless they wanted to be cheerleaders. Such young women often joined the pep squad as an alternative, and a strong esprit de corps developed among the pep squad members. They were a group of 50 young women in costume who came to the games and helped the cheerleaders arouse crowd enthusiasm. The pep squad also helped publicize and decorate the school and town with catchy team-spirit slogans such as "Smash the Seahawks" and "Spear the Javelinos." In addition, they helped organize after-the-game school dances. Their uniforms expressed loyalty to the team, and pep squad members were given a number of small status privileges in the school. They were sometimes released early for pep rallies and away games. . . .

Homecoming: A Rite of Community Solidarity and Status

Ideally, North Town graduates would return to the homecoming bonfire and dance to reaffirm their support and commitment to the school and team. They would come back to be honored and to honor the new generation presently upholding the name and tradition of the community. In reality, however, few graduates actually attended the pregame bonfire rally or postgame school dance. Typically, the game itself drew a larger crowd and the local paper played up the homecoming game more. College-bound youth were noticeably present at the informal beer party after the game. Some townspeople were also at the pregame bonfire rally, something that rarely happened during an ordinary school pep rally. . . .

Three groups of boys with pickup trucks . . . created a huge pile of scrap wood and burnable objects that had been donated. The cheerleaders, band, and pep squad members then conducted the bonfire ceremonies. Several hundred persons, approximately an equal number of Anglo and Mexicano students, showed up at the rally along with a fair sprinkling of older people and others who were not in high school. Nearly all of the leaders were Anglos and they were complaining that not enough students supported the school or them. The cheerleaders led cheers and sang the school fight song after brief inspirational speeches from the coaches and players. . . .

The huge blazing fire in the school parking lot . . . added to the festive mood, which seemed partly adolescent high jinks and partly serious communion with the town's traditions. The collective energy of the youth had broken a property law or two to stage this event. Adults laughed about the "borrowed" packing crates and were pleased that others "donated" things from their stores and houses to feed the fire. The adults expressed no elaborate rationale for having a homecoming bonfire, which they considered nice, hot, and a good way to fire up the team. Gathering around the bonfire reunited all North Towners, past and present, for the special homecoming reunion and gridiron battle. . . .

After the homecoming game, a school dance was held featuring a homecoming court complete with king and queen. The queen and her court and the king and his attendants, typically the most popular and attractive students, were elected by the student body. Ideally they represented the most attractive, popular, and successful youth. They were considered the best of a future generation of North Towners. Following tradition, the queen was crowned during halftime at midfield as the band played and the crowd cheered. According to tradition, the lovely queen and her court, dressed in formal gowns, were ceremoniously transported to the crowning in convertibles. The king and his attendants, who were often football players and dirty and sweaty at that, then came running from their halftime break to escort the young women from the convertibles and to their crowning. The king and his court lingered rather uneasily until the ceremony was over and then quickly returned to their team to rest and prepare for the second half. . . .

The Powder-Puff Football Game: Another Rite of Gender Reproduction

A powder-puff football game was traditionally held in North Town on Friday afternoon before the seniors' final game. A number of the senior football players dressed up as girls and acted as cheerleaders for the game. A number of the senior girls dressed up as football players and formed a touch football team that played the junior girls. The male football players served as coaches and referees and comprised much of the audience as well. Perhaps a quarter of the student body, mainly the active, popular, successful students, drifted in and out to have a laugh over this event. More boys than girls, both Anglo and Mexicano, attended the game.

The striking thing about this ritual was the gender difference in expressive manner. Males took the opportunity to act in silly and outrageous ways. They pranced around in high heels, smeared their faces with lipstick, and flaunted their padded breasts and posteriors in a sexually provocative manner. Everything, including the cheers they led, was done in a very playful, exaggerated, and burlesque manner.

In sharp contrast, the females donned the football jerseys and helmets of the players, sometimes those of their boyfriends, and proceeded to huff and puff soberly up and down the field under the watchful eyes of the boys. They played their part in the game as seriously as possible, blocking and shoving with considerable gusto. This farce went on for several scores, until one team was the clear winner and until the females were physically exhausted and the males were satiated with acting in a ridiculous manner.

. . . Anthropologists . . . call such serious practices "rituals of inversion," specially marked moments when people radically reverse everyday cultural roles and practices. During these events people break, or humorously play with, their own cultural rules. Such reversals are possible without suffering any sanctions or loss of face. These moments are clearly marked so that no one familiar with the culture will misread such reversals as anything more than a momentary break in daily life.

Males of North Town High used this moment of symbolic inversion to parody females in a burlesque and ridiculous manner. They took great liberties with the female role through this humorous form of expression. The power of these young males to appropriate and play with female symbols of sexuality was a statement about males' social and physical dominance. Conversely, the females took few liberties with their expression of the male role. They tried to play a serious game of football. The females tried earnestly to prove they were equal. Their lack of playfulness was a poignant testimony to their subordinate status in this small town. . . .

Prominent Citizens and Their Booster Club: Reproducing Class Privileges

North Town was the type of community in which male teachers who had athletic or coaching backgrounds were more respected than other teachers. For their part, the other teachers often told "dumb coach" jokes and expressed resentment toward the school board's view of coaches. North Town school board members, many of them farmers and ranchers—rugged men of action—generally preferred that their school leaders be ex-coaches. Consequently a disproportionate number of ex-coaches became school principals and superintendents. . . . School board members invariably emphasized an ex-coach's ability to deal with the public and to discipline the youth.

Once gridiron warriors, coaches in small towns are ultimately forced to become organization men, budget administrators, and public relations experts. . . . Ultimately they must appease local factions, school boards, administrators, booster clubs, angry parents, and rebellious teenagers. The successful North Town coaches invariably become excellent public relations men who live a "down home" rural lifestyle; they like to hunt and fish and join local coffee klatches or Saturday morning quarterback groups. They must be real men who like fraternizing with the entrepreneurs, politicians, and good ole' boys who actually run the town. This role as a local male leader creates a web of alliances and obligations that puts most coaches in the debt of the prominent citizens and their booster club.

North Town's booster club, composed mainly of local merchants, farmers, and ranchers, had the all-important function of raising supplementary funds for improving the sports program and for holding a postseason awards banquet. The club was the most direct and formal link that coaches had with the principal North Town civic leaders. North Town had a long history of booster club and school board interference in coaching the team. One coach characterized North Town as follows: "One of the toughest towns around to keep a job. Folks here take their football seriously. They are used to winning, not everything, not the state, but conference and maybe bidistrict, and someday even regional. They put a lot of pressure on you to win here." . . .

The pattern of community pressures observed in North Town was not particularly exceptional. A good deal of the public criticism and grumbling about choices of players had racial overtones. The debate over which Anglo varsity quarterback to play also reflected community class differences among Anglos. North Town students and adults often expressed their fears and suspicion that racial and class prejudices were operating. It would be an exaggeration, however, to portray the North Town football team as rife with racial conflict and disunity. Nor was it filled with class prejudice. On a day-to-day basis there was considerable harmony and unity. Mexicanos and Anglos played side by side with few incidents. A number of working-class Mexicano youths and a few low-income Anglos were also members of the football program. At least in a general way, a surface harmony and equality seemed to prevail. . . .

Local sports enthusiasts are fond of arguing that coaches select players objectively, without class or racial prejudices, because their personal interest, and that of the team, is served by winning. Unfortunately, this free-market view glosses over how sport actually functions in local communities. Small-town coaches are generally subjected to enormous pressures to play everyone's child, regardless of social class and race. Success in sport is an important symbolic representation of familial social position. Men can reaffirm their claim to leadership and prominence through the success of their offspring. A son's athletic exploits relive and display the past physical and present social dominance of the father. In displaying past and present familial prominence, the son lays claim to his future potential. Every North Town coach lived and died by his ability to win games *and* his social competence to handle the competing status claims of the parents and their children.

Socially prominent families, who want to maintain their social position, promote their interests through booster clubs. The fathers of future community leaders spend much time talking about and criticizing coaches in local coffee shops. These fathers are more likely to talk to the coaches privately. Coaches who have ambitions to be socially prominent are more likely to "network" with these sportsminded community leaders. A symbiotic relationship develops between coaches, especially native ones, and the traditional community leaders. Preferential treatment of the sons of prominent community leaders flows from the web of friendships, hunting privileges, Saturday morning joking, and other such exchanges.

The booster club that coach Trujillo had to deal with was run by a small clique of Anglos, . . . "good ole' boys and redneck types." They became outspoken early in the season against their "weak Mexican coach." They fanned the fires of criticism in the coffee-drinking sessions over which of the two freshman quarterbacks should start, the "strong-armed Mexican boy" or the "all-around, smart Anglo boy." The Anglo boy was the son of a prominent car dealer and . . . booster club activist. The Mexican boy was a son of a migrant worker and small grocery store manager. The freshman coach, Jim Ryan, chose the Anglo boy. . . . In a similar vein, conflict also surfaced over the selection of the varsity quarterback. Coach Trujillo chose the son of an Anglo businessman, an underclassman, over a senior, the son of a less prominent Anglo. The less educated Anglo faction lambasted the coach for this decision, claiming he showed his preference for the children of the more socially and politically prominent [families].

Moveover, considerable pressure to favor the sons of prominent citizens comes from within the school as well. The school and its classrooms are also a primary social stage upon which students enact their social privilege. These youths establish themselves as leaders in academic, political, and social affairs, and teachers grant them a variety of privileges. This reinforces the influence of their parents in the PTA, the sports and band booster clubs, and the school board. Both generations, in their own way, advance the interests of the family on many fronts.

The Spectators: Male Socialization Through Ex-players

Another major aspect of the football ritual is how the spectators, the men in the community, socialize each new generation of players. In North Town, groups of middle-aged males with families and businesses were influential in socializing the new generation of males. These men congregated in various restaurants for the morning coffee and conversation about business, politics, the weather, and sports. Those leading citizens particularly interested in sports could be heard praising and criticizing "the boys" in almost a fatherly way. Some hired the players for part-time or summer jobs and were inclined to give them special privileges. Athletes were more like to get well-paying jobs as road-gang workers, machine operators, and crew leaders. Most players denied that they got any favors, but they clearly had more prestige than other high school students who worked. Nonplayers complained that jocks got the good jobs. On the job site the men regaled players with stories of male conquests in sports, romance, and business.

Many players reported these conversations, and I observed several during Saturday morning quarterback sessions in a local restaurant and gas station. One Saturday morning after the all-important Harris game, two starters and their good buddies came into the Cactus Bowl Café. One local rancher-businessman shouted, "Hey, Chuck, Jimmie, get over here! I want to talk to you boys about the Harris game!" He then launched into a litany of mistakes each boy and the team had made. Others in the group chimed in and hurled jokes at the boys about "wearing skirts" and being "wimps." Meanwhile the players stood slope-shouldered and "uh-huhed" their tormentors. One thing they had learned was never to argue back too vociferously. The players ridiculed such confrontations with "old-timers" privately, but the proper response from a good kid was tongue-biting deference. . . .

Some ex-players led the romanticized life of tough, brawling, womanizing young bachelors. These young men seemed suspended in a state of adolescence while avoiding becoming responsible family men. They could openly do things that the players had to control or hide because of training rules. Many of these ex-players were also able to physically dominate the younger high school players. But ex-players no longer had a stage upon which to perform heroics for the town. Consequently they often reminded current players of their past exploits and the superiority of players and teams in their era. Current players had to "learn" from these tormentors and take their place in local sports history.

Players Talking About Their Sport: The Meaning of Football

The preceding portrayal of the community sports scene has already suggested several major reasons why young males play football. Many of them are willing to endure considerable physical pain and sacrifice to achieve social prominence in their community. Only a very small percentage are skilled enough to play college football, and only one North Towner has ever made a living playing professional football. The social rewards from playing football are therefore mainly local and cultural.

However, there are other more immediate psychological rewards for playing football. When asked why they play football and why they like it, young North Town males gave a variety of answers. A few openly admitted that football was a way for them to achieve some social status and prominence, to "become somebody in this town." Many said football was fun, or "makes a man out of you," or "helps you get a cute chick." Others parroted a chamber of commerce view that it built character and trained them to have discipline, thus helping them be successful in life. Finally, many evoked patriotic motives—to beat rival towns and to "show others that South Texas plays as good a football as East Texas."

These explicit statements do not reveal the deeper . . . lessons learned in sports combat, however. In casual conversations, players used phrases that were particularly revealing. What they talked most about was "hitting" or "sticking" or "popping" someone. These were all things that coaches exhorted the players to do in practice. After a hard game, the supreme compliment was having a particular "lick" or "hit" singled out. Folkloric immortality, endless stories about that one great hit in the big game, was what players secretly strove for. For most coaches and players, really "laying a lick on" or "knocking somebody's can off" or "taking a real lick" was that quintessential football moment. Somebody who could "take it" was someone who could bounce up off the ground as if he had hardly been hit. The supreme compliment, however, was to be called a hitter or head-hunter. A hitter made bone-crushing tackles that knocked out or hurt his opponent.

Players who consistently inflicted outstanding hits were called animals, studs, bulls, horses, or gorillas. A stud was a superior physical specimen who fearlessly dished out and took hits, who liked the physical contact, who could dominate other players physically. Other players idolized a "real stud," because he seemed fearless and indomitable on the field. Off the field a stud was also cool, or at least imagined to be cool, with girls. Most players expected and wanted strong coaches and some studs to lead them into battle. They talked endlessly about who was a real stud and whether the coach "really kicks butt."

The point of being a hitter and stud is proving that you have enough courage to inflict and take physical pain. Pain is a badge of honor. Playing with pain proves you are a man. In conventional society, pain is a warning to protect your body, but the opposite ethic rules in football. In North Town bandages and stitches and casts became medals worn proudly into battle. Players constantly told stories about overcoming injuries and "playing hurt." A truly brave man was one who could fight on; his pain and wounds were simply greater obstacles to overcome. Scars were permanent traces of past battles won, or at the very least fought well. They became stories told to girlfriends and relatives. . . .

Many players, particularly the skilled ones, described what might be called their aesthetic moments as the most rewarding thing about football. Players sitting around reviewing a game always talked about themselves or others as "making a good cut" and "running a good route," or "trapping" and "blindsiding" someone. All these specific acts involved executing a particular type of body control and skill with perfection and excellence. Running backs made quick turns or cuts that left would-be tacklers grasping for thin air. Ends "ran routes" or a clever change of direction that freed them to leap into the air and catch a pass. Guards lay in wait for big opposing linemen or aggressive linebackers to enter their territory recklessly, only to be trapped or blindsided by them. Each position had a variety of assignments or moments when players used their strength and intelligence to defeat their opponents. The way this was done was beautiful to a player who had spent years perfecting the body control and timing to execute the play. Players talked about "feeling" the game and the ball and the pressure from an opponent.

Team sports, and especially American football, generally socialize males to be warriors. The young men of North Town were being socialized to measure themselves by their animal instincts and aggressiveness. Physicality, searching for pain, enduring pain, inflicting pain, and knowing one's pain threshold emphasize the biological, animal side of human beings. These are the instincts needed to work together and survive in military combat and, in capitalist ideology, in corporate, academic, and industrial combat. The language used—head-hunter, stick 'em, and various aggressive animal symbols—conjures up visions of Wall Street stockbrokers and real estate sharks chewing up their competition.

Other Males: Brains, Farm Kids, and Nobodies

What of those males who do not play high school football? Does this pervasive community ritual require the participation of all young males? Do all non-athletes end up in the category of effeminate "band fags"? To the contrary, several types of male students did not lose gender status for being unathletic. There were a small number of "brains" who were obviously not physically capable of being gridiron warriors. Some of them played other sports with less physical contact such as basketball, tennis, track, or baseball. In this way they still upheld the ideal of being involved in some form of sport. Others, who were slight of physique, wore thick glasses, lacked hand-eye coordination, or ran and threw poorly, sometimes ended up hanging around jocks or helping them with their schoolwork. Others were loners who were labeled nerds and weirdos.

In addition, there were many farm kids or poor kids who did not participate in sports. They were generally homebodies who did not participate in many extracurricular activities. Some of them had to work to help support their families. Others had no transportation to attend practices. In the student peer groups they were often part of the great silent majority called "the nobodies."

Resistance to the Football Ritual: The Working-Class Chicano Rebels

There were also a number of Mexicano males who formed anti-school oriented peer groups. They were into a "hip" drug-oriented lifestyle. These males, often called "vatos" (cool dudes), made it a point to be anti-sports, an activity they considered straight. Although some were quite physically capable of playing, they rarely tried out for any type of team sports. They made excuses for not playing such as needing a job to support their car or van or pickup. They considered sports "kids' stuff," and their hip lifestyle as more adult, cool, and fun.

Even for the vatos, however, sports events were important moments when they could publicly display their lifestyle and establish their reputation. A number of vatos always came to the games and even followed the team to other towns. They went to games to be tough guys and "enforcers" and to establish "reps" as fighters. The vatos also went to games to "hit on chicks from other towns." During one road game, after smoking several joints, they swaggered in with cocky smiles plastered on their faces. The idea was to attract attention from your women and hopefully provoke a fight while stealing another town's women. Unlike stealing watermelons or apples from a neighbor, stealing women was done openly and was a test of courage. A man faced this danger in front of this buddies and under the eyes of the enemy.

. . . [A]fter the game the vatos told many tales about their foray into enemy territory. With great bravado they recounted every unanswered slight and insult they hurled at those "geeks." They also gloried in their mythical conquests of local young women. . . . As the players battled on the field, the vatos battled on the sidelines. They were another kind of warrior that established North Town's community identity and territoriality through the sport of fighting over and chasing young women.

The Contradiction of Being "In Training"

In other ways, even the straight young men who played football also resisted certain aspects of the game. Young athletes were thrust into a real dilemma when their coaches sought to rationalize training techniques and forbade various pleasures of the flesh. Being in training meant no drugs, alcohol, or tobacco. It also meant eating well-balanced meals, getting at least 8 hours of sleep, and not wasting one's emotional and physical energy chasing women. These dictates were extremely difficult to follow in a culture where drugs are used regularly and where sexual conquest and/or romantic love are popular cultural ideals. Add a combination of male adolescence and the overwhelming use of sex and women's bodies to sell commodities, and you have an environment not particularly conducive to making sacrifices for the coach and the team. North Town athletes envied the young bachelors who drank, smoked pot, and chased women late into the night. If they wanted to be males, American culture dictated that they break the rigid, unnatural training rules set for them.

. . . [M]any North Town football players . . . broke their training rules. They often drank and smoked pot at private teen parties. Unlike the rebellious vatos, who publicly flaunted their drinking and drugs, jocks avoided drinking in public. By acting like all-American boys, jocks won praise from adults for their conformity. Many of them publicly pretended to be sacrificing and denying themselves pleasure. They told the old-timers stories about their "rough practices" and "commitment to conditioning." Consequently, if jocks got caught breaking training, the men tended to overlook these infractions as slips or temptations. In short, cool jocks knew how to manage their public image as conformists and hide their private nonconformity. . . .

Fathers who had experienced this training contradiction themselves . . . gave their sons and other players stern lectures about keeping in shape, *but* they were the first to chuckle at the heroic stories of playing with a hangover. They told these same stories about teammates or about themselves over a cup of coffee or a beer. As a result, unless their youth were outrageously indiscreet—for example passing out drunk on the main street or in class, getting a "trashy girl" pregnant—a "little drinking and screwing around" was overlooked. They simply wanted the school board to stop being hypocritical and acknowledge that drinking was all part of growing up to be a prominent male.

In the small sports world of North Town, a real jock actually enhances his public image of being in shape by occasionally being a "boozer" or "doper." Indeed, one of the most common genres of stories that jocks told was the "I played while drunk/stoned," or the "I got drunk/stoned the night before the game" tale. Olmo, a big bruising guard who is now a hard-living, hard-drinking bachelor, told me a classic version of this tale before the homecoming game:

> Last night we really went out and hung one on. Me and Jaime and Arturo drank a six-pack apiece in a couple of hours. We were cruising around Daly City checking out the action. It was really dead. We didn't see nobody we knew except Arturo's cousin. We stopped at his place and drank some more and listened to some music. We stayed there till his old lady [mom] told us to go home. We got home pretty late, but before the sun come up, 'cause we're in training, ha ha.

[Conclusion]

. . . [T]he football ritual remains a powerful metaphor of American capitalist culture. In North Town, football is still a popular cultural practice deeply implicated in the reproduction of the local ruling class of white males, hence class, patriarchal, and racial forms of dominance. Local sports, especially football, are still central to the socialization of each new generation of youth and to the maintenance of the adolescent society's status system. In addition, this ritual is also central to the preservation of the community's adult status hierarchy. The local politics of the booster club, adult male peer groups, and Saturday morning coffee klatches ensnare coaches and turn a son's participation in the football ritual into an important symbolic reenactment of the father's social class and gender prominence. . . .

36 Beauty and the Beast of Advertising

JEAN KILBOURNE

The most recent social institution to develop, and rapidly becoming one of the most powerful, is the mass media. The *mass media* consist of those forms of communication that reach mass audiences—radio, television, movies, newspapers, magazines, and books. The Internet is the most recent form of the mass media, with millions of people simultaneously reading the same news articles and ads transmitted via satellite across the world.

On a commonsense level, the primary functions of the media are to entertain and inform. Certainly, they do this. But have you noted the prevalence of advertising in the mass media (with the exception of most books)? There are those who claim that advertising has become *the* primary purpose of the mass media; the real reason for our entertaining and informative television programs, for example, is to round up an audience for the advertising. Perhaps so. The mass media are certainly a primary tool of business.

A second primary purpose of the media is social control. Seldom is this purpose so obvious as its heavy-handed use by Goebbels in Nazi Germany, Stalin in communist Russia, and Hussein in totalitarian Iran. The social control function of *our* media, though more covert, is nonetheless similarly powerful. The mass media are used not only to keep us in line politically, but also to influence our ideas, attitudes, and behavior in all realms of life. As advertising continually bombards us, it plants ideas and massages our attitudes, giving them subtle shape and direction. That advertising is highly effective becomes apparent from Kilbourne's analysis of how it influences our ideas of beauty. (You may wish to compare this article with the findings Eder reported on middle-school girls in article 14 and Katz's observations in article 27.)

"YOU'RE A HALSTON WOMAN from the very beginning," the advertisement proclaims. The model stares provocatively at the viewer, her long blonde hair waving around her face, her bare chest partially covered by two curved bottles that give the illusion of breasts and a cleavage.

The average American is accustomed to blue-eyed blondes seductively touting a variety of products. In this case, however, the blonde is about five years old.

Advertising is an over $130 billion a year industry and affects all of us throughout our lives. We are each exposed to over 1500 ads a day, constituting perhaps the most powerful educational force in society. The average adult will spend one and one-half years of his/her life watching television commercials. But the ads sell a great deal more than products. They sell values, images, and concepts of success and worth, love and sexuality, popularity and normalcy. They tell us who we are and who we should be. Sometimes they sell addictions.

Advertising is the foundation and economic lifeblood of the mass media. The primary purpose of the mass media is to deliver an audience to advertisers.

Adolescents are particularly vulnerable, however, because they are new and inexperienced consumers and are the prime targets of many advertisements. They are in the process of learning their values and roles and developing their self-concepts. Most teenagers are sensitive to peer pressure and find it difficult to resist or even question the dominant cultural messages perpetuated and reinforced by the media. Mass communication has made possible a kind of nationally distributed peer pressure that erodes private and individual values and standards.

But what does society, and especially teenagers, learn from the advertising messages that proliferate in the mass media? On the most obvious level they learn the stereotypes. Advertising creates a mythical, WASP-oriented world in which no one is ever ugly, overweight, poor, struggling, or disabled either physically or mentally (unless you count the housewives who talk to little men in toilet bowls). And it is a world in which people talk only about products.

Housewives or Sex Objects

The aspect of advertising most in need of analysis and change is the portrayal of women. Scientific studies and the most casual viewing yield the same conclusion: Women are shown almost exclusively as housewives or sex objects.

The housewife, pathologically obsessed by cleanliness and lemon-fresh scents, debates cleaning products and worries about her husband's "ring around the collar."

The sex object is a mannequin, a shell. Conventional beauty is her only attribute. She has no lines or wrinkles (which would indicate she had the bad taste and poor judgment to grow older), no scars or blemishes—indeed, she has no pores. She is thin, generally tall and long-legged, and above all, she is young. All "beautiful" women in advertisements (including minority women), regardless of product or audience, conform to this norm. Women are constantly exhorted to emulate this ideal, to feel ashamed and guilty if they fail, and to feel that their desirability and lovability are contingent upon physical perfection.

Creating Artificiality

The image is artificial and can only be achieved artificially (even the "natural look" requires much preparation and expense). Beauty is something that comes from without: more than one million dollars is spent every hour on cosmetics. Desperate to conform to an ideal and impossible standard, many women go to great lengths to manipulate and change their faces and bodies. A woman is conditioned to view her face as a mask and her body as an object, as *things* separate from and more important than her real self, constantly in need of alteration, improvement, and disguise. She is made to feel dissatisfied with and ashamed of herself, whether she tries to achieve "the look" or not. Objectified constantly by others, she learns to objectify herself. (It is interesting to note that one in five college-age women has an eating disorder.)

"When *Glamour* magazine surveyed its readers in 1984, 75 percent felt too heavy and only 15 percent felt just right. Nearly half of those who were actually underweight reported feeling too fat and wanting to diet. Among a sample of college women, 40 percent felt overweight when only 12 percent actually were too heavy," according to Rita Freedman in her book *Beauty Bound.*

There is evidence that this preoccupation with weight begins at ever-earlier ages for women. According to a recent article in *New Age Journal,* "even grade-school girls are succumbing to stick-like standards of beauty enforced by a relentless parade of wasp-waisted fashion models, movie stars, and pop idols." A study by a University of California professor showed that nearly 80 percent of fourth-grade girls in the Bay Area are watching their weight.

A recent *Wall Street Journal* survey of students in four Chicago-area schools found that more than half the fourth-grade girls were dieting and three-quarters felt they were overweight. One student said, "We don't expect boys to be that handsome. We take them as they are." Another added, "But boys expect girls to be perfect and beautiful. And skinny."

Dr. Steven Levenkrom, author of *The Best Little Girl in the World,* the story of an anorexic, says his blood pressure soars every time he opens a magazine and finds an ad for women's fashions. "If I had my way," he said, "every one one of them would have to carry a line saying, 'Caution: This model may be hazardous to your health.'"

Women are also dismembered in commercials, their bodies separated into parts in need of change or improvement. If a woman has "acceptable" breasts, then she must also be sure that her legs are worth watching, her hips slim, her feet sexy, and that her buttocks look nuder under her clothes ("like I'm not wearin' nothin'"). This image is difficult and costly to achieve and impossible to maintain—no one is flawless and everyone ages. Growing older is the great taboo. Women are encouraged to remain little girls ("because inno-cence is sexier than you think"), to be passive and dependent, never to mature. The contradictory message—"sensual, but not too far from innocence"—places women in a double bind: somehow we are supposed to be both sexy and virginal, experienced and naive, seductive and chaste. The disparagement of maturity is, of course, insulting and frustrating to adult women, and the im-plication that little girls are seductive is dangerous to real children.

Influencing Sexual Attitudes

Young people also learn a great deal about sexual attitudes from the media and from advertising in particular. Advertising's approach to sex is pornographic: it reduces people to objects and de-emphasizes human contact and individuality. This reduction of sexuality to a dirty joke and of people to objects is the real obscenity of the culture. Although the sexual sell, overt and subliminal, is at a fevered pitch in most commercials, there is at the same time a notable absence of sex as an important and profound human activity.

There have been some changes in the images of women. Indeed, a "new woman" has emerged in commercials in recent years. She is generally pre-sented as superwoman, who manages to do all the work at home and on the job (with the help of a product, of course, not of her husband or children or friends); or as the liberated woman, who owes her independence and self-esteem to the products she uses. These new images do not represent any real progress but rather create a myth of progress, an illusion that reduces complex sociopolitical problems to mundane personal ones.

Advertising images do not cause these problems, but they contribute to them by creating a climate in which the marketing of women's bodies—the sexual sell and dismemberment, distorted body image ideal, and children as sex objects—is seen as acceptable.

This is the real tragedy, that many women internalize these stereotypes and learn their "limitations," thus establishing a self-fulfilling prophecy. If one accepts these mythical and degrading images, to some extent one actualizes them. By remaining unaware of the profound seriousness of the ubiquitous in-fluence, the redundant message, and the subliminal impact of advertisements, we ignore one of the most powerful "educational" forces in the culture—one that greatly affects our self-images, our ability to relate to each other, and ef-fectively destroys awareness and action that might help to change that climate.

37 Men Who Share "The Second Shift"

ARLIE HOCHSCHILD
ANNE MACHUNG

The fast moving currents of social change have not left the U.S. family untouched. We all are familiar with many of the consequences—postponing marriage, smaller families, two paychecks, divorce, teenage pregnancy, unwed mothers and fathers, nursing homes, abortion, and cohabitation. Family violence may also be higher, but this is speculation for we have no firm figures to measure the present, much less the past. Some of us come from broken homes; others of us have been divorced. Hardly any of us expects our marriage to be the way our grandparents' was, and many of us even anticipate that our approach to being a husband or wife will differ markedly from that of our own parents.

Although we can mentally project ourselves into anticipated roles, we have little idea of what we will really face. Certainly, with the rapid pace of change, many of our attitudes and ideas will be different in a few years. It seems certain, however, that increasing pressures will be brought to bear on husbands to share what the authors call the *second shift*, the housework and family and home duties that remain to be done after the day's work-for-pay is completed. To gather data for their study, Hochschild and her colleagues interviewed fifty families, following a dozen in depth. In these families, from different social classes and racial–ethnic groups, the wife was usually a "supermom," working the second shift herself with little assistance from her husband. She averaged an extra *month* more of work a year on the second shift than her husband. About 20 percent of the men, however, shared the second shift. In this selection, we examine differences between the men who shared the second shift and those who did not, and the effects this had on the marriage and the children.

ONE OUT OF FIVE MEN in this study was as actively involved in the home as their wives—some were like Greg Alston, working the same hours as their wives but sharing in a more "male" way, doing such things as carpentry; others, like Art Winfield, shared the cooking and being a primary parent. In my study the men who shared the second shift had a happier family life, so

395

I wanted to know what conditions produce such men. How do men who share *differ* from other men?

The men in this study who shared the work at home were no more likely than others to have "model" fathers who helped at home. Their parents were no more likely to have trained them to do chores when they were young. Michael Sherman and Seth Stein both had fathers who spent little time with them and did little work around the house. But Michael became extremely involved in raising his twin boys, whereas Seth said hello and goodbye to his children as he went to and from his absorbing law practice. Sharers were also as likely to have had mothers who were homemakers or who worked *and* tended the home as non-sharers. . . .

Did the men who shared the work at home love their wives more? Were they more considerate? It's true, egalitarian men had more harmonious marriages, but I would be reluctant to say that men like Peter Tanagawa or Ray Judson loved their wives less than men like Art Winfield or Michael Sherman, or were less considerate in other ways. One man who did very little at home said, "Just last week I suddenly realized that for the first time I feel like my wife's life is more valuable than mine, because my son needs her more than he needs me." Men who shared were very devoted to their wives; but, in a less helpful way, so were the men who didn't.

Two other, more external factors also did *not* distinguish men who did share from men who didn't: the number of hours they worked or how much they earned. Husbands usually work a longer "full-time" job than wives. But in the families I studied, men who worked fifty hours or more per week were just *slightly* less likely to share housework than men who worked forty-five, forty, or thirty-five hours a week. In addition, fifty-hour-a-week *women* did far *more* childcare and housework than men who worked the same hours. Other national studies also show that the number of hours a man works for pay has little to do with the number of hours he works at home.

Of all the factors that influence the relations between husbands and wives, I first assumed that money would loom the largest. The man who shared, I thought, would need his wife's salary more, would value her job more, and as a result also her time. . . .

I assumed that the man who shares would not earn more, and that the wage gap between other husbands and their wives might *cause* the leisure gap between them. Both spouses might agree that because his job came first, his leisure did, too. Leaving childcare aside (since most men would want to do some of that), I assumed that men who earned *as much or less* than their wives would do more housework. I assumed that a woman who wanted fifty-fifty in the second shift but had married a high-earning man would reconcile herself to the family's greater need for her husband's work, set aside her desires, and work the extra month a year. By the same token, a traditional man married to a high-earning woman would swallow his traditional pride and pitch in at home. I assumed that money would talk louder than ideals, and invisibly shape each partner's gender strategy.

If money is the underlying principle behind men's and women's strategies, that would mean that no matter how much effort a woman put into her job, its lower pay would result in less help from her husband at home. Research about on-the-job stress suggests that jobs in the low-level service sector, where women are concentrated, cause more stress than blue-and-white-collar jobs, where men are concentrated. Although working mothers don't work as long hours as working fathers, they devote as much *effort* to earning money as men, and many women earn less for work that's more stressful. Thus, by using his higher salary to "buy" more leisure at home, he inadvertently makes his wife pay indirectly for an inequity in the wider economy that causes her to get paid less. If money is the key organizing principle to the relations between men and women in marriage, it's a pity for men because it puts their role at home at the mercy of the blind fluctuations of the marketplace and for women because if money talks at home, it favors men. The extra month a year becomes an indirect way in which the woman pays *at home* for *economic* discrimination *outside* the home.

The Limits of Economic Logic

Money mattered in the marriages I studied, but it was not the powerful "invisible hand" behind the men who shared. For one thing, this is clear from the family portraits. Michael Sherman earned much more than Adrienne but his job didn't matter more, and he shared the work at home. For years Ann Myerson earned more than her husband but put her husband's job first anyway. John Livingston valued his wife's job as he did his own, but she took more responsibility at home.

A number of researchers have tried to discover a link between the *wage* gap between working parents and the *leisure* gap between them, and the results have been confusing. All but one study found no significant relation between the amount a man earns relative to his wife and how much housework or child care he does. Among couples in this study, these two factors were not related in a statistically significant way.

An intriguing clue appeared, however, when I divided all the men into three groups: men who earn more than their wives (most men), men who earn the same amount, and men who earn less. Of the men who earned more than their wives, 21 percent shared housework. Of the men who earned about the same, 30 percent. But among men who earned less than their wives, *none* shared.

If a logic of the pocketbook is only a logic of the *pocketbook*, it should operate the same whether a man earns more or a woman earns more. But this "logic of the pocketbook" didn't work that way. It only worked as long as men earned as much or more than their wives. Money frequently "worked" for men (it excused them from housework) but it didn't work for women (it didn't get them out of it).

Another principle—the principle of "balancing"—seems to be at work. According to this principle, if men lose power over women in one way, they make up for it in another way—by avoiding the second shift, for example. In this way they can maintain dominance over women. How much responsibility these men assumed at home was thus related to the deeper issue of male power. Men who earn much more than their wives already have a power over their wives in that they control a scarce and important resource. The more severely a man's financial identity is threatened—by his wife's higher salary, for example—the less he can afford to threaten it further by doing "women's work" at home.

Men who shared the second shift weren't trying to make up for losing power in other realms of their marriage; they didn't feel the need to "balance." Michael Sherman had given up the *idea* that he should have more power than Adrienne. Art Winfield talked playfully about men being "brought up to be kings."

But Peter Tanagawa felt a man *should* have more power, and felt he'd given a lot of it up when Nina's career rose so dramatically. He's adjusted himself to earning much less, but to a man of his ideas, this had been a sacrifice. By making up for his sacrifice by doing more at home, Nina engaged in "balancing." Among other couples, too, it's not only men who "balance"; women do too.

Thus, more crucial than cultural beliefs about men's and women's *spheres,* were couples' beliefs about the right degree of men's and women's *power.* Women who "balanced" felt "too powerful." Sensing when their husbands got "touchy," sensing the fragility of their husbands' "male ego," not wanting them to get discouraged or depressed, such women restored their men's lost power by waiting on them at home.

Wives did this "balancing"—this restoring power to their husbands—for different reasons. One eccentric Englishman and father of three children, aged six, four, and one, took responsibility for about a third of the chores at home. A tenured member of the English department of a small college, he taught classes, and held obligatory office hours, but had abandoned research, minimized committee work, avoided corridor conversations, and had long since given up putting in for a raise. He claimed to "share" housework and childcare, but what he meant by housework was working on a new den, and what he meant by childcare was reflected in this remark, "The children do fine while I'm working on the house; they muck about by themselves." He was touchy about his accomplishments and covertly nervous, it seemed, about what he called the "limitless" ambitions of his workaholic wife. Without asking him to do more, perhaps his wife was making up for her "limitless ambitions" by carrying the load at home. In the meantime, she described herself as "crushed with work."

I looked again at other interviews I'd done with men who worked less than full time. One architect, the fourth of four highly successful brothers in a prosperous and rising black family, had lost his job in the recession of the late 1970s, become deeply discouraged, taken occasional contracting jobs, and otherwise settled into a life of semi-unemployment. His wife explained: "Eventually we're going to have to make it on my salary. But it's awfully hard on my husband right now, being trained as an architect and not being able to get a job. I take that into account." Her husband did no housework and spent time with his son only when the spirit moved him. "I do very little around the house," he said frankly, "but Beverly doesn't complain, bless her heart." Meanwhile, they lived in near-poverty, while Beverly worked part time, cared for their baby and home, and took courses in veterinary science at night, her overload the result of their economic need added to her attempt to restore a sense of power to her discouraged husband. As she let fall at the end of the in-terview, "Sometimes I wonder how long I can keep going."

Other men earned less and did less at home but weren't "balancing." They were going back to get a degree, and their wives were temporarily giving them the money and the time to do this. The husband's training for a job counted as much in their moral accounting system as it would if he already had that more important job. For example, one husband was unemployed while studying for a degree in pediatric nursing. His wife, a full-time adminis-trator, cared for their home and their nine-month-old baby. The rhythm of their household life revolved around the dates of his exams. His wife ex-plained: "My husband used to do a lot around here. He used to puree Stevy's carrots in the blender. He used to help shop, and weed the garden. Now he studies every evening until ten. His exams come first. Getting that "A" is im-portant to him. He plays with the baby as a study break." She said she didn't mind doing the housework and caring for the baby and got upset when he complained the house was messy. She said, "I keep myself going by reminding myself this is *temporary*, until Jay gets his degree."

I heard of no women whose husbands both worked and cared for the family while the wives studied for a degree. For a woman, getting a degree was not so honored an act. There was no tradition of "putting your wife through college" analogous to the recent tradition of "putting your husband through college." A wife could imagine being supported or being better off when her husband got his degree. Husbands usually couldn't imagine either situation. One husband *had* shared the work at home fifty-fifty when his wife worked, but came to resent it terribly and finally stopped when his wife quit her job and went back to school to get a Ph.D. A job counted as legitimate rec-ompense, but working toward a degree did not. Feeling deprived of attention and service, one man shouted into my tape recorder—half in fun and half not: "You can't eat it. You can't talk to it. It doesn't buy a vacation or a new car. I *hate* my wife's dissertation!" Women who put their husbands through school may have resented the burden, but they didn't feel they had as much right to complain about it.

Taken as a whole, this group of men—semi-unemployed, hanging back at work, or in training—neither earned the bread nor cooked it. And of all the wives, theirs were the least happy. Yet, either because they sympathized with their husbands, or expected the situation to improve, or because they felt there was no way to change it, and because they were, I believe, unconsciously maintaining the "right" balance of power in their marriage, such women worked the extra month a year. Meanwhile, their lower-earning husbands often saw their wives as intelligent, strong, "a rock"; at the same time these men could enjoy the idea that, though not a king at work, a man still had a warm throne at home.

Some women had other ways of accumulating more power than they felt "comfortable" with. One woman I know, an M.D., not in this study, married a former patient, a musician who earned far less than she. Perhaps the feeling that her status was "too great" for their joint notion of the "right" balance, she—a feminist on every other issue—quietly did all the second shift and, as her husband put it, "She never asks." Another woman, a teacher, secretly upset the power balance by having a long-term extra-marital affair almost like another marriage. Life went on as usual at home, but she quietly made up for her secret life by being "wonderful" about all the chores at home.

In these marriages, money was not the main determinant of which men did or didn't share. Even men who earned much more than their wives didn't get out of housework *because* of it. One college professor and father of three, for example, explained why he committed himself to 50 percent of housework and childcare:

> My wife earns a third of what I earn. But as a public school teacher she's doing a job that's just as important as mine. She's an extraordinarily gifted teacher, and I happen to know she works just as hard at her teaching as I do at mine. So, when we come home, she's as tired as I am. We share the housework and childcare equally. But [in a tone of exasperation] if she were to take a job in insurance or real estate, she'd just be doing another job. She wouldn't be making the contribution she's making now. We haven't talked about it, but if that were the case, I probably wouldn't break my back like this. She would have to carry the load at home.

Ironically, had his wife earned *more* at a job he admired less—had she worked only for *money*—he would *not* have shared the second shift. . . .

That doesn't mean that money has nothing to do with sharing the second shift. In two different ways, it does. In the first place, couples do need to think about and plan around financial need. Most of the men who shared at home had wives who pretty much shared at work. The men earned some but not much more. And whatever their wives earned, working-class men like Art Winfield really needed their wives' wages to live. Second, future changes in the general economy may press more couples to do "balancing." Some experts predict that the American economy will split increasingly between an elite of highly paid, highly trained workers and an enlarging pool of poorly paid, unskilled workers. Jobs in the middle are being squeezed out as companies lose out to foreign competition or seek cheaper labor pools in the Third World. The personnel rosters of the so-called sunrise industries, the rapidly growing, high-technology companies, already reflect this split. Companies with many jobs in the middle are in the so-called sunset industries, such as car manufacturing. As the economist Bob Kuttner illustrates: "The fast food industry employs a small number of executives and hundreds of thousands of cashiers and kitchen help who make $3.50 an hour. With some variation, key punchers, chambermaids, and retail sales personnel confront the same short job ladder." In addition, unions in the sunrise industries often face companies' threats to move their plants to cheap labor markets overseas, and so these unions press less hard for better pay.

The decline in jobs in the middle mainly hits men in blue-collar union-protected jobs. Unless they can get training that allows them to compete for a small supply of highly skilled jobs, such men will be forced to choose between unemployment and a low-paid service job.

The "declining middle" is thus in the process of creating an economic crisis for many men. This crisis can lead to two very different results: As economic hardship means more women have to work, their husbands may feel it is "only fair" to share the work at home. Or, there may be a countervailing tendency for men and women to compensate for economically induced losses in male self-esteem by engaging in "balancing." If the logic of the pocketbook affects the way men and women divide the second shift, I think it will affect it in this way, through its indirect effect on male self-esteem.

All in all, men who shared were similar to men who didn't in that their fathers were just as unlikely to have been model helpers at home, and just as unlikely to have done housework as boys themselves. But the men who shared at home seemed to have more distant ties with their fathers, and closer ones with their mothers. They were similar to non-sharing men in the hours they worked, but they tended not to earn a great deal more or less than their wives.

Sharing men seemed to be randomly distributed across the class hierarchy. There were the Michael Shermans and the Art Winfields. In the working class, more men shared without believing it corresponded to the kind of man they wanted to be. In the middle class, more men didn't share even though they believed in it. Men who both shared the work at home and believed in it seemed to come from every social class. Everything else equal, men whose wives had advanced degrees and professional careers—who had what the sociologist Pierre Bourdieu calls "cultural capital"—were more likely to share than men whose wives lacked such capital. Men with career wives were more likely to share than men with wives in "jobs." All these factors were part of the social backdrop to the working man's gender strategy at home.

Added to these was also the strategy of his wife. Nearly every man who shared had a wife whose strategy was to urge—or at least welcome—his involvement at home. Such women did not emotionally hoard their children, as Nancy Holt came to do with Joey. When Evan had been about to leave to take Joey to the zoo for a father-son outing, Nancy had edged Evan out by deciding at the last minute to "help" them get along. At first awkward and unconfident with children, Michael Sherman could well have developed a "downstairs" retreat had it not been for Adrienne's showdown and continual invitation to join in the care of their twins. Often, something as simple as the way a mother holds her baby so he or she can "look at Dad" indicates her effort to share. Adrienne Sherman didn't just leave her twins with Daddy; she talked to them about what Daddy could do with them; consciously or not, she fostered a tie to him. She didn't play expert. She made room.

As a result, such men were—or became—sensitive to their children's needs. They were more realistic than other fathers about the limits of what their wives provide, and about what their children really need.

Limiting the Idea of Fatherhood

Involved fathers had a much fuller, more elaborate notion of what a father was than uninvolved fathers did. Involved fathers talked about fathering much as mothers talked about mothering. Uninvolved fathers held to a far more restricted mission—to discipline the child or to teach him about sports. For example, when asked what he thought was important about being a father, one black businessman and father of two said:

> Discipline. I don't put up with whining. It bothers me. I'm shorter tempered and my wife is longer tempered. I do a significant amount of paddling. I grew up with being paddled. When I got paddled I knew damn good and well that I deserved it. I don't whip them. One good pop on their bottom and I send them down to their room. I've scared them. I've never punched them. And I'll spank them in front of people as well as not in front of them.

To him, being a disciplinarian *was* being a father. As a result, his children gravitated to their mother. She had worked for an insurance company but, under the pressure of home and work, finally quit her job. In a strangely matter-of-fact way, she remarked that she didn't "feel comfortable" leaving the children with her husband for long periods. "If I go out to the hairdresser's on Saturday, I might come back and find he didn't fix them lunch; I don't leave them with him too much." If it wasn't a matter of discipline, he didn't think caring for children was his job.

Other fathers limited their notion of fathering mainly to teaching their children about the events in the newspaper, baseball, soccer. When I asked uninvolved fathers to define a "good mother" and "good father," they gave elaborate and detailed answers for "good mother," and short, hazy answers for "good father," sometimes with a specific mission attached to it, like "teach them about cars."

I asked one man, "What's a good mother?" and he answered: "A good mother is patient. That's the first thing. Someone who is warm, caring, who can see what the child needs, physically, who stimulates the child intellectually, and helps the child meet his emotional challenges."

"What is a good father?" I asked. "A good father is a man who spends time with his children." Another man said, "A good father is a man who is around."

It is not that men have an elaborate idea of fatherhood and then don't live up to it. Their idea of fatherhood is embryonic to begin with. They often limit that idea by comparing themselves only to their own fathers and not, as more involved men did, to their mothers or sisters, or to other fathers. As a Salvadoran delivery man put it, "I give my children everything my father gave me." But Michael Sherman gave his twins what his *mother* gave him.

Curtailing the Idea of What a Child Needs

Men who were greatly involved with their children react against two cultural ideas: one idea removes the actual care of children from the definition of *manhood*, and one curtails the notion of how much care a child needs. As to the first idea, involved fathers' biggest struggle was against the doubts they felt about not "giving everything to get ahead" in their jobs. But even when they conquered this fear, another cultural idea stood in the way—the idea that their child is "already grown-up," "advanced," and doesn't need much from him. A man's individual defense against seeing his children's need for him conspires with this larger social idea.

Just as the archetype of the supermom—the woman who can do it all— minimizes the real needs of women, so too the archetype of the "superkid" minimizes the real needs of children. It makes it all right to treat a young child as if he or she were older. Often uninvolved parents remarked with pride that their small children were "self-sufficient" or "very independent."

I asked the fifth-grade teacher in a private school how she thought her students from two-job families were doing. She began by saying that they did as well as the few children she had whose mothers stayed home. But having said that, her talk ran to the problems: "The good side of kids being on their own so much is that it makes them independent really early. But I think they pay a price for it. I can see them sealing off their feelings, as if they're saying, 'That's the last time I'll be vulnerable.' I can see it in their faces, especially the sixth-grade boys."

Throughout the second half of the nineteenth century, as women were increasingly excluded from the workplace, the cultural notion of what a child "needs" at home correspondingly grew to expand the woman's role at home.

As Barbara Ehrenreich and Deirdre English point out in *For Her Own Good*, doctors and ministers argued strongly that a woman's place was at home. The child needed her there. As the economic winds have reversed, so has the idea of a woman's proper place—and the child's real needs. Nowadays, a child is increasingly imagined to need time with other children, to need "independence-training," not to need "quantity time" with a parent but only a small amount of "quality time." As one working father remarked: "Children need time to play with other children their age. It's stimulating for them. Nelson enjoyed it, I think, from when he was six months."

If in the earlier part of the century, middle-class children suffered from overattentive mothers, from being "mother's only accomplishment," today's children may suffer from an underestimation of their needs. Our idea of what a *child* needs in each case reflects what *parents* need. The child's needs are thus a cultural football in an economic and marital game.

An Orwellian "superkid" language has emerged to consolidate this sense of normality. In a September 1985 *New York Times* article entitled "New Programs Come to Aid of Latch Key Children," Janet Edder quotes a child-care professional as follows: "Like other child-care professionals, Mrs. Selgison prefers to use the phrase 'Children in Self Care' rather than 'Latch Key Children,' a term coined during the depression when many children who went home alone wore a key around their necks." "Children in Self Care" suggests that the children *are* being cared for, but by themselves, independently. Unlike the term "Latch Key Children," which suggests a child who is sad and deprived, the term "Children in Self Care" suggests a happy superkid.

Another article, in the August 1984 *Changing Times*, entitled "When You Can't Be Home, Teach Your Child What to Do," suggests that working parents do home-safety checkups so that a pipe won't burst, a circuit breaker won't blow, or an electrical fire won't start. Parents should advise children to keep house keys out of sight and to conceal from callers the fact that they're alone at home. It tells about "warm lines"—a telephone number a child can call for advice or simple comfort when he or she is alone. Earlier in the century, advice of this sort was offered to destitute widows or working wives of disabled or unemployed men while the middle class shook its head in sympathy. Now the middle class has "children in self-care" too.

The parents I talked to had younger children, none of whom were in "self-care." The children I visited seemed to me a fairly jolly and resilient lot. But parents I spoke to did not feel very supported in their parenthood; like Ann Myerson, many parents in the business world felt obligated to hide concerns that related to a child. Many female clerical workers were discouraged from making calls home. Many men felt that doing anything for family reasons—moving to another city, missing the office party, passing up a promotion—would be taken as a sign they lacked ambition or manliness. As for John Livingston's coworkers, the rule of thumb was: don't go home until your wife calls.

For all the talk about the importance of children, the cultural climate has become subtly less hospitable to parents who put children first. This is not because parents love children less, but because a "job culture" has expanded at the expense of a "family culture."

As motherhood as a "private enterprise" declines and more mothers rely on the work of lower-paid specialists, the value accorded the work of mothering (not the value of children) has declined for women, making it all the harder for men to take it up.

My Wife Is Doing It

Involved fathers are aware that their children depend on them. Every afternoon Art Winfield knew Adam was waiting for him at daycare. Michael Sherman knew that around six A.M. one of his twins could call out "Daddy." John Livingston knew that Cary relied on him to get around her mother's discipline. Such men were close enough to their children to know what they were and weren't getting from their mothers.

Uninvolved fathers were not. They *imagined* that their wives did more with the children than they did. For example, one thirty-two-year-old grocery clerk praised his wife for helping their daughter with reading on the weekends—something his wife complained he didn't make time for. But when I interviewed her, I discovered that her weekends were taken with housework, church, and visiting relatives.

Sometimes I had the feeling that fathers were passing the childcare buck to their wives while the wives passed it to the baby-sitter. Each person passing on the role wanted to feel good about it, and tended to deny the problems. Just as fathers often praised their wives as "wonderful mothers," so mothers often praised their baby-sitters as "wonderful." Even women who complain about daycare commonly end up describing the daycare worker as "great." So important to parents was the care of their child that they almost had to believe that "everything at daycare was fine." Sadly, not only was the role of caretaker transferred from parent to baby-sitter, but sometimes also the illusion that the child was "in good hands."

The reasons men gave for why their wives were wonderful—for example, that they were patient—were often reasons women gave for why the baby-sitters were wonderful. Just as uninvolved fathers who praised their wives often said they wouldn't want to trade places with their wives, so wives often said they wouldn't want to trade places with their daycare worker.

As one businesswoman and mother of a three-year-old boy commented: "Our baby-sitter is just fantastic. She's with the kids from seven o'clock in the morning until six o'clock at night. And some kids stay later. I don't know how she does it. *I* couldn't." Another working mother commented: "I couldn't be as patient as Elizabeth [the daycare worker] is. I love my child, but I'm not a baby person."

The daycare worker herself was often in a difficult spot. She depended economically on the parents, so she didn't want to say anything so offensive it might lead them to withdraw the child. On the other hand, sometimes she grew concerned about a child's behavior. Typical of many daycare workers, Katherine Wilson, who had cared for children for fifteen years, remarked:

> One out of five parents just drop their children off and run. Another three will come in and briefly talk with you. Then the last person will come in and talk to you quite a bit. Not too many call during the day. A lot of parents aren't too concerned with day-to-day activities. They just trust we know what we're doing.

Some daycare centers even established a policy of check-in sheets that required parents to come inside the daycare center and sign their child in each morning, thus preventing the hurried few who might otherwise leave their children off at the sidewalk.

Pickup time was often hectic, and not a good time to talk. As one daycare worker observed:

> It's a hell of a life the parents lead. Every time I see them they're in a rush. It's rush in the morning and rush in the evening. They barely ask me what Danny had for lunch or how he seemed. I think they might feel bad when they see him around four o'clock in the afternoon. He gets kind of restless then. He's waiting. He sees the parents of the other children come and each time the doorbell rings he hopes its his parents. But, see, they come in the last—six-thirty.

Sometimes a daycare worker becomes worried about a child. As Alicia Fernandez confided:

> I've had Emily for a year and a half now. She's never been real open with me and I don't think she is with her mother either. I think, in a way, Emily was hurt that her former sitter had to give her up. It was a hard adjustment coming in to me and in fact I don't think she has adjusted. One day she took the money out of my wallet—the money her mother had given me—and tore it up. I was so shocked. It was my pay. I slapped her across the knees. She didn't even cry. I felt bad I'd done that, but even worse that she didn't even cry. I thought, hey, something's wrong.

Had she mentioned this to Emily's mother and father? I asked. She replied quickly and quietly: "Oh no. It's hard to talk about that. I feel badly about it but on the other hand if I told her mother, she might take Emily away."

The daycare worker, who could best judge how Emily's day had gone, felt afraid to confide her concerns to Emily's parents, who badly needed to hear them. Other daycare workers also kept their opinions to themselves. As another daycare worker noted: "You can feel sorry for them. I have Tim for nine hours. I have Jessica for ten and a half—now Jessie's mother is a single mother. Like I say, at the end of the day they cry." "Do you talk to their parents about the crying?" I asked. "They don't ask, and I don't bring it up." She continued, echoing a thought other daycare workers expressed as well:

Don't get me wrong. These children are adaptable, They're pliant. As long as there's a sense of love here and as long as you feed them, they know I'm the one who satisfies their needs. That's all I am to them. The children love me and some little children, like Nelson, don't want to go home. He's three now, but I've had him since he was seven months old; Stephanie's three and I've had her since she was six weeks. But I do feel sorry for the children, I do. Because I know there are days when they probably don't feel like coming here, especially Mondays.

When daycare workers feel sorry for the children they care for, something is wrong. This woman, a thirty-year-old black mother of three, was gentle and kindly, a lovely person to care for children. What seemed wrong to me was the overly long hours, the blocked channels of communication, and the fathers who imagined their wives were "handling it all."

A Father's Influence

In a time of stalled revolution—when women have gone to work, but the workplace, the culture, and most of all, the men, have not adjusted themselves to this new reality—children can be the victims. Most working mothers are already doing all they can, doing that extra month a year. It is men who can do more.

Fathers can make a difference that shows in the child. I didn't administer tests to the children in the homes I visited nor gather systematic information on child development. I did ask the baby-sitters and daycare workers for their general impressions of differences between the children of single parents, two-job families in which the father was uninvolved, and two-job families in which the father was actively involved. All of them said that the children of fathers who were actively involved seemed to them "more secure" and "less anxious." Their lives were less rushed. On Monday, they had more to report about Sunday's events: "Guess what I did with my dad. . . ."

But curiously little attention has been paid to the effect of fathers on children. Current research focuses almost exclusively on the influence on children of the working *mother*. A panel of distinguished social scientists chosen by the National Academy of Sciences to review the previous research on children of working mothers concluded in 1982 that a mother's employment has no consistent ill effects on a child's school achievement, IQ, or social and emotional development. Other summary reviews offer similar but more complex findings. For example, in charting fifty years of research on children of working mothers, Lois Hoffman, a social psychologist at the University of Michigan, has concluded that most girls of all social classes and boys from working-class families, whose mothers worked, were more self-confident and earned better grades than children whose mothers were housewives. But she also found that compared to the sons of housewives, middle-class boys raised by working mothers were less confident and did less well in school. But what about the influence of the fathers?

Apart from my study, other systematic research has documented a fact one might intuitively suspect: the more involved the father, the better developed the child intellectually and socially. Professor Norma Radin and her students at the University of Michigan have conducted a number of studies that show that, all else being equal, the children of highly involved fathers are better socially and emotionally adjusted than children of noninvolved fathers and score higher on academic tests. In Professor Radin's research, "highly involved" fathers are those who score in the top third on an index comprised of questions concerning responsibility for physical care (e.g., feeding the children), responsibility for socializing the child (e.g., setting limits), power in decision-making regarding the child, availability to the child, and an overall estimate of his involvement in raising his preschooler. In one study of fifty-nine middle-class families with children between the ages of three and six, Professor Radin found that highly involved fathers had sons who were better adjusted and more socially competent, more likely to perceive themselves as masters of their fate, and a higher mental age on verbal intelligence tests. A 1985 study by Abraham Sagi found Israeli children of highly involved fathers to be more empathetic than other children.

A 1985 comprehensive and careful study by Carolyn and Phil Cowan, two psychologists at the University of California, Berkeley, found that three-and-a-half-year-old children of involved fathers achieved higher scores on certain playroom tasks (classifying objects, putting things in a series, role-taking tasks) than other children. When fathers worked longer hours outside the home, the Cowans found in their observation sessions, the three-and-a-half-year-olds showed more anxiety. The daughters of long-hours men were, in addition, less warm and less task oriented at playroom tasks, although they had fewer behavior problems. When fathers worked long hours, mothers tended to "compensate" by establishing warm relations with their sons. But when mothers worked long hours, husbands did not "compensate" with their daughters. In spite of this, the girls did well in playroom tasks. When fathers *or* mothers worked more outside the home, the parent established a closer bond with the *boy*.

Finally, the results of active fatherhood seem to last. In one study, two psychologists asked male undergraduates at the University of Massachusetts, Amherst, to respond to such statements as "My father understood my problems and worries and helped with them, hugged or kissed me goodnight when I was small, was able to make me feel better when I was upset, gave me a lot of care and attention." They were also asked to describe his availability ("away from home for days at a time, . . . out in the evening at least two nights a week, . . . home afternoons when children came home from school," and so on). The young men who ranked their fathers highly—or even moderately—

nurturant and available were far more likely to describe themselves as "trusting, friendly, loyal, and dependable, industrious and honest."

In the end, caring for children is the most important part of the second shift, and the effects of a man's care or his neglect will show up again and again through time—in the child as a child, in the child as an adult, and probably also in the child's own approach to fatherhood, and in generations of fathers to come. Active fathers are often in reaction against a passive detached father, a father like Seth Stein. But an exceptionally warmhearted man, like the step-father of Art Winfield, could light the way still better. In the last forty years, many women have made a historic shift, into the economy. Now it is time for a whole generation of men to make a second historic shift—into work at home.

38 India's Sacred Cow

MARVIN HARRIS

Although its form varies widely from one culture to another, religion is
one of humanity's fundamental social institutions. A generation ago,
some "experts" predicted that with the rise of science and the secular-
ization of U.S. culture religion would fade quietly into the background.
On the contrary, religion is as vital for Americans today as it was in the
past. Church membership is even higher now than at any time in U.S.
history. Tens of millions of Americans continue to seek solace in religion. They look to religion for answers to many of the perplexing questions that social life poses and that science cannot answer.

Like the other social institutions, religion is interconnected with
the other parts of society. It sometimes is difficult to recognize these
interconnections when we refer to our own religion, for we tend to
focus on its smaller aspects, such as our own congregation, synagogue,
or mosque. It often is easier to see this point, however, when we look
at unfamiliar religions, those whose practices are far removed from our
experiences. There, since we are not immersed in taken-for-granted
assumptions, we may be prompted to ask basic questions. For example,
why are cows allowed to wander India's city streets and country roads?
Why don't deprived and hungry Indians kill them? Essential interconnections between religion and culture become evident as Harris analyzes such questions.

NEWS PHOTOGRAPHS that came out of India during the famine
of the late 1960s showed starving people stretching out bony hands to beg for
food while sacred cattle strolled behind undisturbed. The Hindu, it seems,
would rather starve to death than eat his cow or even deprive it of food. The
cattle appear to browse unhindered through urban markets eating an orange
here, a mango there, competing with people for meager supplies of food.

By Western standards, spiritual values seem more important to Indians
than life itself. Specialists in food habits around the world like Fred Simons at
the University of California at Davis consider Hinduism an irrational ideology
that compels people to overlook abundant, nutritious foods for scarcer, less
healthful foods.

What seems to be an absurd devotion to the mother cow pervades Indian
life. Indian wall calendars portray beautiful young women with bodies of fat
white cows, often with milk jetting from their teats into sacred shrines.

Cow worship even carries over into politics. In 1966 a crowd of 120,000 people, led by holy men, demonstrated in front of the Indian House of Parliament in support of the All-Party Cow Protection Campaign Committee. In Nepal, the only contemporary Hindu kingdom, cow slaughter is severely punished. As one story goes, the car driven by an official of a United States agency struck and killed a cow. In order to avoid the international incident that would have occurred when the official was arrested for murder, the Nepalese magistrate concluded that the cow had committed suicide.

Many Indians agree with Western assessments of the Hindu reverence for their cattle, the zebu, or *Bos indicus,* a large-humped species prevalent in Asia and Africa. M.N. Srinivas, an Indian anthropologist, states: "Orthodox Hindu opinion regards the killing of cattle with abhorrence, even though the refusal to kill vast number of useless cattle which exist in India today is detrimental to the nation." Even the Indian Ministry of Information formerly maintained that "the large animal population is more a liability than an asset in view of our land resources." Accounts from many different sources point to the same conclusion: India, one of the world's great civilizations, is being strangled by its love for the cow.

The easy explanation for India's devotion to the cow, the one most Westerners and Indians would offer, is that cow worship is an integral part of Hinduism. Religion is somehow good for the soul, even it if sometimes fails the body. Religion orders the cosmos and explains our place in the universe. Religious beliefs, many would claim, have existed for thousands of years and have a life of their own. They are not understandable in scientific terms.

But all this ignores history. There is more to be said for cow worship than is immediately apparent. The earliest Vedas, the Hindu sacred texts from the second millennium B.C., do not prohibit the slaughter of cattle. Instead, they ordain it as part of sacrificial rites. The early Hindus did not avoid the flesh of cows and bulls; they ate it at ceremonial feasts presided over by Brahman priests. Cow worship is a relatively recent development in India; it evolved as the Hindu religion developed and changed.

This evolution is recorded in royal edicts and religious texts written during the last 3,000 years of Indian history. The Vedas from the first millennium B.C. contain contradictory passages, some referring to ritual slaughter and others to a strict taboo on beef consumption. A.N. Bose, in *Social and Rural Economy of Northern India,* 600 B.C.–200 A.D., concludes that many of the sacred-cow passages were incorporated into the texts by priests of a later period.

By 200 A.D. the status of Indian cattle had undergone a spiritual transformation. The Brahman priesthood exhorted the population to venerate the cow and forbade them to abuse it or to feed on it. Religious feasts involving the ritual slaughter and consumption of livestock were eliminated and meat eating was restricted to the nobility.

By 1000 A.D., all Hindus were forbidden to eat beef. Ahimsa, the Hindu belief in the unity of all life, was the spiritual justification for this restriction. But it is difficult to ascertain exactly when this change occurred. An important event that helped to shape the modern complex was the Islamic invasion, which took place in the eighth century A.D. Hindus may have found it politically expedient to set themselves off from the invaders, who were beefeaters, by emphasizing the need to prevent the slaughter of their sacred animals. Thereafter, the cow taboo assumed its modern form and began to function much as it does today.

The place of the cow in modern India is every place—on posters, in the movies, in brass figures, in stone and wood carvings, on the streets, in the fields. The cow is a symbol of health and abundance. It provides the milk that Indians consume in the form of yogurt and ghee (clarified butter), which contribute subtle flavors to much spicy Indian food.

This, perhaps, is the practical role of the cow, but cows provide less than half the milk produced in India. Most cows in India are not dairy breeds. In most regions, when an Indian farmer wants a steady, high-quality source of milk he usually invests in a female water buffalo. In India the water buffalo is the specialized dairy breed because its milk has a higher butterfat content than zebu milk. Although the farmer milks his zebu cows, the milk is merely a by-product.

More vital than zebu milk to South Asian farmers are zebu calves. Male calves are especially valued because from bulls come oxen, which are the mainstay of the Indian agricultural system.

Small, fast oxen drag wooden plows through late-spring fields when monsoons have dampened the dry, cracked earth. After harvest, the oxen break the grain from the stalk by stomping through mounds of cut wheat and rice. For rice cultivation in irrigated fields, the male water buffalo is preferred (it pulls better in deep mud), but for most other crops, including rainfall rice, wheat, sorghum, and millet, and for transporting goods and people to and from town, a team of oxen is preferred. The ox is the Indian peasant's tractor, thresher, and family car combined; the cow is the factory that produces the ox.

If draft animals instead of cows are counted, India appears to have too few domesticated ruminants, not too many. Since each of the 70 million farms in India require a draft team, it follows that Indian peasants should use 140 million animals in the fields. But there are only 83 million oxen and male water buffalo on the subcontinent, a shortage of 30 million draft teams.

In other regions of the world, joint ownership of draft animals might overcome a shortage, but Indian agriculture is closely tied to the monsoon rains of late spring and summer. Field preparation and planting must coincide with the rain, and a farmer must have his animals ready to plow when the weather is right. When the farmer without a draft team needs bullocks most, his neighbors are all using theirs. Any delay in turning the soil drastically lowers production.

Because of this dependence on draft animals, loss of the family oxen is devastating. If a beast dies, the farmer must borrow money to buy or rent an ox at interest rates so high that he ultimately loses his land. Every year foreclosures force thousands of poverty-stricken peasants to abandon the countryside for the overcrowded cities.

If a family is fortunate enough to own a fertile cow, it will be able to rear replacements for a lost team and thus survive until life returns to normal. If, as sometimes happens, famine leads a family to sell its cow and ox team, all ties to agriculture are cut. Even if the family survives, it has no way to farm the land, no oxen to work the land, and no cows to produce oxen.

The prohibition against eating meat applies to the flesh of cows, bulls, and oxen, but the cow is the most sacred because it can produce the other two. The peasant whose cow dies is not only crying over a spiritual loss but over the loss of his farm as well.

Religious laws that forbid the slaughter of cattle promote the recovery of the agricultural system from the dry Indian winter and from periods of drought. The monsoon, on which all agriculture depends, is erratic. Sometimes, it arrives early, sometimes late, sometimes not at all. Drought has struck large portions of India time and again in this century, and Indian farmers and the zebus are accustomed to these natural disasters. Zebus can pass weeks on end with little or no food and water. Like camels, they store both in their humps and recuperate quickly with only a little nourishment.

During drought the cows often stop lactating and become barren. In some cases the condition is permanent but often it is only temporary. If barren animals were summarily eliminated, as Western experts in animal husbandry have suggested, cows capable of recovery would be lost along with those entirely debilitated. By keeping alive the cows that can later produce oxen, religious laws against cow slaughter assure the recovery of the agricultural system from the greatest challenge it faces—the failure of the monsoon.

The local Indian governments aid the process of recovery by maintaining homes for barren cows. Farmers reclaim any animal that calves or begins to lactate. One police station in Madras collects strays and pastures them in a field adjacent to the station. After a small fine is paid, a cow is returned to its rightful owner when the owner thinks the cow shows signs of being able to reproduce.

During the hot, dry spring months most of India is like a desert. Indian farmers often complain they cannot feed their livestock during this period. They maintain the cattle by letting them scavenge on the sparse grass along the roads. In the cities the cattle are encouraged to scavenge near food stalls to supplement their scant diet. These are the wandering cattle tourists report seeing throughout India.

Westerners expect shopkeepers to respond to these intrusions with the deference due a sacred animal; instead, their response is a string of curses and the crack of a long bamboo pole across the beast's back or a poke at its genitals. Mahatma Gandhi was well aware of the treatment sacred cows (and bulls and oxen) received in India. "How we bleed her to take the last drop of milk from her. How we starve her to emaciation, how we ill-treat the calves, how we deprive them of their portion of milk, how cruelly we treat the oxen, how we castrate them, how we beat them, how we overload them" [Gandhi, 1954].

Oxen generally receive better treatment than cows. When food is in short supply, thrifty Indian peasants feed their working bullocks and ignore their cows, but rarely do they abandon the cows to die. When cows are sick, farmers worry over them as they would over members of the family and nurse them as if they were children. When the rains return and when the fields are harvested, the farmers again feed their cows regularly and reclaim their abandoned animals. The prohibition against beef consumption is a form of disaster insurance for all India.

Western agronomists and economists are quick to protest that all the functions of the zebu cattle can be improved with organized breeding programs, cultivated pastures, and silage. Because stronger oxen would pull the plow faster, they could work multiple plots of land, allowing farmers to share their animals. Fewer healthy, well-fed cows could provide Indians with more milk. But pastures and silage require arable land, land needed to produce wheat and rice.

A look at Western cattle farming makes plain the cost of adopting advanced technology in Indian agriculture. In a study of livestock production in the United States, David Pimentel of the College of Agriculture and Life Sciences at Cornell University, found that 91 percent of the cereal, legume, and vegetable protein suitable for human consumption is consumed by livestock. Approximately three quarters of the arable land in the United States is devoted to growing food for livestock. In the production of meat and milk, American ranchers use enough fossil fuel to equal more than 82 million barrels of oil annually.

Indian cattle do not drain the system in the same way. In a 1971 study of livestock in West Bengal, Stewart Odend'hal [1972] of the University of Missouri found that Bengalese cattle ate only the inedible remains of subsistence crops—rice straw, rice hulls, the tops of sugar cane, and mustard-oil cake. Cattle graze in the fields after harvest and eat the remains of crops left on the ground; they forage for grass and weeds on the roadsides. The food for zebu cattle costs the human population virtually nothing. "Basically," Odend'hal says, "the cattle convert the items of little direct human value into products of immediate utility."

In addition to plowing the fields and producing milk, the zebus produce dung, which fires the hearths and fertilizes the fields of India. Much of the estimated 800 million tons of manure produced annually is collected by the farmers' children as they follow the family cows and bullocks from place to place. And when the children see the droppings of another farmer's cattle along the road, they pick those up also. Odend'hal reports that the system operates with such high efficiency that the children of West Bengal recover nearly 100 percent of the dung produced by their livestock.

From 40 to 70 percent of all manure produced by Indian cattle is used as fuel for cooking; the rest is returned to the fields as fertilizer. Dried dung burns slowly, cleanly, and with low heat—characteristics that satisfy the household needs of Indian women. Staples like curry and rice can simmer for hours. While the meal slowly cooks over an unattended fire, the women of the household can do other chores. Cow chips, unlike firewood, do not scorch as they burn.

It is estimated that the dung used for cooking fuel provides the energy-equivalent of 43 million tons of coal. At current prices, it would cost India an extra 1.5 billion dollars in foreign exchange to replace the dung with coal. And if the 350 million tons of manure that are being used as fertilizer were replaced with commercial fertilizers, the expense would be even greater. Roger Revelle of the University of California at San Diego has calculated that 89 percent of the energy used in Indian agriculture (the equivalent of about 140 million tons of coal) is provided by local sources. Even if foreign loans were to provide the money, the capital outlay necessary to replace the Indian cow with tractors and fertilizers for the fields, coal for the fires, and transportation for the family would probably warp international financial institutions for years.

Instead of asking the Indians to learn from the American model of industrial agriculture, American farmers might learn energy conservation from the Indians. Every step in an energy cycle results in a loss of energy to the system. Like a pendulum that slows a bit with each swing, each transfer of energy from sun to plants, plants to animals, and animals to human beings involves energy losses. Some systems are more efficient than others; they provide a higher percentage of the energy inputs in a final, useful form. Seventeen percent of all energy zebus consume is returned in the form of milk, traction, and dung. American cattle raised on Western rangeland return only 4 percent of the energy they consume.

But the American system is improving. Based on techniques pioneered by Indian scientists, at least one commercial firm in the United States is reported to be building plants that will turn manure from cattle feedlots into combustible gas. When organic matter is broken down by anaerobic bacteria, methane gas and carbon dioxide are produced. After the methane is cleansed of the carbon dioxide, it is available for the same purposes as natural gas—cooking, heating, electric generation. The company constructing the biogasification plant plans to sell its product to a gas-supply company, to be piped through the existing distribution system. Schemes similar to this one could make cattle ranches almost independent of utility and gasoline companies; for methane can be used to run trucks, tractors, and cars as well as to supply heat and electricity. The relative energy self-sufficiency that the Indian peasant has achieved is a goal American farmers and industry are now striving for.

Studies of Odend'hal's understate the efficiency of the Indian cow, because dead cows are used for purposes that Hindus prefer not to acknowledge. When a cow dies, an Untouchable, a member of one of the lowest ranking castes in India, is summoned to haul away the carcass. Higher castes consider the body of the dead cow polluting; if they handle it, they must go through a rite of purification.

Untouchables first skin the dead animal and either tan the skin themselves or sell it to a leather factory. In the privacy of their homes, contrary to the teachings of Hinduism, untouchable castes cook the meat and eat it. Indians of all castes rarely acknowledge the existence of these practices to non-Hindus, but most are aware that beefeating takes place. The prohibition against beefeating restricts consumption by the higher castes and helps distribute animal protein to the poorest sectors of the population that otherwise would have no source of these vital nutrients.

Untouchables are not the only Indians who consume beef. Indian Muslims and Christians are under no restriction that forbids them beef, and its consumption is legal in many places. The Indian ban on cow slaughter is state, not national, law and not all states restrict it. In many cities, such as New Delhi, Calcutta, and Bombay, legal slaughterhouses sell beef to retail customers and to restaurants that serve steak.

If the caloric value of beef and the energy costs involved in the manufacture of synthetic leather were included in the estimate of energy, the calculated efficiency of Indian livestock would rise considerably. As well as the system works, experts often claim that its efficiency can be further improved. Alan Heston [et al., 1971], an economist at the University of Pennsylvania, believes that Indians suffer from an overabundance of cows simply because they refuse to slaughter the excess cattle. India could produce at least the same number of oxen and the same quantities of milk and manure with 30 million fewer cows. Heston calculates that only 40 cows are necessary to maintain a population of 100 bulls and oxen. Since India averages 70 cows for every 100 bullocks, the difference, 30 million cows, is expendable.

What Heston fails to note is that sex ratios among cattle in different regions of India vary tremendously, indicating that adjustments in the cow population do take place. Along the Ganges River, one of the holiest shrines of Hinduism, the ratio drops to 47 cows for every 100 male animals. This ratio reflects the preference for dairy buffalo in the irrigated sectors of the Gangetic Plains. In nearby Pakistan, in contrast, where cow slaughter is permitted, the sex ratio is 60 cows to 100 oxen.

Since the sex ratios among cattle differ greatly from region to region and do not even approximate the balance that would be expected if no females were killed, we can assume that some culling of herds does take place; Indians do adjust their religious restrictions to accommodate ecological realities.

They cannot kill a cow but they can tether an old or unhealthy animal until it has starved to death. They cannot slaughter a calf but they can yoke it with a large wooden triangle so that when it nurses it irritates the mother's udder and gets kicked to death. They cannot ship their animals to the slaughterhouse but they can sell them to Muslims, closing their eyes to the fact that the Muslims will take the cattle to the slaughterhouse.

These violations of the prohibition against cattle slaughter strengthen the premise that cow worship is a vital part of Indian culture. The practice arose to prevent the population from consuming the animal on which Indian agriculture depends. During the first millennium B.C., the Gange Valley became one of the most densely populated regions of the world.

Where previously there had been only scattered villages, many towns and cities arose and peasants farmed every available acre of land. Kingsley Davis, a population expert at the University of California at Berkeley, estimates that by

300 B.C. between 50 million and 100 million people were living in India. The forested Ganges Valley became a windswept semidesert and signs of ecological collapse appeared; droughts and floods became commonplace, erosion took away the rich topsoil, farms shrank as population increased, and domesticated animals became harder and harder to maintain.

It is probable that the elimination of meat eating came about in a slow, practical manner. The farmers who decided not to eat their cows, who saved them for procreation to produce oxen, were the ones who survived the natural disasters. Those who ate beef lost the tools with which to farm. Over a period of centuries, more and more farmers probably avoided beef until an unwritten taboo came into existence.

Only later was the practice codified by the priesthood. While Indian peasants were probably aware of the role of cattle in their society, strong sanctions were necessary to protect zebus from a population faced with starvation. To remove temptation, the flesh of cattle became taboo and the cow became sacred.

The sacredness of the cow is not just an ignorant belief that stands in the way of progress. Like all concepts of the sacred and the profane, this one affects the physical world; it defines the relationships that are important for the maintenance of Indian society.

Indians have the sacred cow, we have the "sacred" car and the "sacred" dog. It would not occur to us to propose the elimination of automobiles and dogs from our society without carefully considering the consequences, and we should not propose the elimination of zebu cattle without first understanding their place in the social order of India.

Human society is neither random nor capricious. The regularities of thought and behavior called culture are the principal mechanisms by which we human beings adapt to the world around us. Practices and beliefs can be rational or irrational, but a society that fails to adapt to its environment is doomed to extinction. Only those societies that draw the necessities of life from their surroundings without destroying those surroundings inherit the earth. The West has much to learn from the great antiquity of Indian civilization, and the sacred cow is an important part of that lesson.

References

Gandhi, Mohandas K. 1954. *How to Serve the Cow*. Bombay: Navajivan Publishing House.

Heston, Alan, et al. 1971. "An Approach to the Sacred Cow of India." *Current Anthropology* 12, 191–209.

Odend'hal, Stewart. 1972. "Gross Energetic Efficiency of Indian Cattle in Their Environment." *Journal of Human Ecology* 1, 1–27.

39 The World of the Hospital

DANIEL F. CHAMBLISS

To most of us, the distinction between professionals and non-professionals is vague. But not to sociologists, who view professionals as people who have been rigorously educated in the theory underlying their work. In addition, professionals are self-regulated; that is, they establish the criteria for entering the profession, oversee and evaluate the performance of their members, and discipline their rule breakers. Professionals also exercise authority over their clients: Being the expert, the professional tells the client what to do. Supposedly at least, professionals are also motivated by service to society rather than by self-interest. Certainly this is an idealized list of traits, and various groups of workers can be classified as having "more" or "less" of these characteristics.

Sociologists view medicine as the prime example of a profession, stressing how it exhibits these characteristics the best of any group. In this article, we get to look over the shoulder of medical professionals as they do their work. From this analysis, it becomes clear why the professional's view veers so sharply from that of the client. What for the patient is an emergency, is for physicians and nurses only routine—another part of their daily work. Chambliss' analysis helps us understand how, for professionals, even tragedy can become routine.

How the Hospital Is Different

... MUCH [IN A HOSPITAL] is the same as in other organizations: the daily round of paper processing, answering the phone, making staffing decisions, collecting bills, ordering supplies, stocking equipment rooms; there are fights between departments, arguments with the boss, workers going home tired or satisfied. And medical sociology has made much of these similarities, using its research to create broader theories of, for instance, deviance or of the structure of professions.

But in one crucial respect the hospital remains dramatically different from other organizations: *in hospitals, as a normal part of the routine, people suffer and die.* This is unusual. "[A] good working definition of a hospital is that place where death occurs and no one notices; or, more sharply, the place where others agree to notice a death as a social fact only so far as it fits their particular purposes." Only combat military forces share this feature. To be complete, theories of hospital life need to acknowledge this crucial difference, since adapting themselves to pain and death is for hospital workers the most distinctive feature of their work. It is that which most separates them from the rest of us. In building theories of organizational life, sociologists must try to see how hospitals resemble other organizations . . . but we should not make a premature leap to the commonalities before appreciating the unique features of hospitals that make a nurse's task so different from that of a teacher or a businessman or a bureaucrat.

A quick survey of typical patients in one Surgical Intensive Care Unit on one Saturday evening should make the point. The words in brackets are additions to my original field notes:

Room 1. 64-year-old white woman with an aortic valve replacement: five separate IMEDs [intravenous drip-control devices] feeding in nitroglycerine, vasopressors, Versed [a pain killer which also blocks memory]. Chest tube [to drain off fluids]. On ventilator [breathing machine], Foley [catheter in the bladder], a pulse oximeter on her finger, a[rterial monitoring] line. Diabetic. In one 30-second period during the night, her blood pressure dropped from $160/_{72}$ to $95/_{50}$, then to $53/_{36}$, before the nurse was able to control the drop. N[urse]s consider her "basically healthy."

Room 2. Man with pulmonary artresia, pulmonary valvotomy [heart surgery].

Room 3. Woman with CABG [coronary artery bypass graft; a "bypass operation"]. Bleeding out [i.e., hemorrhaging] badly at one point during the night, they sent her back to the OR [Operating Room]. On heavy vasopressors [to keep blood pressure up].

Room 4. Older woman with tumor from her neck up to her temple. In OR from 7 a.m. until 2 a.m. the next morning having it removed. Infarct [dead tissue] in the brain.

Room 5. 23-year-old woman. MVA [motor vehicle accident]. ICP [intracranial pressure—a measure of brain swelling] measured—terrible. Maybe organ donor. [Patient died next day.]

Room 6. Don't know.

Room 7. Abdominal sepsis, possibly from surgery. DNR [Do Not Resuscitate] today.

Room 8.   Big belly guy [an old man with a horribly distended abdomen, un-controllable. Staff says it's from poor sterile technique in surgery by Dr. M., who is notoriously sloppy. This patient died within the week.] [Field Notes]

This is a typical patient load for an Intensive Care Unit. Eight beds, three patients dead in a matter of days. "Patients and their visitors often find the ICU to be a disturbing, even terrifying place. Constant artificial light, cease-less activity, frequent emergencies, and the ever-present threat of death create an atmosphere that can unnerve even the most phlegmatic of patients. Some are so sick that they are unaware of their surroundings or simply forget the ex-perience, but for others the ICU is a nightmare remembered all too well," On floors—the larger, less critical care wards of the hospital—fatalities are less common, and patients are not so sick; even so, one-third of the patients may have AIDS, another one-third have cancer, and the rest suffer a variety of seri-ous if not immediately lethal diseases. The ICUs just get patients whose deaths are imminent.

It is interesting that this density of disease presents one of the positive at-tractions of nursing. People don't become nurses to avoid seeing suffering or to have a quiet day. Everyday nurses respond to and share the most intense emotions with total strangers. "People you don't know are going through the most horrible things, and you are supposed to help them. That's intense," says one nurse. And another enthuses about coming home as the sun is coming up; the rest of the world thinks things are just starting, and here you're coming off a big emergency that lasted half the night: "[T]here's a real adrenaline kick in all this stuff. If you deny that, you're denying a big part of [nursing]."

The abnormality of the hospital scene liberates the staff from some niceties of everyday life and allows them a certain freedom. . . . Two small, even silly, examples may illustrate the point. (1) Many nurses wear scrub suits—the pajama-like pants and tops worn in operating rooms and on some units. Written on the suits are phone numbers, vital statistics, or even doodles drawn during surgery. It's more convenient than finding a piece of paper. One observer, Judith André, has commented, "It's like a childhood fantasy" to scribble things on your clothes. (2) During a "code," as a patient was being re-suscitated, one nurse who was having her period began to leak menstrual fluid. She ran into the patient's bathroom to change her sanitary pad. When she came out, another nurse seeing the stain on her pants, yelled, "Well, J. got her period!"—a comment unthinkable in the everyday world. But this isn't the everyday world. As Everett Hughes (1958: 79) wrote, "All occupations—most of all those considered professions and perhaps those of the underworld—in-clude as part of their very being a licence to deviate in some measure from common modes of behavior." In this sense, the hospital is like a war zone, in which common niceties and rules of decorum are discarded in the pursuit of some more immediate, desperate objective. There is an excitement, and a pressure, that frees hospital workers in the "combat zone" from an array of normal constraints on what they say and do.

And yet, for them their work has become normal, routine. On a medical floor, with perhaps two-thirds of the patients suffering eventually fatal diseases, I say to a nurse, "What's happening?" and she replies, walking down the hall, "Same ol' same ol'. Nothing new, nothing exciting." Or an Intensive Care Unit in the same hospital, "What's going on?" The resident replies, with a little shrug of the shoulders, "People are living, people are dying." Again, no surprises, nothing new. The routine goes on.

As other writers have noted, the professional treats routinely what for the patient is obviously not routine. For the health worker, medical procedures happen to patients every day, and the hospital setting is quite comfortable: "The staff nurse . . . belongs to a world of relative health, youth, and bustling activity. She may not yet have experienced hospitalization herself for more than the removal of tonsils or the repair of a minor injury. Although she works in an environment of continuous sickness, she has been so conditioned to its external aspects that she often expresses surprise when someone suggests that the environment must be anxiety evoking." (Brown 1966: 202). Everett Hughes's (1958: 54, 88) formulation of this divergence of experience is classic: "In many occupations, the workers or practitioners . . . deal routinely with what are emergencies to the people who receive their services. This is a source of chronic tension between the two." Or, more precisely, "[O]ne man's routine of work is made up of the emergencies of other people."

To the patient, though, the hospital world is special, frightening, a jarring break from the everyday world. For the nurse, it's just the "same ol' same ol'." How extreme the gap is was observed in an ICU one evening:

> Three residents were attempting an LP [lumbar puncture—a "spinal tap" in which a long needle is inserted into the spinal column to draw out spinal fluid]. This is a very painful procedure and is difficult to perform. The television over the foot of the patient's bed was turned on, and "LA Law" was playing. While the resident was inserting the needle, she kept glancing up at the television, trying to simultaneously watch the show and do the LP. The patient, curled into the fetal position to separate the vertebrae, was unaware of this. The other two residents as well were glancing back and forth from procedure to television. The resident tried for several minutes drawing out blood instead of fluid. Eventually, she called the head resident, who came in and successfully finished the LP. [Field Notes].

This illustrates how casual staff can become, to the point of malfeasance.

How do staff, nurses in particular, routinize the abnormal? Or more fundamentally, what do we even mean by routinization?

What Routinization Entails: The Operating Room

The most egregious violation of commonsense morality—the profound physical violation of another person's body—is made completely routine in the hospital operating room. To help the reader understand routinization, we will consider this example in some detail.

In large teaching hospitals like Northern General or Southwest Regional, there are some twelve to twenty operating rooms in the "OR suite," with the rooms organized in a long hallway around a central equipment and supply area. The entire suite is "sterile," that is, everyone coming in and out wears scrub suits and face masks, shoe covers, and hair bonnets. Each operating room is furnished with a narrow padded table on which the patient lies during surgery, as well as with huge movable overhead lights and rolling tables for equipment of all sorts. Certain rooms are typically reserved for cardiac, neurological, orthopedic, and other special types of surgery, and the peculiar equipment for each of these is always available in those rooms. There are also one or two "crash rooms," for emergency surgery of the sort associated with the automobile wrecks or shootings frequently seen in large urban medical centers. Each room may be scheduled for one to six operations in a day; several dozen surgeries are scheduled for the hospital each weekday morning, usually starting at 6:00 and running until 2:00 or so in the afternoon.

Nurses manage these rooms between operations, supervising the flow of patients and the resupply of equipment (sponges, surgical tools, clean linens, etc.), answering the telephone or intercom and letting the physicians know when it is time to begin. There are typically at least two such nurses, the "scrub nurse" who assists the surgeon, handing tools and dealing directly with the sterile field, and the "circulating nurse" who can move in and out of the OR, touch nonsterile areas (such as the telephone), and keep the supplies flowing as needed to the surgical team. The circulating nurse is a kind of stage manager and fills in as needed, solving problems arising outside the surgery itself.

During surgery, the circulating nurse has several duties. First, she must document everything that happens: the time when surgery begins, what specific procedures are being conducted, what personnel are participating, when the procedure is done and "closing" begins, and when the patient is wheeled out of the room. Working together with the scrub nurse, she repeatedly counts and recounts the number of "sponges" (absorbent pads) used in the operation (there may be dozens). She must account for all of them, both before and after the operation, to ensure that none are mistakenly left in the patient's body. She does the same for the surgical needles used, making certain that all are accounted for and disposed of properly, a serious concern since the advent of AIDS. The best circulating nurses, it would seem, are precise to the point of obsessiveness. The scrub nurse shares in these duties, counting sponges and accounting for all equipment, as well as passing to the surgeon, quickly and reliably, the specific tools needed at different stages of the operation. The scrub nurse also "preps" the patient: she drapes the patient with sterile cloths, leaving bare the shaved area to be cut open, disinfecting the body surface with an iodine solution, and covering the skin with a clear plastic film called "Opsite" which protects the uncut area. A screen of cloth is usually set up between the patient's head and the rest of the body, so conscious patients will not see what's going on. This also means that the operating area is detached from the patient as a person, an important feature of the scene. The nurses carry out routine tasks dozens of times in a single day—for instance, the one-by-one counting of sponges, carried with tongs from a table to a waste bucket, perhaps two dozen of them counted aloud. The failure to perform these tasks conscientiously could be disastrous.

Once both room and patient are "prepped," the medical team can begin. The patient's body, fundamentally, is transformed into an object. An anesthesiologist (a physician), or a nurse anesthetist, will administer either a spinal anesthetic, which numbs the body below the injection point on the spinal cord, or a general anesthetic, which puts the patient to sleep. From then on, the operative area, screened from the patient's head and deadened of all feeling, effectively becomes to the surgeons a piece of nonhuman meat. The target area is isolated and immobilized; the patient is either asleep or, with a spinal, may be chatting away up at the head of the table with the anesthesiologist. In one case, a man's leg was being removed at one end of the table while at the other he was telling the anesthesiologist about his recent vacation trip. Looking at the operating area, the skin being cut or bone being sawed, you think, "No one I know has ever looked like this." Anesthetized flesh doesn't respond as the flesh of a living human being would. In amputations, the flesh being removed is usually dead and looks it—dark, hard, lifeless. But living flesh, too, on the table, looks more like what it "objectively" is, that is, meat. Human fat looks like the chicken fat you see on the stove; human skin peels back the way a chicken's does when peeled. An old man's tanned skin, when cut, looks like leather—which, precisely speaking, it is: old, tanned, animal skin. Surgeons working inside the body cavity remind one of cooks stuffing the Thanksgiving turkey, pulling open a section here, pushing a hand deep inside, feeling around for something there, stretching back tendons, trimming the fat, snipping pieces here and there with a small pair of scissors. The fine details of surgery are remarkably complex and refined, but its basic principles are brutally simple:

> To amputate this diabetic lady's toes, Dr. R., a small woman, used a thing like a big pair of bolt cutters to actually cut the bones, one toe at a time—with the big toe she had some difficulty, and she was almost lifted off the floor squeezing the big handles together before the "crunch" and the blades snapped through the toe. Then the last flesh was snipped away and five toes, all together, like a section of beef or chicken, came off in a single piece, and the scrub nurse laid it into a specimen tray. [Field Notes]

This primitive business is executed with simple tools: a razor-edge knife to cut open the skin (the scalpel); scissors to trim away flesh inside the body; smooth hooks to pull back the skin while the operation is under way (retractors); needle-nose pliers to shut off blood vessels (hemostats); and a small electric probe, essentially a soldering iron, used to cauterize the open ends of small blood vessels (the "Bovie"). Tools come in many sizes and specialized shapes, but this is the basic array. Orthopedic surgery adds its various saws, drills, and bits; the equipment table looks like a bench in an immaculate hobbyist's workshop, which in a sense it is.

To the senior staff, these tools and their uses become commonplace. During one routine orthopedic operation (routine for the staff, not for the patient), a group of young residents were working on a teenage patient's shoulder. The supervising attending physician, nominally in charge, popped in occasionally during the three-hour operation to see how things were going. On one visit he stopped for fifteen minutes to flip through the "swimsuit issue" of *Waterski* magazine, which one of the residents had brought. His pointed air of "no big deal" was more than casual; it seemed almost an assertion of his own power and sophistication, contrasted with the barely concealed anxiety of the residents he was monitoring. When he left, the residents visibly relaxed and resumed openly discussing how to perform the operation. One actually shuttled back and forth to a table against the wall to look at the diagrams in his textbook to see how the surgery should be done. Then the attending anesthesiologist came in to check on his resident and to sign a form ("So I'll get my cut," he said smiling) and walked out again. Music by popular musicians Phil Collins and Los Lobos was on a portable tape cassette player as the residents worked. The residents were learning to do highly skilled surgery and how to regard it as part of everyday life.

Routinization in the OR or elsewhere in the hospital seems to mean that actions are repeated, and that they violate normal taboos. Each operation is not the first of its kind; most in fact are done several times each day and hundreds of times each year, even by a single team of surgeons, nurses, and technical aides. What the team sees, they have seen many times. Gallbladder removals, hernia repairs and shoulder operations on athletes—these are all very common procedures in the major medical center.

And those repeated procedures take place against the even less dramatic background of the repeated daily events of the nurse's work: starting intravenous lines, taking blood pressure four times a day on every patient on the floor, drawing blood samples, charting vital signs, writing nurses' progress notes, passing food trays, helping patients on and off the bedpan. Both trivial and consequential activities are repeated over and over until each one becomes much like the next; indeed, as Hughes (1958: 54) says, the professional's "very competence comes from having dealt with a thousand cases of what the client likes to consider his unique experience." Says one nurse, "You get to the point where you don't really care for the patients anymore and one GI [gastrointestinal] bleeder gets to be the same as the next GI bleeder."

In a Medical Intensive Care Unit, death itself becomes an often-repeated event:

Another MICU patient just coded and died; that's five in the past six days. Incredible. The docs are here one month—N[urse]s are here for good . . .

I just came in unit; first N[urse] says, "You just missed it." They said that to me a few days ago. It's not that I "just miss," I think, but rather that so much [is] going on. You'll always "just miss" something. [Field Notes]

Death becomes a routinized part of daily life, incorporated into the flow. "Mr. Smith died last night," says one nurse to another. "Oh, that's too bad. He was such a nice man"; a casual exchange. One day is like another, if not for Mr. Smith, then at least for the rest of us. For the nurses, Mr. Smith will be replaced by another man, a Mr. Jones, with similar ailments and a similar end. . . .

After a middle-aged woman died late one night in room 5 of a medical ICU, her family, loudly crying and hugging each other, came into the room to see their dead mother. Outside the room, three nurses who had tried for thirty minutes to resuscitate the patient sat around a table eating corn chips and gossiping, as if nothing had happened. One of those nurses said to me, "We're pretty dehumanized, huh?" But it wasn't true: if she were dehumanized no such comment would even be made. She knew what was happening, and eating corn chips, even then, is in fact quite human. In a unit where three patients die each week, to get upset with every death would be humanly unacceptable.

Sometimes routinization goes beyond mere commonplace into an attitude of detachment, unconcern, or sheer boredom—one of the more common emotions of the nurse's life, to the surprise of laypersons. Indeed, one of the most frequent questions nurses asked me during my research was, "Aren't you bored?" . . .

How Routinization Is Accomplished: Creating Conditions for Ordinary Life

Thus, for the nurse, hospital life is ordinary—not extraordinary, or mystical, or even an object of thoughtful scrutiny. This is what we mean by saying the nurse has routinized the world of the hospital. Her life here has taken on a quality of mundane sameness, often to the point of sheer boredom.

The first time I had to interview a patient in my first year of nursing school, he said he had a scar [on his chest]. I asked to see it, he just pulled up his gown [around his neck; she gestures to show how he was bare]. I was . . . [rolls her eyes, embarrassed] "Oh, my God." And now . . . [waves her hand, flutters eyes to indicate her totally blasé attitude]. [Field Notes]

No layperson would experience such exposure so casually. And nudity is simple; witnessing open heart surgery, or an endotracheal intubation, or CPR, is far more threatening to one's everyday reality. But nurses see these events every day, without becoming upset. The nurse's view—or more accurately, the nurse's very way of *living* here and dealing with such trauma—is different from ours.

How does this casual attitude develop? How does this abnormal become routine? The conventional answer is that "you just get used to it." This implies that over time, with enough exposure, one adapts, willy-nilly, to whatever is happening in the environment. This may be true, but it is insufficient. "Getting used to it" suggests that routinization is purely a matter of the passage of time, with repetition as the implied causative agent. Yes, routinization happens "over time," but time alone is insufficient to cause routinization. Some nurses never become accustomed, as we will see, to deformed newborns, or psychotic teenagers, or incontinent geriatric patients. Then, too, some people "get used to it" virtually immediately. Before my own first witnessing of surgery, I conscientiously followed all the head nurse's instructions to avoid physical or emotional upset: I rose early, ate a full breakfast, and was wide awake before going to the OR suite. After donning the scrub suit, bonnet, and shoe covers, I went into the OR and asked the circulating nurse what the first case would be, hoping for something "easy," maybe a wrist or ankle operation. She looked at the chart and said, without missing a beat, "leg amputation." I nearly panicked, but I stayed. To my own amazement, I was not in the least upset by the amputation or any of the surgeries I witnessed, including the repair of a ruptured ectopic pregnancy that drove at least two experienced nurses from the OR in dismay. For some reason, there seemed to be no period of "getting used to it" at all. So repeated exposure as a means of routinization is insufficient; more is at work.

At least four phenomenological tasks go into the routinization of the hospital world: learning one's geographical surroundings, so that the routine is physically manageable; learning the language so one can meet and work with other people; learning the technique of the work being done (if you don't know how to start an IV, it's hard to be casual about it); and learning the "types" of patients and standard procedures for recognizing and dealing with them. . . . There is also, harder to define, a fifth task, a perceptual "leap," which I will describe after presenting these components. . . .

1. *Learning the geography.*   The first step in the routinization of a world is simply to learn one's way around the physical setting. It's difficult to be casual when rooms are unfamiliar, hallways look long and forbidding, and one can't find the bathroom. Supplies are often kept in unexpected places, telephones sometimes work in strange ways ("You have to dial 8 first"), even chairs may have traditional claims on them (until recently in American hospitals, nurses stood while physicians sat). Hospital beds come in various models, and working them isn't always easy.

This geography has social meanings and implications too, which must be learned. One has to know that "this is Joanne's chair," or that the clerk always gets the phone, or that everyone cleans their own coffee cup. The physical setting, that is, must be known in its social ramifications. . . .

2. *Learning the language.* To move easily in the world of the hospital, the nurse must learn its peculiar language, the technical jargon, and the informal slang. The jargon is technically complex, even daunting. DNR: an order to Do Not Resuscitate a terminal patient when his or her breathing or heartbeat stops. CABG: pronounced "Cabbage," a coronary artery bypass graft, what the layperson calls bypass surgery. Or consider this description of the possible causes of one common symptom.

> [It is found] accompanying diaphragmatic pleurisy, pneumonia, uremia, or alcoholism . . . abdominal causes include disorders of the stomach, and esophagus, bowel diseases, pancreatitis, pregnancy, bladder irritation, hepatic metastases, or hepatitis. Thoracic and mediastinal lesions or surgery may be responsible. Posterior fossa tumors or infarcts may stimulate centers in the medulla oblongata . . . [Merck 1987: 1356–1357]

Pity the poor layperson who overhears such language to discuss his or her symptom—which in this case is hiccups.

Besides medical jargon, informal slang is highly developed, as the staff live in an experiential world far different than the layperson. Here, a dying patient is "going down the tubes," "circling the drain." The dead have "bought the farm," "straight-lined," or perhaps "Marshalled"—a reference to the name of the building that houses the morgue. An older patient who violently resists the nurses is "confused" and after drug sedation becomes much more "appropriate." Every emergency room has its "Gomers"—one of the most ubiquitous cases of hospital slang, derived from "Grand Old Man of the ER," or variants, and referring generically to old people with no treatable problems who are virtually permanent residents of the hospital. On the acute psychiatric unit, there is the "quiet room": what once was called a padded cell, where a suicidal teenage girl huddles in the corner, crying, visible through the peephole in the door. The patient is regularly technicized in discussions of "input" and "output" (of food and waste). Learning the peculiar language is a vital part of becoming an insider. To understand what people are talking about, much less to become comfortable here, you need to learn the slang. And even when no special jargon is used, the very matter-of-factness of the talk can be disarming: "Well, he had a stool; it was soft, but he said there was some diarrhea." Most of us simply don't talk in that way with fellow workers.

3. *Learning the techniques.* Routinization requires learning the techniques of one's work: the job itself must be familiar. One reason that I was immediately "used to" seeing surgery was that I was only observing it, not participating. Observing is a skill at which, as a sociologist, I have had much practice. There was no further technical learning necessary.

Nursing entails a great number of specific technical skills, and until one learns them the job can be overwhelming. "Being organized" is a prime job skill for nurses. The staff nurse dispenses hundreds of pills a day to dozens of patients, starts and maintains intravenous lines, gives bed baths, documents on paper virtually everything she does, monitors temperatures, blood pressures, and urine "outputs," delivers food trays, and responds more or less to all the miscellaneous patient and family requests that, from her point of view, often get in the way of her finishing her basic required work. Simply getting through an eight-hour shift without mistakenly giving Mrs. Jones the pills for Ms. Smith, or forgetting to check Mr. Martin's IV line, or not helping Miss Garcia eat her lunch is challenge enough. And these are the everyday, nonemergency tasks, the basics of the job.

4. *Learning the patients.* Patient types, too, become routine to the nurse. Despite an outsider's first impression of a multitude of different medical problems, most patients suffer one of a fairly small number of predictable ailments: cancer, heart disease, COPD (chronic obstructive pulmonary disease, such as emphysema or bronchitis), and now AIDS. These cover most of the severe cases. Treatments are relatively predictable as well, from the nursing staff's perspective: surgery, intravenous therapy, the usual medications. In heart disease, there are perhaps a half-dozen routinely used drugs; for cancer, there is surgery and the usual chemotherapy or radiation. So patients quickly become typed: the COPD lady in room 8, the AIDS guy in 2. . . .

An advantage of being used to seeing pain is that one can then work with suffering people. The "detached concern" that Merton writes about allows a nurse to lose the embarrassment many of us feel in front of sick people and allows her to talk with sick or dying patients. A dying woman can tell a nurse her fears; she may hesitate to burden a friend with them. A nurse, one may believe, has seen it all, so seeing one more thing perhaps won't upset her. It's probably true. One nurse told me that a friend said to her, "My dad is on oxygen!" and she, the nurse, thought to herself, "What would these people think if they saw someone in the unit with IV lines, an NG [nasogastric] tube, chest tubes, a catheter stuck in the bladder, and another tube stuck up the rectum? Ye gods, everyone I *know* is on oxygen!" She has become familiar with the patients.

Having learned the geography of the hospital, the language, the techniques of work, and the types of patients, a nurse is well prepared to convert what was a chaos of disasters into a routine, well-organized round of daily activities.

5. *Routinization of the world.* But learning the specifics of the job—the geography, the jargon, the techniques, the patients—does not automatically produce an acceptance of the hospital world as normal. Some nurses learn the techniques but still never accept the daily disasters; they leave the profession,

or move to less acute care settings, working in a school, a physician's office, or perhaps a home health care agency. More is demanded than simply accruing new information about work, or people, or the setting. Routinization itself demands a qualitative transformation in one's thinking, an entirely new way of relating to events and people. It can happen suddenly. Some nurses say that after six months or so on the job, having struggled through the heavy demands, often near to despair, one day they realize that the work no longer bothers them; they are "into" it.

> When I [first] walked into that unit, I had never seen any of these machines . . . there are 15,000 machines, they all have different alarms, they all have different ways to work them, different trouble-shooting things, and here you are expected to take care of this patient who's crumping every minute . . . it's just overwhelming.
>
> And then all of a sudden, one day, you say, Gee, I've survived this shift, and all of these things happened, and it was OK. . . .
>
> [So what happened that you got used to it?]
>
> You know, I have absolutely no idea . . . You go in and you do it again and again, and your patient codes for the fifth time . . . I can't even tell you when it happens, it's different for different people . . .
>
> Then the scary thing happens. You start to *like* it. [Field Notes]

What this nurse describes is not just a gradual transition over time, not a simple accumulation of experiences that finally equals "getting used to it." The accumulation of experiences is part of it, to be sure. But these only make possible the major shift, a qualitative transformation of consciousness, a *routinization of the world*. It is as if one takes the proverbial journey of a thousand single steps and discovers that the final step is in fact a fifteen-foot jump over a deep mountain gorge. Without the final leap, the journey is incomplete, almost a waste. But even that analogy doesn't quite fit, since many nurses "jump the gorge" without ever realizing what they have done. Usually, it just happens ("How did you get used to it?" "I have absolutely no idea."). Still, it is the nurse who "does" this happening, who makes the leap, even if subconsciously. . . .

References

Brown, Esther Lucille, "Nursing and Patient Care," in Fred Davis, *The Nursing Profession: Five Sociological Essays* (New York: John Wiley & Sons, 1966), p. 202.

Hughes, E. C., *Men and Their Work* (Westport, CT: Greenwood Press, 1958), p. 79.

The Merck Manual of Diagnosis and Therapy, 15th ed. (Rahway, NJ: Merck Sharp & Dohme Research Laboratories, 1987). pp. 1356–1357.

40 Police Accounts of Normal Force

JENNIFER HUNT

My personal contacts with the police have been infrequent and brief. Nevertheless, I have seen a policeman handcuff a rape suspect to a tree and then slap him in the face in front of a group of citizen-witnesses. I have heard another threaten the life of a suspect he was escorting near a stream, saying he wished the suspect would attempt to flee so he "could shoot her and watch her body float down the river." And in Mexico, after recovering my billfold and apprehending the two men who had picked my pocket, the secret police offered to hold the culprits while I beat them. They felt that I *ought* to beat them because, as they said, the men had caused me (and presumably them) so much trouble. (I didn't, in case you are wondering.)

These events have convinced me that police violence is no random matter but is a regular part of the occupation. Sociological research bears this out. Why should this be? Is it because the police recruit people with sadistic tendencies? As a sociologist, Hunt does not look for explanations lodged *within* people, such as "personality types." Rather, she examines the occupational culture, *external* conditions that affect people's orientations, in this instance how occupational norms influence the behavior and attitudes of recruits.

If you were a social reformer and you wanted to decrease police violence, where would you start? Keep in mind what Hunt found—the virtual absence of differences by gender, the distinction between formal and informal expectations, and the strong support for "normal" violence that is built into this occupation—and the lessons from the Zimbardo experiment in Part VI.

THE POLICE ARE REQUIRED to handle a variety of peacekeeping and law enforcement tasks including settling disputes, removing drunks from the street, aiding the sick, controlling crowds, and pursuing criminals. What unifies these diverse activities is the possibility that their resolution might require the use of force. Indeed, the capacity to use force stands at the core of the police mandate (Bittner, 1980). . . . The following research . . . explores how police themselves classify and evaluate acts of force as either legal, normal, or excessive. Legal force is that coercion necessary to subdue, control, and restrain a suspect in order to take him into custody. Although force not accountable in legal terms is technically labeled excessive by the courts and the public, the police perceive many forms of illegal force as normal. Normal force involves coercive acts that specific "cops" on specific occasions formulate as necessary, appropriate, reasonable, or understandable. Although not always legitimated or admired, normal force is depicted as a necessary or natural response of normal police to particular situational exigencies. . . . Brutality is viewed as illegal, illegitimate, and often immoral violence, but the police draw the lines in extremely different ways and at different points [from] either the court system or the public. . . .

The article is based on approximately eighteen months of participant observation in a major urban police department referred to as the Metro City P.D. I attended the police academy with male and female recruits and later rode with individual officers in one-person cars on evening and night shifts in high crime districts.[1] The female officers described in this research were among the first 100 women assigned to the ranks of uniformed patrol as a result of a discrimination suit filed by the Justice Department and a policewoman plaintiff.

Learning to Use Normal Force

The police phrase "it's not done on the street the way that it's taught at the academy" underscores the perceived contradiction between the formal world of the police academy and the informal world of the street. This contradiction permeates the police officer's construction of his world, particularly his view of the rational and moral use of force.

In the formal world of the police academy, the recruit learns to account for force by reference to legality. He or she is issued the regulation instruments and trained to use them to subdue, control, and restrain a suspect. If threatened with great bodily harm, the officer learns that he can justifiably use deadly force and fire his revolver. Yet the recruit is taught that he cannot use his baton, jack, or gun unnecessarily to torture, maim, or kill a suspect.

When recruits leave the formal world of the academy and are assigned to patrol a district, they are introduced to an informal world in which police recognize normal as well as legal and brutal force. Through observation and instruction, rookies gradually learn to apply force and account for its use in terms familiar to the street cop. First, rookies learn to adjust their arsenals to conform to street standards. They are encouraged to buy the more powerful weapons worn by veteran colleagues as these colleagues point out the inadequacy of a wooden baton or compare their convoy jacks to vibrators. They quickly discover that their department-issued equipment marks them as new recruits. At any rate, within a few weeks, most rookies have dispensed with the wooden baton and convoy jack and substituted . . . the more powerful plastic nightstick and flat-headed slapjack.[2]

Through experience and informal instruction, the rookie also learns the street use of these weapons. In school, for example, recruits are taught to avoid hitting a person on the head or neck because it could cause lethal damage. On the street, in contrast, police conclude that they must hit wherever it causes the most damage in order to incapacitate the suspect before they themselves are harmed. New officers also learn that they will earn the respect of their veteran co-workers not by observing legal niceties in using force, but by being "aggressive" and using whatever force is necessary in a given situation.

Peer approval helps neutralize the guilt and confusion that rookies often experience when they begin to use force to assert their authority. One female officer, for example, learned she was the object of a brutality suit while listening to the news on television. At first, she felt so mortified that she hesitated to go to work and face her peers. In fact, male colleagues greeted her with a standing ovation and commented, "You can use our urinal now." In their view, any aggressive police officer regularly using normal force might eventually face a brutality suit or civilian complaint. Such accusations confirm the officer's status as a "street cop" rather than an "inside man" who doesn't engage in "real police work."

Whereas male rookies are assumed to be competent dispensers of force unless proven otherwise, women are believed to be physically weak, naturally passive, and emotionally vulnerable.[3] Women officers are assumed to be reluctant to use physical force and are viewed as incompetent "street cops" until they prove otherwise. As a result, women rookies encounter special problems in learning to use normal force in the process of becoming recognized as "real street cops." It becomes crucial for women officers to create or exploit opportunities to display their physical abilities in order to overcome sexual bias and obtain full acceptance from co-workers. As a result, women rookies are encouraged informally to act more aggressively and to display more machismo than male rookies. . . .

For a street cop, it is often a graver error to use too little force and develop a "shaky" reputation than it is to use too much force and be told to calm down. Thus officers, particularly rookies, who do not back up their partners in appropriate ways or who hesitate to use force in circumstances where it is deemed necessary are informally instructed regarding their aberrant ways. If the problematic incident is relatively insignificant and his general reputation is good, a rookie who "freezes" one time is given a second chance before becoming generally known as an untrustworthy partner. However, such incidents become the subject of degrading gossip, gossip that pressures the officer either to use force as expected or risk isolation. Such talk also informs rookies about the general boundaries of legal and normal force.

For example, a female rookie was accused of "freezing" in an incident that came to be referred to as a "Mexican standoff." A pedestrian had complained that "something funny is going on in the drugstore." The officer walked into the pharmacy where she found an armed man committing a robbery. Although he turned his weapon on her when she entered the premises, she still pulled out her gun and pointed it at him. When he ordered her to drop it, claiming that his partner was behind her with a revolver at her head, she refused and told him to drop his.[4] He refused, and the stalemate continued until a sergeant entered the drugstore and ordered the suspect to drop his gun.

Initially, the female officer thought she had acted appropriately and even heroically. She soon discovered, however, that her hesitation to shoot had brought into question her competence with some of her fellow officers. Although many veterans claimed that "she had a lot a balls" to take her gun out at all when the suspect already had a gun on her, most contended "she shoulda shot him." Other policemen confirmed that she committed a "rookie mistake"; she had failed to notice a "lookout" standing outside the store and hence had been unprepared for an armed confrontation. Her sergeant and lieutenant, moreover, even insisted that she had acted in a cowardly manner, despite her reputation as a "gung-ho cop," and cited the incident as evidence of the general inadequacy of policewomen.

In the weeks that followed, this officer became increasingly depressed and angry. She was particularly outraged when she learned that she would not receive a commendation, although such awards were commonly made for "gun pinches" of this nature. Several months later, the officer vehemently expressed the wish that she had killed the suspect and vowed that next time she would "shoot first and ask questions later." The negative sanctions of supervisors and colleagues clearly encouraged her to adopt an attitude favorable to using force with less restraint in future situations. . . .

At the same time that male and female rookies are commended for using force under appropriate circumstances, they are reprimanded if their participation in force is viewed as excessive or inappropriate. In this way, rookies are instructed that although many acts of coercion are accepted and even demanded, not everything goes. They thereby learn to distinguish between normal and brutal force. . . .

Accounting for Normal Force

Police routinely normalize the use of force by two types of accounts: excuses and justifications. . . .

EXCUSES AND NORMAL FORCE

Excuses are accounts in which police deny full responsibility for an act but recognize its inappropriateness. Excuses therefore constitute socially approved vocabularies for relieving responsibility when conduct is questionable. Police most often excuse morally problematic force by referring to emotional or physiological states that are precipitated by some circumstances of routine patrol work. These circumstances include shootouts, violent fights, pursuits, and instances in which a police officer mistakenly comes close to killing an unarmed person.

Police work in these circumstances can generate intense excitement in which the officer experiences the "combat high" and "adrenaline rush" familiar to the combat soldier.[5] Foot and car pursuits not only bring on feelings of danger and excitement from the chase, but also a challenge to official authority. As one patrolman commented about a suspect: "Yeh, he got tuned up [beaten] . . . you always tune them up after a car chase." Another officer normalized the use of force after a pursuit in these terms:

> It's my feeling that violence inevitably occurs after a pursuit. . . . The adrenaline . . . and the insult involved when someone flees increases with every foot of the pursuit. I know the two or three times that I felt I lost control of myself . . . was when someone would run on me. The further I had to chase the guy the madder I got. . . . The funny thing is the reason for the pursuit could have been something as minor as a traffic violation or a kid you're chasing who just turned on a fire hydrant. It always ends in violence. You feel obligated to hit or kick the guy just for running.

Police officers also excuse force when it follows an experience of helplessness and confusion that has culminated in a temporary loss of emotional control. This emotional combination occurs most frequently when an officer comes to the brink of using lethal force, drawing a gun and perhaps firing, only to learn there were no "real" grounds for this action. The officer may then "snap out" and hit the suspect.[6] In one such incident, for example, two policemen picked up a complainant who positively identified a suspect as a man who just tried to shoot him. Just as the officers approached the suspect, he suddenly reached for his back pocket for what the officers assumed to be a gun. One officer was close enough to jump the suspect before he pulled his hand from his pocket. As it turned out, the suspect had no weapon, having dropped it several feet away. Although he was unarmed and under control, the suspect was punched and kicked out of anger and frustration by the officer who had almost shot him.

Note that in both these circumstances—pursuit and near-miss mistaken shootings—officers would concede that the ensuing force is inappropriate and unjustifiable when considered abstractly. But although abstractly wrong, the use of force on such occasions is presented as a normal, human reaction to an extreme situation. Although not every officer might react violently in such circumstances, it is understandable and expected that some will.

SITUATIONAL JUSTIFICATIONS

Officers also justify force as normal by reference to interactional situations in which an officer's authority is physically or symbolically threatened. [In contrast to excuses, which deny responsibility for the act but recognize that the act is blameworthy, justifications accept responsibility for the act but deny that the act is blameworthy.—Ed.] In such accounts, the use of force is justified instrumentally—as a means of regaining immediate control in a situation where that control has become tenuous. Here, the officer depicts his primary intent for using force as a need to reestablish immediate control in a problematic encounter, and only incidentally as hurting or punishing the offender.

Few officers will hesitate to assault a suspect who physically threatens or attacks them. In one case, an officer was punched in the face by a prisoner he had just apprehended for allegedly attempting to shoot a friend. The incident occurred in the stationhouse, and several policemen observed the exchange. Immediately, one officer hit the prisoner in the jaw and the rest immediately joined the brawl.

Violations of an officer's property such as his car or hat may signify a more symbolic assault on the officer's authority and self, thus justifying a forceful response to maintain control. Indeed, in the police view, almost any person who verbally challenges a police officer is appropriately subject to force. . . .

On rare occasions, women officers encounter special problems in these regards. Although most suspects view women in the same way as policemen, some seem less inclined to accord female officers *de facto* and symbolic control in street encounters, and on a few occasions seem determined to provoke direct confrontations with such officers, explicitly denying their formal authority and attempting none too subtly to sexualize the encounter. Women officers, then, might use force as a resource for rectifying such insults and for establishing control over such partially sexualized interactions. Consider the following woman officer's extended account providing such situational justifications for the use of force:

> . . . I'm sitting at Second Street, Second and Nassau, writing curfews up. And this silver Thunderbird . . . blows right by a stop sign where I'm sitting. And I look up and think to myself, "Now, do I want to get involved?" And I figure, it was really belligerent doing it right in front of me. So I take off after him, put my lights on and he immediately pulls over. So he jumps out of the car. I jump out of the car right away and I say, "I'm stopping you for that stop sign you just blew through. . . . Let me see your cards, please." Then he starts making these lip smacking noises at me everytime he begins to talk. He said, (smack) "The only way you're seeing my cards is if you lock me up and the only way you're gonna lock me up is if you chase me." And I said to him, "Well, look, I will satisfy you on one account. Now go to your car because I will lock you up. . . . And just sit in your car. I'll be right with you." He smacks his lips, turns around and goes to his car and he sits. And I call a wagon at Second and Nassau. They ask me what I have. I say, "I've got one to go." So as the wagon acknowledges, the car all of a sudden tears out of its spot. And I get on the air and say, "I'm in pursuit." And I give them a description of the car and the direction I'm going. . . . And all of a sudden he pulls over about a block and a half after I started the pursuit. So I got on the air and I said, "I got him at Second and Washington." I jumped out of my

car and as I jumped out he tears away again. Now I'm ready to die of embarrassment. I have to get back on the air and say no I don't have him. So I got on the air and said, "Look, he's playing games with me now. He took off again." I said, "I'm still heading South on Second Street." He gets down to Lexington. He pulls over again. Well, this time I pulled the police car in front of him. . . . I go over to the car and I hear him lock the doors. I pull out my gun and I put it right in his window. I say, "Unlock that door." Well, he looked at the gun. He nearly liked to shit himself. He unlocked the door. I holster my gun. I go to grab his arms to pull him out and all of a sudden I realize Anne's got him. So we keep pulling him out of the car. Throw him on the trunk of his car and kept pounding him back down on the trunk. She's punching his head. I'm kicking him. Then I take out my blackjack. I jack him across the shoulder. Then I go to jack him in the head and I jack Anne's fingers. . . . The next thing they know is we're throwing him bodily into the wagon. And they said, "Did you search him?" We go to the wagon, drag him out again. Now we're tearing through his pockets throwing everything on the ground. Pick him up bodily again, threw him in. . . . So I straightened it out with the sergeant. . . . I said, "What did you want me to do? Let any citizen on the street get stopped and pull away and that's the end of it?"

In this instance, a male suspect manages to convey a series of affronts to the officer's authority. These affronts become explicitly and insultingly sexual, turning the challenge from the claim that "no cop will stop me" to the more gender specific one, "no woman cop will stop me." Resistance ups the ante until the suspect backs down in the face of the officer's drawn revolver. The force to which the culprit was then subjected is normalized through all the accounts considered to this point—it is situationally justified as a means to reestablish and maintain immediate and symbolic control in a highly problematic encounter and it is excused as a natural, collective outburst following resolution of a dangerous, tension-filled incident. And finally, it is more implicitly justified as appropriate punishment, an account building upon standard police practices for abstract justification, to which I now turn.

ABSTRACT JUSTIFICATIONS

Police also justify the use of extreme force against certain categories of morally reprehensible persons. In this case, force is not presented as an instrumental means to regain control that has been symbolically or physically threatened. Instead, it is justified as an appropriate response to particularly heinous offenders. Categories of such offenders include: cop haters who have gained notoriety as persistent police antagonizers; cop killers or any person who has attempted seriously to harm a police officer (Westley, 1970:131); sexual deviants who prey on children and "moral women"; child abusers; and junkies and other "scum" who inhabit the street. The more morally reprehensible the act is judged, the more likely the police are to depict any violence directed toward its perpetrator as justifiable. Thus a man who exposes himself to children in a playground is less likely to experience police assault than one who rapes or sexually molests a child.

"Clean" criminals, such as high-level mafiosi, white-collar criminals, and professional burglars, are rarely subject to abstract force. Nor are perpetrators of violent and nonviolent street crimes who prey on adult males, prostitutes, and other categories of persons who belong on the street.[7] Similarly, the "psycho" or demented person is perceived as so mentally deranged that he is not responsible for his acts and hence does not merit abstract, punitive force (Van Maanen, 1978:233–34).

Police justify abstract force by invoking a higher moral purpose that legitimates the violation of commonly recognized standards. In one case, for example, a nun was raped by a seventeen-year-old male adolescent. When the police apprehended the suspect, he was severely beaten and his penis put in an electrical outlet to teach him a lesson. The story of the event was told to me by a police officer who, despite the fact that he rarely supported the use of extralegal force, depicted this treatment as legitimate. Indeed, when I asked if he would have participated had he been present, he responded, "I'm Catholic. I would have participated."

Excessive Force and Peer Responses

Although police routinely excuse and justify many incidents where they or their co-workers have used extreme force against a citizen or suspect, this does not mean that on any and every occasion the officer using such force is exonerated. Indeed, the concept of normal force is useful because it suggests that there are specific circumstances under which police officers will not condone the use of force by themselves or colleagues as reasonable and acceptable. Thus, officer-recognized conceptions of normal force are subject to restrictions of the following kinds:

1. Police recognize and honor some rough equation between the behavior of the suspect and the harmfulness of the force to which it is subject. There are limits, therefore, to the degree of force that is acceptable in particular circumstances. In the following incident, for example, an officer reflects on a situation in which a "symbolic assailant" (Skolnick, 1975:45) was mistakenly subject to more force than he "deserved" and almost killed:

> One time Bill Johnson and I . . . had a particularly rude drunk one day. He was really rude and spit on you and he did all this stuff and we even had to cuff him lying down on the hard stretcher, like you would do an epileptic. . . . So we were really mad. We said let's just give him one or two shots . . . slamming on the brakes and having him roll. But we didn't use our heads . . . we heard the stretcher go nnnnnBam and then nothing. We heard nothing and we realized we

had put this man in with his head to the front so when we slammed on the brakes his stretcher. . . . I guess it can roll four foot. Well, it was his head that had hit the front. . . . So, we went to Madison Street and parked. It's a really lonely area. And we unlocked the wagon and peeked in. We know he's in there. We were so scared and we look in and there's not a sound and we see blood coming in front of the wagon and think " . . . we killed this man. What am I gonna do? What am I gonna tell my family?" And to make a long story short, he was just knocked out. But boy was I scared. From then on we learned, feet first.

2. Similarly, even in cases where suspects are seen as deserving some violent punishment, this force should not be used randomly and without control. Thus, in the following incident, an officer who "snapped out" and began to beat a child abuser clearly regarded his partner's attempt to stop the beating as reasonable.

> . . . I knock on the door and a lady answers just completely hysterical. And I say, "Listen, I don't know what's going on in here," but then I hear this, just this screeching. You know. And I figure well I'm just going to find out what's going on so I just go past the lady and what's happening is that the husband had. . . . The kid was being potty trained and the way they were potty training this kid, this two-year-old boy, was that the boyfriend of this girl would pick up this kid and he would sit him down on top of the stove. It was their method of potty training. Well, first of all you think of your own kids. I mean afterwards you do. I mean I've never been this mad in my whole life. You see this little two-year-old boy seated on the top of the stove with rings around it being absolutely scalding hot. And he's saying "I'll teach you to go. . . . " It just triggered something. An uncontrollable. . . . It's just probably the most violent I ever got. Well you just grab that guy. You hit him ten, fifteen times . . . you don't know how many. You just get so mad. And I remember my partner eventually came in and grabbed me and said, "Don't worry about it. We got him. We got him." And we cuffed him and we took him down. Yeah that was bad.

Learning these sorts of restrictions on the use of normal force and these informal practices of peer control are important processes in the socialization of newcomers. This socialization proceeds both through ongoing observation and experience and, on occasion, through explicit instruction. For example, one veteran officer advised a rookie, "The only reason to go in on a pursuit is not to get the perpetrator but to pull the cop who gets there first offa the guy before he kills him."

Conclusion

The organization of police work reflects a poignant moral dilemma: For a variety of reasons, society mandates to the police the right to use force but provides little direction as to its proper use in specific, "real life" situations. Thus, the police, as officers of the law, must be prepared to use force under circumstances in which its rationale is often morally, legally, and practically ambiguous. This fact explains some otherwise puzzling aspects of police training and socialization.

The police academy provides a semblance of socialization for its recruits by teaching formal rules for using force. . . . [T]he full socialization of a police officer takes place outside the academy as the officer moves from its idealizations to the practicalities of the street. . . .

. . . [J]ustifications and excuses . . . conventionalize but do not reform situations that are inherently charged and morally ambiguous. In this way they simultaneously preserve the self-image of police as agents of the conventional order, provide ways in which individual officers can resolve their personal doubts as to the moral status of their action and those of their colleagues, and reinforce the solidarity of the police community.

Notes

1. Nonetheless masculine pronouns are generally used to refer to the police in this article, because the Metro P.D. remained dominated by men numerically, in style, and in tone. . . .

2. Some officers also substitute a large heavy duty flashlight for the nightstick. If used correctly, the flashlight can inflict more damage than the baton and is less likely to break when applied to the head or other parts of the body.

3. As the Metro City Police Commissioner commented in an interview: "In general, they [women] are physically weaker than males. . . . I believe they would be inclined to let their emotions all too frequently overrule their good judgment . . . there are periods in their life when they are psychologically unbalanced because of physical problems that are occurring within them."

4. The woman officer later explained that she did not obey the suspect's command because she saw no reflection of the partner in the suspect's glasses and therefore assumed he was lying.

5. The combat high is a state of controlled exhilaration in which the officer experiences a heightened awareness of the world around him. Officers report that perception, smell, and hearing seem acute; one seems to stand outside oneself, and the world appears extraordinarily vivid and clear. At the same time, officers insist that they are able to think rationally and instantly translate thoughts into action; when experienced, fear is not incapacitating but instead enhances the ability to act.

6. This police experience of fear and helplessness, leading to a violent outburst, may be analogized to a parent's reaction on seeing his child almost die in an accident. Imagine a scene in which a father is walking with his six-year-old son. Suddenly, the boy runs into the street to get a red ball on the pavement. The father watches a car slam on the brakes and miss the boy by two inches. He grabs his son and smacks him on the face before he takes him in his arms and holds him. . . .

7. The categories of persons who merit violence are not unique to the police. Prisoners, criminals, and hospital personnel appear to draw similar distinctions between morally unworthy persons; on the latter, see Sudnow (1967:105).

References

Bittner, E. (1980). *The Functions of the Police in Modern Society*. Cambridge, MA: Oelgeschlager, Gunn & Hain.

Hunt, J. (forthcoming). "The development of rapport through the negotiation of gender in field work among police." *Human Organization*.

Skolnick, J. (1975). *Justice Without Trial*. New York: John Wiley.

Sudnow, D. (1967). *Passing On: The Social Organization of Dying*. Englewood Cliffs, NJ: Prentice-Hall.

Van Maanen, J. (1978). "The asshole." In P. K. Manning and J. Van Maanen (eds.), *Policing: A View from the Street*. Santa Monica, CA: Goodyear.

Westley, W. A. (1970). *Violence and the Police: A Sociological Study of Law, Custom and Morality*. Cambridge, MA: MIT Press.

41 The My Lai Massacre

HERBERT KELMAN
V. LEE HAMILTON

War is a part of politics. When a nation's leaders are frustrated as they see other strategies for reaching international goals fail, war becomes a possibility. *War,* then, can be considered a technique—albeit a most violent one—to accomplish political objectives.

Nations vary in their willingness to go to war. Switzerland, for example, has vowed to never go to war, and for over 200 years has been at peace. The Swiss, however, require that their men learn to handle weapons in case another nation should attack them. The United States, in contrast, is very willing to invade other nations—in recent years Somalia, Haiti, Panama, Grenada, Desert Storm, and Bosnia. To paraphrase the Allies' slogan for World War I, "to make the world safe for capitalism" seems to be the reason for these wars. Seldom is the matter put this crassly, of course, for the goal of controlling oil, although it sells well on Wall Street, doesn't go down well on Main Street—which provides the sons (and, increasingly, the daughters) to be sacrificed on the altar of profits.

While war can bring out the best in people—such as soldiers throwing themselves onto live grenades in order to save their buddies—it often brings out the worst. *Dehumanization,* considering opponents as less than human and treating them as such, is one of the unfortunate consequences of prolonged wars. In this selection, Kelman and Hamilton analyze the case of dehumanization that received the most publicity in the war in Vietnam.

MARCH 16, 1968, WAS A BUSY DAY IN U.S. HISTORY. Stateside, Robert F. Kennedy announced his presidential candidacy, challenging a sitting president from his own party—in part out of opposition to an undeclared and disastrous war. In Vietnam, the war continued. In many ways, March 16 may have been a typical day in that war. We will probably never know. But we do know that on that day a typical company went on a mission—which may or may not have been typical—to a village called Son (or Song) My. Most of what is remembered from that mission occurred in the subhamlet known to Americans as My Lai 4.

The My Lai massacre was investigated and charges were brought in 1969 and 1970. Trials and disciplinary actions lasted until 1971. Entire books have been written about the army's year-long cover-up of the massacre (for example, Hersh, 1972), and the cover-up was a major focus of the army's own investigation of the incident. Our central concern here is the massacre itself—a crime of obedience—and public reactions to such crimes, rather than the lengths to which many went to deny the event. Therefore this account concentrates on one day: March 16, 1968.

Many verbal testimonials to the horrors that occurred at My Lai were available. More unusual was the fact that an army photographer, Ronald Haeberle, was assigned the task of documenting the anticipated military engagement at My Lai—and documented a massacre instead. Later, as the story of the massacre emerged, his photographs were widely distributed and seared the public conscience. What might have been dismissed as unreal or exaggerated was depicted in photographs of demonstrable authenticity. The dominant image appeared on the cover of *Life:* piles of bodies jumbled together in a ditch along a trail—the dead all apparently unarmed. All were Oriental, and all appeared to be children, women, or old men. Clearly there had been a mass execution, one whose image would not quickly fade.

So many bodies (over twenty in the cover photo alone) are hard to imagine as the handiwork of one killer. These were not. They were the product of what we call a crime of obedience. Crimes of obedience begin with orders. But orders are often vague and rarely survive with any clarity the transition from one authority down a chain of subordinates to the ultimate actors. The operation at Son My was no exception.

"Charlie" Company, Company C, under Lt. Col. Frank Barker's command, arrived in Vietnam in December of 1967. As the army's investigative unit, directed by Lt. Gen. William R. Peers, characterized the personnel, they "contained no significant deviation from the average" for the time. Seymour S. Hersh (1970) described the "average" more explicitly: "Most of the men in Charlie Company had volunteered for the draft; only a few had gone to college for even one year. Nearly half were black, with a few Mexican-Americans. Most were eighteen to twenty-two years old. The favorite reading matter of Charlie Company, like that of other line infantry units in Vietnam, was comic books" (p. 18). The action at My Lai, like that throughout Vietnam, was fought by a cross-section of those Americans who either believed in the war or lacked the social resources to avoid participating in it. Charlie Company was indeed average for that time, that place, and that war.

Two key figures in Charlie Company were more unusual. The company's commander, Capt. Ernest Medina, was an upwardly mobile Mexican-American who wanted to make the army his career, although he feared that he might never advance beyond captain because of his lack of formal education. His eagerness had earned him a nickname among his men: "Mad Dog Medina." One of his admirers was the platoon leader Second Lt. William L. Calley, Jr., an undistinguished, five-foot-three-inch junior-college dropout who had failed four of the seven courses in which he had enrolled his first year. Many viewed him as one of those "instant officers" made possible only by the army's then-desperate need for manpower. Whatever the cause, he was an insecure leader whose frequent claim was "I'm the boss." . . .

The Son My operation was planned by Lieutenant Colonel Barker and his staff as a search-and-destroy mission with the objective of rooting out the Forty-eighth Viet Cong Battalion from their base area of Son My village. Apparently no written orders were ever issued. Barker's superior, Col. Oran Henderson, arrived at the staging point the day before. Among the issues he reviewed with the assembled officers were some of the weaknesses of prior operations by their units, including their failure to be appropriately aggressive in pursuit of the enemy. Later briefings by Lieutenant Colonel Barker and his staff asserted that no one except Viet Cong was expected to be in the village after 7 A.M. on the following day. The "innocent" would all be at the market. Those present at the briefings gave conflicting accounts of Barker's exact orders, but he conveyed at least a strong suggestion that the Son My area was to be obliterated. As the army's inquiry reported: "While there is some conflict in the testimony as to whether LTC Barker ordered the destruction of houses, dwellings, livestock, and other foodstuffs in the Song My area, the preponderance of the evidence suggests that such destruction was implied, if not specifically directed, by his orders of 15 March" (Peers Report, in Goldstein et al., 1976, p. 94). . . .

Charlie Company's Captain Medina was briefed for the operation by Barker and his staff. He then transmitted the already vague orders to his own men. Charlie Company was spoiling for a fight, having been totally frustrated during its months in Vietnam—first by waiting for battles that never came, then by incompetent forays led by inexperienced commanders, and finally by mines and booby traps. In fact, the emotion-laden funeral of a sergeant killed by a booby trap was held on March 15, the day before My Lai. Captain Medina gave the orders for the next day's action at the close of that funeral. Many were in a mood for revenge. . . .

As March 16 dawned, much was expected of the operation by those who had set it into motion. Therefore a full complement of "brass" was present in helicopters overhead, including Barker, Colonel Henderson, and their superior, Major General Koster (who went on to become commandant of West Point before the story of My Lai broke). On the ground, the troops were to carry with them one reporter and one photographer to immortalize the anticipated battle.

The action for Company C began at 7:30 as their first wave of helicopters touched down near the subhamlet of My Lai. By 7:47 all of Company C was present and set to fight. But instead of the Viet Cong Forty-eighth Battalion, My Lai was filled with the old men, women, and children who were supposed to have gone to market. By this time, in their version of the war, and with whatever orders they thought they had heard, the men from Company C were nevertheless ready to find Viet Cong everywhere. By nightfall, the official tally was 128 VC killed and three weapons captured, although later unofficial body counts ran as high as 500. The operation at Son My was over. . . .

But what could have happened to leave American troops reporting a victory over Viet Cong when in fact they had killed hundreds of noncombatants? It is not hard to explain the report of victory; that is the essence of a cover-up. It is harder to understand how the killings came to be committed in the first place, making a cover-up necessary.

Mass Executions and the Defense of Superior Orders

Some of the atrocities on March 16, 1968, were evidently unofficial, spontaneous acts: rapes, tortures, killings. For example, Hersh (1970) describes Charlie Company's Second Platoon as entering "My Lai 4 with guns blazing" (p. 50); more graphically, Lieutenant "Brooks and his men in the second platoon to the north had begun to systematically ransack the hamlet and slaughter the people, kill the livestock, and destroy the crops. Men poured rifle and machine-gun fire into huts without knowing—or seemingly caring—who was inside" (pp. 49–50).

Some atrocities toward the end of the action were part of an almost casual "mopping-up," much of which was the responsibility of Lieutenant LaCross's Third Platoon of Charlie Company. The Peers Report states: "The entire 3rd Platoon then began moving into the western edge of My Lai (4), for the mop-up operation. . . . The squad . . . began to burn the houses in the southwestern portion of the hamlet" (Goldstein et al., 1976, p. 133). They became mingled with other platoons during a series of rapes and killings of survivors for which it was impossible to fix responsibility. Certainly to a Vietnamese, all GIs would by this point look alike: "Nineteen-year-old Nguyen Thi Ngoc Tuyet watched a baby trying to open her slain mother's blouse to nurse. A soldier shot the infant while it was struggling with the blouse, and then slashed it with his bayonet." Tuyet also said she saw another baby hacked to death by GIs wielding their bayonets. "Le Tong, a twenty-eight-year-old rice farmer, reported seeing one woman raped after GIs killed her children. Nguyen Khoa, a thirty-seven-year-old peasant, told of a thirteen-year-old girl who was raped before being killed. GIs then attacked Khoa's wife, tearing off her clothes. Before they could rape her, however, Khoa said, their six-year-old son, riddled with bullets, fell and saturated her with blood. The GIs left her alone" (Hersh, 1970, p. 72). All of Company C was implicated in a pattern of death and destruction throughout the hamlet, much of which seemingly lacked rhyme or reason.

But a substantial amount of the killing was *organized* and traceable to one authority: the First Platoon's Lt. William Calley. Calley was originally charged with 109 killings, almost all of them mass executions at the trail and other locations. He stood trial for 102 of these killings, was convicted of 22 in 1971, and at first received a life sentence. Though others—both superior and subordinate to Calley—were brought to trial, he was the only one convicted for the My Lai crimes. Thus, the only actions of My Lai for which *anyone* was ever convicted were mass executions, ordered and committed. We suspect that there are commonsense reasons why this one type of killing was singled out. In the midst of rapidly moving events with people running about, an execution of stationary targets is literally a still life that stands out and whose participants are clearly visible. It can be proven that specific people committed specific deeds. An execution, in contrast to the shooting of someone on the run, is also more likely to meet the legal definition of an act resulting from intent—with malice aforethought. Moreover, American military law specifically forbids the killing of unarmed civilians or military prisoners, as does the Geneva Convention between nations. Thus common sense, legal standards, and explicit doctrine all made such actions the likeliest target for prosecution. . . .

The day's quiet beginning has already been noted. Troops landed and swept unopposed into the village. The three weapons eventually reported as the haul from the operation were picked up from three apparent Viet Cong who fled the village when the troops arrived and were pursued and killed by helicopter gunships. Obviously the Viet Cong did frequent the area. But it appears that by about 8:00 A.M. no one who met the troops was aggressive, and no one was armed. By the laws of war Charlie Company had no argument with such people.

As they moved into the village, the soldiers began to gather its inhabitants together. Shortly after 8:00 A.M. Lieutenant Calley told Pfc. Paul Meadlo that "you know what to do with" a group of villagers Meadlo was guarding. Estimates of the numbers in the group ranged as high as eighty women, children, and old men, and Meadlo's own estimate under oath was thirty to fifty people. As Meadlo later testified, Calley returned after ten or fifteen minutes: "He [Calley] said, 'How come they're not dead?' I said, 'I didn't know we were supposed to kill them.' He said, 'I want them dead.' He backed off twenty or thirty feet and started shooting into the people—the Viet Cong—shooting automatic. He was beside me. He burned four or five magazines. I burned off a few, about three. I helped shoot 'em" (Hammer, 1971, p. 155). Meadlo himself and others testified that Meadlo cried as he fired; others reported him later to be sobbing and "all broke up." It would appear that to Lieutenant Calley's subordinates something was unusual, and stressful, in these orders. . . .

Among the helicopters flying reconnaissance above Son My was that of CWO Hugh Thompson. By 9:00 or soon after, Thompson had noticed some horrifying events from his perch. As he spotted wounded civilians, he sent down smoke markers so the soldiers on the ground could treat them. They killed them instead. He reported to headquarters, trying to persuade someone to stop what was going on. Barker, hearing the message, called down to Captain Medina. Medina, in turn, later claimed to have told Calley that it was "enough for today." But it was not yet enough.

At Calley's orders, his men began gathering the remaining villagers—roughly seventy-five individuals, mostly women and children—and herding them toward a drainage ditch. Accompanied by three or four enlisted men, Lieutenant Calley executed several batches of civilians who had been gathered into ditches. Some of the details of the process were entered into testimony in such accounts as Pfc. Dennis Conti's: "A lot of them, the people, were trying to get up and mostly they was just screaming and pretty bad shot up. . . . I seen a woman tried to get up. I seen Lieutenant Calley fire. He hit the side of her head and blew it off" (Hammer, 1971, p. 125).

Pfc. Gregory Olsen corroborated the general picture of the victims: "They were—the majority were women and children, some babies. I distinctly remember one middle-aged Vietnamese male dressed in white right at my feet as I crossed. None of the bodies were mangled in any way. There was blood. Some appeared to be dead, others followed me with their eyes as I walked across the ditch" (Goldstein et al., 1976, p. 502). . . .

It is noteworthy that during these executions more than one enlisted man avoided carrying out Calley's orders, and more than one, by sworn oath, directly refused to obey them. For example, Pfc. James Joseph Dursi testified, when asked if he fired when Lieutenant Calley ordered him to: "No. I just stood there. Meadlo turned to me after a couple of minutes and said 'Shoot! Why don't you shoot! Why don't you fire!' He was crying and yelling. I said, 'I can't! I won't!' And the people were screaming and crying and yelling. They kept firing for a couple of minutes, mostly automatic and semi-automatic" (Hammer, 1971, p. 143). . . .

Even those who obeyed Calley's orders showed great stress. For example, Meadlo eventually began to argue and cry directly in front of Calley. Pfc. Herbert Carter shot himself in the foot, possibly because he could no longer take what he was doing. We were not destined to hear a sworn version of the incident, since neither side at the Calley trial called him to testify.

The most unusual instance of resistance to authority came from the skies. CWO Hugh Thompson, who had protested the apparent carnage of civilians, was Calley's inferior in rank but was not in his line of command. He was also watching the ditch from his helicopter and noticed some people moving after the first round of slaughter—chiefly children who had been shielded by their mother's bodies. Landing to rescue the wounded, he also found some villagers hiding in a nearby bunker. Protecting the Vietnamese with his own body, Thompson ordered his men to train their guns on the Americans and to open fire if the Americans fired on the Vietnamese. He then radioed for additional rescue helicopters and stood between the Vietnamese and the Americans under Calley's command until the Vietnamese could be evacuated. He later returned to the ditch to unearth a child buried, unharmed, beneath layers of bodies. In October 1969, Thompson was awarded the Distinguished Flying Cross for heroism at My Lai, specifically (albeit inaccurately) for the rescue of children hiding in a bunker "between Viet Cong forces and advancing friendly forces" and for the rescue of a wounded child "caught in the intense crossfire" (Hersh, 1970, p. 119). Four months earlier, at the Pentagon, Thompson had identified Calley as having been at the ditch.

By about 10:00 A.M., the massacre was winding down. The remaining actions consisted largely of isolated rapes and killings, "clean-up" shootings of the wounded, and the destruction of the village by fire. We have already seen some examples of these more indiscriminate and possibly less premeditated acts. By the 11:00 A.M. lunch break, when the exhausted men of Company C were relaxing, two young girls wandered back from a hiding place only to be invited to share lunch. This surrealist touch illustrates the extent to which the soldiers' action had become dissociated from its meaning. An hour earlier, some of these men were making sure that not even a child would escape the executioner's bullet. But now the job was done and it was time for lunch—and in this new context it seemed only natural to ask the children who had managed to escape execution to join them. The massacre had ended. It remained only for the Viet Cong to reap the political rewards among the survivors in hiding.

The army command in the area knew that something had gone wrong. Direct commanders, including Lieutenant Colonel Barker, had firsthand reports, such as Thompson's complaints. Others had such odd bits of evidence as the claim of 128 Viet Cong dead with a booty of only three weapons. But the cover-up of My Lai began at once. The operation was reported as a victory over a stronghold of the Viet Cong Forty-eighth.

William Calley was not the only man tried for the event at My Lai. The actions of over thirty soldiers and civilians were scrutinized by investigators; over half of these had to face charges or disciplinary action of some sort. Targets of investigation included Captain Medina, who was tried, and various higher-ups, including General Koster. But Lieutenant Calley was the only person convicted, the only person to serve time.

The core of Lieutenant Calley's defense was superior orders. What this meant to him—in contrast to what it meant to the judge and jury—can be gleaned from his responses to a series of questions from his defense attorney, George Latimer, in which Calley sketched out his understanding of the laws of war and the actions that constitute doing one's duty within those laws:

LATIMER: Did you receive any training . . . which had to do with the obedience to orders?

CALLEY: Yes, sir.

LATIMER: . . . what were you informed [were] the principles involved in that field?

CALLEY: That all orders were to be assumed legal, that the soldier's job was to carry out any order given him to the best of his ability.

LATIMER: . . . what might occur if you disobeyed an order by a senior officer?

CALLEY: You could be court-martialed for refusing an order and refusing an order in the face of the enemy, you could be sent to death, sir.

LATIMER: [I am asking] whether you were required in any way, shape or form to make a determination of the legality or illegality of an order?

CALLEY: No, sir. I was never told that I had the choice, sir.

LATIMER: If you had a doubt about the order, what were you supposed to do?

CALLEY: . . . I was supposed to carry the order out and then come back and make my complaint (Hammer, 1971, pp. 240–41).

Lieutenant Calley steadfastly maintained that his actions within My Lai had constituted, in his mind, carrying out orders from Captain Medina. Both his own actions and the orders he gave to others (such as the instruction to Meadlo to "waste 'em") were entirely in response to superior orders. He denied any intent to kill individuals and any but the most passing awareness of distinctions among the individuals: "I was ordered to go in there and destroy the enemy. That was my job on that day. That was the mission I was given. I did not sit down and think in terms of men, women, and children. They were all classified the same, and that was the classification that we dealt with, just as enemy solders." When Latimer asked if in his own opinion Calley had acted "rightly and according to your understanding of your directions and orders," Calley replied, "I felt then and I still do that I acted as I was directed, and I carried out the orders that I was given, and I do not feel wrong in doing so, sir" (Hammer, 1971, p. 257).

His court-martial did not accept Calley's defense of superior orders and clearly did not share his interpretation of his duty. The jury evidently reasoned that, even if there had been orders to destroy everything in sight and to "waste the Vietnamese," any reasonable person would have realized that such orders were illegal and should have refused to carry them out. . . .

A jury of combat veterans proceeded to convict William Calley of the premeditated murder of no less than twenty-two human beings. (The army, realizing some unfortunate connotations in referring to the victims as "Oriental human beings," eventually referred to them as "human beings.") . . .

Lieutenant Calley was initially sentenced to life imprisonment. That sentence was reduced: first to twenty years, eventually to ten (the latter by Secretary of the Army Callaway in 1974). Calley served three years before being released on bond. The time was spent under house arrest in his apartment, where he was able to receive visits from his girlfriend. He was granted parole on September 16, 1975.

Sanctioned Massacres

The slaughter at My Lai is an instance of a class of violent acts that can be described as sanctioned massacres (Kelman, 1973): acts of indiscriminate, ruthless, and often systematic mass violence, carried out by military or paramilitary personnel while engaged in officially sanctioned campaigns, the victims of which are defenseless and unresisting civilians, including old men, women, and children. Sanctioned massacres have occurred throughout history. Within

American history, My Lai had its precursors in the Philippine war around the turn of the century (Schirmer, 1971) and in the massacres of Native Americans. Elsewhere in the world, one recalls the Nazis' "final solution" for European Jews, the massacres and deportations of Armenians by Turks, the liquidation of the kulaks and the great purges in the Soviet Union, and more recently the massacres in Indonesia and Bangladesh, in Biafra and Burundi, in South Africa and Mozambique, in Cambodia and Afghanistan, in Syria and Lebanon. . . .

The occurrence of sanctioned massacres cannot be adequately explained by the existence of psychological forces—whether these be characterological dispositions to engage in murderous or profound hostility against the target— so powerful that they must find expression in violent acts unhampered by moral restraints. Instead, . . . it is more instructive to look not at the motives for violence but at the conditions under which the usual moral inhibitions against violence become weakened. Three social processes that tend to create such conditions can be identified: authorization, routinization, and dehumanization. Through authorization, the situation becomes so defined that the individual is absolved of the responsibility to make personal moral choices. Through routinization, the action becomes so organized that there is no opportunity for raising moral questions. Through dehumanization, the actors' attitudes toward the target and toward themselves become so structured that it is neither necessary nor possible for them to view the relationship in moral terms.

AUTHORIZATION

Sanctioned massacres by definition occur in the context of an authority situation, a situation in which, at least for many of the participants, the moral principles that generally govern human relationships do not apply. Thus, when acts of violence are explicitly ordered, implicitly encouraged, tacitly approved, or at least permitted by legitimate authorities, people's readiness to commit or condone them is enhanced. That such acts are authorized seems to carry automatic justification for them. Behaviorally, authorization obviates the necessity of making judgments or choices. Not only do normal moral principles become inoperative, but—particularly when the actions are explicitly ordered—a different kind of morality, linked to the duty to obey superior orders, tends to take over.

In an authority situation, individuals characteristically feel obligated to obey the orders of the authorities, whether or not these correspond with their personal preferences. They see themselves as having no choice as long as they accept the legitimacy of the orders and of the authorities who give them. . . . The basic structure of a situation of legitimate authority requires subordinates to respond in terms of their role obligations rather than their personal preferences; they can openly disobey only by challenging the legitimacy of the authority. . . .

An important corollary of the basic structure of the authority situation is that actors often do not see themselves as personally responsible for the consequences of their actions. Again, there are individual differences, depending on actors' capacity and readiness to evaluate the legitimacy of orders received. Insofar as they see themselves as having had no choice in their actions, however, they do not feel personally responsible for them. They were not personal agents, but merely extensions of the authority. Thus, when their actions caused harm to others, they can feel relatively free of guilt. A similar mechanism operates when a person engages in antisocial behavior that was not ordered by the authorities but was tacitly encouraged and approved by them—even if only by making it clear that such behavior will not be punished. In this situation, behavior that was formerly illegitimate is legitimized by the authorities' acquiescence.

In the My Lai massacre, it is likely that the structure of the authority situation contributed to the massive violence in both ways—that is, by conveying the message that acts of violence against Vietnamese villagers were *required*, as well as the message that such acts, even if not ordered, were *permitted* by the authorities in charge. The actions at My Lai represented, at least in some respects, responses to explicit or implicit orders. Lieutenant Calley indicated, by orders and by example, that he wanted large numbers of villagers killed. Whether Calley himself had been ordered by his superiors to "waste" the whole area, as he claimed, remains a matter of controversy. Even if we assume, however, that he was not explicitly ordered to wipe out the village, he had reason to believe that such actions were expected by his superior officers. Indeed, the very nature of the war conveyed this expectation. The principal means of military success was the "body count"—the number of enemy soldiers killed—and any Vietnamese killed by the U.S. military was commonly defined as a "Viet Cong." Thus, it was not totally bizarre for Calley to believe that what he was doing at My Lai was to increase his body count, as any good officer was expected to do.

Even to the extent that the actions at My Lai occurred spontaneously, without reference to superior orders, those committing them had reason to assume that such actions might be tacitly approved of by the military authorities. Not only had they failed to punish such acts in most cases, but the very strategies and tactics that the authorities consistently devised were based on the proposition that the civilian population of South Vietnam—whether "hostile" or "friendly"—was expendable. Such policies as search-and-destroy missions, the establishment of free-shooting zones, the use of antipersonnel weapons, the bombing of entire villages if they were suspected of harboring guerrillas, the forced migration of masses of the rural population, and the defoliation of vast forest areas helped legitimize acts of massive violence of the kind occurring at My Lai. . . .

ROUTINIZATION

Despite these forces, however, given the nature of the actions involved in sanctioned massacres, one might still expect moral scruples to intervene, but the likelihood of moral resistance is greatly reduced by transforming the action into routine, mechanical, highly programmed operations. Routinization fulfills two functions. First, it reduces the necessity of making decisions, thus minimizing the occasions in which moral questions may arise. Second, it makes it easier to avoid the implications of the action, since the actor focuses on the details of the job rather than on its meaning. The latter effect is more readily achieved among those who participate in sanctioned massacres from a distance—from their desks or even from the cockpits of their bombers.

Routinization operates both at the level of the individual actor and at the organizational level. Individual job performance is broken down into a series of discrete steps, most of them carried out in automatic, regularized fashion. It becomes easy to forget the nature of the product that emerges from the process. When Lieutenant Calley said of My Lai that it was "no great deal," he probably implied that it was all in a day's work. Organizationally, the task is divided among different officers, each of which has responsibility for a small portion of it. This arrangement diffuses responsibility and limits the amount and scope of decision-making that is necessary. There is no expectation that the moral implications will be considered at any of these points, nor is there any opportunity to do so. The organizational processes also help further legitimize the actions of each participant. By proceeding in routine fashion—processing papers, exchanging memos, diligently carrying out their assigned tasks—the different units mutually reinforce each other in the view that what is going on must be perfectly normal, correct, and legitimate. The shared illusion that they are engaged in a legitimate enterprise helps the participants assimilate their activities to other purposes, such as the efficiency of their performance, the productivity of their unit, or the cohesiveness of their group (see Janis, 1972).

Normalization of atrocities is more difficult to the extent that there are constant reminders of the true meaning of the enterprise. Bureaucratic inventiveness in the use of language helps to cover up such meaning. For example, the SS had a set of *Sprachregelungen,* or "language rules," to govern descriptions of their extermination program. The code names for killing and liquidation were "final solution," "evacuation," and "special treatment." The war in Indochina produced its own set of euphemisms, such as "protective reaction," "pacification," and "forced-draft urbanization and modernization." The use of euphemisms allows participants in sanctioned massacres to differentiate their actions from ordinary killing and destruction and thus to avoid confronting their true meaning.

DEHUMANIZATION

Authorization processes override standard moral considerations; routinization processes reduce the likelihood that such considerations will arise. Still, the inhibitions against murdering one's fellow human beings are generally so strong that the victims must also be stripped of their human status if they are to be subjected to systematic killing. Insofar as they are dehumanized, the usual principles of morality no longer apply to them.

Sanctioned massacres become possible to the extent that the victims are deprived in the perpetrators' eyes of the qualities essential to being perceived as fully human and included in the moral compact that governs human relationships. . . . Thus, when a group of people is defined entirely in terms of a category to which they belong, and when this category is excluded from the human family, moral restraints against killing them are more readily overcome.

Dehumanization of the enemy is a common phenomenon in any war situation. Sanctioned massacres, however, presuppose a more extreme degree of dehumanization, insofar as the killing is not in direct response to the target's threats or provocations. It is not what they have done that marks such victims for death but who they are—the category to which they happen to belong. They are the victims of policies that regard their systematic destruction as a desirable end or an acceptable means. Such extreme dehumanization becomes possible when the target group can readily be identified as a separate category of people who have historically been stigmatized and excluded by the victimizers; often the victims belong to a distinct racial, religious, ethnic, or political group regarded as inferior or sinister. The traditions, the habits, the images, and the vocabularies for dehumanizing such groups are already well established and can be drawn upon when the groups are selected for massacre. Labels help deprive the victims of identity and community, as in the epithet "gooks" that was commonly used to refer to Vietnamese and other Indochinese peoples.

The dynamics of the massacre process itself further increase the participants' tendency to dehumanize the victims. Those who participate as part of the bureaucratic apparatus increasingly come to see their victims as bodies to be counted and entered into reports, as faceless figures that will determine their productivity rates and promotions. Those who participate in the massacre directly—in the field, as it were—are reinforced in their perception of the victims as less than human by observing their very victimization. The only way they can justify what is being done to these people—both by others and by themselves—and the only way they can extract some degree of meaning out of the absurd events in which they find themselves participating (see Lifton, 1971, 1973) is by coming to believe that the victims are subhuman and deserve to be rooted out. And thus the process of dehumanization feeds on itself.

References

Goldstein, J., B. Marshall, and J. Schwartz, eds. 1976. *The My Lai Massacre and Its Cover-up: Beyond the Reach of Law?* (The Peers Report, with a supplement and introductory essay on the limits of law). New York: Free Press.

Hammer, R. 1971. *The Court-Martial of Lt. Calley.* New York: Coward, McCann, & Geoghegan.

Hersh, S. 1970. *My Lai 4: A Report on the Massacre and Its Aftermath.* New York: Vintage Books.

———. 1972. *Cover-up.* New York: Random House.

Janis, I. L. 1972. *Victims of Groupthink: A Psychological Study of Foreign-Policy Decisions and Fiascoes.* Boston: Houghton Mifflin.

Kelman, H. C. 1973. "Violence without Moral Restraint: Reflections on the Dehumanization of Victims and Victimizers." *Journal of Social Issues* 29 (4): 25–61.

Schirmer, D. B. 1971, April 24. "My Lai Was Not the First Time." *New Republic,* pp. 18–21.

PART IX Social Change

$\mathbf{W}$HAT IMAGERY SHOULD WE USE? We are in a small, drifting boat on a tumultuous sea of social change. Like a mighty wind, unpredictable events swirl around us, at times seeming to sweep us away. Like an out-of-control fire, change threatens to devour us.

Regardless of the imagery, vast social change is a basic fact of contemporary life—and that change can be ominous, threatening to cast us into the unknown. Nothing seems to remain the same. Familiar landmarks are torn down and replaced, seemingly overnight, by a supermarket or another of an endless chain of fast-food outlets. Farm fields and woods are paved over as they sprout malls and shopping centers. Computers change so rapidly that the one you bought a year or two ago seems hopelessly out of date. Afraid of divorce—and of making a commitment—the young postpone marriage.

C-cash for purchases on the Internet. A plane propelled by human muscle-power, and another that goes around the world without refueling. "Smart cards" to control access and security. Interactive television and "virtual reality." Long distance surgery, with patient and surgeon 3,000 miles apart. A wallet computer that functions as a credit/cash card, a checkbook, a fax, and an e-mail communicator—and also dispenses tickets for airlines and concerts, and, not incidentally, will pop a coke out for you from the soda machine.

Although change is an essential part of today's society, it is anything but new. Twenty-five hundred years ago, Heraclitus said, "Everything flows;

nothing stands still." Six hundred years later, Marcus Aurelius Antoninus wrote, "The universe is change." A more recent observer of the social scene put it this way: "The only thing constant is the certainty of change."

Social change was indeed a part of past civilizations, too, but an essential difference distinguishes those changes and what we are experiencing today. Barring catastrophe in the form of human or natural disaster, change in ancient times was slow and orderly—sometimes so slow that even over generations its effects were barely perceptible. In all societies of the world, in fact, it was routinely the case that the father passed his occupation down to his son, who, in turn, passed it on to his son, and so on. Mothers, too, passed their occupation to their daughters. The society that children lived in was practically identical to that into which their parents had been born. Although the players had changed, the basic social institutions, with their routine ways of handling things, remained the same over generations.

The contrast with our situation is stark. Most children today take it for granted that they are different from their parents—some even being amazed if they notice similarities with them. Adolescents routinely assume that their parents will not understand them, for each represents a different world. With worlds so dissimilar, it is not uncommon for a grown child visiting his or her parents, following an absence of months or even years, to find that after "catching up"—about an hour or so—they have little or nothing left to talk about. Social change has sorted them into different worlds, their differing experiences imparting contrasting orientations to life and, in effect, making them different kinds of people.

"Adapt or die" may be the maxim under which living creatures exist. Only the organisms that adapt to changing circumstances survive, and humans are no exception. Confronted with challenge, humans adapt. They change their social institutions to match changing circumstances. The effects are highly visible as people modify their outward behaviors. But the consequences are hardly limited to the external, for they also penetrate people's inner life, changing their ideas, attitudes, and beliefs, their basic orientations to the world.

In the opening selection, George Ritzer examines what is perhaps the broadest change affecting society today. He aptly calls it *McDonaldization,* meaning a rationalized efficiency that is taking over many of the routine aspects of everyday life. Not everyone welcomes social change, of course. Jerry Savells focuses on the Amish, analyzing how this religious group resists social change in order to maintain its way of life. Laura Miller then continues this theme by looking at men's resistance to the gender integration of the military. We close the book with an analysis by Kenneth Smith and Linda Belgrave of how people adjust to natural disaster, a particularly unwelcome form of change.

In conclusion, I would like to add that you, the reader, are the future. Certainly you cannot escape being shaped by your experiences of the vast changes occurring in society. For you to make better sense of your transformative experiences, however, I highly recommend the sociological imagination—the idea with which we began this book.

42 The McDonaldization of Society

GEORGE RITZER

A key term in sociology is *rationalization*. This term refers to choosing the most efficient means to accomplish tasks. In business it refers to the bottom line, calculating costs to produce the most gain. With rationalization, profit becomes king, while people, valued for what they bring to the bottom line, become expendable.

The rationalization of society, said Max Weber, the sociologist who first analyzed this process, is extremely significant, for it tends to ensnare us all. The traditional ways of doing things—which may be inefficient but which are also the source of huge satisfactions—are passing. In their place come bureaucracies with time and motion studies, cold analyses of every act, with profits placed higher than the people who make up the work setting. Weber didn't know how far reaching and accurate his analysis would prove. Rationalization threatens to engulf all of society, locking us all in what Weber called an iron cage of rationality. College administrators, for example, want to evaluate instructors not by how they challenge students to think, by how they stimulate originality and creativity, or by how they open minds to new perceptions, but, rather, by the sheer number of students they churn out each semester. Even traditional, routine, everyday aspects of family life are not impervious to this change, as becomes evident in Ritzer's analysis.

MCDONALD'S HAS SOUGHT to construct highly efficient systems, and *McDonaldization* implies the search for maximum efficiency in increasingly numerous and diverse social settings. *Efficiency* means the choice of the optimum means to a given end, but this definition requires some clarification. Although we use the term *optimum,* it is rare that the truly optimum means to an end is ever found. Rather, there is a search for a . . . far better means to an end than would be employed under ordinary circumstances. . . .

Wireless Keyboards and Self-Service Slurpees

The emphasis of McDonaldization on efficiency implies that contrasting, nonrational systems are less efficient, or even inefficient. The fast-food restaurant grew as a result of its greater efficiency in comparison to alternative methods of obtaining a meal. In the early 1950s, at the dawning of the era of the fast-food restaurant, the major alternative was the home-cooked meal made largely from ingredients previously purchased at various markets. . . .

But the home-cooked meal was, and still is, a relatively inefficient way of obtaining a meal. The restaurant has long been a more efficient alternative. But restaurants can be inefficient in that it may take several hours to go to the restaurant, consume a meal, and then return home. The desire for more efficient restaurants led to the rise of some of the ancestors of the fast-food restaurant—diners, cafeterias, and early drive-through or drive-in restaurants. The modern fast-food restaurant can be seen as being built on the latter models and as a further step in the direction of more efficient food consumption. . . .

Above all else, it was the efficiency of the McDonald brothers' operation that impressed Ray Kroc [the individual behind the franchising of McDonald's], as well as the enormous profit potential of such a system if it were applied in a large number of sites. Here is how Kroc described his initial reactions to the McDonald's system:

> I was fascinated by the simplicity and effectiveness of the system. . . . Each step in producing the limited menu was stripped down to its essence and accomplished with a minimum of effort. They sold hamburgers and cheeseburgers only. The burgers were . . . all fried the same way.

Kroc and his associates looked at each component of the hamburger in order to increase the efficiency with which it could be produced and served. For example, they started with only partially sliced buns that were attached to one another. However, it was found that buns could be used more efficiently if they were sliced all the way through and separated from one another. At first, the buns arrived in cardboard boxes and the griddle workers had to spend time opening the boxes, separating the buns, slicing them, and discarding the leftover paper and cardboard. In addition to separating and preslicing them, buns were made efficient to use by having them shipped in reusable boxes. Similar attention was devoted to the meat patty. For example, the paper between the patties had to have just the right amount of wax so that the patties would readily slide off the paper and onto the grill.

Kroc makes it clear that the goal of these kinds of refinements was greater efficiency:

> The purpose of all these refinements, and we never lost sight of it, was to make our griddle man's job easier to do quickly and well. And the other considerations of cost cutting, inventory control, and so forth were important to be sure, but they were secondary to the critical detail of what happened there at the smoking griddle. This was the vital passage of our *assembly-line,* and the product had to flow through it smoothly or the whole plant would falter. (Italics added.)

. . . Once diners enter the fast-food restaurant, the process continues to appear to be efficient. Parking lots are adjacent to the restaurant and parking spots are readily available. It's a short walk to the counter, and although there is sometimes a line, food is usually quickly ordered, obtained, and paid for. The highly limited menu makes the choice of a meal's components quite easy. This contrasts to the many choices available in many of the alternatives to the fast-food restaurant. With the food obtained, it is but a few steps to a table and the beginning of the "dining experience." The fare almost always involves an array of finger foods (for example, Chicken McNuggets and french fries) that can be popped into the diner's mouth with the result that the entire meal is ordinarily consumed in a few minutes. Because there is little inducement to linger, the diners generally gather the leftover paper, styrofoam, and plastic, discard them in a nearby trash receptacle, and are back in their car and on their way to the next (often McDonaldized) activity.

Not too many years ago, those in charge of fast-food restaurants discovered that there was a way—the drive-through window—to make this whole process far more efficient for both themselves and the consumer. Instead of the "laborious" and "inefficient" process of parking the car, walking to the counter, waiting in line, ordering, paying, carrying the food to the table, eating, and disposing of the remnants, the drive-through window offered diners the choice of driving to the window (perhaps waiting in a line of cars), ordering, paying, and driving off with the meal. It was even possible to engage in the highly efficient act of eating while driving, thereby eliminating the need to devote a separate time period to dining. The drive-through window is also efficient from the perspective of the fast-food restaurant. As more and more people use the drive-through window, fewer parking spaces, tables, and employees are needed. Further, consumers take their debris with them as they drive away, thereby eliminating the need for additional trash receptacles and employees to periodically empty those receptacles. . . .

"Home-Made" Fast Food and the StairMaster

Given the efficiency of the fast-food restaurant, the home kitchen has had to grow more efficient or it might have faced total extinction. Had the kitchen not grown more efficient, a comedian could have envisioned a time when the kitchen would have been replaced by a large, comfortable telephone lounge used for calling Domino's for pizza delivery. The key to the salvation of the kitchen was the development and widespread adoption of the microwave oven. The microwave is simply a far more efficient means than its major alternative, the convection oven, for preparing a meal. It is usually faster than the old oven and one can prepare a wider array of foods in it than the old-fashioned oven. Perhaps most importantly from the point of view of this chapter, it spawned the development of a number of microwavable foods (including soup, pizza, hamburgers, fried chicken, french fries, and popcorn) that permit the efficient preparation of the fare one usually finds in the fast-food restaurants. For example, one of the first microwavable foods produced by Hormel was an array of biscuit-based breakfast sandwiches "popularized in recent years by many of the fast-food chains," most notably McDonald's and its Egg McMuffin. Banquet rushed to market with microwavable chicken breast nuggets. In fact, many food companies now employ people who continually scout fast-food restaurants for new ideas for foods that can be marketed for the home. As one executive put it, "Instead of having a breakfast sandwich at McDonald's, you can pick one up from the freezer of your grocery store." As a result, one can now, in effect, enjoy fast food at home without venturing out to the fast-food restaurant. . . .

Another factor in the continued success of the fast-food restaurant is that it has many advantages over the "home-cooked" microwave dinner. For example, a trip to the fast-food restaurant offers people a dinner out rather than just another meal at home. For another, as Stan Luxenberg has pointed out in *Roadside Empires,* McDonald's offers more than an efficient meal, it offers fun—brightly lit, colorful, and attractive settings, garish packaging, special inducements to children, give-aways, contests—in short, it offers a kind of carnival-like atmosphere in which to buy and consume fast food. Thus, faced with the choice of an efficient meal at home or one in a fast-food restaurant, many people are still likely to choose the fast-food restaurant because it not only offers efficiency but a range of other rewards.

The microwave oven (as well as the range of products it spawned) is but one of many contributors to the increasing efficiency of home cooking. Among other obvious technological advances are the replacement of the hand beater by the electric beater; slicers, dicers, and even knives by the Cuisinart; and the presence of either stand-alone freezers or those that are an integral part of the refrigerator.

The large freezer has permitted a range of efficiencies, such as a few trips to the market for enormous purchases rather than many trips for small purchases. It has permitted the storage of a wide range of ingredients that can be readily extracted when needed for food preparation. It has allowed for the cooking of large portions which can then be divided up, frozen, and defrosted periodically for dinner. The widespread availability of the home freezer led to the expansion of the production of frozen foods of all types. The most notable frozen food from the point of view of efficiency is the "TV dinner." People can stock their freezers with an array of such dinners (for example, Chinese, Italian, and Mexican dinners as well as a wide variety of "American" cooking) and quite readily bring them out and pop them into the oven, sometimes even the microwave. . . .

The McDonaldization of food preparation and consumption has been extended to the booming diet industry. Diet books promising all sorts of efficient shortcuts to weight loss are often at the top of the best-seller lists. Losing weight is normally difficult and time-consuming, hence the lure of various diet books that promise to make weight loss easier and quicker, that is, more efficient.

For those on a diet, and many people are on more or less perpetual diets, the preparation of low-calorie food has been made more efficient. Instead of needing to cook diet foods from scratch, they may now purchase an array of prepared foods in frozen and/or microwavable form. For those who do not wish to go through the inefficient process of eating those diet meals, there are the diet shakes, like Slim●Fast, that can be mixed and consumed in a matter of seconds.

A fairly recent development is the growth of diet centers like Nutri/System and Jenny Craig. Nutri/System sells dieters, at substantial cost, prepackaged freeze-dried food. All the dieter need do is add water when it is time for the next meal. Freeze-dried foods are not only efficient for the dieter but also for Nutri/System, because they can be efficiently packaged, transported, and stored. Furthermore, the dieter's periodic visit to a Nutri/System center is efficiently organized. A counselor is allotted ten minutes with each client. During that brief time the counselor takes the client's weight, blood pressure, and measurements, asks routine questions, fills out a chart, and devotes some time to "problem-solving." If the session extends beyond the allotted ten minutes and other clients are waiting, the receptionist will buzz the counselor's room. Counselors learn their techniques at Nutri/System University where, after a week of training (no inefficient years of matriculation here), they earn certification and an NSU diploma.

There is a strong emphasis on efficiency in modern health clubs, including such chains as Holiday Spas. These clubs often offer, under one roof, virtually everything needed to lose weight and stay in shape, including a wide array of exercise machines, as well as a running track and a swimming pool. The exercise machines are highly specialized so that one may efficiently increase fitness in specific areas of the body. Thus, working out on running machines and the StairMaster—one kind of exercise machine—increases cardiovascular fitness, whereas using various weightlifting machines increases strength and muscularity in targeted areas of the body. Another efficiency associated with many of these machines is that one can do other things while exercising. Thus, many clubs have television sets throughout the gym allowing people to both watch television and exercise. The exerciser can also read, listen to music, or even listen to a book-on-tape while working out. The exercise machines also offer a high degree of calculability, with many of them registering miles run, level of difficulty, and calories burned. All of this in the kind of clean, sterile environment we have come to associate with McDonaldization.

"Selling Machines" and L. L. Bean

Shopping has also grown more efficient. The department store obviously is a more efficient place in which to shop than a series of specialty shops dispersed throughout the city or suburbs. The shopping mall increases efficiency by bringing a wide range of department stores and specialty shops under one roof. Kowinsky describes the mall as "an extremely efficient and effective selling machine." It is cost-efficient for retailers because it is the collection of shops and department stores ("mall synergy") that brings in throngs of people. And it is efficient for consumers because in one stop they can visit numerous shops, have lunch at a "food court" (likely populated by many fast-food chains), see a movie, have a drink, and go to an exercise or diet center.

The drive for shopping efficiency did not end with the malls. In recent years, there has been a great increase in catalogue sales (via L. L. Bean, Lands' End, and other mail-order companies), which enables people to shop while never leaving the comfort of their homes. Still more efficient, although it may require many hours in front of the tube, is home television shopping. A range of products is paraded in front of viewers who may simply phone each time a product catches their eye and conveniently charge their purchase to their credit card accounts. The latest advance in home shopping is the "scan-fone," an at-home phone machine that includes "a pen-sized bar-code scanner, a credit card magnetic-strip reader, and a key pad." The customer merely "scans items from a bar-coded catalogue and also scans delivery dates and pay-ment methods. The orders are then electronically relayed to the various stores, businesses, and banks involved." Some mall operators fear that they will ulti-mately be put out of business because of the greater efficiency of shopping at home.

Video Rentals and Package Tours

With the advent of videotapes and video rental stores, many people no longer deem it efficient to drive to their local theater to see a movie. Movies can now be viewed, often more than one at a sitting, in one's own den. For those who wish even greater efficiency, viewers can buy one of the new televisions sets that enable viewers to see a movie while also watching a favorite television program on an inset on the television screen.

The largest video rental franchise in the United States is Blockbuster, which, predictably, "considers itself the McDonald's of the video business." Blockbuster has more than 2,000 outlets. . . . However, there may already be signs that Blockbuster is in danger of being replaced by even more efficient al-ternatives. One is pay-per-view movies offered by many cable companies. Instead of trekking to the video store, all one need do is turn to the proper channel and phone the cable company. Another experimental alternative is an effort by GTE to deliver movies to one's home through fiber-optic cables. Just as the video store replaced many movie theaters, video stores themselves may soon be displaced by even more efficient alternatives.

. . . [T]ravel to exotic efficient locales has also grown more efficient. The best example of this is the package tour. Let us take, for example, a thirty-day tour of Europe. To make this efficient, only the major locales in Europe are visited. Within each of these locales, the tourist is directed toward the major sights. (In Paris, the tour would definitely stop at the Louvre, but perhaps not at the Rodin Museum.) Because the goal is to see as many of the major sights as possible in a short period of time, the emphasis is on the efficient transportation of people to, through, and from each of them. Buses hurtle to and through the city, allowing the tourist to glimpse the maximum number of sights in the time allowed. At particularly interesting or important sights, the bus may slow down or even stop to permit some picture-taking. At the most important locales, a brief stopover is planned; there the visitor can hurry through the site, take a few pictures, buy a souvenir, and then hop back on the bus to head to the next attraction.

There is no question that this is a highly efficient way of seeing the major tourist attractions of Europe. Indeed, the package tour can be seen as a vast people-moving mechanism that permits the efficient transport of people from one locale to another. If tourists attempted to see the major sights of Europe on their own, it would take more time to see the same things and the expense would be greater. There are, of course, costs associated with the package tour (for example, does the tourist ever really have time to experience Europe?), as there are with every other highly rational system, but we will reserve a discussion of them for later. . . .

Customized Textbooks, Books-on-Tape, "News McNuggets," and Drive-in Churches

Turning to the educational system, specifically the university, one manifestation of the pressure for greater efficiency is the machine-graded, multiple-choice examination. In a much earlier era, students were examined on a one-to-one basis by their professors. This may have been a very good way of finding out what students know, but it was (and is) highly labor intensive and inefficient. Later, the essay examination became very popular. While grading a set of essays was more efficient from the professor's perspective than giving individual oral examinations, it was still relatively inefficient and time-consuming. Enter the multiple-choice examination, the grading of which was a snap in comparison to giving oral tests or reading essays. In fact, the grading could be passed on to graduate assistants, an act that was very efficient for the professor. Now we have computer-graded examinations that maximize efficiency for both professors and graduate students.

The multiple-choice examinations still left the professor saddled with the inefficient task of composing the necessary sets of questions. Furthermore, at least some of the questions had to be changed each semester because new students were likely to gain possession of old exams. The solution: Textbook companies provided professors with books (free of charge) full of multiple-choice questions to go along with the textbooks required for use in large classes. Professors no longer had to make up their own questions; they could use those previously provided by the publisher. However, the professor still had to retype the questions or to have them retyped by the office staff. Recently, however, publishers have been kind enough to provide their sets of questions on computer disks. Now all the professor needs to do is select the desired questions and let the printer do the rest.* . . .

Publishers have provided other services to make teaching more efficient for those professors who adopt their textbooks. With the adoption of a textbook, a professor may receive many materials with which to fill class hours— lecture outlines, computer simulations, discussion questions, videotapes, movies, even ideas for guest lecturers and student projects. With luck, professors can use all of these devices and do little or nothing on their own for their classes. Needless to say, this is a highly efficient means of teaching from a professor's perspective, and it frees up valuable time for the much more valued activities (by professors, but not students) of writing and research. . . .

Another example of efficiency in publishing is the advent of books-on-tape. There is a number of companies that now rent or sell books recorded on audiotape. The availability of such tapes permits greater efficiency in "reading" books. Instead of doing nothing but reading, one can now engage in other activities (driving, walking, jogging, watching TV with the sound off) while listening to a book. Greater efficiency is also provided by many of these books-on-tape being available in abridged form so that they can be devoured far more quickly. Gone are the "wasted" hours listening to "insignificant" parts of novels. With liberal cutting, a book such as *War and Peace* can now be listened to in a sitting.

Most "serious," nontabloid newspapers (for example, *The New York Times* and *The Washington Post*) are relatively inefficient to read. This is especially true of stories that begin on page one and then carry over to one or more additional pages. Stories that carry over to additional pages are said to have "jumped," and many readers are resistant to "jumping" with the stories. *USA Today* eliminated this inefficient way of presenting and reading stories by starting and finishing most of them on the same page, in other words, by offering "News McNuggets." This was accomplished by ruthlessly editing stories so that narrative was dramatically reduced (and no words wasted), leaving a series of relatively bare facts. . . .

In the realm of religion, McDonaldization is manifest, among other places, in drive-in churches. Another is the widespread development of televised religious programs whereby people can get their religion in the comfort of their living rooms. A particularly noteworthy example of such religious rationalization occurred in 1985 when the Vatican announced that Catholics

---

*Some publishers also offer a "call–in testing service." An instructor can call a toll–free number, specify the desired questions, and the publisher ships the test to the professor—all free. —Editor.

could receive indulgences through the Pope's annual Christmas benediction on TV or radio. ("Indulgences are a release by way of devotional practices from certain forms of punishment resulting from sin.") Before this development Catholics had to engage in the far less efficient activity of going to Rome for the Christmas benediction and manifesting the "proper intention and attitude" in order to receive their indulgences in person. . . .

[*Destroying Relationships*]

The fast-food restaurant offers its employees a dehumanizing setting within which to work. Few skills are required on the job. Said Burger King workers, "A moron could learn this job, it's so easy" and "Any trained monkey could do this job." Thus workers are asked to use only a minute proportion of all their skills and abilities. Employees are not only not using all of their skills, but they are also not being allowed to think and to be creative on the job. This leads to a high level of resentment, job dissatisfaction, alienation, absenteeism, and turnover among those who work in fast-food restaurants. In fact, the fast-food industry has the highest turnover rate—approximately 100 percent a year—of any industry in the United States. That means that the average worker lasts only about four months at a fast-food restaurant; the entire workforce of the fast-food industry turns over three times a year. . . .

The fast-food restaurant is also dehumanizing as far as the customer is concerned. Instead of a human dining experience, what is offered is eating on a sort of moving conveyor belt or assembly line. The diner is reduced to a kind of overwound automaton who is made to rush through the meal. Little gratification is derived from the dining experience or from the food itself. The best that can usually be said is that it is efficient and it is over quickly.

Some customers might even feel as if they are being fed like livestock in a highly rationalized manner. This point was made a number of years ago on television in a *Saturday Night Live* skit entitled "Trough and Brew," a take-off on a small fast-food chain called Burger and Brew. In the skit, some young executives learn that a new fast-food restaurant called Trough and Brew has opened and they decide to try it for lunch. They are next seen entering the restaurant and having bibs tied around their necks. After that, they discover a long trough, resembling a pig trough. The trough is filled with chili and is periodically refilled by a waiter scooping new supplies from a bucket. The customers bend over, stick their heads into the trough, and begin lapping up the chili as they move along the length of the trough making high-level business decisions. Every so often they come up for air and lap some beer from the communal "brew basin." After they have finished their "meal," they pay their bills, "by the head." Since their faces are smeared with chili, they are literally "hosed off" before they leave the restaurant. The young executives are last seen being herded out of the restaurant, which is being closed for a half-hour so that it can be "hosed down." *Saturday Night Live* was clearly pointing out, and ridiculing, the fact that fast-food restaurants tend to treat their customers like lower animals.

"Get Lost" and Wheel of Fortune

Another dehumanizing aspect of fast-food restaurants is that they minimize contact among human beings. Let us take, for example, the issue of how customers and employees relate. The nature of the fast-food restaurant turns these into fleeting relationships. Because the average employee stays only a few months, and even then only works on a part-time basis, the customer, even the regular customer, is rarely able to develop a long-term personal relationship with a counterperson. Gone are the days when one got to know well a waitress at a diner or the short-order cook at a local greasy spoon. Gone are the days when an employee knows who you are and knows what you are likely to order.

Not only are the relationships with a McDonald's employee fleeting (because the worker remains on the job only a short period of time), but each contact between worker and customer is of a very short duration. It takes little time at the counter to order, receive one's food, and pay for it. Both employees and customers are likely to feel rushed and to want to move on, customers to their dinner and employees to the next order. There is virtually no time for customer and counterperson to interact in such a context. This is even more true of the drive-through window, where thanks to the speedy service and the physical barriers, the server is but a dim and distant image.

The highly impersonal and anonymous relationship between customer and counterperson is heightened by the employees having been trained to interact in a staged and limited manner with customers. Thus, the customers may feel that they are dealing with automatons who have been taught to utter a few phrases rather than with fellow human beings. For their part, the customers are supposed to be, and often are, in a hurry, so they have little to say to the McDonald's employee. Indeed, it could be argued that one of the reasons for the success of fast-food restaurants is that they are in tune with our fast-paced and impersonal society. People in the modern world want to get on with their business without unnecessary personal relationships. The fast-food restaurant gives them precisely what they want.

Not only are the relationships between employee and customer limited greatly, but also other potential relationships. Because employees remain on the job for only a few months, satisfying personal relationships among employees are unlikely to develop. . . .

Relationships among customers are largely curtailed as well. Although some McDonald's ads would have us believe otherwise, gone are the days when people met in the diner or cafeteria for coffee, breakfast, lunch, or dinner and lingered to socialize with one another. Fast-food restaurants are clearly not conducive to such socializing. If nothing else, the chairs are designed to make people uncomfortable and interested in moving on to something else. The drive-through windows are a further step toward McDonaldization, by completely eliminating the possibility of interacting with other customers. . . .

Fast-food restaurants also tend to have negative effects on other human relationships. There is, for example, the effect on the so-called "family meal." The fast-food restaurant is not conducive to a long, leisurely, conversation-filled dinnertime. The family is unlikely to linger long over a meal at McDonald's. Furthermore, as the children grow into their teens, the nature of fast-food restaurants leads to separate meals as the teens go at one time with their friends, and the parents go at another time. Of course, the drive-through window only serves to reduce the possibility of a family meal. The family that gobbles its food while driving on to its next stop can hardly be seen as having what is called these days "quality time" with each other. Here is the way one journalist describes what is happening to the family meal:

> Do families who eat their suppers at the Colonel's, swinging on plastic seats, or however the restaurant is arranged, say grace before picking up a crispy brown chicken leg? Does dad ask junior what he did today as he remembers he forgot the piccalilli and trots through the crowds over to the counter to get some? Does mom find the atmosphere conducive to asking little Mildred about the problems she was having with third-conjugation French verbs, or would it matter since otherwise the family might have been at home chomping down precooked frozen food, warmed in the microwave oven, and watching *Hollywood Squares?*

There is much talk these days about the disintegration of the family, and the fast-food restaurants may well be a crucial contributor to that disintegration.

In fact, as implied above, dinners at home may now not be much different from meals at the fast-food restaurant. Families tended to stop having lunch together by the 1940s and breakfast altogether by the 1950s. Today, the family dinner is following the same route. Even when they eat dinner at home, the meal will probably not be what it once was. Following the fast-food model, people are growing more likely to "graze," "refuel," nibble on this, or snack on that, than they are to sit down to a formal meal. Also, because it is now deemed inefficient to do nothing but just eat, families are likely to watch television while they are eating, thereby efficiently combining two activities. However, the din, to say nothing of the lure, of dinnertime TV programs such as *Wheel of Fortune* is likely to make it difficult for family members to interact with one another.

A key technology in the destruction of the family meal is the microwave oven and the vast array of microwavable foods it helped generate. It is striking to learn that more than 70 percent of American households have a microwave oven. A recent *Wall Street Journal* poll indicated that Americans consider the microwave their favorite household product. In fact, the microwave in a McDonaldizing society is seen as an advance over the fast-food restaurant. Said one consumer researcher, "It has made even fast-food restaurants not seem fast because at home you don't have to wait in line." As a general rule, consumers are demanding meals that take no more than ten minutes to microwave, whereas in the past people were more often willing to spend about a half hour or even an hour cooking dinner. This emphasis on speed has, of course, brought with it poorer taste and lower quality, but people do not seem to mind this loss: "We're just not as critical of food as we used to be." . . .

Fast Food [and Homogenization]

Another dehumanizing effect of the fast-food restaurant is that it has contributed to homogenization around the country and, increasingly, throughout the world. Diversity, which many people crave, is being reduced or eliminated by the fast-food restaurant. This decline in diversity is manifest in the extension of the fast-food model to all sorts of ethnic foods. The settings are all modeled after McDonald's in one way or another and the food has been rationalized and compromised so that it is acceptable to the tastes of virtually all diners. One cannot find an authentically different meal in any of these ethnic fast-food chains.

The expansion of these franchises across the landscape of America means that one finds little difference among regions and among cities throughout the country. Tourists find more familiarity and predictability and less diversity as they travel around the nation, and this is increasingly true on a global scale. Apparently exotic settings are likely to be overrun with both American fast-food chains as well as indigenous varieties. The new and world's largest McDonald's and Kentucky Fried Chicken in Beijing are but two examples of this. . . . The spread of American and indigenous fast food throughout much of the world means that there is less and less diversity from one setting to another. The human craving for new and diverse experiences is being limited, if not progressively destroyed, by the national and international spread of fast-food restaurants. The craving for diversity is being supplanted by the desire for uniformity and predictability. . . .

Conclusion

Although I have emphasized the irresistibility of McDonaldization, my fondest hope is that I am wrong. Indeed, a major motivation is to alert readers to the dangers of McDonaldization and to motivate them to act to stem its tide. I hope that we are able to resist McDonaldization and can create instead a more reasonable, more human world.

McDonald's was recently sued by the famous French chef, Paul Bocuse, for using his picture on a poster without his permission. Enraged, Bocuse said: "How can I be seen promoting this tasteless, boneless food in which everything is soft." Nevertheless, Bocuse seemed to acknowledge the inevitability of McDonaldization: "There's a need for this kind of thing . . . and trying to get rid of it seems to me to be as futile as trying to get rid of the prostitutes in the Bois de Boulogne." Lo and behold, two weeks later, it was announced that the Paris police had cracked down on prostitution in the Bois de Boulogne. Said a police spokesman, "There are none left." Thus, just as chef Bocuse was wrong about the prostitutes, perhaps I was wrong about the irresistibility of McDonaldization. Yet, before we grow overly optimistic, it should be noted that "everyone knows that the prostitutes will be back as soon as the operation is over. In the spring, police predict, there will be even more than before." Similarly, it remains likely that no matter how intense the opposition, the future will bring with it more rather than less McDonaldization. . . . [F]aced with Max Weber's iron cage imagery of a future dominated by the polar night of icy darkness and hardness, the least the reader can do is to follow the words of the poet Dylan Thomas: "Do not go gentle into that good night. . . . Rage, rage against the dying of the light."

43 Social Change Among the Amish

JERRY SAVELLS

With change in contemporary society so common, and so extensive, how is it possible to hold it back? Most of us are engulfed in social change so vast that it sweeps over us like a tide. Like it or not, we have little choice but to adapt. Isn't this the situation for everyone who lives in an industrialized society? Vast changes occur, and rapidly so, and our only choice seems to be how to adapt.

But not so for everybody. The Amish are an outstanding exception. This group of people, who broke from the Swiss-German Mennonite church in the late 1600s and settled in Pennsylvania around 1727, can now be found in about twenty states and Ontario, Canada. About 75 percent, however, live in just three states: Pennsylvania, Ohio, and Indiana. To protect their values, the Amish carefully control change. They maintain customs of dress, music, transportation, and morality from the 1600s and continue to reject "worldly ways." How do they manage to resist such pressure? That is the focus of Savells's article.

THE AUTHOR VISITED EIGHT Amish communities in six states from 1982 to 1986: Berne and Milroy, Indiana; Ethridge, Tennessee; Intercourse and Bird-in-Hand, Pennsylvania; Kalona, Iowa; Plain City, Ohio; and Montezuma, Georgia. Face-to-face interviews were conducted with a select number of the local Amish population and some of the non-Amish population who have frequent contact with the Amish, i.e., local merchants who sell to the Amish, craftpersons, farmers, mail carriers, drivers of the local milk trucks who travel to Amish farms almost daily, and others. A structured twelve-page questionnaire has been used to collect research data using a stratified random sample selected from the New American Almanac (1983) and the Ohio Amish Directory (1981). At this time, 130 questionnaires and/or personal interviews have been completed with selected Amish families. An additional fifty interviews have also been completed among so-called "conservative Mennonite" families for future comparisons.

Although the sample is small, it is encouraging since the Old Order Amish have spurned many efforts from the scientific community to investigate their lifestyle. This particular effort gave new meaning to the term "field research," since it represents approximately 6,500 miles of driving, spread over thirty months.

The Amish interviewees were polite and cordial, but they typically do not welcome outsiders intruding into their lives. They were both retiring and private in their demeanor, since they have not been socialized to desire interaction with strangers. Their lifestyle and religion promote voluntary isolation and this has been a major obstacle to anyone intent on collecting research data via personal interviews. Since the religious concerns of the Amish hold top priority, they would not engage intentionally in any activity that would have the potential of embarrassing members in the same church district.

Sociological Considerations

A brief visit to the public library will reinforce the observation that the Amish cherish many social values once widely embraced in our agrarian society of the Colonial period—values which are largely the antithesis of those that emerged in a modern urban, industrialized society. The Amish typically emphasize the importance of humility, modesty, strong obedience to God, and social conformity; they abhor pride, social snobbery, individualism, and winning through competition. Family bonds and their faith are indeed the cornerstones of the Amish lifestyle.

Unfortunately, what limited information is available to the lay public about the Old Order Amish is often sensationalized and distorted. Yet, there is a distinct feeling of "separateness" and "difference" with numerous references to their horse-and-buggy transportation, somewhat drab clothing, and their aloofness (or overt resistance) to those things considered "trendy" or fashionable.

The Amish are very ethnocentric with a strong sense of social solidarity. There is a consciousness-of-kind evident in their thinking and quick sanctions directed toward the non-believer or those displaying evidence of weakness in their faith. Indeed, some sociologists might argue that the Amish practice of insularity—with a limited tolerance of any deviation—is a major reason why they have survived as a model of the extended family of the past.

In his professional writing, journalist Alvin Toffler has pointed out the disastrous consequences of modern materialism, self-serving lifestyles, hedonistic behavior, the transience and rootlessness of this culture, and extreme emphasis upon competition, money, and careerism to determine one's self-worth. The latter suggest experiences both alien and repulsive to Amish tradition; they abhor the concept of personal achievement rather than seeking to express God's will, the modern habit of "powerbrokering" to gain social advantages, and mutual manipulation. . . . Social change is evident—but carefully controlled and monitored. They work to preserve traditions of the past, emphasize the importance of humility and divine guidance in controlling their own destiny, and maintain a strong posture of serving God rather than the interests of humanity.

An Operational Definition of Change

The Amish do not live within a social vacuum. They are surrounded by accelerating currents of social, political, and economic changes which directly influence their quality of life. One reasonably expects the Amish to be vulnerable to pressures toward modernization. For example, many have been asked to sell their land for commercial development at inflated prices. The changing economic climate in these eight communities and the frustration of competing in a money market where "megabucks" and agri-business threaten the small farmer are having a definite impact upon the Amish way of life.

Amish farmers and the future of their children are often adversely affected by soaring land prices, and the foreign trade imbalance can mean a restricted market for some of their farm exports. Furthermore, when the Amish farmer needs to borrow money for spring planting, the interest rate at the local bank can be especially painful for the small farmer with a limited cash flow.

The Amish are forced to compete in a "money market" where agri-business and the profit motive often threaten some of their most cherished values. For example, our society promotes maximum efficiency, quality control through standardization, the accumulation of capital or wealth, competition among workers for career advancement, and the merits of mass production—basic trends essentially alien to the Amish pursuit of "devotedness, simplicity, and peace."

The Amish strongly advocate the "therapeutic value of real work." They believe that physical labor is good for mind, body, and soul in keeping with the biblical admonition of earning one's bread by the sweat of one's brow. Their work is labor-intensive, in contrast to the national marketplace dominated by the forces of technology and profit margins. Thus, the Amish do not view every new labor-saving device as desirable or progressive. . . .

Since life in any Amish community is ongoing, it is not possible or practical to totally isolate units of analysis, i.e., families, without the influence of outside variables. The Amish do not constitute an experimental group in a laboratory situation. Hence, one must be careful not to treat all indicators of social change as evidence of modernity. Some changes may be basically unique to one church district or community, and cannot be considered universal to all Amish. For example, the New Order Amish in both Kalona and Intercourse have accepted the practice of having closer contact with the outside world; some own cottage industries that cater to tourists and some have given their business cards to this researcher. In many Old Order communities this behavior would be unacceptable.

Pressures That Influence Modernization

The five major social institutions—family, religion, economics, education, and politics—were studied in this sample of Amish interviewees as an ethnographic method to identify and document patterns of modernity. Caution is both recommended and prudent to avoid the pitfalls of making global generalizations regarding the Amish lifestyle, since rules of behavior may vary among church districts or regions. The Amish define the behavioral expectations and boundaries of their communities through the *Ordnung*, the official rules of the Amish community. Any member found to have disobeyed the *Ordnung* would be subject to *Meidung*, or shunning. It is a measure of social and religious control still considered an acceptable practice by over eighty percent of the respondents in this study. This has the avowed purpose of encouraging the offender to seek forgiveness from God and other members of the church district as quickly as possible.

FAMILY

This institution is still greatly cherished by the Amish. It is not unusual to see three generations living together in either of the eight research sites. The average Amish family in this sample had seven children, but this researcher talked with some Amish families that had as many as thirteen children. Family size would appear to be more a reflection of age and economic security than sheer desire, since almost all Amish parents profess to want large families. Modern means of contraception are forbidden, unless medically prescribed to protect the health of the mother.

Several Amish parents were concerned that economic factors beyond their control represent a serious challenge to their children and may cause many of their youth to accept employment in occupations provided by outsiders. In Milroy, Indiana, several of the young married males commuted to Indianapolis with the assistance of a non-Amish driver to work as carpenters in the building industry—a situation that forces them to accommodate the expectations of a non-Amish employer. Being away from hearth and home was clearly not their first choice; it reduces the opportunities and time to share family activities. The subtle pressures of this experience can undermine cherished Amish values in the name of economic survival.

Amish parents prefer that their families remain self-supporting, since the daily sharing of work assignments tends to give prolonged contact between parent and child, with a "solidifying effect." The Amish still grow much of their food, provide for their own energy needs, and assume responsibility for their own well-being, rather than relying upon insurance companies, welfare programs, or Social Security to shield them from the hazards of life.

To help preserve this family-centered focus, Amish parents are careful to shield their children from the information explosion of our technological society—particularly as it is disseminated by the mass media and in the public schools. However, where outside employment is essential for survival, accommodation may become necessary through learning new skills or pursuing an advanced education.

The Amish family is still strongly patriarchal. The women's liberation movement has made very few incursions into any of these eight Amish communities. However, Amish women today are by no means totally subservient in a traditional sense. This researcher discovered that Amish women in some church districts can accept modest change without severe reprisals or shunning. For example, in Berne, it was a common practice for Amish women to use polyester cloth rather than 100 percent cotton for their family's clothing. Also, many of these clothes are now purchased, rather than handsewn. Some of the Amish wives in Berne used Mary Kay cosmetics, but only the creams, not the make-up. The latter is considered too "worldly."

RELIGION

The Amish in this sample show some gradual change in their religious practices. Over ten percent of the respondents had changed their religious preference from Old Order to New Order within the context of one generation. This change will definitely have a ripple effect for their children, grandchildren, and great-grandchildren. . . .

The Old Order Amish prohibit ownership of automobiles, telephones, and electricity in the home. However, farm tractors are now being used by the New Order Amish in some areas; in Kalona, tractors were acceptable if they had steel wheels, not rubber tires. The adoption of the latter would create too much mobility.

In both Plain City and Intercourse, diesel generators are now considered an acceptable innovation to supply the barn (not the house) with electricity. The Amish dairy farmer—like all other dairy farmers—must meet state health standards regarding proper refrigeration of milk which is sold commercially. Hence, it is very difficult to pinpoint where the Old Order Amish religious practices actually end and their lifestyle begins since the two are often "one and the same."

A few of the Amish in Berne are now beginning to use cameras, especially to photograph their children, a practice that would have brought immediate censure a few years ago. Even when this practice is known to other family members, it is regarded as a taboo topic for everyday conversation. Most of the Old Order Amish interviewed in Berne still believe that the Bible forbids taking "graven images" of persons.

ECONOMIC CHANGES

The economic security in some of the families interviewed appeared to be more fragile than that of previous generations. Wherever possible parents are still subdividing their farms so that their children will have the chance to enjoy the fruit of their labor in farming. However, with a shortage of affordable and available land for farming, the younger generation has found itself increasingly dependent upon ties with the non-Amish sector of the local economy. In Berne and Intercourse, some of the local Amish men work in craft-related industries, such as factories that manufacture furniture (mostly handcrafted), coal or wood burning stoves, and carriages. In Kalona some of the Amish girls work in a local cheese factory that purchases the bulk milk produced on Amish farms. The waitresses in some of the local restaurants are also members of the local Amish community.

This trend toward outside employment leaves the Amish especially vulnerable to forces of economic recession and a stagnant national economy. Since the Old Order Amish prohibit their members from pursuing an advanced education which would make them more competitive in the national job market, they are often underskilled in jobs that require moderate levels of technological sophistication.

The Amish are also forbidden to accept employment where joining a labor union is a condition of the workplace; thus, they have minimal job security in a formal sense. However, the Amish in this sample remained cheerful and optimistic that God would provide for their daily needs.

EDUCATION

As one moves from the environment of the Old Order Amish to the New Order Amish, one expects that the number of years of formal education might increase with each successive generation. There is a definite trend in that direction, since some of the New Order Amish want to develop marketable skills at a trade school or by taking correspondence courses. In Montezuma this researcher interviewed a young female from a New Order Amish family who is a registered nurse.

The Old Order Amish still maintain their own schools in most of the communities studied. In Berne the Old Order Amish can send their children to the eighth grade in an Amish school where funds for operating the school are provided by the parents of the children who attend, and an Amish teacher is provided, or they are permitted to send their children to a public school in Berne—only through the ninth grade.

Very few of the children in Old Order Amish families remain in school after reaching age sixteen—the age at which they can quit according to most state laws. In order to comply with legal requirements some Amish children voluntarily repeat the ninth grade—a sacrifice to the expectations of their Amish parents.

One Old Order Amish mother of several children indicated that she wanted her sons and daughters to consider going to college, preferably a Mennonite college, where they could receive training to become a member of a "noble" profession. Then they could serve the Amish community directly in professions such as teaching, and medical or veterinary practice.

This researcher found that most of the Amish adults were reasonably well informed about news events on a global scale. Some Amish families subscribe to both *The Budget,* an Amish-related newspaper, and a local or regional newspaper. Some have subscriptions to such mass circulation magazines as *Time, Newsweek, U.S. News and World Report, Reader's Digest, and National Geographic.* Most of the Amish adults do travel out-of-state to visit relatives and for recreation. In Montezuma, one respondent had recently returned from a trip to Australia.

POLITICS

The Old Order Amish in each of these eight communities do not permit their members to pursue or hold public office. To say that the Old Order Amish are politically uninvolved is not accurate. For example, they have petitioned the Congress of the United States to be exempt from payment of Social Security taxes since they do not allow their members to collect Social Security benefits. They have also sought a favorable hearing in the courts to have their children exempt from both mandatory attendance at public secondary schools and conscription into the military service.

The Old Order Amish in this sample showed an aloofness to affiliation with either major political party. Less than fifteen percent of the male interviewees had voted in either the 1980 or 1984 United States presidential election, when one of the most conservative candidates in recent history was representing the Republican Party. The Amish fear that politics with either party would certainly invite reprisals from the opposite party. Thus, it is in their best interest to remain neutral—a strong statement for the separation of church and state.

MODERNIZATION

This researcher found that the majority of the social changes that are occurring in these eight Amish communities are the result of very careful, selective, conscious deliberation, i.e., planned change. . . . One respondent added a word of caution regarding their non-use of so-called modern technology: "We do not feel that electricity, the telephone, and the automobile are evil in themselves; rather, our non-use helps us to keep from being drawn into the mainstream of the world."

Thomas Foster, a respected scholar of the Old Order Amish, has suggested that one of the most significant factors reinforcing Amish self-sufficiency is their reliance upon appropriate technologies that complement their lifestyle and religious beliefs, i.e., their sustained, practical use of human labor and power from wind, water, horses, wood, and the sun. These small-scale, labor-intensive technologies greatly reduce the need for large capital investments while keeping a lid on operating costs compared to their non-Amish peers. Foster maintains that in Ohio, for example, the Old Order Amish can earn profits on 75 to 150 acres of land at a time when Ohio's non-Amish farmers, who use diesel tractors and other costly equipment, have difficulty making a decent profit on acreage twice as large.

Social Change Among the Amish

Change has been regarded as neither evil nor good among the Amish. It can work for betterment, or it can create havoc. The Amish perceive that much of what is regarded as "modern" or "progress" by contemporary standards remains a source of temptation for their young, and potential conflict and disharmony for their communities if not kept at a proper distance. For example, the Amish do not believe electricity, telephones, and driving an automobile are inherently evil, but they realize that these so-called modern conveniences would alter the Amish lifestyle and that of future generations. The effects of this technology, e.g., high mobility with an automobile, would offer too much temptation and less concern for maintaining tradition.

Simply speaking, the Amish prefer not to become dependent upon these inventions, but prefer to maintain a quiet and simple life unfettered with the high-level complications of the modern world. Some outsiders feel the Amish have essentially avoided the acceptance of social change in order to maintain the pursuit of a Nirvana or heaven on earth. The Amish, on the other hand, rarely convey that they feel cheated by denying themselves in this life. . . .

Historians and sociologists have been aware that in other historical periods, religious ideology and practice have fueled powerful motivations for creating change—as seen in the kinship between the growth of Protestantism and industrialism in the Western World. Yet, the Amish have cited their religion as one of the most important reasons why they have essentially and successfully avoided much of the social change identified with the Industrial Revolution. Change is *not* welcome if it adversely affects their religious beliefs, their family stability, their nonresistant lifestyle, or if it creates too much conflict.

Where change has been accepted—and this can be measured figuratively more in inches than yards—it has ordinarily been seen as either an improvement of their ability to provide economically for their families or as reasonable for public safety and the public good. Two examples of the latter were the adoption in some states of batteries on horsedrawn transportation to provide flashing taillights at night as a safety precaution, and the adoption in some districts of diesel generators in their barns, primarily to cool and agitate milk in bulk tanks. To the Amish this is a preference, not a paradox. If it confuses outsiders, they do not feel a need to explain.

Although the vast majority of my sample had routine (daily or weekly) contact with outsiders, most felt that the average outsider did not understand their Amish lifestyle or values and the religious justification for the way they prefer to live. Thus, from an outsider's perspective, the Amish are resisting change simply to preserve tradition—but the Amish understand their actions to be "the will of God."

Summary and Conclusions

. . . Each generation experiences a certain amount of trial and error in finding norms and values that will best serve their unique needs. Tradition for the sake of tradition is hardly an answer to the complex problems facing the Amish. Although the Amish honor important traditions regarding their faith and their people, they also recognize that social and economic survival necessitates that some acceptance of change will be both normal and inevitable. As one Old Order Amish man remarked, "You cannot put a ship in the middle of the ocean and expect the deck to always stay dry."

Acculturation *is* occurring in the majority of Old Order Amish communities visited by this researcher, but it is neither rampant nor whimsical. Rather, social change has consistently been scrutinized carefully and accepted gradually—where the results could be monitored for any possible unwanted side effects. The Old Order Amish enclave is not so much a model of "paradise lost" as it is a model of "evasive innovation" to save and protect a small, but significant, religious minority who wish to be "in the world, but not of the world."

44 Women in the Military

LAURA L. MILLER

That we are immersed in rapid social change has become a taken-for-granted assumption of contemporary life. But the pinch of change is not felt to the same degree by everyone. A change may affect one person's life profoundly, while for others it merely provides an interesting topic of conversation. Some change is so moderate that we can adjust to the new aspect of life with little difficulty. Others upset us because they challenge our taken-for-granted assumptions about the way the world is and should be. Some gain by change, and like what is happening; others lose, and can't stand it. With perspectives so vastly different in our pluralistic society, some view the same change as long overdue; others insist that it should never have come about in the first place.

The women's movement represents profound social change. It has challenged taken-for-granted assumptions and brought deep consequences for our lives. But, as with other social change, not everyone has been touched in the same way. In this article we look at the integration of women in the military, where women now occupy positions from which they were excluded just a generation ago. Miller focuses on how men react to the presence of women in formerly all-male jobs, noting that they are using techniques of resistance more commonly associated with the protests of minorities.

THE DATA PRESENTED HERE are taken from multiple stages of field research on active-duty Army soldiers from early 1992 to late 1994. I used a multimethod strategy to capture both large-scale attitudinal patterns and individual viewpoints. To collect the data, I traveled to eight stateside Army posts and two national training centers, where soldiers conduct war games on a simulated battlefield. I also lived with Army personnel for 10 days in Somalia during Operation Restore Hope, for seven days in Macedonia during Operation Able Sentry, and for six days in Haiti during Operation Uphold Democracy. . . .

Given the military context and the sensitive nature of some of the issues, [in my discussion groups and interviews] I relied on written notes rather than tape-recording. . . . I also collected large-scale survey data in order to analyze the relationships between soldiers' demographics and their attitudes on a wide array of issues. The ethnographic data were cross-validated by multiple stages of questionnaires totaling more than 4,100. . . .

In *Domination and the Arts of Resistance,* James C. Scott (1990) provides an extensive historical analysis explaining how powerless groups resist and subvert the efforts of those with power over them. His work demonstrates that people's fear of negative sanctions often drives them to resist in ways that cannot be traced to the initiator, or are lost in the anonymity of crowds. The greater the power exerted from above, the more fully masked the resistance from below. Scott provides numerous examples of the art of political disguise, including gossip, rumor, grumbling, folktales, possession by spirits, mass defiance, anonymous threats, symbolic inversion of the social order, and rituals of reversal such as carnival. Like much of the research on which he draws, Scott continues the Marxist tradition of dividing the world in two: those with economic power (the bourgeoisie, landlords, kings, the ruling class, employers) and those who depend on them or must serve them (the proletariat, peasants, serfs, slaves, workers). . . .

Scott's examples closely parallel behavior that I found in gender relations in the Army, except for one very significant anomaly: It is the structurally dominant group, Army men, who employ the strategies of resistance that are generally seen as the weapons of the weak. My research shows that some men devote a great deal of energy to resisting their women coworkers and commanders through methods such as sabotage, name-calling, foot-dragging, and spreading rumors. Women, paradoxically, do not appear to be using any of these strategies of the weak to gain power from men, according to either their accounts or men's.

What explains the use of weapons of the weak by the structurally dominant group but not by the subordinate minority? My investigation led me to social psychological studies of power. In this literature it is argued that people act according to perceptions of power based on their own experiences and knowledge, not according to some objective analysis of resources. . . . Frequently military men described themselves as unjustly constrained or controlled by military women. Furthermore, these men tend to believe that women's power is usually gained illegitimately and that women take advantage of their gender to promote their own careers. . . .

For example, enlisted men may not enjoy the privileges of their sex as much as men at the higher command levels, particularly in relation to women officers; also, in this era of organizational downsizing, male career officers sometimes blame their limited opportunities on increased participation by women. Thus not all military men experience male privilege, and even some of the more privileged members are constrained within the organization. . . .

In this article I first describe men's resistance in the form of gender harassment. Then I examine who is likely to oppose expanded or even current roles for women soldiers, and why gender harassment is a product of this opposition. I conclude with the implications of this case for gender and other minority relations as well as for the study of power and resistance.

Gender Harassment

DISTINGUISHING GENDER HARASSMENT FROM SEXUAL HARASSMENT

> Sexual harassment implies that you can only be harassed through sexual means. Women can also be harassed through the job in other ways. If your commander doesn't like you, you will encounter harassment, i.e., the shit details, made to work later than everyone else, constant field problems, low efficiency ratings, etc. It's more prejudice than harassment towards females in the Army. (black NCO [Non-Commissioned Officer] in administrative support)

Sexual harassment is not an analytically useful category because it may refer to situations as disparate as sexual assault, discrimination in promotion or assignment, sexual comments, and gender harassment. . . . In my analysis, I limit the term *sexual harassment* to unwanted sexual comments or advances.

Gender harassment refers to harassment that is not sexual, and is used to enforce traditional gender roles, or in response to the violation of those roles. This form of harassment also may aim to undermine women's attempts at gaining power or to describe that power as illegitimately obtained or exercised. Examples include men proclaiming "Women can't drive trucks" in the presence of female drivers or refusing to follow a superior's directives simply because that superior is a woman. Many Army women report that gender harassment on the job is more prevalent than sexual harassment.

Gender harassment also can be used against men who violate gender norms. For example, men who fail to live up to the "masculine ideal" by showing insecurity or hesitation during maneuvers may be called "fags" or "girls" by their comrades. . . . Because behavior that conflicts with one's gender role is stereotypically associated with homosexuality, both heterosexuality and traditional gender roles are enforced through gender harassment.

Because of the prevalence of gender harassment, workshops and policies that address only sexual harassment miss much of the picture. Women report that gender harassment can be just as disruptive in their lives as sexual harassment: It can interfere with their ability to do their work, with their private lives, and with their opportunities to receive some recognition and promotions. Gender harassment is often difficult to attribute to individuals, may not be recognized by command as a problem, and is often invisible in debates about harassment of women in the military. . . .

Gender harassment is hardly unique to military men and women; it is found in many studies of women in sex-atypical work. Examples of what I call gender harassment are scattered throughout studies of job climate, male coworkers' reactions to women, and subtle or covert sex discrimination:

[We] also face another pervasive and sinister kind of harassment which is gender-based, but may have nothing to do with sex. It is a harassment aimed at us simply because we are women in a "man's" job, and its function is to discourage us from staying in our trades. (M. Martin 1988: 10)

SOME FORMS OF GENDER HARASSMENT

Below are some illustrative examples of gender harassment.

Resistance to Authority. Women who are officers or NCOs commonly complained of male subordinates, especially older enlisted men, who "just don't like answering to a woman." When given orders, they feign ignorance about what is expected of them, or engage in foot-dragging. This method is effective because the men do not risk the official reprimand warranted by an outright refusal to obey orders; yet they challenge women's authority by not complying completely. As one white NCO hypothesized, "Men are intimidated by women superiors and most try to undermine their work." Several women leaders reported having to "pull rank" more often than their male counterparts to get things done. . . .

Constant Scrutiny. Hostile men use constant scrutiny to catch individual women making mistakes, and then use the mistakes to criticize the abilities of women in general. Because of this scrutiny women often feel obligated to work harder than those under less supervision. Women report that they experience such scrutiny as relentless harassment, and that it can make them feel self-conscious and extremely stressed.

Both enlisted and officer women report that as women they are subject to closer scrutiny than men. When women are singled out for observation by suspicious peers and superiors, they often feel they have to work harder than their coworkers just to be accepted as equal members of the unit. . . .

The behavior of a few women is often projected onto the entire gender, but the same is not true for men. To illustrate, some women soldiers serving in the early phases of operations in Haiti pointed out that if the three soldiers who committed suicide there had been women, a discussion would have ensued: People would have asked whether women could handle the stress of deployments or separation from their families. Yet because they were "just men," they were reported as *soldiers*, and the suicides were not interpreted as saying anything about men in general. . . .

Women leaders are rendered less flexible than men because of the constant scrutiny. Sometimes they believe that the people watching them are waiting for them to make mistakes or deviate from regulations; this is a disconcerting environment in which to make decisions. As a result, some men as well as some women classify female superiors as unfair or "too hard." They prefer to serve under men, who have more freedom to bend the rules in favor of their troops: "Women seem to feel they have something to prove. They do, but should not abuse their soldiers [in the process]" (white enlisted man in electronics).

Scrutiny as a harassment strategy is particularly safe in the military because it fits into the functioning of the organization. One cannot be punished for seeking out and correcting errors, and it would be quite difficult to prove that women are being watched more closely than men.

Gossip and Rumors. Army women are often the subject of untrue gossip about their sex lives. Repeatedly I heard that if a woman dates more than one man in the Army, she is labeled a "slut." If she doesn't date, she is labeled a "dyke." Unlike men, women who are promoted quickly or who receive coveted assignments are often rumored to have "slept their way to the top." At every post I visited, soldiers had heard the rumor (which has never been verified) that a few women soldiers in the Persian Gulf War made a fortune by setting up a tent and serving as prostitutes for their male counterparts.

Young Army women in particular feel that their personal lives are under intense scrutiny at all times, and that ridiculous lies can emerge from the rumor mill for no apparent reason. One enlisted woman was shocked when her commander took her aside one day and said, "Look, I know you're sleeping with all the guys in your unit." She could not imagine why he said that to her; who would have started such a rumor, or why; or why fellow soldiers—her friends—would have contributed to spreading the stories. . . .

Because rumors are usually untraceable, they cannot be addressed through a formal complaint system. Scott discusses the power of such strategies:

> Gossip is perhaps the most familiar and elementary form of disguised popular aggression. Though its use is hardly confined to attacks by subordinates on their superiors, it represents a relatively safe social sanction. Gossip, almost by definition, has no identifiable author, but scores of eager retellers who can claim they are just passing on the news. Should the gossip—and here I have in mind malicious gossip—be challenged, everyone can disavow responsibility for having originated it. . . .
>
> The character of gossip that distinguishes it from rumor is that gossip consists typically of stories that are designed to ruin the reputation of some identifiable person or persons. If the perpetrators remain anonymous, the victim is clearly specified. There is, arguably, something of a disguised democratic voice about gossip in the sense that it is propagated only to the extent that others find it in their interest to retell the story. If they don't, it disappears. (1990:142)

Sabotage. I found evidence of sabotage, as a form of gender harassment, only in work fields that are nontraditional for women. Because these nontraditional occupations can be strenuous and dangerous, the sabotage of equipment can be quite threatening. . . . .

In one instance of sabotage from my research, two women new to an all-male vehicle maintenance and repair unit arrived at work every morning to find that the heavy, difficult-to-change track had been removed from their assigned vehicle. After a few weeks, during which they patiently replaced the track each day, the harassment ended. They had earned the men's respect by proving their skills and their willingness to work hard. The men's doubts were dispelled when they decided that the women's abilities had earned them a position in the unit, and that they would not use their gender to exempt themselves from dirty and difficult work.

Sabotage of equipment and tools was reported by women in mechanical fields, but I never heard of sabotage in the form of disappearing files, erased computer data, jammed typewriters, hidden medical supplies, or misplaced cooking utensils.

Indirect Threats.   Some soldiers reported that some of their fellow men would rape women who dared to enter infantry or armor units. The comments written on surveys include these remarks by a black enlisted man in the combat arms:

> The majority of men in the Army are sexist. I know, because I'm a man. Women in combat units would be harassed, if not raped. I say this because I've seen it and have nothing to hide. If you want the truth about issues, don't ask NCOs or officers. They'll tell you everything is all peaches and cream!! If you want the truth ask an E4 that's been in about 5 years. Women only have a fair shake as cooks or nurses. They'll be extremely harassed, if not molested, if they enter combat arms. I know, trust me.

Another infantryman echoed that assessment, although he proposed that male violence toward women is due to the conditions of deployments, not to sexism:

> In a situation where times are hard—less food, no showers, road marching, with 70–100 lbs ruck on your back, and [you] don't know when the next supply shipment will be in, the male soldiers will start thinking of sex and the female soldiers may be raped or something.

Why Gender Harassment? Perceptions of Power and Limited Forms of Protest

Some men resort to gender harassment to protect changing gender norms, either because they personally prefer traditional norms or because they think that men and women are not capable of successfully working outside traditional roles. Many of these men believe that women's attempts to claim equality have resulted in favorable treatment for women who have been largely unwilling or unable to fully meet the demands of being a soldier. Gender harassment is an attempt to push women back into their more "natural" roles, restore the meritocratic order of the organization, and ensure that all soldiers on the battlefield can do their jobs and assist the wounded in times of war. Certainly these views are considered sexist by many, and potentially could cause problems for any soldier who expresses them openly in mixed company. Thus gender harassment is preferred as an often unattributable way to protest the expansion of women's roles and to attempt to balance scales that are perceived to be tilted in women's favor.

HOSTILE PROPONENTS AND ANOTHER VERSION OF EQUALITY

"Women should be given totally equal treatment and standards. But I don't see it happening." This assertion by a male Army captain expresses the views of many Army men. Rather than championing women's rights, however, this officer is among the men who feel that women, not men, are the privileged and powerful group in the military. These men oppose expanding women's opportunities because they believe that women already enjoy too many advantages in the organization and have not yet met the requirements of the roles they already fill.

Some men believe that women use the term *equality* to advance their personal interests, and that they would object if true equality were offered:

> My opinion is that if women want the right to be in combat roles, they should have to register with selective service. Also, if women want to be treated and have the same rights as men, they should be treated equally all of the time and not just when it is convenient for them. (white enlisted man)

Interview data reveal that most of the men who favor opening combat roles to women on the same terms as men do so only because they are confident that women will fail in those roles. I term this group "hostile proponents" of women in combat. Such hostile proponents reason that the issue of women in the combat arms will not be put to rest until women have been given the opportunity to prove their incompetence. For example, a male driver agreed that women should be allowed to volunteer for combat roles—until he dropped off the female officer who was traveling with us. As soon as she left our group, he added that he thought women should be allowed into combat because they would see how hard the combat arms really are, and no one would have to listen any longer to their complaints about wanting to be included. This "treat women the same to watch them fail" attitude was expressed in writing by a white NCO in the combat arms:

> My feelings are that women just want a door open that is closed. If they want to be totally equal with us, shave their head in basic training [and] give them the same [physical training] test as men. Women in the infantry would ruin male bonding and get soldiers killed or hurt trying to cover for them in combat. Try an all female infantry basic training and [advanced individual training] with the exact same standards as males.

These hostile proponents have found that they can voice their objections by appropriating the language of the feminist activists. Arguments that women should stay home and raise children can be denounced as sexist; agreeing with activists that women and men are "equal" and should be expected to be treated equally cannot. When women are kept out of certain occupations, feminists can continue to argue that women, given the chance, could perform as well as men. Hostile proponents believe that admitting women is a better strategy for reducing the credibility of such arguments because, they insist, the reality will prove the arguments false.

One resistant male soldier provided the formula "(Equal pay = equal job = equal responsibility = equal risk) = equal opportunity" to stress that equality should be sought across the board, not only in pay or opportunity. He was one of the many men who believed that the differential policies actually work in women's favor, disrupt the meritocratic order, and are likely to imperil soldiers in times of war.

A few combat soldiers in my survey were motivated by self-interest to support admitting women to their Military Occupational Specialties (MOSs). One such man, a black NCO, wrote:

> If women are allowed in combat they should be made to shave their heads like men, or let men grow their hair like women. And if women are allowed, field duty would become better for men, because of [women's] needs. So therefore, I'm for them in combat. Yes, let them in.

MEN'S PERCEPTIONS OF WOMEN'S PRIVILEGES

Why do some Army men perceive themselves, and not women, to be the disadvantaged gender in the military? Although other respondents offer counterarguments to these men's opinions, I focus here on the viewpoint of men who regard themselves as underdogs. In this section I demonstrate how a structurally dominant group can perceive itself to be a disadvantaged group, and therefore resort to the types of resistance strategies that Scott attributes to the weak. The unifying theme of these examples is the belief that most military women do not take the same risks or work as hard as do military men, and yet are promoted more quickly than men because of their gender.

Easier Physical Training Standards. Both men and women reported that women's physical training requirements are not only different from men's, but easier for most women to meet than men's are for most men. Although this training is supposed to maintain physical fitness, most soldiers interpret it as a measure of strength. That the women's requirements are easier than the men's is seen by many as proof that women are less well qualified for physically strenuous work:

> I can't be adamant enough. There is no place for women in the infantry. Women do not belong in combat units. If you haven't been there, then you wouldn't understand. As far as equal rights, some women say they are as physically strong as a

man. Then why are the [physical training] standards different? (white NCO in the combat arms)

Thus some soldiers argue that only one standard should exist for men and for women, and that such a standard should reflect the requirements of the job. A white lieutenant in intelligence and communications explained his view:

> The standards are never the same for men and women. The [Army Physical Fitness Test] is a perfect example. [W]hat most junior leaders feel (that I have discussed the topic with) . . . there should be no difference for either sex. [The Department of the Army] has established minimum standards and they should apply across the board, regardless of sex. Which means the female standards would have to go out the window. A man who can only do 18 pushups is unfit for service, so it should be [the same] for females. If a female can meet the same standards as me, I will gladly serve with, for, or over her. But if she can't I will also gladly chapter her out of the Army as unfit for service. I've seen action in Grenada and Iraq and know there are females who could've done my job. Few, but some. However my wife, who went to Saudi, is 104 lbs., 5'4" and couldn't carry my 201 lbs. across the living room, much less the desert if I was wounded. Whose standards should apply?

In deployments and field exercises, the differences are most apparent. Some commanders find them difficult to know how to handle:

> The topic about women in combat MOS's has finally cleared up with me, I have completed [platoon leadership training], and found that the women on my patrol team could not perform their squad duties. For example, being a 60-gunner, or radio operator I was patrol leader. I assigned the females on my team the 60 and the radio. After about 2 miles of patrolling, the females could not do their jobs. I was accused of being sexist, but when it came down to it, men had to take those assigned jobs in my squad from these women. I'm sure that there are some females that could "keep up" or "hang" with the men, but the fact is that women are not physically strong enough. (white enlisted man in the combat arms)

Pregnancy as an Advantage. Some men find it unfair that women have an honorable option out of the service, deployments, or single barracks that men do not have: pregnancy. A white enlisted man in intelligence and communications wrote:

> There seems to be a trend that females in the Army take advantage of free medical and have kids while serving. The 9 months of pregnancy limits them to no physical labor and is bad on morale. They are still a soldier, but they are only working at about 30% of their potential, forcing men or non-pregnant women to compensate.

A white lieutenant in the medical field noted, "I am currently in a unit with female soldiers, about 60–75% are pregnant or on some type of profile." "Profile" is a standing in which soldiers' physical abilities are limited; therefore they are exempt from physically strenuous tasks, including daily physical training. Pregnant women are among the most common sources of resentment and thus are targets of harassment. Pregnancy then, is another way in which some men feel that women are receiving equal pay and promotion, but are not doing equal work and not taking equal risks and responsibilities.

Better Educational Opportunities.   Many men feel that restrictions on women's roles are unfair not because they limit women, but because they appear to give women opportunities to receive more schooling than men, thus improving their chances for promotion. A white enlisted man wrote, "Most women are in rear units and have the chance to go to school and complete correspondence courses." A black NCO viewed these opportunities as tipping the balance in women's favor in competitions for promotion: "Of most of the units that I've served, the female soldier is more apt to attend schools, i.e., military and civilian. This constant trend allows them better opportunities for career progression."

Some men feel that with this extra training, women will be more qualified than men, with the result that "Most women are promoted above their peers" (white NCO). One white enlisted man expressed the view that it is wasteful to allow women to take coveted slots in combat-related training to help their careers when they are currently restricted from performing those tasks in the event of a real war:

> Each person male or female will perform according to his or her gifts. We cannot make that determination. Congress needs to get off its lazy butt and make a decision one way or the other. Until that time, it remains a waste of time and taxpayer's money to send women to combat related schools (jump schools and air assault, etc.) just for the sake of being "stylish" and to appease those women who whine about discrimination when they're not allowed to do something a male soldier does.

Exemption from Combat Arms as a Way to Faster Promotion, Better Assignments, and "Cushy" Jobs.   In some units there is a hierarchy of assignments, which is sometimes disrupted by the way women are integrated. The lowest jobs are often the "grunt work"—hard, mindless labor. Some men protested to me that when women are assigned to such a unit, they are spared the grunt work and placed (often by male superiors) ahead of men for more desirable assignments. Not only are they excused from doing what men have to do; they also delay men's progress into better positions and sometimes have authority over the men they have bumped. A white lieutenant cited an example of the problems created because a man in a signal MOS can be assigned to a combat unit and required to do grunt work, but a woman is always assigned elsewhere:

> Currently, females in combat support roles (e.g., signal, chemical, [military police], medical services) can not hold a designated position in Combat Units. For example, females are allowed to serve in the signal corps, but they are not allowed

to serve as a signal [platoon leader] in a combat arms unit. There is too much animosity towards females in a specific branch if they can't hold the same positions
that their male counterparts [do]. The females are seen as getting the "cushy" jobs
and interesting jobs as the males have to fulfill the combat roles. If a female can
not hold a position in their designated specialty, they should not be allowed in
that specific specialty.

These men view women not only as obtaining easier work, but as jumping up
the hierarchy without earning it. As a white lieutenant explains, this can breed
resentment:

Chemical corps: females should not be allowed in this branch if they cannot serve
in all positions. For example, they get sent to this division, but cannot serve in the
infantry, armor, or forward artillery units. This leaves very few slots for them to
fill. [The Army] does not manage this very [well] at all. As a new lieutenant, we
must put in our time at the battalion staff level, first, then we are awarded a platoon at the chem company. (One company per division). [The Department of the
Army] sends us more females than we have slots for, so they wind up being
platoon leaders at the company ahead of the males who have put in their time at
the battalions. A lot of hard feelings about this. They (females) should not be
branched chemical or some of the other combat support branches.

Men complained that women are not required to do the heaviest or dirti-
est part of any job, and that they can get away with it without reprimand because of their sex. Although men may find it humorous when Beetle Bailey
shirks his assignments, they may become resentful when women have an unfair advantage based on their sex. One black enlisted man wrote: "Today all
you hear in the Army is that we are equal, but men do all the hard and heavy
work whether it's combat or not."

According to some men, women's current behavior is proof that most are
unable or unwilling to do the work required of soldiers in the combat arms.
Thus they resist putting their lives on the line with such soldiers: "I feel
women are useless to the Army, most do not do their part when it comes to
real work! Most won't change a tire, or pick up a box if it weighs more than 5
lbs. I would not go to war with women in or out of a combat role." Some of
these conclusions are based on experience in the States:

When given the same opportunity, most [women] look for excuses not to do the
work. You in your position can not see it. However, I am exposed to it daily. The
majority of females I know are not soldiers. They are employed. Anything strenuous is avoided with a passion. I would hate to serve with them during combat! I
would end up doing my job and $2/3$ of theirs just to stay alive. (black NCO in administrative work)
    I feel as if women in the military are ordered to do less work, get out of
doing things such as field problems, and when it comes to doing heavy work, they
just stand around and watch the work until it is completed. This is part of the reason I feel they could not handle a combat role because of a weaker physical and

mental capability under such a stressful situation. I say this because it is proved in an everyday day of work. (black enlisted man in a technical field)

Women's gender identity traditionally has been tied to "delicacy," while men's identity has been tied to the ability to be tough and strong. So men may try to avoid work in general, but avoiding heavy labor in particular would make them look weak, cast doubt on their masculinity, and draw ridicule from other men about their "femininity." Thus many men resent that women can avoid a great deal of dirty, heavy work and still succeed in the military, while men's lives are considerably tougher. Although men tend to lay most of the blame for "getting by" on women, this behavior could not persist unless the leaders allowed it.

Paternalism Allowing Women to Get Away With More. Both men and women may try to bend the rules, but when women succeed because of their gender, male coworkers may hold it against them. Several times women told me how they could avoid certain duties by complaining of cramps to particular male commanders. At the first mention of anything "menstrual" their commander would grimace and wave them away. (This did not work with women superiors, who sent them to sick call if they thought the cramps were serious.) Two women told me that they could hide off-limits items such as candy by placing tampons or underwear on top of the contents of their lockers or drawers. During inspections, their male commander took one look at their belongings, saw the personal items, and moved on, apparently too embarrassed to examine the rest of the contents.

As another example, one man wrote on his survey.

I don't think women can withstand not being able to take showers for as long as men. When I was in the Gulf, we were ordered to use the water that we had only for drinking. But after one week the women were using our drinking water to take bird baths. This made me very upset.

This problem is framed as a matter of women's behavior, not the command's enforcement of rules.

Male commanders enforce rules differently for women, for several reasons. In the case of the water, the leader may have made this exception for women because he perceived them as more fragile than men, or felt that some sort of chivalry was appropriate. Padavic and Reskin (1990) call such behavior "paternalism," which they measured in their study of blue-collar workers according to whether women "had been relieved of some hard assignments, whether male coworkers had given them special treatment because of their sex, and whether their supervisors had favored them because of their sex" (p. 618).

Men in command positions sometimes fear disciplining women or pushing them to excel. These men worry that they will be accused of harassing women soldiers because of their gender, or of being insensitive to women's needs or limitations. Also, some are too embarrassed about women's under-wear or hygiene to perform the ritual invasion of privacy men must undergo. As a result, even when sensitivity to women is intended, women receive privi-leges that men do not; this situation breeds disdain for women soldiers among some of the men.

In the military, some believe that male leaders' unwillingness to push women to excel creates a weakness among the troops that could have grave consequences during a war:

> The more fundamental question is whether women should be in the military at all. They have served well, but are victims of a male dominated system which has always demanded less of them than they would (hopefully) of themselves. If every soldier in the U.S. Army today had been trained at the same low level of expecta-tion that female soldiers routinely are, the U.S. Army today would either be dead or in Prisoner of War camps. (an "other race" major)

Quotas, Sex, and Other Paths to the Top.   As noted earlier, some men believe that women can "sleep their way" to the top, and that quotas allow women to receive undeserved promotions and assignments because of their minority status. Some men also believe that women can and do challenge poor perfor-mance reviews by claiming discrimination, and that they can use false harass-ment claims to punish or remove men they do not like. The perception is that women usually are believed over men in harassment cases; as a result, men's careers are ruined by the whims of ambitious or vengeful women.

Most of these perceptions reinforce the view that women want the pres-tige and promotions that come with serving in the combat arms, but do not in-tend to make the same efforts as men: "They want equal rights, but don't want to do what it takes to become equal" (white enlisted man in administration).

LIMITED FORMS OF PROTEST

When I asked men who opposed women in combat roles what they thought would happen in the future, they all asserted that integration was inevitable. They concluded that women eventually would "have their way" despite any reasonable objections. Perhaps because women's gains have been made gradu-ally over the years, men perceive this progression not as a series of slow, incre-mental change toward one goal but as a string of victories for women over men.

One white major said, "As minorities, women have advantages." White men were likely to have a similar attitude about race; for example, they tended to think that nonwhite soldiers unfairly charge racial discrimination to chal-lenge negative performance reviews. One white NCO spoke for many of his comrades in defining himself as a member of the oppressed minority: "I feel that the white enlisted male has more prejudice against him than any other sector in the military." He specified not only his gender but also his race and rank as contributing to his position.

Scott analyzes both the micro interactional forms of resistance by subjugated people and the outward rebellion of the powerless that occurs when "an entire category of people suddenly finds its public voice no longer stifled" (1990:210). I found the reverse among military men: a category of people who have assumed and enjoyed gender privilege, and who rebel because their public voice has been deemed sexist and has been silenced.

Because of the nature of the military organization, many forms of protest are not realistic options for men who contend that they are disadvantaged. Army men cannot strike, circulate petitions, organize rallies or demonstrations, walk out during the workday, or quit collectively in response to a policy change. (Before quitting they would have to meet their enlistment obligations or complete time-consuming formal exit procedures and paperwork.) Boycotts and "client preference" arguments are generally irrelevant here. Thus men who are silent in mixed-sex environments may be channeling their frustrations into underground grumbling.

I experienced firsthand evidence of men's perception that they must hide their opinions. Often the men who eventually voiced their objections to working with women were not initially forthright. When asked about gender issues, they first told me what they imagined I wanted to hear, or recited the "party line" that would keep them out of trouble should any statements be attributed to them. After calculating my opinion on the basis of my status as a young civilian woman conducting research on military women, they hesitated at my opening questions and then said reluctantly that they thought women should and could serve in any military roles. Then, when I raised an opposing argument (such as "So you don't see any problem with close contact between men and women serving in tanks together?"), their true feelings burst forth.[1]

In mixed-sex groups (particularly groups of officers), some of the men squirmed, rolled their eyes, or shook their heads, but did not speak up during discussions about gender. After I dismissed the group, I privately asked those men to stay behind, and asked them why they were silent but seemingly dissatisfied. They revealed that they refrained from participating because they believed that organizational constraints prohibited them from stating their true opinions, particularly in the presence of officer women. In this way I learned which arguments were considered legitimate in the organization (at least when women were present) and which would be censured. The opportunity to write anonymous comments on the formal questionnaires may have been particularly appreciated by soldiers who felt their views were controversial. Men were concerned that they would be held accountable for any

---

[1]Men who I believe truly support women in combat roles responded to this probing technique with assertions such as "No. I don't think it would be a problem. Men and women can work together without having sex all the time: I've seen it."

statements that could be considered sexist; they feared an official reprimand and negative consequences for their career.

These soldiers' perceptions are evidence that the Army has made some headway in controlling men's willingness to make openly sexist statements. (Soldiers' self-censorship about gender contrasted sharply with their comments about allowing open gays and lesbians to serve in the military; men did not hesitate to make loud, violent threats against any gays they might discover.) Many of these men resent the inability to speak their minds. They believe that even if they could speak candidly, their concerns would not be addressed formally because they think women have the advantage in gender-based disputes. Therefore they express their resentment in ways that the institution cannot control.

Male soldiers interpret the "suppression" of some arguments against women as proof that those arguments are valid and that women have no legitimate counterargument. Thus some men are angry because they perceive women as having gained their power in the military illegitimately or as having taken advantage of that power. Others simply object to changing gender norms and increasing participation of women in non-traditional roles. This tension is exacerbated by the perceived prohibition against expressing their dissatisfaction. Therefore many men hold their tongues in public, but complain among themselves and retaliate with gender harassment. Although grumbling is certainly a part of military culture, the resistance strategies I found directed against women are rarely employed for similar complaints against male leaders or fellow soldiers in general.

Implications of Gender Harassment

The Army's formal sexual harassment [policies] in the 1990s have taught many men the definitions and the possible consequences of this behavior.

Yet improvements in controlling sexual harassment do not necessarily mean that women are now working in a supportive or even a tolerant environment. Although women can be hurt by public sexist comments that express doubts about their abilities, it is also debilitating when such comments are forced underground, where they cannot be challenged. In addition, because many men perceive themselves as unable to safely voice their concerns about women as coworkers, some men feel that gender harassment is a justified means of registering their complaints.

As previously disadvantaged groups gain some power in legislating discriminatory behavior, their opponents may come to rely on forms of resistance that are difficult to regulate. These implications go beyond gender and affect areas such as race, ethnicity, and sexual orientation. Even as minorities enjoy increased success in controlling overt harassment, they must recognize that people will seek other ways to express hostility. When minority groups call for equality, they should be prepared to be informed about inequities that favor them, and to learn how the language of equality might be used against them.

Underlying the cases in the resistance literature is the assumption that the reader is sympathetic to the oppressed groups; groups claiming oppression in fact are oppressed and are justified in their resistance. Resistance, then, has been treated as something constructive, which preserves human dignity and may lead to the overthrow of an unjust system. Thus nobody has asked how to eliminate the "hidden transcript" and dismantle underground forms of resistance. In the traditional dichotomous framework of resistance studies, that question would have been asked only by oppressors seeking compliance— seeking to use their power for manipulation or indoctrination.

But what do we say when the resisting group is not entirely powerless and does not wish to relinquish one of the realms in which it holds power? The powerful can appropriate for themselves the language and framework used to explain dominance and resistance. They can portray themselves as victims, as "silenced," when *they* suddenly are required to monitor their behavior in the presence of others. Is the attempt to regulate racist, sexist, and homophobic speech and behavior equivalent to the past suppression of minority groups' voices? Are we to be sympathetic when previously powerful groups develop underground resistance because their behavior is suppressed?

In this paper I have sought to demonstrate that in order to effectively examine power dynamics, studies of resistance must supplement cultural and structural analyses. Future work must recognize the importance of perceptions of power because such perceptions do not necessarily correspond to objective measures of power. These perceptions, however, strongly influence people's attitudes and behavior. In the military, soldiers' experience of gender varies according to rank, age, race, and occupational specialty.

Resistance studies also must move beyond seeing the world in terms of only two classes: the oppressors and the oppressed. This dichotomy cannot fully explain the dynamics of a world in which multiple hierarchies can make people simultaneously powerful and powerless relative to others. Future research must account for people's multiple statuses which result in a much more varied distribution of power than a dichotomous model would allow. The behavior of some military men toward women soldiers demonstrates that researchers must look for "weapons of the weak" in the hands of people at all levels of both perceived and structurally measured power.

References

Martin, Molly, ed. 1988. *Hard Hatted Women: Stories of Struggle and Success in the Trades*. Seattle: Seal Press.

Padavic, Irene, and Barbara F. Reskin. 1990. "Men's Behavior and Women's Interest in Blue-Collar Jobs." *Social Problems*, 37:613–628.

Scott, James C. 1990. *Domination and the Arts of Resistance: Hidden Transcripts*. New Haven: Yale University Press.

45 After Hurricane Andrew

KENNETH J. SMITH
LINDA LISKE BELGRAVE

Collective behavior is a catch-all term that refers to a wide variety of human activity. It is often used to refer to groups of people who are doing extraordinary things, such as participating in riots and lynchings. This term is so broad, however, that it also refers to fads, even to a food fight in a cafeteria. Its breadth makes collective behavior one of the less useful terms in sociology, as it lumps together young women who get ankle tattoos with an enraged mob bent on lynching someone. The term is so unsatisfactory that even to try to make the extraordinary its common element fails, for it also includes fashions, often not unusual at all.

As you can see, however, despite its limitations, collective behavior refers to some of the most interesting of human activities. One of the many topics encompassed by this term is the behavior of people following a disaster. In this article, we examine the aftermath of a devastating hurricane in Florida. Smith and Belgrave focus on how people attempted to rebuild their normal realities, the obstacles they encountered, and how lives were changed by this catastrophic event. If you compare the findings reported here with how people's lives were changed due to the disaster at Buffalo Creek (article 20), the significance of the twin themes of this book—social structure and social interaction—will become apparent.

AT MIDNIGHT, August 24, the winds hit Miami. The high winds are 140 miles an hour and gusting to 180 miles an hour. In every inhabited South Dade County home, people are hiding in closets, hallways, and bathrooms. By 8 AM Monday, people were coming out of their shelters and homes. The storm had cut a twenty-by-twenty-mile swath of destruction through the inhabited part of South Dade County. A total of 63,000 houses were destroyed, 250,000 people were homeless, and 39 people were dead (Lyskowski et al. 1992; Christie 1992). . . .

Theoretical Considerations

Natural (Mount St. Helena) and technological (Chernobyl) disasters destroy, at least temporarily, the rituals and routines that make up everyday life. They impose the necessity of reorienting and reorganizing the responses to the primary world of family and neighbors and the secondary world of community relationships (Goode 1992).

Quarantelli and Dynes (1985) note that the primary and secondary interactions of disaster victims can be viewed, over time, as moving through three phases: a disaster phase, transition from disaster to normality, and a postdisaster recovery period. If one views this formulation as proceeding through three phases at two different levels of interaction, one can describe the process in the following way. The initial phase is the disaster as an event requiring an extraordinary mobilization of available energy and resources to face the onslaught or sequelae of the event itself. Following the disruption and dislocation caused by the disaster is a transition toward normality where "approximate versions" of the work, school, shopping, and other routines of the ante-disaster period are reinstated. This transition to normality leads to a postdisaster recovery period. In this third period, new routines and rituals of everyday life are reconstructed to redefine the new meaning of everyday life. Recovery, however, does not mean returning to the status quo ante. The hurricane's impact can be a lasting one and can affect life course changes as well as gender role relations and generational relationships. The focus of this article is on the transition and recovery periods rather than on the disaster itself.

Research Design

Our data consist of forty accounts collected during the weeks and months following Hurricane Andrew. These accounts include twenty-one individual interviews, two focus group interviews involving eight people, three first-person accounts, and eight interviews conducted by our students for a special class project. The interviews were in-depth and lasted approximately two hours. They were taperecorded (with permission) and transcribed verbatim, thereby preserving the respondents' own use of language. . . .

The majority of respondents were selected from a list of University of Miami employees and from the staff of a nearby community mental health center who had suffered some hurricane damage. Respondents were chosen so as to include administrators, faculty, and staff. Acquaintances of the authors (and their students) from other social settings whose stories included additional features of the hurricane experience were also interviewed. . . .

Time Out from Everyday Life: Getting By and Digging Out

Time out from everyday life is a period of unreality that follows the destruction of everyday life and continues until the establishment of a new taken-for-granted reality is under way. While this was in some ways a hiatus, it also involved tasks for which many had little or no preparation. During the first few days after the hurricane, those who suffered significant damage devoted much of their energy to simply getting by. *Getting by* is the process of obtaining the basic necessities for survival (water, food, shelter), which became a major undertaking. For some, words such as "adventure" and "pioneering" were used to describe their situations. Not everyone, however, was successful at getting by beyond mere survival. Alternating with getting by is a process that we have described as *digging out*. By this expression, we mean the initial attempts to reconstruct the intimate territory of everyday life. The hiatus and disorientation of getting by merges into a more future-oriented set of tasks designed to reestablish a normal and continuing everyday life.

Basic survival needs that had been part of the mundane world the day before could no longer be taken for granted . . . The water supply was contaminated and was not potable for as long as six weeks in some areas. Some had no running water at all. One respondent, Paul, reported,

> The water we had to drink and the water that was outside could have been contaminated, so we couldn't go for a swim or anything. People were actually dumping sewage into it because they couldn't use their toilets. . . . I think that was the worst part, not even being able to get cleaned up after you were doing all the things you were doing.

Some had no food but were able to get to open stores. Others had food but could not wash, cook, or store it. For those who had come through the storm with well-stocked freezers, the concern was what to do with it:

> We had a freezer full of food with no power, and so I spent a lot of that first day sorting the refrigerator and we cooked what we thought would perish. . . . We did everything to lengthen the life of this food and make it ready to eat at a moment's notice. So we ate some really neat stuff those first few days. (Wendy)

Loading up supplies on a trip north was common. It was not unusual to see someone arrive home, open the car's trunk, and call the neighbors over to get what they needed. In the heavily damaged areas, people were dependent on friends or relatives who lived further north to supply them with food and other necessities. Sharing, accepting, and even requesting food from friends and neighbors quickly became normal.

Even for those who had the means to cook, such as Dixie, "Just the little bit of cooking you did became a major problem." Potable water was purchased from the store. Others used tapwater after boiling it or treating it with bleach for washing or cooking food. One solution was to rely on open restaurants. Another was to subsist on foods that did not require cooking. An adequate but boring diet had some drawbacks. As one respondent exclaimed, "I thought if I saw another can of tuna fish or peanut butter and jelly, I would scream."

Hurricane Andrew left 250,000 people homeless (Lyskowski et al. 1992). While some defined shelter as their most pressing concern, others made do with whatever they had left even though it might be uninhabitable. Rachel's family had few options:

> We were so tired and so cold, so wet and filthy. And all we could do was lay down and go to sleep. We went and laid down in all the debris. . . . [We] tried to get some comforters, and of course they were all soaking wet. And we just went to sleep.

The day after the hurricane, they went to stay with a relative who lived in Fort Myers.

The need for alternative housing, combined with the destruction of rental units, created tremendous difficulties for those who did decide to look for temporary housing. Moves were generally to smaller, less desirable housing or into shared housing. Dean's family, forced by their contractor to vacate their house, moved twice: "We rented a place on Miami Beach, a little one-bedroom apartment. . . . That was just much too small, so we [found] a place a month and a half later in Key Biscayne which is still small, but much better."

Those with fewer resources moved in with family, friends, or even strangers, and families were separated. Thelma and her three children, whose apartment was destroyed, first moved into her ex-husband's one-bedroom apartment. A few days later, she and her oldest son moved in with a neighbor she had just met in her complex's laundry room while her daughter moved to a friend's home and her younger son stayed with his father. Two weeks later, her landlord found her a small apartment. Thelma, her three children, and a friend of her daughter moved into it with no furniture except a twin bed. The daughter's friend, whose own family had only a few inhabitable rooms in their apartment, stayed with Thelma until after Christmas.

For those in devastated areas, the processes of getting by and digging out focused on the present and immediate future, and the tasks involved meeting basic needs. Despite the difficulties of getting by, it could hold a certain appeal and a test of individual resourcefulness:

> We thought we were pioneers. . . . I almost began to love the lifestyle because it was so simple. It was just survival. I must get water to these animals. And then I found I could wash all my clothes in the horse tub and stomp on the clothes. . . . If I stretched fifty foot of hose and let it lay all day in the sun, I could have hot water for a bath. (Barrie)

Of course, not everyone found "roughing it" to be charming. Although she survived, Rachel was not successful at getting by. In describing severe marital problems during the first few weeks after the hurricane, she explained,

> He kept on riding me. "Why don't you have this place liveable? Why don't you clean this place up? Why don't you cook? . . . I lost thirteen pounds in three weeks. I didn't eat at all. . . . I wasn't drinking anything at that time either, no water or soda. I was dehydrated. My lips were starting to crack. . . . My husband said I looked as if I'd been drinking. I know that is why he accused me of it; I

looked so bad. . . . I looked like a banshee and I had no self-esteem and I kind of felt the way I used to feel in my drinking days.

Digging out emerged alongside efforts required for getting by. Activities tended to be centered around cleaning up and salvaging belongings, although some were dealing with insurance almost immediately. Almost everyone who had suffered substantial damage reported cleaning up as a top-priority task. Despite the everydayness of the terms used, this cleaning up was far removed from the mundane, as indicated by Wendy's colorful description of the process. Her family "used a shovel and went and threw the living room out in the front yard."

In addition to cleaning up, there was the task of salvaging anything that could be saved. Those often involved "scrounging" or even literally digging through the remains of one's home to find whatever might be left. While many focused on salvaging items that had more personal meaning than material value, for those who faced virtually total loss items with neither material value nor personal meaning could become important. Rachel recalled, "We had so few things that made it through the storm that no matter what it was, even a bath brush, I was going to take it 'cause it meant that much to me."

Whatever activities one engaged in were undertaken with unusual constraints. The lack of electricity meant more than an inability to use labor-saving devices, many of which would have been useless for the tasks at hand. A vacuum cleaner is of no help when the carpeting is under water. The loss of electric light meant that everything had to be done during daylight hours. Sam explained, "We'd work, eat dinner, and go to bed. There was no electricity and no flashlights, so after sunset just about everybody in the area was going to bed." The lack of supplies, combined with the number of people needing them, increased greatly the effort required for many tasks. One respondent noted that "everywhere you went you had to wait forever." As Angela explained,

> There was nothing that was easy to do. If you attempted anything, there was diffi-culty. You didn't have nails. The store did not have nails. So you would ask your neighbor, "Could you spare three nails?" So everything was hard.

Time out from everyday life did not end abruptly but began to dissolve as the "unreal" became routinized and people returned to at least some of their prior daily routines. Thus aspects of the unreality of the time-out phase continued even after the hiatus ended.

Life in "the Zone"

Life in "the zone" is an expression of one of our informants that seemed an apt way of describing the contrast between everyday life prior to Hurricane Andrew and in undamaged areas compared to the cultural ambience that was established as a result of the hurricane. Essentially, life in the zone consists of emergent ways of doing daily life in the absence of the usual supports that maintain taken-for-granted reality; it is routinization of the nonroutine. . . .

Life in the zone was the daily trek to buy ice and bottled water, dealing with contractors, being apprehensive about transient construction workers who roam the countryside, and living out the day in the unrelenting sunshine and dust (alternating with mud) in a country flattened by a devastating hurricane. . . .

Individuals and families in their automobiles gawking at the misery of others for their own entertainment and the continual helicopters (media or relief going elsewhere) were also a part of the problem:

> They didn't bring us food. . . . They didn't come down and say, "May we help you?" or something. They were just rubbernecking and I wanted to, if I had a bazooka I'd have blown them out of the sky. They just made me so mad, one after the other, providing no assistance, no nothing. We got nothing. (Marie)

This frequent linking of the offensiveness of being observed with the observers' neglect to bring help suggests that the tourists might have been better tolerated had they carried down needed supplies. This was not a short-term problem. During the Christmas holidays, the height of the tourist season for South Florida, a local radio personality brought the wrath of the community on himself by suggesting to listeners that the devastation in South Dade County was something you just had to see for yourself.

In the face of extensive devastation, interruption of services, and changed living arrangements, people developed new routines for handling what had once been mundane tasks. Communication was particularly problematic yet important enough for extensive efforts. In some areas, neighborhood mail delivery was interrupted for six weeks. Martha recalled, "You had to go down and wait in line for two or three hours to get your mail. [I went] once a week, on Saturday. How often do you have three hours to wait for your mail?" Likewise, telephone service was unavailable for months in some areas:

> Every Sunday morning, we'd go someplace to use a pay phone and call both sets of relatives. It was part of the routine. We would go to the grocery store then. The first month or so, it was a pain 'cause there weren't any restaurants open, but afterward we would go and have breakfast and call. (Ed)

The return of services that were once taken for granted was sometimes treated as a major event; their expressed importance helped characterize people's situations. Dixie's response to the return of electricity was not unusual:

> We were waiting for them to get it plugged in, you know, to fix the line. That was a night of absolute celebration. I mean, now you could vacuum. Your refrigerator would get cold. Watch television. All these modern, wonderful things. . . .

A continuing thread running through people's attempts to endure was the desire, or even need, to talk about their experiences. This need was not always easily met:

> I feel like it was yesterday. I cry almost every night. I can't cry in front of my husband because he can't take it. I don't care if people don't want to talk about it at all. That's all I can think about. I came to work every day and I talked there. We all did, though. For about a month, none of us worked. We all just talked about it. (Rachel)

After a while, those who wanted to talk about the storm began to experience disapproval for this behavior. According to Bridget, "We were in the bathroom and talking about the hurricane, and this one lady said, 'I can't believe it! Six weeks after the storm, and they are still talking about it.'"

Dixie, who still wanted to talk about the storm in January, explained that it depends on how badly you were damaged: "The ones that got a lot of damage are all the same way. The ones that didn't get any damage are probably bored with this conversation." Efforts to reconstruct a social reality, especially with those who did not experience the intensity of the hurricane, were met with a lack of empathy, if not outright hostility, perhaps because the non-victims lived in a different social world. Such impatience with hurricane conversation was, if not a flat-out denial of victims' subjective reality, at least a refusal to help validate it. . . .

The Return to Work

For some, the return to work took on unusual importance. Dixie reported that going back to work felt "wonderful! It was so nice to get back to something that was normal. . . . It was a saving grace to go back to familiar jobs." This sentiment was echoed by Bob, even though he had been all but dragged back by his employer:

> They said, "Hey, you got to come back to work . . ." and I was happy 'cause that was like coming to civilization. One week later, there was electricity here. There was running water; you couldn't drink it, but that was pretty close.

Similarly, Derry reported that at first she "spent more time at work than normally I would, but I didn't do much work. [I just wanted] to be there because it was so much more comfortable than at home."

Even some of those who were not personally employed outside the home commented on the impact of the return to work. In reference to her husband, one woman reported, "Once he went back to work, he was a little bit better 'cause he could be around his friends at work and talk and [it was] more of a normal routine for him." . . .

For those living in hard-hit areas, the return to work took place within the context of on-going digging out and getting by. New routines emerged, routines that involved not only continual movement between devastation and normal life but often conflicting demands between these two worlds. Child care was a primary concern. One subject, May, said, "I didn't come back full-time. I came in a little at a time because we didn't have power and I had a lot of problems with finding daycare for Katya." Joe, who along with his wife was putting in twelve- and thirteen-hour days, said, "I sent my daughter over to my mother, who lives in Deland [approximately 100 miles north of Dade County], and she stayed there for about ten or twelve days." Many found that the demands of rebuilding interfered with their ability to meet their own standards for job performance even when those around them were understanding of the difficulties:

> She's always been like my best friend, and she is so supportive. But no matter how great or wonderful your boss is, you have this horrible guilt all the time because I am always saying, "Do you mind if I leave work early? I've got to be there or they won't deliver the tar paper." I feel like I'm always having to ask, and I hate that because I am very conscious of wanting to do a good job. (Barrie)

And a professor echoed similar sentiments:

> Because you are trying to keep on top of everything and keep your appointments and keeping track of tests and classes, and you are also trying to think, "What do I need? I need plywood, and where should I get it?"—because it wasn't always easy to get. . . . I am telling you, I have taught two semesters poorly, and I am not proud of it. (Ed)

Altered Lives

. . . Some of our respondents talked about the impact of Hurricane Andrew in initiating and retarding critical decisions that altered former lives or interfered with desired, anticipated changes in future lives. For example, Ruben was unable to put his former life back together again. The economic burden of rebuilding the prehurricane life was too expensive:

> I would say I go there three to four times a week. It has been very painful; part of the difficulty in selling the house was the neighborhood. The kids had friends there; they were used to walking down the street, talking to the neighbors, and knowing the place. That's probably why we hung on to it as long as we did. When people started talking about the six-month anniversary of the hurricane, that is, when we realized this is the time we were supposed to be back in this house and none of this [had] happened. There is no way we can carry two mortgages and a lease for another six months. . . . So it was painful, but economics drove the decision to sell our house. We do feel a tremendous amount of guilt for having sold the house.

Rachel succeeded in restoring the physical and domestic aspects of her life but was acutely disappointed with the result. Many of her neighbors moved. Homes were sold to speculators, who in turn rented the houses. Even though Rachel rebuilt her house, many of her neighbors did not:

> If I'd known that we [would] have to still be looking at this mess and not having friendly neighbors and having a whole different group of people [neighborhood], I wouldn't have [rebuilt]. . . . Well, we know that we are going to sell this in a year or two anyway and leave. . . . Yeah, we have already decided that. It's just that we don't have the same feeling about this house as we did when we first moved in.

For others, posthurricane circumstances altered responses to existing or anticipated family relationships and life-course situations. . . . In one instance, we found a significant change in the relationship between a mother and her son:

> About five weeks after the hurricane . . . David, my son, had a car accident. . . . I dumped [responsibility for] the whole thing on him. It's his accident, it's his license, his ticket, his driver's school, his insurance, and his problem to get the car fixed. My [only] contribution is that I'm going to a car rental agency to sign some papers so that he has wheels to drive while the car is in the shop. I'll always be his mother. But if the hurricane hadn't happened, then I would have been right in there minding his business for him. [The hurricane] moved things along a little quicker. I have the definite feeling that we crammed about eighteen months of living into the last three months. (Wendy)

. . . It must not be assumed that the problem and complexity of re-creating an everyday life of routines, plans, and goals is the same for the whole family. One's prehurricane life-course situation could be a critical factor in whether the trajectory of the former life was maintained or altered. Talking about his wife eighteen months after the hurricane, Lance explained,

> I think the problem, big problem, is that my wife was just finishing her internship. She is trying to get a degree, a Ph.D. in psychology. She was just finishing her internship at Miami Children's Hospital, and she had to write her dissertation; she had finished all her exams. . . . She had various arrangements for offices and contacts and this and that and [had] plans for what she was going to work out for her dissertation, and the hurricane destroyed all of that. I think a lot of the papers got wrecked because [in] the room she had things in, [the papers] just blew out of the window and we found things floating in the neighbor's pool. So all her connections were ruined, especially since for two months we weren't even in Dade County. So I think that the effect on her, the real effect—I'm not talking about just the psychological effect—was much bigger than on me. . . . It wasn't just a year, because . . . everything was built up to a point and then it was [destroyed]. It wasn't that you were at the same point for a year and you went back another year. So maybe it wiped out two years of her life.

Conclusions

The experience of our respondents highlights dramatically the destruction of the taken-for-granted world and the profound alteration of identity and self. Hurricane Andrew not only destroyed the physical environment but also undermined the plausibility of reality itself. Those who endured the full catastrophe had to rebuild their sense of reality as well as their homes.

The alteration of identity and sense of self was illustrated in reports of stressed and conflicted relationships between our respondents and their spouses, children, and friends. Old relationships and assumptions were blown away by the wind. The trust that had been built up between a recovering alcoholic wife and her husband was challenged by accusations of drinking. Parents redefined their relationships with their children. One's emotional ties to neighbors and homes were changed significantly. Dangerous traffic and fear of looters and strangers turned familiar neighborhoods into hostile places.

Those who remained in South Dade County to reconstruct their social worlds experienced the alienating impact of being identified as "victims," or as estranged others, at whom the "real" people gawked as they drove by in their air-conditioned cars. People who thought of themselves as competent and independent found their resources strained to the limit as they struggled to put food on their tables. Most of the people interviewed were employed both before and after the hurricane. Many, for the first time in their lives, were fearful about their next meals. In their topsy-turvy world, the work and workplace became the context of recreation and relaxation. Home was a place of drudgery, stress, and unrelenting demands.

In attempts to reconstruct and reintegrate the reality of their lives, the hurricane was the principal theme in all of their conversations. Those who shared the experience empathized with and valorized each other's experiences. They needed to talk about it; they exchanged information about contractors, food preparation, and where to buy lumber. To communicate, they drove miles to find working telephones and stood in line for hours in post offices. Those whose sense of reality was not challenged and undermined by the hurricane remained aloof and uninvolved. It was as though they did not understand the language that was being spoken.

Large-scale disasters destroy fundamental aspects of everyday life and the taken-for-granted reality on which it is based, leaving survivors in an untenable situation. The reconstruction of reality is not primarily an intentional process but rather emerges as new routines are developed to deal with the changed situation. In the face of overwhelming destruction of their physical environment and taken-for-granted social structures, disaster victims go to extraordinary lengths to reestablish some semblance of their past routines. Such efforts provide evidence of the tenacity of socially constructed reality, once internalized.

References

Christie, John, ed. 1992. *Andrew: Savagery from the sea.* Orlando, FL: Tribune Publishing. (Collection of published articles)

Goode, E. 1992. *Collective behavior.* Fort Worth, TX: Harcourt Brace Jovanovich.

Lyskowski, Roman, et al. 1992. *Hurricane Andrew: The big one.* Kansas City, MO: Andrews & McMeel. (Collection of published articles)

Quarantelli, E., and R. R. Dynes. 1985. Community responses to disasters. In *Disasters and mental health,* (pp. 158–68), ed. B. J. Sowder. Washington, DC: U.S. Department of Health and Human Services, Public Health Service, Alcohol, Drug Abuse, and Mental Health Administration.

Glossary

Account One's version of an incident; often an excuse or justification for unexpected or inappropriate behavior. See *Excuse* and *Justification*.

Achieved status A person's position or ranking achieved at least partly through personal efforts (such as becoming a college student) or failings (such as becoming a skid row alcoholic).

Aggregate People grouped together for the purpose of social research because of characteristics they have in common. An example is U.S. females between the ages of 18 and 23 who wear contact lenses.

Alienation Used in a couple of different meanings. The first is Weberian, a sense of separation, of not belonging, of being estranged. This meaning includes the idea that one has little control over the social world; may also include the feeling that one's world is meaningless. The second is Marxian, a sense of being separated from and not identifying with the product of one's labor.

Anomie Normlessness; conflict between norms, weakened respect for norms, or absence of norms.

Anticipatory socialization Learning the perspectives of a role before entering it. See *Role* and *Socialization*.

Ascribed status A person's position or ranking assigned on the basis of arbitrary standards over which the individual has little or no control, such as age, race, or sex.

Authority Power that is regarded as legitimate or proper by those over whom it is exercised.

Background expectancies (or assumptions) The taken-for-granted assumptions people have about the way the world is. See *Social construction of reality*.

Belief An idea about some part of the natural or social world; a view of reality.

Body language Giving and receiving messages through the movement or positioning of the body; includes gestures and facial expressions.

Bureaucracy A form of organization characterized by multiple "layerings" of authority, usually depicted by a pyramid. Decisions flow downward, accountability for fulfilling orders goes upward, rules are explicit, emphasis is placed on written records, resources are directed toward efficiently reaching the goals of the organization, the "bottom line" is of utmost concern, and the personal is kept strictly separate from that which belongs to the organization. The reality of any particular organization does not necessarily match this *Ideal type*.

Case study An in-depth investigation of a single event, experience, organization, or situation in order to better understand that case or to abstract principles of human behavior.

Charisma Extraordinary personal qualities that attract followers. It varies from simply a "magnetic" personality to qualities so extraordinary that they are assumed to be supernatural.

Charismatic authority Leadership exercised on the basis of charisma. See *Charisma* and *Traditional authority*.

Class See *Social class*.

Class conflict Karl Marx's term for the struggle between social classes; generally thought of as the struggle between the rich (and powerful) and the poor (and powerless), or those who own the means of economic production and those who do not.

Coding Fitting data into classifications so they can be more easily analyzed.

Collective behavior Relatively spontaneous, unstructured, and transitory ways of thinking, feeling, and acting that develop among a large number of people.

Community Its primary meaning is that of people inhabiting the same geographical area who share common interests and feel a sense of "belonging." From this sense comes a derived meaning of people who share common interests and have a sense of "belonging" but who do not inhabit the same geographical area, such as in the phrase "a community of scholars."

Conflict theory The theoretical view (or school) which emphasizes conflict as the inevitable outcome in society due to its various groups competing for limited resources. See *Functionalism* and *Symbolic interactionism*.

Conformity Following social norms or expectations.

Conspicuous consumption Thorstein Veblen's term for a change from an orientation toward saving in the Protestant ethic to showing off wealth by the elaborate consumption of goods.

Content analysis The classification of the content of documents in order to identify its themes; such as presidential speeches, a series of medical novels, situation comedies, and so on.

Control group The subjects in an experiment who are not exposed to the independent variable, as opposed to the experimental group who are subjected to this variable. See *Experiment*, *Experimental group*, *Independent variable*, and *Variable*.

Covert participant observation See *Participant observation*.

Crime An act prohibited by law.

Cultural diffusion The process by which the characteristics of one culture are adopted by members of another culture.

Cultural relativity The view that one cannot judge the characteristics of any culture to be morally superior to those of another. See its opposite, *Ethnocentrism*.

Culture A way of life, or shared ways of doing things; includes nonmaterial culture (such as norms, beliefs, values, and language) and material culture (such as art, tools, weapons, and buildings). See *Ideal culture* and *Real culture*.

Culture lag (Cultural lag) A term developed by William F. Ogburn to refer to the material culture changing more rapidly than the nonmaterial culture. Thought to be a primary factor in social change.

Culture of poverty The distinctive culture said to exist among the poor of industrialized societies; its central features of defeatism, dependence, and a present time orientation are thought to trap people in poverty and to perpetuate it from one generation to the next.

Culture shock The disorienting effect that immersion in a strange culture has on a visitor as he or she encounters markedly different norms, values, beliefs, customs, and other basic expectations of social life. One no longer is able to rely on the basics of one's socialization.

Data The information scientists gather in their studies.

Definition of reality A view of what the world or some part of the world is like. See *Social construction of reality*.

Dehumanization The act or process of reducing people to objects that do not deserve the treatment given humans.

Demography The study of the size, distribution, composition, and change in human populations.

Dependent variable That which is being explained as the result of other factors; a variable or social phenomenon thought to be changed or influenced by another variable. See *Independent variable*.

Deviance Violation of social norms or expectations.

Deviant One who violates social norms or expectations. As used by sociologists, a neutrally descriptive rather than a negative term.

Deviant career The main course of events during one's involvement in deviance; generally refers to those who are habitually, or at least for a period of time heavily, involved in some deviant activity.

Differential association If a person associates with one group of people, he or she will learn one set of attitudes, ideas, and norms; associating with a different group teaches a different approach to life. Thus such differential association is highly significant in influencing people either to conform or to deviate.

Diffusion The spread of an invention or discovery from one area or group to another.

Disclaimer An excuse or justification for inappropriate behavior that is *about* to take place. Examples are: "Now don't get me wrong, but . . . ;" and "Let me play the devil's advocate for a minute."

Discrimination The denial of rights, privileges, or opportunities to others on the basis of their group membership. See *Minority group*, *Racism*, and *Sexism*.

Division of labor A concept developed by Emile Durkheim to refer to the work specializations in a society (the various ways in which work is divided, with some people specializing in financing or production, others in advertising or distribution, and so on).

Documents In its narrow sense, written sources that provide data; in its extended sense, archival material of any sort, including photographs, movies, and so on.

Double standard More stringent expectations being applied to one group than to another. *The* double standard refers to attitudes and ideas more favorable to males than to females—often to males being allowed more sexual freedom.

Downsizing A fancy way of saying that to reduce costs a company is firing workers.

Downward social mobility Movement from a higher to a lower social position. See *Social class*.

Dramaturgical analysis Developed by Erving Goffman, this term refers to viewing human interaction as theatrical performances. People are seen as actors, their clothing as costumes, what they do as parts they play, what they say as the delivery of lines, where they interact as a stage, and so on.

Dramaturgy Refers to theatrical performances. The same as *Dramaturgical analysis*.

Ecology The study of reciprocal relationships between organisms and their environment.

Education One of the primary institutions of society whereby teaching of values, skills, and knowledge is transmitted from one generation to the next.

Ego Commonly used as a term to refer to the self; technically, Freud's term for the conscious, rational part of an individual.

Endogamy A cultural pattern of marrying *within* one's own social group. See *Exogamy*.

Ethnic cleansing   A recent term for killing people because of their ethnicity, with the goal of "cleaning out" an entire area for one's own ethnic group to inhabit.

Ethnic group   A group of people with a sense of common ancestry, who generally share similar cultural traits and regard themselves as distinct from others.

Ethnic stratification   Groups of people who are stratified on the basis of their ethnic group membership. See *Social stratification*.

Ethnocentrism   Using the standards of one's own group, culture, or subculture to evaluate the characteristics of other groups, cultures, or subcultures, generally from the point of view that one's own are superior. See its opposite, *Cultural relativity*.

Ethnography   A report or study that details the major characteristics of the way of life of a group of people; can be of an entire preliterate tribe, an entire village, or a smaller group within a large society, such as a study of urban cabdrivers.

Ethnomethodology   Developed by Harold Garfinkel, the term refers to the study of the worlds of reality that people construct, their taken-for-granted background assumptions, and the ways by which different people make sense out of their experiences.

Excuse   An account of an event in which one acknowledges that an act is blameworthy, but denies responsibility for the act. See *Account* and *Justification*.

Exogamy   A cultural pattern of marrying *outside* one's social group. See *Endogamy*.

Experiment   A study in which the researcher manipulates one or more variables (independent variables) in order to measure the results on other variables (dependent variables). See *Variable*.

Experimental group   The subjects in an experiment who are exposed to the independent variable, as opposed to the control group who do not experience this variable. See *Experiment*.

Extended family   A family consisting of two or more generations (extended beyond the nuclear family), usually living together. See *Nuclear family*.

False consciousness   A term developed by Karl Marx to refer to a person's understanding of his or her social class membership that does not square with objective facts; often used to refer to members of the working class identifying with capitalists.

Family   People related by ancestry, marriage, or adoption who generally live together and form an economic unit, and whose adult members assume responsibility for the young. The form of the family varies remarkably from one culture to another.

Family of orientation   The family into which one is born. See *Family* and *Family of procreation*.

Family of procreation   The family created by marriage. See *Family* and *Family of orientation*.

Femininity   Our behaviors and orientations as females. Assumed in sociology to be an expression not of biology but of cultural or social learning. See *Masculinity*.

Feral children   Children who have been found in the wilderness, supposedly raised by animals. Not only do they possess no language, but they also exhibit few behaviors that we ordinarily associate with humans.

Field research   Another term for *Participant observation*.

Field study   Another term for *Participant observation*.

Field work   Another term for *Participant observation*.

Folk society   A term developed by Robert Redfield to refer to small, traditional societies in which there is little social change.

Folkways   Developed by William G. Sumner, this term refers to norms people are expected or encouraged to follow, but whose violation is not considered immoral; the ordinary rules, usages, conventions, and expectations of everyday life, such as, in U.S. society, the use of deodorant. See *Mores*.

Formal organization   A social group brought into existence to reach specific goals; often utilizes a bureaucratic mode of operation to achieve those objectives. See *Bureaucracy*.

Formal sanction   A social reward or punishment that is formally applied, often a part of ritual recognition for achievement (such as receiving a passing grade in school, or being promoted at work) or failure (such as receiving a failing grade in school, or being fired from one's job). See *Informal sanction* and *Sanction*.

Functionalism   The theoretical view (or school) that stresses how the parts of a society or social group are interrelated. Emphasis is placed on the contributions (functions) that one part makes for the adjustment or well-being of other parts. Each part, working properly, is seen as contributing to the stability of the whole. See *Symbolic interactionism* and *Conflict theory*.

Future shock   A term developed by Alvin Toffler to refer to the dizzying disorientation brought on by the rapid arrival of the future.

Gender   The social expectations attached to a person on account of that person's sex. Sex is biological, while gender is social. See *Femininity* and *Masculinity*.

Gender socialization   Learning one's gender. See *Gender*.

Generalize   To conclude that the research findings from a sample apply to a broader group.

Generalized other   The ideas we have of the expectations of a major reference group, or even of society in general.

Genocide   Killing an entire population, usually because of the group's biological and cultural traits.

Gentrification   The process by which the relatively affluent move to decaying urban neighborhoods, renovate buildings, and displace the poor.

Gestures   The movement and positioning of the body to communicate meaning. See *Body language*.

Heterosexuality   Sexual acts or feelings toward members of the opposite sex. See *Homosexuality*.

Hidden curriculum   The unwritten goals of schools, such as teaching obedience to authority and conformity to cultural norms.

Holocaust   The Nazi destruction, in death camps and by means of death squads, of Jews, gypsies, Slavs, homosexuals, the mentally retarded, and others considered threats to the purity of the so-called Aryan race.

Homosexuality   Sexual acts or feelings toward members of the same sex. See *Heterosexuality*.

Horizontal mobility   Movement from one social position to another that is approximately equivalent.

Human ecology   Study of the reciprocal relationships between people and their environment.

Hypothesis   A prediction about how two or more variables are related. See *Variable*.

Ideal culture   The way of life represented in people's values and norms, rather than by their actual practices. See *Real culture*.

Ideal type   Developed by Max Weber, this term refers to a model or description of something that is derived from examining a number of real cases and abstracting what appear to be the essential characteristics of those cases.

Identity formation   The process by which we develop a personal identity; our internalization of social expectations. The end result is that we come to think of ourselves in a certain way; that is, as we internalize people's reactions to us, we develop a "self."

Ideology   Statements or beliefs (especially of reasons and purposes) that justify a group's actions or interests; they buttress, uphold, or legitimate the existing social order.

Incest   Sexual intercourse with forbidden categories of kinfolk. See *Incest taboo*.

Incest taboo   The social prohibition against sexual intercourse with specific categories of kinfolk. See *Incest*.

Independent variable   That which is thought to affect or to cause change in some other factor; the variable thought to influence another variable. See *Dependent variable*.

Informal sanction   A social reward or punishment informally applied, often being a spontaneous gesture of approval or disapproval. Examples include staring, smiling, and gossip. See *Formal sanction* and *Sanction*.

Ingroup   The group to which an individual belongs, identifies, and feels loyalty. See *Outgroup*.

Institution   See *Social institution*.

Institutional(ized) racism   The use of social institutions to discriminate, exploit, or oppress a racial (or ethnic) group. See *Discrimination* and *Racism*.

Institutional(ized) sexism The use of social institutions to discriminate, exploit, or oppress either males or females as a group. See *Discrimination* and *Sexism*.

Interaction See *Social interaction*.

Interactional sociology An emphasis on the study of social interaction. See *Participant observation, Qualitative sociology,* and *Structural sociology*.

Internalization Experiences becoming part of one's "internal" consciousness.

Interview Asking a respondent questions; can be face-to-face, by writing, or by some form of electronic communication such as by telephone or fax. See *Respondent*.

Interview bias Effects that interviewers have on respondents that tilt answers in some direction.

Involuntary associations Groups to which people belong, but about which they have little or no choice. Examples include grade school for youngsters and military service during periods of conscription. See *Voluntary associations*.

Justification An account of an event in which one accepts responsibility for an act, while denying that the act is blameworthy. See *Account* and *Excuse*.

Kin People who are related by birth, adoption, or marriage.

Kinfolk See *Kin*.

Kinship The network of people who are related to one another by birth, adoption, or marriage.

Labeling theory (or perspective) The focus on the effects of labels (or terms) on people. This perspective stresses that acts are not inherently deviant (or criminal) but are such only because those acts have been so labeled (or defined). Deviants are those on whom the label of deviant has been successfully applied.

Life chances The likelihood that an individual or group will benefit from their society's opportunities, goods and services, and other satisfactions in life.

Life course The biological and social sequencing through which individuals pass; these cluster around birth, childhood, maturity, old age, and death.

Life expectancy The average number of years a person can expect to live.

Life style The general patterns that characterize an individual or group, including their clothing, manners, recreation, mating, and childrearing practices.

Looking-glass self Charles Horton Cooley's term for the process by which people see themselves through the eyes of others. As people act, others react. In those reactions people see themselves reflected. Perceiving this, they interpret its meaning, which yields a particular self-image.

Masculinity Our behaviors and orientations as males. Generally assumed in sociology to be an expression not of biology but of cultural or social learning. See *Femininity*.

Mass media Forms of communication that reach a large audience, with no personal contact between the senders and receivers of the message. Examples are movies, radio, television, newspaper, magazines, plays, and books.

Master status (or trait) A social role (or achieved or ascribed status) that cuts across most other social roles and provides a major basis for personal and public identity.

Material culture See *Culture*.

Meanings The significance that something has to someone. Also called symbols, mental constructs, ideas, and stereotypes. See *Qualitative sociology*.

Methodology (Methods) The procedures scientists use to conduct their studies.

Military-industrial complex The relationships between top leaders of the Pentagon and U.S. corporations by which they reciprocally support one another and thereby influence political decisions on their behalf.

Minority group A group of people who are treated unequally because of their physical or cultural characteristics. See *Discrimination*.

Mores (Pronounced MORE-rays) Developed by William G. Sumner, this term refers to norms whose violation is considered a moral transgression. Examples are the norms against murder and theft. See *Folkways*.

Negative sanction Punishment for disapproved behavior. See *Sanction*.

Neutralization (techniques of) Words and ways of thinking that help to deflect social norms and avoid social disapproval. An example is saying, "The circumstances required it" or, "I didn't know what I was doing."

Nonmaterial culture See *Culture*.

Nonverbal communication Communication by the use of symbols other than language. Examples are *Body language* and traffic lights.

Norms Rules concerning appropriate and inappropriate behavior by which people are judged and sanctions applied. See *Sanction*.

Nuclear family A family consisting of a husband, wife, and their children. See *Extended family*.

Operational definition The way in which a variable in a hypothesis is measured.

Organization A social unit established for the purpose of attaining some agreed-upon goals.

Outgroup A group toward which an individual feels hostility, tension, or dislike. See *Ingroup*.

Overt participant observation See *Participant observation*.

Participant observation A method of studying social groups in which the researcher participates in the group being studied. If the people being studied know the researcher is in their midst, this method is called *overt participant observation*; if they do not know they are being studied, it is called *covert participant observation*.

Peer group Associates of similar social status who are usually close in age. Examples are one's playmates as a child and workmates as an adult.

Personal identity   Our ideas of who we are. Roughly equivalent to self concept. See *Public identity* and *Self*.

Personality   An individual's tendency over time to act (and think and feel) in ways similar to those he or she did in the past; the stable behavior patterns we come to expect of people.

Population   The target group to be studied.

Positive sanction   A reward for approved behavior. See *Sanction*.

Power   The ability to get your way, even over the objections of others.

Power elite   C. Wright Mills' term to refer to a small group of people with interlocking interests who appear to make a nation's most important political decisions.

Prejudice   Attitudes, ideas, and feelings, often negative and about people one does not know. See *Discrimination* and *Ethnocentrism*.

Prestige   Favorable evaluation, respect, or social recognition.

Primary group   People whose relationship is intimate, face-to-face, expressive, and extended over time. Examples are one's family and close friends.

Prostitution   The exchange of sexual favors for some gain, usually money.

Public identity   The ideas that others have of what we ought to be like. Roughly equivalent to the public social roles we play. See *Personal identity* and *Self*.

Qualitative sociology   Studies of social life in which the emphasis is on the *meanings* of people's experiences. The goal is to determine how people construct their worlds, develop their ideas and attitudes, communicate these with one another, and how their meanings affect their behavior, ideas about the self, and relationships to one another. See *Meanings* and *Quantitative sociology*.

Quantitative sociology   Studies of social life in which the emphasis is on precise measurement, or numbers. Sociologists who have this orientation stress that proper measurement by the use of statistical techniques is necessary if one is to understand human behavior. See *Qualitative sociology*.

Questionnaire   An interview by means of a written form.

Race   A large number of people who share visible physical characteristics on the basis of which they regard themselves as a biological unit and are similarly regarded by others.

Racism   One racial or ethnic group dominating or exploiting another, generally based on seeing those they exploit as inferior. See *Discrimination* and *Ethnocentrism*.

Random sample   A sample in which everyone in the target population has the same chance of being included in the study.

Rapport   A feeling of trust and communication between people.

Rationalization (of society)   Weber's term for the process by which a society or other group adopts a bureaucratic orientation, with emphasis on efficiency, impersonal relations, and the bottom line.

Real culture A people's actual way of life, as contrasted with the way of life expressed by their ideals. See *Ideal culture*.

Reference group A group to which people refer when they evaluate themselves, their behavior, or actions they are considering.

Relative deprivation Feeling deprived relative to what others have; the sense that the gap between the resources or rewards that one actually has and what others have is unjust.

Reliability The extent to which studies produce consistent results.

Replication The repetition of a study in order to test its findings.

Research methods See *Methodology*.

Resocialization Learning norms, values, and behaviors that contrast with one's previous experiences.

Respondent A person who has been interviewed or who has filled out a questionnaire. (He or she has *responded* to the request for data.)

Rising expectations A situation in which people who have accepted existing conditions in the past now feel they have a right to better conditions.

Rites of passage Formal, customary rituals marking someone's transition from one social status to another. Examples include bar mitzvahs, confirmations, first communions, weddings, graduation ceremonies, and funerals. Also known as *rites de passage*.

Role The part played by a person who occupies a particular status. See *Status*.

Role conflict If a person finds himself or herself torn between conflicting demands of two or more roles, that person is said to be experiencing role conflict. Examples include a student wanting to date on the same night that he or she is supposed to study for a final examination.

Role taking Putting yourself in the shoes of someone else and seeing how things look from that perspective.

Sample The individuals intended to represent the population to be studied.

Sanction A social reward for approved behavior, or punishment for disapproved behavior. See *Negative sanction* and *Positive sanction*.

Secondary analysis The analysis of data already collected by other researchers.

Secondary group The more formal, impersonal, and transitory groups to which people belong, such as an introductory course in sociology.

Self The sense of identity that individuals have of themselves as a distinct person; this sense, idea, or conception is acquired through social interaction. See *Identity formation*.

Self-fulfilling prophecy   A false definition of a situation ("The bank is in trouble") that causes people to change their behavior ("People rush to the bank to withdraw their savings") and makes the originally false statement come true ("The bank is now in trouble as it does not have enough cash on hand to meet the unexpected demand for immediate withdrawals").

Sex role   The behaviors and characteristics that a male or female is expected to demonstrate, based on stereotypical cultural concepts of masculinity or femininity; assigned on the basis of one's sex organs.

Sex role socialization   Learning one's sex role. See *Sex role*.

Sexism   Males or females dominating or exploiting the other, with the exploitation generally based on seeing the other as inferior; usually used to refer to males dominating females. See *Discrimination* and *Ethnocentrism*.

Social change   Alteration in society, in its patterns of social structure, social institutions (or some small part of them), culture, and people's behavior.

Social class   A large number of people who have about the same amount of social power. In our society, some sociologists see the primary bases as the amount of people's income and education and the prestige of their occupation. Other sociologists see the essential difference as people's relationship to the means of production—whether they are capitalists (own the means of production) or workers (work for capitalists).

Social class mobility   Changing one's social class, usually in relationship to that of one's parents. See *Social mobility*.

Social construction of reality   The process by which definitions of reality (views of what some part of the world is like) are socially created, objectified, internalized, and then taken for granted.

Social control   The techniques used to keep people in line or, if they step out, to bring them back into line. Examples include persuasion, coercion, ridicule, education, and punishment. See *Sanction*.

Social group   Any human group.

Social inequality   Any inequality between or among groups of people; sometimes used to refer to *social stratification*.

Social institution   Standardized practices (clustered around a set of norms, values, beliefs, statuses, and roles) that develop around the attempt to meet a basic need of society. Examples include government and politics (for social order), education (for training in conformity and the transmission of skills and knowledge), and the military (for protection from external enemies and the implementation of foreign policy).

Social interaction   People acting and reacting to one another; as they do so, they influence each other's feelings, attitudes, and actions.

Social mobility   Movement from one social position to another. See *Downward*, *Horizontal*, and *Upward social mobility*.

Social stratification   Large groups of people ranked in a hierarchy that gives them different access to the rewards their society has to offer.

Social structure   The ways in which the basic components of a group or society are related to one another.

Socialization   Refers to learning; the process of social interaction by which people learn the way of life of their society, or learn to play specific roles.

Society   A group of interacting individuals who share the same territory and participate in a common culture.

Sociobiology   The study of the biological bases of human behavior.

Sociology   The scientific study of human society and social behavior.

Status   One's position in a group or society, such as woman, mother, and plumber.

Stereotypes   A generalization (or idea) about people (or even animals and objects); a mental image that summarizes what is believed to be typical about these people.

Stigma   An indelible mark of social disgrace.

Stratification   See *Social stratification*.

Structural sociology   The emphasis is on the influence of social structure on human behavior, with a focus on social institutions and other group memberships. See *Aggregates, Qualitative sociology*, and *Social structure*.

Structured interview   An interview that uses closed-ended questions.

Subculture   A group that shares in the overall culture of a society but also has its own distinctive values, norms, beliefs, and life style. Examples include cabdrivers, singles, prostitutes, muggers, and physicians.

Subjective interpretation   See *Verstehen*.

Survey   The collection of data by having people answer a series of questions.

Symbol   Any act, object, or event that represents something, such as a traffic light, a gesture, or this definition. See *Symbolic interactionism*.

Symbolic interaction   People's interaction based on symbols. See *Symbolic interactionism*.

Symbolic interactionism   Developed by Herbert Blumer, this term refers to the school of thought (or theoretical perspective) that focuses on symbols as the basis of human behavior—the signs, gestures, and language by which people communicate with one another and change or refine their courses of action in anticipation of what others might do. See *Conflict theory* and *Functionalism*.

Techniques of neutralization   See *Neutralization*.

Technology   Tools or items used to accomplish tasks.

Theory A statement that organizes a set of concepts in a meaningful way by explaining the relationship between them.

Total institution Erving Goffman's term to refer to a place in which people are confined, cut off from the rest of society, and under the almost absolute control of the people in charge. Examples include prisons, the military, and convents.

Traditional authority Authority that is legitimated by custom and practice. The explanation for something is, "We have always done it this way." See *Charismatic authority*.

Trust The willingness to accept the definition someone offers of oneself or of a situation and to play a corresponding role based on that definition.

Unobtrusive measures Techniques of observing people who do not know they are being studied.

Unstructured interview An interview that uses open-ended questions.

Upward social mobility Movement from a lower to a higher social position.

Validity The extent to which an operational definition measures what it is intended to measure.

Value conflict Disagreement over goals, ideals, policies, or other expressions of values.

Value judgment A personal, subjective opinion based on one's own set of values.

Values An idea about what is worthwhile.

Variable Any condition or characteristic that varies from one situation or person or group to another. Examples include age, occupation, beliefs, and attitudes. See *Dependent variable*, *Experiment*, and *Independent variable*.

Verstehen A term used by Max Weber to refer to the subjective interpretation of human behavior; that is, because we are members of a group or culture, we gain insight and understanding into what others are experiencing, allowing us to interpret those experiences. See *Qualitative sociology*.

Vertical social mobility Movement to a higher or a lower social position.

Voluntary associations Groups that people join voluntarily, often because they wish to promote some goal or to be with like-minded people. Examples include a church, a college class, and a bowling league. See *Involuntary associations*.

War Armed confict between nations or politically distinct groups.

White-collar crime Crimes committed by "respectable" persons of high status, frequently during the course of their occupation.

Appendix:
Correlation Chart

To help you integrate this eleventh edition with whatever main text you use, I have matched the articles with the chapter themes common to introductory texts. Because some selections in *Down to Earth Sociology* have several themes, an article may be listed for more than a single chapter. To make it easier to draw up your syllabus, I have listed the article number, its author and title, and the page number on which the article begins.

Some instructors build their introductory course around the articles in *Down to Earth Sociology*. They supplement these readings with a few chapters of what is usually the main text. In this way, their students concentrate on primary sociological materials, rather than on secondary analyses. Regardless of your approach, because of the inherent interest of most of these readings, *Down to Earth* helps make sociology come alive. Instructors report that these articles help them give their students a more engaging introduction to sociology.

I have also written an instructor's manual. In it, I not only include sample test questions but I also suggest in-class activities that you may wish to try. These activities are designed to make your class more lively, to arouse your students' interest in sociology, and to stimulate their sociological imagination. From the feedback that I have received from instructors, these in-class activities accomplish their purpose. I welcome any suggestions you might have for other in-class activities.

Again, my best wishes for your classroom success.

Jim Henslin

TOPIC: FORMAL ORGANIZATIONS

TOPIC: MARRIAGE AND FAMILY

TOPIC: MASS MEDIA

TOPIC: MEDICINE

TOPIC: POLITICS

TOPIC: RACE AND ETHNICITY

TOPIC: RELIGION

TOPIC: RESEARCH METHODS

TOPIC: SEX AND GENDER

TOPIC: SOCIAL CHANGE

TOPIC: SOCIAL CLASS

TOPIC: SOCIAL GROUPS

TOPIC: SOCIAL INTERACTION

TOPIC: SOCIAL MOVEMENTS

TOPIC: SOCIAL STRATIFICATION

TOPIC: SOCIALIZATION

TOPIC: THE SOCIOLOGICAL PERSPECTIVE

TOPIC: SPORTS

Name Index

Subject Index